Samuel Sewall.

THE

HISTORY OF WOBURN,

MIDDLESEX COUNTY, MASS.

FROM THE GRANT OF ITS TERRITORY TO CHARLESTOWN, IN 1640, *TO THE YEAR* 1860.

BY SAMUEL SEWALL, M.A.

OF BURLINGTON, MASS., SOMETIME PASTOR OF THE CHURCH THERE.

WITH A MEMORIAL SKETCH OF THE AUTHOR

BY REV. CHARLES C. SEWALL.

Boston:

WIGGIN AND LUNT, PUBLISHERS,

WASHINGTON STREET.

1868.

ALFRED MUDGE & SON,
Printers,
No. 34 School Street, Boston.

TO

THE INHABITANTS OF WOBURN

THIS HISTORY

IS MOST RESPECTFULLY INSCRIBED,

BY THEIR

FRIEND AND HUMBLE SERVANT,

SAMUEL SEWALL.

MEMOIR.

REV. SAMUEL SEWALL, author of this history of Woburn, was born in Marblehead, June 1, 1785, and died in Burlington, February 18, 1868.

He was a descendant of a long line of worthy ancestors, and bore the name of two, who were honored with the highest judicial office of the State. He traced his lineage, also, to one of the distinguished pastors of the Old South Church, in Boston, whose character he contemplated with reverence, and his sacred office with peculiar interest. Hence, probably, was that soberness of thought and feeling, which was so marked a feature of his early years; and that subsequent purity of aspiration and aim, which led him to the office once filled and adorned by his ancestor. Tradition, also, reports, that he was in infancy consecrated by his mother to the service of God in the Christian ministry; and, certainly, the teachings and discipline of parental love and piety seem to have had that end in view.

Having received preparatory instruction at the Academy, in his native town, he entered Harvard University in 1800, and graduated with unblemished reputation, in 1804. Already decided as to the profession of his choice, he at once commenced the study of Theology, at Cambridge; occupying, at the same time, a minor position in the College government. After the usual period of professional study, and being possessed by nature, education and rigid self-discipline, of fitting qualifications for the ministry, he took orders in the Episcopal church, of which his parents were members, and in which he had been accustomed to worship. Having officiated in this church for a short time, at Cambridge, and elsewhere, he became dissatisfied with its polity and creed, and embraced the principles and service of the Congregational church. He was ordained pastor of the church in Burlington, April 13, 1814. Here, he discharged the duties of the pastoral office with fidelity, and a good measure of success, during a period of twenty-eight years. How great that fidelity and success, though many fruits of it remain, can be fully known only hereafter.

When his connection with the church in Burlington had been dissolved, Mr. Sewall did not relinquish his profession, or relax his interest in the spiritual welfare of his fellow-men. He continued to preach for several years, at North Woburn, and, afterwards, with more or less frequency, in other places. His last sermon was preached at Carlisle, August 11, 1867; and his last public exercise was at the ordination of Rev. Mr. Hudson, now pastor of the church in Burlington, December 19, 1867, when he offered the ordaining prayer.

But, besides the studies and labors of the ministry, which he never neglected, Mr. Sewall was accustomed to pursue, with eagerness and delight, antiquarian and historical researches. In this pursuit, he followed a natural bent of his mind, and was content with only the most thorough and accurate results. His ardent love of truth would not allow him to rest satisfied with any conclusion, respecting which a shadow of doubt remained in his mind. He cherished, in particular, a deep and lively interest in persons and places endeared to him by any special tie, and sought to become familiar with their history. Being pastor of the church in Burlington,—originally a precinct of Woburn,—he felt strong inducement, and used diligent efforts to obtain a precise knowledge of the early settlement and original inhabitants of this town, and of its subsequent municipal and ecclesiastical affairs. He pursued his investigations for many years; foreshadowing, meanwhile, in a series of lectures delivered in Woburn, the results at which he finally arrived. These results were waited for, very naturally, with impatience, by many who were anxious to possess a complete and reliable history of the place of their nativity, or adopted home. The delay, however, to which they have submitted, will now be more than compensated by the fulness and accuracy of the work, and the exceeding interest with which the narrative is clothed. We venture to assert that a more complete and accurate, or more interesting, local history is rarely to be found. As such, it is now presented to the public, and particularly to the inhabitants of Woburn and its vicinity, with confidence that it will be rightly appreciated by all who shall read it.*

To sketch, minutely and with justice, the character of him, whose life is now only a memory, would indeed be pleasing to the writer, and might be profitable to others, should it but inspire them with like ardor of excellence, and like hope of grateful remembrance. But the picture of a character so pure and exalted, and a life so unspotted and saint-like, could not be fitly drawn by one so closely and tenderly allied. The impulses of fraternal affection might give it colorings, which, to another's eye, would seem unreal or be invisible. It shall be only said, therefore, that there was in Mr. Sewall,—as is admitted by those to whom he was most familiarly known, — a singleness and purity of mind, a transparent simplicity and gentleness of heart, a dignity and propriety of deportment, and a tenderness and yet peace of conscience, which made themselves felt wherever he was. He possessed a sound mind, and his intellectual attainments were varied and extensive. He sought, as he desired, only the reputation of a good man and a consistent Christian; and was wholly unambitious of any other distinction. His humility often made him distrustful of himself, and too ready to confide in others. With the meekness of wisdom, he mingled the gentleness of charity. True to his own convictions, he never failed to treat with courtesy and respect the convictions of others, however different they might be. Venerating all genuine goodness and greatness, he inspired an uniform confidence in his own sincerity and unaffected simplicity; a belief that he felt whatever he expressed, and that no interest exhibited by him

* The author died while this work was passing through the press. For himself, it is said, he only wished to live a ew hours longer, that he might see the completion of the work.

was factitious. He lived and moved, he thought and spoke, as if ever in the felt presence of his God. The will of God was the law of his daily life. The strength and joy of his soul sprang from communion with God; and to walk in all the commandments and ordinances of the Lord blamelessly was his constant care and ardent desire. Age shed a ripening influence upon the virtues of his early and maturer years. It gently relaxed the ties which bound him to the world he was soon to leave, while it hallowed the memories and hopes which endeared to him the world he was approaching. It rendered more precious and consoling his own religious belief and trust, while it enlarged his charity and widened his sympathies towards others of every Christian name and sect. Sorrows and the most painful bereavements he had borne with meek submission and unfaltering trust. Sickness and pain could not rob him of the peace of calm, patient, steadfast reliance on the providence of God, and an entire resignation to His will. He knew "Whom he had believed," and his faith in Him never wavered. So death came to him only as an angel of mercy, to release him from mortal pain and decay, and to translate his meek and pure spirit into the blissful presence of his Saviour and his God.

PREFACE.

The History of Woburn, which has been for years in a state of preparation, and long expected by the inhabitants of that town, for whose use it was principally intended, is at last finished, and ready for the press.

Before proceeding to the work itself, it seems proper to state briefly what led me to undertake it, and some of the causes, which have since, for so great a length of time, delayed its completion.

This History originated in a series of historical lectures upon Woburn, begun many years ago, and delivered in that town, at different intervals of time. They were at first undertaken at the suggestion, and under the influence of the friendly, persevering persuasion of the late Dr. Benjamin Cutter, a gentleman eminent in this vicinity for his antiquarian taste, his extensive acquaintance with the localities and ancient affairs of Woburn, and his zeal for advancing its credit and welfare. The first two lectures were delivered on two successive evenings in February and March 1842, in the vestry of Rev. Mr. Bennett's meeting-house, before a large and attentive audience. And so well were they apparently received, that I was encouraged to attempt, from time to time, as I was able, the preparation of others on the same theme. The two lectures just referred to were followed in several succeeding years by seven others, delivered in the same place. And in 1859, a tenth lecture was prepared by special request, and given in Lyceum Hall, bringing down the history to the commencement of the Revolutionary War in 1775.

In 1862, the town of Woburn proposed to me, by a committee, to finish, and make ready for the press, the history I had proceeded in thus far, for a liberal pecuniary compensation. This proposal was agreed to, with the understanding, that the town would take charge of publishing the work, and provide for the expense, and that I should have the inspection of the proof-sheets.

At the time this engagement was entered into, I was confident myself, and encouraged the town to expect, that six months would be amply sufficient for its fulfilment. But certain changes, apparently very necessary or expedient to be made, both in the style, and in the extent of the work, have to my regret, disappointed these anticipations. The Lectures on Woburn history, thus far, had been composed in the style of direct address to a present audience; but now it seemed very desirable to substitute the style of narrative; to publish a history prepared to be read with the eye, rather than one that was apparently designed to be heard with the ear from the lips of the author. The manuscript lectures, too. had hitherto been written on both sides of each leaf; but now, to accommodate the printer, it was deemed advisable to write them over anew, occupying one page only of each leaf, instead of both. Moreover, in the prosecution of the work, it was thought expedient to make certain enlargements beyond what was originally contemplated. In particular, a list of all the men, both citizens and strangers, who were employed by the town as soldiers in the War of the Revolution; and likewise Genealogical Notices of all the known original inhabitants of Woburn down to 1672, and of a certain portion of their descendants in the male line, have been inserted in the Appendix. These additions, and others which might be named, would greatly enhance, it was thought, the value of the work in the estimation of the people of Woburn, and much increase the interest they might take in it. But they have cost me much additional time and labor to prepare them, and have delayed the completion of the history far beyond my own expectations, and the expectations of others. But, through the favor of a kind Providence, my health and strength have held out; and I am able at last to announce to an indulgent community the finishing of a work which I have for years been laboring to prepare for them, and which they for months, or rather, I may say, for years, have been patiently looking to see.

In this Work, with reference to the ecclesiastical affairs of the town, I have aimed to exhibit a complete and impartial history of the First Church and Parish, and a brief account of the other religious societies in the town, down to the present year, 1867. As to matters of civil concern, the principal votes and proceedings of the town, touching the various changes and improvements which have been made in it, since the commencement of the present century till now, will be found embodied, I trust, in the closing chapter. But in regard to the patriotic measures taken and sacrifices made by the town since the year 1860, respecting the late war, and the events particularly interesting to Woburn people which transpired in the course of it, I am not provided with the means of giving a full and satisfactory relation of them. An attempt to make such a relation on my part would render necessary numerous fatiguing and perplexing inquiries; and thus still further protract the finishing of this work (too far protracted already), which I am anxious, for several very important reasons, to bring to a speedy close; and I must therefore leave the narration of this portion of the history of Woburn to other and abler hands.

My principal authority for most of the facts presented in this history have been the Woburn Records. (*a.*) But for various statements made herein, I have been largely indebted to the printed works and written communications of several highly esteemed authors and respected friends, whose names I have generally given, as occasion offered to refer to them, in the foot notes attached to this work. But in this connection, I cannot omit mentioning the Genealogical Dictionary of Hon. James Savage, a standard authority upon the genealogy of the early settlers of New England, and without the aid of which, I must often have been deficient in my Genealogical Notices of the primitive inhabitants of Woburn.

I embrace this opportunity for tendering my grateful acknowledgments to the numerous individuals, who, in one way or other, have kindly lent me their aid and encouragement in the prosecution of

---

(*a.*) The Woburn Records, which are quoted or referred to in this History, are

1. Nineteen volumes in folio, bound and in excellent order; exhibiting the votes and proceedings of the town at all general meetings from the beginning. Volume 11, of this collection, records the doings of the Selectmen at their meetings held monthly for several years from 1672, agreeably to vote of the town April 13, 1644.

2. Proprietors' book of Records from 1739 to 1765, a thin folio, unbound, much shattered, and in some parts defective.

3. A volume of Treasurer's Records, from 1739 to 1772; a folio, bound in parchment, but a cover now broken off.

4. First Parish Records, in folio, 3 volumes, complete from 1730, when Second Parish incorporated.

5. Records of Births, Marriages and Deaths in Woburn, from 1641 to 1841; originally contained in two volumes folio, but now copied with numerous additions from authentic sources, and collected into one large bound folio volume.

this work, which is now brought to a close. In particular, I would thankfully express my obligations to the gentlemen at the State House in Boston, who at divers times have given me free access to public Records and Documents for examination, and thus have opened to me sources of information, which I could nowhere else find, but in the archives of the Commonwealth. I thank the inhabitants of the town of Woburn for the recent generous encouragement they have voluntarily given me to pursue and finish my labors, beyond what they at first led me to depend on; and to the many respected individuals among them, especially to Cyrus Thompson, Esq., and to Mr. John A. Boutelle, who have furnished me from time to time with much desired and important information. I would make my thankful acknowledgments to the clergymen and others of the different denominations in the town, who, by their timely and acceptable communications, made at my request, have greatly furthered my progress in my laborious undertaking. I would present my warmest thanks to Nathan Wyman, Esq., the Town Clerk, and to Lewis L. Whitney, Esq., Clerk of the First Congregational Parish, for the free use they have generously afforded me of the Records in their keeping, without which, I could have made no advances in the work I have been engaged in.

Nor must I here forget or overlook my obligations to Mr. Bartholomew Richardson, senr., and to Dr. Benjamin Cutter, both now deceased. True, they are no longer here to accept my thanks for their services in aid of the work now completed, or to see and examine it, as they once would have been glad to. But to both of them I owe a debt of gratitude, which it would be base on this occasion to ignore or conceal. From the former gentleman, while he was with us, I derived an amount of reliable and interesting information, which but few, if any other men now living could have given me. And without the counsel, help and encouragement of the latter gentleman, this history would never have been undertaken, much less pursued to completion. And now it is finished, should it in any measure contribute to the entertainment or satisfaction of the good people of Woburn, or yield them any interesting or valuable information, let them be assured that they are indebted for it, in part at least, to him, as well as to

Their friend and humble servant,

SAMUEL SEWALL.

BURLINGTON, September, 18, 1867.

CONTENTS.

CHAPTER I.

CHAPTER II.

CHAPTER III.

CHAPTER IV.

CHAPTER V.

CHAPTER VI.

CHAPTER VII.

CHAPTER VIII.

CHAPTER IX.

CHAPTER X.

CHAPTER XI.

CHAPTER XII.

CHAPTER XIII.

CHAPTER XIV.

CHAPTER XV.

CHAPTER XVI.

HISTORY OF WOBURN.

CHAPTER I.

Woburn, originally Charlestown Village, elevated to a Township. — Church gathered; Pastor ordained; Town incorporated, 1642. — Town officers first chosen, 1644. — Streets laid out; common fields authorized. — Johnson's Account of Woburn, 1652. — Successive Divisions of Town's Lands.

WOBURN was originally a grant of land made, 1640, by the General Court of Massachusetts to Charlestown; and, for about two years afterwards, was called "Charlestown Village." The settlement of Charlestown, which is the most ancient town not only in the County of Middlesex, but likewise (Salem and Dorchester excepted) in the Colony of Massachusetts, as distinct from that of Plymouth, had commenced in 1629. In June of that year, Mr. Thomas Graves, a gentleman from Gravesend in Kent, eminent for his skill in surveying and engineering, and in the employ of the Massachusetts Company in London, came there from Salem, with several servants of the Company under his care; laid out the town in two-acre lots; erected a large building for public purposes, called the "Great House;" and with the consent of Gov. Endicott, exchanged the Indian name of the place, Mishawum, for Charlestown, in honor of King Charles I., the then reigning monarch of Great Britain.[1] In the year following, July 1630, a large and select company of Puritans, who had arrived the month preceding at Salem from England, came to Charlestown, with a

---

[1] Prince's N. E. Chronology, pp. 181, 188.

view to build and establish themselves there. Among them were Gov. Winthrop, Dep. Gov. Dudley, Mr. Isaac Johnson, husband of the celebrated lady Arbella, and Rev. Mr. John Wilson. These four persons presently formed themselves into a church, and some accessions being made to their number shortly after, they chose Rev. Mr. Wilson, as their pastor.[2] But a majority of the church and others removing within a few months to Boston to reside, another church, viz: the present First Church of Charlestown, was embodied November 2, 1632,[3] consisting of those members who continued to dwell on the north side of Charles River; and of this church, Rev. Mr. Zechariah Symmes was the pastor, and Rev. Mr. Thomas Allen the teacher, in 1640. And now the foundations both of her civil and of her ecclesiastical prosperity being, to human eye, firmly laid, Charlestown began to look around her; and with a view to the accommodation of her increasing agricultural population, she conceived a desire for the enlargement of her original bounds. And being informed of the conveniency of land adjoining her Western border, she presented a petition to the General Court, in May 1640, for the addition of two miles square to her territory in that quarter.[4] This petition of Charlestown was favorably heard by the Court. The land prayed for was immediately granted her, provided it fell not within the bounds of Lynn Village [Reading], and should be built upon within two years.[5] And at a session of the Court in October next following, the grant was enlarged, upon certain conditions, to four miles square.[6] All

[2] Prince, pp. 240, 243.
[3] Records of 1st Church, Charlestown: Title page.
[4] Woburn Records, Vol. I., p. 3.
[5] Colony Records, Vol. I., p. 290.
[6] Colony Records, Vol. I., p. 306.

(5.) "13 May, 1640. Charlestowne is granted their petition; that is, two miles at their head line, provided it fall nòt within the bounds of Linn village, and that they build within two yeares." — *Colony Records, Vol. I., p.* 290.

(6.) "7 October, 1640. Charles Towne petition is granted them, the proportion of 4 mile square, with their former last graunt, to make a village; whereof 500 acres is granted to Mr. Thomas Coytemore, to bee set out by the Court, if the towne and hee cannot agree," etc. — *Colony Records, Vol. I., p.* 306.

acts of Court were anciently dated from the first day of the session at which they were passed. As the first session of the Court of 1640 commenced on the "13th day of the 3d month" (13th May), and as the land then granted to Charlestown was explored May 15th, only two days after,[4] the precise date of that grant may be confidently fixed to the second day of that session; viz, the 14th of the 3d month, Old Style; or according to New Style, the modern way of computing time, May 24th, 1640. (See Appendix, No. III.)

The territory thus granted to Charlestown seems, before the arrival of the English upon these shores, to have been the abode, or, at least, a favorite place of resort, of numerous Indians. These were perhaps Pawtucket Indians, so named from Pawtucket Falls in Lowell, which was their principal seat; or (which is more probable) those Indians, whom Prince calls Aberginians, and concerning whom he says, that Charlestown Neck was full of them in 1628.[7] Many years have elapsed since Indians of every tribe have entirely disappeared from this town and vicinity, except a few solitary individuals, the memory of whose names and dwelling places are still preserved by some, or have been till recently. But they have left behind them durable memorials of their former residence here, and of their laborious ingenuity. In all the territory within the original limits of Woburn, (comprehending Woburn that now is, with Winchester, Wilmington and Burlington) multitudes of their stone arrowheads have been, and some still continue to be, turned up by the plough; stone heads of their spears and hatchets have not un-

---

[4] Woburn Records, Vol. I., p. 3.

(7.) "Sept. 13, 1628. Among those who arrive at Naumkeak, are Ralph Sprague, with his Brethren Richard and William; who with 3 or 4 more, by Governor Endicot's consent, undertake a Journey, and travel the Woods above 12 miles Westward, light on a Neck of Land call'd Mishawum, between Mistick and Charles Rivers, full of Indians, named Aberginians. Their old Sachem being dead, his eldest son, call'd by the English John Sagamore, is Chief; a man of a gentle and good Disposition; by whose free Consent, they settle here; where they find but one English House, thatch'd and pallizado'd, possess'd by Thomas Walford a Smith."—*Prince's N. E. Chronology, pp.* 174, 175.

frequently been found; and in Burlington, immemorial tradition still points to a spot within the new cemetery there, on the road to Bedford, as the site of one of their wigwams in former days.

The granting to Charlestown of the land she had petitioned for, was quickly followed by repeated attempts to explore it, and to determine its bounds. On May 15, 1640, Mr. Increase Nowell, magistrate, Rev. Zechariah Symmes, Edward Johnson, Edward Convers, Ezekiel Richardson, Mr. "Hubard," an artist, and some others, went from Charlestown to search the land lying within the two miles square.[8] And September 6th, following, Capt. Robert Sedgwick, Ensign Abraham Palmer, Thomas Lynde, Edward Johnson, Edward Convers, John Mousall, and others, went to view the bounds between this grant to Charlestown and Lynn Village, afterwards Reading. In this latter expedition, some of the company experienced a wonderful preservation, which is particularly noticed in Woburn Records by Johnson, who was one of them, as follows: "Lik Jacobits [Like Jacobites; See Gen. 28: 11] laying them downe to rest where night druc one [drew on] [they] were presarued by the good hand of God with cherfull sperits, thought [though] the heauens powred downe raine all night unsessantly. One remarkable prouidence neuer to bee forgotten: sum of the company lying under the body of a great tree (it lying sum distant from the earth) when the daye light appeered, noe sooner was the last man come from under it, but it fell downe to their amasment [amazement], being forced to dige [dig] out their food that was caught under it: it being soe ponderus that all the streneth they had, cold [could] not remoue it." [8]

The use originally designed by Charlestown to be made of this newly acquired territory, was, apparently, to accommodate with farms thereon such useful men as might from time to time be admitted to settle among them, and to promote the building of a village for the improvement of such remote lands as were already laid out.[9] In pursuance of this design, after the land petitioned for was granted and enlarged, a committee of thirteen

---

[8] Woburn Records, Vol. I., p. 3.

[9] Charlestown Records.

was chosen by the town, November 4th, 1640, which was "to sett the bounds betwixt Charlestown and the Village, and to appoint the place for the village."[9] This committee met November 17, 1640, and came to an agreement upon the matters submitted to them. But in this agreement, the committee, it seems, did not concur unanimously. In reference to it, Woburn records, under the date of the meeting, November 17, 1640, observe, that "it was in part assented to, but afterward denyed." A change too in the minds of the people on this interesting subject had now commenced, and was gaining ground. Since the grant of the Court had been enlarged from two to four miles square, a scheme for making a distinct town of it, instead of a village more or less dependent upon Charlestown, had been conceived and was entertained by numbers with favor.

And hence on November 5th, the very day after the appointment of the town committee of thirteen above referred to, the Church of Charlestown chose seven men, viz: Edward Convers, Edward Johnson, Ezekiel Richardson, John Mousall, Mr. Thomas Graves, Samuel Richardson and Thomas Richardson, as commissioners or agents for the erection of a church and town upon the recent grant of Court, where had been designed originally only a village within the limits of Charlestown.[10] By what authority the church took this step, interfering with the action of the town, does not appear. Perhaps they regarded the disposal of

---

[9] Charlestown Records.

(10.) Woburn Town Records commence as follows, from the date of the first grant of Court.

"14 of the 3 month [14 May] 1640. A true Relation of the prosseedings of Edward Conuars, Edward Johnson, John Mousall, Mr. Thomas Graues, Samuwell Richison and Thomas Richison, chosen by the Church of Charlestowne for the Erecting of a Church and Towne; which accordingly by great labor was by them performed, and now cal'd the Towne of Woburne." . . . . . . "the 5 of 9 month [5 November] 1640, the persons aboue specified were chosen by the Church of Charlestowne: chosen for the carring one the affaiers of this new Towne." — *Woburn Records, Vol. I. p.* 3.

Ezekiel Richardson is not named above with the other commissioners, but the omission must have been accidental. He was certainly one of them. For we find the others holding a meeting for consultation at his house, in his turn, on "the 13th of 12th month 1640" [13 February, 1640-1].

the Court's grant as a matter of ecclesiastical as well as civil concernment, and therefore that they were entitled to a distinct voice in it. But however that be, the measure itself seems to have excited no opposition on the part of the town, but rather to have met its entire acquiescence. Six of the seven commissioners chosen by the church were on the committee of thirteen appointed by the town; and it was by the instrumentality of these *commissioners*, not of that *committee*, that the establishment of the town and church of Woburn was at length happily effected.

But many and grievous were the difficulties which they had to encounter, before they saw the accomplishment of their enterprise.

The wild, unsettled state of the country presented many serious obstacles to the discharge of their commission. At the time of their appointment, the whole territory which they were to elevate into a township, as well as all that was adjacent to it for several miles, was an unbroken dreary forest, or a wide uncultivated waste. Hence, beside being frequently exposed to danger or alarm from the wandering savage natives, the commissioners, as they traversed the country in performance of their trust, without beaten roads to travel in, or landmarks to guide them, or houses to shelter them, or friends to extend to them even the most trifling office of hospitality or kindness, must needs have been subjected to hardships, of the severity of which, the present inhabitants of the town can have but faint conceptions. Of their sufferings of this description, one instance on record may be cited as a specimen. As they were engaged, November 9th, shortly after their appointment, in exploring the land about the Shawshin river they were overtaken and lost in a snow storm, and in this sad dilemma they were forced, as night approached, for want of a better shelter, " to lye under the Rockes, whilst the Raine and Snow did bedew their Rockye beds." [11]

Difficulties of this description however they must have anticipated; and fortitude of mind and firmness of bodily constitution abundantly enabled them, in the good cause they were engaged

---

[11] Woburn Records, Vol. I., p. 3.

in, to surmount them. But other troubles awaited the commissioners, which probably they were not prepared to meet, and which proved far more trying. Scarcely had they entered on the labors of their commission, before the church of Charlestown suddenly appeared in opposition. Our Puritan fathers, from motives of piety and benevolence as well as of worldly interest, loved to see the haunts of the savage occupied by civilized men; to see towns planted and churches springing up in the wilderness around them. Accordingly, the church above named appears to have cordially aided in procuring the grant of the newly acquired territory, and took a leading part in the plan of settling it as a distinct town. But at a meeting of her own calling, 23: 9 mo. [23 November] 1640, to see who would go up and become inhabitants of the proposed township, a larger number coming forward than had been expected, she instantly conceived a fear that the loss of so many emigrants would in a manner "depopulate Charlestown," or do her material injury in that day of small things.[11] And now under the influence of this apprehension, which time showed to be groundless, she began to discountenance this enterprise of her own devising or encouraging, and to watch all who were in favor of it or disposed to engage in it, with a jealous eye.[11] But though opposition from such a quarter must have been unlooked for, and very disheartening to the commissioners, yet, happily, it was of but short continuance. The church appears to have soon found that the spirit of emigration which she herself had helped to raise and foster, she could not check or put down at will. She therefore prudently yielded to circumstances; and within a fortnight from the time she began to frown upon their work, full power was given to Edward Convers and Company to go on with it anew.[11]

The obstruction which the church of Charlestown had thrown in their way being thus removed, the commissioners for the erection of the new church and town, resumed with fresh zeal the work of their appointment. Among their first cares for this end, agreeably to the usual practice of our pious ancestors in such

[11] Woburn Records, Vol. I., p. 3.

cases, was the observance of a day for solemn humiliation before God, and for supplication of his aid and blessing in their arduous undertaking. Under date of December 22, 1640, Johnson notes in the records, "considering the waytines [weightiness] of the worke, and the weaknes of the persons, this day was sett appart for humble seecking of God by prayer and fastting for helpe in a worke of soe great consiquence; which was performed at the hows of John Mousall by the forenamed persons and their wiffs [wives], the Lord assisting." [11]

About this time, they commenced a series of meetings, held in rotation, at their respective houses in Charlestown, for consulting on the affairs of the contemplated town, and adopting measures in reference to its settlement. Their first meeting for these purposes was held December 18th, at the house of Mr. Thomas Graves, when they agreed upon Town Orders (Appendix No. 1), and chose Edward Johnson Recorder or Town Clerk.[11] At like meetings in the two following months, they admitted many to set down their dwellings in the proposed plantation; though some of them (to use the words of the Recorder), "being shallow in brayns, fell ofe [off] afterwards." [11] And, on February 10th, 1640–1, they built a bridge over the Aberjona River for their own and the public accommodation, and perhaps too as an earnest of their resolution to go up and possess the land. This bridge, the first that was built in Woburn, they called Cold Bridge. It was in after times better known as the "Convers' Bridge," from the name of the proprietor of the adjacent mill; and as it is said in the records to have been laid "over against Edward Conuars' hows," it is inferred that that house, which continued many years in the occupation of that distinguished family, and the site of which is still well remembered, was either already standing when the bridge was built, or that it was erected immediately after, and before the entry just quoted from the records was made; and that it was the first built dwelling-house in Woburn.[12]

February 8th, 1640–1, the commissioners came from Charles-

---

[11] Woburn Records, Vol. 1., p. 3.

[12] Woburn Records, Vol. I., p. 4.

town to find a suitable location for their projected town. After two days' search, they pitched for this purpose upon a spot at the east end of the Court's grant, which they quickly afterwards laid out. And at a meeting at Ezekiel Richardson's, February 13th, they directed all who intended to become inhabitants, to meet on the ground, February 16th.[12] The place selected as the site of the proposed town, was unquestionably the plain on the borders of the Aberjona River, and near the place which it was designed, at a recent day, to cultivate as a silk farm. But the selection was not made by the commissioners with unanimity. The spot chosen did not meet the views of a considerable proportion of the expected settlers; and at the same time, Mr. Nowell, Mr. Symmes, and other gentlemen of note and principal influence in Charlestown, gave them no small discouragement from going there to build.[12] Hence, when the persons notified came there, February 16th, the day appointed, to the number of forty, though they busied themselves in marking trees, and laying bridges, yet (say the Records) "the way was so playen [plain] backward, that diuers neuer went forward againe."[12] These checks given them by patrons or superiors in standing, and these tokens of fickleness or faint-heartedness on the part of associates in their enterprise, must necessarily have caused the commissioners much perplexity and trouble. But they notwithstanding persevered in their work; and February 29, 1640–1, within a fortnight from the last-mentioned date, by the advice of a committee appointed by Charlestown to confer with them, consisting of Mr. Nowell, Captain Sedgwick, Lieut. Sprague, and others, they abandoned the site which they had first selected for private dwellings and a meeting-house, and decided upon another farther west in its stead. To this spot, which is now in and around the centre of the town, they came in March and May following, and laid out house lots; and, upon some of these lots at least, buildings were doubtless erected in the course of that year.[12]

By this arrangement, another serious obstacle in the way of

[12] Woburn Records, Vol. I., p. 4. See Appendix, No. II.

the commissioners was removed; but their difficulties and trials were not yet terminated. (They were still doomed to suffer repeated and grievous disappointments in their efforts to obtain an able minister for the town, whose foundations they were laying.) This, with our Puritan ancestors, was a point of paramount importance to secure. Their main errand in coming to this country was of a religious, not a secular nature; and hence, as Capt. Johnson, one of the principal founders of Woburn, observes, "it was as unnatural for a right New England man to live without an able ministry, as for a smith to work his iron without a fire."[13] The stated and able ministration of the word and ordinances of the gospel was a privilege for which the first settlers of this land, generally speaking, were ready to make any, even the most costly sacrifices; and scarcely any of them felt willing to seat themselves down in a place where there was not, at least, a comfortable prospect of speedily enjoying it. Of all this, the commissioners for building up Woburn were fully aware. The acquisition of a good and faithful minister of Jesus Christ was not only their own hearts' most earnest desire, but, in their view, it was a matter of essential importance to the prosperity of their infant plantation. Hence the question, Whom should they get for a minister? had been a subject of serious discussion at their meetings in Charlestown the preceding winter. And now, at the present stage of their enterprise, they determined, without delay, to commence vigorous exertions to procure some one, on whom they could rely for the faithful discharge of the sacred office among them. And yet the repeated failure of these exertions was long a cause to them of sore mortification, and at times, to some of their number, almost of despair.

The person to whom they first applied to become their minister was Rev. Jonathan Burr. This gentleman, who came to this country in 1639, had been a clergyman of high repute in England for piety and learning, and had just now received a call to settle over the church in Dorchester, as colleague with Rev.

---

[13] Wonder Working Providence, B. II., Chap. 22.

Richard Mather.[14] But from certain reported differences between him and Mr. Mather, the first settlers in Woburn seem to have imbibed an opinion that he was disposed to quit Dorchester, and might be induced, upon application, to come and be settled over them. Accordingly, " divers " (commissioners and others,) went from here March 17, 1640–1, to speak to him on the subject, to whom he gave " good incorridgment to go one [on]; God would prouid" [provide]; and withal, led them to expect that he might ultimately comply with their wishes.[*] But the differences which had existed between him and his senior colleague, Rev. Mr. Mather, were soon healed;[14] and his friends at Dorchester, after repeated visits to this incipient plantation, being dissatisfied with its local advantages,[15] probably advised him not to remove from where he then was. Influenced doubtless in some measure by their feelings and views in this matter, Mr. Burr returned, May 10, 1641, a negative answer to the invitation given him from this place;[16] and, though afterwards urged anew,[16] he could not be persuaded to revoke it. He remained at Dorchester, and died there, deeply lamented, August 9th of the same year, 1641.[14]

At Mr. Burr's declining a settlement in this place, " most harts grew fainte,"[16] and even a majority of the commissioners began to be discouraged.[17] But there were three, at least, of the seven, whose resolution no adverse occurrences could shake, no obstacles turn from their purpose.[17] Conscious of the rectitude

[14] Allen's Biography. [*] Woburn Records, Vol. I., p. 4.

[15] "The 20th of 1. mo. 1641, Mr. Burr's ffriends came againe, and brought men with them to vew the land, espetially the medow." Wob. Rec. I., p. 4.

"24 of 3d mo. [May] 1641, Mr. Burr's ffreinds came againe with fresh men, whos minds were much for medow, and their jugments short in what they saw." Town Records, Vol. I., p. 4.

[16] " 10: 3d mo. Meeting at Thomas Richison's: Mr. Burr declined; and most harts grew fainte."

" 29: 3d mo. Mr. Thomas Graues and Edward Johnson were sent to Mr. Burr, who was loth to giue a full answer." T. Records, Vol. I., p. 4.

[17] See the several statements in this paragraph, and others connected with it, concerning " a majority of the commissioners," and respecting " three " of their number, illustrated and confirmed in certain Lines in verse, composed by one of them, Captain Edward Johnson, prefixed by him to the Town Records, Vol. I., p. 1, and copied in Appendix, No. II., of this work

of their motives and aims, they repaired again, in that dark and gloomy day, to the Lord, and in return obtained light and encouragement from above. Under date of the 25 of 6 mo. [25 August] 1641, we read in the Records, "Things going heauily one [on], and many Blocks in the waye, espetially sum of their own Company disheartening, this day was set apart for humble seeking the Lord by fasting and prayer: whom they found gratious in keping upp the sperits of sum to the worke."[18] And now, strengthened by the pious exercises of this solemnity, three at least of the commissioners[18] proceeded with their enterprise with fresh resolution and courage. The next day, they built a bridge over Horn Pond River, — a work, at that time, attended with great labor and difficulty. "The place was soe boggy," say the records, "that it swallowed up much wood before it cold [could] bee mad pasable," [passable] and yet they finished the bridge the same day, and called it "Long Bridge."[18]

Shortly after, they made a new effort to procure a minister. Two messengers went to Rowley, October 25, 1641, to make proposals to Rev. John Miller,[18] a clergyman recently from England, and then an assistant to Rev. Mr. Rogers, pastor of the church in that town; but finding Mr. Rogers "loth to part with him," they forbore urging him any further.[18]

In less than a fortnight after, the commissioners spake on the same design to Mr. Thomas Carter, a candidate for the ministry from England, and then a resident at Watertown. And receiving some encouragement of help from him, they proposed to the

[18] Woburn Records, Vol. I., p. 4.

Rev. John Miller had been an ordained minister in England. Upon coming to this country, he was admitted as a member into the Church of Roxbury. After leaving Rowley, about 1642, he was ordained the pastor of the Church of Yarmouth, on Cape Cod, and continued there as late as 1651. Subsequently, he became a preacher of the gospel at Groton; but died, while the people there were taking measures to settle him over them. The following notice of his death is from the Records of 1st Church, Roxbury: "1663, June 14, Mr. John Miller, Preacher of the Gospel at Groyton, sometime pastor of the Church at Yarmouth, rested from his labors." See also Johnson's Wonder Working Providence, Book 11, chap. XI., Butler's History of Groton, p. 155, and American Quarterly Register, Vol. XI., p. 259.

church of Charlestown (of which several of them were members), that they might hold public worship at the village.[19] The church granted their request, and also lent them for one Sabbath the aid of their pastor, Rev. Mr. Symmes; who accordingly, November 21, 1641, preached here the first gospel sermon probably, that had ever been delivered in this portion of the New England wilderness. His text was from those appropriate words, Jeremiah iv. 3. "Thus saith the Lord to the men of Judah and Jerusalem, Break up your fallow ground, and sow not among thorns." [19] Mr. Carter likewise, in fulfilment of the expectations he had raised, preached, December 5th, at this place for the first time, out of Genesis xxii., "incorridging to trust in the Lord for the means." [19] From this time, the people here, by the commissioners, frequently renewed their applications to him to become their minister. And as a pledge of their good will, and of their earnest purpose to sustain him in his work, they set about building a house for the ministry.[20] But it was long before he could be persuaded to enter into any permanent engagement with them. Though solicited again and again, he was for months unwilling to promise anything more than occasional help; and this, the records observe, "was uery [very] seldom." [20] At length their importunity prevailing with him to spend with them a day of humiliation, April 14, 1642, he afterwards gave them good encouragement to hope for his constant services, and passed two Sabbaths with them in succession. Thenceforth their expectations of attaining the great object, which they had so long sought, and labored and prayed for, began to brighten, and with some short interruption [21] continued to increase. At last, hoping to enjoy Mr. Carter's permanent services in the ministry, those among them who were connected by covenant with the church of Charlestown requested, June 5, 1642, that they might be dismissed. That church received their request at first with reluctance, and put them off for a fortnight. Then, after much agitation, she voted them a dismission, and her consent that they might be gathered into a church.[20]

---

[19] Woburn Records, Vol. I., p. 4.

[20] Woburn Records, Vol. I., p. 5.

The First Congregational Church in Woburn was gathered with much solemnity August 14, O. S. or August 24, N. S., 1642, (Appendix III.) The proceedings in this interesting transaction are minutely related by Capt. Edward Johnson, one of the principal founders of this church, and clerk of the town at that time, both in the Town Records [21] and in his celebrated history of New England, entitled "The Wonder-working Providence of Zion's Saviour." [22] From these authorities, we learn that there were present, on the occasion, the elders and messengers of several of the neighboring churches and others; particularly Rev. Messrs. Symmes and Allen of Charlestown, Wilson and Cotton of Boston, Shepard of Cambridge, Dunster, President of Harvard College, Knowles of Watertown, Allin of Dedham, Eliot of Roxbury, and Mather of Dorchester,—ministers, whose praise is still in all the churches of our land. Mr. Increase Nowell of Charlestown, likewise one of the magistrates of the colony, was there, agreeably to an opinion then and long afterwards prevalent, which deemed it a duty for one or more of the magistrates to be present on such occasions, for the prevention of errors and proceedings that might breed disturbance in the Commonwealth; and also for giving countenance and encouragement to so good a work. [22] These all being assembled, about 8 o'clock of the morning on the day just mentioned, Mr. Symmes "continued in prayer and preaching about the space of four or five houres." Then the persons to be embodied in a church state, viz: John Mousall, Edward Johnson, Edward Convers, William Learned, Ezekiel Richardson, Samuel Richardson and Thomas Richardson, stood forth, and made declaration, one by one, of their religious faith and Christian experience; confessing "what the Lord had done for their poor souls by the work of his Spirit in the preaching of his Word and Providences." [22] And here the elders and messengers present had liberty to propound any question to them for their better understanding of them in any point they

[21] "16 of 3 mo. [16 May] 1642. They [the Commissioners] were dishartened by too [two] of their company taking of Councill." Town Records.

[21] Woburn Records, Vol. I., p. 5.

[22] W. W. Prov. B. II., Chap. XXII., p. 175-181.

doubted of; and all at length being satisfied, the persons to be gathered, manifested their consent to their covenant in words expressed in writing to this purpose.

"We that do assemble ourselves this day before God and his people, in an unfeigned desire to be accepted of him as a Church of the Lord Jesus Christ, according to the Rule of the New Testament, do acknowledge ourselves to be the most unworthy of all others, that we should attain such a high grace, and the most unable of ourselves to the performance of any thing that is good, abhorring ourselves for all our former defilements in the worship of God, and other wayes, and resting only upon the Lord Jesus Christ for attonement, and upon the power of his grace for the guidance of our whole after course, do here, in the name of Christ Jesus, as in the presence of the Lord, from the bottom of our hearts, agree together through his grace to give up ourselves, first unto the Lord Jesus, as our only King, Priest, and Prophet, wholly to be subject unto him in all things, and therewith one unto another, as in a Church Body, to walk together in all the Ordinances of the Gospel, and in all such mutual love and offices thereof, as toward one another in the Lord; and all this, both according to the present light that the Lord hath given us, as also according to all further light, which he shall be pleased at any time to reach out unto us out of the Word by the goodness of his grace: renouncing also in the same Covenant all errors and schismes, and whatsoever by-wayes that are contrary to the blessed rules revealed in the Gospel, and in particular, the inordinate love and seeking after the things of the world." "Every Church hath not the same for words; for they are not for a form of words."

And now having entered into covenant, the elders present extended to them the right hand of fellowship, in the name of the churches to which they respectively belonged; thereby acknowledging them to be a true and regularly gathered church of Christ.

The establishment of a church in Woburn was soon followed by the ordination of its first pastor. For some time before the church was gathered, Mr. Thomas Carter had been "exercising his gifts of preaching and prayer among them;" and continuing afterwards to do so with acceptance, the church called him to the pastoral office, and he was ordained over them November 22, O. S. or December 2d, N. S., 1642.[22] On this occasion, the same churches appear to have been sent to for their presence and aid, as at the *gathering* of the church, and the same pastors to have attended that did then, except Rev. Mr. Knowles of Watertown, who was absent on a special mission to preach the gospel in Virginia.[23] This ordination has long been celebrated from the circumstance, that "imposition of hands," the distinctive ceremony of such solemnities, was performed by laymen. Congregational principles, as afterward set forth in the Cambridge Platform, recognize the right of a church to ordain its pastors by the hand of its ruling elders, or other members duly appointed thereto. But they likewise allow the propriety of imposition of hands on the candidate by the elders of other churches present, at the request of the ordaining church, when it has no elders of its own to do it, as was the case in this instance at Woburn.[24] And this latter method of ordination, a little varied, soon became, and still continues to be, the common custom of the country. It was recommended to Woburn church, at the ordination of Mr. Carter. "Some difference there was," observes Gov. Winthrop in his History, concerning this transaction: "Some difference there was about his ordination. Some advised, in regard they had no elder of their own, nor any members very fit to solemnize such an ordinance, they would desire some of the elders of the other churches to have performed it; but others, supposing it might be an occasion of introducing a dependency of churches, and so a presbytery, would not allow it. So it was performed by one of their own members, but not so well and orderly as it ought."[25] Johnson's account of it is, that after Mr. Carter had exercised in preaching and prayer the greater part of the day, "two persons" (of whom he himself was doubtless one) "in the name of the church, laid their hands upon his head, and said, 'We ordain

---

22 W. W. Prov., Book II., Chap. XXII., p. 175–181. For the present Articles of Faith and Covenant in the First Church of Woburn, see Appendix, No. IV.

23 Woburn T. Records, Vol. I., p. 5. Allen's Biog. under Knowles.

24 Platform, Chap. IX., § 3, 4, 5.

25 Savage's Winthrop, Vol. II., p. 109, 110.

thee, Thomas Carter, to be Pastor unto this Church of Christ.'" "Then one of the elders present being desired of the church, continued in prayer unto the Lord for his more especial assistance of this his servant in his work;"[22] and the others held out the right hand of fellowship to him.[20]

In the interval between the gathering of the church, and the ordination of its first pastor, Woburn was incorporated as a town. Its territory was granted originally to Charlestown, on condition that it should be built on within two years.[5] This condition had been fulfilled. And now that a church had been embodied among its inhabitants, and there was a fair prospect of the speedy settlement of a minister over them, (provisions, to which paramount importance was attached by the early legislation of Massachusetts, in their establishment of towns and parishes) the way was fully prepared for granting this people the privileges of a town. Accordingly, at a session of the General Court, which commenced the "8th of 7 mo." or September 8th, 1642, and was continued by adjournment to the 27th of the same month, the town was incorporated. The Act of Court for this purpose is contained in these five words: "Charlestowne Village is called Wooborne."[26] And as the record of this Act of Incorporation is subsequent to the record of the above adjournment, the earliest date that can be assigned to that Act is September 27th, O. S., or October 6th, N. S., 1642.

Thus the permanent settlement of this place, which had been undertaken by the Commissioners for the work, under circumstances of great discouragement, and perseveringly carried on by them and others through the midst of oppressive labors and disheartening difficulties and trials, was at length happily accomplished. By the date of its incorporation, Woburn was the twentieth town in the Massachusetts Colony, as distinct from that of Plymouth; and the twenty-ninth of those three hundred and thirty-one cities and towns which constituted the State of Massachusetts in 1855. At the time it was first legally recognized as a town, not one of those which now immediately border

---

[26] Mass. Col. Records, Vol. II., p. 28. Why this name was given to Woburn at its incorporation, see Appendix, No. V.

upon it, had received a corporate existence. Even Reading, the plantation of which was commenced earlier than that of Woburn, was still known only as Lynn Village. Then, the incorporated towns nearest to Woburn were Rowley and Ipswich on the north, Salem and Lynn on the northeast, Charlestown on the east, Cambridge on the southeast and south; and Concord on the southwest. On the west and northwest, all within the present bounds of Massachusetts, saving Newbury and Salisbury, was as yet a wilderness, uninhabited by man, except by Indians dwelling in scattered wigwams, or in a few denser settlements, such as Nashoba, now Littleton, and Pawtucket, now Lowell.

The first general meeting held in Woburn after the grant to it of corporate privileges was on November 9, 1643. Then an order was passed, imposing a fine of eighteen pence, for the use of the town, upon every one who should absent himself from any public meeting without a reasonable excuse. Committees also were appointed to look after fences, to parcel out meadows, and to lay out a common field, to be afterwards divided by lot among them that should have share therein.[27] But for reasons that can now be only conjectured, there was no general choice of town officers till April 13, 1644, above a year and a half from the Act of Incorporation. At a public meeting on that day, it was voted, with the general consent of all the freemen and other inhabitants then present, that a choice should be made annually, from among the freemen of the town, of seven men (or of a less number in after time, when the town should be more settled), who should have power to order the prudential affairs of the town, and who should continue in office till "the first third day of the weeke in the first month" (that is, till the first Tuesday in March) in the next year, when a new choice should be made. The following Orders likewise were agreed upon for the future direction of their Selectmen:

1. They should always give public notice when any rate or assessment was to be made upon the inhabitants, "to the end, men "may shew their grevance if any bee; and mutual love and agree- "ment may be continued, by takeing ofe [off] the burden from "the opressed."

[27] Woburn Records, Vol. I., p. 5.

2. When any scruples should arise in their minds, in the transaction of the affairs of the town, they should repair to the elder or elders of the church in the said town for advice.

3. They should alter no man's propriety in the town without his free consent.

4. They should meet once a month, at the least, upon the town's business; and keep a record of all orders concluded by the major part of them for the good of the town; and that they should give an account in public at the year's end of their disbursements and disposal of the town's stock and land.[28]

On the same day, they chose Edward Johnson, Edward Convers, John Mousall, William Learned, Ezekiel Richardson, Samuel Richardson and James Thompson for their first Board of Selectmen; William Learned, Constable; and Michael Bacon, Ralph Hill and Thomas Richardson for Surveyors of Highways.[28]

Though Woburn had now acquired the name and privileges of a town, yet much remained to be done to redeem it from its former wilderness condition. House lots had been marked out in the centre and some other places, a house for their minister and a few other scattered dwellings had been built, and a meeting house was either then, or shortly after, erected. But no streets leading to and by their respective places of abode had been completed, no roads for intercourse with other towns had been established, and their territory as yet lay in great measure common. Hence as soon as the incorporation of the town and the settlement of its minister were over, the laying out of streets and highways, and the distribution of the lands, were necessarily among the first subjects of attention to the people. Accordingly, in November, 1645, three streets or highways were laid out, one called Upstreet[29] and the other two running into Upstreet, called Sawpit

[28] Woburn Records, Vol. I., pp. 5, 6.

[29] It would be exceedingly difficult at the present day to determine with certainty the position of the several streets or highways that were first laid out in Woburn.

Upstreet is described in the Records (vol. I, p. 7) as "leading to Shawshin," and there are strong reasons for supposing that it ran from the centre of the town northerly towards Wilmington, and southwesterly from

Lane [30] and Military Lane.[31] In April of the next year, 1646, two other highways were laid out, viz., Plain Street and Driver's Lane. *Plain Street* is described in the Records [32] as "leading to Cambridg mill and towne the one way and to Upstreet and Shawshin the other waye," and seems evidently to be the road which now goes over the plain in the west side of the town to Cutter's mill (formerly so called) in West Cambridge, and which, in coming in the direction towards Woburn, divides near Kendall's mill, into two branches, the easterly branch passing the late Capt. Joseph Gardiner's house, and leading to Upstreet, and the westerly branch into the road towards the Shawshin in Burlington.

---

the same point into Pleasant Street by the house formerly occupied by General Thompson to the George Richardson house, and thence to the house formerly of Benjamin Simonds, now owned by Jesse Cutler, and thence by Mr. John Cummings, jr.'s house to the Shawshin or Hodge Hole meadows in Burlington. But the late Dr. Benjamin Cutter (a gentleman very thoroughly acquainted with Woburn localities) was of opinion that Upstreet, in coming from Wilmington, entered Bedford Street at Mr. George Flagg's, and proceeding thence to the house of Mr. George Richardson, went from there to the houses of Messrs. Jesse Cutler and John Cummings, jr., towards *Shawshin* as mentioned above.

[30] Sawpit Lane, running into Upstreet, according to the Records, appears to have been a highway diverging from the northerly part of Upstreet towards Wilmington through or near what are still called, it is said, the Sawpit Woods, toward Reading.

[31] Military Lane, though long since forgotten, was recognized by name in a Report of the Selectmen made January 28, 1731–2, in the case of a complaint to the Selectmen by Thomas Reed against Jeremiah Center for stopping up the way leading from Reed's house to the meeting-house. In that Report, Military Lane is described as the highway "which leads from our meeting-house through the Training field by the said Jeremiah Center's and Thomas Reed's into that Highway leading to Shawshin, known by the name of Upstreet" [a]. Thomas Reed's house here referred to is presumed to be that lately occupied by Mr. Silvanus Wood, senr., deceased. Military Lane then, after leaving the meeting-house (then standing on the hill east of the Common) and passing over the Training Field into Pleasant Street, proceeded thence to the school-house of the sixth District, lately taken down, and there entering the narrow lane by or back of that school-house, went on by Mr. Center's to Mr. Wood's house, where it met a branch of *Upstreet* coming from Mr. John Cummings, jr.'s corner, and thence went on with that to *Shawshin*.

[32] Records, Vol. I., p. 9.

[a] Woburn Records, Vol. I. *inverted*, p. 69.

Drivers' Lane appears to have been principally intended for the driving of cattle to some common pasture on the plains at the West Side. It was laid out from Kingsford, at the Aberjona River, to Plain Street, one rod wide on the land of Mr. Zechariah Symmes on one side, and one rod wide on the land of Edward Convers on the other,[33] and was probably that road which now goes from the site of the ancient Convers' mill by Winchester meeting-house to "Plain Street," on the road to West Cambridge, at Mr. Loring Emerson's.

In the Summer and Autumn of the same year, 1646, provision was made for the construction of roads to Reading and Mystic Bridge,[33] now South Reading and Medford. In December 1647, a committee was appointed to lay out a highway from "the three Richisons to the Towne meeting-hows one way, and Mr. Thomas Graves the other way," [34] which was doubtless the commencement of the road known from time immemorial as Richardson's Row.

The incorporation of Woburn, 1642, as a distinct town, rendered it very desirable to establish the divisional line between it and Charlestown as soon as possible. And yet for several years this necessary measure, from some cause or other, was still undetermined. While Woburn was yet Charlestown village, an agreement had been entered into by a committee of thirteen, for fixing the bounds between the village and the parent town; but this agreement had been subsequently "*denied*," and the labors of the committee frustrated.[35] When three years and upwards had elapsed from the incorporation of the town, and this important question still remained to be decided, it was agreed at a general meeting at Woburn, March 17, 1646, to send to the Selectmen of Charlestown the following letter.

"To our much Respected and approued good ffreinds of Charlestowne chosen to order the prudentiall affaiers thereof:

"Much Respected and Aintient ffreinds:

"Wee are Bould to interupt your presant pressious Implyments with Request for Issue of those things which Sartaine of our Beloued

[33] Records, Vol. I., p. 9. [34] Records, Vol. I., p. 12. [35] Woburn Records, Vol. I., p. 3.

Brethren among you were Chosen unto. Now our humble Request is, that they may End it forthwith. If otherwise they cannot so doe, our further Request is that sum others unintrested in the things may put a ffreindly Isue (Issue) to the same. Our last Request is, that if nether of these will doe, then in a brotherly and ffreindly way to petistian to the General Court: that wee may not bequeth matter of diferenc to our posteryty. Thus, with hope of a presant answer in writing to our soe Reasanabl Request,

"Wee Remaine yours to bee Comanded
"in all saruis of loue in Christ our Lord." [36]

To this friendly letter, in which Christian courtesy and firmness in insisting upon their just rights are equally conspicuous, no response appears to have been made, and no effectual action taken in the premises by Charlestown for three years more. On the 3: 1 mo: 1649, Edward Johnson, Edward Convers, John Mousall and John Wright, four of the seven Selectmen of Woburn were appointed a committee "to speake with our Brethren of Charlestown about the settling the Bounds sudenly betweene them and us." [37] This quickening message seems to have led soon after to the appointment of a committee mutually chosen by Charlestown and Woburn, who brought to a final issue this and other important questions connected with it, July 29, 1650. Their report was subscribed Dec. 16, 1650, not only by the committee, but by the Selectmen of Woburn, and by two leading members of the church of Charlestown, in token of their approbation of it; and was entered in full upon Charlestown records. The following is a transcript of their return, as copied from those records by Nathan Wyman, Esq., town clerk of Woburn.

"The 29 of the V month, [29 July,] 1650.

"Whereas wee Robt. Sedgwicke, Ralph Sprague, Tho. Lyne and Robt. Hale being chosen by the Ffreemen of Charlestowne & the Ffreemen of Wobourne mutually to settle the bounds bettweene ye two Townes afforesaid, as also to appoint what quantity of Land should be laid to the Lots, & Ffarmes y^t^ are adjoyning to Charles-

[36] Woburn Records, Vol. I., pp. 8, 9.

[37] Woburn Records, Vol. I., p. 14.

towne Common on ye East side of Samll. Richesons; & also to appoint where the Line shall devide the two Townes in all places where ye Land of both Townes doe joyne together, as also to appoint what quantity of Land the said Charlestown shall have from Wobourne in consideration. . . . of Charlestown's resigning up those Lotts & Commons wch. were in the old Bounds of Charlestowne, unto the Inhabitants of Wobourne:

"This first wee agree upon: That the Line of devision bettween the two Townes shall runne from Cambridge Line by ye Northwest end of Mr Nowell's Lott [6] & so all along bettweene Mr. Sims's Ffarme & Edward Convers's Ffarme untill it come to the East side of them adjoyneing to Charlestowne Common.

"Also we have agreed & determined y^t Wobourne shall have five hundred Acres of Land out of Charlestowne Common for the use of those Lotts & ffarmes before mentioned; the which five hundred Acres shall begin at the East Corner of Edward Convers's ffarme, next Mr. Sims's ffarme, & so by all along by the East side of those Lotts, & so up to Charlestowne head Line, of such a breadth as shall take in the five hundred Acres; and y^t the sd. Wobourne (according to theire promise) shall make and maintaine a sufficient ffence of two Railes to runne even in that Line, that shall devide bettweene the five hundred Acres & Charlestowne Common; and that Raile shall bee the bounds bettweene the two Townes on that side.

"Allso wee agree That all the [Tracts?] of Common & Waste Land y^t lye bettweene Cambridge Line & the five hundred Acres (above mentioned) shall belong unto Wobourne.

"Likewise wee agree that Charlestowne shall have three thousand Acres of Land out of the Bounds of Wobourne, in consideration of those Lotts & Commons the which is resigned up to

---

6 This end of the divisional line agreed upon between Charlestown and Woburn, running from Cambridge [West Cambridge] bounds over the hills to the Northwest corner of "Mr. Nowell's lot," remained, till very recently, unchanged; leaving the extensive tract of land, known, till lately by the name of Charlestown End, and including the Gardner Farms, the farm of Mr. Luke Wyman, etc., etc., within the bounds of Charlestown. But by annexing to the other end of the line as here described, the 500 acres of commons with the lots and farms attached, which Charlestown by this agreement ceded to Woburn, and which comprised much of the land at Richardson's Row, and in South Woburn (now Winchester) the actual dividing line in this quarter was carried considerably to the East.

Wobourne out of Charlestowne Lands; and that the three thousand Acres shall lye in the place where Capt. Johnson & Saml. Richeson and others of Wobourne did shew us: That is to say, to begin at the uttermost Corner Northerly next Reading Line, & so to runne Southerly along two miles deepe on the East side of Shawshin [Billerice] Line till the full extent of the three thousand Acres bee out.

"Witness our hands this 16. of the X month [Dec. 16,] 1650. Subscribed by those appointed to order the Prudentiall affaires of the Towne of Wobourne.

"EDWARD JOHNSON	"ROBT. SEDGWICKE
JOHN MOUSALL	THOS. LYNDE
JAMES TOMSON	ROBT. HALE
EDWARD CONVERS	INCREASE NOWELL
RALPH HILL	JOHN GREENE." [38]
SAMLL. RICHESON."	

The appropriation of the town's lands to individual inhabitants was also, of course, another object of deep interest to the people, and of their early attention. The disposal of the land in Woburn, was originally vested in Charlestown, which appears accordingly to have made numerous grants of it to divers of its citizens, before Woburn was erected into a distinct township.[39]

[38] Charlestown Records, Vol. I., pp. 90, 91.
For the ultimate disposal of the 3,000 acres ceded in the above Report by Woburn to Charlestown, see Appendix, No. VI.

[39] Hence the repeated mention in Woburn Records of "Charlestown Lots";[a] and notices also of lots belonging to individual citizens of Charlestown, and bearing their names; as the Dunham lot, apparently near New Bridge, or North Woburn; Frodingham's [Frothingham's] lot, near Horn Pond; Burgess's lot; Davison's lot; and Shepardson's lot, which became eventually the homestead of James Convers, jr.[b] In 1640-1, before the incorporation of Woburn, Messrs. George Whitehand and George Bunker, both of Charlestown, surrendered their respective lots to the disposal of the [intended] town;[c] and the latter gentleman, for a full and valuable consideration paid to him by Woburn, gave Dec. 10th, 1663, a deed of a lot of his, consisting of 238 acres, assigned him by Charlestown, and lying within the bounds of Woburn, for the use of the town forever.[d] In 1654, Mr. Robert Long of Charlestown surrendered for the town's use, a lot or meadow, situate in the centre of Woburn, North and West of Rev. Thomas Carter's, granted him by Charlestown, and still known as *Long's*

[[a] Records, Vol. I., p. 7, 9.] [b] Records inverted, Vol. I., p. 10. [c] Records, Vol. I., 3, 4. [d] Records, Vol. I., p. 30.

At the incorporation of Woburn, this power of granting land within its bounds fell of right to the united body of its inhabitants, who thenceforth disposed of its lands, sometimes by vote in town meeting, and sometimes by their Selectmen in their name, or by committees specially chosen for the purpose. In one or other of these ways, much of the territory of the town was speedily appropriated. In the infancy of the town for instance, there were numerous grants both of upland and meadow to individuals admitted to be inhabitants, as their own proper freehold. To some of these grants was expressly annexed a condition, that they [the grantees] should bring testimonials of their peaceable behavior; or that they should continue in town five or more years. And for all of them, the grantees were required to pay twelve pence an acre for the use of the town. A portion likewise of the common land was reserved, with a pious forethought, very creditable to the first settlers, for succeeding officers of the church. And considerable tracts in various quarters of the town were set apart to be holden and improved by certain individuals in common, as Friendly or Boggy Meadow Field in or near Wilmington, Pleasant Field towards Reading, New Bridge Field in North Woburn, Plain Field on the way from the centre to Convers's mill, Waterfield at the West End, and Hungary Plain Field and Forest Hill Field in and near Burlington. And to prevent injury and hard thoughts among the owners in the use or cultivation of these common fields, it was early ordered that the Selectmen should set off to every proprietor his proportion of fence to maintain, and mark each end of one's share of fence with the initial letters of his name. But the cultivation of

---

Meadow; for which Woburn paid him in recompense thirty shillings.[e] And soon after the incorporation of Woburn, 1642, six of the commissioners for its settlement, viz., Edward Johnson, Edward Convers, John Mousall, and Messrs. Ezekiel, Samuel and Thomas Richardson, in consideration of divers benefits received (particularly meadow, commonage and planting ground) and others expected from the town, gave up all the land therein, which had been granted them "before the placing downe this Towne, near adjoining to the said towne" for the use of the town and the church of Woburn forever.[f]

[e] Records, Vol. I., p. 20. [f] Records, Vol. I., p. 6.

fields held in common having been productive of much uneasiness and contention, they have long since been divided in severalty among their respective proprietors.

And now this town of Woburn, having its affairs put in proper train, and under the direction of suitable officers, soon began to thrive and prosper. This is inferred in part from the increase in the number of its inhabitants and of its church members, during the first ten or twelve years from its incorporation in 1642. Judging from the number of the original subscribers to the Town Orders, which was only thirty-two (and all of them did not eventually become inhabitants), the first settlers in 1642 could hardly have exceeded thirty heads of families, and the founders of the church were only seven in number. But in 1652, the inhabitants of the town had increased to sixty families, and the members of the church to seventy-four. This we learn from the celebrated history of New England, called the "Wonder-working Providence of Zion's Saviour," written, and published in London in 1654, by Capt. Edward Johnson, a principal founder and distinguished citizen of Woburn, who gives in it the following account of the town, as it was at the time he wrote, in 1662.

"There was a Town and Church erected, called Wooburn, the present year [1642]. But because all the actions of this wandering people meet with great variety of censures, the author will, in this Town and Church, set down the manner how this people have populated their Towns, and gathered their Churches, etc., etc. This Town, as all others, had its bounds fixed by the General Court, to the contents of four miles square (beginning at the end of Charlestown bounds): the grant is to seven men of good and honest report, upon condition that within two years they erect houses for habitation thereon, and soe go on to make a Town thereof, upon the Act of Court. These seven men have power to give and grant out lands unto any persons who are willing to take up their dwellings within the said precinct, and to be admitted to all common privileges of the said Town; giving them such an ample portion, both of Medow and Upland, as their present and future stock of cattel and hands were like to improve, with eye had to others that might after come to populate the said Town. This they did without any respect of persons; yet such as were exorbitant, and of a turbulent spirit, unfit for a civil society, they would reject; till they come to mend their manners, such came not to enjoy any freehold. These seven men ordered and disposed of the streets of the Town, as might be best for improvement of the Land, and yet civil and religious society maintained: to which end, those that had land nearest the place for Sabbath assembly, had a lesser quantity at home; and more farther off to improve for corn of all kinds. They refused not men for their poverty, but according to their ability were helpful to the poorest sort in building their houses, and distributed to them land accordingly; the poorest had six or seven acres of Medow, and twenty-five of Upland, or thereabouts. Thus was this Town populated, to the number of sixty families or thereabout: and after this manner are the Towns of New England peopled. The scituation of this Town is in the highest part of the yet peopled land, neere upon the head springs of many considerable rivers, or their branches; as the first rise of *Ipswitch* river, and the rise of the Shashin river, one of the most considerable branches of Merrimeck, as also the first rise of Mistick river and ponds. It is very full of pleasant springs, and great variety of very good water, which the Summer's heat causeth to be more cooler, and the Winter's cold maketh more warmer: their Medows are not large, but lye in divers places to particular dwellings; the like doth their Springs. Their land is very fruitful in many places, although they have no great quantity of plain land in any one place; yet doth their Rocks and Swamps yield very good food for cattel; as also they have Mast and Tar for shipping, but the distance of place by land causeth them as yet to be unprofitable. They have great store of iron ore. Their meeting house stands in a small Plain where four streets meet. The people are very laborious, if not exceeding, some of them." [40]

"Now to declare how this people proceeded in religious matters and so consequently, all the Churches of Christ planted in New England; when they came at once to hopes of being such a competent number of people as might be able to maintain a Minister, they then surely seated themselves, and not before; it being as unnatural for a right N. E. [New England] man to live without an able Ministry, as for a Smith to work his iron without a fire. Therefore this people that went about placing down a Town, began the foundation

[40] Wonderworking Providence, Book II., Chap. XXII., p. 175., etc.

stone with earnest seeking of the Lord's assistance by humbling of their souls before him in daies of prayer, and imploring his aid in so weighty a work. Then they address themselves to attend counsel of the most Orthodox and ablest Christians, and more especially of such as the Lord had already placed in the Ministry, not rashly running together [to gather] themselves into a Church, before they had hopes of attaining an Officer to preach the Word, and administer the Seals unto them; chosing [choosing] rather to continue in fellowship with some other Church for their Christian watch over them, till the Lord would be pleased to provide," etc., etc.

[Here follows the author's account of the gathering of the Church of Woburn, and of the ordination of Rev. Mr. Carter, as summarily given above. He then proceeds as follows:]

"The people having provided a dwelling-house, built at the charge of the Town in general, welcomed him unto them with joy, that the Lord was pleased to give them such a blessing, that their eyes may see their Teachers. After this there were divers added to the Church daily after this manner. The person desirous to joyn with the Church, cometh to the Pastor and makes him acquainted therewith, declaring how the Lord hath been pleased to work his conversion: who discerning hopes of the persons' faith in Christ, although weak, yet if any appear, he is propounded to the Church in general for their approbation touching his godly life and conversation; and then by the Pastor and some brethren heard again, who make report to the Church of their charitable approving of the person. But before they come to joyn with the Church, all persons within the Towne have publike notice of it; then publikely he declares the manner of his conversion, and how the Lord hath been pleased, by the hearing of his Word preached, and the work of his Spirit in the inward parts of his soul, to bring him out of that natural darkness, which all men are by nature in and under; as also the measure of knowledge the Lord hath been pleased to indue him withal. And because some men cannot speak publikely to edification through bashfulness, the less is required of such; and women speak not publikely at all; for all that is desired is, to prevent the polluting the blessed Ordinances of Christ by such as walk scandalously, and that men and women do not eat and drink their own condemnation, in not discerning the Lord's body. After this manner, were many added to this Church of Christ; and those 7 [seven] "that joyned in Church fellowship at first, are now encreased to 74 persons, or thereabout. . . . . . After this manner have the Churches of Christ [in New England] had their beginning and progress hitherto; the Lord continue and encrease them the world throughout." — *W. W. Prov., Book* 11, *Chap. xxii., pp.* 175–181.

It has already been observed, that the original territory of Woburn, as granted to Charlestown in 1640, was four miles square. But this grant was encumbered with another grant of five hundred acres, to be laid out within the bounds of the four miles square, to Mr. Thomas Coytmore, a noted shipmaster, and a highly respected citizen of Charlestown. But before Capt. Coytmore could derive any benefit from this grant to him by the Court, he perished in a storm at sea; and his only son, Thomas Coytmore, jr., dying afterwards in his minority, the General Court, at their session in October 1656, confirmed the grant of 500 acres in Woburn, and also other lands and goods of Capt. Coytmore, to Mr. John Coggan, the then husband of Mrs. Martha, Capt. Coytmore's relict, on condition of his paying £200 to the four daughters of Capt. William Tyng by Elizabeth, Capt. Coytmore's sister.[41] In 1664, Mr. Coggan having deceased, the Coytmore grant in Woburn was claimed by Mr. Joseph Rock of Boston, administrator upon the estate of John Coggan and of Martha, his wife. And now the selectmen of Woburn, considering that even without that incumbrance, Woburn was smaller in point of territory than any other incorporated town in its vicinity, petitioned the Court in 1664, that they would order Mr. Rock's claim of 500 acres in Woburn to be laid out in some other place; and also that they would grant to Woburn four thousand acres of unappropriated land, wherever it might be found in this wilderness, and so do by this town as they had done already by the neighboring towns of Billerica and Reading.[42] In answer to the latter part of this petition, the Court at their session in October of that year, made a grant to Woburn of two thousand acres.[43] But they took no notice of the request in it to order

[41] Colony Records, Vol. IV., Part I., pp. 272, 273, 281.

[42] Woburn Records, Vol. I., p. 29.

[43] Woburn Records, Vol. I., p. 30. Colony Records, Vol. IV., Part II., p. 138. This grant was not laid out to Woburn till upwards of fifty years afterwards; and then, (as will be noted in a future portion of this history) through mismanagement, it proved of no permanent advantage to the town, but a source of contention for a long series of years.

the Coytmore grant, claimed by Mr. Rock, to be laid out elsewhere than in Woburn. And the following year, Mr. Rock sold it for £50 to Messrs. Francis and John Wyman of Woburn, to whom it was laid out by Mr. Jona Danforth, Surveyor, under direction of General Court's Committee, in the westerly and northwesterly parts of what is now Burlington, in October 1667.[44]

Shortly after the above petition to the Court for additional territory was presented, the distribution of a large part of what they already held in common became a subject of intense interest for several years to the citizens of Woburn. At a general meeting, Nov. 14, 1664, it was agreed by a major vote, that there should be a distribution of plough land and swamps, and a particular division of the remote timber; and a committee of seven was chosen to carry this vote into effect, according to justice and equity.[45] But the measure meeting with opposition, this committee did not venture to discharge their commission without further instructions from the town. And now arose a question of importance, Who the proprietors of the town were, among whom the proposed distribution was to be made? This question was decided at a public meeting, Feb. 27, 1665–6, at which it was voted, that "the right proprietors of the common lands of the towne of Woburne" were "those which had their names expressed in the deuiding the herbidg."[46] At the same meeting,

[44] Colony Records, Vol. IV., Part II., p. 356. Middlesex Registry of Deeds, Vol. III., pp. 149, 150.

[44] When Woburn Precinct, now Burlington, was incorporated in 1730, this tract of land was largely dwelt upon and improved by numerous Wymans, the posterity of the above named Francis and John Wyman. But now (1867) and for several years past, there has not been a Wyman in the place to bear up his ancestor's name, and to cultivate this portion of his land.

[45] Woburn Records, Vol. I., p. 29.

[46] Woburn Records, Vol. I., pp. 31, 32. Record of meeting, 27: 12mo. 1665 [Feb. 27, 1665–6]. The decision at this meeting, of the question, Who were the right proprietors? was not improbably grounded on the following order of the General Court, May 30, 1660: "It is ordered, that hereafter no cottage or dwelling place shall be admitted to the privildg of commonage for wood, timber, and herbage, or any other the priviledges that lye in common in any towne or peculiar, but such as are already in being, or hereafter shall be erected by the consent of the towne." — *Colony Records, Vol. V., Part* 1, p. 417.

a vote was passed, "for the diuission of all the lands and timber that belong in common to the said Towne, to the Inhabytance expressed by name as priuilidged by the vote of the Towne in the diuistion of herbidg," and also to three persons (viz: George Brush, John Craggen, and Increase Winn) admitted at that meeting to be inhabitants and "propriety of commonag," and to "noe other."[46] A committee of three likewise was chosen the same day, "to consider of a way of diuistion," to be propounded to the inhabitants at a future meeting, for their approbation and concurrence. The report of this committee was submitted at a meeting of the town, Jan. 28, 1666–7, when it was voted, that the way by which the land should be divided that yet lay in common, should be "by persons and esteats, saruants left out; the head of the family at twenty pound esteat, wifes and children at five pounds esteat." And at another general meeting, March 28, 1667, it was voted by the major part present, "*that all the land that lyeth in common, both land and timber*, shall bee deuided for proprietc [propriety] to the wright proprietors;" and furthermore, a committee of five was appointed at the same meeting, viz: Francis Kendall, John Wyman, Thomas Peirce, John Brooks, and Samuel Walker, sen., who were fully empowered by the town "to laye out the Common to propriety," according to the true intent and meaning of the votes of Jan. 28, 1666–7 and of March 28, 1667; and in order to this end, "to take a List of the persons and esteats of the wright proprietors." In pursuance of their appointment, this committee made out a Table exhibiting the names of all who had right in the common land of Woburn, and their respective proportions in it, according to their several persons and estates; by which Table, not only the present but all future divisions of the town's land were to be regulated. But this committee was not allowed to complete the whole business intrusted to them. Complaint being made, it seems, of some of their proceedings, the General Court chose Oct. 31, 1667, a committee of their own body, viz: Capt. Daniel Gookin, Mr. Thomas Danforth and Mr. Edward Collins, to settle the difficulties which had arisen in Woburn.[47]

[47] Colonial Records, Vol. IV., part II, pp. 354–5.

By these gentlemen, a new committee for the town was nominated, which was empowered to divide the land to be divided, to each proprietor his just proportion, according to his interest in the common land of the town. Accordingly this new committee, consisting of Capt. Edward Johnson, John Carter, Josiah Convers, John Wright and Thomas Peirce[48] did on Sept. 23, 1668, divide all the timber and wood growing or lying on the hither part of the common land in Woburn into eight grand divisions called eighths, each of which was subsequently to be more particularly divided among themselves by the persons expressly named as interested in it, according to the proportion to which each person was entitled in the whole of the common land of the town, and which was annexed to each man's name respectively.[49] In this way, the timber and wood growing or lying on various tracts of land in different quarters of the town, minutely described in the Records,[50] was divided among eighty proprietors, including the widow of Mr. Thomas Graves, of Charlestown, one of the original undertakers for the building up of Woburn; and as each person's proportional part of the timber and wood was confirmed by the committee "to him, his heirs and successors forever, and all hereafter growing on the same land,"[49] it is presumed that the town granted the land itself in progress of time, as it was wanted for cultivation, to those who with their successors were thus made perpetual proprietors of all its future growth; and this conjecture seems to be confirmed by the frequent occurrence, for many years, of the phrase, "where the top is already their own," or some equivalent expression in subsequent grants of land to individual persons.

At the same time, and by the same committee that made distribution of the wood and timber just spoken of, division was made of two extensive cedar swamps, situated in what is now Wilmington, one called Lebanon, the other Ladder Pole Swamp. Both these swamps were first divided into eighths, as nearly equal as might be to each other in their joint contents, that is, the sum of an eighth of one swamp added to an eighth in the

---

[48] Woburn Records, Vol. I., p. 80. [49] Records, Vol. I., p. 45. [50] Records, Vol. I., pp. 45–47.

other. Then one man, on behalf of all those who were named as interested in the same eighth with himself, drew by lot the place of his eighth; and then another man the place of his, etc. etc. After which, each eighth was to be particularly divided among themselves by those to whom it belonged, in proportion to their respective interests therein: the land, as well as cedar and timber, to belong to them and their heirs forever.[51]

To compensate the two committees above named, employed to effect the foregoing grand division of wood, timber and land, agreeably to vote of March 28, 1667, there was granted at a general meeting Feb. 26, 1677–8, by a major vote of the proprietors, as follows: To the Dividing Committee, Capt. Edward Johnson, Capt. John Carter, Mr. John Wright, Dea. Josiah Convers, and Sergeant Thomas Peirce, thirty acres of make meadow or swamp, "to sattisfy the said committee, and those that they sett to worke, for all the truble and pains that they were at, in deuiding the common lands into proprieties." To the proportioning committee, John Wyman, Francis Kendall, Sergeant Thomas Peirce, Samuel Walker and John Brooks, seven acres of make meadow or swamp, "to satisfy them for proportioning every man's right in the common lands."[48]

In 1673, there was another grand division of the common land of the town; viz: of timber land adjoining Billerica line and Maple Meadow in Wilmington. This land, amounting to above 500 acres, was distributed by lot among 80 proprietors, in proportion to their respective rights. For stating the lines of the great lots in which it was laid out, the town allowed the committee of four appointed for the work, twenty-four shillings, or six shillings apiece; and each proprietor was to give William Johnson, for setting off to him his proportion, and marking his lot in three places in every side line with the initials of his name, two pence an acre, in Indian corn at eight groats a bushel, or in other pay to Mr. Johnson's content: and the town was to pay one hand for carrying the chain all the time, two and sixpence a day.[52]

---

[51] Woburn Records, Vol. I., pp. 47-49.

[52] Woburn Records, Vol. I., pp. 41, 42.

Finally, in 1677, a large tract of common land, lying between Billerica line, Maple Meadow River and Reading line, and containing by estimation about four thousand acres, was the greater part of it divided proportionally between seventy-nine proprietors, besides a lot of sixty acres, reserved for a succeeding officer of the church. Provision was made that the Selectmen might from time to time lay out highways through this tract for the mutual accommodation of the proprietors, without allowance given for the land taken for this purpose; and William Johnson was employed to lay out the lots, for which each proprietor was to pay him twopence an acre in Indian corn, barley or rye, he furnishing a plot of the said land.[53] And after the division then made, there being still a residue of this tract undivided, it was granted Feb. 26, 1677–8, by an unanimous vote of the proprietors, to forty-four young men, who petitioned for it; and was divided among them by William Johnson for a compensation agreed upon by them.

This appears to have been the last extensive distribution of the common land in Woburn. More was yet left in various places, in comparatively small parcels, of which grants were occasionally made to different individuals. In a shattered record book still extant, commenced in 1739, and purporting to belong "to the proprietors of the common and undivided lands in Woburn and Wilmington," are recorded their proceedings at their meetings from time to time in relation to those lands; such as the appointment of committees to perambulate their lines, and to establish bounds; to lease their lands to individuals, and to receive their rents: and to prosecute at the law, such persons as trespassed upon their lands, unto final judgment.

At a meeting of the proprietors, May 17, 1739, and continued by adjournment to 1st Monday in September following, Messrs. Jacob Wright, Thomas Carter and Joseph Baldwin were chosen a committee with full power to lay out to each proprietor his just proportion of the common lands.[54] Accordingly with the help of Caleb Brooks, surveyor, this committee laid out a

---

[53] Woburn Records, Vol. I., pp. 77, 78, 79.

[54] Proprietors' book, p. 5.

large portion of these lands as directed; and at a meeting January 4, 1741 [1741–2] they presented a report of their doings in the premises, as far as they had proceeded; which report was accepted and ordered to be recorded.[55] From this report as recorded, it appears that they had laid out about 141 acres, lying in Wilmington "great lot," Wood Hill, on the west side of Clear Meadow brook, and on the east and west sides of Maple Meadow River, in seventy-seven lots to as many proprietors, and one lot retained by the proprietors themselves in common, and called the proprietors' lot. To defray the expense of this survey and division of the common lands, Low's Meadow had been previously sold, by order of the proprietors.[56] At a Proprietors' Meeting, May 26, 1763, voted to grant a place for a burial ground, and one for a pound, if places convenient for these purposes could be found.

The last grants by the proprietors, upon record in this book, were of stable lots near the meeting-house on the common, to Rev. Josiah Sherman, Dea. Eames and others, voted June 10, 1765. At the same time it was voted to grant horse stable lots to no others but proprietors.

At a general meeting of the town, December 7, 1741, and continued by adjournment to January 4, and February 8, 1741–2, it was apparently attempted to nullify the distinction between the proprietors of the common lands in Woburn, and other inhabitants of the town, with a view to prosecute the proprietors' committee, as intruders, in making division of those lands from time to time, as the votes of the proprietors had authorized them. But the town records being examined by a committee appointed for the purpose, it was probably found, that the town had for years recognized and acted upon the distinction, which was founded upon an order of the General Court in 1660, and the attempt failed. See Town Records, vol. VII., p. 380, 381, 382. See also Mass. Records, vol. IV., part I., p. 417: Town Records, vol. I., p. 31, 32.

---

[55] Proprietors' book, p. 9.

[56] Proprietors' book, pp. 7, 14, 15.

CHAPTER II.

Civil customs — Moral and Religious habits of the First Settlers — Town officers — Town meetings — Measures to prevent pauperism — Taxes paid largely in produce of Soil; Schooling, etc., etc., etc. — Death and brief notices of the Seven Commissoners for building up Woburn.

IN the First Chapter of this History of Woburn, we have seen the foundations of the town laid, its government organized, its lands, the larger portion of them, distributed among its early proprietors, and all its affairs, civil and ecclesiastical, brought into a regular and successful train. In this chapter, it may be useful as well as interesting to advert briefly to the civil customs and institutions of the town, and to the literary, moral and religious character of its founders, and of their immediate successors for the first fifty years, before we resume the thread of its history.

At the first election of town officers in Woburn in 1644, there were chosen only Selectmen, a Constable, and three Surveyors of the highways. In the record of that transaction, no mention is made of town clerk, treasurer, assessors, and other officers, whom both law and expediency have now rendered indispensable. The reason is, with regard to the town clerk, that the law did not then expressly require that officer to be chosen annually as it does now; and the people were not disposed to drop from the office one whom they had found hitherto to be faithful. Hence Woburn, for the first forty-eight years, had but two town clerks; Capt. Edward Johnson, chosen by the commissioners for its settlement in 1640, and continued in office by the good will of the people, without re-election, till his death in 1672; and William Johnson, Esq., his son, who was chosen clerk in 1672, and served the town in that capacity, without re-election, till 1688. And as to other town officers, they came gradually into distinct notice and use, as the increase of the public business, or the interest of the people rendered them necessary. For many years, the Selectmen were the keepers of the town's treasure, as well as the local guardians of its rights. In 1695 was the first, and till 1719 the only instance in Woburn, of the election of a town treasurer, distinctively as such; and the person chosen treasurer in 1719, and for several years afterward, was one of the Board of Selectmen.

For upwards of a century too, from the first planting of the town, the Selectmen *ex officio*, or by the uniform choice of the people, discharged the duties of Assessors and School Committee; and the constables were also collectors of taxes. In assessing Town and County Rates, however, the Selectmen used to be assisted by an officer, now unknown by name, but then annually chosen by the people, and called "Commissioner of the Rate."[1] Woburn had likewise in its early days three other commissioners, styled in the records, "Commissioners to end small causes." The appointment of such commissioners was sanctioned by law in all towns where there was no magistrate, and they constituted an inferior Court of Justice, having the powers of magistrates (excepting that of committing to prison); to hear and determine, according to their own best judgment, all causes in which one of the parties belonged to the town in which they presided, and in which, the debt, trespass or damage [did] not exceed forty shillings. In Woburn Records, they appear to have been elected by the people, with other town officers, but the law required them to be licensed by the County Court, or by the Board of Assistants.[2] They continued to be appointed in this town,

---

[1] Colony Laws, 1672, p. 23. Record of Choice of Town Officers for 1653. "Ensigne Carter, Commistionor for the Rate." Town Records, Vol. I., p. 18.

[2] Colony Laws, 1672, p. 20, Colony Records, Vol. II. p. 188. Extract from "Choyce of Town Officers the 25, of 12 mo. 1650." [25 Feb. 1650-1.]

"Commissionor to carry the Votes to Cambridge, James Tompson."

"EDWARD JOHNSON,
EDWARD CONUARS,
JOHN MOUSALL,
JOHN WRIGHT,
JAMES TOMPSON,
SAMUEL RICHISON,
RALPH HILL," *Selectmen.*

"EDWARD JOHNSON,
EDWARD CONUARS, [Convers.]
JOHN MOUSALL,"
"Deputy, EDWARD JOHNSON."
Commissionors to end Small Causes.

Town Records, Vol. I., p, 16.

though not uniformly every year, till 1674; were frequently the same persons as three of the Selectmen; and were always men of great weight of character, and of principal influence in the town.

The time originally agreed upon by the inhabitants of Woburn, 1644, for the choice of town officers, was "the first third day of the weeke in the first month;" that is, the first Tuesday in March. But the very next year, 1645, the people anticipated their appointed time for this transaction. A deep snow falling the latter part of the winter, which proved a great obstruction to other business, some persons from a wish "to redeem time," prevailed to have the town officers elected Febuary 19th, of that year. In 1647, the town voted to choose its officers on the first *Monday* of March annually, instead of the first *Tuesday*. And the next year but one, 1649, the day for this purpose was again altered, by vote of the town, to the last Tuesday in February; on which day, the people were ordered to meet every year for this business without further warning.[3] And this continued to be the day for the election of town officers in Woburn, till 1692, when by a law of the Province, all such elections were required to be made in March.

At the time Woburn anciently chose its town officers, it was likewise accustomed to choose deputies to the General Court. For this service, it rarely employed more than one person, but it sometimes did two. And as the law then allowed towns to elect persons who were resident anywhere within the Colony, to represent them in the Legislature, provided they were freemen, it sometimes happened, that one or both the deputies for Woburn belonged to Boston.[4] As a compensation for his services, the town voted, 1645, to allow their deputy sixpence per day, beside his board.[5] And to save expense in the latter article, they

3 Town Records, Vol. I., pp. 5, 7, 11, 14.

4 Deputies from Woburn for 1670, 1671, Capt. Edward Johnson, Mr. Humphrey Davie of Boston; for 1672, 1673, Mr. Humphrey Davie, Capt. Edward Hutchinson, of Boston. The following record intimates, that deputies were sometimes chosen for only part of a year, or a single session. " Mr. Humphary Dauie was chosen deputy for the whole yeare 1675." —*Town Records, Vol. I., p.* 59.

5 Town Records, Vol. I., p. 7.

sometimes sent him corn, to be made into bread for his own use, if he belonged to Woburn; but if he were a citizen of Boston, or if, though an inhabitant of Woburn, he chose to provide his board in his own way, while attending the Legislature on the town's behalf, they were constrained to pay him for his services in solid coin.[6] But penurious as the people may seem to have been in the stated compensation of their deputy, they could at times be generous. At a General Meeting, Nov. 16, 1674, the inhabitants of Woburn resolved as follows, on behalf of one of their deputies, who had represented them that year and several years before, and who was a resident of Boston. "Voted that there shold bee tenne cord of wood gotten at the town's charge, and delivered on the wharf at boston as a gratuity for the good saruise Mr. Humphary Dauie hath dune this Towne at the generall Courte." — *Woburn Records, Vol. II., p.* 18.

The municipal regulations of the early inhabitants of the town are deserving of the notice, and, in many instances, of the imitation of their successors.

The selectmen were accustomed to meet statedly on the first Monday of every month, for the transaction of public business. And lest the interests of the town should suffer at any time, through their dilatoriness or neglect to attend on such occasions, they agreed, March 11, 1674, that if any Selectman should fail to make his appearance at the place of meeting, by 9 o'clock of the morning, their appointed hour, he should pay three shillings to the use of the town, unless he were detained by some providence of God, which the majority present should account a sufficient excuse. And at their very next meeting, it is recorded, that they fined Capt. John Carter, one of their number, *sixpence,* for "being nere an hour to [too] late;" and shortly after, Francis Kendall, another member of their body, for a like omission of duty, was fined the same sum.[7]

---

[6] "The town Dr. in the year 1674:" To deputy's dyet . £02 : 05 : 00.

"To Gershom Flagg for bringing down Corne for deputy's dyet	00 : 02 : 00.
"To deputy's dyet, silver	01 : 16 : 00.

Town Records, Vol. II., pp. 22,31.

[7] Town Records, Vol. II., p. 167, 168, inverted.

The primitive inhabitants too, of Woburn, were zealous to secure a full and punctual attendance of its citizens at all its general meetings, and to preserve among themselves a due esteem of their civil privileges. As early as 1643, they passed an order, "That if any man shall absent himselfe from a publike meeting without a lawfull excuse, hee shall pay 18*d.* to the use of the Towne."[8] And in February, 1648–9, there was a vote of the town imposing a fine of two shillings, for the town's use, upon any inhabitant who should fail to appear by eight o'clock of the morning at any stated annual meeting for election, though unwarned; or who should withdraw on such an occasion, without leave of the assembly, more than a quarter of an hour before the meeting was dissolved; or who should be absent or tardy at any public meeting whatever, that had been legally warned.[8] And that this vote might not stand on their records a mere empty form of words, without force or effect, it was ordered by the whole town, present at their annual meeting, 1653–4, that the constable for the time being, should call over the persons warned to appear at every town meeting, and should gather up the fines of all such as are found delinquent for non-appearance, agreeably to the vote just cited, changing only the time of appearing from eight o'clock in the morning to nine.[9]

Nor was there less concern manifested to secure a civil, peaceable behavior at public meetings, than constancy and punctuality of attendance. The fathers of the town took care on all occasions to maintain their authority before the people, and failed not to punish any, who shewed openly before them a disposition to contemn or resist it. In 1664, for instance, they passed an order, allowing the inhabitants freely to present their grievances at any general meeting, either by word or writing, provided they did it in a becoming manner, and with the leave of the moderator; but imposing a fine of five shillings for the town's use upon any one who should presume on such occasions to speak disorderly, or go on to take up the time of the town unnecessarily.[10] And a few years afterward, they fined Nathanael

[8] Town Records, Vol. I., pp. 5, 14.

[9] Town Records, Vol. I., p. 19.

[10] Town Records, Vol. I., p. 30.

Richardson, ten shillings for publicly charging them "with trampling him under their feet and wronging him, and for twitting them of putting themselves in place, with a stuborne, unciuill carige."[11]

In the infancy of the town, no one was allowed to become an inhabitant of it, or to acquire in it any freehold, right of common, or other civil privilege, without first producing evidence of his peaceable behavior, and obtaining the approbation of the Selectmen, or consent of the town by vote at some public meeting.[12] And to guard against the intrusion of suspicious characters, and preventing any from gaining a legal settlement here in a clandestine manner, one of the original Town Orders provided that no person should entertain any inmate, whether married or otherwise, for more than three days, without the consent of four Selectmen; and that every one offending in this particular should forfeit sixpence to the use of the town for every day that he should offend herein.

---

[11] Town Records, Vol. II., p. 18. To the above may be added another instance. 1674 : 1 : 10 mo George Polly summoned to appear before the Seclectmen for harbouring Inmates contrary to Town Orders. In answering to the charge, Polly declared that "he wold entertaine them for all the townsmen; and that the woman shold not goe out of towne for any of them." Upon this, the Selectmen granted distress upon Polly's estate to the value of eight shillings. But Polly afterward coming before them, and humbling himself, and "acknowledging his false charges, and promising that he wold clere the Towne of the forsaid Inmates by the next second daye at night, then the Constable was ordered to respet his distress; but in case the said Polly did not goe on to perform his promise, then the Constable was to goe on to leuey (levy) the eaight shillings for the Towne's use." *Town Records, Vol. I., p.* 57. No trifling with such town officers as these.

[12] 6 : 11 mo : 1648, [6 Jan. 1648-9.] "William Chamberlin admited an Inhabitant of this Towne, and permited to by land for his conuenency in any place thereof, prouided he unsetle not any Inhabitant, and bring testimony of his peacibl behauour, which is not in the least mesur [measure] questioned." Town Records, Vol. I., p. 13.

At a generall meetting 27: 12 mo: 1665, [27 Feb. 1665-6.] Gorge Brush, John Craggen and Increse Winne were admited Inhabitance and propriety of comoneg" [commonage].—*Woburn Records, Vol. I., p.* 31.

At a meeting of the Selectmen 5 : 12 mo : 1676, [5 Feb. 1676-7.] "John Hews of Watertowne is permitted to come into Towne, and follow his trade of weauing."—*Records, Vol. II., p.* 52.

This order appears to have been rigorously enforced for a long series of years.[13] And though, in a few instances, it may have operated hardly, and to the public disadvantage, yet it doubtless did much towards securing that freedom from the burdens of pauperism which the town for a long time, with but little interruption, happily enjoyed. The first two instances in which the town had occasion to grant help to any of its inhabitants, occurred in the years 1665, 1673. But the persons here referred to as assisted by the town, were not, strictly speaking, paupers, but insane. They both were possessed of houses and lands in Woburn; but being, by the hand of God, bereft of their reason, and so rendered incapable of managing for themselves, the Selectmen took both of them (one of them by order of the County Court) under their care, and disposed of their property for them to their best advantage. And in this situation, they both lived long enough to exhaust all they had in their maintenance, and were buried at last at the charge of the town. The first decisive pauper case in Woburn did not occur till the town had been settled about forty years, and is that referred to in the following extract from the records; "The Selectmen agreed with John Brooks, for the keeping of Goarge Wilkinson, from this 4 of April, 1681, till next Michealmas; and in case more than ordinary sickness come, then the Towne to consider the charge."[14] Wilkinson had been a soldier in Philip's Indian war, in 1675–76, and there, probably, had exhausted both his

---

[13] "The selectmen mett the 7: of the 4 mo: 1675, and called Joseph Knight, jun. to an accoumpt [account] for entertaining to [two] Inmats; and hee breaking the Towne Order, is fined three shillings, and to giue in a bond of fiuety pounds to free the Towne of all damage that may come to them by these too persons, namely, Jacob Hurd and Nathanell Wilson, his [Hurd's] apprentis." [Here follows his bond.]

"At the same time, the Selectmen caled Dauid Wyman, to answer for entertaining the widow Farmer as an Inmate in his hows: the said Dauid hauing bin conuicted before the Selectmen for breach of a towne order, is sentanced to paye seuen shillings for fourteen days entertainment." — *Record, Vol.* II., p. 26.

Similar instances of enforcing this Town Order may be seen, Record, Vol. I., p. 74, 113, etc., etc.

[14] Town Records, Vol. III., pp. 6, 47.

strength and what property he had in the public service; and now, feeble in health, and poor in estate, he was obliged to throw himself on the care of the town. He died in 1683, and was buried at the town's expense.[14]

Observable, too, are the means employed by the early inhabitants of Woburn, with the sanction of the law,[15] to prevent or break up all those irregular and vicious habits, which usually terminate in pauperism, or lead to confirmed depravity and spiritual ruin. Among these means, was the appointment of Tithingmen, whose office it was, as the records express it, "to have the oversight of their neighbours, and see that they keepe good orders in their houses." The object of their appointment, under the Colony laws, appears to have been to advance the divine honor and the spiritual benefit of the people, by encouraging family worship and government, by checking or preventing disorderly conduct in private families and public houses; by suppressing or checking profanity, Sabbath breaking, idleness, intemperance, and sundry other immoralities. With these ends in view, all the inhabitants were distributed into companies of nine or ten adjacent families each; and then these several companies were committed to the inspection of as many overseers, called tithingmen, or tenth men, from their having a tithing or a company of ten families each to look after, inclusively of their own. These tithingmen appear, in Woburn, to have been annually chosen by the Selectmen;[16] were wont to be men of the

[16] At a meeting of the Selectmen, 9 : 4 mo : [June 9th] 1676, "the tithing men were-chosen, who by law are to haue the oversight of their naighbours, and see that they keepe good orders in their howses : who are decon Josiah Conuars, Sargent Mathew Johnson, Ffrances Kendall, Robert Peirce, Allen Conuars, Henery Bolden, John Russell, Joseph Wright, and Joseph Richison.

[17] "At a meeting of the Selectmen 5. of 5 mo, [5 July] 1680, nine persons are named as Tithingmen, and the names of all the heads of the families, (82 in all) which were severally assigned to them for their inspection in their respective districts.

[18] "Ffebrewary ye, 1st, 1691-2 ye Selectmen of Wobourne met & chose tithingmen (for said Towne) for ye year ensuing: and their names are as follows :

[15] Colony Records, Vol. V., pp. 133, 240, 241, 373. [16] Town Records, Vol. II., p. 37. [17] Town Records, Vol. II., pp. 153, 154. [18] Town Records, Vol. III., p. 31.

first respectability in the town; were required by law to make complaint of what they saw amiss in any under their inspection, to the nearest magistrate, to be dealt with and punished by him, or by the County Court; and being sworn to the faithful discharge of their office, they were often doubtless very serviceable for checking the profanation of God's name, day and house, and for the promotion of peaceableness, sobriety and religion in the families commended to their care and watch.

In the early days of Woburn, taxes were not paid wholly in money or labor, as now. Silver was then scarce; and paper currency had not as yet been introduced. Hence the first inhabitants were accustomed to pay only a certain part of their taxes of every description, in money; and the rest in cattle, in corn, or other fruits of the soil, or in articles of home manufacture.[19] For instance, only a fourth part of the annual salary of their first, and of their second minister, was satisfied with coin; the remainder being made up in grain, or other articles of family consumption, which were called "country pay." And country pay was made great use of, too, in discharging their Town and Colony taxes, which occasioned no small inconvenience to the Constables,

---

"For ye West End of sd Towne, — Thomas Kendall & Benjam. Simons.
For ye South End, — Edwd Convers.
For ye East End, — Samuell Richardson.
For ye Towne, [centre of] — John Mousall, John Berbeen, and Joseph Winn.
For New Bridge End, — Lt. Joseph Peirce.
For Boggy Meadow End, — John Wright, Senr.
For Totman's End, — Joseph Richardson.
For Shawshenn End, — Edward Johnson."

"These eleven persons are chosen to inspect these famalyes near adjasent to each of ye [their] dwellings, according to the law intitled Tithingmen." [18] N. B. May 2d, 1692. The Selectmen chose Jona. Tompson for New Bridge, and Daniel Baldwin and John Brooks for the Centre, in the room of Joseph Peirce, Joseph Winn and John Burbeen, Senr., chosen Selectmen Feb. 23, and unwilling on that account to serve as tithingmen.[18]

[19] "Received of Jacob Wyman, Constable of Woobourne, the summe of £3 : 6s. in Shoos : and £5 : 4s. in and as money, in all is eight pound ten shillings. in or as money, being in full for their Town's County Rate made January 20th, 1692-3. I say Recd by me.

Samll. Andrew, County Treasurer." — *Records, Vol. III., p.* 52.

especially when the articles of country pay were so bulky as to put them to extraordinary expense in conveying them to Boston, or proved, when there, of an unmerchantable quality,—cases in which the Colony Treasurer was not apt to make them any allowance, and the Town (it may be presumed) if it did it, would do it with reluctance. Of the troubles, in which, from this cause, the Constables were liable to be not unfrequently involved, the annexed Treasurer's certificate, and Constable's charge, copied from the records, may serve as illustrations.

"Boston, October 21, 1679. Received of John Ted, (Tidd) and John Barbene, (Burbean,) Constables of Woburne, the whole of the six Rates of June 1677, and of the three Rates of November 1677; save only they detaine in their hands eight pound for transportation; which I cannot allow of, not having allowed it to other townes; and therefore it must be assigned by some superior authority. Otherwise, I say, received and allowed sd. rates. John Hull, Treasurer."[20]

"The Town Dr. 1673. To James Fowle, (Constable in 1672.)

"For loss of Corne, and more than ordinary troupble, £01 : 00 : 00."[21]

Concerning schools, and the attention bestowed on the education of the young, in the early history of Woburn, I find nothing on record prior to 1673. From this circumstance, however, it cannot be certainly inferred that no school had been sustained in this town during the thirty years which had then elapsed from its settlement. For very possibly the records are deficient on this head. The law too of that day, while it strictly required that a school for teaching to read and write should be kept in every town containing fifty householders, still allowed the means of its support to be drawn either from the parents and guardians of the children who attended it, or from the town at large.[15] Hence it is very possible that a school answering to the description of the law, may have been kept for years previous to the above-mentioned date; and yet, the compensation of its instructor coming directly from the parents or guardians of its pupils, and not from the town, there was no necessity of recording it in the Town Book.

In a town account for 1673, the town is made "Dr. to Allen

---

[20] Records, Vol. II., p. 143.

[21] Records, Vol. II., p. 4.

[15] Mass. Colony Records, Vol. II., p. 203.

Conuars' wife and Joseph Wright's wife for scooling, £00. 10s. 00d." [16] From this charge, compared with others presently to be quoted, these dames appear to have taught the same school, each of them half of the time stipulated, in 1673, and to have received from the town ten shillings for their year's work, to be divided equally between them. At a meeting of the Selectmen, Oct. 5, 1674, "they agreed with Jonathan Tomson to tech biger children, and Allen Conuars' wife to tech leser children." [17] And agreeably to this arrangement, goodman Thompson and goodwife Convers took charge, in 1675, of the children respectively assigned them, and were allowed by the Town £1. 00. 00 between them for "teching to reade," as the Records express it.[18] In 1676, the Town stands indebted on the town accounts to Allen Convers £1.00 "for too [two] years scoollinge"; without specifying the years he taught.[19] March 1, 1678, the Town is made debtor, by account, to Allen Convers' wife for schooling, [probably in 1677] £00. 10. 00.; and in 1679, to John Houlton, Sen., "for his wife's schooling, and worke [done by him?] on the 'Meeting hows,' £00. 14. 06." [20] At a meeting of the Selectmen, March 1, 1679–80, the widow Convers was appointed to teach school for that year;[21] and for this service, she was allowed ten shillings in a subsequent town account.[22]

In 1685, the town having increased indisputably to the number of one hundred families, or householders, and so being obliged by law to set up a grammar school, the instructor whereof should be able "to instruct youth so as to fit them for the college," the Selectmen appointed Mr. Samuel Carter, probably a son of Rev. Thomas Carter, their pastor, a graduate of Harvard College in 1660, and then resident in Woburn, to keep a grammar school that year, with a salary of £5. 00 per annum.[23] But, though Mr. Carter was doubtless competent to teach such a school, there were *no scholars to attend it.* The following Spring, the Selectmen appointed the widow Walker

---

[16] Town Records, Vol. II., p. 4. [17] Town Records, Vol. II., p. 166, inverted. [18] Town Records, Vol. II., p. 34. [19] Town Records, Vol. II., 56. [20] Town Records, Vol. I., p. 83, 96. [21] Town Records, Vol. II., p. 152. [22] Town Records, Vol. II., p. 107. [23] Town Records, Vol. I., p. 129.

"to be a school dame for the yeare 1686, and to haue tenn shillings for her labor, as the other [mistresses before her] had."[24] Likewise, at the same meeting, the Selectmen, feeling unwilling to expose the town to the penalty of ten pounds, prescribed by law for neglect to keep a grammar school by towns of one hundred families each, and yet reluctant to obligate themselves to pay a master five pounds the second time for doing nothing, (as they seem to have been apprehensive they should have to, if they positively engaged to give that sum) again employed Mr. Carter to keep such a school in Woburn, in 1686, but promised, *absolutely*, to give him only thirty shillings in pay for that year; but that if he should have any scholars, they would give him five pounds, as they had stipulated to give him the year before.[23] Doubtless Mr. Carter, in consenting to these terms, cherished a confident hope, that there were a few boys, at least, in the town who would discover ambition enough to sit that year under the instructions of a grammar school master, and so his full pay might be secured. But, alas, the apprehensions on this score which the Selectmen seem to have conceived, in making their engagement with him, were but too fully realized. No scholars attended grammar school in Woburn in 1686, as none had attended in 1685. And in a town account for 1685 and 1686, Mr. Carter stands credited £6. 10*s.* for schooling in Woburn during those two years, when he had no scholars to teach, and all the room and time to himself.[25]

In view of the foregoing statements, some perhaps may be ready to conclude, that the inhabitants of Woburn at that day were a boorish race, who had no value for good learning themselves, and grudged the least expense for procuring its benefits for their children. But this, without much qualification, would be a rash and most unjust inference. For in the very infancy of the town, when they do not certainly appear to have had any school for their own children, they contributed £ 5. 13*s.* 7½*d.* [sterling?] for the benefit of the scholars at the College in Cambridge,—a larger sum than was given at that time for this end by any town

[24] Town Records, Vol. III., p. 93.

[25] Town Records, Vol. III., p. 102.

in this County but two, not excepting even Cambridge itself, and larger than by any town in the Colony but five.[26] And in 1669, a little before the time when they commenced paying, as a town, the paltry sum of ten shillings per annum for the support of common schools among themselves, they contributed £ 27. 2*s.* 0*d.* for the erection of a new College in Cambridge[26],—a contribution in which they were not exceeded by any town in Middlesex County, excepting Cambridge, Charlestown, Watertown, Concord and Reading. There can be no question then, that the primitive inhabitants of Woburn were favorable to the cause of education at the college, and disposed to patronize it according to their power. And they were so probably from various motives; and more especially, because, in common with the generality of the first settlers of New England, they regarded a liberal education as a necessary prerequisite to a learned ministry; as an indispensable means of training up a competent number of young men for becoming thoroughly qualified to dispense the word of life to the people, when the accomplished ministers who had accompanied them from England should sleep in the dust. But at the same time, there were but few in the town, who duly appreciated the value of learning to any beside *professional* men.

Through the influence of prejudices imbibed and habits formed on the other side of the Atlantic, the great majority could not perceive the utility of general knowledge, beyond an ability to read and write, to those who were destined all their days to follow the plough, or to work in their shops. And hence they were slow to establish institutions among themselves designed to promote this end, and sparing of their hard-earned money to encourage them. They all unquestionably approved of grammar schools in general, because they would not see the learning taught therein "buried in the graves of (their) forefathers in church and commonwealth;" and particularly because they regarded these institutions as helpful to the advancement of the leading object for which the college was founded. Of common

---

[26] Quincy's History of Harvard University, Vol. I. p. 456, 509.

schools, likewise, they generally approved, as very necessary aids in families in which the parents could not read themselves, for teaching the children to read the Bible, and to repeat the Catechism,—exercises accounted at that time as alike indispensable to the youth of all classes and occupations in society. But then at that day, few or none of the young men of Woburn seem to have manifested a predilection for a professional life; in which alone, it was generally supposed there, that classical literature could be useful. And there were not then many families in the place, especially in the outskirts of the town, but could more conveniently teach their children to read at home, or in small private schools kept in their immediate vicinity, and maintained by themselves, than they could send them to a common school at a distance from their thinly-scattered dwellings, and over their rough and widely separated roads. Hence, when agreeably to law, they founded both a common and a grammar school in or near the centre of their settlement, for such children as might be sent to them, none went at first to the grammar school, and but few seemingly attended the common school. As the labor of teaching these few was comparatively but light, so the compensation allowed for it was but small; and as it was performed, such as it was, quite as ably by women as by men, so the Selectmen made no distinction in the wages of either, but paid instructors of each sex alike.

With regard to the moral and religious character of the early inhabitants of Woburn, the principal source of information at the present day is the Town Records; and these exhibit many traces of that high standard of virtue and piety, drawn from the Word of God, which the Puritan settlers of New England had generally adopted, and of the strenuous measures which they took to secure a prevailing conformity to it. They disclose many facts, which go to show the predominance of a correct moral sense in the primitive settlers of this place, and which indicate an earnest desire on their part, and especially on the part of the civil fathers of the town, for the suppression of vice and irreligion, and for the promotion of good morals and strict piety among themselves and their children after them.

Nor does it detract materially from the weight of their evidence on this head, that these facts do in many instances relate to measures of the Selectmen, taken in compliance with the then existing laws of the country. In arbitrary governments, external obedience to laws even of a good moral tendency, originating as they do solely in the will, and enforced by the coercive arm of the sovereign, is no certain sign of virtue in the people. But in such a government as ours has been from the beginning, where the laws have always proceeded from the will, and been executed with the consent of a majority of the people, ready and prevalent obedience to such laws is a strong token at least of general soundness of morals. Under such a government, the passing of good laws for the prevention and punishment of vice and crime, and for the encouragement of virtuous manners and habits, and the impartial, undisturbed, execution of them, both combined, constitute a powerful argument of the prevalence of correct moral sentiment in any community; for without such a sentiment, they would hardly have been *enacted*, much less would they have been *enforced*, without opposition. And, therefore, whenever in a free community we see such laws for the promotion of virtue and piety made, and not suffered to remain a dead letter on the Statute Book, but promptly, quietly and without resistance carried into effect, there, we may reasonably presume, that sound morals and real religion do generally predominate. And much evidence of this description have we, beside some other, that your early ancestors were generally exemplary in their moral and religious character and habits.

1. The first settlers of Woburn, and their immediate descendants were a very industrious, as well as a hardy, courageous race of men. According to the testimony of Capt. Edward Johnson, who was one of them, and a principal sharer in all their toils and hardships, they were "very laborious, if not exceeding, some of them."[27] They were frugal of their time, diligent in their respective occupations and callings, and gave no countenance to idleness or dissipation. And, accordingly, we

---

[27] Wonderworking Providence, Book II., Chap. XXII.

find the Selectmen of those times exercising their authority, in one instance at least, in passing censure upon an individual of highly respectable connections, who was indolent and improvident in his habits. At a meeting of the Selectmen, Jan. 13, 1698–9, "John Carter, Jun., was sent for, and animadverted [upon] for mispending his time, and admonished to improve it better for the futer, or else he might expect some other cource would be taken."[28] Economy of time was indeed in that day a virtue, to which dire necessity compelled, as well as correct principle inclined them. And as proofs as well as fruits of their prevailing, virtuous industry, great changes were wrought in their condition for the better, during the first fifty years from the settlement of the town. On coming hither to take up their abode, they found no convenient houses to shelter them, or fields prepared for culture. All around them was a dense forest, or a dreary waste, infested with wolves,[29] and traversed as yet by no human beings, except savage Indians, the report or experience of whose occasional cruelties could not but keep

---

[28] Town Records, Vol. IV., p. 125.

[29] The following passages, from the Records, indicate that wolves originally were numerous and destructive in Woburn:—

"Izack Brooks haueing ingaiged to set traps from time to time in a spring betweene Wood hill and Maple medow Playne to *cach Wolues*, hee haueing bin at Charge to alure [allure] the wolues thether; all other persons are prohibited to set any traps at the same place, soe long as Izack Brooks liueth, and shall goe on to improue it for the same end or use." — *Records, Vol. I., p. 52, Genl Meeting 24 : 12 mo : 1673.* [24 *Feb.*, 1673–4.]

The town is Cr., 1676, by cash paid

	"To Francis Kendall for a wolfe	00 :10 :00.
	"To widow Nutting for a wolfe	00 :10 :00.
	"To Izack Brooks for a wolfe	00 :10 :00."
		(*Records, Vol. II., p.* 56.)
1677.	"To Izack Brooks, wolues, by County's order	03 :00 :00.
		(*Records, Vol. II., p.* 65.)
17 :7mo. 1677.	"To Izack Brooks, for a wolfe	00 :10 :00."
		(*Records, Vol. II., p.* 74.)
In 1677.	"To Izack Brooks, for two wolues [two wolves]	01 :00 :00."
		(*Records, Vol. II., p.* 84.)

Among other noted places in Woburn, in former days, was "the Ould Wolfe penne."—*Records, Vol. I., p.* 88.

them in a state of constant anxiety, fear or alarm. Their first dwellings were but mean buildings; and their provision of food for some years, it is likely, was quite as plain, precarious and scanty, as that of the Indians to whom they had succeeded. But in the course of fifty years, the Indians had been beaten and effectually checked in Philip's war, in the dangers and hardships of which, the inhabitants of Woburn (as I may have occasion to show hereafter) bore their part. The ferocious wolves they had driven back in good measure from their borders to remote forests, and kept them at bay there. Their patient, persevering labor had gradually subdued their rough, uncultivated soil. And the close of half a century from the foundation of the town found them, generally speaking, in possession of thriving farms and orchards, of houses far more commodious than the first, and furnished with many of the comforts and delights of life.

2. The records furnish pleasing evidence, that the primitive inhabitants of the town were generally speaking, a just people; lovers of equity and fairness of dealing. We there find the Selectmen repeatedly interposing (as the laws empowered them to do) to punish oppression. And the specimens there exhibited of the bargains and covenants made by the Selectmen themselves with individuals in the town's employ, or to whom they leased its common lands, while they discover great shrewdness and foresight to save the town from harm, do also manifest a commendable disposition to deal honorably and equitably with those with whom they had to do. Take the following, as instances of their dislike of hard dealing.

" The Selectmen mett the 1: 11 mo: 1676: and summonsed Hopestill Foster for inordinate wages, and [he] is refer'd to hering the next Towne meeting."

" The Selectmen meet the 5: of 12 mo: 1676: and fined Hopestill Foster, for opresion [oppression] in a case depending betweene Josiah Conuars and himselfe about making brads; two shillings, eight pence of it to the said Josiah Conuars."

"Also in a case depending betweene Mathew Johnson and the said Foster, for opresion in making streak nayls and putting in riuits [rivets] in cart boxes, eleven shillings; six of it to the complainer." — *Records, Vol. II., p.* 58.

3. Similar tokens do the Records set before us of the mercifulness and compassion of the people of Woburn at that day, towards those who were suffering adversity. In various instances, they present the people, or their agents, the Selectmen, remitting taxes to the aged and unfortunate, commiserating the poor and destitute, and restoring lands to *children*, which, through the hand of God upon their parents, had fallen into the possession of the town. Of this amiable trait in their character, the following instances, among a number that might be produced, may serve both as illustrations and as proofs. At a general meeting, March 1, 1696–7, voted that "considering that Benjn Wilson, having mett with considerable losses, and is very poore, altho' he be found very diligent in his place, he shall goe rate free for this yeare, to all rates and taxes whatsoever." [30]

Sept. 9, 1700. "The Selectmen being informed that the widow Hensher [Henshaw] was in want, they ordered the Constable Holding to pay her fiue shillings for a present supplye, out of the Town Rate comitted to him to collect.[31]

"October the 27th. there was a contribution made for the widow Hensher: there was then gathered 3^{lb} : 15 : 3 : and the Selectmen provided a cow for her supplye with milk, and the cow cost 59 shillings, and the cow remains the town's, only the said widow hath the use of the cow free; and the Selectmen layd out 7^{s} : 6^{d}. for cloth to make her dumb child a coat, and 3^{s} : 6^{d}. for a pair of shoos; and the remainder of the said contribution, being 6^{s} : 3^{d}, it was deliuered to the said widow by the Selectmen." [31]

4. Of the character of the people in general for *sobriety*, we may form some judgment in their favor from the exertions then made and sustained, without complaint or opposition, against the contrary vice. The records furnish repeated testimonials to the zeal and faithfulness of the early civil fathers of the town to carry the laws against intemperance, and practices which lead to

[30] Town Records, Vol. IV., p. 87.

[31] Town Records, Vol. IV., p. 166.

it- into execution. They present them again and again, as summoning before them persons charged with intoxication, and sentencing them, upon conviction, to pay a fine, or to sit in the stocks. The following are instances upon record of their proceedings on this head. "The Selectmen meet the 17. of 7 mo. 1677: William Deane was sumoned for excess in drincke, and [they] ordered him to pay for his ecsess three shillings and fourpence." [32] "The Selectmen mette the 1: of 2 mo. 1678, and by warrant sent for William Deane, who was proved to be in drink the third time; [and] is sentanced to paye ten shillings uppon the Constable's demand." [33] At a meeting of the Selectmen 3: 8 mo. 1682, William Deane was fined the thurd time for being druncke, tenne shillings, or to sitt in the stocks." [34] Jan. 22, 1679, Andrew Pittamy, Indian, and his squaw, and another squaw, being taken drunck, were all brought before the Selectmen of Woburne, and the case heard and proued, were sentenced to paye tenne shillings apeece, or to be whipt tenne lashes, and to defray the charge of Constable and witnesses." [35] "John Johnson, jun. being taken in drinck, was sentenced to paye tenne groats." [35]

Such was the rigor with which the laws were anciently enforced in this town against persons chargeable with intemperance. Nor did the civil authorities frown upon the hard drinker only, but also, in some cases at least, upon those, who were accessary to his bad practices. The first person apparently, that was approved by the Selectmen to keep tavern in Woburn, and recommended for a license to sell spiritous liquors, was Mr. Samuel Walker, Senr., in 1675.[36] Mr. Walker was a highly respectable citizen, and one who was, generally speaking, of an irreproachable character. Nevertheless, for once abusing his license, by allowing a certain noted tippler to come to his house, and there to indulge his vicious appetite after warning, he incurred the censure of the civil fathers of the town alike with the tippler himself. The Selectmen, showing no respect of persons, imposed upon the latter offender a fine of

---

[32] Town Records, Vol. II., p. 74. [33] Town Records, Vol. I., p. 89. [34] Town Records, Vol. I., p. 120. [35] Town Records, Vol. II., p. 147. [36] Town Records, Vol. II., p. 27.

five shillings for going to the tavern, and another fine of five shillings more for tippling there after warning; and a fine of twenty shillings upon Mr. Walker for finding him room and drink to tipple with.[37]

But while the fathers of the town were thus laudably exerting themselves for the prevention and suppression of intemperance and its kindred vices, they were unconsciously giving countenance to one practice which had a tendency to promote it: that of giving drink at funerals. This seems at that day to have been the universal custom, especially in this place. Whoever died here, intoxicating liquor must be distributed among all who attended his burial. They buried their paupers with rum, and they buried their wealthy men and ministers with wine. One of the charges allowed by the Selectmen in 1683, at the death of George Wilkinson, the pauper already referred to, was one for three quarts of rum, to be drank at his funeral.[38] And in an account of the funeral expenses assumed by the town at the death of their beloved pastor, Rev. Mr. Carter, in 1684, there is a charge of £2. 9*s*. 0*d*. for fourteen gallons of wine.[39] This practice originated doubtless in a commendable desire to show

---

[37] Town Records, Vol. II., p. 58. [38] Town Records, Vol. III., pp. 47, 58.

[39] "Charges on Mr Thomas Carter's funarall in 1684.

"By fourteene gallons of wine, at 3*s*. 6*d*. per gallon	02 :09 :00.
"For tarr, two shillings	00 :02 :00.
"For gloues	01 :16 :00.
"For his Coffin, muny	00 :06 :00.
"For his graue, in pay	00 :05 :00.
"For manchester, 6 yards : and Jarr for tarr	00 :01 :06.
	04 :19 :06."

Nor did the custom cease with the 17th century, as appears by the following bill, still extant. — *Town Records, Vol. III., p.* 68.

"Charlestown Anno 1726.

"Mr Jacob Fowl & Mr Thos Reed: Bot of Seth Sweetser

"Sept. 22.	To 7 gallons Sweet wine, at 6 :6d - - - - -	£2 :5 :6
"	To 7½ Fyal at 5s - - - - - - - - -	1 :17 :6
		£4 :3 :0

"For ye funeral of Mr Symons Deceasd." [Mr. Benjamin Simonds, of Woburn, who died 21 Sept., 1726. — *Woburn Records of Deaths.*]

hospitality to those, who manifested their respect for a person deceased, and their sympathy with his surviving friends, by attending his funeral; and especially, when they came for this end from a distance over their rough roads, or in an inclement season of the year. But such an expression of hospitality on funeral occasions is now justly regarded as injurious in its tendency, as well as often burdensome by its expensiveness; and has been wisely suffered to fall into general disuse.

Finally, piety was a distinguishing trait in the character of the early inhabitants of Woburn, as it was generally in that of all the first planters of New England and their immediate successors. The town was settled principally by emigrants from Charlestown; and there is reason to believe that its founders, and a large proportion of its primitive population were associates in travel and suffering with those who accompanied Winthrop and Dudley, Wilson and Phillips, in their perilous voyage across the Atlantic, from a land of privilege and plenty, to this, then, American wilderness, for conscience' sake toward God. And their whole conduct, so far as any particulars of it have been transmitted to us, proves them worthy of being reckoned with that illustrious company of Puritans. Nor did their immediate descendants come far behind them, in respect to their religious character. In many of these, indeed, love had begun to wax cold; and there gradually came on a decay of vital religion, both here and throughout the land, which was observed and lamented by such as had seen New England in her first glory. Still, in a goodly proportion of the inhabitants of Woburn, of the second generation, there yet abode a like spirit of piety and devotion which had been the chief ornament of their fathers. And this excellent spirit was continually manifesting a powerful influence in the civil customs and measures, in the domestic arrangements, and in the general character and manners of the early inhabitants of this town. And the same spirit, I may safely add, had a larger share in moulding the ancient distinctive character of the people of New England, and in originating all those privileges and institutions, which are now their boast, than any other cause or influence whatever, merely secular, that can be assigned.

1. Particularly, this spirit manifested itself in Woburn, in zeal for the public worship of God. A leading object of the primitive settlers in leaving Charlestown to establish themselves in this place was to erect here a church, for the diffusion of the light of God's Word, and for upholding in it the ordinances of his gospel. Hence, notwithstanding a long train of difficulties and discouragements, which they had to encounter successively in their way to this object, they here quickly gathered a church, and procured and settled a minister over it, to lead in the services of the sanctuary. Here too, they had scarcely provided a shelter for themselves and families, before they built a house for the honor of God's name, and the conducting of his public worship. And as soon as this house had fallen into decay, or had become too strait for them, their sons built a second, larger and more convenient than the first. And ere this second house had been erected ten years, they took occasion repeatedly to enlarge it, for the better accommodation of the multitude which thronged it from Sabbath to Sabbath. Nor was it on the Sabbath day only, that they showed their zeal and diligence to assemble together in the Sanctuary to serve the Lord. During the ministry of the first two pastors of the church, there was a stated public lecture in Woburn for prayer and exposition of the Scriptures, similar to those then held in most of the early settled towns in Massachusetts.[40] How often it occurred, is not certain; but it appears, from the records, to have been held on Wednesday,[41] and to have been well sustained upwards of sixty years: and though in the ministry of the second Mr. Fox, there are signs of its falling into disuse, in consequence, probably, of his frequent ill health, and perhaps, too, of a growing indifference on the part

---

[40] In the record of general meeting, 27: 12 mo: [27 Feb.] 1665-6 reference is made to measures to be propounded to the inhabitants at a meeting, 28: 1 mo: 1666 next "after Lecture." — *Town Records, Vol. I.*, *p.* 32.

[41] Under Record of Selectmen's meeting, [Monday] 7 : 5 mo : [7 July,] 1679, mention is made of the next Lecture day on 16: 5 mo: 79. [Wednesday.] At a meeting of the Selectmen, Nov. 23, 1702, they appointed Wednesday ye 30th of December following after Lecture, to be a general meeting, etc. — *Town Records, Vol. IV.*, *p.* 214.

of some of the people, yet even then, attempts were repeatedly made, by a majority of the town, to revive and encourage it, and so to continue it to posterity.[42]

2. Nor was the religious spirit of the early inhabitants of Woburn less conspicuous in their exertions to maintain solemnity and decorum in public worship, than it was in those which they used to establish and continue it among them. Generally speaking, they were, universally, men who reverenced the Sanctuary of the Lord, set an excellent example of becoming seriousness in all its sacred exercises themselves, and could not endure to have them interrupted by anything like trifling or levity in others. Hence, when above thirty years after the settlement of the town, a portion of its youth began to behave themselves disorderly in public worship, the people generally were much aggrieved, and the fathers of the town immediately set themselves to devise a remedy. To put an end to the evil complained of, they passed successively a number of orders and regulations, the motives of all which cannot be too highly appreciated, though at the recital of some of them we can hardly refrain from smiling at their minuteness, and seeming singularity at the present day. At a meeting of theirs, Sept. 7, 1674, they resolved as follows on this subject: "Considering how greatly God is dishonoured by seuerall youths playing at meetting, and the trust that is by the athouryty of this Commonwealth committed to the Selectmen; they doe therefore order that from this time forward, all youths or male persons that shall playe or carry it unciuilly on the Saboth day, or in time of Exercise, they shall bee injoyned to sit in the last sete of the Rainge of mens seats, and all other persons whatsoeuer are prohibited sitting in that seat upon the penalty of halfe a Crowne, they doing it presumptuously."[43] But this injunction not being generally obeyed, or the appeal implied in it, to the shame of these young offenders, not proving so effectual as might have been anticipated, the Selectmen two years after-

[42] At a general meeting, March 4, 1716-17. It was voted to add £20 to Rev. Mr. Fox's salary of £80 for that year, provided that he keep a "Lecture once in six weeks, if he be able."— *Town Records, Vol. V., p.* 357.

[43] Town Records, Vol. II., p. 18.

ward had recourse to another expedient. They first set apart two seats in the meeting-house, particularly described in the records, for all those boys who should be expressly directed to sit in them, and whose names were to be fixed on them in writing, and forbade all other persons over sixteen years old, not expressly allowed, to sit in them, upon a penalty of 2*s.* 6*d.* each time.[44] And then to secure success to this measure, and perhaps likewise to afford some relief to the constables, under whose sole care the boys had hitherto been, in time of public worship, they appointed twenty-six men of respectable character to overlook those boys in the meeting-house, two days each in succession, under penalty of five shillings per day upon each of them who should refuse to serve. The business of this numerous committee, as stated in the records, was, to oversee the boys in the meeting-house, "to haue power to rape [rap] them with a stick," who did not "behave themselves as they ought"; and in case they persisted in their unseemly behavior, to complain of them to the Selectmen.[45] But strict as this measure may seem to have been, it did not at once eradicate the evil. For at a subsequent meeting of the Selectmen, March 1679–80, after making a new assignment of seats for the boys in the meeting-house, they committed them again to the oversight of the men "appointed as formerly," and of the constables[46] with their black staves.[47]

3. Again, the religious disposition of the early ancestors of this people was still further displayed in their equitable and generous treatment of their ministers of religion. For the first pastor of this church, Rev. Thomas Carter, the town built a dwelling-house at their own cost, and presented it to him at his settlement, as a gift. They also made him considerable grants of land soon after his settlement, and in all subsequent general distributions of the public lands, they allowed him his full proportion with the other inhabitants who were proprietors. The salary they originally agreed to give him, viz: £80, was a very liberal one for that day; and in his old age they enlarged it by

[44] Town Records, Vol. II., p. 36. [45] Town Records, Vol. II., p. 41. [46] Town Records, Vol. II., p. 152. [47] Town Records. Vol. II., p. 23. See also Vol. III., p. 119, 121.

an annual donation of twenty cords of wood.[48] And when at length his increased infirmities made the aid of a colleague necessary, they did not turn him adrift upon the world, as some towns have done by their ministers, worn out in their service, in modern times, neither did they put him off with a meagre, insufficient compensation, as has been the practice in many instances since, but they adjusted with him the question of his salary for the time to come, entirely to his own satisfaction; and when he deceased, they discovered their affectionate regard for the dead by their continued kindness to the living, his surviving widow. For Rev. Jabez Fox also, their second minister, the town of their own accord offered to erect a dwelling-house at their own expense, and present it to him as a gift. At his request, they enlarged it in building beyond the dimensions they had proposed, for an allowance he engaged to make them in money towards the cost. They granted him freely, as his own property, a portion of those lots of land, which they had reserved from time to time in disposing of their public lands, for a succeeding officer of the church; and the use of the residue, till they should need it for a successor. And when he died, they did not withdraw their kindness from his widow, but granted her a sum equal in amount to her husband's salary for half a year. These several testimonials of good-will to their ministers, and concern for their temporal comfort and well-being, speak loudly in favor of the religious character of the ancient inhabitants of Woburn. The people showed herein not only an effectual regard for their worthy pastors themselves, but likewise a becoming esteem for their work; love for that holy cause in defence of which they were set, and for the advancement of which among them they labored. Whereas, a mean, hard or unjust treatment of worthy ministers of religion on the part of the people whom they serve is generally speaking, a decisive indication of indifference or hostility toward religion itself.

4. Finally, the pious spirit of the ancient inhabitants of Woburn displayed itself in their care for the religious education of their children and youth. By a law of this colony,

---

[48] Town Records, Vol. I., pp. 54, 98, 101, 102.

passed in 1642, the same year with that in which Woburn was incorporated, the Selectmen of every town were required to see "that all masters of families do once a week (at the least) catechise their children and servants in the grounds and principles of religion; and if any be unable to do so much, that then at the least, they procure such children and apprentices to learn some short orthodox catechism without book, that they may be able to answer unto the questions that shall be propounded to them out of such catechism by their parents or masters, or any of the Selectmen, when they shall call them to a trial of what they have learned in that kind."[49] And although the Court had occasion, about thirty years after, viz, 1671, to complain of the neglect of this and other legal provisions on behalf of children and youth, which had resulted, they say, in the increase of sin and profaneness, and proceeded to enjoin upon the Selectmen anew, throughout this jurisdiction, to attend to their duty in this respect, yet there seems to be no ground for supposing that the neglect of catechising was then extensively prevalent. On the contrary, there is abundant reason to believe that, by the great body of the people, it was practised, even then, with exemplary strictness throughout the Colony; especially have we ground for this conclusion in regard to the inhabitants of this town. The transmission of this pious and laudable custom in the great majority of families in this place, till within a very recent period, affords, of itself, satisfactory proof of the high esteem and general observance of it by the early inhabitants of Woburn. Regarding religion themselves as "the principal thing," they were earnestly solicitous to inculcate the same great truth on the minds and hearts of their offspring. From a principle of piety, as well as from an obedient regard to the law of the land, they were careful to bring them up in the nurture and admonition of the Lord. They did not abound in books; but whatever other books they lacked, they *must* have a Bible (or, at the least, a Testament and a Psalter) and a

---

[49] Colony Laws, published 1672, p. 26; Colony and Province Laws, 1814, p. 74.

catechism in all their houses. They were at much pains to teach their children themselves, or to procure them to be taught by others, to read the Bible while young, and early to reverence and take heed to it, as the Word of God. Nor did they show scarcely less solicitude early to initiate their children into an acquaintance with the great truths of the Bible, both doctrinal and practical, as laid down in the Assembly's Catechism. And lest there might possibly be some families who were negligent of the catechetical instruction of those under their care, the Selectmen of the town appear to have been accustomed, after the injunction of the Court in 1671, to go round among the several families, from time to time, with a view to ascertaining and rectifying what was amiss in any on this head. One instance of their care in this matter we have upon record in their Day Book, as follows: "The Selectmen mette the 5. day of Octob. 1674, and agreed on the 15 day of this instant mo. to goe throo the Towne, and ecsamin the familys about Catichising^{e}."[50] The object of this visitation was doubtless the same as that which the law of that day suggested, viz, to question children whom they thought proper, out of their catechism; to reprove any heads of families whom they found negligent of it; and to use their influence and authority to induce them either to teach it their children themselves, or to employ others to do it for them.

By the time Woburn had been incorporated thirty years, a large proportion of its first settlers had left the world. Within that period especially, those seven commissioners, who had been intrusted with the care of laying its foundations, and had led the way in its settlement, had all rested from their labors. And here some brief notices of these worthies, to whom Woburn is so much indebted, may not be unacceptable.

1. The first of their number I shall mention, Mr. Thomas Graves, distinguished in the "History of Charlestown" as

---

[50] Town Records, Vol. II., p. 166.

Rear Admiral Graves [51] was born at Ratcliff, England, June 6th, and baptized at Stepney, June 16th, 1605.[51] He became a seafaring man, and was master of several ships sailing between England and this country 1632, and the three years following. He married in Charlestown Miss Catharine Coytmore, a daughter of the noted Capt. Thomas Coytmore, to whom a grant of five hundred acres within the bounds of Woburn was made by the Court in 1640.[51] He and his wife Catharine were admitted into the church of Charlestown, October 7, 1639.[52] In 1640, he was made a freeman of the Colony, as his namesake, the Engineer, had been in 1631;[53] and being appointed the same year as a suitable person, with the aid of others, to build up a distinct church and town in the then recent grant of Charlestown Village, he appears, for a while, to have been actively engaged in promoting that design. It was at his house in Charlestown, the commissioners held their first meeting, December 1640, and

---

[51] The family manuscripts, preserved by the descendants of this gentleman in Charlestown, represent him as identical with Mr. Thomas Graves, the celebrated Engineer and Surveyor, who laid out Charlestown in 1629.[51] And this, till recently, was the prevalent opinion on this subject. But it is now, for various reasons, generally given up, particularly on account of the apparent difference in their respective ages, and of the wide and striking dissimilarity of their handwriting. The Engineer, in 1629, the year of his arrival in this country, had left behind him in England a wife and five children, an indication that he was a considerably older man than the Admiral, born in 1605. Moreover, in the subscription of his name to the contract which he made March 1629, with the Massachusetts Company in London, previously to his embarking for New England in their service, the Engineer left a specimen of his handwriting, as did the Admiral of his, in signing his will. Copies of these autographs are presented to view in the History of Charlestown, by Richard Frothingham, Esq., page 140: and so great is the obvious difference between the two, that it can hardly be supposed that they were both written by the same hand.

[51] History of Charlestown, by Richard Frothingham, Esq., pp. 139, 140. "Ratcliff Hamlet, Camden says 'twas in his time a little town inhabited with sailors; and that here was a red Cliff, from whence it had the Name. Since the Houses taken from it, and added to St. Anne's, Limehouse, it contains about 1380. Stepney Church and Village are properly situate in this Hamlet." — *Complete System of Geography. London:* 1747; *Vol. I., p.* 116; *England, County of Middlesex.*

[51] Frothingham's History, p. 26.

[52] Records of 1st Church, Charlestown.

[53] Colony Records, Vol. I., pp. 366, 376.

agreed upon town orders for the contemplated settlement: and it was he who accompained Edward Johnson in his journey to Dorchester, in the final attempt made to procure Mr. Burr for their minister. But at Mr. Burr's declining eventually to come to Woburn, Mr. Graves seems to have become utterly discouraged from making any further effort to build up Woburn. He resumed his old occupation of following the seas, and as Johnson expresses it in his verses prefixed to the Town Records of Woburn, with apparent allusion to him:

—— "He did hie
To foren lands, Free from the Baby's crye,"

which he had undertaken with his associates to nurse and bring up.

In 1643, he was master of the "Trial," the first ship built in Boston, and which had been under the command of Capt. Coytmore. And while sailing, during the Protectorship of Cromwell, as master of a merchantman upon a mercantile voyage, he met and captured a Dutch privateer in the English channel. For this instance of his bravery, the owners of the vessel rewarded him with a present of a silver cup; and Cromwell raised him to the command of a ship of war, with the title of Rear Admiral.[51] He died at Charlestown, July 31, 1653, in the 49th year of his age, sustaining the character of "an able and godly man."[51]

Woburn Town Book, in recording the laying out of Richardson's Row in 1647, describes it as leading "from the three Richardsons to the town meeting house one way, and to Mr. Thomas Graves the other way."[54] By the house of Mr. Graves here referred to, could hardly be intended a dwelling within the limits of Woburn, which he made his ordinary residence. As his name does not occur in the Woburn tax list of 1646, or in any list of town officers, or in any of the numerous allotments of meadow and other land to the inhabitants of Woburn previous to 1653, the year of his death, it is probable that he never occupied any dwelling-house within its limits; but that before

[54] Town Records, Vol. I., p. 12.

its settlement was fully accomplished, he had taken up his residence in some house on the road from Woburn, within the bounds of Charlestown. The people of Woburn, however, appear to have always held in grateful remembrance his early efforts for the settlement of the town in its infancy; and in all the extensive divisions of their common lands made subsequently to his death, his widow had assigned her a liberal proportion.

2, 3, 4. The three Richardsons, — Ezekiel, Thomas, and Samuel, — were brothers, born in England, and for some time after their arrival were in this country, resident in Charlestown, where they had children born to them. Ezekiel, who was probably the eldest, was early admitted into First Church, Boston, which was gathered at Charlestown in 1630. From this church, he was dismissed October 14, 1632, with his wife Susanna and thirty-three others, and was embodied with them, November 2, 1632, into a distinct church at Charlestown, now the First Church in that place.[52] His brothers, Thomas and Samuel, were both admitted as members of Charlestown Church, February 18, 1637-8,[52] and they were all three dismissed from it, June 1642, to help form the church at Woburn. Upon their removal to Woburn, they lived near each other in the same street, which, from its having been the place of their residence, and of many of their posterity, has been known, from time immemorial, as Richardson's Row. They were members of Woburn church at its foundation; men highly respected in their day, and much employed in the business of the town. Their descendants bearing the name of Richardson, long have been, and still are more numerous, than persons of any other name in Woburn; and among them have been found some of the most valued members of the church and citizens of the place. Ezekiel died October 21, 1647; Thomas, August 28, 1651; and Samuel, March 23, 1657-8.

5. John Mousall was a brother of Ralph Mousall, one of the founders of the present First Church, Charlestown, in 1632. He was himself admitted into that church with his wife [Joanna?] Aug. 23, 1634; was one of the seven male members who constituted the church of Woburn at its gathering, Aug. 14, 1642; and afterwards one of its two original deacons till his

decease. He was also much honored in the town, being uniformly one of the "Commissioners to end small causes," in Woburn, and one of the Selectmen for twenty-one years in succession. He died March 27, 1665, leaving his widow, Joanna, a son, John Mousall, who was likewise a distinguished citizen in his day, and a daughter, Eunice, wife of John Brooks; but the name of Mousall, as a surname, is now extinct from the place.

6. Edward Convers was born in England, arrived in New England in the fleet with Winthrop, 1630, and settled in Charlestown. In 1631, grant was made to him of the first ferry between Boston and Charlestown, and of this he had the management several years, under the authority of the General Court. He was made a freeman of the Colony, 1631; served Charlestown as Selectman from 1635 to 1640; and was early admitted a member of First Church, Boston (gathered at Charlestown, 1630). From Boston Church he, his wife Sarah, and thirty-three other members were dismissed Oct. 14, 1632, to be embodied into the present First Church, Charlestown, entering into mutual covenant for this purpose Nov. 2, 1632.[55] His name stands at the head of the seven commissioners appointed by that church for effecting the settlement of Woburn: he appears to have been ever zealous and persevering in his labors for this end, and after the incorporation of the town, in 1642, he became one of its most popular and useful citizens. He was a member of Woburn Church from the beginning, and a deacon in it, one of the first two, till his death. In the civil affairs likewise of the town, he was much employed, serving uniformly as one of the Board of Commissioners for the trial of small causes, and being chosen annually as one of the Selectmen without interruption from the first choice in 1644 till his decease. He died Aug. 10, 1663, aged seventy-three years. His place of residence in Woburn was at the mill once called by his name in the South Village, now Winchester, and there, and in the vicinity, several of his numerous posterity continued to dwell for many years. Among his descendants, there ever have been and still are individuals

---

[55] Church Records of Charlestown.

highly honored and respected; and one of their number, Major James Convers, a gentleman of much distinction in the Commonwealth as well as in the town, there will be occasion particularly to notice hereafter.

By his first wife, Sarah, who accompanied him from England, Deacon Convers had three sons, viz: Josiah, James and Samuel (see genealogy), and a daughter, Mary, who first married Simon Thompson, 19th Dec. 1643, and he dying in May 1658, she married John Sheldon, of Billerica, Feb. 1, 1659. — *Woburn and Billerica Records of Marriages, Deaths, etc.*

Deacon Edward Convers' wife dying, 14th Jan. 1662, after he had made his will (in which he mentions her, and which is dated in Aug. 1659, and recorded Oct. 7, 1663), he married a second wife, Mrs. Joanna Sprague, of Charlestown, relict of Ralph Sprague, Sept. 9, 1662. — *See Woburn Records, and Will of Edward Convers.*

7. Last of all, but not least of this worthy band, died Edward Johnson. He originated from Kent in Old England; in a parish within which county, called in his Will, Heron Hill, that is "Herne Hill," or "Herne,"[56] and at a place in that parish, called "Waterham," he left behind, at coming to New England, both houses and lands, which he retained in possession during life, and divided by his will to six of his grandchildren, when he should be removed by death. According to statements of Hon. James Savage, in his Genealogical Dictionary, he doubtless came to this country in the fleet with Winthrop, 1630; requested admission as a freeman of the Colony, 19 October of that year, and took the Freeman's Oath, 18 May following; and thus after living some time at Charlestown, Salem, or other plantation to satisfy himself, he went back to England, to bring away his wife and children, in 1636, or 7. Upon his return voyage, his name is registered as follows, in a list of those who embarked from

---

[56] "Herne, a town of Kent, 6 miles from Canterbury" etc., etc.— *Brookes's Gazetteer.*

"Sir John Fineux . . . . . died about the year 1526, and lies buried in Christ's Church in Canterbury; who had a fair habitation in this City, and another in Herne in this County" etc., etc.— *Fuller's Worthies, Kent, p.* 76.

the port of Sandwich for the American plantations, in June 1637.

"Edward Johnson, of Canterbury, joiner, and Susan his wife, 7 children, 3 servants." [57]

He arrived in New England in the course of that summer, or early in the autumn of 1637, and took up his abode at Charlestown, where grants of land were repeatedly made to him for his accommodation in 1637, and in April 1638.[58] In the settlement of Woburn, for which he was one of the commissioners appointed by the church of Charlestown, he seems to have taken the leading part. At the first meeting of those commissioners, held at Charlestown, December 18, 1640, he presented a plot of the contemplated town, and was chosen its Recorder, or Clerk; an office he continued to sustain till death. He took a lively interest in the establishment of its church, of which he was a distinguished member from the beginning; and in the settlement of its first minister. His influence in the management of town affairs was great. He was put on almost all important committees for the distribution of the town's lands; and was uniformly appointed one of its Board of Commissioners for *trials of small causes;* and, with but few interruptions, one of its Selectmen till his decease. He was also captain of its military company, no small honor in that age of martial spirit and prowess. And accordingly, in mustering the forces of the Colony in that day, in his History of New England, having mentioned the bands of Concord and Cambridge, as being under two Kentish soldiers, (Captains Willard and Gookin,) he modestly notices "the band of Wooburn," as being commanded by "another Kentish Captain," meaning himself.

Captain Johnson was likewise deputy from Woburn to the General Court almost every year from the first choice of one, in 1646, till his death. And by that Honorable Body he was much distinguished, being chosen Speaker *pro tem.* for a short session in 1655; and appointed repeatedly on important committees. In

---

57 Gleanings for New England History, by James Savage, Esq., in Collections of Massachusetts Historical Society, Vol. VIII., Series III., p. 276.

58 Charlestown Town Records.

1643, before he became a member, he was sent by the Court with Capt. George Cooke and Lieut. Humphrey Atherton to Rhode Island, to apprehend the seditious Samuel Gorton. They had military commissions given them; and were attended by forty men.[59] At the restoration of King Charles II., to the throne of England, when the Charter of the Colony and all its privileges and liberties were apprehended to be in danger, he was one of an important committee, appointed by the General Court, in May 1661, consisting of eight laymen and four clergymen, to consider what was expedient to be done for their preservation, and to make report at the next session.[60] In June 1661–2, he was on a committee of the Court, with Deputy Governor Bellingham, Daniel Gookin, Esq., Thomas Danforth, Esq., and others, for the directing and despatching of Simon Bradstreet, Esq., and Rev. Mr. John Norton to England, as agents to plead the cause of the Colony there.[60] And in 1664, he was one of a committee of four (Hon. Richard Bellingham, Major General Leverett and Capt. Thomas Clark being the other three) to whom the Colony Charter was delivered by the General Court for safe keeping.[60]

He was the undoubted author of the early history of New England, styled, "The Wonder Working Providence of Sion's Saviour, in New England," which has already been often quoted or referred to in this work. That history was published in England in 1654, without the writer's name in the title page; and although it abounds in errors of the press, and has been noted for the indefiniteness or inaccuracy of many of its dates and statements, it still contains a large amount of authentic and valuable information, the want of which could hardly be supplied elsewhere. In it, the author frequently discovers a mind exceedingly embittered against the English prelates, in consequence, not improbably, of having suffered much from their arbitrary proceedings either in his own person, or in his friends. But at the same time, his work furnishes numerous and strong indications on his part, of a sincere, warm zeal for God and religion, an

[59] Colony Records, Vol. II., p. 44. [60] Colony Records, Vol. IV., Part II., pp. 24, 39, 102.

earnest desire for the prevalence of piety and virtue, and a hearty love of his country and good men.

Capt. Johnson died April 23, 1672.[61] In his last will and testament, dated May 15, 1671, and written with his own hand, he expresses, in view of his approaching dissolution, a lively hope "through faith in Christ Jesus," "to have the sight of (his) Saviour to all eternity." From this instrument (still extant in the Probate Office of this County) it appears that he left a widow, Susanna, and seven children; viz: five sons, Edward, George, William, Matthew and John; and two daughters, Susan, (?) wife of James Prentice, and Martha, wife of John Ames (?) or Eames; and grandchildren by them all. Of his children, only three, William, Matthew and John, appear to have been then resident in Woburn. William and Matthew were his executors. *Matthew* was a carpenter by trade, and a much esteemed citizen, chosen repeatedly one of the Selectmen, and deputy from Woburn to the General Court. *John* was proprietor of a saw-mill; but having in his old age become poor, lame and helpless, he and his wife Bethiah were taken, in 1712, to Canterbury, Ct., by their sons, William and Obadiah, of that town, to maintain for life at Woburn's expense. William, son of Capt. Edward, was a man of superior talents and extensive usefulness in his day; and sustained for several years a very honorable station in the Commonwealth. And from him sprang a numerous posterity, who were long distinguished by their general respectability of character, and by the great influence they had in the affairs both of Woburn, and of its precinct, now Burlington; and some do yet survive, who maintain the ancient credit of their family. But more may be expected of William Johnson and his descendants hereafter.

---

[61] Woburn Records of Births, Deaths, etc., etc.

CHAPTER III.

Second Meeting-House — Erection of, 1672 — Description of — Settlement in, of Rev. Jabez Fox, 1679 — a Sabbath day's services in, 1680.

THE year 1672 is memorable in Woburn, as being the year in which Capt. Edward Johnson, the father of the town, died; and also as that in which the second house for public worship was erected. The precise time when the first meeting-house was built, has not been transmitted. It was certainly completed before September 14th, 1646, when the Selectmen agreed to call a meeting of the town to reckon about its expense.[1] And the probability is, that it was begun not long after the house lots and place for the meeting-house, originally laid out on the East end of the plantation, were transferred, February 1640–1, by advice of Hon. Increase Nowell and other gentlemen of Charlestown, to the present centre of the town; and that it was finished about the time of Rev. Mr. Carter's ordination in 1642. The memory of the place where it stood, has been better preserved. This, as one of the most intelligent citizens of Woburn, Mr. Batholomew, Senr., now deceased, once told me, was distinctly marked out by a slight banking, which was raised originally about the foundations of the house, and which was plainly visible till about 1788, when the ground was levelled for the accommodation of a military muster. According to his report, moreover, this bank was erected on the common in the centre of the town, about opposite the middle of the space between the town-house and the late Mr. John Fowle's store; and at such a distance northwardly from that interval, as would be sufficient for a road to pass between. And this description of the situation of the first meeting-house in this town agrees well with that which Johnson gives of it, in his "Wonder-working Providence," etc. In

[1] Town Records, Vol. I., p. 9.

that History of New England, published in 1654, he observes that the meeting-house in Woburn stood in "a small plain where four streets meete."[2] These four streets could have been no other than "Hilly Way," or the road over the hill east of the common, where Deacon Mousall and other early settlers erected their habitations; "South Street," leading to Convers's mill and Mistick bridge, now the main road from Woburn to Medford; "Up Street," or "High Street," on which Rev. Mr. Carter's house then stood, now Mr. Silvanus Woods'; and "Military Lane," an ancient way, of which not a vestige now remains, but which is described in the Records,[3] as late as 1732, as coming down from the then meeting-house on Hilly Way, and as crossing the training field, (now the common in the centre) into Up Street or the most ancient road to the Shawshin. Now these several streets or ways, did meet together, as Johnson says, upon or near the "Small Plain," or common, now in the centre of the town: Hilly Way with South Street and Military Lane at or near the southeastern corner of the Plain; and Military Lane with Up Street, or High Street, upon or near its southwestern corner. And they all thus came together within a few rods distance from the banking described by Mr. Richardson, and so indisputably designate the site of the first meeting-house in Woburn.

But the earliest meeting-houses in New England, erected commonly by the people, in their zeal for the worship and ordinances of God, before they had scarcely provided a comfortable shelter for themselves and families, were of necessity but frail, temporary edifices; buildings more noted for the beauty of holiness within, than for external adorning, or skill in their construction. Concerning the first house for public worship in Boston, built in 1632, we are told by the Reverend historian of the First Church in that city, that "its roof was thatched, and its walls were of mud."[4] And it cannot be reasonably supposed, that this of Woburn, erected but about ten years after, was any better than that, or even hardly so good. The highly respectable gentle-

[2] Wonder Working Providence, Book II., Chapter XXII., pp. 175, 181.

[3] Town Records, Vol. I., p. 69, inverted.

[4] Emerson's History.

man, referred to by name in the beginning of this chapter, once informed me, that, judging of its dimensions by those of the banking at its foundations, it was a much smaller building than the second meeting-house; and that its posts, instead of being firmly mortised into substantial sills, according to the present mode, were made fast by their ends being driven into the ground. To such an humble house of prayer, and mean to look to, did your fathers love to resort weekly for the worship of their Maker: and they were notified of the hour by a bell hung on a hill in the neighborhood, (probably that back of the old Fowle tavern stand,) which was called from this circumstance many years after, Bell Hill.[5]

When this first meeting-house in Woburn had stood about thirty years, its visible decay, or its contracted dimensions making it too straight for the people to assemble in with convenience, rendered evident the necessity of another. At a general meeting of the inhabitants, Nov. 1, 1671, a committee was appointed to confer with several carpenters on the subject, and to report at another meeting, to be held on the 20th day of the same month. On that day, the town voted to build a new meeting-house, forty feet square, and of proportionate height, by contract. In pursuance of this vote, they chose Lieut. John Carter, William Johnson, John Wyman, and Thomas Peirce, for a Building Committee, and appointed the Selectmen and five other respectable citizens as a committee to contract with the Building Committee on behalf of the town, for raising and completing the house, to see them paid, and to engage to them £320 of town property, as security.[6] The meeting-house thus contracted for, the undertakers soon commenced building; and it was so far finished during the autumn of 1672, as to be then ready for occupation as a place for public worship. Accordingly, it was doubtless used for this purpose immediately, without previous ceremony; the present laudable custom of solemnly dedicating meeting-houses, before assembling in them for the ordinary services of the Sabbath, not having then been introduced into New England, nor

---

[5] Town Records, Vol. I., p. 80.

[6] Town Records, Vol. I., p. 36.

for many years after.[7] To defray the expense of building this house of God, a tax was levied upon all the polls and estates in Woburn in 1672.[8] And at a final settlement with the undertakers, the town allowed them £334, which was a little more than was originally pledged them, in full satisfaction of all their cost and charge.[9] Reckoning the value of New England silver currency at that period (for paper money was then unknown) to have been what it seems from good authority it actually was, twenty-five per cent less than sterling money, just what it is now, the sum paid for the meeting-house was nominally equal to $1,113.33. But as the usual price of Indian corn and other necessaries of life was then but just about half of what it is now, the real cost of the meeting-house to the town must have been equivalent to $2,226.67 at the present day.

Above a century has elapsed since this meeting-house, erected in 1672, was taken down, with the design of building a town-house of smaller size out of its remains. Hence, there is no one now living in Woburn who remembers it when used for a place of public worship, or can give any information respecting either

[7] The first settlers of New England, and their posterity for several generations after them, as they did not observe Christmas, so they did not consecrate burying-grounds, or dedicate their meeting-houses, by any special religious services. When a house for public worship was built and made ready for its intended use, they noticed the occurrence, generally speaking, only by an appropriate discourse on the first Sabbath they occupied it. For instance, when the present Old South Church, Boston, was first opened, on Sabbath day, April 26, 1730, for public worship, Rev. Mr. Sewall, the senior pastor, preached, A. M., from Haggai ii. 9, "The glory of this latter house," etc.; and Rev. Mr. Prince, his colleague, P. M., from Psalm v. 7, "I will come into thy house," etc. The first meeting-house in Brattle Street was first opened for public worship on Lord's day, Dec. 24, 1699, on which occasion, Rev. Dr. Colman, its first minister, preached from 2d Chron. vi. 18, "But will God in very deed dwell with men on the earth?" etc. And so late as 1773, when the present house of that society was first opened on Sabbath day, July 25th, Dr. Cooper preached in the morning from Gen. xxviii. 17, "This is none other than the house of God," etc.; and Rev. Dr. Chauncy (with whose people the Brattle Street Society had met while their own house was building) preached in the afternoon from Psalm xxvi. 8, "Lord, I have loved the habitations of thy house," etc. — See *Palfrey's Historical Discourse, Appendix, Notes, pp.* 39, 63.

[8] Town Records, Vol. I., p. 38.

[9] Town Records, Vol. I., p. 41.

its external appearance or its internal structure, from his own recollection. On both these topics, however, numerous particulars may be gleaned from the Town Records; some have been handed down by credible tradition, and a few may be very plausibly conjectured, in view of other ancient meeting-houses which were erected about the same time with this, and which were left standing till within a recent date, the striking memorials of the customs and fashions of olden times. Availing myself of all these several sources of information, especially of the two named first, I have attempted to draw up a description of this forgotten house of worship, as like the original as possible, and which may not be uninteresting to the present inhabitants of Woburn to read.

The second meeting-house of Woburn stood, it is well known, upon the hill on the southeast side of the common. Around it grew a number of shade trees, which the prudent care of the fathers of the town had saved from the axe in felling the surrounding forest, and which now served both for ornament and for use.[10] Beneath the pleasant shade of these trees, or close by them, were successively erected, with the leave of the town, and under the direction of the Selectmen, some thirty or forty sheds, for the accommodation of the horses of numerous individuals on Sabbath days and other occasions of public assembly.[10] The meeting-house itself was an edifice forty feet square, facing south, and having the pulpit on the north side.[11] Its frame was of solid, massive oak, some portions of which were long preserved in the town, and are still, or were recently, to be seen.

---

[10] The Selectmen, Dec. 25, 1712, laid out to Robert Convers, Josiah Convers, Jr., William Johnson, Jr., and Thomas Reed, a spot of ground on the south side of the Meeting-House Hill, thirty-six feet in length, "for Stables to set horses in on Saboth dayes and such like occasions." By direction of the Selectmen, these stables were to be erected nine feet square, adjoining each other, and in a range with one another, about six feet "South of the most Southerly Shade Tree," and not to be extended westward within sixteen feet "of the now Horse Block," etc., etc. — *Town Records, Vol. V., p.* 242. Numerous other grants of ground for stables, for the same purpose, are upon record.

[11] Zebadiah Wyman, Esq.; Mr. William Fowle.

Its roof, like that of its venerable contemporary, taken down a few years since upon Lynn plain, was surmounted by a small cupola or *turret*,[12] in which was hung a bell that was rung, probably, as at Lynn,[13] by a rope attached to it, and descending through a hole in the roof into the centre of the broad aisle.[13] And that the hour for ringing the bell and commencing divine service might be known, a sun-dial was procured shortly after the building of the meeting-house, which being set upon or near it, supplied the place of a clock in fair weather.[14] The windows were casements hung like doors upon iron hinges, and otherwise well fortified with iron;[15] and the lights were set with lead, and probably of the diamond shape, as is the case with windows still to be seen at the back of several of the most ancient dwelling-houses of the town. Galleries there were on the sides of the meeting-house, within; yet not all built at once, but as circumstances rendered them expedient. At a general meeting, Feb. 27, 1677–8, the town granted leave to the young men of the place, upon certain conditions, to build a gallery for their accommodation on the east side.[16] The same year, (26 August,

---

[12] "Joseph Richardson Sen." Cr. "By Cills [Sills] for the Meeting hous territt & door cill, as money 00 :10 :00." — *Town Records.*

[13] Letter of Rev. Parsons Cooke, of Lynn. 1674. The Town Dr. to John Tead for ringing the bell £1 :10 :00. — *Town Records, Vol. II., p.* 22. In a reckoning with Gershom Flagg, Oct. 2, 1676, he was allowed by the Selectmen for "the *belrope*," etc. — *Town Records, Vol. II., p.* 48.

[14] Town Records, Vol. II., p. 31. The Town Dr. in 1675, To Gershom Flagg, "for the dyall post." — *Town Records, Vol. II., p.* 23.

[15] March 8, 1699–1700. The Selectmen "agreed with Simon Tompson to ring the bell, sweep the Meeting hous, see to shut the Casements and doors, as need requires," etc., etc. — *Town Records, Vol. IV., p.* 158.

Feb. 9, 1701–2. The Town Dr. to "Daniel Baldwin for Iron work for a Casement for ye Meeting house: £00 :02 :06." — *Town Records, Vol. IV., p.* 196.

"To Serjt Saml Waters for a Casement for ye Meeting house, £00 :03 :00." — *Town Records, Vol. IV., p.* 197.

"Novbr 1729. For mendin of the meetnes [meeting-house] glas:
"For maken of 2 foot of new glas 00 :04 :04."
"For new *leden* [leading] 3 foot of old glas: 00 :04 :00."
etc., etc., etc. — *An old Account on file.*

[16] Town Records, Vol. I., pp. 73, 93.

1678,) one instruction given by the town to a committee for repairing the meeting-house was, to build what galleries might seem to them convenient.[16] In 1707, "the hinde seat in the East galery next the staiers," was granted to eight young men to sit in, they to repair it at their own charge.[17] And in 1694, mention is made in the Records of an "upper gallery,"[18] which was doubtless built over one of the others, and designed for the negroes, who were then far more numerous in Woburn than they are now. The floor of the house was not originally covered with pews, as was recently the universal practice. For upwards of forty years, only two of these aristocratic privileges (as they were probably deemed) were to be seen in Woburn meeting-house, — one the minister's pew, the other for the deacons' wives, the deacons themselves having an appropriate seat of their own.[19] In 1713, the town, by special favor, allowed Col. Jonathan Tyng, a gentleman from Boston, who had been one of Governor Sir Edmund Andros's Council, and who, more recently, had married the widow of Rev. Jabez Fox, of Woburn, and come home to reside, to erect a pew in the meeting-house, at his own cost, which was to be the town's property after his own and his lady's decease.[19] Three years after, viz, March 1716, leave was given by the town to the daughters of four principal families to build a pew to sit in, with the proviso that it was to be the town's, whenever they saw fit to leave it.[20] But so much disturbance did the grant of this privilege excite, that the town within six months revoked their grant.[20] And in 1738, upon the petition of Nathaniel Saltonstall, Esq., Jonathan Poole, Esq., and Capt. Isaac Dupee, gentlemen of distinction in the town from abroad, that they might each of them be allowed to build pews for themselves, the town voted liberty to the former gentleman to sit in the pew once occupied by Col. Tyng; but denied all of them liberty to build any more.[21] Only three pews, then, were ever permitted to be erected and to stand permanently in this second meeting-house in Woburn, as the seats

---

[17] Town Records, Vol. V., p. 43.
[18] Town Records, Vol. IV., p. 41.
[19] Town Records, Vol. V., p. 254.
[20] Town Records, Vol. V., pp. 336, 364.
[21] Parish Records, Vol. I., p. 97.

of individual families, in distinction from the rest of the congregation. The remainder of the lower floor, as likewise the whole of the gallery floors, was taken up by seats, which were under the control and at the disposal of the whole town. Under the windows by the wall on the east and west ends, there ran two long benches, which at one time were the appointed seats of the boys.[22] The rest of the ground on each side of the broad aisle was taken up with ranges of seats facing the pulpit, and having backs to them, like those of the old-fashioned settles, though not so high; those on the east side being for the male, and those on the west side for the female portion of the congregation.[23] And that each individual might know and take his own place without confusion in time of public worship, the town at a general meeting, October 8, 1672, as soon as the meeting-house was ready for occupation, chose five men of character and influence as a *seating committee*, to appoint to all the other inhabitants their respective seats in the house of God; and at the same time was appointed another committee of two, to seat the seating committee themselves with their wives.[24] To aid the seating committee in the discharge of their perplexing duty, they were on this occasion expressly instructed by the town to have respect in it to three things, viz: estate, office, and age.[24] And as death and other causes were continually operating to break up the arrangements of this committee, and to make new ones necessary, the town was accustomed in after years, to choose from time to time a new seating committee, whose business it was to repeat the invidious, difficult task of their predecessors; the doing of which was often the source of much bitterness, and in some instances of hot contention among the inhabitants, as there may be occasion to notice hereafter.

At the head of the broad aisle, there once stood a table, designed no doubt for the communion service; and that so large a one, that it was found necessary, in order to make room for it, to crowd the seats back towards the front of the house.[25] Before the pulpit and adjoining to it, were, I presume to say,

---

[22] Town Records, Vol. II., p. 36.

[23] Town Records, Vol. V., pp. 219, 254.

[24] Town Records, Vol. I., pp. 37, 38.

[25] Town Records, Vol. I., p. 93.

two seats; of which the lower and front one of the two was occupied by the deacons.[26] The other and more elevated one was styled, like a corresponding seat to be seen, till within a few years, in the Congregational meeting-house in South Reading, the elders' seat, because designed originally for ruling elders of the church. For although, from some cause, neither the church in Woburn, nor that in South Reading, is known to have been ever served by officers of this denomination, yet, doubtless, both these churches formerly recognized the office as of divine institution.[27] In ascending the pulpit stairs, there rose, fixed to that end of the pulpit, or of the elders' seat adjoining it, a tall, slender iron rod, with a little enclosure of iron or wooden painted balusters at the top, in which rested an hour glass; placed there, not to show the preacher how soon he might with decency leave off, but to be a silent monitor to warn him how long without offence he might hold on.[28] At the head of the pulpit stairs, against the wall, there was probably a narrow seat, where sat in service time the sexton, that he might be at hand to turn the hour-glass when its sands had run out, and also to receive any communications from the minister for which there might be occasion. In the pulpit itself, there was a cushion in front, as in modern pulpits, which served as a convenient resting-place for the preacher's notes.[29] But no Bible in folio was to be seen there, from which a portion might be read in the regular services of the sanctuary. For though our Puritan fathers accounted the Holy Scriptures as a complete and sufficient, as well as the sole rule, not only of faith and practice, but likewise for the worship

---

[26] Town Dr. 1681. "To Joseph Richardson in timber and pay to Houlton for worke he did on the deacons' seate, £00 :12 :00."— *Town Records, Vol. III., p.* 19.

[27] See "Proposals," or Declaration of the Church of Woburn, 1703; copied in Chapter V.

[28] Town Dr. 1673. "To Josiah Conuers for the Iron for the houer glasse - - - - - - - - £00 :04 :00."

"At Selectmens meeting 3 :12 :1678 [Feb. 3, 1678–9]
Due to decon Conuers 'for the bying an houer glas'" etc.. etc. 00 :02 :00.
Town Records, Vol. II., pp. 4, 114.

[29] 1677 Town Dr. "to Matthew Johnson for a cushen - £01 :9 :4."
Town Records, Vol. II., p. 75.

of the Lord's house, yet by a strange inconsistency, and it is to be feared from a measure of prejudice against the usage of the Church of England, from which they had separated, they esteemed the simple reading of the Word of God in public worship as an unedifying practice, unless it were accompanied with some exposition of man.[30]

At the time this meeting-house was finished, it was unquestionably capacious enough to seat all the inhabitants of Woburn with ease. But so fast did the population increase, that it speedily became necessary to increase its accommodations. As early as 1678, it was found expedient to make to it certain additions.[31] And subsequently to this period, much labor and cost were bestowed on repairing and enlarging this house of God. In 1694, for instance, the town voted at March meeting, that their meeting-house should be repaired withinside and without; seats mended, and new ones erected, at the discretion of a committee then chosen for the purpose.[32] And this vote appears to have been punctually executed. And again in 1709, the meeting-house was not only repaired anew, but an addition made to it of twenty feet on the East end.[33] And it deserves to be mentioned, as a testimony to the zeal for God's house with which a large proportion of the inhabitants of Woburn at that day were animated, that the expense of the repairs in 1694 was defrayed chiefly, and that of the addition just spoken of in 1709, entirely, by a voluntary subscription.[33] And thus, through a constant care bestowed on its preservation and keeping it in good repair, this second meeting-house in Woburn, which I have been endeavoring so much at length to describe, stood eighty

[30] "In Boston, after prayer and before singing, it was the practice for several years for the minister to read and expound a chapter. Whether it was because this carried the service to too great a length, or any other reason could be given for it, in a few years it was laid aside, except when it came in place of a sermon. Exceptions, may we not say cavils, have been made by some learned, serious ministers, against reading the Scriptures, as part of the divine service, without an exposition." — *Hutchinson's History of Massachusetts, Vol. I., Chap. iv., pp.* 427, 428.

[31] Town Records, Vol. I., p. 93.

[32] Town Records, Vol. IV., pp. 19, 21, 25.

[33] Town Records, Vol. V., p. 120.

years. Fifty-eight years of this period, it served as the house of worship for the whole of the then town, comprehending Wilmington, Burlington and Winchester with what is now Woburn within its bounds; and then as the place of solemn assembly for the first parish, till the erection of the third meeting-house in 1752. Concerning its subsequent demolition, with a view to making a town-house of its materials, and the eventual failure of that scheme after the building was raised anew, there may be occasion of speaking hereafter.

It has often been observed, that the building of a new meeting-house is quickly followed by the settlement of a new minister. But in the present case, the remark was not verified. After the meeting-house I have so long been speaking of was completed, instead of treating their aged minister, Rev. Mr. Carter, with unkindness or neglect, or manifesting impatience to see a successor in his room, the people of Woburn gave him substantial evidence of increased attachment. At a general meeting, Nov. 16, 1674, called expressly to confer about Mr. Carter's maintenance, it was agreed by a major vote, say the Records, "that the Towne wold yerly bringe Mr. Thomas Carter, our Reuerant Pastor, twenty Cord of wood, and deliuere it at his dore, ouer and aboue his fower score pound, prouided that those that will, may haue leaue to take the said wood off his own land." [34] The singular proviso annexed to this vote was doubtless added on behalf of a few, who were ready enough to do their part in this act of generosity to their pastor, by giving their labor in drawing his wood to his house, but whose poverty, or distance, or both, might make it too burdensome to take it from their own lots, if they had any.

At length, however, Mr. Carter's advanced years and growing infirmities rendered it evident that aid was needed by him, and would probably be welcome. At a general meeting, Aug. 26, 1678, the town voted unanimously, that they would procure a minister to help Mr. Carter. They also granted four single rates, amounting to about £120, (one quarter part of which was to be paid in silver) for the maintenance of the ministry: viz. £50 for

[34] Town Records, Vol. I., p. 54.

Mr. Carter's assistant, and £70 for Mr. Carter himself, who, in view of the increased burdens of his people on his account, consented to be satisfied with that sum, and with his wood, as agreed upon in 1674, instead of £80, his original compensation.

At the same time, they appointed a committee to wait on Mr. Jabez Fox, a graduate of Harvard College, and then a resident licentiate at Cambridge, and to invite him to Woburn, as an assistant to Mr. Carter for one year.[35] Mr. Fox accepted the invitation. And so well satisfied were the people with his services, that before the term of his engagement expired, they unanimously agreed and voted at a town meeting, July 16, 1679, that they would give him "a call to the ministry, with an intent he may be called to office, in time, if God make waye; and also agreed that for this yeare they will allow him fiuety pounds, one quarter of it in silver; his house rent and his firewood, and afterward inlarge, as God shall inable them."[36] This invitation to a temporary engagement in the work of the Ministry was soon followed by a call to the pastoral office in the church, and to a permanent settlement as a minister of the Gospel in the town. The proceedings of the church on this occasion cannot be specified, as its ancient Records have long been missing. But at a meeting of the town, Nov. 5, 1679, it was voted "that they wold giue the Reuerant Mr Jabiz ffoxe a Call to be their minister for his life time": and the Town, on that consideration, agreed to give him half of several pieces of land, which they had prudently reserved for the benefit of the future officers of the church, in the general distribution of their common lands a few years before; and the use of the whole, till the town should need the other half for another officer.[36] And to crown the indubitable tokens of esteem and affectionate regard which they had already given for this minister of their choice, the people at a meeting, called Nov. 10, 1679, agreed, it seems, to build a house for him, and to present it to him as a gift.[36] And Mr. Fox wishing for some alterations in the dimensions of this house as then determined, to gratify his wishes in this respect, another

[35] Town Records, Vol. I., p. 93. [36] Town Records, Vol. I., pp. 98, 101, 102.

meeting was called a month after, Dec. 8th, when they voted as follows:

"Whereas the Town had formerly agreed to buld the Reuerant Mr foxe a dwelling hows twenty foure feet in laneth, eaighteene feet wide, and thurteene feet stud, a stack of three brick chimnies, a cellar under it, and a leanetwo at the chimney end, and so to finish the said hows and giue it him: now the Towne did agree, upon Mr Foxe's desire, to build the said hows fourty feet long, eaighteene feet wide and thurteene feet stud, a stack of three chimnys and cellar and finish it; Mr foxe being willing to allow toward the worke twenty and fiue pounds, and fiue pounds more, in case that be not suffistiant for what is expended for the making the said hows sixteene feet longer than was agreed of by the Towne in the first place: and decon Josiah Conuars, Ensigne James Conuars and William Johnson are appiointed a Committee to oursee the worke and order the same till it be finished," etc.[36]

According to minutes preserved in the records, the materials of this house, and the labor in framing, erecting and completing it, cost about £133, of the then currency of Massachusetts.[37]

To meet this expense, the town granted in December 1679, four single rates, amounting to £122.15*s*.[38] They also ordered, at the meeting Dec. 8, 1679, just referred to, "that the pece of land reserued for an officer near Tottingham's should be sould to carry an end the bulding of Mr. Foxes hows."[39] The sum which Mr. Fox agreed to give toward it was never actually paid into the town treasury; but was allowed in a settlement with the Selectmen, May 9th, 1698, toward the payment of certain arrears for salary that had long been due.[40] The house thus built by the town and given their minister is known to have stood where the house of Jonathan B. Winn, Esq., now stands, and was occupied by Rev. Mr. Jabez Fox, and by Rev. Mr. John Fox, his son and successor in the ministry, for about seventy-six years. The precise time of the ordination of Rev. Jabez Fox, as colleague with

[37] Town Records, Vol. III., pp. 167, 168, 169.
[38] Town Records, Vol. I., p. 104, 5.
[39] Town Records, Vol. I., p. 101.
[40] Town Records, Vol. III., p. 117.

Rev. Mr. Carter, is not stated in the Town Records; but is supposed to have been not far from November 15, 1679.[a]

Thus were the inhabitants of Woburn provided with a house for God's worship in the room of that wherein their fathers kept Sabbath at the first in this then wilderness; and with a man to conduct the services of the sanctuary, when their aged pastor should be taken away. And now, that I may present a more vivid display of the interesting peculiarities of their public worship, for which all these means and instrumentalities were procured, may I be permitted to relate the particulars of a visit which I once paid them *in imagination*, to keep Sabbath with them in their new meeting-house, and to hear their new minister.

Borne then aloft on the wings of fancy over the current of time, and retracing its stream with an indescribable velocity, I suddenly alighted one fine Sabbath morning, about the 20th of June, Old Style, in the year of our Lord one thousand six hundred and eighty, at New Bridge in Woburn; and taking by instinct, as it were, the road which led to the centre of the town, I began at once slowly to wend my way thither. The sky was serene, the air warm, and the surface of the meadows and grass-g ounds was clad in the richest green. But a solemn stillness presided over the bright scene which nature had spread around me. Neither man nor beast was to be seen at work in the field. No sound of the hammer, or of the woodman's axe saluted my ear; no rumbling carriage of travellers on business or pleasure met my eye. Almost the only tokens of animal life abroad, that I perceived in my walk, were the motions and notes of hundreds of birds, whose songs, together with the fragrant odors diffused by the blossoms and a rich variety of flowers in the gardens and orchards I passed, seemed like a morning offering of praise and sweet incense to the great Lord of the Sabbath, by whose decree summer and winter, seed-time and harvest never cease. Nor, amidst the homage paid by the inanimate

---

[a] In Town Records, Vol. I., p. 105, Major Johnson, the then Town Clerk, makes the following remark in the margin: "The midle of the 10th. mo. 1680, apeered a uery great blazing starr, to the wonder of the world."

and by the irrational portions of the creation, was man their lord insensible to the claims of the Creator. As I went by the low and thinly scattered dwelling-houses of this then humble village, whose doors and windows the warmth of the morning had caused to be opened, I heard, before some, the voice of prayer from within; and at the windows of others, I observed flocks of little boys and girls reading to their pious mothers in the Testament or Psalter, or answering the questions of that far-famed compend of Christian truth and duty, the Assembly's Catechism. While I thus proceeded along, endeavoring to compose my mind into a suitable frame for the exercises of a day, to whose sacredness all that I saw and heard, as well as all that I did not, seemed to bear witness, I was suddenly overtaken on the common by a man, who afterwards made himself known to me as goodman Jonathan Thompson, the sexton for that year,[41] who had just been at the minister's to receive from him certain directions before the hour of prayer arrived, and was now on his way to open the meeting-house. Perceiving me to be a stranger, he civilly accosted me; and learning that I wished to worship with them that day, he kindly offered to conduct me to the house, and find me a seat. We went by the way of Military Lane:[42] and as we walked up the hill, several honest couples passed us on horseback, who severally eyed me with a keen look of yankee-like inquisitiveness, but said nothing; and, nodding respectfully, jogged on. These, my guide told me, were the Jaquiths, and the Butters's from Goshen, and the Reeds, and the Walkers and the Wilsons from Shawshin; who, he shrewdly remarked, though farthest from the Sanctuary, were always first to be there.

Having reached the meeting-house, as I stood in front of it a few minutes, admiring the beauty of the lofty trees with which it was surrounded, numerous other couples arrived on horseback, a large proportion of whom, I observed, drove up to a stone horse-block, about a rod from the southernmost shade,[43]

---

[41] The Town Dr., in the year 1680, "To Jonathan Tompson for ringing the Bell, and sweeping the meeting hows, £01 : 10 : 00." — Town Records, Vol. I., p. 107.

[42] See Chapter I., note 31.

[43] See note 10. This horse-block is still preserved.

and there successively alighting, tied their horses to a long row of stakes set in the ground, and then leisurely advanced toward the meeting-house. As they overtook one another in their approach to where I stood, they saluted each other with a friendly smile and a cordial shake of the hand. But I overheard in their conversation not a word dropped upon politics or the prospect of crops; scarcely anything, in fact, but certain observations and questions which seemed to be dictated by pious gladness, or by a spirit of benevolence and affectionate sympathy for their neighbors or one another. "What a beautiful Sabbath 'tis!" exclaimed one to another; "and how thankful ought we to be for such a lovely morning as this, to come to meeting!" "What," inquired another, "does the doctor say to Brush's child, poor thing; does he think he'll ever get well of his fall?" "Are the neighbors," asked a third, with an anxious pitiful look, — "Are the neighbors attentive to visit poor goody Gilson in her trials, and to carry her in supplies?" "How," questioned a fourth, with much solemnity of countenance, — "How did goodman Farrar appear in his last moments? Did his faith and patience hold out to the end? Did he give evidence to the minister of a good hope?" and, "When, good man, will he be buried?"

And thus, having finished the few brief remarks and inquiries of this sort which they had occasion to make, they tarried no longer at the door; but uncovering their heads the instant they stepped on the threshold, they reverently entered the house of God, and quietly took their appointed seats. And now my friend, the sexton, pointing to the dial, which showed it was almost nine o'clock, and saying it was time to ring the bell, I followed him in to a seat, where I had good view both of the ministers and hearers, and where, while the people were gathering, I improved the opportunity to look around, and survey the novel, interesting scene.

In the front row of seats facing the pulpit, on the east side of the broad aisle, were the Selectmen. At the head sat William Johnson, whom I knew by his open, ingenuous countenance and robust, vigorous frame, such as I have seen in some of his posterity. Next came Ensign James Convers, grave, thoughtful and attentive in his looks, resolute and energetic in his whole demeanor. At his side sat Sergeant Matthew Johnson, a brother of William; and, next to him, John Wright, Jr., and Francis Kendall — all honored names in their day. In the opposite row of seats, on the west side, were the wives of the Selectmen, all fair in appearance and becoming in behavior; and yet whose silk dresses, or the addition of a few extra ribbons to their attire, showed that they had not forgotten the lessons touching the necessity of maintaining distinctions of rank by distinctions of dress, which their mothers had taught them on the other side of the Atlantic. The second and third ranges of seats on the east side were occupied by men whose hoary locks and bending forms proclaimed them to be the surviving few of those who had come up to Woburn at the first to take possession of the land; but whose fixed eyes and laboring ears and solemnity of air were strong indications that their thoughts were now set on a better country, and that they had come to the Lord's house to-day, seeking direction and encouragement in their pilgrimage to it. As my eyes ran from this interesting class of men across the aisle, and surveyed for a moment the venerable matrons, the wives of their youth, or the widows of their early associates now deceased, who filled the two opposite rows of seats, methought I saw a striking exemplification of the Apostle's counsel, "Whose adorning let it not be that outward adorning of plaiting the hair and of wearing of gold, or putting on of apparel; but let it be the hidden man of the heart, in that which is not corruptible, even the ornament of a meek and quiet spirit, which is, in the sight of God, of great price." Next to the aged men's seats came those appropriated to the substantial farmers and tradesmen of the town, who were all arranged in them with some regard both to their years and to the proportion they paid of the public taxes. There, in dense, crowded ranks sat the Converses and Johnsons, the Richardsons and Thompsons; the Mousalls and the Winns, the Wrights and the Baldwins; the Kendalls and the Carters, the Russells and the Walkers; the Peirces and the Wymans, the Fowles and the Simonds; the

Brooks and the Teeds, the Flaggs and the Reeds; the Snows and the Cutlers, the Lockes and the Butters's, and many other respected names, all or most of which are borne to this day by descendants in Woburn and vicinity. There, too, were to be seen the Brushes, now turned into Bruces; and there, too, the Pollys and the Greenes, the Henshaws and Berbeanes, the Cleavelands and the Farrars, the Lepingwells and Bakers, — names once familiar to the ancient inhabitants of Woburn, but which, with others, are now quite extinct in the town, having long since given place to the Parkers and the Cummings's, the Tays and the Skeltons,— names common here in succeeding generations, and now better known. In the corresponding seats on the west side of the aisle sat the wives of these worthy men, — helps meet for them indeed, — who, arrayed in plain homespun garments of the most perfect neatness, defended from soiling by tidy aprons of the purest white, carried evidence in their dress that they came to the house of God to pray and to praise, rather than to see and be seen.

In the remotest seats on the floor of the house, and in the east and west galleries, sat the young men and women, — the flower of Woburn. And, last of all, upon the two long benches against the wall, on the east and west sides of the broad aisle, were seated the boys of the congregation, whom, full of life and playfulness as they were, a grave overseer, with a rod, and a constable, with a staff of office in his hand, at the end of each seat, made out to keep in tolerable restraint; although some of them, I observed, as they looked or winked at one another, could hardly, at times, suppress a whisper or a rising smile. In the deacons' seat sat John Wright, Sen., one of the earliest settlers of the town, but now stooping under the weight of three score years and ten; and Josiah Convers, a brother of the ensign, and like him, of a grave, intelligent, and active appearance. The elders' seat was empty; for, though the church of Woburn held to the Cambridge platform, which represents the office of ruling elder in the church as of divine institution, yet no one of her sons, whom she may have thought worthy of the office, was ever found willing to accept it. In the pulpit, at the left hand, sat Mr. Fox, the recently ordained colleague of the senior pastor, now in the vigor of manhood, a sedate, solid preacher, and much beloved by his flock, both old and young. At the head of the pulpit was Mr. Carter, the senior pastor himself, whose furrowed cheeks and hoary locks signified to all that his work was almost done; and who, as with placid eye and benevolent countenance he looked round upon the people of his charge, seemed to be bidding them all, one after another, farewell; as though he thought that the present might possibly be the last time he should ever meet them there. But while my eyes had thus been moving over this numerous assembly, and were fixed for a moment on their venerable senior minister, the congregation had all collected, the bell had ceased tolling, and the sexton had taken his wonted seat at the head of the pulpit stairs. Divine service was presently commenced by Mr. Carter with a short invocation; praising God for the light and privileges of another of his holy days, and fervently imploring his presence and aid in the prayers and praises now to be offered, and his blessing upon his Word now to be dispensed. The introductory prayer being over, I was expecting to hear the Scriptures read, as I had been used to. But after waiting a few moments, looking for this portion of Divine service to begin, Deacon Wright arose to announce singing; and, holding in his hand the Collection, entitled the "New England Psalms, Hymns and Spiritual Songs," that now forgotten, but once favorite version of our fathers, both in their private and public devotions, he read five stanzas of the 5th Psalm, as follows:

"Jehovah, to my words give ear,
  My meditation weigh;
My King, my God, my cry's voice hear,
  For I to thee will pray.

"Thou in the morn my voice shalt hear;
  Lord, in the morning I
Will unto thee direct my prayer,
  And will look up on high.

"For thou art not a God that will
  In wickedness delight;
Nor shall with thee dwell any ill,
  Nor fools stand in thy sight.

"Craftsmen of sin, thou hat'st all them,
Thou shalt him 'stroy that lies:
The Lord will loath the bloody man,
And them that guile devise.

"But I will to thy house draw near
In thine abundant grace;
And I will worship in thy fear
Towards thy holy place."

When he had finished reading, I was right glad to hear him give out Windsor, as the tune to be sung; for that is a tune, which, like others of the same class, such as plaintive Canterbury and Little Marlborough, and mournful Bangor and Isle of Wight, and stately Rochester and Wells, grave Colchester and Wantage, sweet-toned Barby and Mear, cheerful York and St. Martin's, and majestic Winchester and Old Hundredth, I am always delighted to hear sung on suitable occasions; but which, from the general change of the public taste in Sacred Music, I am seldom or never likely to hear again. The deacon, having announced the tune, read the first line again, and then, with a tremulous voice commenced singing, in which he was instantly joined by almost the whole of the congregation, sitting, both by old and young, males and females. These, as he read severally a line of the portion he had given out, would catch the words from his lips, and fall in with him in singing it. And never, thought I, had I heard singing, that was on the whole quite equal to this. There was no exact harmony in it, no perfect keeping of time, and much otherwise, at which a critical ear might justly take offence. And yet there was in it that, which to me was exceedingly interesting and impressive. The sound coming from such a multitude of voices, seemed as the roar of thunder and the voice of many waters. And then, there was such a seriousness in the appearance and manner of the great majority, such an evident engagedness in this act of praise to the Most High, as caused a deep solemnity to pervade the whole congregation, and in my humble opinion much more than compensated for all the musical faults and deficiences of the performance. Here, thought I, if anywhere, is a specimen of singing to the Lord with the Spirit and with the understanding also, of that melody of the heart which makes even the meanest attempts at melody with the voice an acceptable offering to God through Jesus Christ, and insures his favorable presence in the assemblies of his saints.

To singing succeeded what is commonly termed with us *the long prayer.* And it might very significantly be called so in the present case; for it occupied, as it seemed to me, at least three-quarters of an hour. And yet it was made, I am confident, from better motives than the long prayers of the Pharisees, and without any visible signs of weariness or impatience on the part of the congregation. It was offered by Mr. Carter, who, previously to commencing it, read a large collection of little bills, or notes, as they were called, expressive either of thanksgiving to God on the part of sundry individuals for various mercies which he had recently vouchsafed them, or of desire on the part of others for the prayers of the congregation, that the Lord would be pleased to grant help or relief in sundry exigencies of trouble or suffering there particularly enumerated. Nor did I understand that the notes read this day were more numerous than common, but only a fair sample, in this respect, of what used to be presented every Sabbath. For the first planters of New England, and in a good degree their immediate successors, were eminent for their practical belief in a particular Providence; such as extends not merely to the general interests and concerns, but to the minutest affairs and events of this lower world. They had a firm, realizing, ever present persuasion of the truth of those declarations of the Saviour, that the very hairs of our heads are all numbered with God, that not a sparrow, much less an individual of his human family, falls to the ground without his direction or permission. And they were well assured, too, of the efficacy of humble, fervent prayer for obtaining relief in any exigence into which the hand of his Providence might bring them, so far as would be consistent with his infinite rectitude, wisdom and goodness. Hence their aptness to make almost every event of life a foundation of prayer or praise, both in private and in public. And hence, too, a wonderful minuteness in the devotional exercises of the sanctuary in this place, on the occasion I am speaking of.

The prayer then offered by Mr. Carter, as mentioned above, differed not materially from such as we are accustomed to hear from orthodox pulpits at the present day, in its general acknowledgments of dependence, guilt and spiritual necessity, and in the leading spiritual mercies which it implored. But when he came to present the various special cases and circumstances of his people at the throne of grace, he became minute and particular, far beyond what is now commonly witnessed. Here he grew very fervent in spirit; and from the fulness of his heart, showed great fulness as well as plainness of speech. His mouth was filled with arguments; and he seemed hardly to know when he had said enough, and where to make a stop. He spread all the wants, all the trials and temptations and prevailing sins of his people before the Lord. Scarcely anything could be conceived having a bearing upon their present or future well-being, but he made it a matter of supplication to the Most High. And while he fervently deprecated the Divine judgments, he earnestly implored for his people all manner of blessings, both spiritual and temporal; or, as he quaintly termed them, "blessings of the upper, and blessings of the nether springs." He praised the Lord for granting to his people of this place a favorable seed-time the present spring thus far; and besought him to perfect his mercy in this kind toward them; to give them due measures of sunshine and of the rain of heaven in due time; to suffer no blight or mildew, locust or caterpillar to blast their expectations; but to bless the springing of the earth, to cause their grass to grow, and their land to yield its increase, and to give them their corn, and their flax, and the wine of their orchards in their season. He made devout acknowledgments of God's hand in certain melancholy casualties, and in all the signal occurrences, whether of sorrow or of joy, which had taken place in the town the week preceding; and prayed that God would sanctify to all concerned the visitations of his providence, whether in judgment or mercy. He presented with special minuteness of description the thanksgivings and the requests of those, who had expressly desired particular mention in the prayers of the sanctuary that day. He besought God to accept the thank-offerings of all those, whom he was permitting, after long restraint by sickness, to visit that day with recovered health the courts of his house once more; of his handmaids to whom he had recently granted safe deliverance in childbirth; and of his servants, whom, in their distant journeys by land or by sea, he had protected from enemies and from the perils of the great deep, had prospered them in the way they went, and had now restored them in peace to their homes and families again; and to vouchsafe to all and to each of them a deep and abiding sense of their obligations to the Divine favor; that so they might glorify him in the lives which he had preserved, and with the mercies which he had bestowed. Finally, he prayed the great Lord of Life, that he would sanctify all bereavements by death in this place to those who had lately been afflicted therewith, and had now expressly implored in the assembly of his people support, consolation and grace from above: that he would spread the everlasting arm beneath all who were sick; make their bed in their sickness; abate the violence of their respective diseases, allay the fever in their veins, make whole the bones that were broken; send healing mercy to them all; and above all, if the sickness of any of them who had asked the prayers of the congregation that day was unto death, that he would give them grace to be prepared for the solemn change that awaited them; that so they might meet it in peace, sustained with the blessed hope of pardon and acceptance with Him through the Divine Redeemer, and of eternal life and felicity beyond the grave.

The prayer was followed by singing the 15th Psalm from the same obsolete version as at the first singing.

Then came the sermon by Mr. Fox. While he was announcing his text, there was a most profound stillness. But, immediately after, I heard a slight rustling noise from different quarters of the house; and looking round to discover the cause, I spied the deacons, selectmen and others, who seemed to carry for that day the pens of ready writers, preparing to take down the texts and prominent heads of the discourse. This reminded me, it might be well for me to do the same; and I now copy from the entries then made in my note-book as follows:

The text was 2 Tim. ii: 19. "And let every one that nameth the name of Christ depart from iniquity." After observing that by those who name the name of Christ must here be understood, those who professedly believe in Christ, the preacher went on to deduce from these words of the Inspired Apostle the following doctrine: viz, "That it is the duty of all that profess themselves to be Christians to depart from iniquity." This important doctrine was then explained and made intelligible to the lowest capacities by answers to three pertinent questions, was confirmed by several Scriptural and convincing reasons, and applied to the spiritual benefit of his hearers by a single use for information, which was still further enlarged upon, under four distinct considerations. The questions, by way of explication, were, briefly, 1, "What is meant by iniquity?" 2, "What is meant by departing from iniquity?" 3, "Why is it so, that every one that names the name of Christ must depart from iniquity?" Among the seven "reasons," in confirmation of the doctrine deduced from the text, and implied in the last question, were briefly, 1, "Because God is a holy God, and of purer eyes than to behold iniquity." 2, "Because the Lord Jesus Christ himself is holy, and therefore will not suffer any to live in the profession of his name, and not depart from iniquity." 5, "Because Christians are called with a holy calling." 6, "Because of the great dishonor and reproach that sin casts upon the Lord Jesus Christ." 7, "Because it is the will of God that those that name the name of Christ depart from iniquity." The use "for information" was, "Hence learn the folly of those that make a profession of the name of Christ, and (depart not) from iniquity." "Let such consider, 1, 'that they have not as yet taken one true step towards a true reformation;'" 2, "that neither their persons nor services are accepted before God;" 3, "that it is a bold and daring presumption to name the name of Christ, and not to depart from iniquity." From all which considerations, the preacher deduced one more by way of "conclusion," viz: "Whoever are found under a profession of the name of Christ, and depart not from iniquity, Christ will one day not think them worthy to be named among professors. They shall not be found to be sealed ones, that day."

[44] Such is a brief specimen of the mode in which one of the earliest pastors of this church used to feed the flock of Christ committed to his charge. The spiritual food ministered by him on this occasion was plain food, served up in a homely, and, as some may think, in too precise and starched a style. Still it was wholesome food, the pure milk of the Word, and adapted, with the Divine blessing, to nourish the souls of his flock unto eternal life. The *doctrine* inferred from the text, and inculcated in this discourse, was sound and important; the *reasons* advanced in support of it were clear and sufficient; the *use* or application ever seasonable; and if there were any of his hearers who were not profited by it, the fault was not the preacher's, but their own.

Sermon being over, a short prayer by the preacher for the blessing of God on his Word dispensed, and a solemn benediction, closed the services of the forenoon.

In the afternoon, they were commenced with singing a portion of the 148th Psalm, H. M., to the tune expressly adapted to that Psalm, and thence called the "Old 148th." In the prayer by Mr. Fox which followed, was observed the same particularity of enumeration, and minuteness of description of the mercies implored, as that by which the prayer of the morning was distinguished. After reverend, adoring acknowledgments of the Divine perfections and works, love and mercy to the children of men, and after a more minute confession of prevailing sins (especially among his own people) than is now common, and earnest supplications for pardon and spiritual healing through the grace of God in Christ, he commended anew the special cases and wants of his people, and the interests of Zion among them, to Him that heareth prayer. And then, giving his thoughts a wider range than Mr. Carter had extended his in the morning, so as to take in all the proper subjects of prayer which his senior colleague had omitted, he began to offer earnest intercessions for his country, for all mankind, for the church of God throughout the world. He prayed that the inhabitants of New

---

[44] See skeleton of a discourse by Rev. Jabez Fox, delivered at Cambridge, July 1678, in Alden's Collection of Epitaphs, Vol. I., No. 236, p. 225.

England, especially of the Bay, might never forget the errand upon which their fathers crossed the ocean to this then dreary wilderness, that so they might enjoy the ordinances of God in their purity, and gather churches according to his Word: that they might still pursue the design and work which their progenitors had begun, still adhere to the Holy Scriptures in doctrine, worship and practice, neither adding to nor taking aught from the Divine requirements therein laid down, either by word or example: that so New England might continue New England, and that the Lord God might still condescend to dwell among them, and defend them, and multiply them, and build them up, as he had hitherto, forevermore. He thanked God for the endeavors of the Synod of the Elders and Messengers of these churches, lately convened in the city of our solemnities,[45] with a view to the reformation of those manifest declensions and crying sins, for which, it was to be feared, God had a controversy with the people of this land; and earnestly prayed, that the means and measures which the Synod had recommended for promoting reformation, and averting the Divine displeasure, might be prospered and blessed. And to this end, he earnestly besought of God, that he would pour out his Spirit, and rain down righteousness upon the whole Colony (especially upon this town of Woburn): that so this and all the churches of our land might awake from their slumbers, return to their first love, and do their first works; that godly discipline according to their Scriptural Platform might be kept up in them, the truth of the gospel be maintained in them, holiness and peace abound: that ministers might cry aloud, and spare not to show the people their transgressions, and the house of Jacob their sins; that our honored Magistrates might diligently attend the execution of the salutary laws and orders of the Government for the suppression and punishment of profaneness, Sabbath breaking, drunkenness, oppression, and all manner of wickedness and vice; and be themselves examples of piety and virtue: that the religion of the gospel might revive in power and purity among all ranks and

---

[45] Synod assembled in Boston, 1679, 1680.

conditions of men: that so God might lift on us once more the light of his countenance: that righteousness might dwell in our land; that mercy and truth might here meet together, righteousness and peace kiss each other.

He prayed for God's direction and blessing upon our honored Governor, Deputy Governor and the Magistrates of this jurisdiction; that he would at all times aid and prosper them in all their consultations and measures for preserving unimpaired the then threatened liberties of the country. He praised the Lord for inclining the Great and General Court of this Colony in their recent session to countenance the proceedings of the late Synod, by ordering the Confession of Faith drawn up by it, together with the Platform of Discipline agreed upon in 1648, to be printed "for the benefit of these Churches, in present and after Times;" [46] and prayed, that as Moses and Aaron kissed each other in the Mount of God, so the Lord would direct and dispose our civil and our spiritual fathers always to act in concert wlth each other in all designs for the reformation of the people, and the furtherance of the common welfare. And now, extending his views to the mother country, (or, as our ancestors were accustomed to call it, their home,) he prayed God to preserve and bless our dread Sovereign Lord, King Charles; that he would effectually incline him to remove from his presence all Popish and maliciously affected counsellors, who were laboring for the destruction of these his Majesty's Colonies by suggesting to his royal ear false and malicious insinuations against them; that he would move his princely heart to favor his poor but loyal subjects in these goings down of the sun, and to bestow on them his promised protection; and that so his Majesty ruling in righteousness and mercy, God would clothe all his adversaries with shame; but cause upon him and his royäl house the crown of these kingdoms to flourish, so long as the sun and the moon shall endure. He implored too the Divine benediction upon the High Court of Parliament, the Legislature of the realm of England; that by their laws, and by all their proceedings and measures,

---

[46] Resolve of Court, May 19, 1680.

they might not only maintain justice, mercy and truth at home, but also approve themselves the zealous and successful defenders of British rights and liberties, and of their common Protestant religion in all lands where the dominion of Britain was acknowledged, and over which its sceptre was swayed. And finally, he earnestly besought the Lord that he would protect and deliver his persecuted churches and people throughout the world; that he would hasten the end of all idolatry, superstition and imposture; restrain the violence and defeat the crafty counsels of the man of sin and his abetters; that he would everywhere extend the triumphs of the cross, and give efficacy to the word of his grace, and speed the accomplishment of the blessed time foretold in his lively oracles, when Babylon should fall to rise no more; when the kingdoms of this world should become the kingdoms of our God and of his Christ.

After prayer, succeeded the second singing, which was followed by a sermon from Mr. Carter. But this was not a written, but, in considerable measure at least, an extempore discourse, founded upon the same text that was treated of in the morning. As then, Mr. Fox displayed to all, especially to the members of his church, their obligations to depart from all iniquity; so now, Mr. Carter enforced those obligations. In a kind, affectionate exhortation, he earnestly charged all his hearers, especially professors of religion, to forsake all sin, to practise holiness of heart and life: thus happily illustrating the distinction anciently made by our ancestors between the teacher and the pastor of a church; assigning to the former officer the explanation and defence of the truth; to the latter, the enforcement of it upon the conscience and the heart.[47]

When the good man had ceased from this labor of love, Deacon Wright arose and said, "Brethren, if any one among you have a word of exhortation to offer, let him say on." All eyes, I perceived, were instantly turned toward me; and I felt myself constrained, in a manner, to get up, and, after making my respects to the ministers, to address the people briefly as follows:

---

[47] See Cambridge Platform, Chap. VI., § 5.

My Christian friends: you conclude, I presume, from the singularity of my dress, that I am a stranger in this region; and indeed, I am a stranger, come from a land of many days journey hence. And yet it sometimes seems, as if I were acquainted here: for there's a surprising resemblance in many respects between your country and mine. The climate is the very same. The natural scenery of both places is almost exactly alike. Your town bears the same name as one next to that I live in, when at home. The names of Charles River, Shawshin River, Horn Pond, and other waters, so common I find among you, are also perfectly familiar to me. Nay, your own names, which have been oft repeated in my hearing to-day, are the very same as those most prevalent in the town just referred to, and within whose ancient limits I myself dwell. In view of all these circumstances, I have at times to-day been almost forced into the conclusion, that I have been travelling ever since I left home in a circle; and now that I have come round again to the place I started from, some great alterations in the fashions of our dress, which have occurred in the interval of my absence, prevent me and my old friends and neighbors from recognizing one another. And yet, on the other hand, this supposition seems at once rendered inadmissible by the striking differences, which are everywhere apparent between your Woburn, and the Woburn in my vicinity. Here, in the midst of your village, I see no academy, as I do there, seated like a city on a hill which cannot be hid. Here the dwelling-houses are comparatively few, and scattered and unadorned; there the houses in the principal village are very numerous, and many of them, large and elegant to look to. Here, I see but one house of public worship; and hear of but one denomination of worshippers; there, in the centre alone, there are at least three or four meeting-houses, appropriated to the use of Christians of as many different names. So that considering these and other points of difference, I am driven to the conclusion after all, that I stand now in a very different Woburn from that I have been long acquainted with. And yet it is a satisfaction to find, that great as the interval is between us, we still worship the same God, acknowledge the same Saviour, and profess to take the same Holy Scriptures for our guide, both in faith and practice. Let us all then only adhere to that Sacred Rule, and live up to, and act out our profession of submission and obedience to it, and both you and I and the people I dwell among, cannot fail of being finally happy together forever.

Brethren, it has been highly gratifying, and I hope will be lastingly profitable to me, to have spent this holy Sabbath with you. I have been edified, I trust, by the prayers in which I have joined with you. I have been edified by the dispensation of God's Word in this his house; by the plain and forcible exposition of truth and duty therefrom, to which we all have had opportunity of listening to-day; and certainly, if our hearts are right with God, we none of us can miss of being benefited by what we have heard. Particularly have I been pleased with your singing. It has forcibly brought back to mind the days of my childhood and youth, when I was accustomed to hear sung, from Sabbath to Sabbath, by the congregation generally, the very same or the like simple tunes that I have heard to-day; though then by fewer voices, and sometimes with the aid of an organ, which I am aware you abhor, or at least much dislike. Concerning those days, I well remember what feelings of awe and devout reverence the sight and hearing of my elders, and of my elders' elders, all singing the high praises of God, though with unequal time and occasionally with somewhat discordant voices, used to excite in my breast. Of late, I have but seldom had an opportunity of hearing the songs of Zion sung after this sort. Hence, I have enjoyed listening to them to-day, as a feast, and I regret that it may be long before I am gratified in the same way again. But you, my friends, who are favored with this privilege every Sabbath, do prize it highly, I trust, and will not lightly give it up. And that you may long retain it, beware of multiplying the tunes to be sung. By adhering constantly to the use of a few plain, substantial tunes, which are easily learnt, you are all capable, in one degree or other, of sounding forth the praises of the God of Heaven.

Do not render then this delightful duty impossible to a large majority of your fellow-worshippers (as I have known it done in my own country), by the introduction of a multitude of new and difficult tunes, or by changing singing books once a year. And should your present aversion to instrumental music ever give way (as I doubt not it eventually will), and should you begin to use the harp, the viol and the organ in the worship of the sanctuary, let no one, capable of singing, be willing on this account to excuse himself from the duty, and shift it off upon a few paid individuals, with their instruments, in the gallery. For if singing the praises of Jehovah be a duty to any, it is to all who have a voice and an ear, and any tolerable skill to sing in concert with others. A select choir may be a great help in singing. Still its members cannot be supposed capable of doing the work of praise for others, so well as others, who have any ear for sacred music, can do it for themselves. Excuse, I pray you, the freedom of these remarks by a stranger, proceeding, as I trust they do, from a disinterested desire for your good. A few improvements I might here suggest in your present mode of singing; but I forbear. For in changing there is always risk, I am sensible, of doing harm instead of good; and I fear, that in attempting to make *good* in some measure *better*, I should, as often happens in other cases, mar or spoil the whole.

Brethren, I must repeat the high satisfaction I have taken in the services of this sanctuary this day. The only deficiency I have felt worth mentioning is, the omission to read the Holy Scriptures without comment; an exercise that is common in my own country, and one, it seems to me, that has a Divine warrant for it, and is both profitable in itself, and in accordance with the practice of the church in every age. But I will add no more on this point; assured that your own good sense and pious regard to the will of God, will eventually lead you, on reflection, to correct the error, if it be one. As to all other things, I can with truth express my entire approbation. As I have sat here this day, and attended to the several exercises of Divine worship, and witnessed the propriety and fervor and engagedness with which they have all been performed, I have been ready to exclaim, as did Jacob of old, "How dreadful is this place! this is none other but the house of God, and this is the gate of heaven!" May you ever find it to be so, by your own happy experience! And so may every house of worship that your posterity may hereafter erect in this place, prove to them and their children! I rejoice in seeing you do so much as you do, to teach the rising generation the truths and duties of the Gospel of Christ, and to lead them, both by precept and example, to prize the institutions of God's worship.

In particular, I was glad to perceive in the intermission that you are in the habit of catechising your children, — a good old custom, warranted by Scripture authority, and recommended by early Christian usage, but now (I regret to own it) much neglected in my own land! But there seems to be no need of exhorting you, brethren, to see that it be not neglected among you. I am confident that you will keep up the practice with the same diligence that it was transmitted to you by your fathers; and that you will enjoin upon your children likewise to do so hereafter, for the benefit of those who shall arise after them. You will charge them, whatever other means and methods of instruction they call in to their aid for the religious education of their children, on no account to let this be overlooked or slightly performed; that they will never leave it entirely even to their ministers, much less to other friends of less knowledge and experience than they; that they will keep the matter in their own hands, though they admit others to share in the labor of it with them; and discharge it faithfully according to the light and skill and experience which God severally gives them; and then the result, through the Divine blessing, they may reasonably hope will be, that there shall ever be a generation in this place who shall be taught of God to acknowledge, love and serve him, and whom he will own and build up and rejoice in, — a people for his praise.

Dear Christian friends, this is the first time I was ever with you, and it will, doubtless, be the last. I must presently leave you, and we shall meet no more on this side the grave. But sure I am that, if I am ever prepared myself through grace for a part in the resurrection of the just, I shall meet many, very many, of this congregation again at the right hand of the Son of Man; and shall be admitted to praise and rejoice with you in that better temple above, whence there is no more going out, and where we shall dwell forever with the Lord. The Lord grant that we may all of us find mercy of the Lord in that day! and till then I bid you, one and all, *a cordial farewell.*

Upon my saying these words, which were heard with attention, and were apparently welcome, Mr. Carter offered a short prayer, in which he implored a blessing upon the services of the day, and upon the words uttered by their unknown friend according to God's Word: and then, with singing four stanzas of the 119th Psalm, long metre, to the tune of "Hundredth," and with a Scripture benediction by Mr. Carter, the public worship for that day was ended. As for me, as soon as I could conveniently after leaving the house, I took the conveyance by which I came, and was instantly transported over the current of one hundred and eighty years and upwards, from Hilly Way, in Woburn, in his Majesty's Colony of Massachusetts Bay, in New England, to my own quiet home, near Vine Brook, and within the ancient bounds of the Second Precinct of Woburn, Massachusetts, one of the Independent United States of America.

CHAPTER IV.

Philip's War. — Persons murdered by Indians in Woburn during that War. — Small-Pox in Woburn, 1678. — Arbitrary proceedings of Sir Edmund Andros in Woburn, 1687–88. — Death of Rev. Thomas Carter. — Medford Bridge. — Death of Rev. Mr. Fox.

SHORTLY after the second meeting-house in Woburn was finished (the building, accommodations and weekly worship of which form a prominent subject of the Chapter foregoing), broke out that scourge of New England, Philip's War. It is so called from Philip, the Indian chief, who was its principal instigator. It began in Plymouth Colony, June 24, 1675, and quickly extending itself into Massachusetts, it spread its horrors and devastations in every direction, and seemed to threaten at times the utter ruin of the country.

In this destructive contest, Woburn was not assaulted by the enemy in great numbers at any one time. Nor was it burnt, pillaged and laid waste, either totally or in part, as Marlboro', Sudbury and Groton in the same county were. Still, it was not exempt from a large share of the common burdens and sufferings of that gloomy period.

Its proportion of the public taxes, necessary to sustain the warfare undertaken, was oppressive in the extreme. In 1674, the Colony tax for Woburn was but a trifle over £30.[1] But within fourteen months from the commencement of hostilities to the death of Philip, which occurred August 12, 1676, and which was virtually the conclusion of the war called by his name,[2] no less

---

[1] Town Records, Vol. I., pp. 55, 56.

[2] But war with the Eastern Indians, however, continued many years after. It was distinguished as King William's War, and cost much treasure and many lives to bring it to an end. In the course of it, the following instance occurred, in which Woburn people were involved. On the 6th of July, 1690, as two companies of English were scouting, under Captains Floyd and Wiswall, they came upon a party of Indians at Wheelwright's Pond in Lee, N. H. A bloody engagement ensued, in which Capt. Wiswall, his Lieutenant, Gershom Flagg, of Woburn, Sergeant Edward Walker, a son of the elder Dea. Samuel Walker, of Woburn, and twelve others, were killed and several wounded. —*Belknap's New Hampshire*, in one volume, p. 134.

than twenty single rates were ordered by the Court to be levied for the prosecution of the contest on the part of the Colonists, viz: three rates at their Session, July 9, 1675; seven, October 13, 1675, and ten, May 3, 1676.[3] But burdensome as these large and quickly repeated demands by the Legislature were, for money to carry on the war in which the country was involved, the inhabitants of Woburn, from patriotic motives, appear to have submitted to them all, without murmuring or complaint, and to have made ample and timely provision for answering them.

On the "23: 6 mo:" (23 August) 1675, the Selectmen met with the commissioner, and assessed "a rate for the Country"; and in giving it, on the 4th of the month following, to the constables to collect, they ordered them to gather it of every inhabitant "twice over," thus making it equivalent to two single rates. They also directed them to "demand of the old troopers two shillings and a penny upon each rate, as the Court hath ordered";[4] and likewise "to demand and gather of every person one fourth part of a single rate, for to provide ammunition with for a Town's stock; and to demand of every old trooper sixpence farthing more than what is set down in the said rate."[5]

---

[3] Colony Records, Vol. V., pp. 45, 55, 56, 81.

[4] At their session in July 1675, the Court passed the following resolve: "Whereas the troopers and their trooping horses are wont to be exempted in ordinary country rates, it is heereby declared, that they are not to be freed in the rates granted by this Court for the defraying the charge of the present expedition against the Indians."[a] In the foregoing order of the selectmen, by "old troopers" are meant those who belonged to some troop before the present war began, in distinction from new troopers, who had enlisted since, and of whom, at one time, there were twelve.[b] There were, at this period, five troops of horse within the jurisdiction of Massachusetts, viz: the Suffolk troop, the Essex troop, the Middlesex troop, the Norfolk troop (belonging to the northerly part of Essex County), and the "Three County troop," comprehending all who had enlisted from "the county of Dover and Portsmouth," from the settlements "in and near York, called Yorkshire, and from the settlements upon and near the Kennebeck, erected, 1674, into a county by the name of Devonshire.[c] Troopers from Woburn were attached to the Middlesex troop, commanded by Capt. Thomas Prentice, of Cambridge Village, now Newton.[c]

[a] Colony Records, Vol. V., p. 45.

[b] Town Records, Vol. I., p. 64.

[c] Colony Records, Vol. V., pp. 73, 295.

[5] Town Records, Vol. I., pp. 64, 65, 66, 67, 68, 69.

The amount of the rate thus assessed, and given to the collectors to gather "twice over," added to what was demanded of "fower ould troopers," for their persons and horses, was £60 :19 :10

do. of the quarter rate for ammunition 7 :06 :11

On the 23: of the 9 mo. (23d Nov.) 1675, the selectmen met and levied a rate on the inhabitants "for the charge of the Indian warr," amounting to £120 :00 :00

On the 18 :11 mo. 1675, (18th Jan. 1675–6,) the selectmen met again, and "ordered another Rate for the Indian warr," amounting to - - - £119 :01 :06

These last two assessments doubtless answered to the seven single rates called for by order of the court, Oct. 13th, 1675, and also to the third of the three single rates ordered July 9, 1675, but which, it seems, had not yet been assessed.[5]

On the 14: 4 mo. (14th June) 1676, the selectmen, to satisfy the ten single rates ordered in May of that year, levied what is called in the records, "a Warr Rate," being a single rate ten times doubled, amounting to - - - - - £325 :17 :6

Sum total - - - - £633 :05 :9

Of this sum, about £100, as nearly as can be ascertained, was reserved for the payment of town debts and expenses, such as schooling, support of poor, county tax, etc., etc. — (See *Records.*) - - 100 :0 :0

£533 :05 :9

The balance was paid to the Colony Treasurer, or to others, with his knowledge and allowance, towards defraying the expenses of the war.[5]

To afford some ease to the people in the payment of such heavy taxes, at a period of great scarcity of money, they were allowed by the court to pay them in various necessary commodities, and especially in grain, viz: in wheat at six shillings, rye

[5] Town Records, Vol. I., pp. 65, 66, 68.

at four shillings and sixpence, barley and pease at four shillings, Indian corn at three shillings and sixpence, oats at two shillings, per bushel; provided these articles were delivered to the treasurer without cost to the country. To encourage, however, the payment of taxes in silver, the court ordered an abatement of one-fourth part to such as paid in money.[6]

1675. "Paid in to the Treasurer by John Richison, Constable, by shoose and barly - - - - - - £8 :11 :6."
1675. "Paid by Jonathan Tomson [Constable] in oats and otherways - - - - - - 1 :5 :8."[7]

In settling for taxes during this war, an allowance was made for what were called "debentors"; that is, certificates from some acknowledged authority, of wages due to soldiers for their services. Whenever a constable presented a debentor to the Colony Treasurer, in payment of taxes, he was allowed for it the same as for silver.

"Paid by Jona. Tomson . . . . in silver and debentors, the full sum of all advanced - - £67 :19 :02."
"Paid in to the Treasurer by John Richison, Constable, in silver and debenturs, etc. - - 68 :16 :03."
"Paid by Joseph Wright in his debentor - - 01 :07 :07."[7]

As to the quarter rate for ammunition spoken of above, the Records inform how it was disposed of, as follows:

"Paid to the Captaine [John Carter], of the ammunition Rate, the just sum of - - - - £6 :02 :6

Capt. Carter paid Mr. Richards for a barell of powder, the sum of - - - - - -	£5 :0 :0
By musket bullets and pistoll bullets - - -	0 :17 :0
By to [two] Runlets to put these bullets in - -	0 :1 :4
By the porterige and ferridge [ferryage] - -	0 :02 :0
To Capt. Carter for buying powder - - -	0 :04 :0
For flints by Capt. Carter - - - -	00 :00 :11."[8]

[6] Colonial Records, Vol. V., p. 55.
[7] Town Records, Vol. I., p. 64.
[8] Town Records, Vol. II., p. 23.

But the pecuniary cost of this war, incurred by taxation and in other ways, burdensome as it was to the inhabitants ot Woburn, was nothing compared with the risk and loss of life which it occasioned many of them, the various and grievous hardships to which it subjected them, and the consternation and terror which it caused to prevail in the midst of them, as well as throughout the Colony, both by day and by night, lest they should be waylaid or suddenly assaulted, their houses burned or plundered, and themselves and families either killed, or captivated and reserved for future torture by their savage foes.

August 2, 1675, an order came from Edward Rawson, Secretary of the Colony to the constable of Woburn, "to impresse five able and sufficient horses, well shod and furnisht with bridles and saddles, fitt for the service of the Country; and bring them to Capt. Davis' [9] house in Boston by eight of the clock in the morning." [10] About December 1st, 1675, when preparations were making for the Narraganset expedition, thirteen soldiers were impressed from Woburn, viz: John Baker, John Baldwin, Peter Bateman, John Berbeane, John Cutler, Thomas Hale, Jeremiah Hood, William Peirce, John Polly, John Preist, John Sheldon, Caleb Simonds and Zechariah Snow.[10] February 24, 1675–6, nine horses more, with suitable equipments, were ordered to be impressed from Woburn.[10] And, March 22d following, Woburn was directed to furnish six draught horses and three men by way of impressment [10] "to carry provisions and ammunition to the garrison at Brookfield." [10]

In addition to the thirteen men, expressly named above, as forced into the war from Woburn by impressment, this town appears from its Records, from the Records of Hon. John Hull, Esq., Treasurer of the Colony in 1676,[11] and from other reliable authorities, to have furnished for the war forty-five others, who voluntarily enlisted in the service, or who were drafted for it by lot, viz: John Bateman, Isaac Brooks, John Brooks, William

---

[9] William Davis, Capt. of the Suffolk troop of horse, who died shortly after.

[10] Letters of Rev. Joseph B. Felt, from the State archives.

[11] A folio, once in possession of Nathaniel G. Snelling, Esq., Boston, but now, it is understood, in the rooms of the Historical and Genealogical Society.

Butters, Jacob Chamberlin, Moses Cleaveland, Jr., Samuel Cleveland, Josiah Clopson (or Cloyson), John Coddington, Jonathan Crisp, Paul Fletcher, William Green, John Kendall, Benoni McDonald, John Moloony, Richard Nevers, Abraham Parker,[11] Thomas Parker, Joseph Peirce, Thomas Peirce, Jr., William Reed, Samuel Read, John Richardson, Joseph Richardson, Nathaniel Richardson, Samuel Richardson, David Roberts, John Seirs, Benjamin Simonds, James Simonds, Joseph Simonds, Robert Simpson, Eliah Tottingham, John Walker, George Wilkinson, Joseph Waters [or Wallis], John Wilson, Jr., Increase Winn, Joseph Winn, John Wyman, Jr., Francis Wyman, Jr., and Joseph Wright. To these may be added three other soldiers in that war, named by the Treasurer, viz: William Dean, Thomas "Hincher" (Henshaw), and Benjamin Wilson, who may be confidently presumed to have been the three well known citizens of Woburn answering to those names respectively.

Of the fifty-eight persons above expressly named, as enlisted from Woburn in Philip's War, it may be remarked of fourteen of them, viz: of Peter and John Bateman, Chamberlin, Clopson, Coddington, Crisp, Fletcher, Hood, the two Parkers, Roberts, Simpson, Wallis, and Wilkinson, that they were probably not citizens of Woburn at the commencement of the war, but servants, or hired laborers from abroad, who were persuaded to enlist for this town in the service of the country. Simpson was apparently a Scotchman, one of those who, for espousing the cause of Charles II., were sent over to this country by Cromwell to be sold, after he had defeated them at the battle of Dunbar, 1650, or of Worcester, 1651; and, being a tanner by trade, was bought by Lieut. John Wyman, tanner, of Woburn, "on purpose for the management of his tan yard." Mr. Wyman, his master (having had his son slain in the fight at Narraganset) petitioned the General Court, May 16, 1676, that his servant,

[11] An Abraham Parker, according to the Records, was married in Woburn, in 1644, and had children. A son, Abraham, was born to him, March 8, 1650, but died Oct. 20, 1651. No mention is made subsequently of the father in the records, nor is his name on the tax lists of 1666, 1672, 1674, '75, '76, whence it is inferred that he had removed from the town.

Simpson, then a garrison soldier at Hadley, and needing clothes, might be released and come home, that "so his lether now in the fatts may not be spoyled.[10] Of the other thirteen, Peter Bateman, originally from Concord,[11] died at Woburn, Feb. 13, 1675–6, not improbably of sickness contracted at Narraganset the December before. Chamberlin, Coddington, Crisp, Fletcher, Hood, Abraham and Thomas Parker, do not appear to have returned to Woburn to remain there after the war was over. John Bateman (a brother, perhaps, of Peter: See *Savage's Genealogical Dict.*) came back, married, and reared up a family in Woburn. Clopson, also Roberts, Wallis, and Wilkinson returned, and were taxed here after the war had ended; Wilkinson died in the place, a pauper, 1683; and Roberts married and had a family in Woburn, lived much respected in the place, and died as late as 1724.

The other forty-four soldiers in Philip's War from Woburn, named above, were all citizens of the town, or the minor sons of citizens, when the war began; were most of them here born and brought up; descendants of a majority of them, are still remembered, or yet live in the place, and they constituted almost a third part of all the male ratable persons in the town in 1675, who were then in number only 140.[12]

December 19, 1675, was fought that memorable battle between the English and the Indians, called the Swamp Fight, or Narraganset Fort Fight, from the circumstance of its being fought at a fort in the midst of a swamp in the Narraganset country, within the present bounds of South Kingston, Rhode Island. As all the soldiers impressed about the first of that month from Woburn, and also a considerable proportion of the others enlisted in the war from the same place, appear to have taken part in that bloody engagement, a brief account of it here may not be amiss.

The Commissioners of the United Colonies of New England (viz., Massachusetts, Plymouth and Connecticut) having determined, in November 1675, to undertake an expedition in the

---

[11] Savage's Genealogical Dictionary.

[12] Woburn Town Records, Vol. I., pp. 62, 63.

midst of winter into the enemy's country, they ordered a thousand men to be raised for this service with all possible despatch. Of this army, Massachusetts furnished 527 men, viz, six companies of foot, containing 465 men, under the command of Major Appleton, and Captains Mosely, Gardener, Davenport, Oliver and Johnson, and a troop of horse led by Capt. Prentice. Plymouth found 158 men, in two companies under Major Bradford and Capt. Gorham. Connecticut's quota was originally set at 315 men, but she sent, eventually, into the field 300 English, and 150 Mohegan and Pequot Indians, distributed into five companies commanded by Major Treat, and by Captains Seely, Gallop, Mason, Watts and Marshall. The whole army, now amounting to 1,135 men, English and friendly Indians, was commanded by Major Josiah Winslow, Governor of the Colony of Plymouth. The Massachusetts forces marched from Boston, Dec. 8th, and from Dedham, Dec. 9th, and were joined by those of Plymouth soon after, and by those of Connecticut, Dec. 18th, about evening. After spending that night, which was cold and stormy, in the open air, they moved on at break of day, Dec. 19th, wading through the snow, fourteen or fifteen miles, "without either fire to warm them, or respite to take any food, save what they could chew in their march."

At one o'clock, P. M., they arrived at the edge of the swamp, the place of their enemy's retreat, whither they were conducted by Peter, a disaffected Indian, who told them that here "they should find Indians enough before night." In the midst of this swamp, which was large, the Indians had made, upon a rising ground of five or six acres, a fort, or an enclosure of palisades, surrounded by a hedge of about a rod in thickness. The only way by which our forces could venture to attempt an entrance into it, with any chance of safety and success, was over a long tree elevated four or five feet from the ground; and even this had a log house erected over against it, in which many Indians were stationed, ready to defend the passage against all who should approach it. By this passage, the Massachusetts men, who were in advance of the rest upon entering the swamp, made a bold effort to throw themselves into the fort: but two of their captains, Johnson and Davenport, were instantly shot down mortally wounded; the former upon the tree, the latter upon getting within the palisades. And here commenced a long and sharp conflict between the English and Indians. For a considerable time, the former were obstinately resisted by the Indians, who fought with a desperate resolution against their assailants, as they attempted an entrance into their fort, or when they had succeeded in throwing themselves into it. But nothing could daunt the English, or repress the ardor of their attack. As fast as one company was driven back, another stood ready to take its place, and to renew its efforts. At length, while the main body of the Connecticut forces (who had been stationed in the rear) were strenuously fighting their way over the tree and before the block house, into the fort, another party passed unobserved to the rear of the fort; and there finding a vacancy in the palisades, they clambered over the high and thick hedge, and, rushing along through the opening, "they poured a heavy and well directed fire upon the back of the enemy." And now the Indians, attacked both in front and rear, were gradually compelled to give up resistance, and by one way or another to make their escape from the fort. In the mean while, the English fired their wigwams, in which were collected not only their stores of corn for their subsistence during the winter, but also many of their old men, women and children: and then, having completed this work of destruction, they commenced at dusk marching to their head-quarters fifteen or sixteen miles off, taking with them their wounded, and the greater part of their dead.

But who can describe the horrors of that night! The groans of the dying warriors, as they lay thickly strewed on the ground in the fort; the hideous yells of those who escaped, enraged at their defeat, and at the loss of all that was dear to them; the heart-rending shrieks of old men, women and children perishing in the flames of about six hundred wigwams: all concurred to render the scene inexpressibly shocking, and deeply affected, it is said, the hearts of some of the victors themselves. The loss of the Indians by this battle has been differently estimated.

According to the confession of one eminent among them, who was afterwards taken in Rhode Island, and put to death in Boston, there fell that day seven hundred warriors; and three hundred were wounded, who subsequently, the most of them, died of their wounds. "It was supposed," saith Rev. Dr. Trumbull, concerning the Indians, — "It was supposed that three hundred warriors were slain, besides many wounded, who afterwards died of their wounds and with the cold. Nearly the same number were taken, with three hundred women and children. From the number of wigwams in the fort, it is probable that the whole number of the Indians was nearly four thousand. Those who were not killed in battle, or did not perish in the flames, fled to a cedar swamp, where they spent the night without food, fire or covering." Of the English, "six brave captains fell in the action, and eighty men were killed or mortally wounded. A hundred and fifty men were wounded, who afterwards recovered." Many of the wounded died in consequence of their sufferings from the cold, and from the hardships they endured in their long fatiguing march the night after the battle. "The cold was extreme," saith Dr. Trumbull, "and the snow fell so deep that night, that it was difficult the next day for the army to move. Many of the soldiers were frozen, and their limbs exceedingly swollen. Four hundred were disabled and unfit for duty."[13] Of those returned after the battle from the several companies as dead or wounded, the following six belonged to Woburn, viz:

"Of Major Samuel Appleton's company, Illia Thathane (or, as the name doubtless should have been recorded, Eliah Tottingham)" wounded and left at Rhode Island, January 6, 1675–6.

"Of Capt. Nathanael Davenport's company, Caleb Simonds, Zechariah Snow and John Baker, wounded.

"Of Capt. Prentice's troop, John Wyman, jr., [son of Lieut. John Wyman] slain, and Nathanael Richardson, wounded.[10]

Beside these six officially returned, as dead or wounded,, belonging to Woburn, may be named Francis Wyman, Jr., son

[13] Trumbull's Connecticut, Vol. I., Book 1, Chap. xiv., pp. 337–40. See also Hutchinson's Massachusetts, Vol. I., pp. 298–301. Hubbard's Indian Wars, pp. 100–112.

of Francis, tanner, of Woburn; and Peter Bateman. They were both soldiers in Philip's war from Woburn; the former apparently by voluntary enlistment, the latter by impressment, about Dec. 1st, when preparations were making for the Narraganset expedition; they both appear to have fought in the Fort fight; and they both died shortly after, Bateman 13 Feb., and Wyman 26 April, 1676, not improbably from wounds received, or sickness contracted, in that memorable battle.

But the six soldiers from Woburn, officially returned as killed or wounded at the Fort fight in Narraganset, were not all of its inhabitants whose blood was shed in Philip's war. The town was visited the following spring by two or three of their savage enemies upon a work of death, which they but too successfully accomplished. In the afternoon of April 10, 1676, as Mr. Samuel Richardson, who lived upon what has been recently called the Miller Farm in Richardson's Row, was employed in carting manure into his field, accompaned by his son Samuel, a boy between five and six years of age, he was surprised in looking toward his house, to see feathers flying about it, and other tokens of mischief within. Apprehending that Indians might be there, he hastened home, and there found two of his family murdered, viz: his wife, Mrs. Hannah Richardson, who had been lately confined; and his son Thomas, twin brother to him who had been with him in the field. Upon further search, it was ascertained, that the infant also, a daughter named Hannah, had been killed by the same ruthless hands. The nurse, it appeared, had snatched it up in her arms, upon the alarm of danger, and hurried away to a garrison house in the vicinity for protection. But so closely was she pursued by the enemy, that finding she could not save herself and the babe too, she let the babe drop, and the Indians despatched it upon coming up. Mr. Richardson now rallied some of his neighbors, who went with him in pursuit of the enemy. After following them some time, they espied three Indians sitting together on a rock, and discharged their muskets at them. The Indians instantly fled to a piece of woods hard by; and it being near night, their pursuers fearing that they themselves might be waylaid by them, or decoyed into danger, desisted from following them, and returned home. Upon going afterwards to the place where the Indians entered the woods, they discovered blood on their track; and upon further search, they found an Indian buried under the leaves, who was doubtless one of the three, who had been fired upon by Mr. Richardson and company, and who, being mortally wounded, had died upon the spot where found, and had been buried there by his associates.

To this period, too, may be assigned another occurrence of the same melancholy character with the foregoing, which took place in the opposite quarter of the town. Hubbard, in the Preface to his "Narrative of the Indian Wars," edited in 1677 (as quoted by Drake in his "Biography and History of the Indians of North America"), observes, "a murther was committed at Farmington, another at Woburn, by some Indians in their drunken humors upon a maid Servant or two, who denied them drink." The murder here referred to by Hubbard, apparently as perpetrated a little before Philip's War, was not improbably the same as one committed in the West part of Woburn, now Burlington, the story of which has been transmitted there by creditable, uninterrupted tradition from time immemorial. This story, which differs in some circumstances from that of the Reverend historian just named, is briefly as follows. On a certain Sabbath, an Indian concealed himself in a hop house, the kiln of which is still pointed out, about a mile from Burlington meeting-house, on the road to Bedford, between the house belonging to the Poor Farm, and that of Miss Ruth Wilson. When he supposed the neighbors generally had gone to meeting, he came out from his lurking place, and went to the house, which stood on the spot where Miss Wilson's now is. Upon entering, he asked for cider of a young woman who had been left at home. In compliance with his request, she went to the cellar to draw some; but upon her return, he knocked her in the head with his tomahawk. The cellar door was dashed with her blood, which was never wiped off; and when the house came to be taken down, about 1760, to make way for the erection of the present one on its site, this blood-stained door was removed, as it was, to the barn; and when the barn was afterwards taken down, to make room for a new one in its stead, the door was transferred to another barn in the vicinity; and thus continued to be exhibited in these several places for many years, as a memorial of this instance of savage cruelty.

The period of this war of Philip was one of the darkest, if not the most so, in the history of New England. The thinness of the English settlements in the country at that time, and the thorough acquaintance with their dwellings, fields, roads, and all their common places and times of resort, which the Indians possessed, gave the latter numberless opportunities for attacking them unawares to advantage, which they were not slow to perceive or improve. They were enabled hereby, as Rev. Dr. Trumbull strikingly observes, "not only in small skulking parties, but in great bodies, to make their approaches undiscovered, almost into the very midst of them; and under cover of the night, to creep into their barns, gardens and outhouses; to conceal themselves behind their fences, and lie in wait for them on the roads and in their fields. Sometimes they concealed themselves before their very doors. No sooner did they open them in the morning, than they were instantly shot dead. From almost every quarter, they were ready to rise upon them. At midnight, in the morning, or whenever they could obtain an advantage, they were ready to attack them. While the English were hunting them in one place, they would be slaying the inhabitants and plundering and burning in another." . . . . And thus they "kept the whole country in continual fear and alarm. There was no safety to man, woman, nor child; to him who went out, nor to him who came in. Whether they were asleep or awake, whether they journeyed, laboured or worshipped, they were in continual jeopardy." [14] But happily, this dreadful state of consternation and dismay did not last long. After April 1676, the affairs of Philip rapidly declined; and his death, August 12th, of that year, put a stop to the war which he had been the chief instrument of exciting, about fourteen months from its commencement. Within

[14] Trumbull's Connecticut, Vol. I., Chap. xiv., p. 333.

this short period, according to a statement in Trumbull's History of Connecticut,[15] "About 600 of the inhabitants of New England, the greatest part of whom were the flower and strength of the country, either fell in battle, or were murdered by the enemy." . . . . "Twelve or thirteen towns in Massachusetts, Plymouth Colony and Rhode Island, were utterly destroyed, and others greatly damaged. About 600 buildings, chiefly dwelling houses, were consumed with fire." And even this estimate, the reverend historian just named considers, with reason, as falling short of the truth.

Scarcely was this town delivered from the common burdens, sufferings and terrors of this Indian war, than it was visited by another grievous calamity, (as it was then considered, and really was,) the small-pox. This loathsome distemper, which our ancestors were wont to regard with most painful apprehensions, whenever it appeared among them, before inoculation for it was introduced, was brought at this time into the country by a ship infected with it, which arrived at Nantasket, July 10, 1677.[16] Eight hundred persons in the whole are supposed to have fallen victims to it in different places at this visitation.[16] "*Multitudes*" died of it in Boston in 1678. In Charlestown, among other valuable citizens to whom it proved fatal, was the elder Rev. Mr. Thomas Shepard, one of the most talented and excellent ministers of that town, who caught the disorder from a parishioner whom he ventured to visit on his death-bed, and died of it shortly after himself, December 22, 1677. From Charlestown or Boston, it seems to have gradually spread to Woburn. A number here were sick of it at the close of 1678, which led the selectmen, alarmed by the danger in which it involved all the inhabitants, to pass at a meeting of theirs, January 6, 1678–9, the following order:

"Whereas the hand of God is stretched out against many of the Inhabitants of this Towne in the disease of the small pocks, for the prevention of the spreading of the said disease, it is ordered by the Selectmen of this towne of Woburne, that from this time

---

[15] Trumbull's Connecticut, Vol. I., Chap. xiv., p. 350.

[16] "1677, July 10, the Ship infected with the Small Pox (whereof more than 800 died, came to Nantasket."— *Diary of Rev. Peter Hobart, Hingham.*

forward all and every person that hath been infected with the said disease, shall not goe forth to the Meeting hows or to their neighbours howses before eight weeks are accomplished after they are first taken, or into the streets, or near any person, so as to infect them, and then to have leave from the Selectmen to come forth; also all watchers and tenders with the persons aforesaid are, when they come to the meeting hows, to sit in such seats as are from time to time appointed for that end; and, when meetting is done, to goe forth first, and hasten awaye, and not mix with the assembly: and that there be care had in the hanging out bedding, or cloathes, or throwing out excrements or any other thing, so as may tend to the spreading of the said disease: and that all persons that have not had this disease come not at those howses or persons infected, unless it be those in the same family: and that all visitors be careful in chainging their apparel when they come to the meeting hows: and all persons transgressing this Order, being legally convicted before the Selectmen, shall paye to the use of the Towne twenty shillings for each offence." [17]

But, notwithstanding all the precautions taken by the fathers of the town for preventing the spread of this dreaded disorder, it continued apparently to prevail here, more or less, as late as May 1679. For at a meeting of the Selectmen on the 5th of that month, Eliah Tottingham was fined twenty shillings for a breach of the above Order respecting it.[17] From a memorandum in the Day Book of the Selectmen, (i. e. Town Records, Vol. II.,) it appears that twenty-seven persons in all were sick of it in Woburn at that time, viz: Isaac Brooks, three of his children, and John Cutler, Senr., then a resident in his family; Gershom Flagg; James Thompson and a daughter; three of goodman Houlten's [Holden's?] daughters; goodwife Gilson; David Wyman; Zechariah Convers' wife and child; Edward Farmer, Isabel Farmer; Matthew Johnson and daughter; Salah Adford; Craggen's daughter; Ephraim Buck's wife; Jacob Farrar; Thomas Peirce; George Reed; goodwife Richardson. Of these, four died of the disease, viz: John Cutler, Senr., in the family of Isaac Brooks; Jacob Farrar; David Wyman, and goodwife Convers.[18]

[17] Town Records, Vol. II., pp. 112, 120. [18] Town Records, inverted, Vol. II., p. 163.

September 5, 1684, died Rev. Mr. Thomas Carter, first pastor of the church in Woburn, in the 74th year of his age,[19] and 42d of his ministry. He was born in England, and educated in St. John's College, at the University of Cambridge, where he received the degree of Bachelor of Arts, 1629, and of Master of Arts, 1633.[20] He came to this country, "a young man," and while yet a student in divinity, in 1635 :[20] and may reasonably be supposed to be the Thomas Carter, who (according to a publication of Hon. James Savage, entitled Gleanings for New England "History") was allowed, April 2d of the same year, at the age of twenty-five, to embark with forty others at London, on board the Planter, Capt. Nicholas Travice, bound to New England.[21] This Thomas Carter, it is true, is described in the Register of his permission, as being a servant of Mr. George Giddins, a husbandman, on board the same ship. But then such were the difficulties experienced at that day by men of education and influence, in obtaining liberty to emigrate from England to this country, in consequence of orders from the government, that many were tempted in one way or other to elude those orders, especially by concealing their proper business and profession, or giving but an imperfect description of it.[21] And it is some confirmation of this conjecture, that the age of the emigrant in the Planter above stated exactly agrees with the age assigned to Rev. Mr. Carter at his death. On his arrival in this country, Mr. Carter was admitted an inhabitant of Dedham shortly after its incorporation in September 1636.[22] From Dedham, he removed to Watertown, where he united himself with the church at that place; and where he was employed in some service by the church or town to good acceptance. For, when he was first invited to preach at Woburn, Nov. 3, 1641, it is mentioned as a reason for his not being applied to sooner, that it had been doubted whether Watertown would be willing to part with him.[23] He preached for the first time in this place, December 4, 1641; and was ordained, November 22, 1642.[23]

---

19 Woburn Records, Mr. Boutelle.

20 Savage's Gleanings, pp. 246–248.

21 Savage's Gleanings, pp. 253, 254, 272, 273. Savage's Genealogical Dictionary.

22 Genealogical Dictionary.

23 Town Records, Vol. I., pp. 4, 5.

At his ordination, the town presented him with a house, which they had built for his use, on the spot where the house known as the Coolidge or Silvanus Woods' house now stands.[23] They also engaged to give him a salary of £80 annually, one fourth of which was to be in silver, the remainder in various necessaries of life, at the current price: a compensation, which was enlarged in 1674 by the grant of twenty cords of wood annually, to be delivered at his door. From the time of his ordination, he ministered constantly to this people without aid thirty-six years, till Rev. Mr. Jabez Fox was invited to assist him; and from that time, in connection with Mr. Fox, about six years more, till his death.

Mr. Carter appears to have lived secluded in great measure from the world; and hence he is seldom if ever named in history among the eminent clergymen of his day. Still, there is abundant evidence, that he was a very pious, exemplary man, an able and sound preacher of the gospel, and one whom God honored and prospered in his work. Under his ministrations, the church was greatly enlarged and built up, and the town flourished, and was for the most part, in peace. Capt. Edward Johnson, one of the principal founders both of the church and of the town, speaks of him in his "Wonder-working Providence" (published in 1654) as a "reverend, godly man, apt to teach the sound and wholesome truths of Christ"; and one who had "much encreased with the encreasings of Christ Jesus."[24] And in the following lines addressed by him in the same work to Mr. Carter, he is represented as a plain, but very faithful and successful minister; a pastor of distinguished humility and meekness, and in gentleness towards his flock, as rather exceeding than otherwise.

"Carter, Christ hath his wayes thee taught, and thou
Hast not withheld his Word, but unto all
With's word of power dost cause stout souls to bow,
And meek as lambs before thy Christ to fall:
The antient truths, plain paths, they fit thee best,
Thy humble heart all haughty acts puts by;
The lowly heart, Christ learns his lovely hest,
Thy meekness shews thy Christ to thee is nigh.

---

[24] Wonder-working Providence, Book II., Chap. xxii., pp. 175–181.

Yet must thou shew, Christ makes his bold to be
As lions, that none may his truths tread down;
Pastoral power he hath invested thee
With, it maintain, leest he on thee do frown.
Thy youth thou hast in this New England spent,
Full sixteen years to water, plant and prune
Trees taken up, and for that end here sent;
Thy end's with Christ; with's saints his praises tune." [24]

What the last sickness of this venerable divine was, the Records do not specify. But two charges in the bill for his funeral expenses, presented to the Selectmen, October 6, 1684, give reason to conjecture, that it was some short and violent disease, perhaps a putrid fever. That bill was as follows:

"*Charges on Mr Thomas Carter's funerall in* 1684.

By fourteene gallons of wine at 3s : 6d per gallon	£2.09 : 00
For tarr, two shillings . . .	0 : 02 : 00
For gloves	1 : 16 : 00
For his coffin, money . . .	0 : 06 : 00
For his graue, in pay . . .	0 : 05 : 00
For manchester, 6 yards, and a jarr for tarr	0 : 01 : 06
	£4 : 19 : 06." [25]

At a General Meeting of the inhabitants, October 6, 1684, the same day on which the above bill of funeral expenses was presented to the Selectmen, they voted and agreed unanimously that there should be half a rate made for defraying it and other "Town's debts." They also generously agreed that Mr. Carter's rate for his salary should "be compleated and payd for this yeare as formerly." [25]

By his wife, Mrs. Mary (Dalton) Carter, whom he married before his settlement in Woburn, and who died March 28, 1687, Mr. Carter had eight children, viz: Samuel, Judith, Theophilus, Mary, Abigail, Deborah, Timothy and Thomas. Theophilus and Deborah died young, before their father; Samuel, usually styled in the Town Records, Mr. Samuel Carter, was born August 8, 1640;

[25] Town Records, Vol. III., p. 68.

had a liberal education, was a graduate at Harvard College, 1660, was admitted an inhabitant and a proprietor of the common lands by vote of the town, 4th Jan. 1665–6;[26] sustained at different times several responsible offices in the town, as Selectman, Town Clerk and "Commissioner of the Rate," and was repeatedly employed there as an instructor of youth. By his wife, Eunice [Brooks], whom he married 1672, he had eight children, and died 1693.

Judith married Samuel, son of Deacon Edward Convers, June 8, [alias October 14,] 1660,[27] and secondly, Giles Fifield, May 2, 1672, and died 1676. Mary, born July 24, 1648, married John Wyman, Jr., son of Mr. John Wyman of Woburn, about 1671, and he being killed by the Indians at the Swamp Fight, December 19, 1675, she next married Nathaniel Bachiler of Hampton, N. H., October 31, 1676, by whom she had eight children, and died 1688.[28] Abigail, born January 10, 1649–50, married May 7, 1674, John Smith, and died prior to 1684. Timothy was born June 12, 1653, married Anna Fisk, daughter of David Fisk of Cambridge [Lexington] May 3, 1680, and died July 8, 1727.[28] Thomas was born June 8, 1655, married, 1682, Margery Whitmore, daughter of Francis Whitmore of Cambridge, who died October 5, 1734.[28] Timothy and Thomas Carter were both husbandmen, and proprietors, in their father's right, of several considerable tracts of land in Woburn. Timothy was the father of thirteen children, of whom three died before their parents; and the descendants of Thomas, who had a family of six children, are still numerous in Wilmington, and in that part of Burlington adjoining, which is known by the name of Carter Row.

The same year in which Rev. Mr. Carter died, 1684, the Charter of the Massachusetts Colony, which had long been threatened, was vacated in England; and with their Charter, the people had taken from them, not long after, the invaluable privilege of choosing their own rulers. In December, 1686, Sir Edmund Andros arrived at Boston, as Governor of Massachu-

[26] Town Records, Vol. I., p. 31. [27] Town Records. Savage's Genealogical Dictionary.

[28] Town Records of Marriages, Births, etc., etc. Savage's Genealogical Dictionary. Letter of Thomas B. Wyman, Esq.

setts, by commission from King James II.: a fit servant of a Popish and arbitrary master. Of this Governor, it has been observed, that "Nero concealed his tyrannical disposition more years than Sir Edmund and his creatures did months." He promised fairly at first: but very soon exerted the great power intrusted to him, for ruling as he pleased. He and a few of his Council (appointed also by the King) who resided in or near Boston, passed what laws and raised what taxes they saw fit, without check from any assembly of representatives of the people. They declared the titles to the lands granted under the former Government to be of no validity, under the pretence that the Charter had been vacated, and likewise that those grants had been made without the Colony Seal; and they required the people, if they would enjoy their possessions unmolested, to come to them, and take out new patents for them, at an extravagant price. And when some ventured to complain of oppression, they were insolently told by one of the Council, "that they must not think the privileges of Englishmen would follow them to the end of the world."

This tyrannical government was suddenly put down, in an unpremeditated insurrection of the people, in April 1689. Previously, however, the people had in general been submissive to its measures, because resistance appeared to them both presumptuous and vain. And yet, in some places, murmurs of disapprobation and uneasiness would at times arise, and a disposition to oppose would occasionally manifest itself. The Selectmen of Ipswich, for instance, voted to "petition the King for liberty of an assembly before they [made] any rates"; for which daring act, they were fined and imprisoned. Samuel Appleton, Esq., of the same town, and Rev. John Wise, one of its ministers, were imprisoned for a like offence.

Woburn, too, repeatedly resented the privation of some of its ancient liberties, which it suffered by this government. A law had been passed by Sir Edmund and his Council forbidding town meetings to be held at any time or for any purpose whatever, except once a year for the choice of town officers; and even for this single meeting in any year for this one purpose, it was required, it seems, that it should be called, not by the Selectmen of any town, but by warrant from certain Justices of the County in which the town was located, or by direct authority from the government. But the people of Woburn could not brook this encroachment upon a privilege which they had enjoyed under the old charter from the beginning. Their meeting, for the choice of town officers for 1687, was convened February 22d, the last Tuesday of that month, their long accustomed day for this business, when they chose for Selectmen, William Johnson, Esq. (well known for his warm attachment to the old charter), Francis Kendall, Samuel Walker, William Lock, and Increase Winn. But, within a fortnight, this election was annulled; and the inhabitants were directed to meet, March 7th, for a new choice, by a warrant from Capt. Jonathan Wade, of Medford, Capt. John Brown, of Reading and Lieut. William Symmes, of Medford, three Justices of the Peace for the County of Middlesex, when they chose again the same persons for Selectmen that had been elected in February.[29] No other town meeting is on record for that year. But the next year, to show their continued aversion to the existing law respecting the calling of town meetings, they again ventured to meet on the day they had been used to, February 28th, and re-elected the old Board of Selectmen. But again their proceedings were nullified for being made at a meeting illegally convened; and the people were required, by "Order of the Governour and Councill," to assemble anew for the choice of town officers, May 21, 1688. Accordingly, in obedience to authority, they met again on the day appointed; when William Johnson, Esq., was either purposely dropped from the office of Selectman, and from that of Town Clerk, (which he had holden uniformly since the death of his father, in 1672,) from fear of the resentment of the governor and his creatures; or else, being chosen, he declined accepting; being unwilling to occupy a public

[29] Town Records, Vol. III., p. 121. The name of William Johnson is not mentioned with the others, in the record of the choice of Selectmen, Feb. 22, 1686-7; but he subscribed his name as Selectman with the others to a record of Feb. 6, 1687-8, (Town Records, Vol. III., p. 116,) before the next choice of town officers, Feb. 28, 1687-8, wherein he is expressly named as chosen one of the Selectmen.

station during the existence of a government that had showed itself so arbitrary, and so hostile to the liberties of the people.

In 1694, the town was thrown into a state of violent agitation, in consequence of a summons to answer before the County Court the presentment of Mistick or Medford Bridge. In 1648, the General Court had passed an Order, laying the expense of making and repairing bridges, upon the towns within whose limits they were.[30] But this Order was repealed in 1655.[31] And, subsequently, for a series of years, it became an established custom to assess the repairs of Medford Bridge not on the town of Medford alone, nor on the whole county of Middlesex, but jointly upon the towns of Charlestown, Woburn, Reading, Malden and Medford; even as the great bridge over Concord river at Billerica was wont to be maintained at the united expense of Billerica, Chelmsford and Groton. Woburn, however, had long been growing weary of the incumbrance. As early as October 8, 1672, the town directed the Selectmen to address the General Court by their deputies, or by petition, for granting them "some ease of their burden at Mistick Bridge;" and also authorized them to make an agreement with the other towns united in the support of it, if they saw fit, with the understanding, "that if there come to be County Bridges," their agreement to this end should be void.[32] But no relief was obtained of the General Court, and, apparently, no agreement with the other towns, in pursuance of this vote. The repairs of the bridge being neglected, it was presented in 1675, and from that time Woburn quietly did its part towards keeping it in passable order till 1690. October 16th, of that year, the Selectmen of Woburn, Reading and Malden, met in this town, and agreed to petition the General Court concerning Mistick Bridge.[33] The result of this petition appears to have been the appointment by the Court of a committee to confer with committees of the above named towns, and then, a reference of the whole subject to the County Court for settlement. But the result of this conference is not known. In 1691, the several towns above named were cited to

---

[30] Colony Records, Vol. II., p. 263.
[31] Colony Records, Vol. IV., Part 1, p. 231.
[32] Town Records, Vol. I., p. 37.
[33] Town Records, Vol. III., p. 39.

appear before the County Court, to answer a presentment of the bridge in question. And now the Selectmen of Woburn held a meeting in May 1691, with those of Reading and Malden, to consult with one another how they should conduct their defence.[34] They also chose Sergeant Matthew Johnson to appear before the Court on behalf of Woburn,[34] and appointed a committee of three to measure, previously to the Sessions, all the bridges in the country highways in town, with a view, doubtless, to exhibit to the Court a statement of the cost they were liable to, for maintaining bridges within their own bounds.[35] And, to crown all, the inhabitants at a General Meeting, December 7, 1691, voted as follows: "That the Selectmen of said towne [of Woburn] should withstand the said town's allowing anything more to the repairing of Mistick Bridge; and if they withstand it in law, that the town shall bear all the charge thereof." [36]

In consequence of this bold resolution, nothing seems to have been done by the town for the support of the bridge at Medford for two years. But it did not clear them of their responsibility in this matter. December 22, 1693, the Selectmen received a summons from the Clerk of the Court of Quarter Sessions to send men before said Court on the 26th of that month, "to answer the presentment of Mystick Bridge." In obedience to this citation, Samuel Bloggct, one of the Selectmen, and James Convers 2d (afterwards known as Major James Convers), appeared before the Court on the given day, and made answer, "that Woobourne was not concerned in the presentment of Mistick Bridge; neither would they do anything in order to the repairing thereof, except by Law they were forced thereto; and that they referred themselves to the law in that case; and so left the case for that time." [37] But this resolute stand was easier taken than kept. For, immediately after, came a new citation from the clerk of the sessions, ordering the Selectmen or others on behalf of Woburn to appear before the Court at their

[34] Town Records, Vol. III., p. 149.

[35] "Town Dr. to Mr Carter [Samuel] the 4th. month 1691 for a daye's work taking a Survey of all the Bridges £0:02:10." Town Records, Vol. III., p. 149. Charges for the same service on the same page, by Matthew Johnson and Thomas Peirce.

[36] Town Records, Vol. III., p. 154.

[37] Town Records, Vol. IV., p.

adjournment, January 23, 1693–4, and then "to make returne to said Court of the repairing of Mistick Bridge, on the penalty of five pounds fine to their Majesties for the town's default in that matter." [38] The receipt of this summons threw the whole town into a ferment. The Selectmen immediately called a meeting of the town, January 10, 1693–4, at which they made known to them the above order of Court. Whereupon "the Inhabitants of Woobourne joyntly declared, that what they had formerly done towards the repairing of Mistick Bridge, was only an act of Charity to help Medford when they were low and poore, and to help *those men* that had engaged themselves to help repaire the same; and now Medford was much increased both in number and in estate, and those gentlemen that had formerly engaged themselves as aforesaid being all dead, now therefore the said Inhabitants once more voted with a joynt concurrence, that as by law they were not engaged to help repair Mistick Bridge, so they would do nothing to the same; and furthermore, that they may shew their obedience to authority, the Inhabitants aforesaid nominated and chose Lt. Matthew Johnson and James Convers 2d, both of Woburn aforesaid, to appear for them on the 23d inst. before the said Honored Court at their said adjournment, and make this answer as abovesaid. And further that the said town of Woburn refer themselves to the law in such cases had and provided in this their Majesties Province: also the said Inhabitants do hereby impower the said Matthew Johnson and James Convers to defend the said town in a course of law, either by review, appeal, or any other lawful way or means whatsoever, against the repairing or maintaining of any part of Mistick Bridge, against any who shall demand the same: hereby promising to reimburse all the charges and expenses that they or either of them shall necessarily be at, in and about the premises, granting and allowing unto the said Johnson and Convers full power and authority to appoint and constitute Attorneys one or more under them, and at pleasure to revoke; giving unto the said Johnson and Convers full power to say, execute and do in and about the same whatever is necessary in law; hereby

[38] Town Records, Vol. IV., pp. 5, 6.

promising to ratify and confirm all and whatsoever the said Matthew Johnson and James Convers or their attorneys shall lawfully do or cause to be done in and about the premises and dependances thereof.

"Per order of the Inhabitants of Woburn,
"JAMES CONVERS, Town Clerk."[38]

Thus armed with power and authority from the town, one of its two agents, James Convers, repaired by advice to Boston, and feed a couple of lawyers aforehand, "for fear" (as he expresses it), "of being intercepted"; and both of them appeared before the Court at its adjournment, January 23d, and made defence, as follows: "That Woburn was not presented [presentable?] upon account of Mistick Bridge, nor were they culpable as criminals upon that account. If Medford could plead anything of a Covenant, that was a Civil case, and not a criminal; and they might have their action against us in the Common Law: but at this Court, and in this way, we were not obliged to make any further answer, but to refer ourselves to the law, 'that bridges were to be mended in those towns in whose precincts they lie,' and so left it with the Court; and the Court considered thereof, and gave us the following determination.

"Middlesex, ss: At the Generall Quarter Sessions of the Peace, holden at Charlestown, Jany 23d, 1693–4 ffrom the 20th of December 1693, by their Majesties Justices:

"Whereas there was an Order of the General Court in the year 1691 referring the settlement of Mistick Bridge to ye County Court of Middlesex, and the said Court ordering the repairing of said bridge to be by the respective townes of Charlestowne, Woobourne, Malden, Redding and Medford, according to their wonted manner, till the Generall Court make further provision; and the defects of said bridge having been presented to this Court before the late law respecting Bridges; this Court order that the said respective townes do forthwith make sufficient repaire of the said defects of said Bridge, upon paine and penalty of fiue pounds fine to their Majesties for the respective defaults of each of the said townes, and then to make returne of their doings therein to the next

General Sessions of the peace for Middlesex; and then for the future it shall be left to the determination of the Law."

"Vera Copia Exam^{d} per Samuell Phipps, Cler." [39]

With this decision of the Court, Woburn thought it prudent to comply. "Whereupon," adds the Town Clerk, immediately under his copy of the decision just referred to: "Whereupon the said Bridge was sufficiently mended by Josyah Convers sworne surveyor, and return made as abovesaid and recorded.[39] No doubt, one inducement with the people for thus doing, contrary to their previous resolutions, was the expectation that this was the last time they should ever be called on to repair Mistick Bridge. This expectation was founded on the closing sentence of the decision of the Court, that the repairing of this bridge should in future "be left to the determination of the Law": which they thought would clearly free them and the other towns above named, except Medford, from the burden in question. But in this idea, they soon found themselves mistaken. The law referred to was passed by the Provincial Legislature in 1693, and is entitled "An Act for Highways." Among its numerous provisions is one for the annual choice of two or more Freeholders in each town, who should "take care that all Highways, Private Ways, Causeys and Bridges lying within the Precincts of such Town, be kept in repair, and amended from time to time, when and so often as shall be needful, at the charge of such Town (where it is not otherwise settled)," etc., etc.[40]

"*Where it is not otherwise settled.*" Of this exceptive clause in the law, advantage seems to have been afterwards taken, to defeat the expectations of Woburn, of being freed from all obligation to aid in the repairs of Mistick bridge. It was doubtless insisted upon by Medford, with the countenance of the Court, that it had been so long *settled* by custom, that Woburn should join with Charlestown and the other towns concerned in helping Medford to keep that bridge in repair, that the law referred to did not now release them from

---

[39] Town Records, Vol. IV., p. 6.

[40] Colony and Provincial Laws of Massachusetts Bay, pp. 267–8.

it, and they must still do as they had done. Hence, after the above decision of the County Court, in 1694, Woburn was called upon year after year, again and again, to mend the bridge at Medford, though out of its own limits; again and again it demurred, and passed resolutions against complying; and yet eventually complied:[41] so that nearly seventy years more elapsed, before it was fully released from a burden so long complained of. But, in 1761, an agreement was entered into between Woburn and Medford, by which the long vexed question of Medford bridge was fully put to rest. At a general meeting in Woburn, July 21, 1760, it was voted, "that the Committee chosen at the annual meeting in March last past to manage the affair concerning the Great Bridge at Medford, are hereby directed and impowered to agree with the town of Medford about said Bridge for a certain sum, that so the town of Woburn may be finally discharged from any future charge relative to said Bridge."[42] To this proposal for settlement, Medford showed itself willing to assent. For at a town meeting there, May 13, 1761, six of its citizens were chosen as a committee "to treat with Woburn, Reading and Malden, or either of said towns separate, concerning Medford Great Bridge; that is, to take a certain sum of money of said Town or Towns, and acquit any of them that shall comply, from all further charge."[43] After this manifestation on the part of Medford of its readiness to compromise its difficulty with Woburn in the way of Woburn's own proposing, the committees of the two towns met to confer with one another on this subject, and came to a mutual agreement. This agreement was ratified by Woburn in town meeting, June 25, 1761, when its inhabitants voted "that they would give the sum of two hundred

---

[41] Viz, in 1702. — (Town Records, Vol. IV., p. 204.) In 1706. — (Town Records, Vol. V., pp. 24, 28.) In 1711, Aug. 20th, "The Selectmen of Wooboum were warned to appear at the Quarter Sessions of the Peace . . . . to answer the Presentment of Mistick Bridge. Accordingly, the Selectmen appointed Stephen Richardson to procure Stuff and mend Said Bridge, which he did," etc., etc. — (Town Records, Vol. V., p. 196.) At a general meeting, March 3, 1728–9, chose Mr. Daniel Peirce and Mr. Caleb Blogget, as a Committee to go to the General Court with a Petition that they may be "eased of the burden of Mistick Bridge, or to have liberty of a Landing Place at the River," etc., etc. — (Town Records, Vol. VI., p. 369.) See also Proceedings of the Town at a general meeting, Jan. 28, 1744–5, (Town Records, Vol. VII., p. 462,) and May 19, 1760, (Town Records, Vol. VIII., p. 291.)

[42] Town Records, Vol. VIII., pp. 294, 315. [43] Town Records, Vol. VIII., p. 466.

pounds, Old Tenor, or equivalent in Lawful Money" (the amount agreed upon by their committee), "to the town of Medford."[42] And thus this controversy of nearly a century's standing was brought to a peaceable issue, as stated in the following attested copy of Medford's agreement:

"*Agreement of Medford about ye Bridge.*

"Know all men by these Presents, that we Samuel Brooks Esqr. Stephen Hall Esqr. Zachariah Poole Gentleman, Simon Tufts Gentleman, Seth Blogget Gentleman, and Benjamin Parker Gentleman, being chosen and impowered by the Town of Medford to agree with the Town of Woburn about Medford Bridge, we being all of the Town of Medford in the County of Middlesex and Province of the Massachusetts Bay in New England, DO agree that for and in consideration of the sum of Twenty six pounds thirteen shillings and four pence of Lawful Money paid by the Town of Woburn before the ensealing hereof, do hereby acquit and discharge the said Town of Woburn from all past and future charges arising by reason of said Bridge, and do, in our said capacity take upon the town of Medford all the charge and care of said Bridge, which the Town of Woburn was bound to do or ever shall be: In Witness whereof we in our said capacity have hereunto sett our hands and seals this seventh day of July annoque Domini one thousand seven hundred and sixty one, and in the first year of his Majesty's Reign.

"Signed, Sealed and Delivered	Stephen Hall	[L. S.]
in the Presence of us	Z. Poole	[L. S.]
Willis Hall	Simon Tufts	[L. S.]
Aaron Hall	Benjn Parker	[L. S.]"[43]

An amusing specimen of the town's watchful attention to its minute as well its weighty interests and concerns in former times, occurs in the Records of 1696. At a General Meeting, June 24th of that year, after citing several delinquents in the payment of Rev. Mr. Fox's salary to appear before the Selectmen on the following Monday at the house of James Fowle, "public notice was likewise given to all persons concerned, that have incroached upon the Town's Common and Highways by fencing in yards or the like without Order," that they also appear before the Selectmen at the same time and place, "to agree with the said Selectmen about their severall trespasses, or else some other measures will be speedily taken to redress the same."[44] From the sharp threatening at the close of this warning, uttered in open town meeting, and apparently with the consent and approbation of all the people present, it might naturally be inferred that some grievous trespass upon town property had been committed. What was it, then, and who were the trespassers? Had some covetous householders rendered half of Upstreet impossible to be passed with safety by making large, unauthorized enclosures? Had certain unprincipled wood-dealers presumptuously invaded and fenced in some twenty acres of the town's woodland in Wood Hill? Or had some greedy landholder inclosed, and appropriated to his own use a goodly portion of the Town Common in the plains of Goshen? Oh, no; nothing of the kind. The sum of the encroachments complained of was this. The Rev. Jabez Fox, their minister, and two other highly respectable citizens, Thomas Peirce, Senr., and Daniel Baldwin, happened to be fond of tobacco; and taking a notion to raise enough themselves for their own smoking and chewing, they had each ventured to fence in some unsightly nook or bend in the highway near their respective premises, where the soil was peculiarly favorable for the growth of the noxious weed, and had there set out plants of it, which were now thriving like so many skunk cabbages, promising them a luxuriant harvest. But, in accordance with the warning now given them, backed by such plain threats of a civil prosecution, they all three, like good citizens, came before their Honors, the Selectmen, at the time and place appointed, to make satisfaction for their wrong-doing. And there, having received some gentle reprimand for their unauthorized converting of public into private property for the time, they were let off from any further censure or punishment, and had leave to enjoy "the improvement of those severall bitts of land" for that summer, on condition of agreeing to pay the Selectmen a penny each for the use of the

---

[44] Town Records, Vol. IV., pp. 72, 73.

town, and throwing open their enclosures to the highway by the next "Michaelmas."[44] And so far at least as relates to the money they promised to pay for the town's use, there is evidence upon Record that they were as good as their word. For in the Town Accounts for that year, James Convers, Jr., the Town Clerk, is made Dr. to the town

"For money paid for quittrent for three tobacco yards per Mr ffox, Clark Peirce & Sargt Baldwin . . . . £00:00^s:03^d."[45]

Rev. Jabez Fox appears to have possessed the confidence and affectionate regard of the great body of the people in Woburn, and to have retained the same through life. And yet the men of the generation he served, were not all so punctual to fulfil their engagements to him as their fathers had been to his predecessor in the ministry. Through the pressure of the times (which were confessedly hard), and especially in consequence of the heavy taxes imposed during the Indian and French wars of that period, a number were constantly behind hand in paying their proportions to his salary, so that, at one time, the arrears due to him were about £70, equivalent nearly to his salary for a year. Various were the expedients resorted to by the Selectmen and by the town to cure this evil, but long without the desired success. One method proposed was, that the Deacons for the time being should reckon with Mr. Fox at the end of every year, and warn all who were found delinquent to make up their arrears within two months after the year had expired, and report them to the Selectmen, if they persisted in their neglect; in which case, the Selectmen were to recover their dues in a legal way. But the Deacons proving but inefficient collectors and duns, the whole burden devolved upon the Selectmen, who summoned the delinquents before them at times, when some, say the Records, "that were behind, were brought up to their proportions" (T. R. IV., p. 27). At a General Meeting, January 18, 1696–7, a committee, consisting of Major William Johnson, Deacons Samuel Walker and James Convers, Jr., was appointed to audit Rev.

---

[45] Town Records, Vol. IV., p. 69.

Mr. Fox's accounts, and to make report respecting delinquents at the next General Meeting. At the same time, the Selectmen were ordered for the future to furnish Mr. Fox, in November of every year, with a List of every man's proportion to his salary, and at the end of every year to reckon with Mr. Fox, and give a list of rates unpaid to the Constables to collect them. And, moreover, it was voted at the same meeting, that Rev. Mr. Fox's salary should be paid semi-annually; that so if any persons should be about to remove from the town, the Selectmen, by taking care, might "save the one halfe of their rates, if not the whole." [46]

December 6, 1697, the Selectmen met, say the Records, "to look after Mr. Jabez Fox his arrears, and sent writts to some, and messages to others. Severall came up and paid their arrears . . . others warned to appear the 21st courant" etc.[46] Finally, at a General Meeting, March 3, 1698–9, the following Resolve was passed: "The freeholders and other Inhabitants of this Towne of Wobourne having considered and discoursed the difficulty of bringing up some men to their duty, as to their paying their due proportions to the maintenance of the Rev. Mr. Jabez Fox, annually, according to covenant; divers methods having been taken which did not prove effectual, the said Inhabitants declared their minds in the matter, that the most likely way for the collecting the said Mr ffox his sallery, is to make fair lists thereof (as of other rates) of each and every one's due proportion to the same, and affix warrants thereto, and deliver the same to the severall Constables annually, to collect it by distress, of all such as refuse or neglect to pay their respective parts thereof: and for all those persons that pay their respective parts of the said sallery without such distress, they shall pay no part of the Constables' charge for collecting the same, but the whole charge of the said collection, distress or distresses, shall be paid by those persons only, that by their refusal or negligence occasion the same: and this was voted and passed in the affirmative." [47] Accordingly, three days after the General Meeting, March 6, 1698–9, the Selectmen "mett and perfected the lists for the Reverend Mr.

---

[46] Town Records, Vol. IV., pp. 83, 101.

[47] Town Records, Vol. IV., p. 137.

Jabez ffox his sallery for the year 1698, beginning on the first of November last, and affixed Warrants to the same, and delivered the same to the Constables to collect, as above said" etc.[47] This method seems to have been effectual for the end intended during the remainder of Mr. Fox's life; but still there were large arrears due for the years preceding, which were not collected till after his death. This mournful event took place suddenly, while he was yet in the midst of his days and usefulness. Being at Boston on a visit, he was seized with the small-pox, of which he died there, February 28, 1702–3. A friend of his in Boston thus records his death at the time: "Lord's Day Feb. 28 1702–3. Mr Jabez Fox dies of the Small Pox in the forenoon."[48]

Rev. Mr. Jabez Fox, second pastor of the church of Christ in Woburn, was, according to a family tradition, a lineal descendant of Rev. John Fox, a nonconformist divine in the reign of Queen Elizabeth, and author of the work entitled "Acts and Monuments of the Church"; or, as it is more familiarly known, Fox's Book of Martyrs: a book much read by the Puritan founders of New England, and regarded by them with a reverence and esteem short only of that which they paid to the Bible.

His father, Mr. Thomas Fox, resided first in Concord; and then removing to Cambridge, was one of its Selectmen in 1658, and repeatedly afterwards; and died there April 25, 1693, aged 85. His mother, Mrs. Ellen Fox, previously to her marriage to his father, Mr. Thomas Fox, had been the widow of Mr. Percival Green of Cambridge, a member of the church there, who died Dec. 25, 1639, and by whom she had had two children, John and Elizabeth Green, both baptized in infancy in the church at Cambridge.

Mr. Jabez Fox was born and baptized in Concord, about

---

[48] Diary of Judge Sewall.

[48] At a general town meeting, April 5th, 1703, it was generously voted to pay Mrs. Judith Fox, the relict of their late pastor, forty pounds of the annual salary which had been proportioned for her husband the November preceding, but who had died when but about four months of his year had expired. — See *Town Records, Vol. IV., p. 224.*

1647,[49] and was yet in his minority when his father removed from there to Cambridge; was graduated at Harvard College, in 1665, and appears to have studied divinity there. He had commenced preaching, and had married before application was made to him, in 1678, to go to Woburn, and to preach there statedly a year, as an assistant to Rev. Mr. Carter. This invitation was accepted; and so satisfactory were his services, that, before the term of his engagement expired, the town voted him unanimously, July 16, 1679, "a call to the ministry, with an Intent he may be called to office in time, if God make waye";[50] and, November 5th, 1679, they invited him to settle over them for life; and made generous provision for his comfort and support.[50] The church, too, it is presumed, a little previously to the last date, gave him a call to the pastoral office, as he had been encouraged to expect they would. The precise date of his ordination has not been preserved; but may reasonably be assigned to the middle of November, 1679. His salary year was long reckoned as commencing with November 1st. The whole term of his constant service in the gospel ministry in this place was somewhat over twenty-four years; viz: one year as an assistant to Rev. Mr. Carter, and twenty-three years and upwards as settled minister in Woburn, and pastor of this church.

At his decease, in Boston, his remains were brought to Woburn, and there interred in the Old Burial Ground. For many years, it is understood, the stone which marked the place of his interment, was overlooked, or supposed to have been removed. But, during the past summer (1866), a descendant, Jabez Fox, Esq., of Washington, D. C., made a visit to Woburn; and going upon Burial Hill, found the gravestone of his

---

[49] It has been supposed by some that Mr. Fox was born in Cambridge. But this hypothesis is disproved by the following extract from a "List of Members in the Church of Cambridge," in the handwriting of Rev. Mr. Jonathan Mitchell, its pastor, which purports to have been "taken and registred in ye 11th. month 1658." [January, 1658-9.]

"Thomas ffoxe & Ellen his wife, both in full Comm.

"His son Jabez ffoxe baptized at Concord, but in minority when his ffather joyned here." — See *Cambridge Church Records.*

[50] Town Records, Vol. I., pp. 98, 101.

ancestor, and took down an exact copy of the inscription upon it, as follows:

Memento Mori: Fugit Hora.

HERE LYES Y^{E} BODY OF
Y^{E} REVEREND MR JABEZ FOX.
PASTOUR OF Y^{E} CHURCH OF
CHRIST IN WOBOURN 23 YEARS.
& AGED 56 YEARS, DECESE$_{D}$
FEB^{R} Y^{E} 28th 170$\frac{2}{3}$.

Rev. Mr. Fox's widow, Mrs. Judith Fox, was daughter of the elder Rev. John Reyner, minister of Plymouth and Dover, N. H. After Mr. Fox's death, she married Col. Jonathan Tyng, of Boston, who had been of the Council of Gov. Sir Edmund Andros, and who, coming in his latter days to Woburn to reside, died there suddenly, January 19, 1723–4. The venerable lady, his widow, survived him till June 1736; and the following touching memorial of her excellence is copied from her gravestone:

Here lyes Buried ye Body
of Mrs Judith Tyng, wife
to Col^{l} Jonathan Tyng,
formerly wife to ye Rev^{d}
Mr. Jabez Fox: who Dy'd
June 5th, Anno Dom^{i} 1736,
in ye 99th year of her Age:
A woman of Most Exemplary Vertue
& Piety; Rich in Grace, ripe for Glory.[51]

By this worthy lady, Rev. Jabez Fox had five children; viz:

1. John, born at Cambridge, May 10, 1678, shortly before his father was invited to preach in Woburn, and who afterwards succeeded his father there in the pastoral office.
2. Thomas; born at Woburn July 6, and died July 10, 1680.
3. Thomas; born at Woburn November 13, 1681.
4. Jabez; born December 2, 1684.
5. Judith; born June 19th, 1690, and died the same year.

---

[51] Jabez Fox, Esq., above mentioned. This inscription, furnished by him, differs considerably from that exhibited in Alden's Epitaphs. Vol. I., No. 237, p. 229.

It is not known that Rev. Mr. Fox ever published any of his writings. A skeleton of a sermon, delivered by him at Cambridge, July 28, 1678, from 2 Tim. ii. 19, and committed to writing by Mr. afterwards Rev. Nathaniel Gookin, pastor of the church in Cambridge, is published in Alden's Collection of American Epitaphs, vol. I., No. 236, pages 226–229, and is presented (a good part of it) in Chapter III. of this work. Another skeleton of a discourse, preached by Rev. Mr. Fox at Cambridge, May 11, 1673, from Eph. v., 16, "Redeeming the time," is found in the voluminous manuscript collections of Hon. John Hull, Esq., and of his son-in-law, Judge Sewall. It was probably taken down on paper at the time of delivery, by the latter gentleman, who was then a resident graduate or tutor at the college in Cambridge; and it is here given, not only as a sample of the instructions addressed to his hearers by the second minister of Woburn, but also as a specimen of the manner in which the ancient divines of New England constructed their discourses for the pulpit.

By Mr. Fox, May 11, 1673.

Ephe. 5 :16. Redeem. ye time.

2 motives (1) because such are termed wise.
[See v. 15.] (2) because ye dayes are Evil.

"D." [Doctrine.] It is a duty incumbent on, & much for ye interest of all (especially in evil times) to redeem ye time.

Luke 15. 17. Jonah when his soul fainted, remembered ye L. [Lord.] Hester. Ninevites.

Expli. [Explication: by 3 Questions.]

1 Q. [1Question] When said to be evil dayes?

(1) All ye dayes of our lives are evil, both in respect of sinne & the effects of it.

Special. (1) In ye day of Jacob's *trouble.*
(2) When, notwithstanding our afflictions, there is noe returning to ye L. [Lord.]
(3) When those evils are found among a people which call for evil dayes: as

1. Pride.
2. Lighting [slighting?] ye means of grace: Speak. [Speaking] Smooth things &c.
3. Covetousness, oppression & deceipt. Micæ 2. [Micah, 2, 3.] When these things are incorrigibly persisted in, so yt ye prudent keep silence. Gray haires, & men know it not. Eccl. 12. 1.
Several gray haires: as

1. Decay of first love.
2. When there is a want of life & vigour.
3. A lukewarm spirit; a spirit of neutrality, when men know not whether to be for God, or Mammon: such a Laodicean strain speakes evil times.
4. When God seems to be withholding his converting spirit.

2 Q. [2Question] What to redeeme time?

Nega. [Negatively] time cannot be called back.

It presupps. [presupposes]

1. A sence of ye loss & worth of time.
2. A sence of ye disadvantage accrueing by ye loss of it.

[It implies (1) Knowing ye seasons & opp. [opportunities] Rom. 13. 11.

(2) A dew [due] improving ye time: catching at all opportunityes & parcels of time. Eccle. 9. 7. do it with all thy might.

R. 1. [Reason 1.] 1. From ye *absolute necessity* of it, in respect of what we have lost.
2. With respect unto ye shortness of time.
3. With reference to ye means of redeeming time, which are hastening away.
4. With respect to ye work & buisinesse we have to doe.

R. 2. From ye comand [command] of God.

3. Because ye dayes are evil from ye sinne acted by each of us.

Q. 3. [Question3] Why especially at such a time?

(1) God expects it then.
(2) Evil dayes cut men short of their time.
(3) It is ye only means to prevent ye badnesse of ye times.
(4) Because evil dayes take awaye ye means for redeeming time.
(5) Satan is then most busy.
(6) Else we shall be fools.
(7) At such a time, we do most honour God, if so be then we redeem ye time.

U. Exam. [Use for Examination.] 1. Whether ye evil of ye times have been any motive to us to redeem it.
2. Hath it wrought in us a greater circumspection? hath it stirred up a spirit of prayer in us?

U. 2. Wt. [What] thankfulnesse, yt God gives us a season & opportunity to redeem time? God sumes [sums] up a great deal of love in ys [this;] I gave her space to repent: ye more

1. Because we have neglected ye time.
2. How many cut short of time!

U. Exort. [Use for Exhortation.] Redeem ye time. If we have all lost time, yn [then] it is time for us to redeem time.

(1) Our time is limited to a certain time.

(2) There is notice & account taken of all ye opportunityes we enjoy. 3 years I come &c.

(3) This is ye very end of all ye space we have afforded us.

Direct. [Directions]

1. Bethink yourselves what ye worth of time is.
2. Take heed of resting in dutyes.
3. Do not procrastinate: this, a daring of God. Matt. 24, latter end.

CHAPTER V.

Settlement of Rev. John Fox, November 1703.—Declaration of the Church, 1703.—Occasion of Baptists in Woburn, 1671.—Proceedings in the Law against Them, etc., etc.—Brief Notices of the Six Subscribers to the Church's Declaration, viz: William Johnson, Esq., Dea. Saml. Walker, Joseph Wright, Senr., James Convers, Senr., W. Locke, Senr., James Convers, Jr.

THE last chapter, it will be remembered, brought down the history of Woburn to the death of Rev. Jabez Fox, its second minister, February 28, 1702–3. In April following, agreeably to ancient Puritan custom, a Fast was held by the town, the public services of which were conducted by several of the neighboring ministers, to implore the divine direction in the choice of a successor.[1] At a town meeting, April 5th, 1703, Mr. John Fox, eldest son of Rev. Jabez Fox, who was then keeping the Grammar School in the town, was invited to preach three months on probation; and this invitation was afterwards renewed for three months more. Before this latter engagement expired, the church held several meetings with reference to his permanent continuance among them; at one of which, they chose Mr. Fox, as the Town Records express it, "for their Minister, in order to his full settlement in the worke of the Ministry":[2] by which choice seems to be meant, that they voted him a call to the pastoral office. The town, at a meeting October 4, 1703, confirmed these proceedings of the church; choosing by a major vote, "Mr. John Fox to be the Minister of the town of Woobourne."[2] They also voted to give him £80, one fourth in money, as his salary for the first year; which was the same compensation that his father had been wont to receive; and promised, in case

[1] Paid "to James Fowle . . . . for the Elders Entertainment, for themselves and horses, on the Town Fast in Aprill last [1703] - - £1 :8 :0."
Town Records, Vol. IV., p. 249.

[2] Town Records, Vol. IV., p. 238.

"of his settling in the Worke of the Ministry in Woobourne upon his own Lands,"[3] that they would use their influence with the proprietors of the town[4] to grant him at their next meeting a piece of land lying between his own land and that of Mr. Timothy Carter, son of the first minister. These proposals were accepted by Mr. Fox, and he was accordingly ordained the following month, November 17, 1703, as the pastor of the church, and minister of the town of Woburn. The exercises of this solemnity are preserved in remembrance, in the following brief notice from the diary of Rev. Joseph Green of Salem Village, now Danvers, who was present on the occasion. "17 Nov. 1703. I went with Mr Fitch and Lld. [landlord] to Mr Fox's ordination at Oburn. Mr. Peirpoint [of Reading] began with a prayer. Mr Fox preach'd. Mr. Willard [of Old South Church, Boston] gave the charge. Mr Peirpoint the right hand. I came home at 7 o'clock."[5]

But though Mr. Fox was now considered as permanently settled in Woburn, yet nothing had been determined hitherto respecting his salary beyond the first year. At a meeting called to act on this subject, November 13, 1704, the town voted:

1. To "maintaine their minister, the Reverand Mr John Fox, by a rate or assessment proportioned upon them for that end, according to former custom in Woobourne."

2. To allow him for his encouragement in his work the sum of eighty pounds annually, "forty pounds in money, and forty pounds in corne and other provisions at money price, at the ordinary rate they are sold for between man and man in Woobourne."

3. That this agreement should stand as long "as the said Mr. John Fox shall continue and carry on the whole work of the Ministry in Woobourne."[6]

---

[3] Upon the homestead inherited from his father.

[4] The old distinction between the *proprietors* and the *inhabitants* of the town is here, as it is in other passages of the records, properly observed.

At a meeting of the proprietors, March 6th, 1703-4, they voted unanimously to give Mr. Fox the piece of land referred to, "to be his own proper estate forever." — *Town Records, Vol. IV., p.* 253.

[5] Manuscripts of the late William Gibbs, Esq., of Lexington. Vol. C., No. 10, p. 30.

[6] Town Records, Vol. IV., pp. 269, 270.

But these votes were not passed by the town with unanimity. Twenty-six persons, several of whom were men of great respectability, entered a protest against them; which, with their names, is recorded in the Town Book.[6] Their dissent, however, was not owing apparently to any dissatisfaction they felt with Mr. Fox, but founded expressly upon the alleged poverty of this town in particular, and of the country in general, by reason of the growing charge of the then present war, which rendered them averse to "stating any certain sallery at [that] time," etc.[6]

Mr. Fox being present at this meeting declared his acceptance of what the town then voted, as his permanant annual allowance, and in view of the public burdens then pressing upon his people, he agreed, for the present year, to be satisfied with Seventy pounds, and to make due consideration afterward, "So long as the charge of the present war lay so heavy upon this town." [6]

While the question of Mr. Fox's settlement was pending, a communication was made to him by the church, subscribed by six of its leading members, in behalf, apparently, of themselves and their brethren, which shows decisively what were the sentiments of the great majority of Woburn Church at that day, respecting the doctrines of religion, and ecclesiastical order and government. A copy of this interesting communication was found many years ago in a box of time-worn papers, belonging to the Dean family, in which, probably, it had been quietly resting for upwards of a century. It is seemingly in the handwriting of Major William Johnson, and reads as follows:

"A Coppy of the Proposals of Wooburn Church offered to Mr John Fox, when on his probation among them June y 3d. 1703."

"It is now about three score years since this Church of Wooburn entered into Couenant as a Church of Christ, and haue continued ever since in that ffaith and Order which we were instructed in by our Honourable and Reverend fathers spirituall, political and naturall, and above all, the Word of God, the which we haue perused, and finde it to warrant the same, and wee hope wee shall not depart from it now wee are old.

"Wee do therefore declare the Confession of Faith drawn up by the Rev[d] Synod held at Cambridge in (48) and approued of by the Honoured Gen[ll] Court, and perused again by the Synod held at Boston in the year (79), and that Platform of Discipline agreed upon at the same Synod in (48) and approued of by the Synod in (79) held at Boston, for the Substance of it wee agree with it; and wee do fully comply with that Chapter in the Confession of Faith concerning Baptism, Paragraph (4), that not only those who do actually proffess Faith [in] and Obedience unto Christ are to bee baptized, but allso the Infants of one or both Belieueing Parents are to bee Baptized, and they only. Wee also comply with and hold that a Congregational Church ought to be furnished with Pastours and Teachers, Ruling Elders and Deacons, as in the (7) Chapt. of Discipline. Wee agree allso with the (8) Chapt. concerning the Election of Church Officers, and with the (9) Chapt. concerning Ordination and Impositions of hands, and with the (10) Chapt. concerning Church Power, and with the (12) Chapt. concerning the Admissions of Members: all which wee pray God to keep us stedfast in, that wee may hold out to the End.

" WILLIAM JOHNSON
" SAM[ll] WALKER
" JOSEPH WRIGHT Sen[r]
" JAMES CONUERS Sen[r]
" WILLIAM LOCK Sen[r]
" JAMES CONUERS Jun[r]."

The "Confession of Faith," to which the subscribers to this Declaration for themselves (and probably for the Church at large) profess their assent, is here, through inadvertence, erroneously ascribed by them to the synod assembled at Cambridge in 1648. That synod framed no Confession of their own; but only expressed their approbation of that composed by the Westminster Assembly. The Confession here intended is that which was agreed upon by the Reforming Synod (so called), assembled at Boston 1679 and 1680. Excepting some few variations, it is the same as the Savoy Confession, drawn up and assented to by the Elders and Messengers of the Congregational Churches in England convened at the Savoy Building in London in 1658. It is in sentiment thoroughly Calvinistic. Being adopted by the Reforming Synod in this country, May 1680, as expressing their own views in religion, and those of the churches represented by them, it was immediately submitted to the General Court, then sitting in Boston, for their approbation; and, receiving their sanction, it thenceforth became for many years a common standard of faith to the churches of Massachusetts, especially to such as were gathered during the first half of the last century. In Chapter xxix. of this Confession, entitled "Of Baptism," the fourth paragraph reads as quoted in the Declaration, "Not only those that do actually profess Faith in, and Obedience unto Christ; but also the Infants of one or both believing Parents, are to be baptized, and those only."

This Declaration may reasonably be considered as a decisive testimony to the faith, worship, and order of the church of Woburn at the period it was drawn up; and was, doubtless, made in compliance with a previous request, expressed or intimated, by Mr. Fox. But here the inquiry suggests itself; viz: What led Mr. Fox to present such a request to the church? For, though it is very common for a church to require of a *candidate* for settlement over them a formal statement of his views of religion and ecclesiastical discipline, yet, *churches* have been but very rarely, if ever, asked to make such a statement by the candidates whom they employ, while preaching upon probation among them. No light on this point can be gathered from the records of this church at that day, which have long been missing. The Town Records, too, are entirely silent on the subject. But the ecclesiastical history of the country at that period brings certain facts to view, from which may be deduced a plausible solution, at least, of this interesting inquiry. At the commencement of the last century appears to have been first raised an alarm that innovations were making in the primitive faith and constitution of the churches of Massachusetts. The ancient orthodox standards of religious belief, it is true, were yet acknowledged and retained; still, there is ground for supposing that declension from them was even then creeping into the churches, which some years afterward openly manifested itself. The opinion that the communion was a converting ordinance, and, consequently, that evidence of regeneration was not an indispensable prerequisite for admittance to church fellowship, was now, for the first time, advanced by Rev. Solomon Stoddard, of Northampton, a minister pre-eminent for learning, piety, and the distinguished success of his labors; and, being recommended by his great name and influence, was gaining ground in the churches, and lowering, in many places, the terms of admission to ecclesiastical privileges. Again, sundry novelties in the worship and discipline of Brattle Street Church, Boston, established in 1699, excited, for a while, apprehensions in many of a design to introduce Presbyterianism or Episcopacy on the ruins of Congregationalism.

From the year 1700, likewise, a plan appears to have been ripening, which, with the ostensible design of improving the constitution of the Congregational churches, was, in reality, calculated to subvert it. This plan was published and warmly recommended by one Clerical Association in 1705, and not improbably would have been extensively adopted, had it not been counteracted by the opposition of Rev. Dr. Increase Mather (who, though friendly to its general provisions, warmly objected to some of its peculiarities); and, more especially, by the keen satire, as well as powerful reasoning of Rev. John Wise, minister of Chebacco Parish, Ipswich, in his celebrated work, entitled, "The Churches Quarrel Espoused." Moreover, it appears from documents to be presently adverted to, that about the year 1670, the church of Woburn, itself, was considerably divided on the subject of Baptism, and, although that division was now probably in good measure healed, yet the remembrance of it had not passed away, and might naturally excite some solicitude in the mind of one who was preaching here as a candidate for the pastoral office. It is not surprising, then, that Rev. Mr. Fox, while preaching at Woburn on probation in 1703, should desire of the church some distinct expression of their views, both of the various controversies which were then agitating the public mind, and also of that, which, it was still remembered, had once been debated among themselves. And such an expression was the Declaration above cited. It is a full, definite disclosure of the sentiments of the church, by some of its leading members, in regard to all the points of controversy alluded to; and it was excellently calculated to relieve Mr. Fox of all anxiety which the consideration of them might have occasioned.

The allusion just made to Baptists in Woburn, above a century before the foundations of the present numerous and highly respectable church and society of this denomination were laid, may naturally excite curiosity in the present inhabitants of the town to know who and how many these persons were; what stand they took in relation to their peculiar sentiments and practices; and how long the separation continued before it ceased, and Congregationalists became once more the only publicly known denomination of Christians in town? The great mass of the first settlers of the Bay State were either strictly Congregational at coming to this country, or speedily became so. For about thirty-five years from the settlement of Salem, the oldest town in the Massachusetts Colony, as distinct from that of Plymouth, all the churches that were gathered in it were Orthodox, Pædobaptist, Congregational churches. But in 1663, a Baptist Church was gathered at Rehoboth, now within the bounds of Massachusetts, but then within Plymouth jurisdiction. This church, in 1667, was removed to Swansea, by order of the Plymouth Government, and there flourished under the pastoral care of Rev. John Miles, a clergyman from Wales, in Great Britain. In 1665, the First Baptist Church in Boston was formed at Charlestown, two of the principal members of which, Mr. Thomas Gould and Mr. Thomas Osburn, had previously for years belonged to the Congregational Church of Charlestown. From Charlestown and Boston, the peculiar opinions of the Baptists seem to have quickly spread to Woburn; and several members of the church here either embraced them, or were strongly disposed to favor them, and, consequently, to contemn or to withdraw from the worship and ordinances of the church to which they belonged, and to unite themselves with the church of the new denomination. But such a course of proceeding was then an offence against the Colony laws, and soon involved its abettors in trouble before the judicial tribunals. The following extracts from the Records of the ancient Quarterly Courts for the County of Middlesex [7] show the names, and the number of the persons indicted belonging to Woburn, the nature of their supposed offences, and the methods taken to punish or reclaim them.

"Court at Charlestown, December 19, 1671.

"John Johnson of Oburne [8] appearing according to sumons, to answer the presentment of the Grand Jury for his absenting himself constantly on the Lord's Dayes from the Publick Worship of God — confessed that he had formerly gone to the Anabaptisticall assembly, but now he had left off; and for some time had attended the worship of the Lord with the People of God in the place where he dwells, and was resolved, God continuing life and health, that he would still so do. The Court accepted of his promise; and paying Court fees, he was discharged.

"Hopestill Foster John Peirce of Oburne appearing before the Court to answer presentment of the Grand Jury for turning their back on the holy ordinance of Baptism, confessed the presentment; and being the first time, the Court sentenced them to be admonished; which was accordingly performed in open court; and paying fees of Court, were discharged.

"John Russell of Oburne sen^r^. [8] appearing before the Court to answer the presentment of the Grand Jury for renouncing communion with the Church of Christ in that plase, whereoff he is a member; and this declared of late by his frequent absenting himself from the Public ministry of God's word on the Lord's Dayes, and turning his back on the holy Ordinance of Baptism, and refusing to partake with the Church, in the Sacrament of the Lord's Supper, joiynng himself to the schismaticall assembly of the Anabaptists, and taking office power among them, casting out John Johnson who was a member with them: He the said Russell confessed the presentment; and the Court considering the nature of his Indictment, and the firm [former?] endeavors legally used for his conviction and reformation, and by his obstinacy therein he hath made himself lyable to the judgment and sensure of the Court

[7] Copied from Lib. 3, pp. 11–13, and communicated by Thomas B. Wyman, Esq., of Charlestown.

[8] No uncommon way of spelling *Woburn* in former days; but whence derived, uncertain. Beside John Russell, Senr., his son, John Russell, Jr., was also cited to appear before this Court. But his indictment, and the result of his trial, are not mentioned in these extracts.

of Assistants, do order that he give bond in ten pounds to appear at the next Court of Assistants to answer the aforesaid presentment, and that he stands committed untill this order be fulfilled — John Russell sen^{r}. doth acknowledge himself to stand bound in ten pounds sterling to be forfeited and payd to the crier of the Court, at Boston, On condition that the said John Russell shall appeare at the next Court of Assistants to be held at Boston, to answer the presentment of y^{e}. Grand Jury as is above declared; and that he shall abide the order of the Court therein, and not depart without license.

"Matthew Johnson appearing before the Court to answer the presentment of the Grand Jury for turning his back on the holy ordinance of Infant Baptism, confessed the presentment: and being the first time of his conviction, the Court sentenced him to be admonished; which was accordingly done in open Court: paying costs, he was discharged.

"Whereas John Wright,[9] Isaac Cole, Ffrancis Wiman, John Wiman, Ffrancis Kendall, Robert Peirce, Matthew Smith & Joseph Wright, members in full communion with the Church of Christ at Woburne, were presented by the Grand Jury of the County of Middlesex in New England at the Court in October last for refuseing communion with the Church of Woburne in the Lord's Supper, and rejecting the counsell of neighboring churches, and all other measures for healing the disorder and scandall thereby occasioned: This Court having heard their severall answers, wherein they pretend and alledge that the grounds of their withdrawing are sundry scruples in poynt of conscience, not daring to partake with the church for fear of defilement by sin, giving some reasons of their dissatisfaction, which not being satisfactory to the Court, who are sensible of the scandall thereby redounding to our profession, and considering the directions given by the word of God and laws of this Colony, requiring the attendance of all due meanes for preserving the peace and order of the churches in the wayes of godliness and honesty, that so all God's ordinances may have passage unto edification, according to the rules of Christ.

"This Court do therefore, upon serious consideration of the whole case, order that the respective churches of Charlestown,

---

[9] Not Deacon John Wright, but a son of his; as was also Joseph Wright, presented at the same time. See notice of Joseph, at the close of this chapter.

Cambridge, Watertown, Redding & Billerica be moved and requested from the Court, according to God's ordinance of communion of churches, to send their elders and messengers unto the church of Woburne the day of March next, where the brethren that were presented as above said are ordered and required to give a meeting together with the church there, and shall have liberty humbly and inoffensively to declare their grievances, and the church also to declare the whole case for the hearing of their proceedings: And after the case is fully heard by the said councill, they are to endeavor the healing of their spirits, and making of peace among them, for the issuing of matters according to the word of God, and to make returne of what they shall do herein to the next county Court to be held at Cambridge: And the Recorder of this Court is ordered seasonably to signify the Court's mind herein to the several churches above named. It is ordered that the Court's final determination in the above named case be respited, untill they receive the councill's return, and the above named persons that were presented by the Grand Jury are ordered to attend at the next court at Cambridge."

By these extracts from the above mentioned authentic sources of information, it appears, that thirteen citizens of Woburn were prosecuted before the Middlesex County Court, in Dec. 1671, for publicly manifesting contempt for the ordinance of Infant Baptism, as administered in the church of Woburn; or for withdrawing from the worship or communion of that church, and attending the assemblies of the Anabaptists, (as they were called) which were not then allowed by law. Of these thirteen persons, one was discharged upon his acknowledgment and promise of change of conduct, and paying costs of Court. Three received in Court a public admonition. One deemed more irreclaimable than the rest, (viz: John Russell, Senr.,) was bound over to the Court of Assistants, then the Supreme Court of the Colony, for a final decision upon his case; and sentence upon the remaining eight was deferred by the Court, till the efficacy of the reasonings and persuasions of an ecclesiastical council could be tried for reducing them to terms of peace and unity with the church of Woburn once more. This Council appears to have met at the time and place appointed; for the Court afterwards ordered that its expense should be defrayed by the Church.[10] But there being no known record of its result, or of any further action of the Court in the case, it seems probable, that the report of the Council was so far favorable to the persons indicted, as that the Court deemed it expedient to discharge them.

Two of the eight persons whom the Council had to deal with, viz, Joseph Wright and John Wyman, seem to have been convinced of error by the labors of the Council, or some other instrumentality, and to have become cordially reconciled to the church of Woburn again; for the former person became afterwards a deacon in that church, and was one of the subscribers to the above-cited "Declaration," and the latter took an active part in the settlement of Rev. Jabez Fox, as colleague of Rev. Thomas Carter, in 1679; and in his will, dated March 10, 1683–4, he left a legacy of forty shillings to each of them, styling them his "Reverend Pastors." His brother, Francis Wyman, appears to have always retained his partiality for the sentiments of the Baptists; for, in his will, dated Sept. 5th, 1698, a few months before his death, he bequeathed to the two elders of the Baptist Church in Boston, Mr. Isaac Hull and Mr. John Emblen, "twenty shillings apiece." But in naming these gentlemen in his will, as he does not call them "his pastors," as his brother John does Messrs. Carter and Fox in his will, he gives room for the supposition that he ultimately decided, from prudential considerations, to attend public worship with his neighbors where he lived; and that, keeping his peculiar sentiments on the subject of baptism to himself, as implying nothing in his view essential to the Christian character, he died in communion with the church of Woburn. The course taken by the other five members of the church, with whom the Council was to deal, by order of Court, is unknown. As I have been unable, however, either by tradition or records, to discover

---

[10] "This Court doth order that the charges expended in entertayning the late councill at Woburne shall be satisfied by all the church (apportiond?) as other charges are payd among them by order of the Selectmen; and the constable is ordered to levy the same." — *Quarter Court Records, Vol. III., p.* 37.

any traces of Christians in Woburn, subsequently to this period, who maintained the opinions and worship of the Baptist denomination, in opposition to Congregationalists, or in distinction from them, previously to the troubles with Rev. Mr. Sargent, about 1795, it seems but reasonable to conclude that all belonging to Woburn, who had been summoned before the civil tribunals for their Baptist sentiments and practices, December 1671, except John Russell, Senr., and John Russell, Jr., his son, either renounced those sentiments and practices as erroneous; or else that they worshipped unitedly with their Congregational brethren while they lived, not accounting the differences between them as essential; and that, when they died, their peculiarities died with them in Woburn, or, at least, ceased to be publicly manifested there and insisted upon by any who might hold them.

But there was one person indicted as above, whose resolute spirit no opposition could subdue, no suffering could break down, or cause to swerve from the path which he deemed to be right. John Russell, Senr., was one of the earliest inhabitants of Woburn, being a subscriber to the Town Orders drawn up for it at Charlestown, in 1640. By occupation he was a shoemaker; and, for several years, without interruption, was chosen to the responsible office of Sealer of Leather. He was also one of the Selectmen several years in succession; and, in 1664, was appointed on a highly respectable and important committee of seven for making distribution among the proprietors of the town "of plow lands and swamps, and a particular division of the remote timber, according to justice and equity."[11] He is likewise named in the Town Records of the same year as a deacon of the church; and, at that time, was doubtless an Orthodox Congregationalist, both in profession and practice. But, afterwards, embracing the peculiarities of the Baptists, he was in the latter part of the year 1669, or in the former part of 1670, admitted into the Baptist Church of Boston, which then met for worship at Noddle's Island. Of this church, he was soon after

[11] Town Records, Vol. I., p. 29.

chosen an elder. For in a letter from Edward Drinker, (a leading member of that church, and one of its founders,) directed to Mr. Clarke and his Baptist Church at Newport, and dated November 30, 1670, he takes the following notice of Mr. Russell: "The Lord has given us another elder, one John Russell Senr., a gracious, wise and holy man that lives at Woburn, where we have five brethren near that can meet with him; and they meet together first days, when they cannot come to us; and I hear there are some there looking that way with them." Before this, probably in consequence of the change in his religious views, he had become remiss in his attendance upon public worship at Woburn, was wont to turn his back at the ministration of Infant Baptism, and refused to partake with the church there, of which he then was, or recently had been, both a member and an officer, in the Sacrament of the Lord's Supper. Upon these charges, and likewise for joining the Baptist Church in Boston, which had not been regularly gathered according to the laws of the Colony, and for accepting the eldership among them, and exercising the authority of that office in excommunicating John Johnson, Senr., of Woburn, who had been admitted a member before him, he was summoned and tried before the Court of Quarter Sessions at Charlestown, December 19, 1671: and, by that Court, he was bound over, as we have seen, to appear before the Court of Assistants at their next session. By the decision of this tribunal, which was then the Supreme Judicial Court, as well as principal Legislative body of the Colony, he was committed to prison, but was shortly after released. For in a letter from William Hamlit, a Baptist brother, dated at Boston 14: 4 mo: (14 June) 1672, he is spoken of thus: "I perceive you have heard, as if our brother Russel had died in prison. Through grace he is yet in the land of the living, and out of prison bonds; but is in a doubtful way as to the recovery of his outward health: but we ought to be quiet in the good will and pleasure of our God, who is only wise. I remain your loving brother,

"WILLIAM HAMLIT."

After the death of Elder Gould, first pastor of the Baptist Church in Boston, in October 1675, Elder Miles, of Swansea, seems to have statedly ministered to it till 1679, when he returned to his former charge in Swansea, and Mr. Russell was ordained to succeed Mr. Gould in Boston. It seems to have been long taken for granted that the person thus ordained as Elder Gould's successor in the pastoral office, was John Russell, Senr., who had been an elder in the Baptist Church at Boston, almost from the time of his admission as a member. But the Records of Deaths in Woburn, represent "John Russell" to have deceased June 1, 1676; and that John Russell, Senr., is there intended, inspection of Woburn Records of Births, in which the births of the children of John Russell, Jr., are registered till January 1678, does plainly show. The obvious inference from these statements is, that Elder John Russell, Senr., died at Woburn, June 1, 1676, above three years before he is commonly supposed to have been recognized as the pastor of the Baptist Church in Boston. And this inference is confirmed by the date of his Will in the Probate Office, which is May 27, 1676,[12] five days only before the date of the death referred to as recorded in Woburn Town Book. Reflection upon these and similar recorded facts has induced a firm persuasion, that the successor of Elder Gould, in the pastoral office at Boston, was John Russell, Jr., not John Russell, Senr.; as, through inadvertence to the difference of the persons occasioned by the sameness of name and secular occupation, has been commonly supposed.

John Russell, Jr., was probably born either in England, before his father came to this country, or at Charlestown, where his father resided before Woburn was settled; married Sarah Champney (of Cambridge, it is presumed), 31 October, 1661; followed, doubtless, his father's trade of shoemaking; and, like his father before him, was chosen repeatedly in Woburn, Sealer of Leather.[13] He was admitted to the Baptist Church in Boston

[12] Abstract of Wills, taken from Probate Office, and communicated by Thomas B. Wyman, Esq.

[13] Viz: for 1677 and 1678. Town Records, Vol. I., pp. 72, 79.

some months at least, if not a year or more, before his father, being the fourth male person received into that church after it was constituted, in 1665; and was always regarded by the other brethren, as a very respectable and valuable member. In letters to that church from other churches and ministers of the same denomination from abroad, as quoted in Backus' History of the Baptists, he is repeatedly mentioned with his father in their salutations, in terms of equal respect and affection. He was quite as obnoxious, too, as his father to the civil authorities; and was presented with him to the Court of Quarter Sessions at the same time, December 1671. This fact we learn from a letter from Benjamin Sweetzer, a Baptist member belonging to Charlestown, to Mr Samuel Hubbard, a member of the Baptist Church at Newport, R. I. In that letter, dated at Charlestown, December 10, 1671, he writes, "The persecuting spirit begins to stir again. Elder Russel and his son, and brother Foster, are presented to the Court that is to be this month. We desire your prayers for us, that the Lord would keep us, that we may not dishonor that worthy name we have made profession of; and that the Lord would still stand by us, and be seen amongst us, as he has been in a wonderful manner, in preserving of us until this day."

John Russell, Jr., was ordained, as successor of Elder Gould, to the pastoral charge of the First Baptist Church in Boston, July 28, 1679. At the same time, he removed his residence from Woburn to Boston, according to the historian of the Baptists, with whose statement on this point Woburn Records do well agree. For these, while they record the births of John Russell, Jr.'s children till January 1677–8, and his taxes in Woburn till December 1679, the year of his removal to Boston, make no mention of him afterwards, though they record the death of his widow, Sarah, April 25, 1696; who, it seems, after the death of her husband, removed back from Boston to Woburn. At Boston, Elder Russell appears to have been a zealous and successful laborer in his sacred office; but he was not permitted to continue in it long, being taken away by death, December 21, 1680. Concerning him, Rev. Isaac Backus, the historian of the Baptists, observes, "It is evident, that the gifts and graces of Elder Russell were not small; and his memory is precious."

During the short period Elder Russell was in office, he wrote a treatise in answer to some harsh reflections upon the Baptists, contained in a then recent publication of Rev. Dr. Increase Mather, asserting "The divine right of Infant Baptism." This answer was entitled "A brief Narrative of some considerable passages concerning the first gathering and further progress of a church of Christ in Gospel order, in Boston in New England," etc. It was "dated from Boston the 20th. of May 1680"; and, being approved by his church, it was sent, for publication, to London, where a preface to it was written by seven noted Baptist ministers of that day.

The descendants of Elder John Russell, Senr., who continued in Woburn, seem not to have retained his peculiar sentiments as a Baptist, but to have been of the Congregational persuasion; and when the town was divided into two parishes in 1730, John Russell, his great grandson, was the first Clerk of the First Congregational Parish in Woburn, and also Parish Treasurer and a Parish Assessor for several years in succession. But a granddaughter of Elder Russell, Senr., by his daughter, Mary Brooks, wife of Timothy Brooks of Woburn, was married at Swansea to a gentleman by the name of Mason, by whom she had three sons, Job, Russell, and John Mason, all of whom were esteemed preachers of the Baptist denomination in their day.

In reverting briefly to the civil prosecutions of the Baptists in Woburn above cited, it cannot but be deeply regretted by all who venerate the memory of our pious ancestors, that they should have resorted to the measures they did in this matter. As we view it at this distant day, it would seem that sound policy, as well as consistency with their own professed principles, dictated a far more liberal course. For what had these men done, that they should be compelled to answer for their conduct before the judicial tribunals of the country, and there be admonished as evil doers, fined, and one of them eventually sentenced to imprisonment? Had they committed any flagrant crime? This is not pretended. Had they been chargeable with factious, seditious conduct, by which the peace of the community was infringed, or the public safety endangered? There appears but little or no sound foundation for such an allegation as this. The charge against them, which looks most like a civil misdemeanor, is that of turning their backs in God's house at the administration of infant baptism. This charge, all of them who were presented for it, confessed in Court; and I cannot help thinking, that even our candid Baptist brethren of the present day must own that they were blamable for this, as being a sort of rude, irreverent behavior, very unseemly for the time and place, which faithfulness to their principles did not require them to show, and which was calculated to give needless offence to their pious Pædobaptist brethren; and so was in this view a species of wilful disturbance of public worship. For if this were a right and becoming way of manifesting their conscientious scruples about, or *rejection* of an ordinance, which the great majority of their fellow-worshippers were equally conscientious in *observing*, then some similar method might be properly taken to express our dislike of, or objections against something which might be said in *prayer* or *preaching*; and in such case, what scenes of disorder and confusion might our churches be rendered by something exhibited to the eye only, without any help from the voice or the foot? Even this fault, however, seems quite as proper a subject for animadversion from the pulpit, as before a tribunal of justice. And as to all the other charges for which the first Baptists in Woburn were presented to the Court, I am free to express my apprehensions, that there was more wrong done to them than by them. For absenting themselves from Communion, they were rightfully answerable, not to the civil authorities, but to the church of Woburn, of which they were members. And as to the accusations against them and others of their day, that they had withdrawn from the established public worship, and gathered themselves into conventicles and churches which were without, or against the allowance of the civil government; what had they done in all this, but what our Puritan ancestors had done themselves, or had pleaded for the right of doing, or bitterly complained of as an infringement of the rights of conscience, whenever against their own persuasion of what was right they were forcibly prevented from doing, in their mother country? Consistency, then, required them to show the same tender indulgence to the consciences of their dissenting brethren here, that they had pleaded or claimed should be shown to themselves by the bishops and church officials at home. For otherwise, how could they fulfil the law of love, — to do unto others, as they would have others do to them?

But while we cannot justify our ancestors in their proceedings against the early Baptists in Woburn, it behoves us in equity to moderate our censures, and to make all those allowances for them, which a due regard to their general character, and to the peculiar opinions and customs of those times demands. A large proportion of the magistrates, ministers and other leading men of that day were indeed among the excellent of the earth, men to whose pious care and benevolent exertions, not only their own, but all succeeding generations have been largely indebted. The sin of persecution, which has been often alleged against them, is not one which lies particularly against them, but was a sin of the times in which they lived. The rights of free inquiry, and of liberty of conscience, are matters which were then at best, but imperfectly understood; and a persuasion was almost universally prevalent of the necessity of uniformity in religious faith and worship in order to the public weal, and of the right and duty of the civil magistrate to maintain it by force. These two principles, understood in the extent to which they were formerly carried, are now generally and justly regarded as erroneous. Still, they were embraced by the civil fathers of Massachusetts with all sincerity. And from the practical influence of these principles upon their minds and measures, rather than from an inhuman, persecuting spirit, proceeded all their rigorous laws and hard dealings towards those who dissented from them in some particulars of their faith and practice. In passing those laws, they seem to have aimed at the purity of the churches, and the maintenance in them of truth and peace; and in the execution of those laws, while the edge of them was severely felt, not only by Baptists, but by Episcopalians, Quakers, and by some individuals even of their own denomination, the magistrates who put them in force, appear all the while never to have been sensible that they were violating the rights of conscience, but to have been persuaded that they were only bearing that testimony to the truth, which they were in duty bound to manifest, and by the neglect of doing which, they would not only incur the judgments of heaven themselves, but bring ruin upon the country which they were set to defend and govern. As the renowned father of Woburn, Capt. Edward Johnson, observes in his "Wonder-working Providence," concerning the immediate predecessors of the rulers referred to; "To them it seems unreasonable, and to savour too much of hypocrisy, that any people should pray unto the Lord for the speedy accomplishment of his word in the overthrow of Antichrist, and in the mean time become a patron to sinful opinions and damnable errors that oppose the truths of Christ, admit it be, but in the bare permission of them."

But here lay the error of our pious ancestors and rulers in former days. All men, whether rulers or subjects, are bound to study, and seek after, and embrace and obey the truth of God themselves, and in their several places, and according to their several abilities and opportunities, to promote the reception of it by others. This is the best way of bearing testimony to the truth. But the Word of God nowhere authorizes rulers to employ the sword of persecution or civil force to compel men to believe, profess and follow its sacred dictates. The only sword that is lawful to be used in the Christian warfare against error and sin is the sword of the Spirit, which is the Word of God. All other weapons are only carnal weapons, which are strictly forbidden to be employed, even in defence of the truth. While, then, we admire and honor our ancestors for their many virtues and great excellences, let us not be blind to their faults, or attempt to justify or excuse them. Nor let us be so unjust to them ourselves as to condemn them without measure, after the manner of some, but candidly consider the numerous circumstances which palliate their failings, and willingly allow them all the weight that is their due.

Three years from the date of the memorable Declaration of the Church, in 1703, had but just elapsed, when three of those who subscribed it, viz, Deacon Walker, Major Johnson and Major Convers, had finished their course; so that their subscription to it may with reason be regarded as their dying testimony to the faith and order of the Church of Woburn at that day. And as these gentlemen, as likewise the three subscribers who survived them, were all men of great respectability and usefulness, a brief particular notice of each of them here may not be unacceptable.

William Johnson, Esq., whose name stands at the head of these worthies in their subscription to the Declaration, was the third son of Capt. Edward Johnson, one of the principal founders of the town and church of Woburn. He was born in England about 1630; was brought to New England, when a child, by his father, together with his mother Susanna and six other children of the family, in 1637; and removed with him, in 1641, from Charlestown, his first place of abode on this side of the Atlantic, to Woburn, where he continued to reside the rest of his days in usefulness and honor.

His public spirit and talent for business were early discerned by his fellow-citizens, who duly noticed and availed themselves of them. He was chosen one of the Selectmen in 1664, and again in 1672, and each following year in succession, till 1688. *That year*, also, he was chosen Selectman at the usual time under the Old Charter; but the choice on that day not being allowed to stand by the arbitrary government of Sir Edmund Andros, he appears to have declined a re-election on the day appointed by the Governor and Council for making a new choice; preferring a private station to holding office under the control of a power that was so openly hostile to the liberties of the people.

Shortly before the death of his father, in 1672, he was chosen to succeed him as Recorder or Town Clerk; an office which he held without interruption till 1688, in which year Lieutenant (afterwards Major) Convers was elected. His father had been constantly Town Clerk from the beginning of the town, in 1640, till the year of his death; so that the whole term during which the father and son served the town, in this capacity, was forty-eight years.

He represented the town in the General Court in 1674; and again, eight years in succession, from 1676 till 1683 inclusively, either alone or associated with Humphrey Davie, Esq., of Boston, or with his distinguished townsman, Ensign James Convers.

In 1684, and the two following years, he was chosen one of the Board of Assistants, which, under the First Charter, was not only the Senate of the Colony, but the Supreme Court of Judicature. But the Colonial Government, being superseded, in 1686, by a President and Council, and quickly after, by a Governor and Council of the King's appointment, Major Johnson lived in retirement till the deposition of the Governor, Sir Edmund Andros, at the insurrection of the people in April 1689. At this interesting crisis, he was associated with other leading men in the community as a "Council for the safety of the people and conservation of the peace:"[14] and the old government, being shortly after revived, till a new charter could be obtained of King William, and the government orderly re-settled under it, he resumed his seat at the Board of Assistants, which had been vacated three years before. For his strong attachment to the Old Charter, and his expected opposition to the New, his name was dropped from the List of Councillors appointed by the Crown in the Provincial Charter in 1691. From this time, the part he took in the management of the public affairs of the country appears to have ceased. But the town of Woburn continued, on various occasions, and in various ways, to enjoy the benefit of his experience and services, till his death; which took place, after several months confinement, May 22, 1704.

Like his father before him, Major Johnson was eminently skilful in surveying; and of the numerous grants and extensive divisions of the common lands in the town, which were made during the first sixty years from its incorporation, there were but few which one or the other of these gentlemen was not employed to lay out. He was also the largest proprietor of

---

[14] Hutchinson's History of Massachusetts, Vol. I., pp. 381–2.

land in the town, excepting the brothers, John and Francis Wyman, in his day. In the Town Records, his homestead (situate in "Plain Street," near what has been recently known as Mr. Edmund Parker's farm) and seventy other distinct tracts of land, containing nine hundred acres in all, obtained, some by purchase, and some by inheritance or by grant from the town, are recorded as his. A considerable portion of this great landed estate lay in the northwesterly part of the town, and was eventually settled upon and improved by his children and grandchildren, who were among the principal founders and inhabitants of the Second Precinct, or Burlington.

Major Johnson was highly esteemed for his wisdom and prudence as a magistrate. Tradition relates that several persons were brought before him for examination, accused of witchcraft, probably in 1692, the year of the general delusion on this subject. Papers containing an account of these examinations are said, on good authority, to have been once in the hands of his descendants. These documents are now lost. But as none belonging to Woburn appear to have been arraigned and prosecuted before the Court on this charge, it may be safely inferred that he had penetration enough to discern the imposture or prevailing error in this affair, and refused to commit the accused for trial.

He was distinguished for his undeviating attachment to the Old or Colony Charter, under which the people had enjoyed the right of choosing their own Governor, and other privileges of which they were very tenacious, but which had been condemned, and declared forfeited to the Crown in 1684. Like Cooke, Wiswall, Oakes, and other noted public men of that day, he was for insisting on that charter, or none; expecting probably, that by resolutely refusing to accept from the King any other charter, the people would eventually succeed in obtaining the restoration of the old one.[15] In this expectation, he was disappointed. And by his unwillingness to acknowledge and submit to the government by a President and Council, which

---

[15] Hutchinson's History, Vol. I., p. 414.

immediately succeeded the Old Charter Government, he not only lost his former influence in the direction of public affairs, but was once in danger of being deprived of his personal liberty. On this subject, Judge Sewall, a friend of his, and an associate under the Old Government, thus writes in his Diary:

"1686 July 30. About this time, William Johnson Esq. is sharply reproved by the Council for his carriage on the Fast day, staying at home himself, and having a Dozen Men at his House: Told him must take ye Oath of Allegiance: he desired an hour's consideration; then said he could not take it: but when his Mittimus writing or written, he consider'd again, and took it rather than goe to Prison. Objected against that Clause of acknowledging that to be Lawfull Authority which administered; would see the Seals."

Major Johnson was a professed Christian, and a member of the church of Woburn; and his life appears to have been answerable to his holy profession. In principle, he was a strict Orthodox Congregationalist, as is evident from his subcription to the Declaration of the Church, so often referred to. In his Will, dated May 10, 1695, he distinctly recognizes the doctrine of the Sacred Trinity; and, after making distribution therein of his worldly estate, he concludes with the following pious exhortation: "And thus haveing finished my Will, I doe exort and require all my children to live in peace one with another; and above all, [that] they honor and love the God of their father and grandfather, and to walk in their stepps, so farr as they have walked aright with God; and then I pray the God of love and grace [peace ?] be with you all, Amen."

By his wife, Esther (daughter of Thomas Wiswall, ruling elder of the church of Newton), whom he married May 16, 1655, Major Johnson had nine children, viz: six sons, William, Edward, Ebenezer, Joseph, Benjamin and Josiah; and three daughters: viz, Esther, Susanna and Abigail. Esther was married to Seth Wyman, and became the mother of Lieutenant, afterwards Captain, Seth Wyman, who distinguished himself at Lovewell's Fight. Abigail was married to Samuel Peirce. William, the eldest son, appears to have been at first a shipwright in

Charlestown, and, after his father's death, to have lived on the homestead in Woburn with his mother, agreeably to a codicil to his father's will. The other five sons all resided in that part of the town which afterwards became the Second Precinct; and among them and their children were found some who were zealous movers for the separation of that parish from the first, and principal supporters of public worship in it.

Deacon Samuel Walker, who was the second to sign the foregoing Declaration, and the direct ancestor of the family of his name, which, springing from this town, has been honorably distinguished in all generations by the attainments and public services of many of its members, both near and far off from their original seat, was the eldest son of Samuel Walker, Senr., of Woburn.

John Farmer, Esq., in his Genealogical Register, supposes that this Samuel Walker, Senr., was a son of Augustine Walker, of Charlestown, who had a son Samuel, born in 1642. And this hypothesis of Farmer has been adopted by several others on this point. But a decisive objection to this theory is that Samuel Walker, Senr., of Woburn was a much older man than Samuel, son of Augustine, of Charlestown; being, by a testimony he gave in at Court, December 28, 1658, forty-three years of age at that time.[16] This gentleman may on very plausible grounds be concluded to be a son of Capt. Richard Walker, who was one of the first settlers of Lynn in 1630, was made freeman of the colony, 1634, was chosen ensign of the military company of that town, March 1636–7, and afterwards successively its lieutenant and captain; and was elected, 1640, 1641, and again in 1648, 1649, the Deputy of Lynn to the General Court. He died in May 1687, aged ninety-five years; and his burial is briefly noticed by Judge Sewall in his Diary as follows: "Monday May 16, 1687, I go to Reading, and visit Mr Brock; and so to Salem. This day, Capt. Walker, a very aged Planter, buried at Lin." Besides two daughters, Capt. Walker had two sons, Richard and Samuel, both inhabitants of Reading.

---

[16] Thomas B. Wyman, Esq., from Court files.

Samuel Walker, Senr., of Woburn, presumed above to have been the son of Capt. Richard Walker of Lynn, was born in England; accompanied his father to New England, 1630; and after residing with him a while at Lynn, he removed with his brother Richard to Reading, originally Lynn Village; and thence he subsequently appears, for some reasons, to have removed once more, and to have permanently established himself in Woburn, the adjoining town. He is first mentioned as an inhabitant of Woburn in its Records, at the annual election of town officers, February 25th, 1661–2, when he was appointed a Surveyor of Highways for that year. By occupation, he was a maltster; and was approved by the Selectmen, 1675, in order to obtaining a license for keeping tavern, being the first person known to have followed that business in Woburn. He appears to have been much respected in his day; being chosen Selectman in 1668, and appointed by the town the year before on a very important Committee for taking "a List of the persons and estates of the *right Proprietors*", among whom, it had been voted to divide a large portion of the common lands of the town. He died November 6th, 1684; when, agreeably to a testimony given by him in Court, and referred to above, he must have been in the 69th or 70th year of his age.

His children (the given name of his wife is unknown) were Samuel, Jr., Israel, and probably John, Senr., of Woburn; Hannah wife of James, son of Simon Thompson of Woburn; and Joseph Walker of Billerica.

Samuel Walker, Jr., his son (distinguished likewise in Woburn Records successively by the titles of Corporal, Sergeant, and Deacon Walker), was the second subscriber to the memorable "Declaration" of the church of Woburn above cited, and a gentleman of note and influence in his day. He was Selectman in 1679, and served the town in that office repeatedly afterwards. He was a member of the Convention of the Colony, which met in Boston 1689, upon the deposition of the governor, Sir Edmund Andros; and after the establishment of the government under the Provincial Charter of 1691, he represented Woburn in the General Court, 1694. About 1692, he was chosen a deacon of the church of Woburn, an office which he seems to have retained through life. He died, January 18, 1703–4, aged 61 years.

Deacon Walker married, for his first wife, Sarah "Read," [Reed] of Woburn, 10th September, (or, as the County Records have it, 23d October,) 1662. By her, he had six sons: Edward, John, Samuel, Timothy, Isaac,[17] and Ezekiel; and one daughter, Sarah, married, January 12, 1686, [1686–7] to Edward, son of Major William Johnson. His wife, Sarah, dying November 1, 1681, he married, for his second wife, April 18, 1692, Abigail, widow of Lieut. James Fowle of Woburn: but by her he had no issue.

Among the descendants of Deacon Walker, there have been in all generations numerous individuals useful and respected in their day, and some of them, prominent members of society by their influence, public services, and high standing in the communities in which they have lived. Of this latter description, in the line of John, the *second* son of Deacon Walker, may be named,

I. 1. Mr. Edward Walker, son of John, born October 7, 1694; lived on his father's place (as did after him, his son Josiah, and his grandson Josiah, both reputable farmers in their day); married Esther Peirce, March 31, 1718, represented Woburn in the General Court 1745, 1751, '52, '53, '54; and was so highly esteemed by his fellow citizens for his integrity and soundness of judgment, that it was customary to prefix Mr. to his name, an honor rarely conferred in Woburn at that day. He died December 6, 1787, at the advanced age of 93 years. His wife died before him, September 23, 1761, aged 65 years.

2. General John Walker, a grandson of Edward, above named, and a son of Capt. Joshua Walker. He was born in Woburn

---

[17] The birth of Isaac Walker is recorded in Woburn Town Book, as follows: "Isaac, son of Samuel Walker Senr, born ye 1st. of 9th. mo: 1677." But here, it can hardly be doubted, there is a mistake of the clerk in writing "Senr" for "junr." He married, 20 Feb., 1704-5, Margery Bruce, of Woburn; and he, and his sons by her, Isaac, Jr., Ezekiel, and Timothy, were some time resident at Pennicook, now Concord, N. H. — See *History of Concord, by Rev. Dr. Bouton.*

Precinct, February 7, 1762, and was appointed, 1798, by the elder President Adams, a Major-General, and commander of the army at Oxford,—the country then seeming to be in imminent danger of a war with France. Subsequently, he took a leading part in the measures adopted to procure a legal separation of his native village from Woburn; and, after it was incorporated as a town by the name of Burlington, in 1799, he ever exerted a powerful influence in the management of its affairs. He married, January 22, 1784, Miss Lucy, daughter of Mr. Jonathan Johnson, who was a descendant of the fourth generation from Capt. Edward Johnson, a principal founder of Woburn. He died, June 8, 1814, aged 53.

3. Hon. Timothy Walker of Charlestown, a brother of the General's, noted for his business talents and his wealth, and sometime a member of the Senate of this Commonwealth.

4. Rev. James Walker, D.D., a son of the General's; born in 1794; a graduate of Harvard University, 1814; several years pastor of the Unitarian Church of Charlestown; more recently the accomplished President of the University; and since his resignation of that office, living honored and beloved in retirement.

5. Dr. William Johnson Walker, a son of Hon. Timothy Walker of Charlestown, was graduated at Harvard University, 1810; perfected his medical education in Europe; and, upon his return to his native land, rose to high distinction by his skill and success as a physician and surgeon. He deceased lately in Newport, R. I., whither he had retired from the practice of his profession.

II. Samuel, third son of the first Deacon Samuel Walker, was born January 25, 1667–8; married Judith Howard, June 1st, 1689; occupied many years a house upon Maple Meadow Plain in Goshen, now Wilmington; but, about 1725, he removed to a house, recently standing in the south part of Burlington, where he spent the residue of his days. In 1709, he was chosen a deacon of the First Church in Woburn. But, at the incorporation, 1730, of the Second Precinct of Woburn, now Burlington, within the limits of which he then resided, he became of course a supporter of the public worship there, and aided in gathering the Precinct church, and in ordaining Rev. Supply Clap, its first pastor, October 29, 1735. He was one of the ten brethren (including the minister) who subscribed the "Articles of Agreement," and the "Church Covenant," adopted on that solemn occasion; and November 10th, following, he was chosen one of the first two deacons of that church. In this office, he continued to serve till his death, which occurred September 28, 1744, in the 77th year of his age. A gravestone in Burlington Old Burial Ground marks the place of his interment. His wife, Judith, dying November 14, 1724, he married Mary, widow of Capt. James Fowle, who survived him. She died at Charlestown, October 23, 1748, æt. 80.

1. Capt. Samuel Walker, son of the second Deacon Samuel Walker and Judith, his wife, was born September 3, 1694; lived in the same house his father had lived in, upon Maple Meadow Plain, in Goshen, (so called) after his father had quitted it, about 1725; was a principal mover in the effort to procure the separation of Goshen from Woburn, and erecting it into a distinct town, which resulted successfully in the incorporation of Wilmington in 1730. By his wife, Hannah, he had twelve children, nine of whom died in less than two months, in 1738, of throat distemper. Capt. Walker died February 13, 1771; Hannah, his widow, died May 13, 1788, æt. 99.

2. Rev. Timothy Walker, son of the second Deacon Samuel Walker, and brother of the above Capt. Samuel Walker, was born within the present bounds of Wilmington, July 27, 1705; was graduated at Harvard College, 1725; was ordained first minister of Penacook, (afterwards Rumford, now Concord, N. H.) November 18, 1730; went three times to England, between 1753 and 1762, to appear before the King and Council, as Agent of the Proprietors of Rumford, in a controversy they had with the town of Bow; and died, universally loved and lamented by his people, September 1, 1782, in the 78th year of his age, and 52d of his ministry. His wife, Sarah, daughter of James Burbeen of Woburn, born June 17, 1701, died February 19, 1778, æt. 77, and lies buried by his side.

3. Hon. Timothy Walker, son of Rev. Timothy and Mrs. Sarah Walker, was born in Rumford, June 27, 1737; graduated at Harvard College, 1756; licensed to preach, 1759; but after laboring in the sacred profession about six years, he relinquished it for civil life; was a gentleman of great influence, and often employed both in town and State affairs; accepted the office of Judge of the Court of Common Pleas in New Hampshire, in 1777; was Chief Justice of that Court from 1804 to 1809; and died, May 5, 1822, in the 85th year of his age. By his wife Susanna, daughter of Rev. Joseph and Mrs. Esther Burbeen of Woburn, he had fourteen children, ten of whom lived to grow up.

4. Deacon Timothy Walker, son of Capt. Samuel Walker of Wilmington and Hannah his wife, born July 5, 1732, married, in 1758, Eunice, daughter of Joseph Brewster of Duxbury, who was a descendant of the third generation from Elder William Brewster of Plymouth in 1620; was chosen a deacon of the church of Wilmington, and died there May 9, 1809, æt. 77. Eunice, his widow, died June 2, 1815, æt. 84 years.

5. Hon. Timothy Walker, a grandson of Deacon Timothy, and a son of Benjamin Walker, Esq. and Susanna (Cook) Walker his wife, was born in Wilmington, December 1, 1802, graduated at Harvard College, 1826; studied law; settled as a lawyer in Cincinnati, Ohio, and was eventually promoted to be a Judge in one of the Courts of that State. He received from his Alma Mater, in 1854, the honorary degree of LL.D., and died in 1856.

6. Sears Cook Walker, brother of Hon. Timothy above named, and son of Benjamin, Esq. and Susanna (Cook) Walker of Wilmington, was born in Wilmington; graduated at Harvard College, 1825; eminent on both sides the Atlantic for his scientific attainments, especially in Astronomy; and sometime employed by the Government of the United States in the Coast Survey. He resided, principally, it is believed at Philadelphia, and died in 1853.

Joseph Wright, Senr., was son of Deacon John Wright, one of the first settlers of Woburn, and a subscriber to the Town

Orders, agreed upon at Charlestown, December 18, 1640; a Selectman of Woburn, 1645, and many years afterwards; one of the committee appointed by the General Court's Committee in 1668, for dividing the common lands "into proprieties," and a deacon of the church from 1664 till his death, June 21, 1688. His wife, Priscilla, died April 10, 1687. He left two sons, John and Joseph, born before the settlement of Woburn, and three daughters, Ruth, Deborah, and Sarah, born after. The deaths of his son John and wife are recorded as follows: "John Wright senr. died April 30. 1714 [aged 84 years: Gravestone] Abigail wife of John Wright died Apl. 6. 1726 [aged 84 years. G. S.]

Joseph Wright, third subscriber to the Declaration of the Church in 1703, is called in that Instrument Joseph Wright, Senr., in distinction from his own son, Joseph Wright, Jr., who was born March 14, 1667. Joseph Wright, Senr., was born before the settlement of Woburn in 1641, either at Charlestown, or possibly before his father, Deacon John Wright, had emigrated from England to this country. He married Elizabeth Hasell, November 1, 1661, by whom he had a numerous progeny. He was one of the Selectmen of Woburn 1670, 1673, 1692; and a deacon of the church as early as 1698 (Town Records, Vol. III., p. 124), in which office he continued through life. His death and that of his wife are recorded as follows: "Elizabeth, wife of Dea. Joseph Wright, died June 28, 1713." "Deacon Joseph Wright died 31 March 1724."

In December 1671, Joseph Wright, Senr., was presented by the Grand Jury, with his brother John and six others, to the court sitting at Charlestown, for withdrawing from the communion of the church of Woburn, of which they all were members, and for favoring in other ways the sentiments and practices of the Baptists. But, subsequently, being convinced that he had been in an error, he became reconciled to the church of Woburn, accepted the office of a deacon in it, and subscribed the "Declaration" made by it, which is decidedly Pædobaptist, in 1703.

James Convers, Senr., familiarly distinguished in the Town Records as Ensign or Lieutenant Convers, and whose name stands next to that of Deacon Wright among the subscribers to the above cited "Declaration," was born in England. He came to this country with his father, Deacon Edward Convers, in the fleet which conveyed Governor Winthrop, in 1630; sat down first at Charlestown; and thence removed to Woburn, among its earliest settlers, in 1641. He married, October 24, 1643, Anna Long,[18] daughter of Robert Long, of Charlestown, by whom he he had ten children. Through a long life, he was a very valuable and highly esteemed citizen; was repeatedly honored by the town with the principal offices which it had to confer; and surviving his son, the Major, he died, May 10, 1715, aged 95 years.[19] In his will, dated August 28, 1712, he bequeathed as follows: "To my Reverend Pastor, Mr John Fox, twenty shillings; and to the church of Christ in Woburn, twenty shillings to purchase a large flagon withall." The twenty last years of his life were spent in retirement. But he was not one who under any circumstances could live without care or concern for the good of others. As indicative of this, the following anecdote respecting him seems worth preserving. As Hon. Judge Sewall was once journeying homeward from Newbury to Boston, he took the road through Andover and Woburn, then adjoining towns. His passage through Woburn he notices in his Diary thus: "1702 August 12.——Right [Wright] conducts me to Wooburn through the Land of Nod [in which he was largely interested]. This is ye first time I have seen it. Got late to Fowl's at Wooburn: Sick there, which made me uneasy. Aug. 13. Visit Mr Fox. View ye Hop-yards. Come home: very hot. Met Mr Converse the Father, & discours'd him under a Shady Tree. Won't give his Grandchildren till after his death, for fear of giving offence. Express'd his Grief that Govr Dudley put men in place that were not good."

In this brief extract from the authentic record above referred to, it is strongly intimated that Woburn, the mother, was once as much noted for that now neglected branch of husbandry, the raising of hops, as her daughters, Goshen or Wilmington, and Shawshin or Burlington, have been in recent times. The

---

18 Woburn Records of Births, etc.

19 Gravestone.

"shady tree," likewise there named, was doubtless the far-famed Woburn Elm, which stood near the Convers Mill, in what is now Winchester, and not far from the original house of the Convers family.[20] Beneath the wide spread limbs of that lofty tree, upon some block at its foot, methinks I see those venerable Puritans discussing in a friendly manner some knotty point of divinity; or discoursing with solicitude upon matters which concerned the welfare of their families, or of this, their adopted country; glancing in their conversation, every now and then, with a sigh at that better country, the heavenly Canaan, the longed-for land of every genuine Puritan, as his final abode, the land of his everlasting rest above.

William Lock, Sen., fifth subscriber to the Declaration, was brought to New England, 1635, on board the "Planter," from London, by Nicholas Davis, who, it is believed, was his uncle. He was then a child of but six years old, and was probably born at London, December 13, 1728; seems to have lived at first at Charlestown; came early to Woburn, after its settlement; married Mary, daughter of William Clark, of Watertown, November 27, 1655, by whom he had nine children, one of whom (the first) died in infancy; lived near to Kendall's Mill, in Woburn, on the spot where the late Capt. William Fox had his dwelling; was of the Board of Selectmen, 1687, 1696; was a deacon of the Church in 1700; and died June 16, 1720. His wife, Mary, died before him, July 18, 1715.

His descendants in Woburn, Lexington, and West Cambridge, have been very numerous. Among them was Rev. Samuel Locke, D.D., President of Harvard College. He was the son of Samuel Lock (a grandson of Deacon William) and of Rebecca Lock, his wife; was born at Woburn,[21] November 23,

---

[20] This elm stood in the front yard of Deacon Benjamin F. Thompson, a few steps after crossing the railroad in Winchester, upon the left hand side of the road leading to Medford, and was cut down by that gentleman, (he once told me) some twenty years ago [1866].

[21] Biglow, in his History of Sherborn, claims him to have been a native of Lancaster. But Woburn Records of Births, Marriages, etc., state that his father and mother at marriage were both of Woburn, and record the birth of this their son Samuel, and the births of four other of their children, as occurring in the same town.

1731; graduated at Harvard College, 1755; ordained pastor of the church in Sherborn, November 7, 1759; installed President of the University, March 21, 1770; resigned that office December 1, 1773; removed back to Sherborn, and there died suddenly of apoplexy, January 15, 1778.[22]

James Convers, Jr., the last of those worthies, who subscribed the above Declaration of the church of Woburn in 1703, and familiarly known in his day as Maj. James Convers, was the eldest son of James Convers, Senr., and was born in Woburn November 16, 1645. He was a gentleman that, for a succession of years, appears to have faithfully and acceptably discharged various civil trusts reposed in him by the town.

But he is most celebrated for his services to his country in the military line, and especially for his gallant defence of Storer's garrison at Wells, during the war against the French and Eastern Indians, which began in 1688, and has been called, "The Ten Years War." That exploit of Major (then Captain) Convers, is spoken of, both by Hutchinson and by Belknap in their respective Histories, in terms of commendation.[23] Mather also, in his History of this War, entitled "Decennium Luctuosum," gives a minute and interesting account of this celebrated action, and as it is highly creditable to this distinguished son of Woburn, an abridgment of it may not improbably be gratifying to the citizens of Woburn at the present day.

It seems that on November 29, 1690, six Indian sachems had agreed at Sagadahock with Capt. John Alden upon a truce till the first day of May 1691, on which day they promised to bring all the English captives in their hands into Lieut. Storer's house at Wells, and there conclude upon terms of a firm and lasting peace.

Accordingly, on the day appointed, Deputy Governor Dan-

---

[22] Woburn Records, Savage's Genealogical Register, Biglow's History.

[23] Hutchinson's History, Vol. II., pp. 67, 68, 72. Belknap's History of New Hampshire, p. 135. "But on the tenth day of June, [1691] an army of French and Indians made a furious attack on Storer's garrison at Wells, where Capt. Convers commanded; who, after a brave and resolute defence, was so happy as to drive them off with great loss."

forth and certain other gentlemen came from Boston to Wells, suitably guarded, expecting the fulfilment of this engagement by the Indians. But, as Mather expresses it, "the Indians being poor musicians for keeping of time," Capt. Convers went out, and returned with some of them, who brought in six English captives in company, and promised "that in twenty days more they would bring in to Capt. Convers all the rest." After waiting for the Indians beyond the term agreed upon, the Deputy Governor and company withdrew; and Capt. Convers, suspecting treachery, made earnest application to the County of Essex for help to be sent him as speedily as possible; and received from that quarter thirty-five men. This providential reënforcement saved the place. For scarcely half an hour had elapsed from their entering Storer's house on June 9, 1691, before Moxus, a fierce sachem, beset it, with two hundred Indians. But, receiving a brave repulse from the garrison within, he became discouraged and drew off. This gave occasion to Madockawando, another noted Indian sachem, and a virulent foe to the English, to say, as was afterwards reported, "My brother Moxus has miss'd it now; but I will go myself the next year, and have the dog Convers out of his hole." The event proved that this was no empty threat; that Madockawando meant as he said. For, on June 10, 1692, just a year and a day from the time that Moxus commenced his attack on the garrison of Wells the year before, the cattle of that place came suddenly home from the woods affrighted, and some of them wounded. Warned by this infallible sign that Indians were nigh, the inhabitants of the place fled for refuge to the garrison house; and the next morning, an army of French and Indians, from 300 to 500 in number, commanded by Labocree, a Frenchman, and under him, by Moxus, Madockawando, Egeremet, and other Indian sachems, was discovered lurking around. To defend himself against this host, Capt. Convers had only fifteen men in the garrison, and as many more aboard of two sloops and a shallop in the river hard by, which had recently arrived from Boston with ammunition for the soldiers, and a contribution of supplies for the impoverished inhabitants of that vicinity. So weak and contemptible did the

Indians account these few opponents, and so sure were they of victory, that one of the first things they did after their arrival was to agree upon a division among themselves of the prisoners and of the spoils.

They then made a violent assault upon the garrison. But meeting there a hot reception, and having no cannon, they were glad to leave it for that time, and try their efforts upon the sloops. So narrow was the river or inlet where these lay, that the enemy could approach them within twelve yards of the land; and from hence, behind a pile of plank, and a haystack fortified with posts and rails, they discharged their volleys upon them. By means, too, of fire arrows, they succeeded several times in setting the sloops on fire. But the sailors, "with a swab at the end of a rope tied to a pole, and so dipt into the water," contrived to extinguish the spreading flames; and, encouraged by their resolute commander, Lieutenant Storer, they made such stout resistance, that before night their assailants, disappointed, withdrew. But they soon returned, to try the effect of stratagem and threatening. In the course of the night, they inquired of the men on board the sloops, Who were their commanders? And being answered, "We have many commanders," the Indians replied, "You lie; you have none but Converse, and we will have him too before morning." But morning arrived, and found Convers still alive and well within the walls of Storer's house. On that morning, by daylight, the Indians commenced preparations for another assault upon the garrison. They began to march towards it in a body, with great display; and so terrific was their appearance, that one of the garrison ventured to suggest the expediency of a surrender. But Captain Convers, rendered indignant by such a proposal, "vehemently protested that he would lay the man dead who should so much as mutter that base word any more." When the Indians had come within a short distance from the garrison, they raised a shout that caused the earth to ring: and crying out in English, "Fire, and fall on, brave boys," they all, being drawn into three ranks, fired in a body at once.

But, violent as this onset was, Capt. Convers was prepared to meet it. His men were all ready, waiting his commands; and the female inhabitants of the town, who had fled to the garrison for protection at the approach of the enemy, were not only active in handing ammunition to the men, but several armed themselves with muskets, and discharged them. Capt. Convers had given orders to his men to refrain from firing till they could do it to most advantage; and, when they came to discharge their artillery at his word, such was the execution done, that many of the enemy were swept down before them, and many others were constrained to flee. Baffled in this, their second attack upon the garrison, the enemy now renewed their attempts upon the sloops. They constructed a raft, eighteen or twenty feet square, which they loaded with combustible materials, and then towing it as near as they dared, set fire to it, and left it for the tide to float it towards the sloops. And now the men on board, perceiving their imminent danger of perishing by fire, commended themselves to God for help. And suddenly, it is recorded, the wind shifted, and the raft was driven upon the opposite shore, and so much split as to let in water, with which the fire was quenched. By this time, the enemy's ammunition was nearly exhausted, and numbers of them disheartened with their ill success, began to draw off. The rest, after some consultation, thought best to send a flag of truce towards the garrison advising them to surrender. But Capt. Convers sent them word, that "he wanted nothing but for men to come and fight him." The Indians replied, "Being you are so stout, why don't you come and fight in the open field, like a man, and not fight in a garrison like a Squaw?" The Captain rejoined, "What a fool are you! do you think thirty men a match for five hundred? No: come with your thirty men upon the plain, and I'le meet you with my thirty as soon as you will." Upon this, the Indian answered, "Nay, mee own, English fashion is all one fool; you kill mee, mee kill you! No: better ly somewhere, and shoot a man, and he no see; that the best soldier!"

With this, the Indian enemy, from *daring* Capt. Convers, had recourse to *coaxing* and *flattery*. But, finding him too wise to trust the promises of insidious foes, and that all their devices to induce him to surrender, or to draw him from his stronghold, were ineffectual, they were thrown into a rage, and with a horrid imprecation declared, " We'll cut you as small as tobacco before to-morrow morning." But the only reply which the intrepid captain made to this vaporing threat, was, " to bid them come on; for he wanted work." The enemy themselves, notwithstanding their boast what they would do with him, came near him no more. Having now continued before the garrison and in its neighborhood forty-eight hours, and been disappointed in all their confident expectations, and defeated in all their efforts to get the dog Convers (as they had called him) and his men into their power, they first wreaked their vengeance upon all the cattle they could light upon, and cruelly tortured to death a poor unhappy captive they had taken on the morning they came to Wells, and then marched off, leaving some of their dead behind them, Labocree, their commander-in-chief, among the rest; thus giving cause of joy and thanksgiving unto God to the garrison, and to the country at large, for so wonderful a deliverance.

For this, his brave and successful action, Captain Convers was promoted the following year, by Governor Phipps, to the rank of a Major, and appointed to the command of all the Massachusetts forces then in Maine. Here, and in the Legislature, he still continued to serve his country during the remainder of the war: and shared at last in the honor of bringing it to an end. Towards the close of the year 1698, he and Colonel John Phillips, a member of the Council of the Province, with Captain Cyprian Southack, commander of the Province Galley, sailed from Boston for the Eastern country, intrusted by the Government with full powers for effecting a peace with the Indians. Proceeding to Casco Bay, they there met with the leading Indian sachems, and persuaded them, January 7, 1699, to accede to and solemnly subscribe a treaty, which was the same, in the main, with the one they had entered into at Pemaquid, but which they had broken, as they alleged, through the persuasion of the French. Peace had, previously to this, been made with the French by the treaty of Ryswick, 1697.

In 1699, the year in which peace with the Indians was concluded, and in the four preceding years, and again in 1701, and the four following years, Major Convers was sent a member for Woburn to the General Court; and in three of those years, viz, 1699, 1702, 1703, he was chosen Speaker of the House. In 1706, he was again returned to the lower branch of the Legislature; but did not live to finish the term for which he had been elected. Being seized, apparently, with some sudden, violent sickness, death put an end at once to his usefulness and his life, July 8, 1706, in the 61st year of his age.

Major Convers married, January 1, 1668–9, Hannah, a daughter of Capt. John Carter. By her, he had nine children, six sons and three daughters. Four of these died in infancy or childhood, or in youth unmarried. Two of his sons, Robert and Josiah, the second son of the name, were men of influence and distinction in their day, and descendants of Josiah, of the third and fourth generations from his son Josiah, Jr., still live in Woburn, and maintain a highly respectable position and character in society.

While this distinguished citizen of Woburn was Town Clerk, he performed one piece of service, for which the town doth now, and ever will, owe him a grateful remembrance. After his accession to that office, observing that his predecessors had recorded the Births, Marriages and Deaths in Woburn upon sundry loose papers, which were then in a shattered and perishing condition, he procured a blank folio volume, well bound, at his own expense, and transcribed those Records into it, adding, in his own records of births, the names of both the parents, instead of the father only, as had previously been the custom. By this, his laudable care, and by the subsequent purchase of the new volume by the town, at the recommendation of his successor in the Clerk's office, Lieutenant Fowle, the valuable records of almost fifty years on the above mentioned topics, were preserved for posterity in a fair hand, and in a durable form, which otherwise had long since perished, or been scattered and lost.[24]

[24] The original letters of Major Convers to Governor Joseph Dudley having been put into my hands by J. Wingate Thornton, Esq., of Boston, I have thought it might be gratifying to many of the citizens of Woburn to have copies of them presented in the Appendix; which see, No. VII.

CHAPTER VI.

Seating the Meeting-House. — Location of the Two Thousand Acres. — Province Loan Money. — Woburn's Share of Lovewell's Fight, 1725.

It was observed in a former Chapter of this history, that seating the meeting-house, from time to time, became not unfrequently an occasion of disorder and contention. A memorable instance of this occurred in 1710. The work of repairing and enlarging the house of public worship the year before having been completed, it became necessary to seat it anew. Accordingly, at a general meeting, December 9, 1709, John Brooks, Sergeant Eleazar Flegg, Sergeant John Tidd, Sergeant George Reed, and James Fowle were chosen a committee for this purpose. But so irksome was this office accounted, and at the same time so thankless and invidious, that two of the persons nominated for it on this occasion, Messrs. Tidd and Fowle, immediately declined. To supply their places, Messrs. Peirson Richardson and Ensign Samuel Bloggett, were then elected. But Mr. Bloggett, signifying at once his unwillingness to serve, a vacancy was again made in the committee. This vacancy, the town did not attempt to fill; and the remaining four members went on to perform the work of their appointment. But in the discharge of their office, they were far from giving general satisfaction. At the time of their election, the town had instructed them to have respect, in their official labors, to three things; viz, to age, to what men had done towards building the meeting-house at the first, and towards its recent repairs and enlargement; and finally, to their proportion in the public charges.

But, in seating the people, the committee seem to have paid more regard to the last two of these qualifications than to the first; and to have preferred to the front seats in the temple the wealthy and liberal, though young, before the aged members of the church and community that were poor, and so of necessity but slender contributors towards the cost of the late work upon the house of God. This manner of proceeding laid the foundation of much murmuring and discontent. At a meeting of the Selectmen, February 6, 1709–10, a petition was handed in to them, signed by about fifty-seven inhabitants, alleging that what the Seating Committee had done, in the fulfilment of their trust, was illegal, and greatly prejudicial to the peace of the town; and praying that the town might be called together for the choice of another Committee, who should perform the work anew. Two of the Selectmen were opposed to granting this petition, apprehensive of the difficulties which might ensue. But the other three were so far convinced of the necessity of the meeting petitioned for, that they gave orders for warning one to be held March 6th, the day for the annual choice of town officers, at 8 o'clock in the morning. By fixing upon this early hour for the meeting requested, the Selectmen who called it, doubtless intended to have the petition acted upon under their own supervision and authority, before a new choice of Selectmen was made. Accordingly, the day being come, and the town assembled at the hour specified, as soon as the meeting was opened, and a Moderator chosen, those three Selectmen, at the motion of many of the people, ordered the Moderator, Ensign John Peirce, to call for votes for the choice of a new Seating Committee. But this, he utterly refused to do; and the Selectmen, in consequence, commanded the Town Clerk to record his refusal. A motion was then made and carried, that the Town Clerk should record the reason which the Moderator had rendered for his refusal to make the choice of the Committee petitioned for, the first thing to be done on that occasion; viz: that he thought it most proper, that the choice of town officers, which was the regular business of the day, should be first attended; and then, if there were time left, the petition might be acted upon by the town, if they saw fit.

The consequence of this altercation was, that no seating committee was chosen at this time, and the people were obliged to acquiesce for the present in the arrangements of the committee appointed at the former meeting. Still, the dissatisfaction with those arrangements did not cease. At a meeting of the Selectmen May 7, 1711, a petition was presented them from several of the inhabitants, declaring themselves "much aggrieved at the disorderly seating of many persons, in the House of God, the aintient behind the backs of the youth, which they apprehended not to be according to the Law of God, which requireth the youth to rise up before the hoary head, and to honour the person of the old man:" and, therefore, the petitioners moved the Selectmen to call the town together, "to regulate such disorders, that so peace and order may be in the house of God."[1] In compliance with this request, the Selectmen directed the Constables, in warning a town meeting, May 18th, for the choice of a Representative, to give notice also, that at the same meeting some proper method would be considered for the redress of the irregularites complained of. At the meeting thus notified, the petition referred to was read, and some debate arising respecting it and the disorders alleged therein, it was moved by some, as a good expedient for remedying them, that the town declare the last seating of the meeting-house void. This question was put, and the majority voting in the affirmative, the last seating was annulled, and no provision being made at the same time for a new seating, it is presumed that the people, upon some acknowledged principles of propriety, seated themselves, and probably to better mutual satisfaction, than any committee, in the existing state of feeling, could have done it for them.

In view of this and similar contentions among our ancestors on this subject, we have cause of congratulation that houses of public worship at the present day are constructed, and seats assigned in them, on a plan which supersedes the need of a seating committee. It is readily granted, that respect is always and everywhere due to age, especially in the house of God, and were the floors of our meeting-houses now occupied with long seats, as of old, it might be justly regarded as a gross impropriety, and one that ought to be rectified, if aged and respectable, yet poor members of the church were seated behind the young, who had

---

[1] Town Records, Vol. V., p. 185.

nothing but wealth and a large share in the public taxes to recommend them. But then, while the old custom prevailed, there would unavoidably arise cases, almost innumerable, of persons, whose respective claims to precedence it would be next to impossible to adjust with exactness. And the grievance springing from a supposed erroneous decision in such instances would, doubtless, be greatly increased by the prevailing sensitiveness in former days upon the subject of rank in society. The first settlers of New England were men to be ever deeply venerated for their piety, and their many sterling virtues. But they brought over with them high notions of family rank, and station. Such distinctions, the institutions and customs of the mother country had created and cherished; and under the influence of education and habit, our earliest ancestors here attached an inordinate importance to them themselves, and were jealous of any neglect of them by others. And while their descendants of the first and second generations had much degenerated, it is to be feared, from their praiseworthy qualities, they retained with little or no diminution their sentiments with regard to rank and condition in society. Many illustrations of this state of feeling, at the commencement of the last century, might be given were it necessary. But there is an anecdote showing its existence in Woburn and its vicinity at that period, which may not be amiss to relate. A tradition of unquestionable correctness states, that a certain lady, a daughter of a prominent family in this town, who was married and lived in Billerica, observing one of her sons connecting himself in marriage with a young woman whom she deemed to be of a family far inferior to her own, felt sufficiently chagrined at the circumstance, but thought best, for that time, to keep her feelings to herself. But, hearing afterwards, that another of her boys was following, in this respect, his brother's steps, she could forbear no longer, but vented her mortification with exclaiming, "One slice of the brown loaf to a family is surely enough."

In 1664, it will be recollected, the General Court made a grant to this town of two thousand acres of land, to be taken up wherever they could find it in this then wilderness, clear of any prior claim.[2] Votes had been passed by the town at different times in relation to this grant; but fifty years were suffered to pass, before anything effectual was done towards its location. But, in 1714, the town took up this business in earnest. At a general meeting, May 11th, of that year, a committee was appointed to look out a place for the location of the 2000 acres formerly granted to the town. But that committee neglecting to fulfil their appointment, (possibly from an apprehension that in consequence of the long delay there had been on the part of Woburn, to lay down the land, some new authority from the Court had become necessary or expedient,) a committee of two, viz: Ensign John Peirce and Sergeant John Tidd, was chosen November 14, 1716, "to prefer a petition to the General Court, for the renewal of their grant."[3] Accordingly, a petition was addressed by these gentlemen to the Court, which was favorably accepted. The grant was renewed, and at the annual town meeting, March 4, 1716–17, Messrs. Ebenezer Johnson and Eleazar Flegg were chosen a committee to look out a place where they might take it up.[4] These gentlemen proceeded forthwith to the discharge of their commission. For the location of the tract of land in question, they pitched upon a place, called Turkey Hill, near Lancaster, west of Groton, and within the bounds of what was afterwards incorporated as the town of Lunenburg. Here, with the assistance of others whom they took with them from Woburn, and of a committee from Lancaster, they ran its lines, and established boundaries, which from time to time were subsequently renewed.[5]

Before the location and bounds of this grant were determined, it had been contemplated to sell it, and to let the money upon interest for the benefit of the town; and a committee had been appointed to carry this scheme into effect. But at a meeting, May 15, 1724, the proprietors voted that the land should remain for the present in the hands it was then in. They also forbade any one interested therein, and all others, to cut or carry

---

[2] Town Records, Vol. I., pp. 29, 30.
[3] Town Records, Vol. V., p. 353.
[4] Town Records, Vol. V., p. 357.
[5] Town Records, Vol. VI., p. 20.

off from it either wood or timber; and chose Ensign Josiah Convers and John Russell as a committee to take it into their care, and to prosecute any who might trespass upon it.[6] In this condition, it continued about ten years. How it was ultimately disposed of, will appear in a subsequent chapter.

In 1721, March 31st, to remedy the scarcity of money then much complained of, and to facilitate the payment of taxes, the Legislature of Massachusetts, issued what was called, the £50,000 Loan. By this, was intended that amount in Bills of Credit, which were distributed among the several towns, according to the taxes they paid, and to be returned into the Province Treasury, within a limited time.[7] At a general meeting in Woburn, October 12, 1721, it was voted, that they would take their proportion of "the fifty-thousand pound" out of the public treasury, and would commit it to three trustees, to manage it as the town should direct, and to receive one-sixth part of the interest for their trouble. The persons chosen for this trust were, Major Eleazar Flegg, Mr. John Brooks and Capt. John Fowle; who were instructed by the town to let the money, in sums not less than ten pounds, nor greater than twenty pounds, to any one man; to let it at an interest of five per cent per annum, to be for the town's use; to keep it in their hands till the last of the following May; and that, if by that time, inhabitants of Woburn did not appear to take up the whole upon good security, to let it to any person in the County, who should offer landed or other security satisfactory to the trustees.[8] Woburn's share in this public loan was £624: and much to the praise of the trustees, it was managed by them on the town's behalf with entire fidelity. In volume VII., p. 2, of the Town Books are recorded five distinct receipts, acknowledging their payment of the principal into the Province Treasury, in five equal instalments of £124:16*s.* each; the first being dated July 29, 1726, and the last, July 29, 1730. And there is also upon record, in the same volume, page 1st, a long particular account of their disposal of the interest of this sum,

---

[6] Town Records, Vol. VI., p. 196.

[7] Felt's Massachusetts Currency, p. 77.

[8] Town Records, Vol. VI., pp. 130, 131.

agreeably to vote of the town, for the payment of pauper bills, county tax, representatives, school-masters and hire of preaching, during the frequent indisposition of Rev. Mr. Fox. Never, apparently, was a public trust more faithfully discharged than this; never was there a happier illustration of following the Apostle's example in a like case, of "providing for honest things, not only in the sight of the Lord, but also in the sight of men."

But the town was not so fortunate in its investment, a few years afterwards, of its share in the £60,000 loan so called. The act of the Legislature granting this loan was passed early in the year 1728, and was styled "An act for raising and settling a public revenue for and towards defraying the necessary charges of the government, by an emission of £60,000 in bills of credit." "This was done to bring it within the words of the [king's] instruction, which restrained the governor from consenting to the issuing bills of credit, except for charges of government. The interest of 4 per cent, or £2400, was to be applied annually to the public charges, and gave colour for issuing the principal sum of £60,000."[9] This loan, like the preceding one, was distributed among the several towns in the Province, according to their proportion in the public taxes. The sum to which Woburn was entitled is not upon the Records of the town, but could not have been far from £750. At a general meeting in Woburn, April 4, 1728, it was voted "that the town would take their proportion of the Sixty thousand pound, provided the trustees would be bound to indemnifie the Town."

At the same time, three trustees, viz, Samuel Richardson, Caleb Blogget, and John Fowle, were chosen to receive the town's part of this loan, and to let it out; and the Selectmen were appointed a committee to take security of them against loss by their means. It was also voted, that the trustees should not let more than £20, nor less than £10, to any one person; and should be allowed a sixth part of the interest for their compensation.[10] No mention is made in the Record of the rate of

[9] Felt's Historical Account of Massachusetts Currency, p. 84.
[10] Town Records, Vol. VI., p. 347.

interest to be demanded. But as four per cent of it was to be paid annually into the Province Treasury, and a sixth part of it was to go to the trustees, it appears evident that the money was to be let at the rate of six per cent interest, and that the remaining sixth part was to go towards defraying town charges.[9] No account is to be found in the Records of the manner in which either the principal or interest of Woburn's share of this loan was at any time disposed of; and six years passed away, from the time the town voted to accept it, before any inquiry was instituted as to the manner in which it was managed. At a general meeting, May 16, 1734, a committee of three was chosen to reckon with the trustees "about the lone money of the first and second Banck,"[11] and to give an account of their doings at the next annual meeting in March.[11] But no Report of this committee is upon record; and four years more rolled on before the town awaked to a proper sense of its responsibility on this subject, and to a suitable care for its own security. At a meeting of the freeholders and other inhabitants, November 20, 1738, they chose a committee of three, viz., Messrs. William Tay, Benjamin Johnson, and Samuel Eames, whom they fully authorized "to reckon, receive, and recover in the Law, for the town's use, all such sum or sums of Province Bills as are due from Capt. John Fowle, Mr Samuel Richardson and Capt. Caleb Blogget, as trustees for the town for the £60,000 loan . . . . and also to see that the trustees pay the full parte of said money, that is due to the Province Treasurer, into the Treasury; and also to see that the town have the parte that is due to said town": and to make return of their proceedings at the next general town meeting after the May meeting ensuing.[12]

But before the meeting here designated (which was not held till December 28, 1739,) arrived, Woburn's proportion of the above named loan, or a part of it, was called for into the public treasury; and the sum demanded not being forthcoming from the trustees, the town was obliged to provide for the deficiency. A "Loan Tax," so called, of £250 7*s.* 6*d.* (which was probably

---

[11] Town Records, Vol. VII., p. 113.

[12] Town Records, Vol. VII., p. 286.

about one third part of the whole sum received by the trustees) was assessed upon the inhabitants, February 13, 1739, to be collected and paid by the Constables "unto the Province Treasurer, according to the direction of his Warrant."[13] This sum now became due from the trustees to Woburn, instead of the Treasurer of the Province; and the town seemed determined to recover it, if possible, together with the proportion of the interest of the loan to which it was entitled, but which appears to have been still unpaid. At a meeting, December 28, 1739, it granted anew to the Committee appointed November 20, 1738, full power and authority to demand, and "to recover in the Law all such sum or sums of this Province's Bills of Creditt as are due to the Inhabitants of Woobourn from Mr Samuel Richardson, Capt. John Fowle and Capt. Caleb Bloggett, as they are Trustees for said Town for their part of the Sixty Thousand Pound Loan; and the same to pursue to final judgment and execution."[14] At a subsequent meeting, May 4, 1741, two members of this committee, viz: Lieut. Samuel Eames and Mr William Tay, were re-appointed "to demand and receive the interest of the Loan Bills of Creditt, due to the town from Capt. Caleb Bloggett and Mr Samuel Richardson; and to prosecute that affair in the Law to final judgment, if need be."[15]

And finally, at a meeting, May 7, 1742, in acting upon an article in the Warrant, to "consider whether the Town will remitt all or any part of the interest due from the Committee [Trustees] about the £60.000 Loan on a bond of forty two pounds?" it was decided in the negative.[15] This was taking a firm stand, on the part of the town. But what was the effect of these votes and resolutions, what was actually done by the Committee so amply empowered by them, and what was the result of the measures which the Committee adopted, the Records nowhere show. These, on all the points just named, maintain every where a studied silence. Considering, however, the respectable standing which the Trustees had hitherto occupied in society, the integrity which one of them had manifested as a trustee for

---

[13] Town Records, Vol. VII., pp. 323–330. [14] Town Records, Vol. VII., p. 315.
[15] Town Records, Vol. VII., pp. 368, 399.

the management of the town's part of the preceding loan, the security which they were severally required to give the Selectmen to indemnify the town at their appointment to office, and the apparent omission of the Committee to use their power to commence a suit against them to recover what they owed to the town, it seems more probable than otherwise, that they gradually recovered from the embarrassments, under which they may have labored for a time, and eventually satisfied all the demands of the town against them, as trustees in the affair of the £60,000 loan.

It is lamentable to witness, or to have occasion to relate instances, even of temporary delinquency, in persons intrusted with public money. Such, of all men, are concerned to be faithful to their trust. Generally speaking, a man may do what he will with his own; but he has no right to be careless or lavish of that which is another's, or the property of the community. By unfaithfulness in the latter case, many are injured; many are aggrieved by his abuse of their confidence, and his own reputation and usefulness inevitably suffer. But in the instance before us, powerful reasons demand a charitable construction upon the conduct of the trustees, and forbearance in the sentence we pass on it. For many years, the General Court of the Province had been making issues in paper money from time to time, without any adequate provision to keep up its nominal value. The consequence was, a growing scarcity of specie, and a constant depreciation of their bills of credit. And yet, as these bills were almost the only currency in the market, the people were generally urgent in their calls for an increase of them, and a majority in the popular branch of the Legislature was always ready to gratify the wishes of their constituents in this respect. But the more bills of credit were multiplied, the more and faster did their value diminish: So that whereas, in 1710, eight shillings in bills were accounted equal in value to an ounce of silver, sixty shillings in bills were reckoned, in 1750, but an equivalent to the same standard value.[16] Hence arose

[16] Felt's Historical Account of Massachusetts Currency, pp. 83, 135.

universal embarrassment in the community; and to several descriptions of people, severe and increasing suffering and distress. Avaricious administrators of estates lay under a strong temptation at least to detain the property of widows and orphans in their hands, and to pay it at last in depreciated paper; ministers and other salaried men were reduced to great straits, by being obliged to receive their salaries in a currency not worth half its original nominal value; and creditors were kept out of their honest dues altogether, or compelled to take up with what was far below their just claims. It is no groundless presumption therefore to suppose, that the delinquency of the trustees of Woburn in the present instance was owing to the failure of those to whom, with the town's authority, they had lent the town's loan money to fulfil on demand their obligations, rather than to any intention in the trustees to defraud. Nor is it likely that their case was a singular one. Were inquiry made, it would very probably be found, that the trustees for this loan, in a considerable number of our towns, even men of fair and unimpeachable characters, were rendered unable, by the difficulties of the times to meet, at once, their public responsibilities, and so, through dire necessity, and to their own grief, became, for a season, the unwilling instruments of trouble and loss to their fellow-citizens, and of disappointing the confidence reposed in them.

In 1725 occurred that bloody encounter with Indians, which is commonly distinguished as Lovewell's Fight. It took place, May 8, O. S., and its centennial anniversary was commemorated on the spot, in an address before a large and intelligent audience by Charles S. Davies, Esq., on the corresponding day in N. S., May 19, 1825. As a considerable number of the English, who fought in this engagement, were either inhabitants of Woburn, or had originated from it, and as the event of it was heard by the people of this place, at the time, with bitter lamentation or with deep concern, a particular account of it will not, I presume, be uninteresting to their descendants at this distant day.

During the war carried on by the English against the Abenaquis or Eastern Indians, from 1722 to 1726, the government of Massachusetts, to encourage scouting parties for the defence of the frontiers, offered a bounty for Indian scalps and captives in 1723, which was raised the next year to £100 each. With a view to obtaining this bounty, as well as from motives of patriotism, Capt. John Lovewell, of Dunstable, raised a company of volunteers, and made two successful expeditions in pursuit of Indians in December 1724, and early in 1725. In the latter expedition of the two, he and his men killed ten Indians, whom they surprised lying round a fire asleep near a pond in Wakefield, N. H., since called Lovewell's Pond;[17] and bringing their scalps to Boston, they were paid £1,000 for them out of the public treasury.[17] Emboldened by this repeated success, he quickly after undertook a third expedition for the same object. On the 16th of April, 1725, he and forty-five others, inclusively of a surgeon and a chaplain, marched from Dunstable for the Indian villages at Pigwacket near the upper part of Saco River, once the residence of a powerful tribe of Indians, and since places of their occasional resort.[17] Before he had proceeded far, one of his men disabled by lameness, and another by an old wound, were dismissed and returned home. When they had reached the great Ossipèe pond, another of the company falling sick, they halted, and built a small fort, which might serve as a place of refuge in case of necessity.[17] Here they left the sick man, and the surgeon to take care of him, and eight other men for a guard, together with a considerable quantity of provision for their own use, on their return.[17]

The company was now reduced to thirty-four, inclusively of the captain; and their names (excepting that of one who fled at the beginning of the fight, which it was therefore thought best to consign to oblivion) were as follows: viz, Capt. John Lovewell, Lieutenants Joseph Farwell and Jonathan Robbins, Ensign John Harwood, Sergeant Noah Johnson, Robert Usher and Samuel Whiting of Dunstable; Ensign Seth Wyman, Corporal Thomas Richardson, Timothy Richardson, Ichabod Johnson and

[17] Belknap's New Hampshire, in one vol., pp. 209, 210, etc. See also Hutchinson's History, Vol. II., pp. 314, 315.

Josiah Johnson of Woburn; Eleazar Davis, Josiah Davis, Josiah Jones, David Melvin, Eleazar Melvin, Jacob Farrar and Joseph Farrar of Concord; Mr Jonathan Fry of Andover, Chaplain; Sergeant Jacob Fullam of Weston; Corporal Edward Lingfield of Nutfield, now Londonderry; Jonathan Kittredge and Solomon Keyes of Billerica; John Jefts, Daniel Woods, Thomas Woods, John Chamberlain, Elias Barron, Isaac Lakin and Joseph Gilson of Groton; and Ebenezer Ayer and Abiel Asten of Haverhill.[17] Pursuing their journey northward, about twenty-two miles in a direct course, but forty miles by the indirect road they are supposed to have taken, they came to a pond near the Pigwacket villages by the Saco, and now within the township of Fryburg, by the side of which pond they encamped.[17] On Saturday, May 8 (the day so fatal to many of them—so full of peril to them all), very early in the morning, while they were at prayers, they heard a gun discharge; and, not long after, they espied an Indian standing on a point of land, which ran into the pond, more than a mile distant. This point was a noted fishing place: and, at the present day, there seems good reason to believe that the Indian they observed was not stationed there with any insidious design, but was entirely ignorant of there being any English in the neighborhood, and that the gun which they heard, he had fired at a flock of ducks.[17] But Captain Lovewell and company had been alarmed the night before by sundry noises, which they had attributed to enemies; and now the sight of this solitary Indian confirmed them in the persuasion that their suspicions had been well founded; that a party of the enemy was lying in wait between him and them; and that he had been set where he stood for a decoy to draw them that way. Accordingly, a consultation was held by Captain Lovewell with his men, whether they should attempt a retreat, or venture to face and fight an enemy, whom they could not expect, as they had hoped, to take by surprise. Their answer generally was, "We came out to meet the Enemy; we have all along prayed God we might find 'em; and we had rather trust Providence with our lives, yea, die for our country, than try to return, without seeing them, if we may, and be called cowards for our pains."[18] Upon receiving this bold reply, the captain at once decided, though with some misgivings, and, apparently, against his own judgment, to go forward: and, still supposing the enemy to be before him, he ordered his men to lay down their packs where they were, that they might be as free from incumbrance as possible; to march with the utmost circumspection, and in perfect readiness for an assault at an instant's warning.

But, while Capt. Lovewell, with his men, was moving cautiously onward, expecting that his wily foes lay concealed in his *front,* they were in reality gathering and laying wait for him in his *rear.* For it so happened, that in his march he crossed a carrying place, to which, presently after he left it, came two parties of Indians, with Paugus, a noted chief, and Wahwa at their head, who had been scouting down Saco river, and were now on their return to the lower village of Pigwacket, situate upon a meadow by the Saco, about a mile and a half from the pond.[17] These Indians, perceiving the tracks of Lovewell's company at the carrying place, traced them back to their packs, which they immediately seized upon and removed for their own use; and ascertaining by counting them, that their owners were fewer in number than themselves, they skulked in ambush hard by, and watched for their return. In the mean while, as Capt. Lovewell and men were marching round the pond, to come at the place where they had seen the Indian standing, they met him returning by another path to the village, with his game and two fowling pieces in his hands. Several of the company fired upon him, and he returned the fire, and mortally wounded Capt. Lovewell, it was supposed, though he made but little complaint, and was able to keep on his march. Ensign Wyman then fired and killed the Indian; and another took his scalp. Having discovered no enemy in their march, as they had anticipated, the company now bent their way back toward the place where they had left their packs. But, when they had reached the spot, and while they were looking for their baggage, which had been removed, (it being about 10 o'clock in the forenoon) the Indians

---

[18] Historical Memoirs, etc., by Rev. Thomas Symmes, of Bradford.

rose in two bodies in their front and in their rear; and, with a hideous yell, ran towards them with their arms presented. The English likewise instantly presented arms, and ran to meet them. Both parties fired when they had come within a few yards of each other; and many of the Indians were killed at once, while the English, most of them, escaped the first shot unhurt. But so superior were the Indians to the English in respect to numbers, that nine of the latter were slain quickly after. These were, Capt. Lovewell, Sergeant Fullam, Ensign Harwood, John Jefts, Jonathan Kittredge, Daniel Woods, Ichabod Johnson, Thomas Woods, and Josiah Davis. Three also were badly wounded, viz: Lieut. Farwell, Lieut. Robbins and Robert Usher; and the rest, perceiving the Indians were endeavoring to surround them, retreated to the pond, which now covered their rear, while they were in some measure sheltered in other quarters by a few large pine trees, and by a rocky point running into the pond.

In this position, under the direction of Ensign Wyman, upon whom devolved the command after Capt. Lovewell was killed, and the two Lieutenants, Farwell and Robbins, were disabled by their wounds, they maintained a sharp, resolute contest till about night. To intimidate them, the Indians kept up a constant howling like wolves, and barking like dogs, and all manner of hideous noises; but the English answered them only by frequent shouts and huzzas, such as they had made at firing their first round. At one time, some of the Indians holding up ropes to them, proposed to them to ask for quarter, but they spiritedly replied, they would take none but at the muzzle of their guns. Nothwithstanding their inferiority in number to the Indians, and the faintness they experienced for want of food, of which they had taken none since early in the morning, they continued fighting courageously as men resolved to die rather than yield.

It was apparently during the afternoon fight, that Paugus, a noted Indian chief, was killed by John Chamberlain of Groton, who knew him. In the engagement, their guns having become foul, they both went to the pond about the same time to cleanse them, and there met. The following lively description of their encounter, confirmed in the main by tradition, though embellished probably by fancy in some of its minor circumstances, is quoted by Lemuel Shattuck, Esq., in his History of Concord, from the "Philadelphia Album," in 1828.

"They slowly and with equal movements cleansed their guns and took their stations on the outer border of the beach. 'Now, Paugus,' said Chamberlain, 'I'll have you;' and with the quickness and steadiness of an old hunter, sprung to loading his rifle. 'Na, na, me have you,' replied Paugus; and he handled his gun with a dexterity that made the bold heart of Chamberlain beat quick, and he almost raised his eyes to take his last look upon the sun. They rammed their cartridges, and each at the same instant cast his ramrod upon the sand. 'I'll have you, Paugus,' shouted Chamberlain, as in his desperation he almost resolved to rush upon the savage, with the breech of his rifle, lest he should receive his bullets before he could load. The woods across the pond echoed back the shout. Paugus trembled as he applied his powder-horn to the priming; Chamberlain heard the grains of his powder rattle lightly upon the leaves beneath his feet. Chamberlain struck his gun breech violently upon the ground — the rifle primed herself, he aimed, and his bullets whistled through the heart of Paugus. He fell, and as he went down, the bullet from the mouth of his ascending rifle touched the hair upon the crown of Chamberlain, and passed off without avenging the death of its dreadful master."[19]

The fight was maintained with great obstinacy and resolution on both sides; and continued, with but little intermission, about ten hours. Shortly after sunset, the Indians withdrew, being the first to desist and quit the ground. They carried with them their wounded and most of their dead; and left the bodies of Lovewell, and the others whom they had killed at the commencement of the action, unscalped; and so much had they suffered in the fight, through the firm resistance and skilful manœuvring of the English, that they went off with greatly reduced numbers. In accounts subsequently received, it was stated, that "they were

---

19 Shattuck's History, p. 69.

seventy in the whole, whereof forty were said to be killed on the spot, eighteen more died of their wounds, and that twelve only returned."

About midnight, after the moon had risen, the remnant of Capt. Lovewell's company, who were able to travel, withdrew from the field, and began their march towards the fort, which they had built in coming, for a refuge. They left behind the bodies of their nine companions who were killed at the commencement of the engagement; also Jacob Farrar, who was just expiring; and Lieut. Robbins and Robert Usher, who were mortally wounded, and unable to accompany them. At parting, Lieut. Robbins requested them to load his gun, and leave it with him, saying, "The Indians will come in the morning to scalp me, and I'll kill one more of 'em, if I can." They complied with his request: but the Indians do not appear to have returned to the ground; and his body and those of the other two were shortly after found dead, and lying, apparently, where they severally breathed their last. They who marched from this fatal spot were twenty in number, of whom eleven had been badly wounded. But their troubles did not cease upon quitting the field of battle. They suffered extremely from hunger; their provisions having fallen into the hands of the Indians on the morning of the attack.

They had proceeded but about a mile and a half in their way, when four of them, viz: Lieut. Farwell, Mr. Frye, Eleazar Davis and Josiah Jones, were compelled, by the anguish of their wounds, to stop, receiving encouragement from the rest, that as soon as they reached the fort, they would send some of the guard they had left there, to their assistance. Shortly after, on coming to a thick piece of woods, the fear of making a track, by which the Indians might discover and follow them, led the remainder of this little band to separate into three divisions, and one of these divisions consisting of Ensign Wyman and four others, being actually pursued by three Indians to a considerable distance, Elias Barron, an individual belonging to it, went astray from his companions; and, though his gun case was found afterwards by the side of Ossipee river, yet he himself was never more heard from. The other two divisions, eleven men in all, at length recovered the fort. But to their surprise and grief, they found it abandoned by those whom they had left there, who had been frightened away by a terrific report brought them by the nameless deserter, who had basely run from his post, and forsaken his friends, when they most needed him, at the commencement of the battle. Here, however, they were presently rejoiced by the arrival of Solomon Keyes, who was not with them when they began their march from the battle ground, and who had been preserved to see them by means truly astonishing, as well as unexpected to himself. His report was, that, on the day of battle, after continuing to fight till, through loss of blood from three wounds he had received, he could stand no longer, he crawled to Ensign Wyman, and told him, "He was a dead man: But (says he) if it be possible, I'll get out of the way of the Indians, that they mayn't get my scalp." In his efforts to reach a place where the Indians would not discover him, he lighted, providentially, upon a canoe in the pond: and, rolling himself into it, he was driven by the wind a considerable distance towards the fort; and, then, being wonderfully strengthened, he was enabled to perform the rest of the journey on foot, and so as to come to the fort about the same time that the eleven just referred to did.[20] And now these twelve men, having refreshed themselves with provisions, which they found at the fort, proceeded to Dunstable, where they arrived, May 13, at night, being the fifth day after the engagement. On May 15, they were rejoined by Ensign Wyman and three of his party. By him they were told that they had not tasted food of any sort from Saturday morning, the day of the fight, till the Wednesday following: when two mouse-squirrels, which they caught and roasted whole, seemed a delicious morsel to them; and that, afterwards, partridges and other game which they killed, comfortably supplied their wants the rest of their journey.[20]

In the mean while, their four companions, whom they had left behind shortly after commencing their march from the battlefield, waited patiently several days, in hope of receiving the

[20] Symmes' Memoirs, etc.

assistance from the fort which they had encouraged them to expect, but which they failed to send them, in consequence of their finding the fort deserted. But at length these four forsaken ones, giving up the prospect of help in despair, set out themselves on their way homeward, though their wounds had become corrupt for want of dressing, and they themselves were almost famished with hunger. Two of them, Davis and Jones, after acute suffering, succeeded in their attempts to reach the English settlements, the former coming in at Berwick, the latter at Saco. But the effort proved too great for Lieut. Farwell and Mr. Fry. According to information subsequently given by Davis, who kept with them both as long as they were able to travel, Fry first gave up; but Farwell held out several days, till he had come within a few miles of the fort, and they both doubtless died in the places where they were severally left by Davis, being never seen or heard from more. Both these gentlemen were very highly esteemed, and their deaths were deeply lamented.

But there was something peculiarly affecting in the circumstances of the death of Mr. Fry, the chaplain. He was the son of Mr. James Fry, of Andover, was graduated at Harvard College, 1723; and at his decease had a journal, which he kept of the expedition, in his pocket. He had much endeared himself to the company, both by the excellency of his devotional performances as chaplain, and also by his personal courage and readiness to share with them in their dangers and hardships. In the afternoon of the day of battle, he received a severe wound fighting with the rest; and, being disabled by it from further active service, he was repeatedly heard praying aloud, that God would preserve and prosper his brethren in arms, in their then sharp conflict. After the fight had ceased, he travelled with the rest a little way towards the fort; and, then, with Farwell, Davis, and Jones, was left behind, being unable to go any further. Here he stayed with them several days, looking in vain for help from the fort; and then set forward in company with them again. But, after travelling several miles with them, perceiving his strength fail him, and his end draw near, Mr. Fry lay down, and, addressing Farwell and Davis, desired them not to wait for him, for that he felt himself to be a dying man, and should never rise any more. He likewise charged Davis, if God should spare his life to get home, to go and tell his father, "*that he expected in a few hours to be in eternity; and that he was not afraid to die.*"[20] This is the last that is known of this good man. He probably breathed his last in the place and posture in which his companions left him. No monument marks the spot where his untimely decease took place, and where his remains rest. But an elm tree, which he planted with his own hands before his father's door in Andover, still lives, or did recently, and will be, while it stands, a memorial of him.

Such was the issue of this disastrous conflict. Twelve of our men lay dead or dying on the field of battle: two were left in their retreat to die of their wounds in the wilderness; and one went astray, and was never after heard of. Of the thirty-three English who engaged in the fight, only eighteen lived to return to their families: and of these, only nine, viz., Ensign Wyman, Edward Lingfield, Thomas Richardson, David Melvin, Eleazar Melvin, Ebenezer Ayer, Abiel Asten, Joseph Farrar, and Joseph Gilson, escaped any considerable injury. The other nine, viz, Sergt. Noah Johnson, Timothy Richardson, Josiah Johnson, Samuel Whiting, John Chamberlain, Isaac Lakin, Eleazar Davis, Josiah Jones, and Solomon Keyes, were badly wounded, and some of them were made cripples or invalids for life.

The report of this fight and its lamentable result excited deep concern, as well as sympathy for afflicted survivors, throughout the community. In a message from Lieut. Governor Wentworth of New Hampshire to the House of Representatives there, May 17, 1725, he thus alludes to this melancholy affair. "I received an express from Lieut. Governor Dummer, giving an account that Capt. Lovewell met a party of Indians at or near Pigwacket, which broke Capt. Lovewell's company in pieces. I have sent fifty-two men, under command of Capt. John Chesley, to make the best of his way to Ossapy and Pigwacket, and thence make diligent search for Capt. Lovewell's fort, &c., and to relieve any wounded men they may meet in their way thither or elsewhere." The House, in their answer, May 22, say: "As for the misfortune of Capt. Lovewell and his men, we desire to be humble before God for so great a frown of his Providence, and thank your Honour for sending a company for the relief of any that may be yet alive." But the company of men sent on this benevolent errand by Lieut. Governor Wentworth, some how or other, missed their way, and never reached the scene of the engagement. But Col. Tyng of Massachusetts, with a company of men from Dunstable, went to the spot, and there found and buried beneath an aged pine the twelve men of ours that had been left there, dead or dying, on the night after the battle, and carved their names on the neighboring trees. He also discovered there three graves, one of which being opened was found to contain the body of Paugus, the Indian chief, killed by Chamberlain, as above related. Rev. Dr. Belknap, who visited the place in 1784, observes in a note to his History of New Hampshire,[21] that "the names of the dead, on the trees, and the holes where balls had entered and been cut out, were [then] plainly visible. . . . The trees had the appearance of being very old, and one of them was fallen."

The intelligence of Lovewell's fight was heard at Woburn with bitter mourning and lamentation. Inclusively of Sergt. Noah Johnson (a native of Woburn, though then an inhabitant of Dunstable) six of her sons, belonging to three of her most numerous and respectable families, and four of them grandsons of Maj. William Johnson, had been engaged in it. Of these six men, three were wounded, and one slain. The wounded persons, Timothy Richardson, Noah Johnson and Josiah Johnson seem all to have ultimately recovered. But the death of Ichabod Johnson, who fell in the beginning of the battle, proved too hard a stroke for his fond father. Capt. Edward Johnson, born March 19, 1658, was the second son of Maj. William Johnson, and a grandson of Capt. Edward Johnson, one of the principal settlers of the town, whose name he bore, and who remembered him in his will. He lived about half a mile from where Burlington meeting-house was afterwards built, in a house

[21] Belknap's New Hampshire, p. 212, note.

on the most easterly path to Shawshin, now the road to Bedford, opposite to Mr. Alfred B. Shaw's, the cellar of which was, till recently, visible; and through life he stood high among his fellow-townsmen, in reputation and usefulness. He was many years one of the Selectmen of Woburn; its representative to the General Court in 1700, and about 1720[a] was chosen a deacon of the church. He was also a gentleman of handsome property for that day; and was blessed by his first wife, Sarah Walker, with seven children, and with two by his second wife, widow Abigail Thompson, whose maiden name was Gardiner. But of these nine children, though all were deservedly dear to him, Ichabod, the youngest son by his first wife, appears to have been his Benjamin, the darling of his heart; and when the news of the sudden, bloody death of this favorite child, reached his ear, he was so overcome by it, as that his gray hairs were brought quickly down with sorrow to the grave. Neither honor, nor wealth, nor any worldly blessing could now yield him consolation or support. His surviving sons and daughters, his numerous relatives and friends, all rose up to comfort him, but in vain. Even that holy religion which he professed (for want doubtless of a due application on his part of its blessed truths, promises and exhortations to his own case) failed to minister its soothing, healing balm to his wounded spirit. He seems to have imagined, that with Ichabod the glory of his house had departed (as the name denotes); and to have sunk in grief and despondency. Before three months from the death of his son had fully elapsed, the father went down to the grave mourning. He died August 7, 1725, in the 68th year of his age; and as a venerable granddaughter of his (Miss Abigail Johnson) once told me, he died of a broken heart.

The Legislature of Massachusetts gave prompt and substantial evidence of sympathy for these unfortunate soldiers and their heirs. Soon after the battle, the widow of Capt. Lovewell petitioned, that the Province would allow her for what he paid for the supplies of the men who accompanied him. To this, the

---

[a] Compare Town Records, Vol. VI., pp. 67, 78.

Court agreed; and gave her assurance, that when they came to reward those who fought in the battle, they would consider her case more particularly. Accordingly, June 17, 1725, they voted to allow Capt. Lovewell and company or heirs, £300, for the scalps of the three Indians killed (doubtless those whose graves were found by Col. Tyng), though the scalps were not produced, as the law required; also, £30 to be paid to or for each of the thirty-three men who had fought in the battle, amounting in all to £990; also, £210 to the heirs of the six men killed, Capt. Lovewell's portion to be £60, the rest £30 apiece. By the six men killed, referred to in the last donation, were unquestionably meant the six officers who were killed in the battle, or died quickly after of their wounds, viz: Capt. Lovewell, Lieuts. Robbins and Farwell, Ensign Harwood, Sergt. Fullam, and the Chaplain, Rev. Mr. Fry. They also engaged with regard to the wounded, that the subject of paying their physician's bills, and of granting them pensions out of the public treasury, should be considered the next session.

The result of their deliberations on this question appears to have been in favor of the unfortunate men concerned.[22] And

[22] "1726, June 14. A Petition of Josiah Johnson of Woburne, shewing that the wound he received in the late Battle of Pigwackett is now open, and that he has expended since last November £4 :14s. in order to get a cure, Praying the compassionate consideration of the Court for *such further allowance* in the Premises, as to them in their Wisdom shall be thought meet:

"Read and committed to the Committee for Muster Rolls.

"June 16. Mr Lewis from the Committee for Muster Rolls Reported on the Petition of Josiah Johnson, as Entred on the 14th, which was Read and Accepted; and Resolved that the sum of Eighteen Pounds Fourteen Shillings be allowed and paid out of the Publick Treasury to the Petitioner Josiah Johnson, in Answer to the said Petition: viz. £4 :14s to discharge the Doctor's Bill, the remaining £14 in Consideration of his Pain, and Loss of Time, and Inability for Labour. Sent up for Concurrence." — *Votes of Representatives.*

In December of the same year, in answer to the Petition of Timothy Richardson, another of the wounded men from Woburn, praying the Court for relief "in consideration of the Wounds he received in the Battle of Pigwackett against the Indian Enemy;" a Resolve passed the House (which was sent up, and was doubtless concurred in by the Council) granting five pounds to be paid him out of the public treasury. Similar grants

finally, the General Court, in 1728, made a grant of Suncook, now Pembroke, N. H., then conceived to be within the bounds of Massachusetts, to sixty persons, forty-six of whom were the survivors or heirs of those who were engaged in this fight with the Indians. Among the first settlers of this township was Sergt. Noah Johnson, who had been wounded in that engagement. He was a grandson of Maj. William Johnson, being the third son of his eldest son William and of his wife Esther Gardiner; and is remembered in his grandfather's will, dated April 2, 1700. He was born, 1699, at Woburn, or possibly at Charlestown, where his father, William Johnson, Jr., was living and wrought as a shipwright in 1698. At the time of Lovewell's Fight, he was a resident of Dunstable, whence he removed to Pembroke, after becoming entitled to a share in that grant, and there became a deacon of the church. When advanced in life, he moved his abode once more, to Plymouth, N. H., and there died, August 13, 1798, at the great age of 99 years, 6 months and 11 days, being the last survivor of that little band, who hazarded their lives in the service of their country in the fight at Pigwacket.

Before closing this article, some further notice seems justly due to Ensign Seth Wyman, who had the conduct of Capt. Lovewell's men the greater part of that eventful day. He was a grandson of Lieut. John Wyman, a man of wealth and distinction among the first settlers of Woburn, and the eldest son of Mr. Seth Wyman and Esther, daughter of Maj. William Johnson, his wife. He was born, September 13, 1686, probably on a farm in the westerly part of Burlington, given his father by his grandfather Wyman in his Will: and, January 26, 1715, [1715–6 ?] he married Sarah Ross, of Billerica. At Lovewell's Fight, he greatly distinguished himself by his self-possession, fortitude and valor. All his superior officers having been killed or mortally wounded early in the engagement, he had the com-

---

were subsequently voted by the House to Josiah Johnson, whose wound appears to have been worse and more difficult to be healed than those of Richardson: the last as late as June 15, 1731. — See *Records of General Court.*

mand of our men almost the whole time of its continuance; and, by his prudent management and courageous example, he was doubtless, mainly instrumental, under God, for preserving so many of them as there were from being utterly cut off. Seeing them in danger of becoming dispirited in the contest, in view of the greatly superior numbers and other advantages of the enemy, he animated them to action (it was afterwards reported by Eleazar Davis, who was one of them), by assuring them "that the day would yet be their own, if their spirits did not flag"; and so encouraged were they by his exhortations, and so briskly did they fire in consequence, that several discharged their muskets "between twenty and thirty times apiece." Immediately upon his return, he was honored by Lieut.-Governor Dummer, then Commander-in-Chief of Massachusetts, with a Captain's commission. He had also presented him, in testimony of the public approbation of his valor, a silver-hilted sword. But he did not live long to enjoy his honors. To encourage volunteers to enlist against the Indian enemy, the General Court offered four shillings wages per day, in addition to the bounty of £100 for every scalp. Upon this, many enlisted, and marched under the command of Capt. Wyman and others. But the extreme heat of the weather, and the prevalence of the dysentery, prevented them from going far, and several of them died upon their return, Capt. Wyman among the rest, who deceased September, 5, 1725, before he had completed his thirty-ninth year. His widow survived him but little more than two years, dying November 5, 1727. Worthy descendants of the third and fourth generations from this worthy man are still living in Woburn and West Cambridge.

CHAPTER VII.

Schools from 1690 till 1775, — Wages: Teachers: Master Fowle: School Houses: Moving System: Schools beside Grammar School: School Books: Contention about Masters, 1725.

In the second chapter of this Work, notice was taken of the Schools in Woburn during the first half century from its incorporation. In this chapter, the consideration of this interesting subject will be resumed. It is proposed to give in it a somewhat minute and extended account of the condition and progress of the public schools in the town, from 1690 till the beginning of the Revolutionary War, in 1775.

At the commencement of the period above mentioned, in regard to women's schools, the same ten shillings, or rather six and eight penny per annum system, which had previously prevailed in the town, still continued. For instance, the Selectmen, say the Records, at a meeting of theirs, March 7, 1691–2, "sent to speak with Mrs. Walker in order to keepe a scoole for lesser children to learn them to read; and agreed with her to performe said servis, the Towne allowing her *in pay*, the sum of ten shillings per the year."[1] By pay, is here meant, country produce, as pork, Indian corn, rye, etc., upon which a discount was made in those days of 30 or 33⅓ per·cent for money. Mrs. Walker was the widow of Mr. Samuel Walker, the earliest progenitor in Woburn of that well known and highly respected family of the name, which has furnished the town with many valuable citizens, and the country at large with some of its most distinguished individuals. Leading a solitary life, this lady was willing to keep school, both for company and for employment's sake. She had served as a school teacher before, and living apparently in the centre of the town, she doubtless appropriated a room in her own house for a school-room. The good woman fulfilled the

[1] Town Records, Vol. III., p. 157.

above engagement with the Selectmen; and, two years afterwards, she was credited by Constable Ebenezer Johnson with seven shillings in money on her tax bill for her year's work,[2] the rent of her room being reckoned gratis. This must have been cold comfort to a widow's heart. Still, she ventured to try the business one year more. At a meeting of the Selectmen, May 7, 1694, they agreed, the Records state, "with Mrs. (Mistress) Walker to keep a scoole for the smaller sort of children, to learn them to read, for the year insueing; and the year to begin upon the first of Aprill last past; and she to have ten shillings in pay allowed her by the town for the same."[3] Accordingly, Mrs. Walker went on and completed this engagement, and at a final settlement between her and the town, the account stands recorded thus:

"The Widow Walker is Creditor:

"for scooling small children in the year 1694 until the first of Aprill 1695, according to agreement with her per the Selectmen, pay, 10s: money - - - - - -	£00 :06 :8
"To Widow Walker Dr.	
"her rate to Jams ffoull in money - - - - - -	£00 :02 :03
and to Ben. Simonds - - - - - - - - -	00 :03 :02
paid by James Simonds, Constable in 96 - - - - -	00 :01 :03
	0 :06 :08."[3]

From this authentic document, it appears that this worthy woman, having waited for her wages a whole year from the time her work was done, received, after two years' taxes were deducted, the sum of one shilling and threepence in silver for her toil and pain in teaching a twelve-month all the little boys and girls in Woburn that were sent to her, their alphabet, or reading and spelling; reckoning her room for their accommodation as rent free. A fact like this can hardly fail to strike a modern reader with surprise. One would have supposed, that the least the town could have done in this case would have been, to set off her taxes for the use of her room in their service. No thanks to the Selectmen, that she did not starve long before the term of her engagement with them was half expired.

[2] Town Records, Vol. IV., p. 8.

[3] Town Records, Vol. IV., pp. 24, 28.

Notwithstanding the wide difference between the price of the necessaries of life at that day and this, it is plain she must have had other resources for a livelihood than school-teaching. Had she depended solely on this, she must obviously have soon been forced to relinquish it; or else, like the widow of Sarepta, the meal in her barrel, and the oil in her cruse, (to say nothing of her wood) must have been daily replenished by miracle.

Such was the condition of primary schools in Woburn at the close of the 17th century. Nor did grammar schools fare any better. The studies of such schools were then held in low estimation in the town; and but few, if any of its youth, were willing to attend to them. And hence, schools of this description were but inconstantly kept; and sometimes only after intervals of several years. From the appointment of Mr. Samuel Carter in 1686, as grammar school-master, and his failure to get scholars to teach, no attempt seems to have been made in Woburn to get up a grammar school again, till four years after. At a meeting of the Selectmen, March 3, 1689–90, they agreed with Mr. Carter anew, "to record the Selectmen's acts about towne affaires": and also "to keep a grammar school, paying him thirty shillings for his service."[4] But whether he kept the grammar school as agreed upon, and whether his success was any better than before, there is nothing upon record to show. The person next engaged for this office, was Rev. Jabez Fox, with whom the inhabitants agreed, at a town meeting, March 26, 1694, that "he should teach and instruct any children that belong to this town of Woobourne, to wright, and in the gramer, all and so many as shall be sent unto him now for one year insueing."[5] A similar engagement was made with him by the Selectmen, May 24, 1699, to keep school a year for instruction in grammar alone.[5] But in neither of these engagements is there any mention of compensation; and as none appears from the Records to have been ever paid, there is ground for presuming, that none was ever stipulated; and that Mr. Fox, anticipating he should have but few or no scholars to teach, demanded

[4] Town Records, Vol. III., p. 138.

[5] Town Records, Vol. IV., pp. 22, 146.

nothing for his labor. The next year, at a general meeting, March 1, 1699–1700, a committee of three was chosen to inquire for, and treat with some suitable person to keep a grammar school in the town, and occasionally to assist the Rev. Mr. Fox in the ministry; and to make report to the town of their doings herein, before they agreed with the man.[5] But nothing was done to effect by this committee in fulfilment of their commission; and, within three months from their appointment, the town was presented at the Court of Quarter Sessions, for want of a school according to law. Startled in view of a presentment for such a cause, the town, at a general meeting, May 31, appointed Maj. William Johnson and Lieut. Josiah Convers a new committee "to agree with *Sir ffox* or any other gentleman upon as easy terms as they can," to keep school in Woburn for four months, from June 10, upon trial.[6] Accordingly, this committee applied to "Sir Fox," as Mr. John Fox, son of their minister, was called, in common with all graduates of Harvard College during the interval between taking their first, and their second or Master's degree. With him they agreed to keep a grammar school in Woburn for four months, from the day named, for £9.[6] And so acceptable were his services during the term of his probation, that the inhabitants, at a general meeting, December 4, following, hired him, "by a very clear voat," for this service again, for a year, to begin December 9, at a salary of £28 per annum.[6] These terms were of Mr. Fox's own proposing; and the salary, a handsome one for that day. But it was larger than Woburn had ever as yet paid a master, or than it was willing the next year to grant him again, especially as he had but few pupils to instruct. At a meeting, January 28, 1701–2, the town being notified that they were then destitute of a school-master, voted to choose a committee to procure one forthwith, as the law requires, "provided that a suitable person can be found to officiate in that place, and will undertake the worke for the space of one yeare in, and for said town, for such a sum as may be agreed for, not exceeding twenty pounds, for one year." [7]

---

[6] Town Records, Vol. IV., pp. 165, 167.

[7] Town Records, Vol. IV., pp. 194, 200.

The committee chosen for this purpose reported to the town, March 2, 1701–2 following, that they had agreed with Mr. John Fox, to keep a grammar school for one year from February 2d, preceding; and that, for this service, they had engaged to give him "eighteen pounds certain; and in case he should have more worke in that place than he had the last year, he should have forty shillings more."[7] This report was accepted by the people; and yet, reluctant to pay their worthy school-master even this greatly reduced salary, less by more than a third than that which they had given him the year before, they voted at the same meeting, "that every person that shall send any children or servants to the above said schoole in Woobourne, shall pay in to the selectmen of said town three pence per week for every child or servant that is sent or comes to the said schoole; and the selectmen to improve all such sums so payd in to them towards the discharging the schoolmaster's sallery: but if any shall send their children to said schoole, that in the judgment of the selectmen are not well able to pay as above said, they have their liberty to send their children to said schoole at the publick charge of the town."[7] But this requirement of heads of families, who had children or servants to send to school, to pay tuition money, beside their proportion of the school tax, if indeed it were legal, seems never to have been executed. No mention is made, in the settlement of town accounts for that year, of the payment of any money to the Selectmen from the source here indicated; and the town appears never to have had recourse afterwards to this expedient for lightening the school rates of some, legally and equitably imposed, by laying a double portion of the expense of schooling upon others.

Mr. John Fox continued to keep the grammar school in Woburn quite up to the time of his ordination as their minister, in October 1703, when he became disqualified, by a law then recently enacted, for the office of a school teacher any longer.[8] At March meeting, 1703–4, the inhabitants chose Lieut. Josiah Convers, one of the Selectmen of that year, and Lieut. John

---

[8] Colony and Province Laws, p. 372.

Carter, to inquire for and to hire a suitable person to keep a grammar school. This committee promptly attended to their duty in this matter: and not long after reported to the Selectmen, that, having made an unsuccessful application at the College, they had gone to Andover, and proposed to Mr. Dudley Bradstreet, of that town, to come and do the work of a schoolmaster at Woburn for the present, till they could provide themselves with another; that Mr. Bradstreet had signified his agreement to their proposal under his hand; that he had been "personally at Woobourne at the time of Charlestown Court"; but no scholars presenting themselves as his pupils, he had returned to Andover again; and, having "had his expences borne, while he was in Woobourne, he had eighteen shillings in silver for a gratuity."[9] Here is another striking token of the indifference of the people of Woburn for grammar school instruction at the commencement of the last century. But why is it specified in the Committee's Report, that Mr. Bradstreet was at "Woobourne at the time of Charlestown Court"? He was doubtless here at that particular time by an understanding with the committee, and to answer the same purpose that another teacher, some thirty years afterwards was expected to, who had a consideration made him by the town "for standing in (as the Records express it) School master Two Courts."[10] In both these cases, and in others that might be named, the school committee (though men of good character and very respectable standing), wishing to save the town expense, and yet avoid a legal presentment, resorted to artifice. In making an agreement with a school-master, they would stipulate with him, that he must by all means be at Woburn, and keeping school, in Court time, even if he were to be off the very next week; fearing that otherwise, the Grand Jury, who were the eye of the county, might spy out the deficiency, and present the town; and that the Justices of the Sessions might impose on it

---

[9] Town Records, Vol. IV., p. 255.

[10] "To Mr Ebenr Flegg in full for keeping Grammar School in the year past [1731] and standing in School Master two Courts, £13:10:0." — *Town Records, Vol. VII., p.* 140.

a fine of £20 for its default, as the law required. But, in having recourse to measures of this description, the committee cheated themselves, their children, and the town, more than they did the County and Province; and, for the sake of saving a few paltry shillings or pounds to the town, they defrauded the town and its children of one of the most indispensable means to the prosperity and happiness of both.

In stating, however, the above facts, showing the backwardness of the people of Woburn, at the beginning of the last century, to encourage public schools, it is by no means intended to insinuate that they were singularly faulty in this thing. The like delinquency, in other places, was at that time a matter of complaint. And, hence, the General Court felt it incumbent on them, in 1701, to pass an additional Act relating to Schools and School-masters. In the Preamble to that Act, they declare, that the observance of the "wholesome and necessary Law," then in force, requiring all towns containing fifty families to be constantly provided with a school-master to teach children and youth to read and write, and every town containing a hundred families to establish a grammar school in it, and to procure by suitable encouragement, a discreet person of good conversation, and well instructed in the tongues, to keep it, was "shamefully neglected by divers towns, and the penalty thereof not required, tending greatly to the nourishment of ignorance and irreligion, whereof grievous complaint is made."

And then, for the prevention of this evil, they proceed to enact, among other particulars, that the penalty for the non-observance of the law referred to, should be twenty pounds per annum, instead of ten, as it had been hitherto.[11] And this increased penalty proving insufficient for the end intended, the Court, in 1718, passed another additional act, in which, after setting forth, that "many towns," which were both obliged by law, and abundantly able to support a grammar school, chose to incur and pay the fine for the neglect of the law, rather than maintain one, went on to enact, that fine should be increased to

---

[11] Province Laws, 1702, Chap. lxxxii., pp. 371-2.

thirty pounds, in the case of towns that had one hundred and fifty families, and to forty pounds in the case of those which had two hundred families.[12] No peculiar reproach then attaches itself to Woburn, on account of its occasional failure at that period to observe the law respecting schools and school-masters, or of its reluctant compliance with it. The delinquency complained of was a common one; and in view of the fact, it became an interesting inquiry, How we are to account for it? Whence proceeded the too general neglect at the commencement of the last century, suitably to encourage and cherish Common Schools, that far famed institution of our Puritan ancestors?

One reason of this neglect, it may be plausibly conjectured, was, that the generation then on the stage appreciated learning, and the means of acquiring it, at a much lower rate than their predecessors in general did. A considerable proportion of the first settlers of Massachusetts came to this country an enlightened people, and they were kept so by sitting under the ministry of men, who, generally speaking, were lights in the world, and whom for love, they had followed to these ends of the earth, that they might continue to enjoy the benefit of their instructions. From their pious and learned teachers, they had imbibed exalted conceptions of the importance of learning, as an excellent handmaid of religion, and that high estimate of it which they had brought with them across the Atlantic they still retained amidst their numerous trials and hardships in this their adopted country. Hence, they could not endure the thought (to use an expression of their own), "that learning [should] be buried in the graves of [their] forefathers in church and commonwealth;"[13] but were earnestly desirous, by erecting the college, and founding common schools, to transmit the treasure to their posterity, as the best earthly legacy they could leave them. But the mass of their descendants of the two next generations seem to have been far more absorbed in earthly cares, and in pursuits merely secular, than their fathers were. As they had confessedly declined from the strict piety of their predecessors, so they appear to

---

[12] Province Laws, 1718, Chap. cxxviii., p. 420.

[13] Colony Laws, Chap. lxxxviii., p. 186.

have had but a diminished sense of the importance of knowledge and learning, and hence were less solicitous about providing the means for educating their children in it.

Another reason seems to be, that competent instructors for grammar schools were then scarce; too few, to supply the wants of the whole community. This was a difficulty particularly felt at Woburn. At the commencement of the last century, recent graduates of Harvard College, though not a numerous body of men, were almost the only persons willing and qualified to teach schools of this description. And, as these few would naturally go where they found most encouragement, and as Woburn then too often made a point of engaging teachers who could be got for the lowest wages, the School Committees sometimes experienced great difficulty in procuring masters, even when they earnestly exerted themselves to do it. Take the following instance, particularly noticed in the Records.

"Friday the 3d of November 1710. The Selectmen of Woobourn met to consider how they might obtain a suitable person to keep a grammar schoole in said town, but found it very difficult to do [so] by reason that they heard that there was none to be had at Colledge: whereupon they appointed Ensign John Peirce to goe to Boston, and try if Dr Oaks his son, [14] or Mr. Kallender's son [15] might be obtained for that end" etc.[16] "December the 8th, 1710. The Selectmen of Wooburn being met together, Ensign John Peirce made the following Return: that according to the Selectmen's orders and appointment, he had been at Boston to speak with Dr Oaks his son, and Mr Callender's son, and found that they were already improved, and so could not be obtained: and that he had made inquiry after some other suitable person to keep a grammar schoole in Woobourn, but could not hear of any to be had. Soon after, the Selectmen were informed, that it was probable, that Sir Wigglesworth [17] might be obtained to keep a grammar schoole for our town. Whereupon the said Selectmen appointed Lieut. John Carter to goe to Cambridge, and treat with him about that matter.

---

[14] Mr. Josiah Oakes, Harvard College, 1708, son of Dr. Thomas Oakes, of Boston.

[15] Mr. Elisha Callender, Harvard College, 1710, a son of Rev. Ellis Callender, minister of the Baptist Church in Boston.

[16] Town Records, Vol. V., p. 165.

[17] Edward Wigglesworth, Harvard College, 1710, and afterwards first Hollis Professor of Divinity there.

Accordingly, soon after, Lieut. Carter made return to the Selectmen, that he had been at Cambridge, and had had a discourse with Sir Wigglesworth with reference to keeping a grammar schoole in Woobourn; and that he the said Sir Wigglesworth did give some encouragement in the matter, but could not give a full answer until the beginning of the following week, and then appointed him to come again for an answer. Accordingly the Selectmen ordered Lieut. Carter to attend the time that Sir Wigglesworth had appointed to give his answer, and to wait upon him for it. But when the said Lieut. John Carter came to Cambridge at the time before appointed, he was informed that Sir Wigglesworth was engaged or gone to Casco Bay Fort to keep a schoole there; and there was no further hope of obtaining of him."

"After this, Mr John Turft [Tufts][18] informed that Mr Recompence Wadsworth[19] had left the Schoole at Barnstable; and was in hopes we might obtain him to keep a Grammar Schoole in Woobourn. Whereupon the Selectmen appointed Lieut. John Carter and Mr Josiah Johnson to go to Boston, and discourse with said Mr Wadsworth on Monday the 11th. of December currant, with reference to his keeping a Grammar Schoole in Woobourn. Accordingly on the 12th. currant, agreement was made with the said Mr Recompence Wadsworth to keep a Grammar Schoole in Woobourn for the space of six months, and to begin the Schoole on the 18th. currant, and so six months from that time, for the sum of twelve pounds, and his board found him free by the Town of Woobourn. Accordingly the said Mr Wadsworth came to Woobourn on Saturday the sixteenth day of the same month, and the Selectmen ordered James Fowle to board him upon the Town's accompt. But in case the said Mr Wadsworth should be called off from keeping said schoole by any other business within the said six months, [he is] to give the Town seasonable warning."[20]

Here was an instance in which the Selectmen, who were the School Committee for 1710, were obliged to despatch three of their number in succession upon four several journeys, two to Boston, and two to Cambridge, in order to obtain a person

---

[18] Of Harvard College, 1708; subsequently minister of Newbury.

[19] Son of Timothy Wadsworth, of Boston, and grandson of Capt. Samuel Wadsworth, of Milton; born 1688; Harvard College, 1708; died 1713.

[20] Town Records, Vol. V., p. 170.

suitable to keep the grammar school; and were repeatedly baffled in their expectations, and kept six weeks in suspense before they could secure a teacher to their mind, and get him on the ground. School-masters, or those who sought the employment, were not then to be met at every corner; nor was there a choice of them to be selected from applicants twofold, or even fourfold more numerous than the schools to be kept, as is often the case at the present day. Then, if a committee would obtain a well qualified master, they must, generally speaking, diligently search him out, go from town to town, far and near, and be willing to bear repeated disappointments, and still to persevere in their efforts, before they lighted upon a man who would serve their purpose. But so much difficulty as this, in obtaining a competent teacher, must needs have rendered the office of School Committee a burdensome one, and doubtless often operated as a hinderance or discouragement from duly attempting to fulfil it.

But the principal cause, it is apprehended, why towns were backward at the period mentioned, to sustain schools, or to provide for them competent instructors, was the scarcity of money, the burden of taxes, and the consequent general poverty of the people. Notwithstanding the issues of the mint in Massachusetts, which coined the famous New England shillings and pine tree money for about thirty-six years, from 1652, specie had become so scarce at the close of the 17th century, that many towns found it very difficult, if not impossible, to pay their taxes to the country, except in the produce of their soil, or in articles of their own home manufacture. Thus, Hingham was allowed the privilege, in 1687, of paying their taxes to government in pails;[21] and Woburn paid in part its County tax, for 1693, in shoes.[21] In 1685, the towns of Springfield and Suffield petitioned the Government, setting forth "the difficulty of their paying money taxes, which were assessed, beside those payable in grain." The former town desired Government "to receive their rates as formerly, in corne; and noe more require any money of your moneyless petitioners." And the inhabitants

[21] Felt's History of Massachusetts Currency, p. 47. Town Records, Vol. III., p. 52.

of the latter town, say in their petition, "Doe not for Charitie's sake enjoyne us to pay one penny more in money. Let it be adjudged abundantly enough for us to pay henceforward our country's dues in Corne, when we can raise it, and are not forced to go to other towns to work for corne for our familyes." But not only was money scarce, but the public taxes were excessively burdensome. Notice was taken in a former chapter of the heavy taxes during Philip's war, in 1675–1676, and the distress occasioned thereby to the community. In 1690, to defray the public debt, contracted in the unfortunate expedition of that year to Canada, the government issued the first paper currency in this country.[22] And the next year, to discharge Woburn's proportion of this debt, a tax was assessed, in which every man's single rate was increased twenty-three fold;[23] and which amounted to the enormous sum, for that day, of £532 and upward.[23]

Other instances of very heavy taxes, imposed while the wars against the Indians and French in the reigns of King William III. and Queen Anne were going on, might be produced from the Records. No wonder then, that the people, ground down to

---

[22] Felt's History of Massachusetts Currency, pp. 49, 50.

[23] Town Records, Vol. III., p. 150. "August the 27. 1691. The Selectmen met to make the Country Rate for the year ensuing [present?]; the Commissioner [of the rate] and Constables also joining with them . . . . August the 31. 1691. The Selectmen met at the house of Israel Reed with the Commissioner and Constables, and finished the Country Rate which they had before begun: they then also writ out a List of the said Rate, and delivered it to the Commissioner, to carry to the Commissioners of the County, according to law.

"October the 5. 1691. The Selectmen met and perfected the Rate made for the raising of the 24 thousand pounds; and for the raising of the town's proportion in the said sum, every man's single rate were [was] 23 times doubled. October the 6. 1691. Delivered for Constable John Peirce at his house a List of his part of the 23 rates, containing the sum of £272 :18 :08. with a warrant under the hands of the Selectmen to gather the same. The same day abovesaid delivered for Constable John Teed at his house a list of his part of the aforesaid 23 rates, containing the sum of £259 :05 :06, with a warrant under the hands of the Selectmen to gather the same." The country rate assessed Sept. 30, 1689, was but little over £32. — *Town Records, Vol. III., pp.* 132–135.

the earth, as it were, by the public burdens, should feel unable, and at times disinclined to give due support to institutions, confessedly of the first necessity and importance. In 1704, a considerable number of the inhabitants of Woburn, it has been seen, remonstrated against granting at that time to Rev. Mr. Fox a fixed salary, for the express reason of the pressure of the war then carried on, and the weight of the taxes assessed to sustain it.[24] Much more likely then would they be, under such circumstances, to object to the expense of schooling, and at times be tempted to evade, if possible, the requirements of the law respecting it. In the condition they were then in, they were averse to bestowing the encouragement that was desirable, both upon the preaching of the gospel, and upon their public schools, not because they deemed those institutions of inferior moment, or grudged their expense, but because they were reduced to such straits, as that they could scarcely pay their taxes for their country's defence, and provide bread for themselves and families. And, accordingly, within a few years after, when they had become more numerous and able, and their taxes lighter, they immediately made more liberal grants for schools; and not only punctually paid their minister's stipulated salary, but year after year made voluntary additions to it, especially in seasons when provisions were unusually scarce and dear.[25]

The town being without a school-master the greater part of the year 1706, was presented for that deficiency, in September, at Cambridge Court; and the Selectmen were summoned to answer

---

[24] Town Records, Vol. IV., p. 269.

[25] At a general town meeting, March 5, 1715–16, it was voted to add twenty pounds to Rev. Mr Fox's salary for that year. The original contract was for £80 per annum. At March meeting, 1716–17, it was voted "that the Reverend Mr John Fox should have 20 pounds added to his Fourscore this year, provided that he keep a Lecture once in six weeks if he be able." At the same meeting, provision was made for the supply of his pulpit, when he was "sick and unable to preach." In March 1724–5, by voluntary vote of the town £30 was added to his original salary of £80, without any condition, (Town Records, Vol. VI., p. 213,) and in March 1725–6, and again in March 1726–7, his salary was raised to £120 for each of those years. — *Town Records, Vol. VI., pp.* 265, 296.

the presentment.[26] In this exigency, they authorized Capt. Josiah Convers, one of their number, to appear on their behalf, who informed the Court, that the Selectmen had not been negligent to inquire for a suitable school teacher; and that, though they had hitherto been unsuccessful, yet their efforts to procure one were still continued.[26] This assurance seems to have satisfied the Court for the present. A teacher for the grammar school in Woburn[26] was soon after engaged for six months, from November 9, for £15; and, at the expiration of that term, in 1707, his engagement was prolonged.[26] The year following, the town having learned by experience, that grand jurors would do their duty in this case, according to their oaths, took seasonable care to prevent another presentment. At a general meeting, March 1, 1707–8, they chose the Selectmen as a committee to look out for and agree with some suitable person to keep a grammar school in Woburn; and "to provide one against the next Court, which is the 9th. currant, if possible."[27] Agreeably to the above appointment, the Selectmen employed Capt. Josiah Convers, one of their number, to attend to this business: who reported to the Selectmen, March 12, that he had agreed with Mr. John Tufts to keep a grammar school in Woburn for the space of one year, beginning with March 8: "And to improve and pay him for eight months of the said time; he to stay in Town one month from the said eighth day of March; and then to come again when the town sends for him. And he to receive out of the Town Treasury after the rate of thirty pounds per annum for the time he stays in town as our school master."[28] This arrangement is evidently another instance of contrivance to give the town's money and credit at the same time.

To prevent a presentment of the town, Mr. Tufts, the schoolmaster elect, must be at their call for a whole twelve-month. He must commence his school the day before the Court sat; and after keeping it a month, he might go about his own private occasions, if he pleased, but must come again when the town sent for him, that so they might have him among them, keeping

[26] Town Records, Vol. V., pp. 35, 48. [27] Town Records, Vol. V., p. 76.
[28] Town Records, Vol. V., p. 82.

school, whenever the Court sat during that period, and especially in March Term the next year. But at the same time, the Committee gave him to understand, that he would be actually employed and paid only eight months of the twelve; apprehending, perhaps, that unless he should prove a popular teacher, the town's money for a longer time than that would be no better than thrown away. But, contrary to the Committee-men's fears perhaps in this respect, Mr. Tufts' labors proved so very acceptable, that at the next March meeting, 1708-9, the town as a body voted him an invitation to continue them here the whole of the next year, and authorized the Selectmen to hire him for this end "upon as reasonable terms as may be."[29] And, accordingly, the Selectmen, at a meeting of theirs, March 21st, engaged Mr. Tufts to be the grammar school-master of Woburn for the year ensuing; and, for this service, promised not only to pay him in money, at the same rate as the year preceding, viz: £30 per annum, but also that when he went into the different quarters of the town to keep school, the inhabitants of each quarter "should find him a horse to ride to meeting on"; a privilege which at that day was highly set by, and which was afterwards indulged other masters in like circumstances, as contributing much to their general respectability, and especially as increasing their influence over their pupils.[29] And now, from this time, 1709, till 1775, the year of the Revolutionary war began, Woburn appears to have been uniformly supplied with a grammar school-master, for a longer or shorter portion of every year save one. Influenced not only by desire to escape the penalty of the law, all attempts to elude which they had found to be vain or injurious to themselves, but also, it is to be hoped, by a due regard for their own reputation, and for the best interests of their posterity, they henceforth constantly manifested a disposition to maintain and encourage their grammar school; and so vigilant were they to see it duly provided with a teacher, that they never allowed themselves, as late as 1775, to be again

---

[29] Town Records, Vol. V., pp. 109, 111.

presented for the want of one but once, viz: during the unfortunate circumstances of the town, in 1732.[30]

Their School Committees were careful every year to make seasonable inquiry for a master; they were concerned to find one competent for the work; and seemed willing to pay him an equitable compensation. And the result of this wise policy was an inestimable benefit to the rising generation, and the giving of an impulse to the cause of education that has continued to the present day. The masters whom they employed during this period were commonly young gentlemen of liberal education from abroad, and especially students in theology, resident at Cambridge and in the vicinity; and some of them afterwards distinguished themselves in the Christian ministry or in civil life: as Hon. Nathaniel Saltonstall of Haverhill; Hon. Jonathan Sewall, Esq., the noted Attorney General at the commencement of the Revolution; Rev. John Hancock of Braintree, now Quincy, father of Governor Hancock; Rev. Habijah Weld of Attleborough; and that profound theologian and eminent minister of the Gospel, Rev. Peter Clark of Danvers. But a considerable proportion of their grammar school-masters were Woburn's own sons, who were born and instructed in the first rudiments of learning within her own precincts, and then completed their education at the College in Cambridge. Of these, some were honored in civil life: as Col. Jabez Fox of Portland, son of Rev. John Fox of Woburn. Some eventually preached, and became respected ministers of the gospel: as Rev. John Gardner of Stow, Rev. Timothy Walker of Pennicook, now Concord, N. H.; Rev. Ebenezer Flegg of Chester, N. H., and Rev. Ebenezer Wyman of Union, Ct. And others still of them were either school-masters by profession, or at least, excellently qualified for the employment, judging by the frequency with which

---

[30] In an account of the disposal of money raised by the town, March 1732–3, for the payment of the town's debts and expenses, is the following item: "Paid to Mr Josiah Johnson, due last year, £1.0.0. and for . . . . money he paid at the Court for the Town's being presented for want of a Schoole master, and about the Highway £11 :14 :10." — *Town Records, Vol. VII., p.* 168.

they were engaged in it, in their native town. Such were Mr. Isaac Richardson, Mr. Adam Richardson, Mr. Jabez Richardson, Mr. Ebenezer Thompson, Mr. James Fowle, and more particularly, Mr. John Fowle; a gentleman for many years distinguished by way of eminence in Woburn, by the title of Master Fowle; one whose stern manners, strict discipline and aptness to teach, rendered him the terror of all idlers and rogues in his school, but recommended him to the esteem of the diligent and ingenuous, and whom such eminently scientific men as Col. Loammi Baldwin and Benjamin Thompson, Count Rumford, were not ashamed, in their younger days, to attend upon his instructions, and to call their master.

This noted teacher was a son of Maj. John Fowle, and of Mrs. Mary (Convers) Fowle, his wife; was born in Woburn, February 1, 1726, [1726–7] graduated at Harvard College, 1747; commenced keeping school in Woburn, 1758, and from that year till 1770, was constantly employed there in that work. He died of a nervous fever, October 15, 1786. The following anecdote, illustrative of his management and discipline in school, was told me by Mrs. Mary, widow of Mr. James Bennett, and daughter of Capt. Joshua Walker, of Woburn Precinct, who in her childhood, attended Master Fowle's school, when it was keeping in the Precinct, and who died, 1857, in the 94th year of her age. He had a class of young men, studying Latin, who, presuming upon their advanced age and standing, ventured to take unwarrantable liberties in school hours. Master Fowle saw and watched them for some time without making complaint. But he at length broke out, and addressed them in such words as these:

"Ho, you Latiners, up there: you seem by your actions to think, that because you sit in a higher seat, and are more forward in your studies than the rest of the school, you may do here as you like. But I'll quick let you know that you shan't. I have had my eyes upon you for some time, though you did not know it. And now I tell you what, boys. You, every one of you, deserve for what I've seen in you a sound thrashing; and a sound thrashing every one of you shall have, unless you instantly come forward, and upon your knees on the floor ask pardon of me and of the whole school for your misbehaviours. Come on then, I say; come at once, and no waiting; or I'll be at you."

This command was dreadfully humiliating to the young rogues. But, knowing that their master in his threats always meant as he said, and that with him, it was but a word and a blow, they at once reluctantly came forward, and ashamed and mortified, did as they were bid. And we may be sure that Master Fowle had never afterwards occasion to speak to them for the like offence.

Schools in Woburn seem to have been kept originally in the dwelling-houses of their instructors, or of other persons interested in the promotion of learning, who severally fitted up a room in their homes for this use at their own cost. The first distinct notice on record of a place provided by the town to keep school in was in 1700. After the town, at a general meeting, December 4th, of that year, had agreed with Mr. John Fox to keep the grammar school a twelve-month, the Selectmen hired for his accommodation the house of George Reed, Jr., nigh the meeting-house, at twenty shillings rent per annum.[31] This house was accordingly fitted up as a school-house, at the town's expense, and continued to be used for this purpose several years afterwards.[32] In 1707, when the grammar school began to be moved occasionally into different quarters of the town, other private houses were hired by the town for the time they were needed to keep it in. At a general town meeting, March 2, 1712–13, liberty was granted to any persons, who should be disposed, to erect at their own cost a convenient school-house for

---

[31] Town Records, Vol. IV., p. 167.

[32] The Town Dr. Oct. 1, 1700, for "Boards and Nayls for a table and bench for ye Scoolhous two shillings and fiue pence." — *Town Records, Vol. IV., p.* 166.

The Town Cr. 1705. "By Cash paid to Serg^t^ Geo. Reed for his house rent last year, 8 shillings."

The Town Cr. 1705. By cash paid "to Constable Thos. Peirce for work about repairing the forms & tables of the Schoole House," etc. — *Town Records, Vol. V., p.* 21.

The Town Dr. 1705. "To Serg^t^ George Read for the rent of his house for the Schoole this present year 0 :9 :0." — *Town Records, Vol. V., p.* 22.

the town's use upon the town's land, "at any convenient place between. the meeting house & Lieut. John Coggin's"; the particular spot to be stated by the Selectmen.[33] Accordingly, a subscription paper for this purpose was put in circulation, which obtained eighty subscribers. Rev. Mr. Fox headed the list with £1. Among other principal subscribers, Mr. Jacob Wyman put down £1 15*s.*; Capt. Josiah Convers, £1 5*s.*; Col. Jonathan Tyng, £1 5*s.*; Mr. William Symmes, 16*s.* 6*d.* The whole amount of the subscription was £41 15*s.* 6*d.* With this encouragement, the undertakers proceeded to build a school-house, which, when completely finished, cost £43 18*s.* 4*d.*, a trifle over the sum subscribed for this end at the first. This school-house, by direction of the Selectmen, was erected, say the Records, "on the East side of the highway [to Wilmington?], over against Thomas Leppingwells."[34] In compliance with the request of sundry petitioners, liberty was given them at March meeting, 1735–6, to remove it from its original location "down near the meeting house," on condition of their being at the cost of removing it, and fitting it up again "in good order to keep schoole in."[35] But this, it seems, was not its final resting place. For, at March meeting, 1744, it was voted, that the stated place for the grammar school in the Old Parish, for that year, should be as near the meeting-house as a spot to set a school-house on could be procured.[36]

Accordingly, in 1748, and other subsequent years, reference is repeatedly made in the Records to the School-house in the First Parish, as standing near the Meeting-house. And as this school-house was the first one erected in the town, so, as late as 1760, it appears to have been the only one, unless that in the Precinct, the date of whose erection is not known, be an exception. In 1736, it was furnished not only with benches, a table etc., as is usual, but also with a "Great Chair", designed, no doubt, to add dignity to the master, in presiding over the miniature kingdom under his rule.[37] This chair was probably a

[33] Town Records, Vol. V., p. 254.
[34] Town Records, Vol. V., p. 279.
[35] Town Records, Vol. VII., pp. 217, 224.
[36] Town Records, Vol. VII., p. 440.

[37] 1736, Sept. 13. The Town Dr. "To Ebenezer Johnson for a great Chear for the Schoole House £0 :10 :0." — *Town Records, Vol. VII., p.* 247.

large flag bottomed one, with a high back, and with legs and arms all curiously wrought and carved, like other chairs manufactured in those days, that are yet occasionally to be seen. And such a favorite was this important article of school-house furniture with the master, and so constantly used by him, that, within eleven years, it had come to need seating anew. For at a meeting of the Selectmen, September 25, 1747, an order was granted on the Treasurer to pay Mr. Isaac Richardson £27 10s. Old Tenor for keeping school that year; and 10 shillings Old Tenor more that he paid to Mr. Samuel Kendall for "Bottoming the School House Cheer."[38]

From the time that a grammar school was established and constantly kept in Woburn, the town seems to have considered this school as fully answering the design of the law, and so to have neglected the maintenance of other schools for teaching children to read and write: for the Records make no mention, after 1700, of the appointment of any teachers, male or female, for this office, or of granting them any compensation. There can be no doubt, however, that women's schools, for this purpose, were still kept here by private subscription. For, at a general meeting, March 1, 1724–5, liberty was voted and given "to several of the inhabitants that should agree to set up a school house for children to learn to read in, upon the town's land in the street, where it may be most convenient; and the Selectmen to set out the place."[39] And the liberty granted by this vote not being, apparently, for some reason, improved, another vote was passed at a general meeting, March 4, 1733–4, by which leave was given to several persons who had petitioned for that end, to erect a small school-house near the meeting-house, where the Selectmen shall appoint, for the accommodation of a school-mistress to instruct their children to read, and other things that are necessary to learn.[40] And such a house, it is probable, was built, and employed for the use intended, though the Records are afterwards silent respecting it.

The grammar school in Woburn was originally kept, year

[38] Town Records, Vol. VII., p. 521.
[39] Town Records, Vol. VI., p. 213.
[40] Town Records, Vol. VII., p. 171.

after year, in one place only, viz, in the centre of the town. But at a general meeting, March 3, 1706–7, it was agreed as follows: "Forasmuch as our Town of Woobourne (is) situated very scattering and remoat, so that the whole Town (cannot) be benefitted alike, by the Schoolmaster's keeping the Schoole in the Senter of the Town at all times, that therefore the Schoole Master for the time being (shall) keep the Schoole one quarter of the year in the Center of the Town, and the other three quarters of the year in three of the remoat Quarters of the Town, according to the direction and appointment of the Selectmen for the time being."[41] This vote laid the foundation of the moving school system, which was much, though not uniformly practised in this town during a large part of the last century. By this, the grammar school and its instructor were moved round into the different sections of the town, for lengths of time proportionate to the taxes they paid, by order of the Selectmen, or some other committee of the town's appointment. At first, only three of the remote quarters were named for the school to be moved to; and in each of these it was to be kept an equal time as in the centre. But as settlements in the town extended and multiplied, the school seems to have been wholly omitted some years in the centre; and the number of places in which it was kept in the outskirts was increased.

The erection of a school-house in the centre, by private individuals, in 1713, caused a temporary check to the moving system, as it was probably intended to; for we read nothing in the Records of keeping school in the quarters for six years afterwards. But at the annual meeting, March 2, 1718–9, it was voted that the grammar school-master for the time to come should "goe into the quarters of the Town": from six weeks to two months into the end of the town where Deacon Walker lives [Goshen, or Wilmington]; as long as that, into the end where Deacon Johnson lives [Shawshin, or Burlington]; and as long as that into the West, and then as long into the East end.[42] At March meeting, 1728–9, it was voted "that the School Master

[41] Town Records, Vol. V., p. 42.

[42] Town Records, Vol. VI., pp. 48, 49.

should move;" and further, "that the School should be moved so far as Mr. Thomas Belknap's [on the road to South Woburn, or Winchester] their proportion; and to Sergeant Thomas Reed's house [West end] their proportion; and to Sergt. Benjamin Johnson's [Burlington] their proportion; and to the School house at Goshen [Wilmington] their proportion; and to the house of Samuel Eames [East Woburn] their proportion." [43] At a town meeting, February 2, 1737–8, after resolving that the school should be a movable one, the present and the ensuing year (that is, the remainder of 1737, as then calculated, and through 1738), it was voted that (1) the Precinct, (2) the Richardsons and the Carters at the southerly part of the town, (3) the West, (4) the East, (5) New Bridge, should each have the school among them according to what they pay; that the school should move to the southerly part of Richardson's Row for them and the Carters; and that the Selectmen should state the place where the school should be kept.[44] And at March meeting, 1741–2, the town having appointed the Selectmen a committee to provide a master for the grammar school that year, and voted that he should move into the different quarters, proceeded to choose Lieut. Joseph Richardson, Lieut. James Proctor, Lieut. Samuel Carter, Ensign Samuel Wyman, Mr. Ebenezer Flagg, Mr. William Tay and Mr. Timothy Brooks, as a committee "to agree and determine on the severall places the Schoolmaster shall keep the Schoole at, in said Town, and the time at each place, the year ensuing"; and to report to the Selectmen, who were empowered to direct the master to go to the places, and to keep the terms of time agreed upon, agreeably to the committee's Report.[45] Accordingly, the Selectmen immediately engaged Mr. James Fowle to keep the grammar school in Woburn a year, for £70, Old Tenor; and shortly after, the committee for determining the places where the school should be kept, and how long in each place, reported to the Selectmen as follows: That the school should remove:

---

[43] Town Records, Vol. VI., p. 369.

[44] Town Records, Vol. VII., p. 267.

[45] Town Records, Vol. VII., pp. 394–396.

1. To Lieut. Samuel Kendall's (Kendall's Mill) on the 22d day of March inst. and there keep till May 9th.
2. Thence to the School house (in the Centre) till July 11th.
3. Thence to New Bridge, "house of Martha Tidds', or elsewhere," till August 8th.
4. Thence to the house of Lieut. Joseph Richardson Jr. till Septr 19th.
5. Thence to the Precinct, at some place that they shall agree upon, till Decr 31st.
6. Thence to the Carter's Quarter (South Village) house of Mr. Ebenezer Convers, till (1st) Monday in March next.

Signed by the Committee, March 18, 1741–2.[45]

In this brief view of the operation of the moving school system in Woburn, from its commencement in 1707 till 1742, we may observe, that while the school-house, in the centre of the Old Parish, is mentioned only once among the places, in which, in the different years enumerated above, the grammar school was ordered to be kept, the places in the outskirts for keeping it in had increased from three to five. While some conveniences resulted from this plan of conducting the school, its inconveniences to all parties concerned were many and serious. So much trouble was it wont to occasion the teacher, that Master Fowle petitioned the town one year, 1760 (but without success), to make him some additional allowance besides his salary, "in consideration of the fatigues he hath had by reason of there being so many removals of (his) school."[46] The frequency of these removals in the course of a year, and the shortness of the time the school was kept in some of the quarters, (viz: from a month to six weeks only) were both of them unfavorable circumstances to the comfort and improvement of the scholars. The appointments, too, of time and place for the school by the committee (judging of them as well as we can at this distance of time) appear to have been, in some instances, injudicious, and in others to lie open to the suspicion of partiality. For example, by the last quoted arrangement for January and February, 1742–3, a season of the year, when the severity of the weather, the badness of the travelling, and the superior opportunities which children in the country then usually enjoy for attending

[46] Town Records, Vol. VIII., pp. 285, 288.

school, would naturally have led the committee, one would suppose, to fix upon the school-house in the centre, as the most eligible place for keeping the school, and calculated to accommodate the largest number of pupils, it was ordered to the southernmost extremity of the town, and where, in going to it, a very large proportion of the children and youth, probably a majority of the whole, must have been obliged to travel from two to five miles, or relinquish the privilege of attending school altogether. At times, too, the several committees for fixing the location of the school year after year, gave cause to the inhabitants of some of the quarters to conceive themselves to be slighted. There is on file an original petition to the Selectmen without date, but written probably about 1742, and subscribed by twenty-eight inhabitants of Button End, complaining that they had not had the school among them for nearly thirty years; and earnestly requesting that it might be kept that year in their neighborhood, at the house of Capt. Joseph Richardson, Jr., where accommodations were provided for it.

All these circumstances caused a growing dissatisfaction with the system, and eventually a powerful opposition to it, although many years a majority was found in town meeting who voted in favor of it. At March meeting, 1744, the town voted that the Precinct should have their proportion of the school the year ensuing; and their proportional part of the time being deducted, the school should be kept the remainder of the year in the Old Parish, in one place as near the meeting-house as a spot to set a school-house on could be procured.[47] And at March meeting, 1748, it was voted, (1) that the Precinct should have the school that should be kept the present year, their proportionate part of the time; and, (2) that the school should not be removed about in the First Parish the ensuing year, "but be kept in the School House near the Old Meeting House in said town the rest of the year," after deducting the Second Parish's proportionable part.[48] Votes to the same purpose with this last were passed in the years 1749, 1750, 1751, 1752, 1753, 1754 and 1755.

---

[47] Town Records, Vol. VII., p. 440.

[48] Town Records, Vol. VII., p. 538.

In 1756, the town reverted, in part, to the moving plan. After voting, March 1, that the school should be kept in the Precinct, and in the school-house near the new meeting-house (of the Old Parish), their proportional part, voted, that it should also be moved to the East and West sides, as the Selectmen should proportion the time; but, if either side neglected to provide a house for the school, it was to be kept in the Centre School-house.[49] And, although the three next years the school was ordered again into the quarters, yet, the year following, 1760, this plan was again abandoned, and the grammar school confined to the Precinct, and the centre of the Old Parish. And between that year and 1775, the system of moving the Grammar School into the several different quarters of the town was laid aside, excepting the years 1762, 1767 and 1768, and the school was kept only in the Precinct, and at the school-house in the centre of the First Parish.

In 1760 commenced the institution of schools different from the grammar school, and inferior to it, in the remote parts of the town. That year, after voting, at March meeting, that the Precinct should have its proportional part of "the School," (meaning, the grammar school) the year ensuing, and that the rest of the time the school was keeping, it should be kept in the school-house in the First Parish, and not be removed, and after choosing a committee to provide a person suitable to take the charge of such school, it was voted in May, that "they would allow to each of the extream parts," (meaning the East, South and West parts) "of the first parish in said town the sum of thirty-three pounds six shillings and eight pence, Old Tenor, or equivalent in Lawfull Money, to be draughted out of their Treasury by each part, provided they appropriate said money in hireing some suitable person to keep a school for the instruction of their children before the first day of March next."[50] Votes, of a similar purport, were passed by the town, several of the subsequent years previous to 1775. In 1761, for example, £400, Old Tenor, was raised "for maintaining the Grammar School and other Schools"

---

[49] Town Records, Vol. VIII., p. 172.

[50] Town Records, Vol. VIII., p. 291.

in the town that year. Of this sum, £100 was granted, to be equally divided between the extreme parts of the First Parish, "provided they hire some suitable person to keep a school for the instruction of their children," in the course of that year.[51] In 1773, £40, lawful money, was raised for schools in Woburn; of which sum, £3 6*s.* 8*d.* was allotted expressly to each of the easterly, southerly and westerly extremes, £10 in all, for the instruction of the children in those quarters; and a committee was chosen to procure a suitable person or persons, for performing this service among them, and for determining the times and places of each school, while another committee was chosen to provide a suitable master to keep the grammar school nine months, viz, five months in the school-house in the First Parish, and four months in the Precinct.[52] In March 1774, £40, lawful money, was raised for the grammar school, to be kept in the Precinct its proportional part, and the rest of the time in the school-house near the meeting-house in the First Parish; and in May, £15 more, lawful money, was raised for schools in the remote parts of the town; whereof, £5 was appropriated to the Precinct, as their proportionate part, and the remaining £10, to the instruction of children in the extreme part of the First Parish.[53] And, finally, in 1775, forty pounds was raised for schooling that year, of which sum each parish was to take its proportionate part, and had liberty to unite with each other in hiring a grammar schoolmaster to serve the town in that capacity nine months that year, and "the remaining part of said forty pounds to be appropriated for the instruction of the children in the extream parts of the parishes, as each parish shall think will be for their best interest, and to no other use." [54]

Thus was inaugurated a system of graded schools in Woburn, which had apparently much influence in setting aside the old custom of a *moving grammar school,* and in laying the foundations of the school districts which followed. As late as 1775, there were no school-houses in which to keep the schools in the outskirts; but they were kept in such private houses, and for

[51] Town Records, Vol. VIII., p. 312.
[52] Town Records, Vol. IX., p. 198.
[53] Town Records, Vol. IX., pp. 235, 239.
[54] Town Records, Vol. IX., p. 276.

such lengths of time, in proportion to their taxes, as a committee, appointed by the town for the purpose, was pleased to determine. They were taught by male teachers, engaged for this employment by a committee nominated by the town at March or May meeting; and as the pay of these teachers was smaller, so it is to be presumed that their work was less laborious and diversified than that of the instructors of the grammar school.

It would be gratifying to exhibit here a complete list of the books used in the Woburn schools during the period of the above survey; but such a list, it would now be hardly possible to find or collect. But the following school-books are still extant in Burlington (Woburn precinct), inscribed, some of them, with the names of their former owners, natives of Woburn, and pupils of its schools before 1775, and all of them furnishing strong tokens of having been studied in those schools previously to the year just named.

1. "The Universal Spelling Book" etc. (place and date of printing lost): Part II. of which is styled "An easy Guide to English Grammar, by Way of Question and Answer etc. etc.

> Let all the foreign Tongues alone,
> Till you can read and spell your own."

2. "The Youth's Instructor in the English Tongue: (Title page wanting) In three parts; of which part III. contains "Rules in Arithmetic, with Forms of Bills, Bonds, Releases etc. etc."

3. "A New Guide to the English Tongue: In Five Parts:
The Twenty Second Edition:
By Thomas Dilworth, School Master etc.
London 1760."

[With a likeness of the author prefixed, dressed in the costume of an English school-master of that day.]

N. B. The work last mentioned has lost a number of pages. Part III. contains "A short, but comprehensive Grammar of the English Tongue, delivered in the most familiar and Instructive Method of Question and Answer," etc. etc. Part IV. "An useful Collection of Sentences in Prose and Verse; Divine, Moral and Historical," etc.; and Part V. "Forms of Prayer for Children, on several Occasions."

Such was the condition of the public schools in Woburn, and the progress evidently made in them, between 1690 and 1775. At the commencement of the above term of time, primary schools were but feebly and meanly sustained by the town; and as to a grammar school, scholars could not be found to attend one. But long before the completion of that period, a grammar school was constantly maintained in Woburn; highly respectable teachers were encouraged to take charge of it; and parents manifested much solicitude that their children might enjoy its privileges, and that it might be located where they could conveniently attend it.

And here it may not be amiss to give some account of a contention respecting one of the masters of the grammar school during that period, with which the whole town was agitated. In July 1725, the Selectmen, being the School Committee, hired Mr. Ebenezer Flegg, a nephew of their chairman, Col. Eleazar Flegg [Flagg], to keep the grammar school three months.[55] But it appears that previously to this, one or more of the Selectmen, or some one authorized by them, had spoken to Mr. Timothy Walker, a son of Deacon Samuel Walker, in such terms as that he considered the school as engaged to him, and was unwilling to give it up. Mr. Flegg commenced keeping the school July 26, according to agreement; and Mr. Walker still insisting upon his right, the Selectmen were requested to call a meeting of the town to settle the difficulty; but this they refused to do. Whereupon, application was made to Oliver Whiting, Esq., of Billerica, a justice of the peace, who granted a warrant for the meeting of the inhabitants of Woburn, "to reconcile the difference that has happened relating to their Schoolmasters, and to determine which of them shall keep the said Town Schoole."[56]

---

[55] Col. "Flegg's" name and that of his nephew are here spelt as they are found in Woburn Records, although Gershom, the Colonel's father's name, and that of his remoter descendants in Woburn to this day, is spelt Flagg. Dr. Bond, however, in his "Genealogies" and History of the Early Settlers of Watertown, where the Woburn Flaggs originated, observes, that there can be but very little doubt that the spelling of their name Flagg, though now universally prevalent, is erroneous, and that the correct orthography is Flegg. — See *Bond's Genealogies, etc., p. 762.*

[56] Town Records, Vol. VI., p. 224.

At that meeting, August 27, 1725, "after considerable debate," the Moderator, Mr. Ebenezer Johnson, ordered Capt. Fowle, the Town Clerk, to put upon record the warrant by which they were then met, and also to record Mr. Timothy Walker as school-master for the current year. At the same time, forty-three persons entered a protest against passing, at that meeting, any votes to be put upon the Town Book.[56] In accordance, however, with the above injunction given by the Moderator to the Town Clerk, Mr. Walker seems now to have been forcibly put in possession of the town school-house. But as the Selectmen, who were the School Committee, still refused to acknowledge his claims, he appealed to the law, by entering a complaint in the Supreme Court against them and the Town Clerk. Mr. Flegg appears to have continued keeping school in some private dwelling, under the patronage of the Selectmen; and when his first engagement expired, they prolonged it one month more;[57] and then hired a different master for the remainder of the year. They also, in opposition to the meeting in August preceding, or in order to justify themselves and the course they had taken in view of the community, called another meeting, January 6, 1725–6: the warrant for which is not upon record, but at which it was voted, among other particulars,

1. "That the publick schoole and schoolehouse in said Town should be under the care and regulation of the Selectmen of said Town as formerly.

2. "That the Selectmen should prosecute in the Law any person or persons that shall pretend and doe keep possession of the publick Schoolhouse of said Town, without their order; and also prosecute in the Law any person or persons that shall demolish or harme the same.

3. "That what was voted at a meeting of some of the freeholders and other inhabitants of said Town upon the twenty-seventh of August last past concerning Schoolemasters should be null and void, it being counted irregular."[58]

But before any votes were taken on this occasion, except that for the choice of Moderator, a large number of the inhabitants

---

[57] Town Records, Vol. VI., p. 262.

[58] Town Records, Vol. VI., p. 245.

present entered a Protest against any further action upon the articles of the Warrant, for the following reasons among others, viz:

"1. Because that in the Preface to the Warrant for this meeting it seems to be intimated, that the Town is to signifie their minds concerning the difference in Town relating to the Grammar Schoole: Whereas we esteem [it] very unnecessary for the Town to give themselves the trouble to signifie their minds concerning a matter that is already in the hand of authority, and waits for a determination; the signification of the Town's mind concerning which will be of no consequence, neither pro nor (con): and also we esteem it high presumption and contempt, for the Town thus to pretend to wrest the sword of Justice out of the hands of the King's Justices.

"2. Secondly, Because that the first Particular mentioned in said warrant seems to be grounded upon a supposition, that private men have hired a Grammar Schoole master, and put him into the publick Schoole house of said Town; which supposition is absolutely false; and therefore for the Town to be convened to signifie their minds concerning a matter that is not, nor as we know of, ever will be, is grossly absurd.

"3. But granting the supposition to be true, yet the Law prescribes that nothing shall be enacted at a Town Meeting, but what is plainly set forth in the warrant, to the end that all men may be well apprised of the occasion of their meeting; but yet in any of the particulars of this warrant they have neither set forth who the schoole master is, nor the private men that have hired him.

. . . . .

"5. Because — what in the second particular of said warrant, "they call the publick Schoole house, is a particular propriety; and for the Town to commit the care and trust of any thing to other men which is not their own, is inconsistant with reason.

"6. Because we do not understand what they mean by Regulating the Town meeting in August: for if they mean to confirm and establish any vote then passed, it is a thing unnecessary;

and if it be, to repeal and disannul any, it is beyond their power."[59]

To this Protest, seventy-eight names were subscribed. Among the subscribers, were many of the most respectable inhabitants of the town, especially of the Johnson and Richardson, the Thompson and Wyman families. And the reasons upon which it was professedly grounded, do all seem weighty and forcible, except the fifth, denying the right of the town to dispose of the school-house, which was certainly lame. For, although that building was erected at the expense of private individuals, yet it was built upon the town's land and expressly for the town's use. But all the conflicting votes, opinions and measures of these two several meetings of the town, on this subject, were soon superseded by the decision of the Court, which was in favor of Mr. Walker, the complainant, and in pursuance of which, a writ of mandamus[60] was quickly issued against the Selectmen and Town Clerk. In compliance with this writ, the town came to an amicable settlement with Mr. Walker not long after. At a town meeting, June 13, 1726, it was voted, "that Mr Timothy Walker should have the sum of twenty seven pounds, ten shillings paid him out of the town treasury for services done in keeping the school in Woburn in the year past: which money was paid for peace and the ending of all former differences."[61] At the same time, Mr. Walker signed a certificate, acknowledging himself fully satisfied; and discharging the Selectmen and Town Clerk of all cost, to which they ever had been or might be liable, in virtue of the writ of mandamus, whether claimed by him, or by any under him.[a]

---

[59] Town Records, Vol. VI., p. 246. [60] See Appendix, VIII.
[61] Town Records, Vol. VI., p. 276.

[a] Mr. Walker's certificate was written and signed by him on a separate piece of paper. The following is a copy of it: —

"Woburne June ye 13th. 1726 at a Town meeting. Whereas ye subscriber entered a Complaint, whereby I obtained a Mandamus against Eliezer Flegg Esqr and ye other Selectmen and Town Cleark of ye said Town in ye yeare 1725, for which I do acknowledge myself fully satisfied for all Trouble and Charge, and Ingage to discharge ye sd. Selectmen & Towne Cleark of any charge that hath or shall ever arise concerning sd. Mandamus, or shall arise by me or any under me: as Witness my hand

"TIMOTHY WALKER."

And thus an end was put to the contest, which had kept the whole town in a state of turmoil and confusion almost a twelvemonth. In reviewing it by the best light we can obtain at this remote period of time, it seems a striking illustration of those words of Solomon,[b] "The beginning of strife is as when one letteth out water." The source of this contention was in the beginning, like a shallow outlet, scarcely a hand's breadth wide, to a large pond, which may be easily stopped. By some unaccountable oversight, the Selectmen had hired two masters, both of them gentlemen of unexceptionable character, to keep the same school at the same time. Or else, for reasons now impossible to ascertain, they had suddenly determined to pass by Mr. Walker, whom they had engaged first, and to take Mr. Flagg in his stead. But even now that they had opened a way for a stream of contention, it seems as though a disposition to do exactly right by Mr. Walker, and a little praiseworthy condescension to apologize to Mr. Flagg for the disappointment they might occasion him, would have quickly rectified their error· But no. Having once taken a wrong step, the Selectmen acted as though they thought they must go on, be the consequence what it would: And now the bitter waters of Meribah began to run apace: and urged on with the harsh surmises and stinging reproaches of both parties, that which was at first an insignificant rill, soon swelled into a mighty stream, bearing down all before it, and burying the peace of the town, till checked by the mound erected by the strong arm of the Law. This gave the passions of men time to cool; and now a survey of the trouble and expense in which they had involved themselves and the town, doubtless led the aggressors in this affair to regret that they had not better heeded the words of the Wise Man just cited; and better followed his counsel attached to them, "to leave off contention before it be meddled with."

---

[b] Prov. xvii. 14.

CHAPTER VIII.

Separation of Goshen (Wilmington) as a Town, and of Shawshin (Burlington) as a Precinct or Parish, in 1730: Ordination of Rev. Edward Jackson, 1729: Ordination Dinner.

We have now arrived at a period in the history of Woburn, when it was fast becoming a comparatively populous and wealthy town. The number of persons rated there in the Province tax of 1700 was only 187:[1] but in the Province tax for 1725,[2] it had increased to 305. According to a Valuation for the County of Middlesex, taken by order of the General Court in 1708, Woburn was the fourth town in the county for numbers and real estate; ranking, in both these respects, next after Charlestown, Cambridge, and Watertown; taking the precedence of Concord; and leaving Medford, its present flourishing rival, far behind.[3]

But a change was now impending, by which the population of

---

[1] Town Records, Vol. IV., pp. 170–173.

[2] Town Records, Vol. VI., pp. 248–255.

[3] Town Records, Vol. V., p. 82. In the valuation here referred to, returns are made from twenty towns, including Lancaster, now in the county of Worcester. The number of polls, and the comparative estimate of "real estate" in each of the towns above named, are as follows: —

	Polls.	Estate.
Charlestown	270	£53. 7. 8.
Cambridge	260	27. 9. 9.
Watertown	250	26.12.10.
Woburn	225	22. 8. 3.
Concord	223	16.19. 5.
Medford	46	4.11. 7.

The commissioners, however, to whom these returns were submitted, thought fit, upon examination, to abate from the estimate of "real estate" —

In Charlestown	£8.0.0.
In Cambridge	1.0.0.
And to add to that of "real estate" in Watertown	2.0.0.
" " " " in Concord	4.0.0.

the town was very considerably diminished, and its prosperity for a while, seriously checked. The change alluded to, was the erection of Goshen, or the northerly quarter of Woburn, into a distinct town; and of Shawshin, or the northwesterly quarter, into a precinct or parish. This alteration did not originate in any disaffection to Rev. Mr. Fox: for at the very time it was in contemplation, or in being made, the people were giving him almost every year fresh tokens of their favor and respect by voluntary additions to his salary, and by generous provision for the supply of his pulpit, when he was taken off by sickness from preaching himself.[4] But it grew out of the inconvenience to which the inhabitants of those quarters were subjected, by their remoteness from the place of public worship. There can be no question, that when the second meeting-house in Woburn was built on the hill in 1672, its situation was central, or nearly so, to the great mass of the population. But, since that time, new settlements had been continually making at the north and north-west. And hence the distances of the people in the several quarters of the town from the meeting-house had now become very unequal. For while the inhabitants of the south village (now Winchester) were only between two and three miles from the meeting-house, the dwelling-house of Sergeant Abraham Jaquith, in Goshen, was quite seven miles off; and the Wymans' farms in Shawshin, on the borders of Billerica, not less than five miles.

These were long distances for the inhabitants of those quarters of the town to travel on Sabbath morning, especially in midwinter, when their narrow roads were apt to be blocked up with snow, and next to impassable. But such was the zeal in those days for attendance on public worship and the ordinances of God's house, that, notwithstanding these inconveniences, the people in those parts of the town *would go to meeting*, and be there *punctually* too, at the appointed hour. Authentic tradition

---

[4] One such addition, among others that might be named, is the following: At March meeting, 1727–8, *voted*, "that the Revd Mr John Fox should have fourty pounds added to his sallery this present year; so as to make his sallery six score pounds this year." — *Town Records, Vol. VI., p.* 335.

relates, that the inhabitants of the remotest corner of Goshen, near Billerica line, would often travel to meeting in winter on snow-shoes; and that one of them, Deacon James Thompson, would always be there by 8 o'clock in the morning, (in summer, it is presumed) which was an hour at least before the public services commenced. But, though the people of both the most distant quarters of the town attended meeting on the Sabbath from choice, notwithstanding the inconveniences above alluded to, rather than stay away, yet they accounted their subjection to these difficulties by reason of their location, as a great hardship, because they viewed it as *unnecessary*, and therefore *unjust*; and, after bearing it patiently for years, they at length decided to seek relief from it in a legal way.

The first step taken apparently for this end was a petition to the town from both "the Northwardly branches" thereof, which was read at a town meeting called for the purpose, January 19, 1724–5.[5] The subject of this petition is not stated in the Records: the consideration of it, when read, was deferred till the annual meeting in May; and then it was answered in the negative, as follows: "Voated that they would not grant the Petition that was offered to the Town by the two Northwardly Branches of said Town, as it is set forth in said Petition."[6] But though the petitioners were defeated in this their first effort, they were not discouraged from pursuing the object they had in view. After waiting a twelvemonth, they united in another joint petition to the town. But the Selectmen refusing to call a meeting to consider it, they applied to Oliver Whiting, Esq., of Billerica, a justice of the peace for Middlesex county, who granted them a warrant for a town meeting at Woburn, to be held February 10, 1725–6. At that meeting, "the Question being put, Whether the Town would proceed at present . . . . . ? it was past in the negative": and further, it was then voted, "that the Town would consider of the premises contained in Justice Whiting's Warrant . . . . . at March Meeting next."[7]

The original drafts of the two joint petitions just mentioned,

---

[5] Town Records, Vol. VI., p. 208.
[6] Town Records, Vol. VI., p. 218.
[7] Town Records, Vol. VI., p. 261.

and the warrants calling meetings of the town to consider them, have long since been missing. And the Town Clerk, in recording the action of the town upon them, seems not to have cared that posterity should know anything respecting the subject of them. In his record of the two meetings, January 19 and May 11, 1725, at which the first of these two petitions was considered, he dropped not a word from which might be gathered what the prayer of the petitioners was. But in his record of the meeting, February 10, 1725–6, just noticed, called by Justice Whiting to consider their second petition, he was not quite so successful in shutting out the light on this matter. After writing, "the Question being put, 'Whether the Town would proceed at present?'" he inadvertently added three other important words,. which, upon further reflection, he saw fit to efface, leaving only, "it was past in the negative." Fortunately, however, in drawing his pen twice across the three words referred to, he did not do the work of obliteration so effectually, as to prevent our reading distinctly beneath the erasure, "about a meeting house:" and these three words, when considered with the vote passed at March meeting, to which were adjourned the several articles of Justice Whiting's Warrant not acted upon, and with the subsequent proceedings of the town, September 22 and October 2, 1727, let in abundance of light upon the subjects of the petitions referred to. At the meeting, March 7, 1725–6, it was voted, that sixteen pounds should be paid out of the town treasury towards the support of preaching in both the northerly parts of the town in the three shortest months of the winter, "In case they do provide a minister to preach amongst them; and if they have not a minister to preach amongst them, they are not to have any money out of the treasury."[8] This vote was passed, apparently, to silence the complaints made about the distance of the meeting-house, and to prevent, if possible, any further importunity from the complainants for the grant of their obnoxious petitions, which the town had negatived at the two preceding meetings. Comparing, therefore, the doings of the town,

[8] Town Records, Vol. VI., p. 265.

February 10, and March 7, 1725–6, above recorded, with its subsequent proceedings September 22, and October 2, 1727,[9] there can be but little doubt, that the prayer of the first joint petition of the two northerly parts of the town was, that the meeting-house built on the hill might be removed to a more central situation; and that of the second joint petition was, that the meeting-house might be removed, as above; or otherwise, that the town would erect a new one on a site that would better accommodate the petitioners, its remote inhabitants.

In pursuance of the vote of March 7, 1725–6, the sum of eight pounds of the town's money was paid to the inhabitants of each of the remote quarters respectively, viz: to Dea. James Thompson, on behalf of Goshen; [10] and by Mr. Samuel Kendall, Constable and Collector, to Mr. Benjamin Johnson and others, on behalf of Shawshin, [10] to defray the expense of preaching within their respective bounds during the winter of 1726–7. The grant of the above sums by the town, to these respective portions of her population, for the purpose designated by her vote, was a virtual acknowledgment on her part, that the grievance they complained of had a real, and not an imaginary foundation. And, accordingly, it was renewed the year following to the inhabitants of Goshen, at their request, that they might provide themselves with preaching in the winter of 1727–8. [11] But there is no record of a similar grant to Shawshin for that winter. Whence it would seem, either that the town had some special reason for denying the people of that quarter the favor referred to, or else (which is more probable) that those people themselves had omitted to ask it of the town, as they of Goshen had done; being dissatisfied with it, thinking themselves entitled to some higher consideration, and having already made up their minds to seek a more effectual remedy for the disadvantages they labored under, than the temporary grant of a few pounds year by year could yield them. In accordance with these sentiments, they presented a petition to the General Court at their

---

[9] See onward, the doings of the town on those respective dates.

[10] Town Records, Vol. VI., pp. 293, 294.

[11] Town Records, Vol. VI., p. 309.

session, in August 1727, the substance of which is stated in the following extract from the Court Records:

"At a Great and General Court or Assembly, begun upon Wednesday May 31. 1727, and continued by adjournment to Wednesday August 16th 1727, and then met.

"Thursday Aug. 24. 1727.

"A Petition of the Inhabitants of the North Westerly Part of the Town of Woburn, Shewing, that the Meeting House for the publick Worship of God in the said Town is situated so as to be very far from the Center of the said Township, and by the increase of the Inhabitants the House is too small to receive them with convenience: And forasmuch as the Petitioners are put to great difficulties & inconveniences by reason of their remoteness, especially in the Winter Season, and in stormy Weather; And therefore Praying that either the Meeting House may be removed to the Center of the Town, or that the Petitioners may be set off a distinct Township or Precinct, and that a Committee of this Court may be appointed to view that Part of the Town; and that they may be set off, as follows: viz. To be bounded Westerly two miles & an half on Lexington Line; on Billerica Line four miles; to run from the Lines of Lexington & Billerica into the Town of Woburn four miles in Length: The Committee to make their Report to this Court thereon.

"In the House of Representatives Read, and Voted that the Petitioners forthwith serve the Town of Woburn with a Copy of this Petition, that so they shew forth their Reasons, if any they have, why the Prayer thereof should not be granted.

"In Council, Read & Concur'd.

"Consented to, Wm. Dummer."[12]

Aroused by these proceedings of Shawshin, and by the order of Court in relation to them, the town held a meeting September 22, 1727, at which, after choosing Mr. Joseph Wright, Moderator, they passed the following votes:

"First, that they would choose a committee to agree with a surveyor and two chainmen, to measure the township of Woburn all round, and to find out the centre of the town.

---

[12] Records of Court, Vol. XIII. ? p. 415.

"2dly. Voted that the Selectmen of Woburn were chosen a Committee by themselves, or men whom they should appoint to be a Committee, to agree with a surveyor and two chainmen: which surveyor and chainmen should be upon oath to measure the town of Woburn all round, and find out the centre of the town, and to give a plan of the same; and that the surveyor and chainmen should measure that piece of land petitioned for to be a Township by the Northwesterly part of the Town, and to give a plan of the same also." [13]

They then, for the sake, no doubt, of receiving the surveyor's return before they proceeded to further action, adjourned the meeting with "the subject matter contained in the warrant for the calling of" [it] to October 2.

The gentleman employed by the Committee, as above directed, was Capt. Joseph Burnap, a noted surveyor of Reading, who, with two chainmen of his providing, went to work, measured the town, and made out a plan of it, for which service he was afterwards duly paid.[14] How soon his plan was completed, and where, according to it, the centre of the town was found to be, the Records do not state. Apparently, however, he began his work immediately, and finished in season to communicate the result of his labors to the town at their adjourned meeting, October 2, when they passed the following votes.

1. "First, Voted that they were not for having the meeting house removed from the place where it now stands.

"2ly. Voted that they were not "for building a meeting house for the Westerly part of the Town, as they have set forth in their petition."

"3ly. Voted that the Town was not willing that the land petitioned for in the Westerly part of the Town should be a separate Township.

"4ly. Voted that they would choose a Committee to give in answer to the Great and General Court, why the prayer of the petition [i. e. of Shawshin] 'should not be granted.'

"5ly. Voted, that they would choose three men to be the

---

[13] Town Records, Vol. VI., p 311.

Committee to goe to the Great and General Court to make answer to the above said petition.

"6ly. The men voted and chosen are Mr Caleb Blogget, John Fowle, Mr Joseph Wright." [14]

From the decisive tone and character of these votes, the matter in controversy between Woburn and its Northwesterly district seemed to be now in a fair way of being speedily determined. But in this expectation, both parties were disappointed. For it so happened, that in copying the Order of Court, issued in consequence of the Petition of Shawshin, above referred to, the day appointed by the Court of Woburn, to appear before them, and assign its reasons against granting the prayer of that petition, was, by some oversight, omitted. Of course, the Committee, chosen to make answer to the Court, on behalf of the town, not being duly notified of the time set for their appearance there, accounted themselves discharged from the duty of their appointment, and the petition of Shawshin for that time fell through.

Before another petition could be presented, and another Order of Court be duly served, the town made an attempt to adjust her difficulties with her uneasy children upon her northern and northwestern bounds, upon terms of her own proposing. At a general meeting of the freeholders and other inhabitants, November 15, 1727, after the nomination of Mr. Joseph Wright as Moderator, it was voted as follows: "That the town of Woburn is willing, that the inhabitants of the North and Northwesterly part of the town, should have half the land on that side of the town set off to them either in a Precinct or a Township, Provided they will build for themselves, and maintain the publick worship of God amongst themselves, without the help of the town for time to come." [15] This sounds like a fair offer; and with certain additional qualifications, it might have been satisfactory at the time to those inhabitants of the town, on account of whom it was made. But, expressed as it was, they regarded the vote conveying it with distrust. They could not

[14] Town Records, Vol. VI., pp. 331, 333.

[15] Town Records, Vol. VI., p. 310.

help observing, that, while the town took care by this vote to secure *herself* from all expense in erecting a meeting-house and supporting the gospel among *them,* she did not propose to free them from all liability to charge, for enabling *her* to settle a colleague with Rev. Mr. Fox. A plan for such a settlement was now beginning to be talked of.[16] And the inhabitants of the northern and northwestern quarters were jealous (and as the event proved, not without reason) that the town was disposed to hasten the measure, as a means, if speedily consummated, of embarrassing the Court about consenting to their projected separation; and of retaining it in her power, if they should eventually be set off, to tax them their full proportion of the ordination expenses, and settlement money of the colleague. In view of these considerations, the people, both of Goshen and Shawshin, appear from the first to have listened to the above proposals of the town with dissatisfaction and neglect; and those of Shawshin, disregarding the prospect of an adjustment of difficulties which it held out, determined to embrace the earliest opportunity for renewing the application to the General Court, which it had made during its previous session in August, but which, from causes already explained, had failed of its hoped for issue. Accordingly, at the commencement of the next winter session, January, 1727–8, they addressed the Legislature, as follows:

"To the Honble. William Dummer Esqr. Lieut. Governour & Commander in Chief, the Honble. the Council, and Representatives for his Majesty's Province of the Massachusetts Bay in New England in Gen^ll. Court assembled at Boston the 4th Day of January Anno Dom. 1727": (1727–8).

"The renewed Petition of the Inhabitants of the North Westerly part of the Town of Woburn within the County of Middlesex

Humbly sheweth:

"That whereas your Petitioners at the session of the Gen^ll.

---

[16] At town meeting, April 4, 1728, "Voted, that it was high time to be in a way to settle another minister among us.

"Further it was voated that the town would hear three or four ministers several Sabbath days, in order to settle one to help Mr Fox." — *Town Records, Vol. VI., p.* 347.

Court in August last preferred their Petition, therein setting forth the Difficulties they labour under with respect to their attending the publick Worship of God, at the Meeting House where it now stands in the said Town, and praying to be relieved in such Manner as is therein set forth: Upon which Petition the said Court were pleased to Order that the Petitioners should serve the Town of Woburn with a Copy of said Petition, that so they shew forth their Reasons (if any they have) why the Prayer thereof should not be granted; And the Petitioners, above Twenty Days before the sitting of the Generall Court in October last, served the Town with a Copy of the said Petition, pursuant to the Direction in the said Order: But so it happened, that in penning thereof, there was no Day fix'd for the Respondents to give in their Answer, by Means whereof the same has never to this Day been done, and your Petitioners are without Remedy, unless aided by your Honours:

"Wherefore your Petitioners humbly pray, that their said Petition may be Revived; and Inasmuch as they have already served the Town with a Copy thereof, as aforesaid, they may be obliged to give in their Answer in some short limited time, and in default thereof, the Petitioners may be relieved, agreeable to the Prayer of their said Petition, as to the Wisdom and Justice of this Honble. Court shall seem meet.

"And your Petitioners (as in Duty bound) shall ever pray &c.

"Ebenezer Johnson

"Benjamin Johnson

"In the Name and by Order of the Rest of the Petitioners.

"In Council Jan. 4th. 1727.

"Read & Ordered that the former Petition here referred to be reviewed; and that the Petitioners now serve the Town with a Copy of this Petition & Order, that they may give in their Answer, if they see Cause, on Thursday y^e. 11th. Instant.

"Sent down for Concurrence,

"J. WILLARD, Secr^y.

"In the House of Representatives, Jany. 6. 1727.

"Read & Concur'd, with y^e. Amendment: vizt. Dele, on Thursday y^e. Eleventh Instant, and add the second Thursday of y^e. next Session.

"Sent up for Concurrence

"W^m. DUDLEY, Spec^r.

"In Council Jan . 8th. 1727.

"Read and Concur'd.

"J. WILLARD, Secr[y].

"Consented to:

W[m]. DUMMER.

"Copy Examined "p[r]. J. WILLARD, Secr[y]." [17]

From the authoritative minutes on the back of the attested copy of the above cited petition, it will be perceived that both branches of the Legislature agreed to revive the petition, which had been presented to the Court at their session in August preceding, agreeably to the request of the petitioners. But their deferring of the time set by the Council, at which Woburn was required to respond to this revived petition, from January 11, 1727–8, to so late a day as the second Thursday of the next session in May, seems to have proved a fatal blow to the taking of any further effective proceedings upon it.[a]

Discouraged and baffled by the failure of this, their second application to the Court, and yet uneasy to remain in their

---

[17] Attested copy on file.

[a] The following is a copy of the action of the Court at their next session upon the two petitions of Shawshin above cited.

"Friday, June 14. 1728.

"On the Petition of the North West Part of the Town of Woburn, Enter'd August 24 [1727] and January 4. 1727 [1727–8].

"In Council, Read again, together with the Petition herein referred to, and the Answer of the Town of Woburn; and the same being duly considered,

"Ordered, that the Prayer of the Petition be so far granted, as that Jonathan Dowse, Esq[r]. with such as shall be appointed by the Hon'[ble] House of Representatives, be a Committee to view the Town of Woburn, and consider the Situation & Circumstances of the Inhabitants of the Northwesterly Part of the said Town, and report at the next Fall session what they judge proper for the Court to do, in answer to these Petitions.

"In the House of Representatives Read and Non-Concur'd; and Voted that the Petition be dismiss'd.

"In Council Read." [b]

[b] Court Records, Vol. XIV., pp. 83, 84.

present condition, the inhabitants of Shawshin now turned their attention anew for relief to the town's vote of November 15, preceding.[15] And if the town would have sanctioned such a construction of that vote as would in any measure have met their feelings and views, and assured them of the like exemption from taxation for the support of its own public worship that it had demanded in that vote for itself in support of theirs, in case of a separation between them, both they and their neighbors of Goshen would now, it is very likely, have been glad to accept the proposal of that vote, and have readily complied with the condition annexed to it. To put the disposition of the town on this head to the test, the people of Shawshin and Goshen handed in to the Selectmen the following joint petition:

" Oborne July the 18 daye in the year 1728.

" To the Selectmen of Woborne: Wee the Inhabitants of the Northwesterly and North Branches of said towne, commonly called Shawshin and Goshen, desier you the Selectmen, in your next Warrant to call a towne meeting, [to propose] that the Towne explayne their vote concerning setting off half of the towneship to the said Branches; and that in case these two Branches are set off in order to support the Gospell among themselves, [to see whether] the town will reimburse what charge they the said Branches are att, in settling another Minister with the Reverend Mr Fox, to them.

"Jeams Tompson — Simon Tompson
Ebenezer Johnson — Samuell Butter
Samuel Peirce — Benjamin Harnden
Benjamin Johnson — John Jacqueth
Edward Johnson — James Simonds
James Proctor. — Samuell Jones
Kendall Pearson." [18]

But this petition never received any reply; or, at least, any that can be found on record. It is dated the same day that a town meeting was held, to decide whether the inhabitants would give a call to Mr. Edward Jackson to be their minister, as a

---

[18] See original petition and signatures, in a bound volume of "Miscellaneous Records and papers of Woburn," p. 106.

colleague with Rev. Mr. Fox. This was then a favorite measure with the majority of the people of Woburn, and one which they were very earnest to hasten to its consummation. For reasons, therefore, which have been already intimated, and may be easily conjectured, they did not care to hurry, in answering the foregoing petition, or to give such an explanation of the vote referred to in it as would satisfy the petitioners.

But there was still another, and a plausible reason for not answering the above-quoted joint petition of Shawshin and Goshen. A month before its date, viz, June 17, 1728, the people of Goshen and of the adjoining part of Reading had preferred a petition to the General Court, setting forth the difficulties they lay under, by reason of their remoteness from their respective places of public worship; and praying they might be erected into a "separate & distinct Precinct." This petition had been read with favor in each branch of the Legislature; and the petitioners had been ordered to serve the towns of Woburn and Reading with copies of their petition, that they might show cause on the first Friday of the next Fall Session why the prayer thereof should not be granted.[19] Of this petition of Goshen, the inhabitants of Woburn had been doubtless notified, agreeably to Order of Court, as they had long before been aware of the two previous petitions of Shawshin to the Court for the like purpose. It is not surprising, therefore, that these petitions from both the remote quarters of the town to the Court should be regarded as acts of opposition to the majority of the inhabitants of Woburn; and that the Town should not be forward to gratify the petitioners by explaining their vote of November 15, or giving them the assurance they expressed a wish for, in their note to the Selectmen of July 18.

To defend the town, however, against the above petition of Goshen, it was voted at a town meeting in Woburn, October 14, 1728, to choose a committee "to go to the Great and General Court, to give the reasons why the prayer of the petition of Goshen (so called) should not be granted." The committee

[19] Records of Court, Vol. XIV., p. 88.

chosen for this end were Messrs. Jacob Wyman, Caleb Blogget, and Jonathan Thompson.[20] Nothing, however, was done in Court that year, or certainly nothing decisive, in regard to that petition: and the people of Goshen were soon made to smart for presuming to send it. Two months after they had presented it to the Court, they preferred to the Selectmen, for the sake of securing, for one winter more, the benefit of the allowance which the town had made them the three years past, to procure preaching within the winter, the following humble request:

"Woborne August the 19th. 1728.

"To the Seelectmen of Woborne: Wee the Inhabitants of Goshen, as in time past, so now allso wee renew oure humble Request to the Towne for a sum of money to support preaching the next winter; and Pray you the selectmen to signifie this our humble Request to the Towne in youre next Warrant.

"Presented by the subscribers hereto in behalf of the Rest.

"DANIEL PIERCE,
JAM^s. TÓMPSON,
KENDEL PARSON,
JOSEPH LEWES."[21]

A like application seems to have been made at the same time by the inhabitants of Shawshin. But they who hold the purse strings of any public treasury, hold a rod in their hands, which they find very convenient to chasten opposition with, and which has often been administered for that purpose. At an adjourned meeting of the town, November 11, 1728, it being put to vote "whether the Town would grant a sum of money to Goshen and Shawshin to pay for preaching among them in the Winter season?" it passed in the negative:[22] and, though it was immediately carried, to reconsider this vote at the next meeting, so far as it related to Goshen, yet it does not appear to have been ever actually reconsidered, or that any money was ever paid to Goshen again out of the treasury of the town, for the above-named purpose.

[20] Town Records, Vol. VI., p. 351.

[21] The original draft of this petition was to be seen, a few years ago, pasted between the pages 91, 92, of Records, Vol. I., but it is now missing.

[22] Town Records, Vol. VI., p. 351.

In this unhappy posture, the affairs of the petitioners remained for a twelvemonth longer. During this period, while the town taxed them their full proportion, not only of Rev. Mr. Fox's salary, but of the settlement money and salary of his colleague, Rev. Mr. Jackson, (who had been ordained August 1, 1729,) it denied them even the small pittance, by which, in view of their distance from the meeting-house, it had once aided them, in the depth of winter, to provide for the public worship of God among themselves.

But a prospect of permanent relief at length broke in upon them. The following summer, another petition was preferred by Shawshin to the General Court, subscribed by Ebenezer Johnson, Benjamin Johnson, Edward Johnson, James Proctor and Simon Thompson, on behalf of themselves and others, and praying to be set off from Woburn, either as a town or a precinct.[23] This petition, dated July 9, 1729, appears to have been presented to the Court during an adjourned session at Cambridge in August and September, and due order was taken for furnishing Woburn with a copy of it, and for their giving answer to the Court December 5, why the prayer of it should not be granted.

September 5, 1729, there was presented to the Court a "Petition of Samuel Eames, John Harnden, and sundry other inhabitants of the towns of Woburn and Reading; setting forth their difficulties, by reason of their remote situation from the places of publick worship in their respective towns, and that they are commodiously situated to make a distinct *Precinct* of the North-easterly part of Woburn & the Westerly part of Reading; And therefore Praying that they may be set off from their respective towns accordingly by certain lines particularly set forth and described in the Petition."

"In Council: Read and dismiss'd."[24]

But though the above petition, for reasons not assigned, was rejected, yet it was soon followed by another from the same people, praying to be made a *Town*, which found more favor; as appears by the following minutes of the Court:

---

[23] Town Records, Vol. VII., p. 10. Records of Court, Vol. XIV., pp. 393, 394.
[24] Records of Court, Vol. XIV., pp. 293, 294.

"At a General Court, begun & held at Salem Wednesday May 28, 1729, and thence by sundry prorogations & adjournments to Harvard College, Cambridge; and thence continued by prorogation to Boston Wednesday Nov. 19th. then met.

"Wednesday Nov. 26. 1729.

"A Petition of Daniel Pierce, Benjamin Harding [Harnden] and Samuel Walker, a Committee appointed by sundry Inhabitants of the North East part of Woburn and the Westerly part of Reading; Setting forth the difficulties they are under by reason of their remoteness from the Places of publick Worship in their respective Towns, And Praying to be sett off and constituted a distinct Township, according to their former Petition to this Court.

"In the House of Representatives Read & Ordered that the Petitioners serve the Towns of Woburn & Reading with a Copy of the Petition, that they shew cause on Fryday the sixth [fifth] of December next, why the Prayer thereof should not be granted.

"In Council Read & Concur'd."[25]

At a General Town Meeting in Woburn, December 3, 1729, two days before the day appointed by the Court for the parties to give in their answers to the above petitions; Messrs. Joseph Wright and Jacob Wyman, were chosen a Committee to answer on behalf of the town to the petition of the "Northeasterly part," or Goshen; and Dea. George Reed, Capt. Robert Convers and Mr. Caleb Bloggct to answer to the petition of the "Northwesterly part," or Shawshin.[26] From the Town Accounts for 1729[27] it appears, that the hearing of the parties, December 5, before the Court, occupied two days; and the result was so far favorable to the petitioners, as that the Court chose a Committee from their own body to go upon the ground and judge for themselves concerning their ability to sustain municipal and parochial institutions, and then to make report to the Court, at their next session, what they considered right and proper to be done.[28] Notice was given to Woburn of the appointment of this Committee, and of the object of their coming; and at a meeting of the

---

[25] Records of Court, Vol. XIV., p. 323.
[26] Records, Vol. VII., p. 39.
[27] Records, Vol. VII., pp. 42, 43.
[28] Records of Court, Vol. XIV., pp. 330, 331.

Selectmen, December 16, 1729, they appointed Messrs. Jacob Wyman and Jacob Wright "in behalf of the Selectmen to attend the General Court's Committee, upon their view to Goshen & Shawshin; and Mr. Caleb Blogget to attend the Committee on their view upon Shawshin."[26] The Court's Committee, consisting of Hon. Jonathan Dowse and Hon. Spencer Phips, Esquires of the Council, and of Mr. John Hobson of Rowley, Maj. Daniel Epes of Salem, and Mr. Joseph Hale of Boxford, of the House, appear to have come to Woburn in the summer of 1730, and to have spent several days here upon the business of their appointment; and their report to the Court, given in at the fall session, being in favor of granting the prayer of the petitioners, Shawshin was incorporated as the Precinct or Second Parish of Woburn, September 16, 1730, O. S.; and Goshen with the westerly part of Reading, as a distinct town, by the name of Wilmington, September 25, 1730, O. S.; or September 27, and October 6, according to the present reckoning of time. The following is the report of the Court's Committee respecting Shawshin:

"Province of the Massachusetts Bay:

"Sept. 16th. 1730.

"Jonathan Dowse Esqr., from the Committee of both Houses, on the petition of divers inhabitants of the Westerly and Northwest parts of Woburn, praying for a new Precinct, gave in the following Report: Viz.

"The Committee appointed on the petition of the inhabitants of the Westerly and Northwesterly parts of Woburn, praying to be erected into a Township or Precinct: in obedience to the within order repaired to the land petitioned for, the Selectmen of said town as well as the Petitioners being first seasonably notified of the time of the Committee's going. And after having taken a full and careful view of the land, and heard the parties on the subject matter of the petition at large, and maturely and deliberately considered the same, and how far the town of Woburn may be hereby affected; are humbly of opinion, that it will tend greatly to the advancement of the public worship of God, that the lands within mentioned be erected into a separate and distinct Precinct, by the following Bounds; (there being a sufficient number of inhabitants therein to support and maintain the preaching of the Gospel there.)

Beginning at a great rock on John Lilley's land to the Northward of his Barn, extending thence on a line to a Bridge, about ten rods to the Southwesterly side of Timothy Snow's house, thence Southwesterly till it comes to Lexington line, two miles and an half to the Eastward of Billerica Corner; from thence Westerly to Billerica Corner; thence Northerly till it comes within one hundred poles of Abraham Jaques' land; thence to the Cold Spring Stone Bridge, near the figure of Four Tree 4; and from thence Easterly to the Rock first mentioned; excluding the house and barn of the said Timothy Snow, and [excepting?] whom, the Petitioners shall be erected into a Precinct. The Committee cannot but be of opinion, that the charge of supporting the Minister in the town or first Parish in Woburn, will still be very easy on the Inhabitants of that Parish.

"Which is submitted — In the name and by order of the Committee

"July 1, 1730. "Jonathan Dowse."

"In Council Read and Ordered That this Report be accepted; and that the lands above bounded and described be erected into a separate Precinct accordingly, and that the Inhabitants thereof be vested with the powers and priviledges that the inhabitants of other Precincts within this Province are or ought by law to be vested with.

"In the House of Representatives, Read and concurred.

"Consented to: J. Belcher."[29]

"Report of the Court's Committee on the Petition of Goshen, etc., etc.

"Thursday Sept. 17. 1730.

"Jonathan Dowse Esq'r. from the Committee of both Houses on the Petition of the Inhabitants of the North Easterly Part of Woburn & the Westerly Part of Reading for a Township, gave in the following, viz:

"The Committee appointed to repair to the North Easterly Part of Woburn & Westerly Part of Reading, to hear all Parties within named, and view the land within described & petitioned for, to be a Township: Having first seasonably notified the Selectmen of Woburn & Reading, as also the Petitioners, of their going, have repaired to said Land, and taken a careful View of the same, and

---

[29] Records of Court, Vol. XIV., pp. 393, 394.

fully heard all the Parties therein concerned for & against the Prayer of the Petition; And after mature consideration thereon in all its circumstances, are humbly of opinion, It is highly reasonable that the Prayer of the Petition be granted, and that the Lands within mentioned & describ'd, be erected into a separate & distinct Township, by those Metes & Bounds accordingly, with the following additional Bounds: The Line to extend from one hundred Rods to the Southerly side of Jaques's Farm to the Stone Bridge called the Cold Spring Bridge, near the Tree called the figure of Four Tree 4; thence on a Line to the Southerly Corner of John Townsend's land, lately & now in the possession of Timothy Townsend, about sixty rods Easterly from Woburn West Line: Which is submitted.

"In the Name & by the Order of the Committee:

"JONATHAN DOWSE.

"In Council Read: and Ordered that this Report be Accepted, and that Order [be taken] thereon [that] the Petitioners bring in a Bill accordingly.

"In the House of Rep. Read & Concur'd." [30]

Thus was accomplished a separation, very important in its consequences to the town of Woburn, after it had been in agitation five years. By it, of three hundred and twelve persons who had been taxed to pay Rev. Mr. Jackson's salary in August 1730, while the town yet remained undivided, forty-three had been set off, in 1731, to Wilmington, and eighty-two were included within the bounds of the Precinct or Second Parish; making in all, two-fifths of the whole number of persons who had belonged to the First Parish in Woburn in 1730, and been then taxed in it, but who now paid their minister tax elsewhere: inflicting a blow on the First Parish in Woburn, from which it did not recover for many years, as we shall see hereafter.

While steps were taking for the legal accomplishment of this separation, the majority of the town were busily engaged, and finally succeeded in promoting the settlement of a colleague with the senior pastor, Rev. Mr. John Fox. This had become a strictly necessary measure, although the urgency of its friends to complete it, before the then contemplated separation of a very numerous

[30] Court Records, Vol. XIV., p. 395.

and respectable portion of their fellow citizens from the town or First Parish could be carried into effect, could not but give rise to suspicions that were injurious to their reputation. For a number of years, Mr. Fox had been in a feeble state of health, and often unable to perform his ministerial duties. As far back as 1722, there are four charges in the Town Accounts, for that year, for the hire of preachers, "when Mr Fox was sick."[31] At a meeting of the Selectmen, December 13, 1725, after agreeing with Mr. Samuel Jennison (subsequently minister of Shrewsbury) to keep the grammar school in Woburn, three months, from December 15, they add in the Records, "And we do expect that the said Samuell Jennison should assist to preach for ye Rev. Mr Fox, as often as occasion should serve, he being often indisposed and uncapable to preach."[32] And, accordingly, the Town Accounts for 1725 do show that Mr. Jennison preached for Mr. Fox, while keeping school, ten Sabbaths and one-half day, at the town's expense;[33] and in 1726, the same Mr. Jennison preached two Sabbaths more; and Mr. Habijah Weld, sixteen Sabbaths, at the expense of the town.[34] And at subsequent periods, the charges are not uncommon for the supply of the pulpit by the town, in consequence of Mr. Fox's illness, and the prospect seemed to be, that unless stated, settled help were soon provided for him, he would become ere long, altogether unable to carry on the work of the ministry.

Accordingly, at a general meeting, April 4, 1728, the town voted, first, "that it was high time to be in a way to settle another minister among us;" and 2dly, "that the town would hear three or four ministers preach severall Sabbath days, in order to settle one to help Mr. Fox."[35] The only prominent candidate for this office, whom they appear to have employed, was Mr. Edward Jackson of Newton, a graduate of Harvard College in 1719. In him, the people became speedily so far united, that at a town meeting, July 18, 1728, the church having previously informed the inhabitants of their choice of him "for

31 Town Records, Vol. VI., p. 157.
32 Town Records, Vol. VI., p. 146.
33 Town Records, Vol. VI., p. 262.
34 Town Records, Vol. VI., pp. 292, 294.
35 Town Records, Vol. VI., p. 347.

their minister, in order to his further settlement with them in convenient time," the town immediately chose him, "by 145 votes, for a Minister for the town of Woburn."[36] They also appointed a committee of ten to inform Mr. Jackson of the choice of him by the church and town for their minister, viz: the four deacons, Samuel Walker, William Lock, George Reed, and James Thompson; also, Messrs. Joseph Wright, Samuel Richardson, John Fowle, Jonathan Poole, Jacob Wyman and Capt. Stephen Richardson; and having directed this committee to see to the supply of the pulpit in the mean while, they adjourned the meeting to the first Tuesday in September next ensuing.

At this adjourned meeting, September 3, 1728, it was voted to grant "to Mr. Edward Jackson two hundred and fifty pounds settlement, if he settle in the work of the Ministry in Woburn;" and also "one hundred and twenty pounds salary per year in Bills of Credit, as the money now is, so long as he carrys on the work of the ministry in Woburn."[37] After re-appointing the former committee, and requesting some of them to go to Mr. Jackson, and persuade him to come to Woburn and preach the next Sabbath day, they adjourned the meeting to September 23, and then again to October 14, 1728.

In the mean while, Rev. Mr. Fox had begun to manifest uneasiness at the proceedings going on. What the cause of his uneasiness was, we are not told. But when it is considered, that, according to well substantiated tradition, these two ministers showed afterwards a rooted antipathy to each other, it seems no improbable supposition, that Mr. Fox had already imbibed a personal prejudice against Mr. Jackson, and that he felt averse to receive him as his colleague. To obviate the difficulty, whatever occasioned it, the town, at their adjourned meeting, October 14, 1728, chose a committee of nine, "to goe to the Rev. Mr Fox to see if they can make things easy with him; and if there be need, they shall goe to some of the neighbouring ministers." The committee chosen for this pur-

---

[36] Town Records, Vol. VI., p. 349.

[37] Town Records, Vol. VI., p. 350.

pose were Ensign Samuel Blogget, Messrs. Jonathan Thompson, Josiah Johnson, John Tidd, Senr., Deacons Lock, Thompson, Walker, and Reed, and Lieut. Peirson Richardson, who were also to go and treat with Mr. Jackson "to supply the pulpit for the present": and to the above numerous committee, they voted at an adjournment of this meeting, November 11, 1728, to add four men more, viz, Mr. Jacob Wyman, Jonathan Poole, Esq., and Messrs. John Peirce and Joseph Wright.[38]

This large, overwhelming committee of thirteen (with help from neighboring ministers, if needed) appears either to have persuaded Rev. Mr. Fox freely to give his consent to Mr. Jackson's settlement with him as a colleague, or (which is more probable) to have extorted from him a reluctant, unwilling assent to it. And Mr. Jackson seems to have given an affirmative answer to the call he had received from the church and town to the pastoral and ministerial office, in the course of that winter. For, at the annual town meeting, March 3, 1728–9, it was voted that the former committee, chosen October 14, and November 11, 1728, "should be a committee still, in power to proceed with the Church in bringing forward the ordination of Mr. Edward Jackson; and to proceed in calling such help of Elders and Churches, as should be necessary in that case: and that they be a committee to proceed to supply the pulpit, untill the matter be accomplished, or further order of the Town be given them."

And, further, it was voted, that "the Town would by a free Contribution pay for preaching for the present, to Mr. Edward Jackson, if he supply the pulpit, till the Town see cause to come into some other method."[39]

Agreeably to the vote at March meeting, 1729, due preparations for the solemnity having been made by the committee, Rev. Mr. Edward Jackson was ordained as colleague pastor with Rev. Mr. John Fox over the church of Woburn, August 1, 1729.[40] What churches were sent to on the occasion, and what the exercises were of the solemnity, and by whom conducted,

---

[38] Town Records, Vol. VI., pp. 350, 351. [39] Town Records, Vol. VI., p. 370.
[40] Town Records, Vol. VII., p. 11.

no known memorial has been preserved. The Town Records however have transmitted some account of the splendid and costly entertainment made by the town at the ordination, in a bill of Jonathan Poole, Esq., who was employed to provide it. The following is a copy:

"To Mr Jonathan Poole Esqr for subsisting the Ministers and Messengers and Gentlemen in the time of Mr. Jackson's Ordination:

"To 433 Dinners a 2^s: 6^d a Dinner .	£54: 2: 6^d
"To Suppers & Breakfasts, 178: . .	08:18:0
"To keeping 32 horses 4 days: . .	3: 0:0
"To Six Barrils & ½ of Cyder . .	4:11:0
"To 25 Gallons of wine . .	9:10:0
"To 2 Gallons of Brandy & 4 Gallons Rhum	1:16:0
"To Loaf Suger, Lime Juice & Pipes .	1:12:0
	"£83: 9:6." [41]

Here is a bill, amounting to more than two-thirds of a year's salary pledged to Mr. Jackson, for articles consumed at his ordination entertainment. Our fathers were, generally speaking, very prudent men in their use of money; and more apt to be parsimonious than profuse in their expenses for public purposes. But here is an instance, that, in a comparative view, seems to be well entitled to the charge of extravagance. And such was the general character of ordination expenses during the last century. How came it to be so? Ordinations in the times of the Apostles, were solemnized with prayer and fasting.[42] Such, too, was the custom in the Church of England, from which, for greater purity's sake, our ancestors separated. In that Church, all ordinations are appointed to be held, exclusively, upon the Sundays immediately following the Ember

---

[41] Town Records, Vol. VII., p. 42. Esquire Poole's bill against the town for expenses at Mr. Jackson's ordination was not the only one. Another follows: "To Mr Noah Richardson for keeping the Ministers' & Messengers' horses, in the time of Mr Jackson's ordination . . . £2.0.0." — *Town Records, Vol. VII., p.* 43.

[42] Acts xvi. 3.

weeks, (as certain stated quarterly solemnities were called,) that were set apart for this purpose among others, to implore, with fasting and prayer, the divine blessing upon the candidates, then to be brought to the bishop to be ordained.[43] Such, also, was the custom of the Presbyterians, who rose upon the ruins of Episcopacy in the time of the Westminster Assembly. Through their influence, an ordinance was made by Parliament, directing that all ordinations should be performed with prayer and fasting.[44] And such, too, was the custom of our Puritan ancestors themselves, at their first settlement in this country. Their earliest ordinations were wont to be celebrated on days of solemn fasting and prayer.[45] Whence then the change? This can be accounted for, it seems, only in this way. The earliest ordinations here were performed by the churches themselves, over which candidates were to be ordained, without the aid of the elders of other churches. But when it became common for churches, over which pastors were to be ordained, to ask sister churches abroad to aid by their elders and messengers in the solemnity, then it became necessary to provide for their hospitable entertainment. And entertainments on such occasions, at first probably plain and simple, and by no means to be censured, came at length to be sumptuous: and hence ordinations, from being solemn religious services, degenerated in too many instances, into occasions of excessive feasting and noisy dissipation. An aged minister in this county once said in my hearing, that at his ordination, about half a century previous, such was the noise and confusion on the common before the meeting-house, that the exercises within it could scarcely be heard. And ordinations and commencements, where it might be reasonably expected that good order and decorum would prevail, became too often scenes of noisy mirth and excess.

---

[43] Wheatly on the Book of Common Prayer, Appendix to Chapter IV., Section 2; and Chapter V., Section 2.

[44] Neal's History of the Puritans, Vol. III., Chap. vi., pp. 281, 282.

[45] Winthrop's History, by Savage, Vol. I., pp. 36, 114, 135, 259.

CHAPTER IX

Variance between Rev. Messrs. Fox and Jackson. — Lawsuits of Rev. Mr. Fox, and of Rev. Mr. Jackson, against the Town, 1732, 1740. — Sale of the 2,000 Acres in 1734. — Management of the Committee of Trust till 1772.

THE preceding chapter of this history of Woburn gives an account of the settlement of Rev. Edward Jackson, as colleague pastor with Rev. John Fox, in 1729; and of the incorporation of the northerly quarter of the town, or Goshen, as a distinct town, by the name of Wilmington, and of its northwesterly quarter, or Shawshin, as its Second Precinct, in 1730. These measures had been rendered in a degree necessary, by the failure of Mr. Fox's health, and by the remoteness of the districts just named from the place of public worship. Still, their immediate consequences to Woburn were embarrassing or disastrous, and gave an apparent check to its previous prosperity, from which it did not fully recover for many years.

The separation of Wilmington from Woburn gave rise at once to numerous perplexing questions, respecting taxes for the ministry, paupers, and the undivided lands of Woburn that lay within the bounds of Wilmington. In one or two instances, these questions were settled by mutual agreement. But most of them were put to rest only by the decision of the judicial tribunals of the County, or by the positive refusal of Woburn to act upon the petitions of Wilmington in relation to them. For example, at the first town meeting held in Wilmington, October 20, 1730, a committee of three was appointed to attempt the recovery from Woburn of their proportion of Rev. Mr. Jackson's settlement money and first year's salary.[1] This had been assessed upon those inhabitants of Wilmington who belonged originally to Woburn, within a month after Mr. Jackson's ordination, and but

[1] Wilmington Town Records, Vol. I., p. 2.

little more than a year before their incorporation into a separate town. But as the money was assessed and demanded of them after they had petitioned to be erected into a distinct township, and while the General Court actually had their petition under consideration, they thought themselves fairly entitled to a reimbursement of what had been exacted of them under such circumstances. Accordingly, a petition to this end from Wilmington was exhibited at town meeting in Woburn, March 1, 1730–1, with a request that an article, correspondent to it, might be inserted in the warrant for their meeting in May. But this unwelcome petition was at once summarily disposed of. No sooner was it read, than the inhabitants of Woburn refused by vote to notice it in the warrant referred to; and the subject does not appear to have been ever brought before them by Wilmington again.[2]

In the mean while, the inhabitants of the precinct could not rest content with their newly acquired parish privileges, but aspired at those of a town, like those of their neighbors at Wilmington. At a precinct meeting, January 24, 1733–4 (which was less than four years after their legal separation from the First Parish), they chose a committee to apply to the Selectmen for a town meeting, to see if Woburn would consent to their being set off as a town by themselves, with their proportionate share in its lands, revenues, etc.[3] And so zealous were they for this measure, that within a little more than seven years from this time, two other committees were successively chosen by them with this end in view.[3] Whether the town was harassed with applications from each of these three committees does not appear from the Records. The petition presented by the one first elected, and laid before the town at a meeting February 19, 1733–4, received so much attention, that a committee of five was then chosen to confer with the Precinct Committee, and agree upon proposals to be acted upon at an adjourned meeting. But when the town came together at the adjournment, they negatived the precinct's request.[4] And though the scheme

[2] Wilmington Records, Vol. I., p. 2. Woburn Records, Vol. VII., p. 86.

[3] Precinct Records, Vol. I., pp. 49, 99, 119. [4] Town Records, Vol. VII., p. 165.

of being erected into a separate township was afterwards repeatedly revived in the precinct, yet it was without success till about the close of the last century.

All these and other like questions and petitions, arising out of the measures alluded to in the beginning of this chapter, were in themselves sufficiently annoying; and whether founded in reason and equity or not, yet being urged with zeal, and some of them with a persevering importunity, they must needs have been to the town a source of much perplexity and vexation.

But there were ill consequences to Woburn, growing out of Mr. Jackson's ordination, and the incorporation of Wilmington and the Second Parish, which were far more serious than those just mentioned.

One was, the well known unhappy dissension between the ministers of the First Parish, Rev. Messrs. Fox and Jackson, and the consequent division of their people into parties. On what precisely this dissension was founded, has not been transmitted for our information. Not improbably, Mr. Fox conceived early a personal dislike to Mr. Jackson, or took offence at something advanced in his preaching; and this was afterwards, perhaps, increased by viewing him as the occasion of diverting his people's affections and kind attentions from himself, and possibly, too, by Mr. Jackson's neglecting to show him all the respect and deference to which he thought himself entitled as the senior pastor.

But however the difference between them originated, it certainly commenced with Mr. Jackson's ministry at Woburn:[5] and, instead of diminishing as time progressed, and acquaintance with one another increased, it grew into a settled, thorough aversion; so that, as tradition says, they would not speak to each other in the pulpit. And this mutual alienation of these two professed servants of the Prince of peace, had a most baleful effect upon his cause in this place. Particularly, it became an occasion of division and bitter animosity among the people of their charge. Every man in the parish had his

[5] First Parish Records, Vol. I., p. 238. Petition.

preference for one minister or the other. And these partialities set the friends of each in hostile array against the friends of the other, and long made the town a scene of frequent strife and contention. An aged and very intelligent citizen of Woburn, now deceased,[6] once observed to me, that his parents used to tell him in his youth, that these parties far exceeded those which arose more recently in Rev. Mr. Sargeant's day, in their bitterness towards one another; so that when two opponents met in the street, both would often be ready to fight, before one would give the other the wall. With such feelings towards one another in the week time, it is not surprising, that they could not always worship comfortably together on the Sabbath; nor that the lamentable alienation of these two ministers, and its consequences upon their people, should furnish, as it eventually did, a successful plea for a further division of the First Parish into the First and Third.

Another most serious evil to Woburn, resulting from Mr. Jackson's ordination, and from the separation of Wilmington, and of the Second Parish from the First, was the increased difficulty of sustaining the ministry in the First Parish, and the consequent repeated and unsuccessful lawsuits with Mr. Fox. From 1716 to 1728, when the town was rapidly advancing, both in numbers and wealth, and Mr. Fox was its only minister, the burden of his salary was comparatively light; and, repeatedly during that period, the town, of its own accord, voted a handsome and continually increasing addition to his stated compensation, corresponding to the increasing depreciation of the currency in which it was paid. But as soon as the infirm health of Mr. Fox had made it evident that a new minister must be settled, and the prospect opened of the success of Goshen and Shawshin in their attempts at separation, the accustomed generosity of this people towards their aged minister ceased, and was soon followed by a seeming reluctance even to do him justice. For each of the years, 1729 and 1730, they granted him only £80, his nominal salary, paid in depreciated bills of credit;

---

[6] Mr. Bartholomew Richardson.

and in 1731 and 1732, when the incorporation of Wilmington and the Second Parish had left them with two ministers to maintain, and diminished means for doing it, they wholly neglected to raise any sum whatever for his support.

This ungenerous (not to say unjust) treatment of their senior pastor, was not, however, without plausible pretexts to palliate or excuse it, and perhaps, in the eye of some, to justify it. In 1704, when the town covenanted to give Mr. Fox an annual salary of £40 in money, and £40 in corn and other provisions at market price, paper money (then but recently introduced into the country) had fallen but little below its nominal value; and hence no clause was inserted in their contract with him, as there was afterwards in that with Mr. Jackson, providing against depreciation in the currency, and engaging to make his salary always as good as it was when first granted. Moreover, in regard to the continuance of that contract, it was expressly stipulated in it, that it was "to remaine so long as the said Mr John Fox shall continue and carry on the whole work of the Ministry in Woobourne:"[7] and, therefore, when blindness and sickness rendered him unable, for the time, to labor in his vocation, and Mr. Jackson was ordained as a colleague pastor to assist him, or supply his place, this contract became in law, strictly speaking, null and void. Hence, when the town voted him, in 1729 and 1730, £80 per annum in bills of credit, which had then sunk more than one-half below their nominal value,[8] the people still did as much as the letter of their contract required; and when they failed the two following years to grant him any salary whatever, they might still plead in their defence, with some color of reason, that they had broken no engagement: that their original contract with Mr. Fox had expired, and there was no other to fulfil.

This difficulty, arising from the failure of his contract, Mr. Fox seems to have anticipated with uneasiness, and to have

[7] Town Records, Vol. IV., p. 270.

[8] Felt on Massachusetts Currency, pp. 83, 135. "In 1710, Bills were worth at the rate of 8/ for an ounce of silver." "In 1730, Bills were in proportion of 21/, 20/, and 19/ for one ounce of silver."

objected, in view of it, to the ordination of Mr. Jackson as his colleague, unless the town would come into some new engagement with himself respecting his future support. For, at a town meeting, October 14, 1728, shortly after the inhabitants had given to Mr. Jackson a call to the ministry, and while they were treating with him about his settlement, they chose a large and highly respectable committee of nine, which was subsequently enlarged to thirteen, "to goe to the Rev$^{d.}$ Mr Fox to see if they can make things easy with him; and if there be need, they shall goe to some of the neighbouring ministers."[9] What the uneasiness of Mr. Fox was, which this committee was to attempt allaying, is no where explained in the Records. Possibly, it arose from the disaffection he had felt, from the beginning, towards Mr. Jackson, and the dreary prospect of being connected in the ministry for life with one whom he could not cordially approve. It is more likely, however, that his uneasiness was occasioned by anxiety respecting his support after Mr. Jackson should be settled, and his own contract should cease. But if this were so, this committee had no authority from the town to enter into any new engagement on their behalf with Mr. Fox respecting his compensation. All they were expected to do was, by fair words, to persuade him to waive his objections to Mr. Jackson's ordination for the present: and when that solemnity was over, the town would be left at liberty to act on this subject as it pleased.

But though the town's contract with Mr. Fox at settlement was now expired, and could avail him nothing to compel his people to pay him annually the salary stipulated therein, yet they were not released hereby in *equity* from all obligations to him. He was still their ordained, settled minister. No dismission from office had ever been asked on his part, or granted on theirs. No charge of immorality, no complaint of incompetency or unfaithfulness in the discharge of his ministerial duties had been alleged against him. He had labored for their good nearly thirty of the best years of his life, without complaint on their

---

[9] Town Records, Vol. VI., pp. 350, 351.

part, and apparently to their general acceptance: and now that the hand of God was upon him, afflicting him with weakness of body, and blindness of eyes, this surely was no valid reason for casting him off in his declining days, and turning him adrift on the world, to get his living as he could. Under the circumstances of his case, both the law of equity held them bound to make some competent provision for his support, and the then law of the land obliged them to do it.

Of these, his claims both in law and equity upon his people, Mr. Fox was well aware. And, therefore, having repeatedly remonstrated with them for their neglect, and waited patiently for the desired result without success, he was at length compelled, by his necessities, to commence a legal prosecution. In the spring of 1732, he entered a formal complaint with the Court of Sessions for this County, praying for their interference on his behalf. This received a hearing at Cambridge in July: and hereupon an Order of Court was duly issued for serving the Town Clerk of Woburn with a copy of Mr. Fox's complaint or petition, and for citing the town to appear and answer to it at their next session. At a town meeting in Woburn, November 2, 1732, called, apparently, on purpose to consider what should be done in the case, a motion was made by some for the choice of a committee to settle the difficulty with Mr. Fox, before any further proceedings of the Court were had: but the majority were for standing a trial. And, accordingly, Messrs. Josiah Johnson, Samuel Richardson and Jacob Wyman were chosen a committee on behalf of the town, "to answer the Revd Mr Fox's Complaint, [then] depending in Court, and to appeal, if they saw cause, from Court to Court," unto a final issue.[10] Both parties had a hearing before the Court of Sessions at Charlestown in December; and the case was decided in favor of Mr. Fox. The subjoined extract from the records of that Court, to which are added the names of the places where the Judges belonged) exhibits a concise view of Mr. Fox's complaint, of Woburn's defence by its committee, and of the judgment of the Court, with the grounds upon which it was based.

---

[10] Town Records, Vol. VII., p. 123.

"Middlesex ss. At his Majesty's Court of General Sessions of the Peace, begun & held for & within the County of Middlesex at Charlestown on the Second Tuesday in December, being the twelfth day of said Month Anno Domini One thousand seven hundred and thirty two, In the sixth year of His Majesty's Reign, By His Majesty's Justices of said Court:

"JONATHAN REMINGTON [Cambridge]
JONATHAN DOWSE, CHARLES CHAMBERS [Charlestown]
FRANCIS FULLAM [Weston]
JOSEPH BUCKMINSTER [Framingham]
THOMAS GREAVES [Charlestown]
FRANCIS BOWMAN [Cambridge]
ELEAZAR TYNG [Dunstable]
Esq^rs^. "Justices of Said Court."

"Upon reading the Petition and Complaint of the Rev. Mr John Fox of Woburn in the County of Middlesex, Clerk, Showing that whereas the Petitioner has been settled in the work of the Ministry in said Town for more than twenty eight years past, Which work and duty your Petitioner chearfully discharged in said Town for many Years, but God having in his Providence so ordered it that for more than four Years past the Petitioner has been labouring under great bodily pains and weakness, insomuch that he hath thereby been almost wholly taken off the duties of his function: And whereas there has been a neglect of the Inhabitants of said Town in makeing sufficient provision for the support of the Petitioner for some years past, Viz^t^. Seventeen hundred twenty nine & Seventeen hundred thirty, At or before which time the Contract between the Petitioner & said Town was expired, Allowing him but Eighty Pounds per Annum in Province Bills, as may be made to appear by Town Records: And whereas there has been a total neglect of makeing any Provision at all for the support and maintenance of the Petitioner for almost this year and half last past, Viz^t^. from the year Seventeen hundred thirty, Notwithstanding his repeated Applications for relief; the Petitioner with the greatest Concern and Sorrow is obliged from the most pressing Necessities as a Gospel Minister now to address the Court that they would consider his condition so far as to order him a Competent Allowance for his relief and maintenance as the Law has made provision for remedy & redress where such neglects have been, As by the Petition or Complaint on file: Which Petition was preferred at the Court of the General Sessions of the Peace holden by Adjournment at Cambridge on the first Tuesday of July last, When it was ordered that the Selectmen of Woburn be served with a Copy of the Petition by the Petitioner that they appear at the then next Court to shew Cause (if any they have) why the Prayer of the Petition should not be granted, When the Consideration of the Petition was continued to this Term:

"The Parties by their Attorneys now appearing, and after a full hearing of the Pleas and Allegations of the Petitioner together with the Answer of the Committee of the Town of Woburn, who Insist upon an Agreement made by the said Town with the Petitioner some time after his settlement amongst them, it appearing by the Confession of the said Committee that no Allowance has been made for the Support of the Petitioner since the fourth day of March seventeen hundred thirty thirty one, And that the Petitioner is & continues to be a Settled Minister in said Town, and was never as yet discharged therefrom, And that by the Providence of God, and for no other reason the Petitioner is disabled from dischargeing his Office as a Minister of the Gospel amongst them, And no Contract appearing (now in force) whereby any Support or Maintenance is provided for the Petitioner during such his Inability as aforesaid, or that can Enervate the force of the Law of this Province, enabling the Court of General Sessions of the Peace effectually to provide for the Support of Ministers not otherwise provided for: It's therefore Considered by the Court that the Sum of Eighty Pounds in Money or good Bills of Credit on this Province for the Year Seventeen hundred thirty one, As also the Sum of Eighty pounds in like money for the Year Current, Viz^{t}. Seventeen hundred thirty two be allowed to the Petitioner for his Support and Maintenance. And Ordered that a Warrant from this Court Issue out to the Selectmen of said Town requireing them forthwith to Assess the Several Sums before mentioned on the Inhabitants of said Town in manner & proportion as the Law in that Case provided doth direct, And Cause the same to be Levyed by the Constables of said Town by a warrant under the hands of the said Selectmen or of the Town Clerk by their Order, And that they pay the same unto the Petitioner on or before the first day of May next. Also that the Petitioner shall Recover and have of the said Town of Woburn his Costs of prosecution taxed at two pounds sixteen shillings & six pence." [11]

[11] Records of Court of Sessions for Middlesex, Vol. from 1723 to 1735, p. 291.

From this judgment of the Court of Sessions, the Committee for Woburn saw fit to appeal to the Superior Court of the Province. But their appeal was to no purpose. At the next session of the Superior Court, holden at Charlestown, January 30, 1732–3, both parties appearing, and being fully heard, the Court decided as follows: "It's Considered & Ordered by the Court, that the former Order or Judgment of the Court of General Sessions of the Peace be and hereby is confirmed with additional Costs of this Court." [12] Accordingly, the next month, £164 15*s.* 6*d.*, the whole amount recovered by Mr. Fox in this suit, including costs, was assessed upon all the inhabitants of Woburn in both Parishes, and then paid over to Mr. Fox, agreeably to Order of Court of Sessions.[13]

But now arose a new difficulty in relation to this subject. The inhabitants of the precinct felt aggrieved by the decision of the Court of Sessions, ordering them virtually (being inhabitants of Woburn) to be taxed for the years 1731, 1732, for the support of a minister of the First Parish, from which they had been set off upwards of two years.[14] And when they found that decision was confirmed by the Superior Court, and was actually being carried into execution, they resolved to apply to the Legislature for redress of this conceived violation of their corporate privileges. At a precinct meeting, March 7, 1732–3, it was voted, "that Lieut. Edward Johnson, and Ensign James Proctor be a Committee to address the Great and General Court in the name and behalf of the Inhabitants of said Precinct, that they may be dismissed from paying any part of the eight score pounds of money that the Court of General Sessions of the Peace ordered the town of Woburn to pay to the Reverend Mr Fox, one of the Ministers of the first parish in said Woburn."[15] This committee preferred a petition to the Legislature in June, 1733, which was read a second time, "together with the Answer of the first Parish in Woburn," August 16, of the same year. And both parties being heard

[12] Records of Sup. Court for Middlesex, kept at Boston, 1730—1734, leaf 230, p. 2.
[13] Town Records, Vol. VII., pp. 136–139.
[14] Precinct Records, Vol. I., p. 36.
[15] Precinct Records, Vol. I., p. 39.

thereon, the Court decided that the prayer of the petition should not be granted. The Court ordered, however, at the same time, that the Second Parish in Woburn should be "exempted from any charge in the maintenance of the Rev. Mr John Fox from the end of the year 1732"; throwing hereby, for the future, the whole burden of Mr. Fox's support, as well as of Mr. Jackson's, on the First Parish. In consequence of this order of the Legislature, the union which had subsisted hitherto from the beginning, in the ordering of the parochial and of the municipal affairs of Woburn, was now dissolved. All questions concerning the settlement and salaries of ministers, which, till this time, had been considered and determined in meetings of the town, were henceforth to be decided, as at the present day, in meetings of the several parishes or societies; and their votes respecting them to be registered, together with all ministerial taxes, in their own proper records.

The claims of Mr. Fox upon his people for a competent support had now been established both by the Legislative and by the Judicial authorities of the Province. Still, a majority of the First Parish of Woburn persisted to overlook or contest them. Nothing was raised in Parish meeting for his maintenance during four years, from March 1732. And the consequence was, two more complaints to the Court of Sessions by Mr. Fox, in 1734 and 1736;[16] and two more judgments by that Court in his favor; the former of which judgments was likewise confirmed, upon appeal, by the Superior Court.[17]

Thus, within the space of four years, the principal Religious Society in Woburn had three lawsuits with their senior pastor respecting his salary. But notwithstanding the great expense of these altercations, and the irritation and bitterness usually attendant upon such contests, the prevailing party in the parish was not yet quite satisfied. No money was raised for Mr. Fox at the annual meeting in March 1737; and hence another complaint was made by him to the Court of Sessions at Cambridge, in May. This complaint was subsequently withdrawn from Court, in pursuance of an accommodation effected between Mr. Fox and the

[16] First Parish Records, Vol. I., pp. 38, 63. [17] First Parish Records, Vol. I., pp. 47, 48, 71, 74.

parish at a meeting, where, happily more pacific counsels than usual prevailed.[18] But at the annual meeting in March of the next year, the old spirit of contention revived, and the claims of Mr. Fox were once more utterly disregarded. Within a few weeks, however, and apparently before there was opportunity for lodging another complaint with the Court of Sessions, a parish meeting was called, at the instance of certain peaceably disposed persons, to see what sums of money the parish would grant for the support of the Rev. Mr. Fox, or otherwise to "do that which may be to the satisfaction of the said Mr. Fox, and the peace and safety of the Parish." At this meeting, which was held May 15, 1738, the majority being well aware of the uselessness of contending with Mr. Fox in the law, had recourse to artifice to carry their point. They voted "that they would give the Reverend Mr John Fox seventy pounds in good passable Bills of Credit for the present year as a Gift, provided he will discharge the parish in full until the fourth of June 1738."[19] The motives which prompted this vote were obviously an unwillingness to own their obligations to him in equity, by granting him anything as salary; and also a desire to draw from him, unawares, an implicit acknowledgment that what he received from them was a gratuity, and not his just due. But their Fox was too cunning to be caught in the trap thus insidiously set. At their adjourned meeting, four days after, he sent them, by their committee appointed to inform him of the above vote, the following letter in reply.

"Woobourn May ye 19th. 1738.

"To the Freeholders and other Inhabitants of the First Precinct or Parish in Woobourn now convened at the meeting house: First. As to your late vote of the seventy pounds by way of Gift, I am always ready with thanks to acknowledge your goodness therein: And I shall receive it as a Gift, and no otherwise; but can by no means upon my receiving it, discharge the parish of my salary to the fourth of June 1738: which is the hard condition of the voted Donation.

"2ly. If you will allow me for this present year (which expires the fourth of June next ensuing) the sum of Eighty pounds as salary for my support, I will accept of it for the sake of peace, rather than contend in

---

18 First Parish Records, Vol. I., pp. 81, 82.
19 First Parish Records, Vol. I., pp. 99, 100.

the Law, and discharge the parish for said year. I can uprightly say it is very grievous to me that I should be any ways burthensome to my people, when I can be no more serviceable in the station in which God has placed me. I shall at all times be ready to serve you to the utmost of my power.

"3dly. As to the year coming on, I offer the parish to be at the charge of supplying the pulpit one half of the time, for the same allowance which of late you have made to the Rev. Mr Jackson, my Colleague.

"Thus praying that the God of peace would give you peace allways and by all means, I remain "Your affectionate Pastor

"JOHN FOX."[19]

Upon the reading of this letter, the same day it was written, the Parish voted, after some debate, to give Mr. Fox £75 for his support the then current year, if he would give them a discharge in full to its close on June 4th; and to this proposal, Mr. Fox appears to have afterwards consented, although the sum voted fell somewhat short of his offer.[19] And now commenced a remarkable change in the Parish for the better, in their treatment of their senior pastor. True, both church and parish saw fit to decline his offer to be at the charge of supplying the pulpit half the time that year for the same compensation they allowed Mr. Jackson. But in other respects, they showed themselves wonderfully compliant. Weary of fruitless contention with him in the law, disappointed in all their expectations of getting the advantage of him, and influenced too, it is probable, by respect for his age and the remembrance of his former usefulness, and by a returning sense of their obligations to him in equity, which recent unhappy occurrences had weakened or interrupted, they henceforth, for several years, and with apparent readiness, made honorable provisions for his maintenance. At March meeting, the year following, 1738–9, they granted him £80, in Bills of Credit; and this sum they gradually enlarged to £90, £95 and £100 of the same currency, in some measure corresponding to its constantly declining value. And this course, so honorable to themselves, they continued to pursue, till the separation of the Third Society from the First gave rise to new difficulties and distractions, and led to new arrangements for Mr. Fox's support, as there will hereafter be occasion to show.

But the contentions of Woburn with the ministers of its First Parish at that period were not yet at an end. Now that Mr.

Fox had passed the ordeal, Mr. Jackson's turn came next. At the time this gentleman was settled in Woburn, (viz: August 1729,) the town contracted to give him a salary of £120 per annum "in Bills of Credit, as the money now is"; or, as its vote on another occasion expressed it, £120 in Bills of Credit, "as they now pass."[20] These phrases, "as the money now is," and "as they now pass," in the town's contract with Mr. Jackson, or explanatory of it, were doubtless intended, and for years were understood to signify, that if there should be in future any further depreciation in the Bills of Credit in which Mr. Jackson's salary was to be paid, they would annually add enough to his compensation to make it equal in value to what it was at his settlement, in 1729. As was probably anticipated, these Bills continued from that date to decline from their nominal value.

No remuneration, however, on this account was either asked by Mr. Jackson, or offered by his people, till 1735. That year, at the request of Mr. Jackson, the Parish Committee called a meeting of the parish, to be held on the 1st of July, to consider and act upon the subject. To the warrant issued by them on this occasion, the preamble reads thus: "Whereas considering the great fall of the paper currency, or Bills of Credit since the year 1729, the year the Rev$^{d.}$ Mr Jackson settled in the work of the Ministry here, and he having never had allowance or consideration therefor, according to the vote then passed, relating to his annual support, that he should have 120 pounds per annum *as the money then was*," etc., etc., etc. These words of this preamble plainly show how the Parish Committee, and probably all Woburn, understood the provisions of Mr. Jackson's contract at that day.[21] At the meeting then called, it was voted (and, apparently, without debate or opposition) that Mr. Jackson should have £100 in Bills of Credit, as a recompense for their depreciation during the six years he had been settled in the place: and Mr. Jackson, being present, expressed his satisfaction with the grant, and did freely remit £20 of it to

[20] Town Records, Vol. VI., p. 350; VII., p. 11.
[21] First Parish Records, Vol. I., pp. 51, 52.

the parish. Similar grants, in view of the diminished and constantly diminishing value of the paper currency of that day, were made to Mr. Jackson the next four years, amounting in all to £140; and were all accepted by him in full satisfaction of his demands on this account. But here the harmony, which had hitherto subsisted between minister and people upon this subject, was, for a while, broken up. In a warrant for a parish meeting, December 7, 1739, respecting the two ministers, one article was, "To see whether the inhabitants of said parish will make the Rev$^{d.}$ Mr. Jackson's salary so good as it was when he first settled here in the Ministry, according to Contract," etc. At this meeting, after refusing to grant £50 for the purpose stated in the above article of warrant, the inhabitants finally voted "to give the Rev. Mr Edward Jackson forty & five pounds in good passable Bills of Credit the present year, besides his Annual Salary of one hundred and twenty pounds, provided he will discharge the parish for the present year."[22] This was a larger addition than they had ever raised before, for one year; and, if not a full equivalent for the depreciation which it was designed to compensate, could not have been far from it.[19] But it did not satisfy Mr. Jackson; and, when waited upon by a committee appointed at a parish meeting, March 24th, following, to acquaint him, officially, with what the parish had voted him, December 7th, before, and to inquire whether it would be acceptable, he sent the people word by them, immediately, that he did not accept it; and that he desired no more of them "than for them to make good their contract or agreement with him when he first settled amongst them in the work of the Ministry."[23] This tart, abrupt reply seems to have much irritated the inhabitants, who at once made choice of a committee to examine the contract made with Mr. Jackson at his settlement; to ascertain what the public Bills of Credit had depreciated since that time, and to make return to the inhabitants of the parish at their adjournment of this meeting. The committee selected for this purpose were Roland Cotton, Esq., Capt. Isaac Dupee, and

[22] First Parish Records, Vol. I., p. 124. Felt on Massachusetts Currency, p. 135.

Capt. Stephen Richardson, of which gentlemen it is proper to observe, that the first two were comparatively strangers, but recently settled in Woburn; and that the former of these two, Roland Cotton, Esq., chairman of the committee, was decidedly inimical to Mr. Jackson a few years afterward, and probably was so at the time of this appointment. The committee thus composed, instead of inquiring, as they were directed, how much the currency had fallen in value since the settlement of Mr. Jackson, seem to have set themselves at work to discover in his contract, if possible, some plea by which the parish might be released from all obligations to make him any allowance whatever on the score of depreciation. And the result of their labors they communicated to the parish at its adjourned meeting, April 7, 1740, in the following report:

"The Committee, to whom was referred the examination of the Contract or Agreement made by the Town of Woobourn with the Rev^{d}. Mr. Edward Jackson in September 1728 [1729?] relating to his support, having considered the same, Report as their opinion, that it was not the design and intention of that vote, to fix the Salary to a silver standard, but only to distinguish the Currency as it then was, from the Lawfull or Proclamation Currency at 6s. 10d. per ounce: Consequently, they intended to give but one hundred and twenty pounds Paper Currency, and are not obliged by said Contract to advance any more per annum.

"Yet the Parish being sensible of the depreciation of those Bills of Credit, have from time to time made an additional grant to the Rev. Mr Jackson by Contributions and other ways; which has been truly laudable: And we trust the Parish will still from time to time (as usual) encourage the heart and hands of the Rev^{d}. Mr Jackson, notwithstanding the great and pressing difficulties the Parish labours under (as well as the whole Province) for want of a medium.

"All which is humbly submitted.

"ROLAND COTTON
ISAAC DUPEE
STEPHEN RICHARDSON } Committee.[23]

"Woobourn April the 4th. 1740."

[23] First Parish Records, Vol. I., pp. 145–148.

The construction here put on the contract in question was palpably contradictory to the sense in which it had been understood in Woburn from the beginning, and which the parish had repeatedly put on it in their action within the last five years. But so vexed do the inhabitants appear to have been with Mr. Jackson at this meeting, for refusing to accept what they had voted him, December 7th, and for insisting upon a strict fulfilment of their contract, that they voted to accept the report of their committee, inconsistent as it was with their own declarations and doings upon record. Still, in accordance with the recommendation at the close of the report, they appointed a committee to wait on Mr. Jackson, "to know of him what (would) sattisfie him for the present year beside his annual salary"; and then adjourned to May 19th, to hear his answer.[23] At that adjourned meeting, what reply the committee brought from Mr. Jackson is not found upon record. After repeated motions, however, to add fifty-five pounds, and fifty pounds, to his stated compensation, it was at length voted to add £45, "in good passable Bills of Credit," for that present year, (ending August 1, 1740) on condition that he would discharge the parish to that time.[23] The meeting was then dissolved; and the parish Assessors proceeded, July 10th, to assess the addition of £45, voted as above, together with Mr. Jackson's stated salary of £120, without any notice from that gentleman of his satisfaction therewith. But Mr. Jackson well understood his rights; and not being willing to accept any sum whatever as a donation, (according to the late accepted report) which he could claim as his just and legal due, and especially one which he considered as coming short even of that, he entered a complaint with the Court of Sessions at Concord in August, and by their order, duly served the Parish Committee with a copy.[24]

When notified of this step of their pastor, the people perceived they were in an evil case. They well knew that the addition to Mr. Jackson's stated salary, which they had voted to give him, May 19th, though now assessed, had never been

---

[24] First Parish Records, Vol. I., p. 152.

acknowledged by him as satisfactory. And they were probably convinced too, now that their excited feelings had given way to calm reflection, that the interpretation which had lately been put upon their contract with him by their committee, and approved by their own vote upon Record, would not bear examination in a Court of Justice. They now, therefore, began to wish for an accommodation of their difference with their junior pastor, before any further proceedings were had upon his complaint. And, happily, at a meeting called to consider what should be done in their present situation, and held November 25, 1740, a mutual agreement between minister and people was harmoniously accomplished. The parish voted to add £15 to Mr. Jackson's stated salary of £120, for the year ending August 1, preceding, besides the £45 granted him May 19th, making his salary, in all for that year, £180 in Province Bills. And this sum, Mr. Jackson, who was present, signified his acceptance of, and promised, in consideration of it, to give a discharge to the parish for that year, and to withdraw immediately his complaint from Court. At the same meeting likewise, the parish voted the same addition to his stated compensation for the year which had commenced as for that which had recently ended.[25] And though an effort was made by some disaffected persons, at a meeting December 8th, to obtain a reconsideration of the above votes, under pretence that the meeting at which they were passed was illegal, yet it did not succeed.[25] And here was a termination of all differences between the First Parish of Woburn and Rev. Mr. Jackson respecting his salary, till the separation of the Third Parish in 1746. Henceforth till then, the Parish annually made additions of £60, £65, £80 and £100, Old Tenor, to Mr. Jackson's salary, originally stated at £120, in order, according to contract, to make it "as good as it was when he was first settled in Woburn."[26] And these additions were severally accepted by Mr. Jackson; and thus a lamentable and unedifying contention was amicably settled in a manner that was honorable to the parish, and conducive to the peace and usefulness of their junior pastor.

[25] First P. R., Vol. I., pp. 154, 156, 157. [26] First P. R., Vol. I., pp. 186, 188, 205, 206, 221, 234.

While Woburn, First Parish, was involved in these costly, unhappy contentions with its ministers about their salaries, and burdened with an additional weight of taxes, in consequence of the incorporation of Wilmington and the Second Precinct, the town found some relief in the sale of its two thousand acres at Turkey Hills, now Lunenburg, in the County of Worcester. Concerning this tract of territory, it has already been related, that though granted to Woburn by the General Court, in 1664, it was not located till 1717. But little was done respecting it for seven years after. At a general town meeting, May 15, 1724, the proprietors voted, "that it should lie as it does, until the town or proprietors of the same should see cause to alter it, or pass some other vote upon it."[27] Accordingly, for about ten years longer from this date, it lay in a state of nature, unimproved; and though the town was repeatedly called upon to pay taxes for it to Lunenburg,[27] yet it derived but little or no benefit from it, except occasionally from the rent of its meadows. Measures were taken, however, from time to time, to run its lines, and renew its bounds, and to prevent the spoliation of its timber; and a committee was appointed to take care of the land, and to prosecute any persons who might trespass upon it. But at a general meeting of the inhabitants, May 22, 1733, it was voted, "that the 2000 acres of land lying in Lunenburg should be put upon sale, and the interest of the money be improved for the use of the Town." Accordingly, a committee of five, viz., Mr. Josiah Johnson, Capt. John Fowle, Mr. Samuel Richardson, Lieut. Edward Johnson, and Lieut. Samuel Kendall, was then chosen to sell this land to the highest bidder, giving inhabitants of Woburn the first offer of it.[28] And, at a subsequent meeting, January 21, 1733–4, the town directed the committee to sell it altogether, in one body, and empowered them, or any three of them, to give a warrantee deed of it, in their capacity of town's committee; and voted, that the town (would) defend them in their so doing, they returning the interest of the purchase money to the use of the town, or sufficient security to the town's acceptance.[28]

In pursuance of these votes, three of the committee, viz: Mr.

[27] Town Records, Vol. VI., p. 196; VII., pp. 45, 140.
[28] Town Records, Vol. VII., pp. 151, 164, 165.

Josiah Johnson, Capt. John Fowle and Lieut. Edward Johnson, made on the day last mentioned, a conditional sale of the land to Ensign Israel Reed of Woburn, for £3,300, in Bills of Credit on the Province, eight respectable fellow-citizens offering to be his bondsmen.[28] The price for the land, and the security tendered by Mr. Reed for the payment of the money, were both accepted by the town at a meeting, February 19th, of the same year;[28] and the bargain was completed by the committee's giving a deed to Mr. Reed on the town's behalf. The purchase money for the land, viz: £3,300, in depreciated Bills of Credit, was worth in 1734, (the year of sale) about £1,100, lawful money, or $3,666.67, in the currency of the present day.[29] As portions of this sum were paid in, from time to time, by Ensign Reed, it was loaned by the committee to divers inhabitants of Woburn, chiefly, in sums of £100, to any two individuals, secured by their mutual or joint bond.[30] And as fast as the interest accruing from these loans, or from the portion of the purchase money still remaining in the hands of Mr. Reed, was received by the committee, or by Capt. Fowle, who was one of them, and also Town Treasurer, it was appropriated to the payment of taxes and town charges, by order of the town.[31] By this wise arrangement, a large proportion of the taxes in Woburn, for County and Province, and also of its town expenses of every description, were defrayed several years out of the proceeds from the sale of its 2,000 acres. For instance, it was voted at March meeting, 1735, to raise two rates for the payment of town debts and necessary charges; but, at a meeting in November following, that vote was reconsidered: the rates were never assessed, and the charges they were designed to meet, for schools, support of paupers, county tax, and a multitude of other expenses, were paid out of the town's interest money.[32] And from the same resource, was paid by order of the town, its Province tax for 1736, amounting to £244 15*s*. 0*d*. after it had been actually proportioned upon the inhabitants; as were likewise various other town expenses for the same year.[33]

[29] Felt on Massachusetts Currency, pp. 83, 135.

[30] Town Records, Vol. VII., pp. 218, 222.

[31] Town Records, Vol. VII., p. 219.

[32] Town Records, Vol. VII., pp. 242, 246.

[33] Town Records, Vol. VII., p. 250.

But where public money is intrusted to the care of individuals, it may always be expected that there will be many who will be watching them with a jealous eye; and some, who in their eagerness to be handling it themselves, will each think they know of one, at least, in whose care it would be safer and better managed than where it is. Though the committee who sold the two thousand acres, and had the charge of receiving and letting out the pay, took bonds of those to whom they loaned it, yet they were not under bonds themselves. For the purchase money being secured by Mr. Reed's sureties, and the money loaned being secured by joint bonds from the several borrowers, the town had not deemed it necessary to demand security of their committee likewise, so long as they regularly paid over, as they received it, the interest of the money they had loaned to the town's use. But this circumstance of their not being under bonds themselves for so large an amount (though expected to be put by loan into other men's hands, not to remain in their own) awakened the apprehensions of many who were, doubtless, unfeignedly anxious for the safety of the town's property, and afforded them, and some others at the same time, who were only watching for an opportunity to promote their own personal interest or influence, a handle for complaint.

In 1735, the very first year after the land was sold, an attempt was made, at May meeting, to choose a new committee to look after the £3,300 which the land at Lunenburg had been sold for, with the interest thereof. But such were the reputation and influence of the existing committee, so prudently had they loaned the portion of the purchase money which had been paid in to them, and so punctual were they to bring the interest which they were now just beginning to receive, to the treasurer for the town's use, that this motion to discharge them was negatived.[34] But the leaders in this effort, nothing baffled by defeat this year, renewed their attempt the next. In the warrant for May meeting, 1736, one article was, "To see whether the Town will choose a Committee to call in the money due to the town from Ensign Israel Reed: or to choose a Committee to take security

[34] Town Records, Vol. VII., pp. 198, 200.

from the Committee in whose hands the Town's Bonds are reposed?" But at that meeting, the majority were still so well satisfied with Mr. Reed's sureties, and so confident of the integrity of the present committee in their management of the town's property, that they passed over this article of the warrant without taking any action upon it.[35] But a continual dropping will wear away stones, and oft repeated insinuations against any individuals in a community, or persevering attempts to infuse jealousies and suspicions of them into the public mind, will hardly fail of making a disparaging impression at last, whether deserved or not. At a meeting, February 2, 1737–8, the town chose a committee of three, viz, Mr. John Russell, Jonathan Poole, Esq., and Mr. Jacob Wyman, "to see what circumstances the money that the 2,000 acres of land at Lunenburg was sold for, is under, and what security there is for the same," etc.[36] And in the warrant for the March meeting ensuing, one article was, "To hear the Report of this committee; and if the town shall think the security of the said money not to be good, to take better security of the standing Committee, if they will give it, or choose a committee that will give security to the town's acceptance by making a Return of the sale of said land to the Town in order to be recorded, and discharge the old Committee."[37]

In this article (a few words being transposed which are evidently misplaced upon the records, as they are here copied) it is plainly implied, that a return from the old or Standing Committee of their sale of the land, to be put upon record, would be deemed sufficient security for their faithfulness in the discharge of their trust. Accordingly, at the meeting, March 6th, such a return was actually made, accepted by the Town, and put upon record, subscribed by each member of the Standing Committee, with his own hand.[38] And yet, at the same meeting, (at the instigation doubtless of some whom nothing done by the old committee could reconcile or please) the town voted, "that the security given by the Committee (of trust) to the Town is not

[35] Town Records, Vol. VII., pp. 226, 227.

[36] Town Records, Vol. VII., p. 267.

[37] Town Records, Vol. VII., p. 276.

[38] Town Records, Vol. VII., p. 151.

sufficient." [39] And, at a subsequent meeting, May 19th, following, they chose a committee of nine, to whom, or to a majority of them, provided they gave security to the Town Treasurer to the Town's acceptance, they gave full power "to call in and take the charge of all the Town's money which the Two Thousand Acres of land lying at Lunenburg was sold for by the Town to Ensign Israel Reed"; and also, "full power to discharge the former Committee (viz: Mr. Josiah Johnson, Capt. John Fowle, and Lieut. Edward Johnson) upon their surrendering up said money." [40] The committee chosen for these purposes, were Jonathan Poole, Esq., Nathan Richardson, William Tay, Benjamin Johnson, Nathan Wyman, Ensign James Procter, Capt. John Fowle, Lieut. Edward Johnson, and Thomas Belknap, Jr.; [40] of whom, two, it will be observed, viz: Capt. Fowle and Lieut. Johnson, were on the original committee that sold the land. And now the grand question was, what shall be the security which the new committee should give? On this point, there was evidently much hesitation, and great division of opinion. A meeting was appointed, November 20, 1738, to decide this matter; but all which could be effected, was barely to vote that they would have security from their new committee for their money, and then to adjourn for a fortnight.

At the adjournment, it was determined, that "those persons that have the Trust of letting out the Town's £3,000 and £300 shall give personal Bonds with lawful Interest for the use of the Town, to a Committee that the Town shall appoint and their successors, and acknowledge their bonds, and said bonds to be recorded in the County Records." [41] A further adjournment was then voted to December 25, when it was probably ascertained that several members of the committee of nine chosen, and especially the two that had belonged to the old committee, would not accept the trust upon the conditions that had recently been prescribed. For, on that day, a new committee of nine was chosen, consisting of Jonathan Poole, Esq., for chairman, Josiah Peirce, Lieut. James Simonds, William Tay, Edward

---

39 Town Records, Vol. VII., p. 275.

40 Town Records, Vol. VII., pp. 282, 297.

41 Town Records, Vol. VII., p. 286.

Walker, Nathan Richardson, Benjamin Johnson, David Wyman, and Quartermaster Timothy Brooks. There was likewise chosen another committee of three, viz, Mr. Timothy Snow, Lieut. Peirson Richardson, and Mr. Nathan Wyman, which was to take bonds and good security, on behalf of the town of Woburn, of the committee of nine for the care and management of the town's money. The following votes were then passed by the Town for the direction of these, its several committees, on this subject:

1. That the committee of nine that day chosen "to receive the money or bonds of the old committee, (to wit, Mr. Josiah Johnson, John Fowle, Lieut. Edward Johnson,") shall have "full power to recover in the law the said bonds or money; and upon their receiving the said money and bonds of the old Committee aforementioned, then by a Receipt under their hands or the major part of them, fully to discharge the said Josiah Johnson, John Fowle, Mr Edward Johnson the aforementioned Committee and their heirs of the full sum of three thousand and three hundred pounds (and) the interest of the same, for which they the said Committee sold the land for, lying in the township of Lunenburg, for the town of Woburn.

2dly. "*Voted*, That the Receipt so given by the said Committee shall be laid upon record in the Book of Records for Woburn.

3ly. "*Voted*, That the above said Committee [of nine] shall upon their receiving the said money or bonds into their hands and under their care and charge, shall let it out unto the inhabitants of the town of Woburn, and that for no more than lawful interest.

4ly. "*Voted*, That the said Committee, upon their receiving the said money or bonds, shall give bond or bonds, to the value of three thousand and three hundred pounds with lawful interest to Mr Timothy Snow, Mr Peirson Richardson and Mr Nathan Wyman, trustees chosen by said town to receive the same, and keep them for and in behalf of the Town.

5ly. "*Voted*, That the bonds for the sum of three thousand and three hundred pound with the interest, given by the above said Committee to the above said Trustees, shall be for one year:" [that is, it is presumed, shall be recoverable in one year].

6ly. "*Voted*, That the said Trustees shall make return of said bonds so received by them for and in behalf of said Town, for the sum above mentioned."[42]

Such was the arrangement made by the town for the security of its money, about to be put into the hands of its newly appointed Committee. And had this arrangement been firmly adhered to, and insisted on by the town, this committee would have been effectually guarded against temptation to deviate from a strictly upright course, and been prompted by motives of interest, as well as of duty and honor, to manage their trust with a single eye to the public benefit. But men are not always willing to be dealt with themselves by the same measure that they would have others dealt by, under like circumstances. No sooner had the old committee been dismissed, upon the plea of insufficient security, and the new one chosen and had accepted, than the latter began to flinch at complying with the conditions of their office, to shrink and hold back from giving themselves such security as that, for the want of which they had raised such a breeze against their predecessors. Accordingly, they and their friends speedily combined to procure a relaxation of the strict terms of their appointment. At the same time, another party arose, which being disgusted with the hollow pretences and fruitless contentions on this subject, with which the town had been so long disturbed, was for procuring the dismission of all the committees in this affair, calling in the money, and distributing it among the several inhabitants of the town, or between the two parishes, according to their respective taxes.[43] But the former party prevailed.

At a meeting, February 21, 1738–9, after confirming its choice of the committee of nine, as a committee of trust to succeed the old committee, and renewing its grant to them of all necessary powers to this end, the town materially changed the security demanded of them at their election two months before. It allowed them to loan its money in the capacity of a town's committee only, without giving personal bonds; and required of them, beside being sworn to the faithful discharge of their trust,

[42] Town Records, Vol. VII., pp. 287, 288. [43] Town Records, Vol. VII., pp. 300, 338.

to give such security for the £3,300 as should be satisfactory to the town.[44] And the better to determine what that security ought to be, a committee was appointed, viz: Mr. Josiah Johnson, Capt. Isaac Dupee, Capt. John Fowle, Jr., Dr. Jonathan Haywood, Ensign James Procter, Mr. Nathan Blogget and Mr. John Russell, to prepare a draft in writing, which, being accepted by the town, should be entered in the Town Book.[44] This committee was expected to report at March meeting, then close at hand. But this expectation was doomed to disappointment. The committee, it seems, could not agree upon any report which the town might be thought willing to accept. And, when the time arrived for submitting their draft to its consideration, provision was suddenly made for substituting something very different in its stead. At that meeting, March 5, 1738–9, Mr. Roland Cotton, Capt. Isaac Dupee, Dr. Jonathan Haywood, Mr. James Procter and Mr. John Russell, were appointed to draft a resolution, by which all persons who should hire the town's Loan Money might be excluded from voting and acting in town meeting, in all questions respecting it. These gentlemen (all of whom, except the chairman, had been on the drafting committee, chosen at the preceding meeting) drew up on the spot the following resolution, which was immediately accepted by the town: "*Voted*, that in all votes touching or in any ways concerning the letting out or calling in of the said monies or security for said monies belonging to said Town, or the appointing committee men to manage the same, or in the removing or displacing of committees or any of them relating to said money or security, no person or persons that holds any part or parcell thereof, or hath taken any part or parcell thereof upon loan, shall have any vote or voice therein; [but] during the time of their being principal for the same or any part thereof shall be from voting debarred and excluded." [45]

This resolve sounds, in reading it, a very stringent one; and, could it have been executed, might have been effectual to answer the end intended. But the difficulty was, to execute it. There is not the least evidence that it was ever even attempted to be

[44] Town Records, Vol. VII., pp. 303, 304. [45] Town Records, Vol. VII., p. 308.

enforced. And when it is considered (as a credible tradition to be referred to hereafter, gives too much reason for supposing) that a large proportion, if not a majority of the voters in town affairs, eventually became debtors to the town for larger or smaller sums of its loan money, it is easy to see how this resolution, so forcible in words, should become a mere dead letter on the Records, utterly impracticable in Woburn at that day. And thus the several provisions made by the town for its security, in respect to the money for its two thousand acres, while in the hands of its new or second committee, were virtually rendered, one after another, null and void. The several members of that committee were pledged, as was understood at their appointment, to give personal bonds for their fidelity in the management of the town's money intrusted to them: but they, or their friends for them, had contrived to evade this obligation, by procuring the substitution of easier terms in its stead. They were ordered to be sworn to the faithful discharge of their trust; but there is no notice on the Records that an oath, to this purpose, was ever administered to them. They were required to give such security as a committee, chosen expressly for this end, should agree upon, and as the town, when it was submitted to them, should accept. But, for reasons that can only be conjectured, that committee never reported. A second committee was then appointed for drafting such security, which did report. But the resolution which they recommended, and the town accepted, was such, that while it bound in words both the committee which let the town's money, and the inhabitants who borrowed it, appears to have been found impracticable to be executed; unequal to hold or restrain either the lenders or the borrowers of the money to be secured. And thus, notwithstanding all the noise and bluster with which, for four years, the town had been agitated about getting better security for the money arising from the sale of the town's land at Lunenberg than the committee who sold it had given, the town was not a whit better off than before. The new committee of nine gave no better security, in effect for their fidelity, than the old committee of three had done, which had been displaced to make way for it. The only difference was, that the responsibility which had once been borne by three, was now divided between nine; and whereas the former committee had given all the security that was originally asked of them by the town, the latter committee had contrived, themselves, or by their friends, to get rid of, or to nullify that which had been successively demanded of them, and which, by not declining at their appointment or confirmation in office, they had virtually agreed, in good faith, to give.

And now the new committee of trust, (or at least, as many of them as saw fit to accept,[40]) being firmly established in their office, and furnished by the town with all requisite powers for the discharge of it, went to work. To this time, the proceeds of the sale of the 2,000 acres, consisting principally of bonds for a portion of the purchase money still due from Ensign Reed, and of bonds for loans to inhabitants of Woburn of moneys received from him, had remained in the hands of the original committee. At a general meeting, Febuary 21, 1738–9, the town by vote ordered that committee to deliver up those bonds and whatever money they had of the town's, into the hands of the new committee.[46] But for some reason, now unknown, they demurred about doing it, and in consequence of their delay, the new committee instituted a suit at law against them, before the Court of Common Pleas for Middlesex, at its session in Concord, the following August. At the trial, the plaintiffs, in the name of the inhabitants of Woburn, alleged that the defendants had often refused and, still continued to refuse, giving them a reasonable account of the money they had received for the land which they had been commissioned to sell for the town's use; and laid the damage at £4,000. On the other hand, the defendants, by their attorney, William Brattle, Esq., averred, that they always had been, and now were ready to account with their employers in this matter. Upon this

[40] Town Records, Vol. VII., p. 282. All of the committee of nine first chosen not accepting, another committee was appointed containing some new names; which see pp. 297, 303. And it subsequently appeared that two or three of those never acted with the rest.

[46] Town Records, Vol. VII., pp. 297, 303, 304.

declaration, the Court appointed Samuel Danforth, Esq., of Cambridge, Thomas Jenner, Joseph Lemmon, and Samuel Cary, Esqrs., of Charlestown, and Judah Morris, the celebrated Jewish convert to Christianity and teacher of Hebrew in Harvard College, or any three of them, as "Auditors of the Account, in this Action, and ordered that the Defendants account before the said Auditors accordingly: and the Action was continued to (the December) Term for their Report." At the session of the Court at Charlestown, in December, the Auditors reported, "that having heard the Parties and examined their papers, they find that there is due to the Inhabitants of the Town of Woburn from the said Committee, the Defendants, three thousand three hundred pounds for Principal, and two hundred thirty seven pounds seven shillings for Interest to this day, in the whole, three thousand five hundred thirty seven pounds seven shillings; which with eight hundred ninety five pounds thirteen shillings they have paid in to the Town Treasurer, and seven pounds now allowed them with fourteen pounds formerly paid them by the Town, is in full for their trouble in *viewing*, selling the Land, and letting out the Money; which several Sums before mentioned we judge to be in full of all dues and demands from the Defendants to the Inhabitants of the Town of Woburn."

This Report, subscribed by Thomas Jenner, Joseph Lemmon and Judah Morris, Auditors, the Court accepted, and ordered it to be recorded; and decided upon the Action as follows: "that the Inhabitants of Woburn aforesaid recover against the said Josiah Johnson, John Fowle and Edward Johnson the sum of three thousand five hundred thirty seven pounds seven shillings money Damage, and Costs of Suit with the charge of Auditing, the whole whereof taxed at twenty eight pounds seven shillings & six pence." [47] From this judgment, the defendants appealed to the next Superior Court for the County. But their appeal was to no purpose. Within a few days after the decision of the Inferior Court, Mr. Josiah Johnson, chairman of the old committee, died.[48] And from his heirs and from the two surviving

[47] Records of Inferior Court at Cambridge; December, 1737 — August, 1740, p. 557.

[48] Records of Births and Deaths in Woburn.

members of that committee, Capt. Fowle and Dea. Edward Johnson, of the Precinct, there was afterwards recovered in the law, for damage and costs, the increased sum of £3,623 11*s*. For this large amount, settlement appears to have been made by the old committee shortly after, by delivering up the bonds and all other property of the town in their hands to the new committee; who accordingly stand recorded as responsible to the town for it, in the Town Book, June 18, 1741.[49]

From the last mentioned date, June 18, 1741, when the new committee had obtained the entire control of the town's money for their 2,000 acres, they seem to have managed it for some time to general satisfaction. The sum taken into their hands, amounted, it was just observed, to £3,623 11*s*. From this deducting £87 14*s*. allowed them by the town for lawyers' fees, and their own time and expenses in attending Court during their suit against the old committee, there remained £3,535 17*s*. to be disposed of by them for the benefit of the town. Of this sum, £3,300 constituted a permanent Loan Fund for the benefit of the town, from the proceeds of the sale of its land in Lunenburg, and now consisted principally of bonds given jointly and severally by individuals for money they had unitedly borrowed from it upon interest, in sums not exceeding £100 each.

The residue, £235 17*s*. seems to have been an accumulation of interest, which had been received by the old committee; and which, being now paid into the treasury of the town, and added to so much of the interest annually due upon the bonds, as the new committee collected and paid, proved sufficient, several years, for defraying all the usual town and county expenses, and saved the necessity of assessing any tax in Woburn for ordinary purposes, except the Province tax, till February 1746-7.

But now the new committee became gradually very dilatory and backward in collecting and paying in the interest due on the town's loan money intrusted to their care. As the Treasurer's book shows, they were accustomed to pay portions of this

---

[49] Town Records, Vol. VII., pp. 371, 372.

interest every year, but, generally speaking, not till it had been due above a twelvemonth; and then in such partial payments, as all of them together did not satisfy the just claims of the town. The failure of the committee in this respect was doubtless owing, in a very considerable degree, to the depreciation of money then prevalent. Province Bills of Credit, in which the interest money from the loan fund was wont to be paid, were not worth so much in 1741, when the committee took that fund into their charge, as they were in 1734, when the land in Lunenburg was sold, and the fund was established from the proceeds of its sale; and this, their diminished value, was continually diminishing.[50] To remove the difficulty, which this constant depreciation must obviously occasion, both to the committee who had the charge of the loan money, and to those who were indebted to them for loans from it, the town, at a meeting, August 27, 1744, voted, that "the Town will not require the Sink of their Money in the hands of the present Committee, neither shall the same be required by the said Committee of those who have said Money in their hands, untill further order from the Town."[51] But this vote (which proved in the end a virtual relinquishment of the fund itself, for the sake of securing the prompt payment of the interest due upon sums loaned from it) did not answer the end intended. While it greatly facilitated the action of the committee in collecting and paying up the interest due to the town, it did not effect any material change for the better in their management on this head. With some honorable exceptions, they still made but partial payments of the interest coming to the town from its loan fund; and were generally a year or more behind hand in doing this. This remissness caused much vexation and uneasiness, and great loss to the people of Woburn. It obliged the town to have recourse once more to taxation (from which, through aid from its loan fund, it had been for several years in good measure free,) for defraying its common necessary charges. It became at length a matter of

[50] Bills in 1734 were in the proportion of twenty-four shillings to one ounce of silver; from 1741 to 1744, as twenty-eight shillings to one ounce; and in 1745, as thirty-five shillings to an ounce of silver in value.—See *Felt on Massachusetts Currency*, p. 135.

[51] Town Records, Vol. VII., p. 451.

public, serious complaint in town meeting; and for a series of years, this community was much occupied in devising, and in some instances adopting, a variety of measures for correcting the negligence of the committee in this matter, and for remedying the inconveniences and troubles which it occasioned. But such were the intrinsic defects in these measures themselves, or the difficulty of carrying them in town meeting, in the face of the opposition which they excited, or the lack of energy or decision in those who were appointed to carry them into effect, or the strong influence exerted to thwart or defeat their execution, that little or nothing was accomplished by them. For instance, (to notice some of these measures in a brief, summary way,) at a town meeting, March 6, 1748–9, the town treasurer was ordered to sue each committee-man at the law, who failed to pay in the interest coming from him, within a year from the time it became due; but this was a delicate business, which the treasurer seems to have been averse to meddling with; and so nothing was done.[52]

It was proposed in the warrant for a meeting, May 22, 1753, to choose a committee to inquire, why the interest of their loan money was not paid in, agreeably to vote of the town? But when the town came together, the article was dismissed, and no inquiry was made.[53]

Again, the town ordered the committee, May 13, 1754, to reduce every bond in their hands to lawful money which had not been reduced before, and then to sue it, unless the interest due on it were paid before the next Inferior Court; but this severe expedient proved, eventually, to be a mere empty threat; or if actually tried, it was without success.[54]

Again, at a meeting, May 12, 1757, the town empowered and directed its treasurer to demand forthwith, of the committee for its Loan Fund, the interest then due from it to the town; and in case of neglect to pay, to sue immediately for the principal, held by each delinquent. But there is no evidence that this order was ever complied with by the Treasurer.[55]

---

52 Town Records, Vol. VIII., p. 16.

53 Town Records, Vol. VIII., pp. 104, 106.

54 Town Records, Vol. VIII., p. 131.

55 Town Records, Vol. VIII., p. 205.

Furthermore, it was once and again proposed to discharge the present committee upon their delivering up the town's property in their care, and then to elect a new committee, or appoint the Town Treasurer for the same trust. But in each instance, the article of the warrant suggesting such change, was either dismissed, or adjourned from one meeting to another, till the design was dropped, and the old committee were still allowed to retain their office.[56]

And finally, a committee of three, viz., Josiah Johnson, Esq., James Fowle, Esq., and Mr. Isaac Snow, was appointed, March 1764, to settle all accounts with the committee for the town's loan money; and in the warrant for May meeting, the same year, one article was, to see whether the town would accept that committee's report? But in the Record of this meeting, a profound silence is observed on this subject; and it does not appear whether the committee ever presented the expected report, or whether it was ever acted upon or not.[57]

In the mean while, changes, from various causes, were taking place in the committee. Three of the nine originally appointed, viz., Messrs. Edward Walker, Josiah Pierce, and Lieut. James Simonds, do not appear to have ever accepted the trust; or if they ever acted with the rest, they did so but for a little while. Capt. Benjamin Johnson was displaced by the town in 1756, and Mr. Nathaniel Brooks put in his room. Death also was beginning to do his work, and to compel some of them to pay the debt of nature, if they could not, or would not, their dues to the town. Jonathan Poole, Esq., chairman of the committee, died about 1755; and Mr. David Wyman about 1762; and Mr. Oliver Richardson and Capt. Benjamin Wyman were chosen respectively to supply their places. And these changes, and the prospect of others like them, seem to have combined with other circumstances to rouse the town at last to efficient action.

At a general meeting, May 18, 1767, it was voted, "that the Town's Loan Money that is in the hands of individuals, and the hands of the Committee, should be transferred into the hands of

---

[56] Town Rec., Vol. VIII., pp. 331, 333, 337, 338. [57] Town Rec., Vol. VIII., pp. 394, 400, 401.

the town treasurer for the use and benefit of said town." A committee also was chosen at the same time, consisting of Capt. Benjamin Johnson, Josiah Johnson, Esq., and Lieut. Samuel Thompson, to assist the treasurer in receiving the town's money of the loan committee, "and taking good security for the same." "Voted also that the Treasurer, and the Committee chosen to assist said Treasurer, be and are hereby authorized and empowered to reckon and settle with the said Committee that has said town's Loan Money in their hands, and said Treasurer to give them a Discharge for their trust in that affair."[58] And at May meeting, the following year, the same gentlemen were chosen and empowered by the town as a committee "to reckon and settle with Deacon Nathan Richardson, Lieut. William Tay, Capt. Timothy Brooks, Mr Oliver Richardson, Mr Nathaniel Brooks, and Capt. Benjamin Wyman for their service and trouble as Committee men for the Town's Loan Money, and make each of them such allowance for their service as they can agree with them for, not to exceed one penny upon the Pound per year, and take a receipt of each and every of them; that so the town may have a full discharge from each and every of them from any further demand that either of them can have upon the town for said service, and Report at the next town meeting."[59]

Here seems to be the winding up of the office of committee for the Town's loan money. Henceforth, its trust and duties devolved upon the Town Treasurer, Eleazar Flag Poole, Esq. At March meeting, 1770, the town directed this gentleman "to sue all those bonds for (its) Loan Money that is (are) not changed into Lawfull money, at the next Inferior Court in the County of Middlesex; he first advising with the Selectmen before he puts said Bonds in Suit."[60] In pursuance of these orders, Mr. Poole commenced, that year and the next, five lawsuits in the Inferior Court; in all which, he recovered his demand on the town's behalf, with costs.[61] In two of these suits, however, Joshua Richardson, the defendant, ventured to

[58] Town Records, Vol. IX., p. 38.

[59] Town Records, Vol. IX., p. 64.

[60] Town Records, Vol. IX., p. 106.

appeal to the Superior Court, and gave bonds to prosecute his appeal.[61] But at a session of that Court in Charlestown, April 14, 1772, he failed to appear: upon which the Court, at the prayer of Mr. Poole, confirmed the judgment of the Lower Court, with additional damages and costs.[62] At March meeting, 1772, that gentleman stated, in his account for the preceding year, then rendered, (attested by the Auditing Committee, and afterwards accepted by the Town,) that he had received as principal of the loan money, £76 0*s.* 3*d.*, and as *interest* for the same, £5 15*s.* 7¾*d.*, total received, £81 15*s.* 10¾*d.*; and that there was still due to the town, as principal, £30 13*s.* 04*d.*, and as interest to March 12, 1772, £8 16*s.* 5*d.*; and also, that by a receipt he had, it appeared that there was still in the hands of Nathaniel Brooks, of the town's loan money, £2 2*s.* 4*d.*, as principal, and £1 18*s.* as interest, in all, £43 10*s.* 1*d.*, due to the town on this account.[63] At May meeting, 1772, an attempt was made to prevail with the Town to remit to certain individuals a portion of what they owed, on account of the loan money, or grant them a longer time to pay their dues in; but, to both these proposals, the Town voted a positive refusal.[64] And at a general meeting, June 15, of the same year, the Treasurer was ordered, by vote of the town, "to put in prosecution the conditional note he (had) in his hands, relative to a part of the (town's) Loan money, given to him by Mr James Wyman"; and also, "to prosecute the Receipt he (had) in his hands, that was given by Mr. Nathaniel Brooks and Mr. David Wyman to Mrs. Esther Poole deceased, relative to said town's Loan money."[65] But on account of some acknowledged illegality in this meeting, the above orders were rendered void, and never afterward renewed. Weary of contending for years about their loan money, and discouraged by the failure of their numerous past efforts to get the management of it again into their own hands, till they saw there was comparatively but little to contend for, they ceased from this time to make it a subject of discussion and action in town meeting; and the

---

61 Records of Court; communicated by Lorenzo Marrett, Esq., of East Cambridge.

62 Records of Superior Court, 1772, leaf 50, 2d page.

63 Treasurer's Book, p. 266.

64 Town Records, Vol. IX., p. 164.

65 Town Records, Vol. IX., p. 168.

events which immediately led to the Revolutionary War soon diverted their attention another way; and their remaining claims for the loan money were speedily forgotten or overlooked.

It is melancholy to witness so large and productive a fund as the Woburn Loan money once constituted, and one that promised originally to be of so great and lasting utility, frittered away in the course of a few years into nothing; and curiosity may incline many to inquire the cause. When that fund was created, at the sale, in 1734, of Woburn's 2,000 acres in Lunenburg, it was worth £3,300, in Massachusetts Bills of Credit. As these Bills then passed at the rate of twenty-four shillings for an ounce of silver at eight shillings, or sixty shillings for two and one-half ounces of silver, equal to twenty shillings, or one pound; the whole value of the fund at its commencement was £1,100, lawful money.[66] In 1741, when the new committee recovered in the law the Loan stock from the old committee, and took the entire charge of it into their hands, the Bills of Credit being then valued at twenty-eight shillings for an ounce of silver,[66] the worth of the fund was diminished to £942 6*s*. But so rapidly did they decline in worth between 1745, 1749 and 1750, that in the two years last named, they had sunk into what was called Old Tenor currency, in which an ounce of silver was reckoned an equivalent for sixty shillings in Province Bills.[66] The committee, aware of the tendency of the money in their care to depreciate, became alarmed, it seems, in 1744. But the town relieved them of their apprehensions, by voting, at a meeting in August 1744, not to exact of their committee "the sink of their money" in the payment of interest accruing upon it, and directed them at the same time not to exact it of those to whom they had loaned it.[67] And now the disastrous effect of the depreciation of the currency upon the Woburn Loan Fund began strikingly to show itself. From 1745, down to 1750, inclusively, when Old Tenor money became no longer a legal tender, and lawful money

---

66 Felt's Massachusetts Currency, p. 135. 67 Town Records, Vol. VII., p. 451.

was substituted in its stead, all payments into the treasury, whether of principal from the Loan Fund, or of interest into it, were in Old Tenor; and thus it continued to be for several years after. For instance, when the town voted, in 1761, to take from its Loan Fund £200, Old Tenor, or its equivalent in lawful money, to pay to Medford, in fulfilment of its agreement, in order to be released in future from all obligation to help maintain Medford Bridge, the whole sum taken from the fund for this purpose was only £26 13*s.* 4*d.*, lawful money.[68] And the full amount of interest paid into the Treasury, by Lieut. William Tay, one of the new Committee, for the portion of the Loan Fund in his care, which had for a series of years been £33 0*s.* 0*d.*, Old Tenor, was reduced to £4 8*s.* lawful in 1749.

In each of these two instances was a depreciation of Province Bills, reckoned in Old Tenor, of £7 10*s.*, for £1 lawful money. Computed by this standard, the whole Loan Fund of Woburn, viz, £3,300, as it was originally, and as it was when taken in charge by the new committee in 1741, was worth, in 1750, only £440 lawful money. Here then, we see the main cause of the constantly diminishing value, and final ruin of Woburn Loan Fund. This sad issue is not to be imputed to the incapacity of the second committee, who had the charge of the fund while its depreciation was principally going on; for there were among them, men highly esteemed for their business talents, as well as integrity and moral worth. It was not the result of their defrauding the town of any portion of its Loan Money, either interest or principal. For the Treasurer's Records exhibit numerous and constant payments by them of the interest of the fund committed to their management, so that a sum less than £10 of the interest accruing upon the fund, remained unpaid at the final settlement of the Treasurer, in 1772. And although their customary failure to pay the interest, till a year had elapsed after it became due, was a source of loss to the town, and of much disappointment and vexation, yet even this failure doubtless arose, in most cases, from the failure of those to whom they had loaned the

[68] Town Records, Vol. VIII., p. 466.

money to pay the interest as it had become due. And as to the principal of the fund, the Treasurer's Records credit the committee with numerous payments of it, between 1761 and 1767, amounting in all to £337 18*s.* 9*d.*, which being added to £76 0*s.* 3*d.*, that the Treasurer himself received, according to his final account, March 1772, after the fund was intrusted to his care, and the £32 15*s.* 8*d.*, of the principal, which he then claimed to be due, amounted to £446 14*s.* 8*d.*, a sum little exceeding that, when the whole fund, in passing from Province Bills to Old Tenor currency, and from that to lawful money, was then accounted to be worth.

The final loss then of Woburn Loan Fund must be regarded as one of the unhappy consequences of issuing, by the Government of Massachusetts, Bills or Notes as money, without a suitable care promptly to redeem them, and thus keep up their credit. This was a very common way of producing money at the commencement of the last century, which the Legislature was in a manner constrained by circumstances to resort to, and which the people themselves were very reluctant should be given up. But the more of these Bills were issued, the greater became the general distrust of them; they continually diminished in value; and the consequence of their depreciation (to say nothing of a great increase of crime and moral evil) was a multitude of losses and calamites both to individuals and to communities at large.

CHAPTER X.

Establishment of Third Parish.—Installation in it of Rev. Josiah Cotton.—Erection of Third Meeting-house of First Parish, and disposal of the Second.—Action at Law of Rev. Edward Jackson against Rev. Mr. Cotton for a Libel.—Death and Character of Rev. Mr. Jackson.

In the chapter preceding, some account was given of the unhappy difference between the two ministers of the First Society in Woburn, Rev. Messrs. Fox and Jackson, and of the consequent alienation of their respective friends from one another. This alienation gradually increased, so as to become the occasion, in 1746, of a secession from the First Parish, and of the legal establishment of a Third Society in the town, commonly distinguished at that day by the title of the "Separatists' Society." The measures for effecting this separation commenced with the friends of Rev. Mr. Fox, who handed in a petition to the Parish Committee, August 31, 1745, requesting them, for reasons therein declared, to call a parish meeting, and to insert in their Warrant for it the prayer of the petitioners, that they and those who might join them within a reasonable time might be allowed by the parish to be set off "a separate & distinct society"; and that they, their families and estates, might be henceforth excused from paying anything toward the maintenance of Rev. Mr. Jackson.[1] This petition, after some consideration, the Parish Committee refused to grant. Whereupon, a petition was presented, September 16, to Hon. Samuel Danforth, Esq., one of the justices for the County of Middlesex, subscribed by Roland Cotton, Jonathan Poole, John Fowle, Ebenezer Flegg, and Joshua Sawyer, setting forth the denial which the petition, subscribed by them and others, had met with from the Parish Committee, and praying him to grant his warrant for calling a parish meeting for the purposes mentioned in that petition.[2] In pursuance of this application, Justice Danforth issued

[1] Parish Records, Vol. I., p. 235.

[2] Parish Records, Vol. I., p. 236.

his Warrant for a parish meeting, to be held September 30, "for the purpose of choosing any parish officers that might be judged necessary; and of considering the petition of sundry of the Freeholders of said Parish, as above expressed." At the meeting thus obtained, it was voted, first, not to choose any new officers; and, then, after adjourning one hour for further consideration, "It was put to vote, whether the Inhabitants would dismiss those Petitioners, according as is set forth in their Petition? and it passed in the negative, that they would not." [3]

In the mean while, the Parish Committee had stolen a march upon the petitioners, with a view either to check them in their attempts at separation, or to extort from them as much aid as possible for the benefit of the parish, before they could be legally set off. During the four years immediately preceding this, three unsuccessful attempts had been made to obtain a vote of the parish to build a new meeting-house, or to repair the old one. The proposal to build had been uniformly negatived; and forty shillings was all the parish would grant to repair.[4] But, suddenly, an entire change of mind on this subject took place. On the 18th of September, this year, (only two days after the date of Justice Danforth's warrant for calling a Parish meeting, to see if the parish would dismiss certain members thereof, that they might become a distinct society,) the parish committee issued a warrant for a parish meeting, to be held on the 26th of September, four days before the meeting called by Justice Danforth. And, at that meeting, after granting the salaries of the two ministers for the current year, the Parish voted to build a new meeting-house as soon as they conveniently could; granted £1,000, Old Tenor, for the purchase of materials, and chose a committee of five for carrying on the work.[5]

And now the petitioners, baffled and irritated by these impolitic, overbearing proceedings of the majority of the parish, and confirmed more strongly than ever in their purpose to get off from it, if possible, apply to the Legislature for redress in the following petition: —

---

[3] Parish Records, Vol. I., p. 237. [4] Parish Records, Vol. I., pp. 167, 205, 218.
[5] Parish Records, Vol. I, p. 234.

"Province of the Massachusetts Bay.

"To His Excellency William Shirley, Esq$^{r.}$ Captain General and Commander in chief in and over the Province of the Massachusetts Bay, the Honourable the Council and House of Representatives, in General Court assembled December y^{e} 11th. 1745:

"Humbly shew the Subscribers, Inhabitants of the First Parish in Woburn;

"That they preferred a Petition to the Committee of the said Parish on the 31st. of August last, setting forth, that the Reverend Mr Edward Jackson had been settled in the Ministry in said Town about sixteen years, ever since which there has been an unhappy and unaccountable difference between their senior Pastor the Rev^{d} Mr John Fox and the said Mr Jackson; and notwithstanding the earnest endeavours of many well disposed Ministers and other Christian Brethren to reconcile these two ministers, and induce them to live together as Ministers and Brethren ought to do, yet that this alienation of affection evidently continues to this day, greatly to the prejudice of Religion in this Parish, and the best welfare of ourselves and Families whilst we remain in these very distressing circumstances: we therefore earnestly desired and requested them to call a Parish meeting according to law, and insert in their warrant that it was the Prayer of us the Subscribers and our Associates that should join to us in a reasonable time, to be allowed by the Parish to be set off a separate and distinct Society, that we our Families and Estates might be for the future excused from paying anything toward the maintenance of the said Mr Edward Jackson; and we did in the said Petition engage to the said Parish, that for the promotion of peace and that we and our families might have the precious and invaluable liberty of worshiping God without confusion and disorder, or any uncharitable reflections upon each other, that we would take upon ourselves our proportionable part of the charge of supporting and maintaining the Reverend Mr John Fox, who is the Senior Pastor of that (this) Church and Parish, and who is in justice entitled to as much or more salary than the younger Pastor, although by the Providence of God he is taken off from the publick ministerial performances; and consequently we must be at the charge of settling another; yet we were heartily willing, though but very unable to be at the extraordinary charge; as we were very sensible this method would tend to restore Peace to the Parish, and (by the Blessing of God) to promote the future Happiness of ourselves and Families here and hereafter.

"That the said Parish Committee, as we are informed, met twice after the Petition was presented, but did not see cause to call a Parish Meeting agreeable to our reasonable Request, which obliged us to apply to one of His Majesty's Justices of the Peace according to Law, who issued a warrant on the 16th of September last requiring the Freeholders & others qualified according to Law to meet together to consider our Petition the 30th — following: which when the Parish Committee perceived, they suddenly met together, as we were informed, and issued their warrant for a meeting to see whether the Parish would build a new Meeting House, and directed the Inhabitants to meet the week before the Parish meeting ordered by the Justice, and would not insert our Petition in their Warrant; and when they met together, they (as we apprehend, to baffle, distress and discourage us from our honest & just design of being a distinct Society and living peaceably together, and to render us unable to build a decent meeting house for the publick worship of God) voted to raise a large sum of money towards building themselves a meeting-house, though your petitioners who were present, and sundry others, entered their Protest against such a vote being put, forasmuch as the warning for said meeting was exceeding short, and a great number of the voters being absent; and further at the meeting appointed by the order of the Justice the week after, the Parish unreasonably refused to grant the Prayer of your Petitioners, as by the Records will appear.

"Now may it please your Excellency and Honours, as these Proceedings manifestly tend to distress your Petitioners, and prevent their enjoying Gospel privileges in Peace and Order, They humbly pray that they with their Associates who shall join with them in a reasonable time, as your Honours shall in your wisdom judge meet, may be excused from paying any taxes for the future either to the building a meeting-house for Mr Jackson, or to his maintenance; and that they may be set off a separate and distinct Society, which is of the greatest consequence to your poor distressed Petitioners, who will as in duty bound ever Pray etc., etc. "JACOB WRIGHT JUN[r] JONATHAN POOLE
JONATHAN FOX JOHN FOWLE
DAVID ALEXANDER JACOB WRIGHT
JOSHUA SAWYER EBENEZER FLEGG
GERSHOM FLAGG JUN[r]."

"In the House of Representatives Dec[r]. 18th. 1745 Read and ordered that the Petitioners serve the Clerk of the first Parish in Woburn with a Copy of this Petition, that so they shew Cause if any they have, on the first Wednesday of the next Session of this Court, why the Prayer thereof should not be granted: and all Proceedings with respect to making Parish Taxes are suspended in the meantime.

" Sent up for Concurrence.

" T. Cushing, Speaker.

" In Council Decr[r]. 18th. 1745.

" Read & Concur[d].

" J. Willard, Secr[y].

" Consented to:

W. Shirley." [6]

A Copy of this Order of Court having been duly served, a parish meeting was called January 2, 1745-6; at which a committee of five was chosen, "to go to the Great and General Court to make answer to a Petition there preferred by sundry of the Inhabitants of said Parish, and shew reason why they should not be set off a separate Society as they have requested." This committee consisting of Lieut. Samuel Kendall, Dea. Josiah Peirce, and Messrs. Josiah Johnson, William Tay and Nathan Richardson, doubtless appeared before the Court, on behalf of the parish at the time appointed.[7] But what pleas they urged against the prayer of the petitioners cannot now be ascertained, the volume of the Court's Records for that year being unaccountably missing. Certain it is, however, that the efforts of the Parish Committee in this business were unsuccessful. At an adjourned Session of the Legislature, apparently in August or September 1746, they passed upon the prayer of the petitioners the following order, which is copied from papers, in the hands of descendants in this town, of Lieut. Kendall, Chairman of the committee. "Ordered that the Prayer of the Petition be so far granted, as that the Petitioners with their Families and Estates, together with such Persons and their Estates belonging to said Parish, that shall hereafter, within twelve months next

[6] Parish Records, Vol. I., pp. 238–240.

[7] Parish Records, Vol. I., p. 242.

coming, signify their desire of joining with them by writing under their hands delivered into the Secretary's Office, be and hereby are made and set off a distinct and separate Precinct, and impowered to hold and exercise the same Privileges as all other Precincts within this Province have, and by Law do enjoy; and also set free from any taxes toward the maintenance of Mr Edward Jackson, and building and repairing said [First] Precinct Meeting-house, since the 11th. of Decr. last, when they exhibited this Petition: Provided they pay annually one half of what has been usually allowed by said Precinct towards the support of the Rev^{d}. Mr Fox their aged Pastor." [8]

The Third Society in Woburn, being thus legally established, proceeded to exercise the privileges with which they had been vested. From a comparison of parish taxes, for Rev. Mr. Jackson's salary, for the years immediately before and after its incorporation, the Third Society appears to have consisted of about eighty heads of families and taxable persons, or very nearly two-fifths of the old Society before the separation.[9] Among them, besides Col. Roland Cotton, their leader, and the reputed father of the Society, were several other men of note; as Jonathan Poole, Esq., Major John and Cornet Jacob Fowle; Captains Stephen and Joseph Richardson; Messrs. John and Elijah Leathe; Messrs. Ebenezer, Gershom and Zechariah Flagg, Mr. Jacob Wright and Son, Mr. John Russell; Capt. Samuel and Mr. Jabez Carter, and Col. Jonathan, son of Rev. Mr. Fox. The aged minister himself (Rev. Mr. Fox) appears, from some circumstances, to have usually assembled with them, when able to come abroad. They never arrived to have a proper, regularly built meeting-house of their own, but met on the Sabbath in an unfinished building that formerly stood opposite the house of Dr. Silvanus Plympton, Senr., deceased, [10] and in which there was a large room or hall, fitted up as a place of public worship. A church was gathered in this Third Society, of which Mr. John Leathe was chosen deacon. And their first and

---

[8] Extract rom Petition of First Parish Committee to General Court, dated June 5, 1747, and subscribed by Samuel Kendall, William Tay, and Nathan Richardson.

[9] First Parish Records, Vol. I., pp. 252, 267.

[10] Mrs. Plympton.

only pastor was Rev. Mr. Josiah Cotton, a brother of Col. Roland, who had previously been a settled minister at Providence, Rhode Island. He was installed at Woburn, July 15, 1747; and the following brief notice of the solemnity appeared the next day in the Boston Weekly News Letter. "Woburn July 15. This Day the Rev. Mr. Josiah Cotton was installed Pastor over the 3d. Church in this Town. The whole Affair was carried on with the utmost Peace and Decency."

A vote was passed (it will be recollected) by the First Parish, September 26, 1745, to build a new meeting-house, and to raise £1,000, Old Tenor, for the purchase of materials. This vote was not then carried into execution, in consequence of the order issued by the General Court, December 18, following, in answer to the prayer of the petitioners for the Third Society: which order suspended for the present "all Proceedings with respect to making Parish Taxes." Still, however, that design was not forgotten; and as soon as the separation of the Third Society was fully accomplished, and the excitement which it had occasioned had subsided, it was revived, and again made a subject of public consideration. At an adjourned parish meeting, October 19, 1747, in regard to an article in the warrant, To see whether the Inhabitants of the Parish would build a new meeting-house, agreeably to their former vote, or repair the old one? it was voted, to build a new one, the front of which should be set "about the middle of the place where the old meeting-house now standeth." A committee of nine, also, was chosen, viz: Mr. Joshua Thornton, (a master carpenter, then recently moved into town,) Lieut. Samuel Kendall, Dea. Samuel Eames, Mr. David Wyman, Lieut. William Tay, Mr. Benjamin Richardson, Capt. Timothy Brooks, Mr. Isaac Snow and Mr. Nathaniel Brooks, "to take care of and carry on the building of said house"; and this committee was instructed to draft a plan, to be submitted to the parish at some future meeting.[11] And, at a parish meeting, the following month, November 20, 1747, It was voted to proceed immediately with the building of a new meeting-house:

[11] Parish Records, Vol. I., pp. 264, 265.

the plan presented by the building committee was approved, except in regard to the porch, which was reserved for further consideration; the building committee was authorized to provide all the necessary materials, to be in readiness the following spring; and £1,000, Old Tenor, was raised to defray the expense.[12]

But now began to be manifested a difference of opinion in regard to the spot where the projected house of worship should stand. It was at first determined (as has been seen) to erect it on the site of the old house on the Meeting-house Hill. But, soon a large and increasing number appeared in favor of building it on the Common, west of that hill. And hence, though it was voted the following spring, April 5, 1748, "that they would not reconsider their former votes respecting the setting (of their New Meeting House," yet this vote was carried but by a bare majority; the minds of the people being very nearly equally divided on the subject. And, hence, at an adjournment of that meeting, three days after, it was mutually agreed by both parties to leave the question of the place for the meeting-house to be decided by lot. The lot was cast: and proving in favor of the Hill, the spot originally agreed upon, it was "concluded to a man," say the Records, by a subsequent vote, that the Hill should be the place, agreeably to their former votes. It was resolved, likewise, to take down the old meeting-house, as soon as they were ready to frame the new one; the building committee were directed to provide materials, and go on with the work as fast as possible; and another tax of £1,000, Old Tenor, was voted to defray the charge of building.[13]

But notwithstanding this seeming expression of unanimous resolve in favor of the old site for the new meeting-house, there were many still who could not be cordially reconciled to that location, or long disguise their opposition to it. And the number and influence of these dissentients appear to have been continually increasing; so as to cause embarrassment and delay about demolishing the old meeting-house, and proceeding to build the

[12] Parish Records, Vol. I., p. 267.

[13] Parish Records, Vol. I., pp. 281, 282.

new one upon its site, agreeably to vote of the parish. And at length, at a meeting, October 10, 1748, it was voted by the parish, that "notwithstanding all their former votes, (they) would set their new Meeting House on the Knoll on the Training Field on the West side of the Country Road, as near the road as it can conveniently be set." It was also voted as a desire of the parish, that the Selectmen would call a town meeting, to see whether the town will let the parish set their new meeting-house in the place that was last determined on. And direction was given their Building Committee to provide all the materials that were yet wanting, and to proceed to frame their new meeting-house as soon as they could with conveniency.[14] Agreeably to the desire of the parish just expressed, a town meeting was called October 26, 1748, when the town granted the First Parish the liberty requested, to set their new meeting-house on the spot which they had recently decided upon; and also liberty "of digging the Meeting House Hill so called, that is on the Easterly side of the Country Road, so much of said hill as is sufficient to straighten the aforesaid Road."[15] From these votes, both of the town and parish it would seem, that the Common in Woburn Centre must have then exhibited a very different appearance from what it now does. Then, on the easterly side of the hill, east of the great road from Wilmington and Billerica to Medford, instead of abruptly terminating almost perpendicularly as it does now, must have sloped gradually toward the road; and on the Common west of the road, where it will be recollected by some that the third meeting-house of the First Parish stood, there must have been then a knoll or small rise of ground, instead of the level which we see there now.

The permanent settlement of the question, Where the proposed meeting-house should stand? seems to have given a fresh start to the enterprise of erecting it. While the minds of the people upon this subject were not made up, a whole year rolled away, and little or nothing was done at framing the timber which had been ordered and collected. But now that this question

[14] Parish Records, Vol. I., pp. 284, 285.

[15] Town Records, Vol. VII., p. 543.

was set at rest, the work of framing went on so rapidly, that about the last of November, 1748, preparations were commenced for raising. To aid in this important operation, Mr. Zebadiah Wyman was appointed to procure tackle from Boston; and to ensure energy enough to make the tackle work briskly, (according to the notions of those days,) he was likewisedirected to provide for the occasion two barrels of cider, twenty gallons of rum, and one-fourth cwt. of sugar to sweeten it with, at the expense of the parish: and Capt. Timothy Brooks was charged with the care of these stores. At the same meeting, also, and at successive adjournments, the parish voted, that the raising of their new meeting-house should be commenced on Thursday, December 1; that Tuesday, December 6, should be the raising day; and that a committee of three then chosen (viz: Capt. Timothy Brooks, Lieut. William Tay, and Mr. David Wyman) should provide a public entertainment on that day for Mr. Joshua Thornton, their master carpenter, and for all strangers attending the raising, that were not invited to private houses.[16]

The meeting-house was, doubtless, raised December 6, 1748, according to appointment. But the work of building and finishing it proceeded with a singular slowness; so that more than three years from that date had passed away before the house was fully completed. This delay appears to have been occasioned, at least in part, by the difficulty found in collecting a tax for the support of the two ministers which had been voted by the parish to raise in September, 1745, three months before the petition for the incorporation of the Third Parish was presented to the Court. It was not till March 22, 1749–50, above a twelvemonth after the raising, that a committee of three was chosen to draft a plan for seats and pews on the lower floor and in the side (end?) galleries; and more than two years had elapsed from that date when such a plan was presented at parish meeting, and accepted, January 22, 1751. At the same meeting, and at an adjournment of it, January 28, the parish voted not to raise any money on their seats and pew lots, but to

---

[16] Parish Records, Vol. I., pp. 287, 288.

distribute them among those who had borne the expense of the building, after the following manner:—

A committee of five was chosen (viz: Dea. Samuel Eames, and Messrs. Nathan Richardson, Josiah Johnson, Isaac Snow and Edward Walker) to draw up a list of what sums each person had been assessed in the £5,000, Old Tenor, which had been raised for building the new meeting-house. The person that should appear from this list to have been assessed the most, in this amount of taxes for the meeting-house, upon his real and personal estate (allowing but one poll to each estate) should have the first choice of a pew lot, or of a seat, as he might prefer; the person taxed the next highest should have the second choice, and so each one should choose successively, till all the pew lots were taken up. Every person that chose a pew lot in preference to a seat was to build a pew upon it, under direction of the parish, at his own cost. He must also finish it, and discharge all his dues upon what he had been taxed towards defraying the charge of building the house, by the last of September 1751, or forfeit his lot to the use of the parish, unless the parish by vote should grant him further liberty.[17] Such was the plan adopted by your fathers for disposing of the accommodations of this their new house of worship. But many obstacles were found in the way of its speedy execution. It was not till July 9, 1751, that the committee for drafting the list of each one's taxes above referred to reported. Their list was immediately accepted, and a committee chosen to "line out the Seats and Pew Lotts"; and July 23 was appointed as the day for the people's choosing their several seats or pew lots, according to their respective taxes.[18] Only a few, however, made their choice on that day. Opportunities for doing it were given August 28, and at subsequent times. And when at last all the pew lots were selected, the owners were slow to build on them. Money was scarce; many appear to have been owing for their meeting-house assessments, and consequently were unwilling, under such circumstances, by finishing their pews as they were required to,

[17] Parish Records, Vol. I., pp. 322, 323.

[18] Parish Records, Vol. I., pp. 329, 330.

to risk the forfeiture both of their lots and all the cost they had laid out upon them. And hence the parish was obliged repeatedly to lengthen out the time agreed upon, for delinquents to pay up their respective assessments, and complete their pews. And yet, by a parish vote passed so late as November 21, 1751, it appears that all the pews were not then built, and probably were not till January 22, following, 1752, the farthest day agreed upon by the parish to allow delinquents to fulfil what was required of them.[19]

This third house of worship for the First Parish in Woburn, as it was, after being enlarged, during Rev. Mr. Sherman's ministry, and when burnt in Rev. Mr. Chickering's, is doubtless recollected by some still living in the town. But as it was originally, when it was built, and before its enlargement, there can be none in Woburn now, who have any remembrance of it. Aided however, by the reminiscences of an aged and very intelligent citizen, now deceased,[20] concerning this house as it was in its latter days, I have been able to deduce from the records the following description of its original structure and accommodations, reserving for a future occasion some account of the enlargement that was afterwards made in it. It was an edifice fifty-eight feet long, forty-two feet wide, with twenty-four feet post, and painted without, or within, or both, by this token; that after it was finished, the parish voted to give £10, Old Tenor, to Mr. John White, in consideration of his hard bargain in painting their new meeting-house.[21] It stood on the east side of the common, in the centre of the town, having its east end close to the road from Wilmington to Medford, very nearly opposite to where the post-office is now kept (1867).[21] It had doors in its east and west ends, and in its south side. To the last named, which was its front door, it was proposed in the original plan, to erect a porch; but the parish, after having had the matter some time under consideration, decided by vote there should be none.[22]

The pulpit, with the deacon's seat in front of it, was on the north side, in the centre; and apparently without any other orna-

[19] Parish Records, Vol. I., pp. 339, 340. [20] Mr. Bartholomew Richardson, Senr.
[21] Parish Records, Vol. I., pp. 346, 347. [22] August 17, 1749. Parish Records, Vol. I., p. 305.

ment or furniture than the cushion from the old meeting-house, for which shortly after was substituted a new one, bought on purpose for it by Capt. Timothy Brooks. The broad aisle leading to the pulpit was four feet wide; and diverging from this, near the front door, were two narrow aisles, one on each side, running by the wall pews all round the meeting-house, and meeting before the pulpit. In the body of the house, fronting the pulpit, were seven rows of high back seats, on each side of the broad aisle, whence they were entered; and back of these seven rows of seats, and at their east and west ends, was a single row of pews, which, from the circumstance of their compassing the seats on every side but in front, were called border pews. The wall pews were raised ten inches, and the border pews five inches, above the floor of the house.[23] And the walls of each pew throughout the house were to be built three feet and nine inches high; and ordered to be finished with balusters or "banesturs," as those little pillars at the top of the pews were then called, of which our fathers were universally so fond, as serving in their view for ornament at least, if not for use, in their houses of worship.[23] The Front Gallery contained four rows of seats running the whole length, except where crossed by an aisle in the centre, by which they were entered. The galleries at the east and west ends contained two rows of pews each, with a narrow aisle between each row. The whole number of pews on the floor was forty-three, viz: twenty-seven wall pews and sixteen border pews: and the pews in the east and west end galleries were twenty-six in number, viz: six front and seven back pews in each gallery. Pew No. 27, next to the pulpit on the west, was reserved for the Ministry; and accordingly was built by the parish, and appropriated by vote to Rev. Mr. Jackson, one of the ministers for the time being, so long as he should carry on the work of the ministry among them.[24] All the other pews above and below, sixty-eight in number, were appropriated to the individuals, who made choice of the lots on which they respectively stood,

---

[23] Parish Records, Vol. I., p. 331.

[24] Parish Records, Vol. I., pp. 348, 349.

according to their taxes, and built on them according to order of the parish. Mr. Francis Johnson, for instance, having been taxed the highest toward the meeting-house, had the first choice of a pew lot therein; and he chose No. 2, the next but one east of the pulpit by the wall, and there built his pew, and the same was confirmed to him by the parish, and put upon record. So likewise the three foremost of the seven rows of seats on each side of the broad aisle, on the floor of the house, calculated to contain thirty persons in all; and the foremost row of seats on each side of the aisle in the front gallery, reckoned capable of accommodating eighteen persons, were the private property of those who made choice of them. The hindmost seat in the front gallery was the place assigned to the negroes to sit in. The remaining four rows of seats below, on each side of the broad aisle, and the two middle rows of seats in the front gallery, were common property, intended for the accommodation of any persons belonging to the parish, who had no particular pew or seat of their own. There was a singular exception to this remark however. For some reason now unknown, the parish voted at a certain meeting, that "Mr Josiah Parker (should) have his seat in the fourth seat on the lower floor of the "New Meeting House on the one side, and his wife (should) have her seat in the fourth seat on the other side." [25]

This meeting-house was probably finished about March 1752; for in a warrant for a parish meeting, March 24th, of that year, one article was, "To see whether the Parish (will) accept the New Meetiug House at the hands of the Committee chosen by the said Parish to build the same; Provided their Accompts shall appear just and reasonable when adjusted." To build it, the parish had raised by tax £5,000, Old Tenor, in five equal assessments. A portion of this amount, however, appears from the records, either to have been never collected, or to have been diverted to some other purpose. The whole cost of the meeting-house (exclusively of the pews, which were built at the charge

---

[25] Parish Records, Vol. I., pp. 331, 333.

of their owners) did not probably exceed £4,500, Old Tenor, a sum equal to £600, lawful money; or $2,000 of our present currency. There is no evidence that it was ever dedicated by any special religious ceremony, or service on a week day, as is now customary. The Episcopal Churches of Rome, and of England hold to the holiness of particular *days and places*; and hence the religious observance by Christians of their communion of Christmas, Good Friday and Easter; and hence the consecration of their churches and burial grounds by certain solemn rites and ceremonies of religion. But our Puritan fathers acknowledged no holiness in *times or places* for which they had no express or clear warrant in the word of God; and hence they denied the religious obligation of observing Christmas, Saints' Days, or any other day as holy except the Sabbath, which they regarded as a permanent divine institution; and hence too, they called their houses of public worship not *churches* or *houses of the Lord*, but *meeting-houses*; houses for men to meet in, whether for the offices of religion, or for the transaction of municipal affairs. And accordingly, when they built a meeting-house, they set it apart for the worship of God, and the dispensation of His word and ordinances, by no other solemnity, than by the preaching of an appropriate discourse by their stated minister on the first Sabbath it was ready to be opened, after its completion.

The old meeting-house in Woburn, erected on the hill east of the common in 1672, continued to be used for town and parish meetings some time after the completion of the new one: but at a meeting May 20, 1754, the parish voted to give their old house to the town, provided that the town would erect a convenient town house, and [or ?] a house for their poor to work in, within two years time.[26] The town took this offer into consideration: and at a meeting in October of that year, they appointed Mr. Isaac Snow, Capt. Timothy Brooks, and Dea. Timothy Winn, as a committee to see what could be done with the old meeting-house advantageously to the town.[27] This committee seems to have reported at May meeting, 1755, when

[26] Parish Records, Vol. II., pp. 6, 7.

[27] Town Records, Vol. VIII., p. 138.

the town chose Mr. David Wyman, Capt. Joseph Richardson and Mr. Benjamin Richardson, as a committee to agree with some mechanic to take down the old meeting-house, and to erect out of the same, and on the same spot, a town house, thirty feet square, with twelve feet post, to be finished within six months.[28] In pursuance of this their commission, the committee contracted with Mr. Thomas Underwood, a carpenter then resident in the town, to do the work. According to engagement, Mr. Underwood took down the old building, (which, it will be recollected, was forty feet square,) and reared up out of its materials the walls of another, of the stipulated dimensions for a town house. But discouraged, not improbably, by the failure of the committee to furnish him with money from time to time, as he needed it, in consequence of the exhausted state of the treasury at that day, and the burdens of the French War which then pressed hard upon the country, Mr. Underwood did not go on to complete his undertaking with the spirit with which he commenced it. Impatient at his neglect, the town, at March meeting, 1757, two years afterwards, directed the building committee to sue his bond at May Court, unless he should finish the town house before. But the committee, thinking perhaps that nothing would be gained by such a suit, omitted, it seems, to prosecute as ordered. At May meeting, the following year, the town voted that their negligent committee should exert themselves, and urge the finishing of their town house as quickly as possible.[29] But without money, the mare can't be made to go by a town vote; and the town house still remained unfinished.

After waiting three years longer for the committee, to no purpose, the town determined to take the matter into their own hands, and see what they could do. At May meeting, 1761, they voted that they would go on and finish their town house as soon as it could possibly be done.[30] But now the town too was found lagging behind its own resolution. In about seven months after passing the last cited vote, so expressive of their haste and impatience for the completion of this favorite project,

[28] Town Records, Vol. VIII., p. 157. [29] Town Records, Vol. VIII., p. 236.
[30] Town Records, Vol. VIII., p. 314.

the inhabitants voted, December 22, 1761, not to proceed to finish their town house so called; but appointed a committee of three (viz: Mr. Benjamin Wyman, Capt. Benjamin Johnson and Lieut. Joshua Walker) to reckon and settle with the committee for building it, and with Mr. Underwood, the contractor, and then sell the building for the most it would fetch, for the benefit of the town.[31] And by way of amendment of this vote, the town, at an adjourned meeting, March 9, 1762, authorized their auditing committee to sell their town house for £4 ($13.33), provided they could obtain an acquittance to the town from all further responsibilities in this affair.[31] Accordingly, this committee obtained a receipt of this description from Mr. Benjamin Richardson on behalf of himself, and the rest of the building committee, April 3, 1762. Whether Mr. Richardson took the town house, as it was called, in compensation for the labor and expense which had been bestowed on it by the building committee (of which he was one); or whether the auditing committee sold it to some one else, and satisfied him out of the proceeds of the sale, does not appear. The building continued to stand, though in a neglected condition, many years after. In the Revolutionary war, it was used as a place of deposit for fish and military stores.[32] Mr. Zebadiah Wyman used it for some time as a barn.[32] At length it was sold, it is believed, to Colonel Loammi Baldwin,[32] who took it down. The materials were dispersed; but one stick at least of its solid oak timber, cut down in the forest nearly two hundred years ago, was recently to be seen on the premises of the late Mr. William Fowle, deceased.

In 1752, about the time the new meeting-house was completed all Woburn was thrown into consternation by an event which affords melancholy proof of the virulence of the parties, into which the town was then divided; and of the iniquitous means to which some men, otherwise deemed respectable, will sometimes resort for the sake of accomplishing their party purposes, or gratifying their party feelings. A Mrs. Keziah Henshaw, (or Hincher, as the name was then commonly pronounced,) widow

---

[31] Town Records, Vol. VIII., p. 333.

[32] Zebadiah Wyman, Jr., Esq. informant.

of Thomas Henshaw, who died in 1747, gave birth to a babe; and at the time of her travail, as was certified by the midwife under her hand, she laid it to Rev. Mr. Jackson. There is abundant reason for believing that this charge was welcome, though surprising news to Mr. Jackson's opposers, the friends of Rev. Mr. Fox. Two of them in particular, according to a tradition derived from a source of high respectability,[33] encouraged Mrs. Henshaw to go before a magistrate, and swear to the truth of the report which she had put in circulation; and that when she had taken an oath to this effect, they were seen by a friend of Mr. Jackson who was looking on, to put money into her lap. Even these persons, however, were too cautious, it seems, openly to assert the fact which that report was designed to prove. But Rev. Josiah Cotton, the acting minister of their party, with astonishing imprudence, did not hesitate to proclaim it abroad. Credulously relying upon the truth of the story certified by the midwife, he on a certain day, in the presence and hearing of divers persons, charged Mr. Jackson with being the father of the widow Henshaw's child; "and called him, a vile, wicked man, a fornicator, and unfit to be a minister." [34] For these and other opprobrious speeches, uttered that day against him, Mr. Jackson commenced an action against Mr. Cotton for a libel: alleging in his declaration, that by means of his false, scandalous words concerning him, he had been brought into disgrace and contempt; and that differences and quarrels had arisen in the church and congregation to which he ministered, by which he had been in great danger of being removed from his pastoral office: and laying his damages in consequence at £1,000.[34]

The case was brought before the Court of Common Pleas, at Concord, in September 1752. At this Court, Mr. Cotton, by his attorney, Benjamin Kent, Esq., of Charlestown, seems to have rested his defence, not upon any direct answer to what had been alleged against him in Mr. Jackson's Declaration, but upon the denial of some promise that Mr. Jackson had

---

[33] Late Mr. Bartholomew Richardson, deceased.

[34] Records of Superior Court, Vol. from 1752 to 1753, leaf 205, p. 2d; and leaf 206.

averred that he (Mr. Cotton) had made him. But Mr. Jackson's attorney, Edmund Trowbridge, Esq., of Cambridge (afterwards Judge Trowbridge), maintained, that the defendant's plea was by no means a sufficient answer to his client's, the plaintiff's Declaration; and that he was not bound to reply to it. This likewise was the opinion of the Court. And, accordingly, they decided that Mr. Jackson should recover against Mr. Cotton "the sum of One Thousand Pounds lawful money, Damage;" and £1 16s. 6d. the costs of suit.[35] From this Judgment of the Inferior Court, Mr. Cotton appealed to the next Superior Court of the Province for this County, holden at Charlestown, 30 January, 1753. At this Court, after a full hearing of both parties the case was committed to a jury, who returned as their verdict, that "they (found) for the appellant Costs of Courts." And this verdict of the jury was affirmed by the Court, who decided that Mr. Cotton, the appellant, should recover Cost of Courts against Mr. Jackson, the appellee.[34]

By this decision, Mr. Jackson was thrown into a truly pitiable condition. The former judgment of the Inferior Court in his favor had now been reversed by the highest judicial tribunal in the land, whence there was no appeal. His friends, many of them, grew discouraged, and hung their heads. His enemies triumphed, and freely uttered their jeers and taunts against him. And to sum up his trials, a Council of churches and ministerial brethren was convened, either just at this time, or at a little earlier period of this difficulty, to consider and advise upon his affairs. The result of this Council, it is understood, was published at the time, and a Copy long preserved in the house of the late Capt. Ishmael Munroe, of Burlington, deceased. But several years before his death, this copy was lost; and as no other is known to exist, the object and doings of the Council referred to can only be conjectured. It seems probable, however, that it was called to consider the expediency of his dismission from his pastoral charge: and it is very possible that Mr. Jackson alludes to the proceedings of this Council, where he speaks, in his

35 Records of Inferior Court of Common Pleas for Middlesex, from Dec. 1750, to May, 1751, pp. 303, 304.

Declaration, of the danger he had been in of removal from office. But whatever the precise time and object of assembling the Council were, the event shows, that in such a dark, suspicious case, they wisely judged it best to defer a decision against Mr. Jackson till time should throw further light upon his conduct, and prove his guilt beyond a reasonable doubt. But even supposing this Council to have resulted in such an expression of forbearance towards an accused suffering Christian brother and friend, yet its bare assembling on such an occasion, and upon such a subject of consideration, must have been severely trying to the feelings of Rev. Mr. Jackson,— must have cost him many a pang. Still, the good man under all these trials was wonderfully sustained. The consciousness of his innocence of the crime laid against him, and his acquittal from it by the All Seeing One, proved to him a rock of support that could not be shaken,—never failed him. Nor was he wholly destitute of earthly friends to encourage him. There were still a few at least among his people who were confident of the falseness and malignity of the accusation against him; and that this would one day be made to appear. And therefore, when his enemies would insultingly demand of them, "If Mr. Jackson be innocent, why is he so silent?" these would reply (tradition says) "Aye: but by and by the cry will be, 'When will Mr. Jackson have done?'" meaning, When will he be satisfied with the revenge he will have it in his power to inflict upon his accusers? Cheered by the countenance and firmness of such friends, Mr. Jackson quietly persevered in the discharge of his ministerial duties; kept his mouth as with a bridle, and said little or nothing in his own defence. When one or another of his people would now and then come, and inquire of him, "Why, Mr. Jackson! Don't you hear what people say of you? And do you say nothing? Won't you offer a word in reply?" His answer commonly was, "Aye, all in good time." And thus this injured minister encouraged himself in the Lord his God. He silently committed himself, in the way of well doing, to Him that judgeth righteously; confident that sooner or later, by one means or another, He would bring forth his righteousness as the light, and his just dealing as the noon day. And in this assurance he was not disappointed. But lit- more than six months after the adverse decision of the Superior Court in his case had passed away, when God, in his providence, wonderfully interposed in his behalf, and by an occurence, apparently the most trifling and accidental, wrought for him the expected deliverance.

It happened one day, that, as Mr. Jackson's negro (Cæsar, I will call him) was at work near his master's house, there came along another negro, the slave of one of Mr. Jackson's principal opposers (whom I will call Cuff); when the following conversation, substantially, ensued between them. "Good morning Cæsar," exclaimed Cuff, "Same to you," cried Cæsar: "Where you gwying?" "Gwying!" replied Cuff, "Gwying to Widder Henshir's: got a letter: can you tell me where her lives?" "Got a letter?" answered Cæsar quickly; "Got a letter? O give me: I'll carry it to Massah Jackson: He'll point you where her lives." Cuff upon this, with all simplicity, yields up the letter, and away bounds Cæsar with it to his master. The letter may reasonably be supposed to have been unsealed; for what the need of seals to letters, carried by the hand of a poor ignorant African, that had never learnt the alphabet, and to whom English and Latin, Greek and Hebrew were all alike? Seeing it to be in this condition, Mr. Jackson ventured to open it; and finding that its contents furnished a complete exposure of the falsity of the charge against him, or a direct clew to such a discovery, he quickly copied it, and keeping the original for his own use, he returned the copy by Cæsar to Cuff; and Cuff, without perceiving or suspecting the change, took it from Cæsar, and quietly went on his way with it where he had been sent.

And now came Mr. Jackson's turn to triumph. He embraced the first opportunity to petition the Superior Court for a review of the case which had there been recently decided against him; concealing apparently, however, for the present, as far as was possible, the source of the information upon which his petition for a review was based. The Court granted his request; and at its next session for this County, which was at Charlestown, January 29, 1854, the same place where just a year before it decided against him, it now came to a decision in his favor; and one which completely vindicated his good name, which by its former judgment came near being ruined. The following is a copy of that decision taken from the records of the Superior Court of this, then province, as it is there briefly expressed.

"At a Court held at Charlestown, Jany. 29. 1754.

"Edward Jackson of Woburn in the County of Middlesex, Clerk, Plaintiff, vs. Josiah Cotton of Woburn aforesaid, Clerk, Defendant. In a plea of Review of a plea of the Case &c^ra as in the Writ (on file) bearing date of sixteenth day of August last at large appears: The Defendant altho' solemnly called to come into Court, did not appear, but made Default, and the Plaintiff (the Defendant having paid him the Costs) Releases his Demand for Damages."[36]

The "Writ on file" referred to in this Record, and which, doubtless, set forth Mr. Jackson's reasons for asking a review of his case allowed him, has been repeatedly sought for on the files of the Court, but without success. The judgment of the Court, however, in their review (or rather, as it may be termed, the judgment of Mr. Cotton against himself) is a complete vindication of Mr. Jackson. Mr. Cotton, feeling he could not defend himself, ventures not now to appear before those judges, who, a year before, had decided in his favor. The Court declares Mr. Jackson entitled to damages. But Mr. Jackson generously relinquishes that demand to his new penitent suffering brother minister, he agreeing to pay the costs of Court. And this account of the matter agrees in the main with the popular tradition concerning the termination of this suit. That tradition is, When the Court was assembled and ready to attend to the Review petitioned for, Mr. Jackson put the letter above referred to into his Attorney's hand. The lawyer shows it to its author, a leading man of the Fox party, then present, and asks him if he knew and would own his own hand? The writer blushed and was confounded. The cause being explained to Rev. Mr. Cotton, he ran out of the Court house, and

---

[36] Records of Superior Court for Middlesex, from 1753–1754, leaf 122, p. 2d.

cried like a child at perceiving how deceived or mistaken he had been. And when it was signified in some way to Mr. Jackson that he had now his adversaries completely in his power, he rose and said, "May it please your Honors, I desire not the money of these men; I have no wish that they should be deprived of their liberty; all I ask of them is, that they stand up and confess before the Court, and this whole assembly, that the accusation they have laid against me, or helped to circulate, is a false accusation." Mr. Jackson's proposal was complied with. And while *they* left the Court house mortified and confounded, *he* left it with honor, and with the applause and sympathy of all good men. And thus were fulfilled, in a portion of his opposers at least, those words of the Psalmist, "He made a pit and digged it, and is fallen into the ditch which he made. His mischief shall return upon his own head, and his violent dealing shall come down upon his own pate."

Mr. Jackson did not long survive, to enjoy the vindication of his character, which the late decision of the Court had established to general satisfaction. During a large portion of the year preceding, anxiety of mind seems to have undermined his bodily health, so that a considerable portion of the time, the parish was obliged to hire preaching; and the remainder of the year, he was still in a languishing condition. The parish improved this opportunity to settle with him for their arrears, in paying up his salary for past years; and granted him a larger sum than usual for the year then current. The restoration of his credit, and the silencing of accusation against him, in consequence of the last judgment of the Court, seem to have somewhat raised his spirits, and renewed his usefulness. But before summer was gone, his health appears to have rapidly declined: so that in September the parish voted to hire preaching again for six weeks; but before that term was gone, their junior pastor was no more.

Rev. Mr. Edward Jackson was a son of Deacon Edward Jackson of Newton, and a grandson of Edward Jackson, who arrived in New England about 1642; was made freeman in 1645, and settled in Newton, then a part of Cambridge, between 1642 and 1645. He was born at Newton, April 3, 1700; graduated at Harvard College, 1719, and was ordained at Woburn, as colleague pastor with Rev. Mr. John Fox, August 1, 1729. Through life, for anything that appears to the contrary, he was sound in doctrine, correct in morals, and his public labors and services were acceptable to his people, though he has left nothing in print, by which the style, matter and manner of his preaching can now be estimated. He lived unmarried; and died September 24, 1754, in the fifty-fifth year of his age, and the twenty-sixth year of his ministry. The parish provided for him at their cost a respectable funeral; and by their invitation, Rev. Messrs. Abbot of Charlestown, Appleton of Cambridge, Cook of Menotomy (now West Cambridge,) Morrill of Wilmington, Jones of Woburn Precinct, and Carnes of Stoneham, accompanied his remains, as bearers, to his grave.

In view of the lamentable transactions recorded in the latter part of this chapter, some, perhaps, may be ready to say that religion and morals were at a low ebb in Woburn at that day. But this would be a rash and unjust inference. It is not right to judge of a whole community by the misconduct of a few of its members. Doubtless, several of the prominent characters in the scenes we have been just surveying were persons astonishingly wanting both in principle and morals. But they were few in comparison with the great body of the people. Many there were, I doubt not, both of men and women then in Woburn, who looked with grief upon some of the things done in the midst of them, which have here been noticed; and could not help passing a judgment of entire disapprobation upon them in one way or another, and sometimes expressing it. But after all, they kept themselves aloof from the stripes, and reproaches, and false accusations which then abounded; and meddled with them as little as possible. They were diligent and exemplary in the discharge of the duties of their several occupations and callings in the week time: they were constant in the worship and service of God upon the Sabbath; they followed habitually the things which make for peace; in a word, they did justly and loved mercy in their intercourse with men; they walked humbly with

God; and left a good example when they died for their children to imitate. Such persons, though in the midst of a crooked and perverse generation, are the excellent of the earth: they were in that day the salt of this town; and for their sakes, I doubt not, a blessing has come down upon their posterity in different generations then unborn.

CHAPTER XI.

Ordination of Rev. Josiah Sherman. — Death of Rev. John Fox. — Reunion of Third Parish with the First. — Rev. Josiah Cotton dismissed, and Third Church disbanded. — Col. Roland Cotton. — Enlargement of First Parish meeting-house. — Woburn in French War, 1755–1763. — Memorials of events in that war by Woburn men. — Dismission of Rev. Mr. Sherman.

THE last chapter of this History of Woburn closed with an account of the death of Rev. Edward Jackson, junior pastor of the First Church. This event occurred September 24, 1754. For above a year previous, in consequence of his declining health, and of the age and infirmities of the senior pastor, Rev. John Fox, the pulpit of the First Church had been supplied by preachers from abroad, at the cost of the parish. And it continued to be so supplied for some weeks after Mr. Jackson's death, without any special reference to the settlement of a colleague with Mr. Fox. But at a meeting, January 6, 1755, the parish took some preliminary steps to this important end. They directed their committee, for the supply of the pulpit, to employ Messrs. Aaron Putnam, Jonas Clark and Stephen Minot, graduates of Harvard College, who had recently commenced preaching, two Sabbaths each; and when these gentlemen had severally completed the term of their respective engagements, the parish gave direction for their continued employment among them, three Sabbaths each in succession; and at a meeting, June 18th, they attempted to make choice of one of them for their minister. But as commonly happens in such cases, the attempt was without effect. Each of the three candidates appears to have had a party among the people in his favor; the vote was a divided one; and there being no prospect of union in either of them, they were all three discharged from further service in Woburn.[1] Mr. Putnam was settled not long after at Pomfret, Conn. as Mr. Clark was in

[1] Records of First Parish, Woburn, Vol. II., pp. 11, 15, 20, 21.

Lexington, Mass. Mr. Minot, a son of the venerated "Master" Timothy Minot of Concord, received and accepted a call to the pastoral care of a church in Portland, Maine, in 1759; but died before the day appointed for his ordination arrived.[2]

The gentleman next employed to preach here as a candidate for settlement, was Mr. Nathaniel Potter, a native of Elizabethtown, N. J., and a graduate of Princeton College, N. J., 1753. At a parish meeting, July 2, 1755, the committee for supplying the desk was directed to hire him for three Sabbaths; the engagement then entered into was subsequently prolonged twice; and the last time, Mr. Potter was requested by the committee (agreeably to instructions from the parish) "to tarry a few days" in the place, in order that he and the people might become better acquainted. At a meeting, September 22, 1755, the parish (in concurrence with the church) chose Mr. Nathaniel Potter for their "Gospel minister"; voted to give him a salary of £80 per annum, and £133 6*s.* 8*d.* settlement; and then, after appointing their standing committee, jointly with the committee of the church, to inform Mr. Potter of their choice of him to the ministry, they adjourned their meeting to October 20th. But at this adjourned meeting, Mr. Potter returned a negative answer to their invitation. Upon the 19th day of November following, 1755, he was ordained the pastor of the church in Brookline, Mass., and after sustaining that relation a term short of four years, he was dismissed June 17, 1759.[3]

But though the citizens of Woburn First Parish, had been thus twice disappointed in their hopes of obtaining a settled minister, yet they still persevered in their efforts to this end. Nor were these efforts long without success. At their meeting, October 20th, above referred to, after voting to leave it with their committee to supply the pulpit at their discretion till further orders, they adjourned for a fortnight, to November 3d. But before that day arrived, Mr. Josiah Sherman, a graduate of the same college with Mr. Potter, and very probably by his

[2] Shattuck's History of Concord, p. 247.

[3] Parish Records. American Quarterly Register, Vol. VIII., p. 42.

recommendation, appears to have come to Woburn, and to have preached one or more Sabbaths, by invitation of the committee. At the adjourned meeting, November 3d, the parish voted to request Mr. Sherman to preach for them as a candidate for settlement, and to tarry in town; and appointed a numerous committee to communicate this their request. By this committee, Mr. Sherman immediately signified to the parish his compliance with their request, and so acceptable did his subsequent services prove, that all hearts seem to have been at once united in his favor. At a parish meeting, December 1st, only four weeks from the time he agreed to preach as a candidate, a call was given Mr. Sherman, apparently unanimous, to settle in Woburn. In this deeply interesting proceeding, the church took the lead, casting twenty-four votes in favor of Mr. Sherman. The parish then concurred, by a vote of eighty-three, in the choice of the church; voted, to grant Mr. Sherman a settlement of £133 6*s.* 8*d.*, lawful money of this Province, and an annual salary of £80 "so long as he shall carry on the work of a Gospel Minister in said Parish:" and having chosen a committee to inform him of these votes, adjourned their meeting to December 22d. On that day, Mr. Sherman communicated his acceptance of the call given him: upon which the parish fixed upon January 28, 1756, as the day of ordination; and then, at an adjournment of one week, December 29th, voted as follows:

1. To accept the offer, made by Mr. Benjamin Flagg, of his house, for the entertainment of the Council; and voted, that Lieut. William Tay, Mr. Nathan Richardson and Mr. Zebadiah Wyman be a committee to provide for the Council there.

2. "Voted by said Parish that the following Ministers and their Churches be sent unto, to assist in the Ordination of Mr Josiah Sherman: viz: the Rev[d] Mr Appleton of Cambridge,
Mr Dunbar of Stoughton,
Mr Turell of Medford,
Mr Hobby, Reading,
Mr Cook, Menotomy [West Cambridge,]
Mr Morrill, Wilmington,
Mr Bridge, Chelmsford,
Mr Carnes, Stoneham,
Mr. Jones, Woburn, 2d Parish,
Mr Potter, Brookline."

3. "Then chose a committee of two, Mr Benjamin Wyman and Mr Jabez Richardson, to assist Mr Sherman in drawing up the Letters missive to the above Churches.

4. Requested Josiah Johnson Esqr. "to get Mr Sherman's Letter of Recommendation from the Church in Milford in Connecticut."[4]

Agreeably to arrangements cited above, Mr. Sherman appears to have been first admitted by Letter, as a member into the First Church of Woburn; and then to have been ordained its pastor, January 28, 1756, the day appointed. For, at the annual parish meeting, March 8, 1756, it was voted that they would raise £80 to pay Mr. Sherman's salary the present year, "which began Jany 28th, 1756"; and £133 6*s*. 8*d*. to pay his settlement.[4]

The ordination of Mr. Sherman was soon followed by the death of the senior pastor, Rev. John Fox, who deceased December 12, 1756, when about seventy-eight years of age.

He was the eldest son of his immediate predecessor at Woburn, Rev. Jabez Fox; and was probably born at Cambridge, where his father resided, and occasionally preached, before he was settled at Woburn, in 1679. He was graduated at Harvard College, 1698; took charge of the grammar school in Woburn in 1700; and apparently continued in that employment at his father's death, in February 1702-3. Shortly after that event, he was invited to preach three months upon probation in his father's place; at the expiration of this term, his engagement was prolonged to three months more, and then receiving an invitation to settle, which he accepted, he was ordained over the church and town of Woburn, November 17, 1703. For twenty years, his services were acknowledged with frequent tokens of acceptance and success: such as repeated voluntary grants from the town, in addition to his salary. But then, his health began to fail, so that he was often indisposed and unable to preach; which brought the town under the unwelcome necessity, first, of frequently hiring preaching from abroad, and then of settling a colleague; and for the last fifteen years of his life, he was totally blind. The loss of health and sight, however, did not wholly put a period to his usefulness. While

---

[4] Parish Records, Vol. II., pp. 22-24, 26.

laboring under these great discouragements, he still occasionally preached; "and often catechised the youth of his parish, who use to resort to his house for this purpose, and to receive his pious counsels and exhortations." In Alden's notice of him, in his Collection of Epitaphs, two sermons of Mr. Fox from I. Samuel XIV. 15, occasioned by the great earthquake October 29, 1727, are spoken of, as then extant.

Mr. Fox married Mary, daughter of Hon. Edward Tyng, (one of Sir Edmund Andros' Council, 1687) who having been appointed Governor of Annapolis, in Nova Scotia, "was captured by the French in his passage to that place, carried into France, and there died. Mrs. Fox survived her husband; and died in Woburn February 1764." Their children were,

1. John, born 13 February, 1703 [1703–4]; "who in early life went to Ireland to live with a wealthy relative."

2. Jabez, born 25 May, 1705, graduated at Harvard College, 1727; studied theology, and commenced preaching; but, on account of feeble health, relinquished his profession; settled at Falmouth [Portland], where he spent an honorable and useful life, and was for a number of years a member of the Provincial Council of Massachusetts. He died 7 April, 1755, in the fiftieth year of his age. Anna, his first wife, died and was buried at Woburn, August 5, 1746, aged forty-five years. For a second wife, he married Ann, widow of Phinehas Jones, who died June 9, 1758, aged forty-three.

3. Mary, born 26 October, 1706: married to Rev. Hebijah Weld, of Attleborough, October 17, 1728.

4. Edward, born 26 October, 1708: lost at sea, in his passage to England.

5. Thomas, born 7 April, 1711; a goldsmith at Boston.

6. Judith, born 10 August, 1712; married to Rev. Nathan Stone, of Southborough, October 31, 1734, being his second wife.

7. Jonathan, born 26 March, 1716: married to Ruth Carter, August 17, 1737; lived and died at Woburn, where he was known as Col. Jonathan Fox.[5]

---

[5] Woburn Town Records. Woburn Records of Births, etc. Alden's Epitaphs, Vol. I., No. 238, and Vol. II., No. 321. Rev. Joseph Green's Diary, in Collections of William Gibbs, Esq.

Shortly after the death of Rev. Mr. Jackson, in 1754, and before that of Rev. Mr. Fox, in 1756, an effort was commenced to re-unite the Third Religious Society in Woburn with the First, which eventually proved successful. As the unhappy differences between those reverend gentlemen and their respective partisans had led to the establishment of the Third Society, so at the death of Rev. Mr. Jackson, one main reason for its continuance was removed. Accordingly, at a legal meeting of the First Parish on Monday, April 14, 1755, Dea. Samuel Eames, Lieut. William Tay, Mr. Josiah Johnson, Mr. Oliver Richardson and Mr. Isaac Snow were chosen a committee to treat with a committee of the Third Parish on the subject of a re-union with the First. This committee of the First Parish reported, after an adjournment of one hour, that "*the Third Parish say they are willing to unite with the First.*" Whereupon it was voted by the First Parish, "that they stand ready and willing (upon their desire) to receive the Third Parish into union upon reasonable & equitable terms: and desire their disposition thereunto in the like manner." And at a subsequent meeting of the Third Parish, April 28, 1755, they voted that they were "willing and desirous to unite with the First Parish in said Town on such terms as the said Parishes shall agree on." But though both parties were thus ready to signify, that a re-union would be acceptable to them, yet it was found very difficult to agree on the precise terms. At an adjourned meeting of the First Parish, May 21, 1755, they voted the following proposal to the Third, viz: That they will let the "Third Parish in Woburn come into their new Meeting House in common with them, in case they will first pay their full proportion of cost of building their new Meeting House: allowing those persons to hold their pews and seats that will not give them up: provided other grievances shall be removed and satisfied." On the other hand, the Third Parish, at a meeting on the same day with the above, passed the following vote. "May 21, [1755] Voted in the Third Parish in Woburn, that they stand ready and willing to pay their just proportion (with the First Parish in said Town) of what the new Meeting House is worth: Provided they can come into said House upon an equal right with the First Parish: and in case the Parishes cannot agree on what the said House is worth, they are willing to leave the matter to men mutually chosen.

Test. JOHN LEATHE, Parish Clerk."

But neither of these two offers was satisfactory to the party to whom it was made. And yet the project of reunion was too advantageous to both parishes to be abandoned or lost sight of. The Third Parish, in particular, found new and strong incentives to continue their efforts for a reunion with the First, in the departure from them of their own minister, and in the settlement over the First Parish of Rev. Mr. Sherman, in 1756. Hence numerous meetings were held, and various proposals were made by both parishes to secure this desirable object, during the years 1756, 1757 and 1758. But nothing effectual was done till March 1759. On the first day of that month, the Third Parish voted as follows:

"Woburn, March the first, 1759. Voted in the Third Parish in said Town, that we of the Third Parish in said Town are willing to unite with the First Parish in said Town, on the following terms. viz: That we will pay into the Treasury of the said First Parish Fifty two Pounds towards the Rev. Mr Sherman's salary in twelve months from the date hereof: Likewise we are willing to be taxed and pay with you of the First Parish towards the Rev. Mr Sherman's salary from the 28th day of January last (1759): Provided the First Parish mutually petition the General Court with us, to be incorporated into one Parish: p^r. JOHN LEATHE, Parish Clerk."[6]

At an adjourned meeting of the First Parish, on the same day as the above, at Mr. James Fowle's, Innholder, voted as follows:

"Having received a Vote from the Third Parish, Voted that they will accept of the vote passed this day in the Third Parish in said Town, in order for uniting the said two Parishes, and be incorporated into one Parish: and chose Josiah Johnson Esqr. Lt. William Tay and Mr. Isaac Snow to be a Committee

6 First Parish Records, Vol. II., p. 44.

to join with a Committee of the said Third Parish to petition the Great & General Court that they may be so united."[6]

In fulfilment of their appointment, the joint committee of both parishes petitioned the General Court to unite them again; and the Court passed on their petition as follows:

"MARCH 28, 1759.

"A Petition of Josiah Johnson and others in behalf of the First and Third Parishes in Woburn, setting forth, that heretofore they were the First Parish in that Town, but by means of some unhappy contentions were divided and made two separate Parishes: That as these contentions with the causes of them are removed, and as the said Third Parish is destitute of a Minister, both Parishes are desirous of reuniting and being made the First Parish in Woburn upon certain terms mentioned in said Petition, And praying that they may be united accordingly:

"In the House of Representatives: *Voted*, that the Prayer of the Petition be granted, and that the said First and Third Parishes in Woburn, aforesaid be and hereby are to all intents and purposes reunited, incorporated and erected into one intire Parish or Precinct, and henceforward to be the First Parish or Precinct in Woburn aforesaid, in the same manner as it was before the division thereof into two Parishes: And that the Inhabitants thereof be henceforward invested with the like privileges, Immunities and Powers that any other Parishes or Precincts within this Province are invested withal, any Law or Order to the contrary notwithstanding.

"Provided, nevertheless, that the said Third Parish shall by the first day of March next pay and deliver into the Treasury of the said First Parish the sum of Fifty two Pounds of lawful money of this Province toward the yearly Salary of the present Minister of the aforesaid First Parish, which became due on the 27th day of January last, and from that day forward to be jointly taxed with the said First Parish for their Minister's Salary, and all other Parish or Precinct charges.

"Provided, also, that each of the Parishes aforesaid may and shall severally adjust, settle and finish their own proper Parish Accounts and Affairs, and pay and discharge their several debts respectively due from them, as heretofore they might have done; and be and hereby are fully impowered for those ends and purposes to lay and impose suitable taxes upon the Polls and Estates within their respective parishes sufficient therefor, and may sue and be sued (for any debts already contracted) by the name of the First or Third Parish, in the same manner as if they had not been thus reunited and incorporated together.

"In Council: Read and Concurred.

"Consented to by the Governor." [7]

By this act of the Legislature, the reunion of the two parishes, so much desired by both parties, and of such mutual advantage to both, was legally accomplished, after a separation of fifteen years. Agreeably, however, to the last provision of the Court's Resolve, the first parish, as such, held one meeting more, in order to finish their own proper business, receive money due to them, and pay their own debts, in distinction from the Third Parish. On February 29, 1760, a warrant was issued by the Clerk of the First Parish to Mr. Jonathan Lawrence, Collector, requiring him "to warn and give notice to all the Freeholders and other Inhabitants of [Woburn] that were of the First Parish in Woburn, before the Third Parish in said Town was united with them, to assemble and convene at the Meeting House in said Parish on Monday the tenth day of March next, at One of the Clock afternoon, then and there to elect and depute Parish Officers, viz. a Parish Clerk, a Parish Committee, Assessors, Treasurer, Collector, and all other Officers needful to serve the said Parish, as in their former capacity, the year ensuing," etc., etc.

Of the meeting thus warned, the record begins thus:

"At a legal Meeting of the First Parish in Woburn, in their capacity before the Third Parish in said Town was united to them, on Monday the 10th. day of March 1760, they proceeded as follows." etc., etc.

Having chosen parish officers, as they had been wont, they passed the following votes among others:

"That the money due from the said First Parish shall be paid out of the fifty-two Pounds, due to them from the Third Parish in said Town.

"That if those that were of the Third Parish in Woburn will

General Court Records, Vol. XXII., 1757-1759, pp. 585, 586.

provide money to enlarge the Meeting House belonging to the said First Parish, equal as those of the said First Parish have paid for said Meeting House, that they shall have room in said House equal and according to their pay with those of the said First Parish. And if the equal proportion of money be not sufficient to finish the said addition, then it shall be finished at the joint charge of both the said Parishes."[8]

This latter vote seems to have been acceded to by the Third Parish: for, from henceforth, both parishes appear to have met and worshipped together in one place, and to have acted together as one society. The above meeting of the First Parish, in distinction from the Third, is the last upon record. The next meeting was held, indeed, on the same day as the above; but at that meeting both societies acted as one.

When the question of a reunion of the First and Third Parishes in Woburn began to be agitated, shortly after the death of Rev. Mr. Jackson, in September, 1754, Rev. Josiah Cotton was the settled minister of the Third Parish. But, perceiving the inclination of his people to join the First Parish again, and that his continuance in office might be an obstacle to this good end, he saw fit to call a Council of several churches to meet June 30, 1756, and "to advise & direct him with respect to his removal," etc.[9] The Records of the Third Church being now unfortunately lost,[10] the particulars of the advice which this Council gave him cannot now be recovered. There can be no doubt, however, that the Council convened at Woburn on the day appointed, advised him, under existing circumstances, to ask a dismission from his people; and that, in compliance with their advice, he asked and obtained an orderly and honorable dismission from his pastoral and ministerial charge; and shortly after removed his residence from Woburn.

Rev. Josiah Cotton, pastor of the Third Church in Woburn, was son of Rev. Rowland Cotton of Sandwich; a brother of Rev. John Cotton of Newton, of Rev. Nathaniel Cotton of

---

[8] First Parish Records, Vol. II., p. 49.

[9] Records of Church of Woburn Precinct, or Burlington, Vol. I., p. 164.

[10] "An extract from the *Chh Book belonging to the third Chh in Woburn*" is copied in the Burlington Church Records, Vol. I., p. 22.

Bristol, R. I., of Col. Roland Cotton of Woburn, and of Rev. Ward Cotton of Hampton, N. H.; a grandson of Rev. John Cotton of Plymouth; and a descendant of the third generation from Rev. John Cotton, the renowned Teacher of First Church, Boston. He was born at Sandwich, in June, 1703;[11] graduated at Harvard College, 1722; ordained, October 23, 1728, pastor of a Congregational church at Providence, R. I., which was gathered the same day,[12] and continued to minister there till after May, 1736.[12] He was installed pastor of the Third Church, Woburn, July 15, 1747;[13] and after his dismission from that people in 1756, he was installed at Sandown, N. H., November 28, 1759;[14] and there died May 27, 1780, aged seventy-seven.

Rev. Mr. Cotton married Susanna ——— before he came to Woburn. It is not known that he had more than two children, viz: 1. a daughter who died in Woburn, and upon whose gravestone in the old Burying Place there is inscribed as follows:

"Susanna, daughter of Rev. Josiah & Susanna Cotton, who died Aug. 3. 1748, aged 10 years."[15]

2. A daughter, Sarah, who was baptized (apparently in the Precinct, or Second Church of Woburn) by Rev. Thomas Jones, pastor, November 28, 1756, after her father's dismission from the Third Church, and before he finally left the town. [See Burlington Chh. Records.]

His brother Roland, it seems, had removed from the town before him. Of this once prominent citizen of Woburn, a brief account may not be unacceptable.

Roland Cotton, Esq., was the third son of Rev. Roland Cotton of Sandwich; was born in that town about 1701;[14] graduated at Harvard College, 1719; and upon his first coming to Woburn, sojourned a while at the house of his uncle, Nathaniel Saltonstall, Esq., who was his mother's brother, and brother to Gurdon Saltonstall, Esq., Governor of Connecticut; and who, at his death, June 23, 1739, is said to have made him

---

[11] Rev. Abel Patten, from Sandwich Town Records.

[12] Journal of Rev. Dr. Sewall, Boston. [13] Boston Weekly News Letter, of July 16.

[14] Genealogy of Cotton Family, N. E. Historical and Genealogical Reg'r, Vol. I., p. 165.

[15] Copies of Inscriptions, by Nathan Wyman, Esq.

sole heir to his large estate.[16] He is first noticed as an inhabitant of Woburn in the Province Tax List for 1737; and then in the list of the same tax for 1744, by the title of Col. Roland Cotton.[17] He was chosen in 1737, and the seven immediately succeeding years, to represent the town of Woburn in the General Court.[17] And in 1739, and perhaps other years, he was appointed Clerk of the House of Representatives; and was said to have discharged the duties of that trust "with fidelity and despatch, and to great acceptance." But in consequence, it is supposed, of alleged inconsistency of profession and conduct in his political career, of seemingly arbitrary (not to say, illegal and unjust) proceedings with which he was charged, in the impressment of men for military service, and of his settled hostility to Rev. Mr. Jackson, his popularity in Woburn after 1744 rapidly declined. He appears to have left Woburn early in 1754, if not before, and to have gone back to Sandwich, where he built for himself a house, and where he probably spent the remainder of his days.[16] He married Deborah Mason, October 3, 1760, who died at Sandwich, August 1766.[16] It is not known whether he left posterity.

To his generosity, while living in Woburn, the church of the Second Parish (now Burlington) became indebted for the gift of two handsome silver cups, dated 1740 and 1741, for the communion service; and also previously to him and his uncle Saltonstall for their joint gift of another like cup for the same use. The kind donors have long since ceased from the earth; but by these sacred offerings, their names inscribed on them, will long be kept in grateful remembrance.

At his house in Woburn, died a maiden sister of his in 1742, of good repute, as "Vertuous, Usefull & Obliging in her Day etc."[16] Upon her grave in the old burying-place in Woburn is engraved the following singular inscription:

---

16 Letter of William G. Brooks, Esq., from Diary of Josiah Cotton, Esq., brother of Rev. Robert Cotton of Sandwich.

17 Woburn Records.

"Here lyes the Remains of
M^rs. ELIZABETH COTTON,
Daughter of the Rev^d.
ROLAND COTTON, late
of Sandwich. Dec^d: who died
A VIRGIN October 12th. 1742,
Ataris 46.
"If a Virgin Marry, She hath not Sinned,
Neverth^ls such shall have trouble in the Flesh:
But he that giveth her not in Marriage doth better:[18]
She is happier if she so Abide."

Comparing the lists of parish taxes, assessed immediately before and after the reunion of the Third Parish with the First, we find that by this transaction exclusively of non-residents, fifty-five were added, as members of the First Parish, to the one hundred and fifty-three that previously belonged to it.[19] So large an addition to the parish of taxable inhabitants, with their families, must obviously render necessary, increased accommodations in their house of public worship. Such necessity had been anticipated while the proposals for reunion were pending, and had been in some measure provided for in the votes that finally decided in its favor. But in consequence, probably, of some division of opinion, how much it would be needful to enlarge the meeting-house, or what proportion of the expense should be borne by those who had belonged to the Third Society, for whose accommodation principally, such enlargement was required, no measures for this end were attempted till 1769. Then the want of more room in the meeting-house was so sensibly felt, especially by those who had been of the Third Parish, that articles were inserted in the warrants for several successive meetings of the parish, having in view the making of more seats in the meeting-house; and committees were successively appointed to consider how this object might best be attained. And in the warrant for a meeting called to be June 14, 1770, there was an article "To see if the Parish will hear the Petition of some men that [had been] of the Third Parish in said Town, in order to consult and

[18] William Gibbs, Esq.; taken from Woburn Old Burying Hill.
[19] Parish Records, Vol. II., pp. 42–46.

agree upon some methods and measures that shall be thought and voted most expedient and beneficial, for their having equal and proper room in the parish meeting-house, agreeable to their Petition."[20] But at that meeting, and at an adjournment of it, September 3, 1770, after many fruitless proposals, nothing was done, and the meeting was dissolved.

Such a result must needs have occasioned much disappointment and irritation of feeling, especially in the former members of the Third Society, who suffered most from the alleged inconvenience. Seemingly to allay such feelings, a meeting was held only a fortnight after, at which a committee of five was chosen "to seat some elderly men and high payers in the Parish Rates, and [who] have no seats assigned them — to be seated in the unappropriated seats during the Parish's pleasure."[21]

But this measure, while it made an invidious distinction, could evidently afford only a partial relief from the evil complained of. Hence the question of enlarging the meeting-house, which alone proposed an adequate remedy, did not cease to be agitated. In the course of the eighteen months immediately following, plans for opening the house of worship twelve feet, eighteen feet and a half, and twenty feet, were submitted to the parish and considered; but not one of them all then obtained general and permanent approbation; for though the plan for opening twelve feet was repeatedly voted acceptance, yet it was not long acquiesced in. It was not till March 30, 1772, that the first effectual step was taken towards the desired and much needed enlargement of this House of God. At a parish meeting on that day, it was voted,

"1. That they will open the Meeting House eighteen feet and a half, and move to the West, the Pulpit being in the Centre.

"3. That the new Pews that shall be made in the addition to the Meeting House, shall be sold to the highest bidder; they paying one-third part of the money they bid for the Pew, at the Pew's being struck off to them; and giving security for the payment of the other two thirds; viz. one third at the closing up said house, and one third at the finishing the same; with sureties.

[20] Parish Records, Vol. II., p. 119.

[21] Parish Records, Vol. II., p. 121.

"4. And if any of the said Pews be sold or struck off to any Person that hath one of the old pews, he shall immediately resign his old pew to the Parish, to be sold in the same manner that the New Pews are sold."[22]

In pursuance of these resolves, the parish voted at an adjournment of this meeting, and at a subsequent one June 8, that they would "have Twenty-two Pews made in the Parish Meeting House, part in the addition of eighteen feet & half, and part in the old house, all on the lower floor; and the Parish Pew moved up to the Pulpit, as it stands now." They also chose Capt. Benjamin Wyman, and Messrs. Jacob and Joseph Wright, a committee to sell the pew ground in the meeting-house, both in the addition, and in the old part of the house, to the highest bidder at a public vendue, he belonging to the parish, and appointed Mr. Loammi Baldwin, vendue master.[23] And at an adjourned meeting, June 22, they appointed a committee of three (viz: Messrs. Jacob Wright, Benjamin Wyman, and Jonathan Fox) to hire workmen to complete the contemplated enlargement; and made provision for defraying the expense, from the money arising from the sale of pew ground. And finally they voted, that the common seats on the lower floor and in the galleries that are made or shall be made in the meeting-house, shall be common for the people of the parish to sit in, during the parish's pleasure.[24]

The committee chosen to sell the pew ground at auction discharged the duties of their appointment June 22, and June 29, 1772. The whole was sold on one or the other of those days: and each purchaser paid down £4 10*s*., Old Tenor, as earnest money; and the remainder with a single exception, by January 1773, or shortly after. The whole amount raised by this sale of pew ground, for twenty-two additional pews on the lower floor of the house, was, £2,125, Old Tenor, or $944\frac{4}{9}$.[25]

The committee for hiring workmen, employed Messrs. John Tay and Bartholomew Richardson. These two gentlemen covenanted on their part with the committee, within three months

[22] Parish Records, Vol. II., p. 129.
[23] Parish Records, Vol. II., p. 130.
[24] Parish Records, Vol. II., p. 131.
[25] Parish Records, Vol. II., pp. 133, 134.

from the date of their contract, viz: July 27, 1772, "to open the Meeting House in said Parish, and move to the West eighteen feet & a half; and move the Pulpit to the middle of the House on the North side; and provide all kind of materials, and fill up the vacancy opened, and finish all parts thereof in the same form & fashion with the Old House, except building the Pews: and wheresoever any part of the Old House is broken or defaced by them, they will make it good, and all the materials for said house and the work shall be good and merchantable to the acceptance of the said Committee."

And the committee covenanted on their part, and in their capacity, with Messrs. Tay and Richardson to pay them, for their labor and expense, £150 lawful money (or $500) in all, at three several payments, the last on or before October 10, following, or at the finishing of the house.

And to insure the faithful performance of this contract on both sides, each party bound itself to the other in the penal sum of £300 lawful money, "to be well and truly paid by the defective party to the party performing."

Although the fact is not recorded, yet there can be no doubt that the enlargement of the meeting-house thus contracted for was faithfully completed by the time agreed upon, viz: October 27, 1772. Nor is there cause to question but that the pews were built in due season by the several purchasers of the pew ground, as was done in this meeting-house at its erection in 1749, 1750.

And now, that nothing might be wanting thoroughly to furnish this house of worship for its intended use, the parish, at a meeting January 18th, the following year, 1773, chose Josiah Johnson, Esq. and Joseph Wright a committee to sell the old bell, and to purchase a new one, that should weigh about four hundred and fifty pounds.[b]

In 1755 began that sharp national contest known in New England as "the last French war;" and which continued, with some abatements, till the definitive treaty of peace, signed at

---

Parish Records, Vol. II., p. 137.

[b] Parish Records, Vol. II., p. 145.

Paris, February 10, 1763. This war was occasioned by encroachments, which the French were constantly making in Nova Scotia, a province ceded by them to Great Britain, or acknowledged to belong to her, by a succession of treaties; and by their commencing a chain of settlements and fortifications, which were designed to extend the whole length of the northern and western frontiers of the English colonies, and which would prove exceedingly embarrassing and detrimental to their interests in time of peace, and might be successfully employed for their utter ruin or subjugation in time of war. Remonstrances against these proceedings having been repeatedly urged in vain, hostilities between the two nations actually commenced in 1755, although war was not publicly declared till the following year.

In this war, in the result of which all the British colonies bordering on the Atlantic were so deeply interested, the inhabitants of New England in general engaged with a hearty zeal, and with a willingness to make every sacrifice in their power, in order to bring it to a successful issue. And although, through the rashness, or imbecility and folly of the military commanders, appointed and sent here by the government in England, these colonists were grieved and mortified the first three years of the war to see a constant series of losses and defeats and disappointments, yet upon a change of men and measures, they were overjoyed to behold the former discouraging prospect entirely reversed; to witness success and victory everywhere attendant upon the arms of Britain and her colonies, especially in the campaign of 1759, when Quebec was taken, and the vast region of Canada subdued. For from the first settlement of New England, Canada had been a perpetual scourge to her inhabitants; a constant source of vexation to her commerce, of war and bloodshed to her people, and of malicious, mischievous interference with her Indian neighbors. Hence they longed to see this settlement of France subdued; they freely offered their persons and their fortunes to the accomplishment of this end in the present war. And "great and universal was the joy (saith Rev. Dr. Trumbull in his History of Connecticut)[26] which spread through the Eng-

[26] Vol. II., Chap. xx., p. 429.

lish Colonies, especially through New England, on the conquest of Canada, which, for more than a century, had occasioned so much alarm, such an expense of blood and treasure to them, as well as to the sister colonies. Many had been their own and their forefathers' fastings and prayers for this great event. Now, they conceived, that they were fully answered. Days of public thanksgiving were generally appointed in New England to recognize the divine goodness, and ascribe due honors to HIM, whose is the greatness and the victory, and whose kingdom ruleth over all."

In order to the accomplishment, however, of this most desirable end, for which so many united devout thanksgivings were offered by a whole people unto God, numerous and costly were the sacrifices, both of treasure and life, which the colonies were called to make to procure it. In relating the close of the war, the Reverend Historian just quoted, thus describes these sacrifices. "For nearly eight years they had been making the most strenuous exertions to carry on the war, and to assist his Majesty to humble the pride of their common enemy. Their burdens and losses had been great. As the provincials enlisted for one campaign only, a new army was to be raised, new bounties given, and new clothing to be furnished, every spring. So great was the expense, that the colonies were obliged not only to emit bills of credit to a great amount, but to tax the people as highly as they could bear. Besides the public bounties given by the colonies, the merchants, farmers, and gentlemen of character were obliged to advance considerable sums to encourage the enlistments, or they must have left their farms, merchandise, and various employments, and gone into actual service. Especially was this the case with the northern colonies. New England, in general, had, during the war, ten thousand men in the field. Some years, the two colonies of Massachusetts and Connecticut furnished that number. Massachusetts annually sent into the field five thousand five hundred men, and one year, seven thousand. Besides her annual quota, this colony, for several years, garrisoned Louisburg and Nova Scotia, that the regular troops might be employed in the expeditions against Canada. On the application of the

British admiral, she furnished five hundred seamen, in the expedition against Louisburg and Quebec. At several times, many others were impressed out of the vessels employed in the fishery. According to the statement made by Governor Bernard, and transmitted to the lords of trade, the colony had expended in the war, eight hundred and eighteen thousand pounds sterling. Of this sum, three hundred and twenty-eight thousand pounds had been replaced by parliamentary grants. Four hundred and ninety thousand pounds [or $2,177,777] were expended, for which the colony had no parliamentary compensation."[27] In the course of this war, too, it has been estimated by the same Reverend Historian, that the colonies lost considerably more than twenty thousand men. "These, in general," continues he, "were their most firm and hardy young men, the flower of their country. Many others were maimed and enervated in the many distant and arduous campaigns during the war. And as the New England colonies furnished much the greatest number of men, so this loss fell with the heaviest weight upon them."[27]

Of the public losses and sacrifices, particularly those sustained by Massachusetts, during this war, Woburn had her full share. During the five years immediately preceding 1755, when the country was at peace, the average amount of her proportion of the Province Tax was only £139 9*s.* 5*d.* lawful money. But from 1755, when hostilities commenced, till 1763, inclusively, when peace was concluded between the two contending nations, the annual average amount of her proportion of the same tax was £518 9*s.* 9*d.*, almost four times as much as the average in time of peace. But, oppressive as these taxes were, yet such was the patriotic zeal of the people, they appear to have been borne by them, and paid without complaint.

But what is still more observable is the large proportion of men furnished by Woburn in that war for military service. From a partial examination of the voluminous muster roll returns of that war, preserved in the archives of Massachusetts, and also from family papers and indisputable popular tradition,

---

[27] Trumbull's Connecticut, Vol. II., Chap. xxii., pp. 453–455.

it appears, that one hundred and twenty-seven of the inhabitants of this town were enlisted or impressed for service, in the successive stages, and for the various enterprises of that long and bloody contest. And, were the examination of the public documents above referred to completed, it would not improbably enlarge that number to one hundred and fifty. In 1755, when the war commenced, fifty-four Woburn men were enrolled for the expeditions set on foot that year against Nova Scotia and Crown Point alone. Now this number is more than two-elevenths of all the males in Woburn that were taxed upon the Province tax lists of that year,[28] and more than one in twenty-eight of all the inhabitants of the town the same year, reckoning its population in 1755 to have been 1500, which is a large estimate.[29] But what a heavy burden would it now appear to be, if two-elevenths of all the taxable males in any town, or if one out of every twenty-eight of its inhabitants, including old and young, men, women and children, were to be drafted and sent off upon active military service in any one year!

Two interesting memorials, one written, the other traditionary, of persons and events in this war, have been handed down to us by Woburn men, and are well deserving notice in this connection.

The written memorial is a journal of Samuel Thompson, Esq., once a well known, highly respected citizen of this place, now deceased, which was kept by him, while serving in this war, as a soldier. In April, 1758, he joined a company enlisted for the Northern campaign, commanded by Capt. Ebenezer Jones, then of Wilmington, but of Woburn three years before, when he was a leader in the expedition against Crown Point. This company started for the place of its destination May 24th, and reached Fort Edward, June 17th. When it began its march, Mr. Thompson was one of the sergeants: but in consequence of the sudden death of its commander and several

---

[28] Viz: 142 on the west list, and 152 on the east list=294. Town Records, Vol. VII., pp. 162-168.

[29] The total population of Woburn, ten years afterwards, viz: 1765, was 1,515. See Report of Town Clerk of Woburn for 1865, p. 31.

other officers, of wounds received in an attack by the Indians, he was advanced to be a lieutenant. The journal referred to is an account kept by him, daily, of his marches, hardships, and the innumerable incidents which befell him or his fellow-soldiers, or which he had occasion to notice in the public service, from the time he left home in May 1758, till his return thither again in November of the same year. The entire document has been accounted as well worth copying and preserving in this connection; and a place has therefore been given to a copy of it in the Appendix to this work, No. IX.

The traditionary anecdote referred to, in connection with the war of 1755–1763, respects Capt. John Wood, son of John and Esther Wood, who was born August 23, 1740, within the limits of Woburn precinct (now Burlington) where he resided all his days, and died there, October 19, 1809.

At the age of sixteen, and in the second year of the war, Wood repaired to Concord to enlist. The enlisting officer, seeing he was but a stripling, passed him by till all other applicants had left. He then addressed Wood in some such terms as these: "Well, youngster: and what have you come here for?" "To enlist, Sir," said Wood, "if you will accept me." "To enlist!" replied the officer: "Why, do you think you can kill an Indian?" "I don't know about that, Sir," said Wood: "but I think I can fire a bullet into an oak stump as far as any other man." The officer perceiving by this time that he was a bold, hardy, ingenuous youth, though not so old as he could wish, at length took down his age, measured him, and going through all the other ceremonies of enlistment, dismissed him to the company in which he was to serve.

At a certain time during the period of his enlistment in the war, being under the command (as he used to say) of Benedict Arnold, the future traitor in the War of the Revolution, as he and his company were marching through the forests of Canada in midwinter, with the snow three feet under them on a level, and the weather exceedingly cold, one of his comrades was seized with a sore on one of his legs, which became so swollen and painful as totally to disable him for keeping up with the rest. This the captain perceived; and being resolved not to leave him behind to perish with cold, or by the hand of the enemy, and yet being unwilling to stop to take care of him, feeling it to be important to hasten to the post he was going to, which was thirty miles ahead, he called his men together, and then bade any one, who might be willing to stop there and take care of the poor lame soldier till he could send relief from the fort he was marching for, to present his arms. But no one answering to his bidding, John Wood stepped forward, and offered himself for this benevolent, yet hard and trying service. The captain gratefully accepted his offer; and after employing some of his men to build him a little shanty for his shelter, and others to collect in the forest sufficient wood for his fuel, he gave him such necessaries as he could spare him, and a two-quart wooden bottle of rum for his comfort and that of the sufferer he was to wait upon, and then proceeded with his men on their march.

Early the next morning, as Wood drew aside a blanket which served for a door to his shanty, and looked out, he spied four or five Indians approaching, and as he had reason to think, with hostile intent. At this sight, he was utterly dismayed for a few moments. But quickly perceiving it would be of no use to attempt either to resist or to run, he resorted to kindness for protection. He instantly takes the bottle of rum which had been given him, into his hands, and, going out and holding it up to the Indians, cries out "Oncapee, Oncapee," their word for *ardent spirit.* Upon this, the Indians stepped up, but refused to drink, fearing it might be poison, till Wood drank himself. But still apprehending that he might treacherously hold in his mouth what he knew would be death to take down, they insisted upon his drinking again, and make it appear to them that he swallowed it. Wood readily took another sip, which made such a motion before their eyes as it passed down his throat, that the Indians instantly dismissed all suspicions of any evil design in his offering them "Oncapee," and drank of it freely, as much as they thought proper. And now Wood takes them into his hovel, and shows them the diseased swollen limb of his comrade under his charge, as he lay helpless upon the leaves or whatever served him for a bed. Upon viewing it attentively, one of the Indians (who, it seems, was an Indian doctor,) signified to Wood, that he could cure that sore, and that he wished for a flint. The flint being brought, the Indian pounded it to pieces as well as he could, and taking the splinters, he stuck the sore with them by their sharp points, very thickly, which soon caused matter or water to ooze from the swollen leg. And now this Indian surgeon repairs to a tall hemlock hard by, and scraping away the deep snow at its foot, he takes a little herb he found there, and gives Wood to understand that he must make of it a wash which he must apply to the diseased leg three times a day. And now the red men of the forest depart, leaving Wood unharmed, he prepares and applies the wash as directed; and in three days, within which time the promised help from the fort arrived, the poor, lame soldier entirely recovered the use of his limb, and was able to go with Wood and the rest to his company again. How much real, disinterested benevolence did Wood display on this occasion! And what evidence did the uncivilized Indians he had to do with furnish, by their forbearance and kind offices towards two defenceless foes, that, notwithstanding the horrid cruelties with which their countrymen were sometimes chargeable, they could and would act at times in a manner that deserves and challenges our warmest praise.

The ministry of Rev. Mr. Sherman (who, it has been already stated, was ordained in Woburn in 1755,) commenced under very favorable auspices, and promised several years to be long, harmonious and successful. But pecuniary embarrassments, incurred by him originally in the purchase of his house and lands, at length produced uneasiness between him and his people. To relieve him in his perplexed situation, recourse was had, but unsuccessfully, to various expedients. At one time, the parish voted to give him £100 as a present; but this vote was presently after reconsidered, and declared null and void. It was also proposed, that they should purchase of him his homestead, and then allow him to occupy it free of rent; but this measure, also for his help, when they came to act upon it, they declined to adopt. They raised for him, however, in 1761, and three years afterward in succession, in addition to his salary, eight or ten pounds in money for procuring his firewood; and in 1765, they voted him a permanent grant of ten pounds per annum, for this purpose, so long as he should "carry on the whole work of a Gospel Minister" among them.[30] But this grant, though very acceptable to Mr. Sherman, did not essentially relieve him, or satisfy his wants. He was very desirous, that beside this help, an addition should be made to his stated salary in money, so long as he continued to preach among them; and that while he retained his pastoral relation to the church in the place, some provision should be made for his support and comfort, in case he should be necessarily taken off from his ministerial labors by any Providential occurrence. And at length a mutual agreement to this effect was entered into between him and the parish, through their committee, which is here copied from the records.

"Whereas the Rev. Mr Josiah Sherman, Pastor of the First Church in Woburn, appeared in a legal Parish meeting of the First Parish in said Town, on the 20th day of October A. D. 1766, and requested of them, that they would make an addition of ten pounds of Lawful Money to his salary, to be paid to him annually so long as he shall carry on the whole work of the Gospel Ministry in said Parish; and state sixty pounds of his salary to be paid to him annually so long as he shall sustain the character of a Pastor to the Church in said Parish, in case he shall be taken off his labours in Providence:

"In answer to which Request (after the said Parish and the Rev[d] Mr. Josiah Sherman had mutually agreed thereto) the said Parish on the said Twentieth day of October A.D. 1766, passed the following votes, which are to take place and be in force from and after the twenty-eighth day of January, Anno Domini 1767.

"Voted, by said Parish, that they will add to the Rev. Mr Josiah Sherman's salary Ten Pounds of Lawful Money, to be paid to him annually, so long as he shall carry on the whole work of a Gospel Minister in said Parish, in case he will be therewith contented for the future.

---

30 Parish Records, Vol. II., p. 86.

"Voted, that they will state only fifty Pounds Lawful Money to be paid to him annually for his support, so long as he is in the Pastoral Office in said Parish, when he shall be taken off his labours in Providence, in case that he shall request no more, unless he is constrained by necessity to ask more: but not to exceed ten pounds.

"In Testimony of our mutual consent to the above agreement, we have hereunto set our hands this seventeenth day of December, Anno Domini one thousand seven hundred and sixty-six.

"JOSIAH SHERMAN, Pastor.

"BENJA. WYMAN
WILLIAM TAY
JOSIAH PARKER
Committee, in the Name of the Parish."[31]

In accordance with this engagement, the parish at a meeting March 16, 1767, voted "to raise £100 Lawful for Mr. Sherman's salary and firewood the present year, which began January 28th, 1767."[32] For more than seven years, Mr. Sherman forbore to make any complaint, upon record, of the provisions of the above agreement. But necessity seems then to have compelled him to open his mouth. In the warrant for a parish meeting, to be held March 14, 1774, one article was, "To see if the Parish will take the Rev. Mr Josiah Sherman's circumstances under their consideration, and grant him proper relief; or vote him a Release from his Ministerial Relation to them, according to his request on February 15, 1774."[33] This renewed application by Rev. Mr. Sherman to his people, for their help, prepared the way for a twelvemonth's debate and altercation among them upon the subject of his affairs. During that period of time, various plans for his relief were proposed and urged by his friends; but these were all, one after another, obstructed or defeated by a party, that now openly appeared in opposition to Mr. Sherman. In view of this opposition, Mr. Sherman became quite disheartened. As matters now were, he saw no prospect of securing a comfortable maintenance for himself and family. His people, he

---

[31] Parish Records, Vol. II., p. 96. [32] Parish Records, Vol. II., p. 98.
[33] Parish Records, Vol. II., p. 152.

thought, now eyed him in the sanctuary with a different look from that which they once used to present in the Sabbath assembly. It seemed to him that his comfort and usefulness in the place were now gone: and hence he felt constrained to address the parish committee in a letter, dated January 18, 1775, expressing an earnest request that they would call a parish meeting as soon as possible, to see if the parish would be pleased to release him from his ministerial connection. In compliance with this request, a meeting of the parish was held February 6, 1775. But though a majority could not be obtained in parish meeting to aid Mr. Sherman in the way he desired, yet so deep rooted was the attachment to him of many, and so strong appears to have been the expectation of retaining him upon some terms or other, that, at this meeting, a majority could not be found willing to part with him. After sending for Mr. Sherman, and conferring with him, and debating the matter some time, the parish decided after he withdrew, by a vote of thirty-seven to thirty-four, not to dismiss him.[34]

Three other fruitless meetings concerning Mr. Sherman were held February 15th, March 20th and March 27th. That on March 20th was convened in answer to the petition of seventeen persons, to see if the parish would relieve Mr. Sherman by purchasing the place he lived on, or by granting him a sum of money, or in any other way they should deem expedient, and would be agreeable to Mr. Sherman. But at the meeting it was voted not to act on the warrant, and the meeting was declared dissolved.[35] And at the meeting, March 27th, (it being the annual parish meeting) an article was inserted in the warrant, at the petition of ten persons, seconded by a written note from Mr. Sherman, earnestly requesting the parish to release him that day; it was voted again, after adjourning to March 28th, and conferring with Mr. Sherman once more, not to release him.[36]

In the mean while, there was a meeting of the church upon Mr. Sherman's affairs, which resulted as follows:

"At a meeting of the first Church in Woburn conven'd at

[34] Parish Records, Vol. II., p. 170.

[35] Parish Records, Vol. II., p. 174.

[36] Parish Records, Vol. II., p. 179.

the meeting house in the first Parish in said Town March 27th. 1775.

"The following Votes were passed.

"1. That they would dismiss and recommend Mr Josiah Sherman, their present Pastor, in answer to his request.

"Then the following Recommendation was read.

"At a Meeting of the first Church in Woburn March 27th. 1775:

"The Rev.[d] Mr Sherman, who hath been for many years Pastor of this Church, having represented that he is under great difficulties respecting his temporal Circumstances, which, he finds, cannot be removed without disturbing the peace and harmony of this Society; that he therefore thinks it necessary, his Pastoral relation should be dissolved; and having accordingly requested a dismission from us as Pastor:

"The Church having taken the said request, and the circumstances which attend it, into their serious and deliberate consideration, cannot but express their sincere regret at parting with a Minister, whose doctrine and morals have been unexceptionable while he hath been with us, and who hath discharged the duties of his office and trust reposed in him with fidelity and diligence. But as there seems to be no way of removing the difficulties under which Mr Sherman labors, without introducing great contentions and divisions among us, We are obliged to consent to his removal; and do accordingly dismiss him from his Pastoral Relation to this Church, and Recommend him, as one who is well qualified for the Gospel Ministry, to any Church who may employ him in that sacred work. We heartily wish him all the comforts of that Gospel which he hath preached to us; and that he may be an Instrument of building up the Redeemer's Kingdom in the world.

"2. Voted that they were willing to subscribe that form of dismission and Recommendation that was then read to them.

"3. Voted that they would appoint and make choice of a Committee to sign said Recommendation in their name.

"4. Voted Deacon Nathan Richardson, Deacon Samuel Wyman, and Brother William Tay to be a Committee for that purpose.

"JOSIAH SHERMAN, Pastor."[37]

---

[37] Church Records.

Quickly after this action taken by the Church, a petition was handed in to the parish committee, signed by Deacon Nathan Richardson and others, to call a meeting on April 11, 1775, to see if the parish would do anything to relieve Mr. Sherman under his present difficulties, and make him comfortable among them; or, if not, to see if they would release him: and also to act upon another request of Mr. Sherman to be released, dated April 3, 1775.

At this meeting of the parish, April 15, 1775, it was voted, "that [they] will not relieve the Rev$^{d.}$ Josiah Sherman (according to his? Request).

"Voted to dismiss the Rev$^{d.}$ Josiah Sherman from his Ministerial Relation to them, according to his Request, upon his giving the Parish full and proper discharges." [38]

And thus, after a year's altercation, was accomplished the dismission of the Rev. Mr. Sherman from his charge in Woburn, much to the grief of a large proportion of the inhabitants, and greatly, it seems, to the detriment of the cause of religion in the place. It caused the parties concerned to be exceedingly embittered one against the other: so that in all subsequent proceedings of the parish, respecting the employment of candidates to preach, or the re-settlement of the ministry among them, whatever pleased one party, excited the distrust or the opposition of the other; and sufficient union among the people could not be obtained to settle a successor to Mr. Sherman for ten years to come.

Rev. Josiah Sherman was a son of William Sherman, and a brother of Hon. Roger Sherman, a signer of the Declaration of Independence, 1776, and of Rev. Nathanael Sherman of Bedford, Mass., and a descendant of the third generation from Capt. John Sherman, a highly respected citizen of Watertown, its representative in the General Court 1651, 1653, 1663, and eminent for his skill as a surveyor of land, in which capacity he was frequently employed by the Colonial Legislature. He was a cousin to the distinguished minister of Watertown, Rev. John Sherman, who

---

[38] Parish Records, Vol. II., p. 181.

died in 1685, as did Capt. Sherman in 1691. They both originated in Dedham, Essex County, England; and both came to New England about 1635.

William Sherman, above mentioned, a son of Mr. Joseph Sherman of Watertown, and a grandson of Capt. John, was a shoemaker by trade; resided successively at Charlestown, Newton, Stoughton and Watertown; and married at Watertown, for his second wife, Mehetabel, daughter of Benjamin Wellington of that place, September 3, (13 ?) 1715. In the record of this marriage, he is said to have been then of Charlestown. But he soon removed to Newton, where his son Roger was born in 1721; and in 1723, he removed to Stoughton, the birthplace probably of his son Nathanael.

Josiah, fourth son of William and Mehetabel (Wellington) Sherman, the future minister of Woburn, was born at Watertown, April 2, 1729; was graduated at Nassau Hall, Princeton, N. J., 1754; studied theology with Rev. Dr. Bellamy of Bethlehem, Conn. and with Rev. Mr. Graham of Southbury, was ordained at Woburn, January 28, 1756, and dismissed April 11, 1775. From Woburn, he went to Milford, (New Milford?) Conn. In 1781, after leaving Milford, and residing a short time with his family at Stratford, he was installed at Goshen, Conn. Being dismissed from Goshen, in 1788, he lived a while at Sheffield, Mass., and then received and accepted an invitation to settle over the church and society in Woodbridge, Ct., but died soon after his arrival there, November 24, 1789.

Rev. Mr. Sherman was much extolled in his day as a very eloquent preacher. "His elocution (writes one) was very distinct, tho' fluent & rapid. His voice was excellent. His mind was discriminating. His eloquence was often pathetic, sometimes very powerful, and always of such a character as to command the respect & attention of his audience." "While at Goshen, he published several discourses. . . . . One was from the text, 'And he fain would have filled his belly with the husks which the swine did eat;' and was addressed to infidels, in consequence of the publication of "Ethan Allen's Theology."

"The others were on 'the Redemption by Jesus Christ;' and the 'History of Melchizedec." In 1760, while at Woburn, he preached the Artillery Election Sermon from Psalm cxlix. 6; but this was not published.

During Rev. Mr. Sherman's ministry in Woburn, and the short period which elapsed from his dismission, April 11, 1775, and November 26th following, the admissions into his church were one hundred and twenty-six; viz, forty-four males, and eighty-two females, of whom one hundred and nineteen were by profession, and seven by letter. The baptisms were three hundred and ninety-one; viz, three hundred and eighty-one infants, and ten adults.

He married January 24, 1757, Martha, daughter of Hon. James Minot of Concord, by his second wife, Elizabeth Merrick, of Brookfield, and by her had issue, viz:

1. Roger Minot, born December 9, 1757: of Fairfield Conn.: graduated at Yale College, 1794: LL.D., Judge of Sup. Court, Conn.
2. Martha, born December 8, 1758.
3. Elizabeth, born March 26, 1761.
4. Mary, born February 3, 1763.
5. Susanna, born April 7, 1765.

CHAPTER XII.

Revolutionary War, — Sacrifices of Woburn in, both of Men and Money. — Depreciation of Money, and exorbitant prices. — Convention at Concord, to remedy this evil. — Constitutions of this State, and of the United States Government approved. — Colonel Baldwin — Count Rumford.

THE declaration of peace between England and France, in 1763, found the inhabitants of Woburn a loyal people. They were strongly attached to the mother country and its government: and during the war, just brought to a close, they had given signal proof of this their attachment, in freely hazarding their lives, and submitting to many and costly sacrifices, to extend and establish the dominion of Britain. But the unconstitutional enactments and oppressive proceedings of the Parliament of England, which quickly followed the restoration of peace, awakened in all her American colonies, especially in Massachusetts, a feeling of distrust and apprehension, which gradually alienated the minds of the people from the mother country, and issued in open dissatisfaction, complaint, and opposition. This feeling occasionally manifested itself in Woburn. For instance, it prompted the people there, at a meeting, October 20, 1766 (in disregard to the King's recommendation or injunction), to direct their representative in General Court, Josiah Johnson, Esq., not to consent to making up the damages, which Lieut. Governor Hutchinson and other crown officers in Boston had sustained the year before, by the violence of a mob, excited by their resentment at parliament's passing the Stamp Act.[1] Again, it showed itself in their sending delegates (at the invitation of the Selectmen of Boston) to a convention assembled at Boston, September 22, 1768, from numerous towns and districts in the province, to confer with one another upon the existing state of public affairs, and to consider what was to be done.[2] Woburn was represented

[1] Town Records, Vol. IX., p. 10, new paging.

[2] Town Records, Vol. IX., p. 78. Massachusetts Gazette, September 22, 1768. Hatfield e clined sending delegates, for reasons. See Massachusetts Gazette, October 6, 1768.

in that Convention by Mr. Oliver Richardson and Deacon Samuel Wyman. The date of their appointment is not recorded. But at a meeting, March 6, 1769, the town voted them twenty shillings each "for their time and expences at the late Convention in Boston." [2]

But the most noticeable tokens of their uneasiness and dissatisfaction at the public condition were exhibited at a town meeting, called January 14, 1773, to consult what measures to take at that "alarming crisis," that would be "most conducive to the public weal."[3] At this meeting, a recent communication from the town of Boston, "relative to the publick affairs of Government" was first read, and then a committee of nine was chosen, consisting of Lieut. William Tay, Lieut. Joshua Walker, Mr. Joseph Wright, Lieut. Samuel Thompson, Deacon Samuel Wyman, Capt. Thomas Peirce, Mr. Robert Douglas, Dr. Samuel Blogget, Deacon Timothy Winn, to take into consideration the important matters suggested by the above communication, and to report to the town at an adjourned meeting.[3] On the day of adjournment, February 1, 1773, this committee presented to the town a report, consisting of twelve resolutions, in which they acknowledge King George to be their rightful sovereign, profess their attachment to his person, and their confidence in his readiness to do justice to his subjects in these colonies, could their complaints be laid before him. They likewise declare their satisfaction with the British constitution; and disclaim all disposition to cast off their allegiance, or to murmur against the rulers set over them, with a view to obstruct their influence, or weaken their authority, so long as their rulers governed their measures by the principles of the constitution from which their authority was derived. At the same time, they assert their right to petition government for the rectifying of wrongs which they endured, in violation of the constitution of the British government; and specify particular grievances which they conceived they were subjected to, by reason of certain proceedings and acts of parliament, contrary to the privileges, to which, as

---

[3] Town Records, Vol. IX., pp. 188-191.

British subjects, they deemed themselves entitled. Among the grievances complained of, were the following, viz:

The assumption, by parliament, of power to bind them by laws, and to impose on them taxes, without their consent either in person, or by their representatives.

The delivery, by the Governor, of Castle William, which they regarded as the property of the province, under its jurisdiction, and the "key of its defence," into the hands of troops, over whom, nevertheless, the Governor himself had declared, that he had no authority or control.

The exorbitant power of the officers of the Customs.

The extending of the power of the Vice Admiralty Court, so as virtually to deprive the people of this province of their right, in many instances, to a trial by a jury.

The appointment of the Judges of the Superior Court of the province, the grant of their salaries, and the term of their continuance in office, by the King, thus rendering the Judges entirely dependent upon the Crown for their creation and support, and independent of the people, whose property, liberty and lives, do often turn upon their opinions and decisions.[3]

This report was unanimously accepted by the town; instructions, in accordance with it, were given to Mr. Oliver Richardson their representative in General Court;[4] the clerk was ordered to return an attested copy of the proceedings of the meeting to the corresponding committee of the town of Boston; and a committee of five was chosen on behalf of Woburn; viz, Deacon Samuel Wyman, Mr. Robert Douglas, Dr. Samuel Blogget, Mr. Loammi Baldwin, and Deacon Timothy Winn, to correspond with Boston, and any other towns they thought proper.[4]

During the interval which elapsed between the proceedings just recorded, and April 19, 1775, the inhabitants of Woburn gave various tokens of their continued distrust of the government over them, and of their dissatisfaction with it. They repeatedly manifested apprehensions of the approaching contest, and concern to be prepared for it in season. At a general

[4] Town Records, Vol. IX., pp. 191, 192.

meeting, December 23, 1773, they voted to build a house to put their stock of ammunition in; and chose a committee of three, to see that the work was done;[5] and subsequently, they appointed the Selectmen a committee to procure an additional stock of ammunition, viz: two barrels of powder, and bullets and flints in proportion, for the use and benefit of the town.[5]

At a meeting, January 4, 1775, the town chose Dea. Samuel Wyman, a delegate to the Provincial Congress, which was to assemble at Cambridge, (or some other convenient place,) February 1st. They likewise directed their constable, to pay the moneys which they then had in their hands, or might thereafter be raised by the town to defray "the publick charges of Government," to Henry Gardner, Esq., of Stow, till further order be given by the town to the contrary. And agreeably to this direction, Woburn's proportion of the province tax, £75 18*s.* 5*d.*, apportioned by the General Court, May 25, 1774, and assessed January 11, 1775, was paid by the constables to the said Henry Gardner, Esq., instead of Harrison Gray, Esq., the treasurer of the province, appointed the year preceding by the General Court.[6]

At the same meeting, a committee of twenty-one was chosen by the town, as a "Committee of Inspection," "to see that the Association of the Continental Congress [the Non Importation Agreement?] be strictly adhered to."[6]

And, finally, at a meeting, April 17, 1775, it was voted "to raise a number of Minute Men so called, not exceeding fifty, and they to meet half a day every week in each month the six succeeding months, viz: May, June, July, August, September and October, for Instructing themselves in the military science of handling the firelock; and if called into service, the town voted to each man a Dollar as a premium for their services, exclusive of what they shall be allowed by the government."[7]

At length, that momentous day, April 19, 1775, arrived, when commenced the conflict, which issued in the acknowledg-

---

[5] Town Records, Vol. IX., pp. 227, 276. [6] Town Records, Vol. IX., pp. 252, 262.
[7] Town Records, Vol. IX., p. 280.

ment of these United States, as an independent nation. Before daybreak, on the morning of that day, the citizens of Woburn had been notified of the march of the British troops towards Lexington with hostile intent, by means of special messengers, beat of drum, etc., etc.[8] At the receipt of this intelligence, while some stayed behind, to protect their terrified families, or to convey them to places of greater safety, others, in large numbers, hastened to Lexington, not in military array, but promiscuously, armed or unarmed, by the road, or across the fields,[9] as happened to be most convenient, to the defence and aid of their countrymen in that hour of peril. Of those who thus went from Woburn, two did not live to return, viz: Mr. Asahel Porter, son of Mr. William Porter, who was shot down by the British in the early part of the day; and Mr. Daniel Thompson, brother of Samuel Thompson, Esq., who was killed by the enemy in their retreat from Concord. They were both young men of promise; and the following notice of their funerals is extracted from a recent reprint of a sheet published at that period, giving accounts of Lexington fight, taken from E. Russell's Salem Gazette, or Newbury and Marblehead Advertiser of April 21st, April 25th, and May 5th. "Same day [Friday, April 21st] the remains of Messrs. Azel [Asahel ?] Porter and Daniel Thompson, of Woburn, who also fell victims to tyranny, were decently interred at that place, attended to the grave by a multitude of persons, who assembled on the occasion from that and the neighboring towns: Before they were interred, a very suitable sermon and prayer was delivered by the Rev. Mr Sherman."

[8] Mrs. Betsey, widow of Amos Taylor, of Burlington, (whose 100th birthday was commemorated at her request by religious exercises and an appropriate address at her house, October 31, 1864,) once told me, that while it was yet dark, on the morning of the 19th of April, a messenger was despatched from Capt. Joshua Walker, commander of the then military company of the precinct, to her father, Mr. Jonathan Proctor, the drummer of that company, to beat an alarm as soon as possible; for that the "*red-coats*" were on the march towards Lexington, etc., etc.

[9] It is matter of authentic tradition, that as Woburn men crossed the fields on their way to Lexington, on the 19th of April, the winter rye waved like grass before the wind; indicating that to be an unusually forward season.

Rev. Mr. Marrett, ordained pastor of the church in Woburn precinct, December 1774, gives the following account of the transactions of this memorable day, in his interleaved Almanacs, "1775, April 19. Fair, windy & cold. A Distressing Day. About 800 Regulars marched from Boston to Concord. As they went up, they killed 8 men at Lexington meeting house: they huzza'd and then fired, as our men had turned their backs (who in number were about one hundred); and then they proceeded to Concord. The adjacent country was alarmed the latter part of the night preceding. The action at Lexington was just before sunrise. Our men pursued them to and from Concord on their retreat back; and several killed on both sides, but much the least on our side, as *we pickt them off* on their retreat. The regulars were reinforced at Lexington to aid their retreat by 800 with two field pieces. They burnt 3 houses in Lexington, and one barn, and did other mischief to buildings. They were pursued to Charlestown, where they entrenched on a hill just over the Neck. Thus commences an important period."

Two incidents of that eventful day, in which persons belonging to Woburn were concerned, and both of which have been transmitted by authentic and reliable tradition, it may not be uninteresting to rehearse.

Mr. Silvanus Wood, then living at Kendall's Mill in Woburn, was awaked while in bed before daybreak that morning, by a messenger who called to him, announcing that a party of British soldiers was on the march towards Lexington, and urging him to go and join Capt. Parker's company then assembled on Lexington Common. He went, and was mustered in Capt. Parker's company, and was in its ranks when the men were fired upon by the British, after they had turned their backs to retreat, in obedience to the orders of their captain.[10] When the British continued their march that morning towards Concord, Wood followed with his gun in their rear, accompanied by another person who was without a gun. Upon or near Park-

[10] Mr. Wood.

hurst's Hill, in Lexington, about a mile from the meeting-house, observing a British soldier turn aside from the ranks upon some necessary occasion, he hastened up to him while he was alone, and pointing his gun to his breast, ordered him immediately to deliver up himself and his weapon to him, or he should instantly be a dead man. The soldier, taken thus by surprise, and when unable to defend himself, or receive help from others, obeyed; and Wood taking his musket to himself, and giving his own gun into the charge of his unarmed associate, bade him take that man to such a person (or place) in Lexington; and then proceeded himself in the track of the British, towards Concord. What became of the British private, who, taken in an evil hour had surrendered himself and weapon to Wood, could never afterwards be satisfactorily ascertained. It has been conjectured that the soldier, having a supply of British gold in his pockets, offered a piece of it to the person who had him in charge, and with it successfully bribed him to give him his liberty. Upon the ground of this seemingly unavailing capture however, Wood always claimed the honor of having taken the first prisoner in the American War. And urging this claim at Washington, about the year 1824, he obtained, with the aid of Hon. Edward Everett, then Representative in Congress for the District of Middlesex, a handsome pension for life.[10]

Mr. Wood was son of John and Esther Wood, of Woburn Precinct, and a younger brother of the Capt. John Wood mentioned in the chapter preceding. He was born January 27, 1749, O. S.; admitted a member of the Precinct Church, July 5, 1772; was a lieutenant in the Continental army, in his brother's company, and in the regiment commanded by Col. Loammi Baldwin; and died on his valuable farm at Woburn, west side, August 12, 1840, at the advanced age of ninety-one years. His son, of the same name, Mr. Silvanus Wood, of Woburn, from whom some of the facts respecting his father in the above brief notice were originally derived, and by whom all were confirmed, still (1867) lives.

Upon the evening of April 18th, Hon. John Hancock and Hon. Samuel Adams, having left the Provincial Congress, which had adjourned from Concord on the 15th, came to the house of Rev.

Jonas Clark, of Lexington, to lodge. But as soon as it was ascertained, very early the next morning, that a party of British soldiers was approaching Lexington, Capt. Parker, Rev. Mr. Clark, or some other friend of the above-named illustrious, but proscribed guests of the minister, put them in charge (it is said) of Sergeant, afterwards Colonel Edmund Munroe, to conduct them to a place of safety; and he, in fulfilment of this charge, directed them (together with Miss Dorothy Quincy, the future wife of Mr. Hancock) to Madam Jones', in Woburn Precinct, widow of Rev. Thomas Jones, the former minister, whose family was on intimate terms with Rev. Mr. Clark's, and whose house was but about four miles from Lexington Centre. And here the good lady of the house, who was a zealous Whig, in honor of her distinguished guests, and to gratify them as highly as possible, exerted herself to the utmost to provide for them an elegant dinner. Among other delicacies prepared for the occasion was a fine salmon, which had been presented to Messrs. Hancock and Adams, as a rare dainty at that early season; but which, having been left behind in their hasty flight from Lexington, the coachman had been sent back, after their arrival at Mrs. Jones', to bring with him on his return.

The hour for dinner being at length come, Mrs. Jones, with her honored guests, and Rev. Mr. Marrett, the recently settled minister of the parish, then boarding at her house, sat down with keen appetites to the repast she had provided for them. But scarcely had they seated themselves at the table, when a man fresh from the bloody scenes at Lexington, rushed into the room where they were, and with uplifted hands and affrighted looks exclaimed, "My wife, I fear, is by this time in etarnity; and as to you, (addressing himself to Hancock and Adams) you had better look out for yourselves, for the enemy will soon be at your heels." Startled by this unexpected, earnest warning, all the company instantly rose from the table, and prepared for concealment or flight. Their first care was, to put the coach out of sight, in which Mrs. Jones' guests had been conveyed from Lexington, and which was then standing by the road side in front of the house. This was hurried into Path Woods, in the northwest part of the precinct, near the road to Billerica. Mr. Marrett next conducted Mrs. Jones' illustrious visitors to the house of Mr. Amos Wyman, situate in an obscure corner of Bedford, Billerica and Woburn Precinct, where were collected the women and children of several of the neighboring families, who had fled thither for safety; fearing that if they remained at home, "the regulars" might come, and murder them, or carry them off. And now, as soon as Messrs. Hancock and Adams had had time to become calm after their flight, they besought Mrs. Wyman to give them a little food; saying they had had neither breakfast nor dinner that day. Their good natured hostess, in ready compliance with their request, took down from a shelf a wooden tray, containing some cold boiled salt pork, and also (it is believed) some cold boiled potatoes unpealed, and brown bread; and upon this plain, coarse fare, they made a hearty meal.[11] Upon their return to Mrs. Jones' the next day, they learned that the enemy had not come there in pursuit of them. Either they had never intended it, or else, being closely pursued from Concord by their exasperated and hourly increasing Yankee foes, they thought it best to take a prudent care for their own safety, rather than to digress in their march, into the neighboring towns, in pursuit of Hancock and Adams. Not many years since, it was a current report in Lexington, that Hancock, in gratitude to Mrs. Wyman for her kindness to him and Adams at her house, in their flight for fear of the British, made a present to her of a cow.

Through the whole contest with the mother country now begun, Woburn acted a decided and zealous part. At the commencement of the war, a few of her citizens were charged with being inimical to the cause of their country.[12] But the great

[11] Report of Madam Jones, confirmed by Madam Hancock, afterwards Madam Scott.

[12] At a town meeting, June 23, 1777, in pursuance of previous arrangements, the Selectmen reported the names of Caleb Simonds and Luther Simonds, as being, in their opinion, "enemies to this and the United States." Whereupon it was voted "that the said Caleb and Luther Simonds be tried, to see whether they be inimical to this and the United States, agreeably to an Act entitled an 'Act for securing this and the United States against the dangers to which they are exposed by the

body of the people were steadfast opposers of the unconstitutional claims and pretensions of Great Britain, and determined to do all in their power to preserve inviolate those rights and liberties for which they were contending.

In particular, a very large number of her citizens, in proportion to her population, enlisted in the war.

In the year 1775, the number of the male inhabitants of Woburn who were taxed in the Province or State tax for that year, was three hundred and eleven. This number was afterwards considerably enlarged each year of the war's continuance, so that at its close, in 1783, the average number of the male inhabitants of Woburn who had been annually taxed in the ordinary State tax, while the war was going on, was three hundred and thirty-two. But from various authentic documents, especially from numerous town orders for the payment of her soldiers, and their receipts for the same, still preserved in the archives of Woburn, it appears, that no fewer than three hundred and seventy-six distinct individuals, from among her own male population, enlisted in the service of their country in this contest, besides forty-six persons from abroad, who were employed and paid by the town for the same purpose. For a list of those persons, see Appendix, No. XII.

At the beginning of the war, men were procured to serve in it, by drafting in equal proportions from the three military companies then belonging to the town. Afterwards, enlistments were obtained by a committee appointed by the town, "to hire men into the War." In this way, the three years' men were enlisted in the Continental army from Woburn in 1777, and the six months' men, in 1780. And subsequently the method of classing was resorted to for this purpose. It seems that, agreeably to Resolves of the General Court, in Feb. 1781, and March 1782, the assessors of every deficient town were authorized to distribute all its taxable inhabitants (where the people had not

internal enemies thereof.'" The meeting was then adjourned to July 7th, when after long debate, it was again adjourned to the last Monday in August, and then again to September 15, when the whole design was abandoned, and the meeting dissolved. — *Town Records, Vol. IX., p.* 377.

already classed themselves) into as many classes as the quota of men required of it amounted to, to assess where necessary, the several members of each class their just proportion of the expense of procuring its man; and, if any one proved delinquent in paying his assessment, to put the amount into the hands of a collector, to collect and pay it over to the treasurer of the town. Several documents, illustrative of this new, unusual mode of obtaining men to serve in war, are still extant in Woburn; from which, as matters of curiosity, the following are selected.

" Memorandum of a Class made out by James Fowle jun^r^, and others, in order to hire Philip Alexander as a Soldier for three years, to fill up the Continental Army, agreeably to Recommendation of the General Court.

Heads.	Names.	Silver Tax.	Heads.	Names.	
			.	. . . . .	£7.12.5
1	James Fowle jun^r^.	£2 :14.0.	1	John Tay	0 :19.7
1	John Bruce	5.0	1	Col. Loammi Baldwin	2 :2 :4
1	John Richardson	13.8	1	Mr Jacob Coggin	10 :8
1	Benjn. Fowle	1 :10.8	1	James Tottingham	6.0
1	David Wyman	9.4	2	Daniel Reed	2 :2 :0
1	Aaron Tay	1 :3 :1	2	Capt. Nathl. Brooks	1 :17 :4
1	John Fox	9.0	1	Philip Alexander	5.0
1.	James Wyman	7.8			
					15 :15 :4
		" 7 :12 :5		Pay to Mr Paul Wyman	4 :6
					"£1510 :10 :

"Double four times"

" Woburn June 7th. 1781.

" SAMUEL BLODGET } Assessors.
" ZEB^h^. WYMAN }

" To Mr James Fowle & Class." [13]

" We the Subscribers [have] assessed the delinquent members belonging to the Class No. 2 (Capt. Nathaniel Brooks head of said Class) the sum of £22 :5 :7 : and committed the same to Mr Paul Wyman, one of the Collectors of Woburn, to collect and pay to the Treasurer of Woburn, according to the Resolve of the Great and General Court, dated March ye 8th. 1782.

" SAMUEL THOMPSON } Assessors. [13]
" JEDUTHUN RICHARDSON }

" Woburn April 26. 1782."

[13] Class Papers on file.

Of the large number above designated of the citizens of Woburn, engaged in the war, all did not serve their country in one way only; but a considerable proportion of them, at different periods of the contest, in more ways than one. In the years 1775, 1776, there were various military services, or "tours of duty," as they were termed, to employ her men, as enlisting for eight months, and afterwards, for one year, in the Continental Army; guarding at the lines of Boston, Charlestown, Cambridge, and Roxbury; serving in detachments sent into the States of New York and New Jersey; and joining the expeditions to Ticonderoga and Canada. In one or more of these ways, during the two years named above, one hundred and eighty citizens of the town enlisted in the war, as appears from orders on the Treasurer still extant, which were given in their favor, and are receipted by them; and which, being dated, for the most part, early in 1777, the year next following, are expressly stated to be in payment of services performed "in the present War," or "before January 1777."

Subsequently to 1776, (as appears from additional orders on file for the payment of soldiers, and from other authentic or reliable documents, still preserved,) numerous individuals, inhabitants of Woburn, and persons who were strangers in the place, were enlisted in the war, for various other services, such as the exigencies of the times required.

But Woburn manifested her zeal in sustaining the War for Independence, not only by furnishing men to contend in the struggle, but also by liberal grants of money for the encouragement of those men, and large supplies, according to their ability, of food and clothing for their support.

At a town meeting, held December 13, 1776, and called "in observance of the Resolves of the Continental Congress now sitting at Philadelphia," it was voted to raise £1,500 lawful money, "to defray the charges that had or may arise, relative to the raising or hiring men in this town for the defence of these American Colonies, relating to the unhappy dispute between them and Great Britain." . . . . .

"*Voted*, to choose a Committee of nine men 'to enquire and

see what each and every one *has paid*[14] and to ascertain the sum total of said charges: and to report to the town upon the adjournment, what each turn or tour of duty shall be set at, for their acceptance.' etc. etc.

"*Also Voted,* that the Town will proportion the necessary charges that have arisen over and above those Encouragements that have been given by the Continent or this State since April y.e 19th. 1775, and all Charges [that] shall arise, during these unhappy disputes with Great Britain, relating to hiring troops for our defence; and to levy the same as all other taxes are levied."[15]

At the adjournment of this meeting, December 27, 1776, the committee of nine, then appointed, reported as follows:

"To each and every Person, which is to be paid out of the Town Treasury, as follows, Viz.

"For the first eight Months in the year 1775, per man	£4: 0:0.
"For the two Months Service in the beginning of 1776.	1: 0:0
"For twelve Months in the Continental Army	8: 0:0.
"For five Months at Ticonderoga	12: 0:0.
"For five Months at or near Boston lines.	0:12:0.
"For two Months at New York	6: 0:0.
"For the three Months at New York [and New Jersey ?]	12: 0:0."[15]

This Report was read and accepted. And now to defray the expenses hitherto incurred by Woburn in the war, and especially to pay her soldiers the bounties which she had engaged to give them, over and above the encouragements that had been given them by this State or the country to expect, the £1,500 lawful money, which it had been voted to raise for these purposes, was

[14] In this expression (has paid) and others which occur in the lists of two of the military companies in Woburn (Documents, Vol. I., II.,) it seems to be implied that several, both of the soldiers and other citizens, advanced money to pay immediate expenses of the war, and had it deducted from their proportion of the tax of £1,500, soon after assessed.

[15] Town Records, Vol. IX., p. 331.

assessed February 18, 1777. And from its proceeds, apparently, there was paid

"To the 22 men who engaged in the two months service at the beginning of 1776	£23 :13 :0
"To those who enlisted for a year in the Continental Army	247 :13 :4
"To the men who marched June 24th, 1776 [to Ticonderoga] under Capt. Samuel Tay	607 :13 :8.
"To 20 men, who served 2 months in 1776 under Capt. Samuel Belknap, in New York—	120 : 0 :0.
"To 21 men, who served three months under the same commander in New York, or New Jersey	303 : 2 :7."
Amounting in all to . .	£1302 :2 : 7 [16]

The residue of the £1,500 lawful money, (equivalent to £1,562 depreciated currency,[17]) voted, December 13, 1776, to be raised by tax for the payment of military expenses, was probably paid in the bounties agreed upon to give the men who enlisted in 1775 for eight months, in the Continental army, and to those who served five months at one time, in 1776, at the Boston lines.

Subsequently to 1776, Woburn paid during the war, in bounties to her soldiers, the nominal sum of £48,944 0*s.* 8*d.* This sounds like an enormous amount of money to be appropriated by a single town to this purpose, at that day. But here it is to be observed that while, previously to the commencement of 1777

---

[16] War Document, XII.

[17] War Document, XVIII., "the whole amount of the expenses [bounties] arising by the War, in Capt. Samuel Belknap's Company, from the beginning of the present War up to the first of January 1777

	£533 : 2 : 8½
" Amount of do in Capt. Jesse Wyman's Company	461 : 1 : 3.
" Amount of ditto in Capt. Joshua Walker's Company	567 :18 :11½
" Amount	1562 :2 :11."

bounties were equivalent in value, or nearly so, to their nominal, amount in lawful money, they were paid from the beginning of that year in depreciated bills of credit; and their depreciation increased with surprising rapidity towards the close of the war. On this head, Lemuel Shattuck, Esq., remarks, in his History of Concord, "The value of money was regulated monthly." . . . . "January 1st. 1777, $100 in silver was worth $105 currency; in 1778 [January 1st?] $328; in 1779, $742; in 1780, $2,934; and in February 1781, $7,500."[18] At this rate of depreciation, it is obvious that the nominal bounties paid by Woburn, after 1776, to the soldiers in her employ, would quickly become greatly diminished in value. To ascertain their real worth in lawful money, let $100 in silver be accounted as equivalent to $105 currency through the whole year 1777, as it was, according to Mr. Shattuck, on the first day of January of that year; let the same sum in silver be estimated equal, agreeably to his statements, to $328 paper, in 1778; to $742, in 1779; to $2,934, in 1780;[19] and to $7,500 paper in February 1781, which was as soon, almost without exception, as the bounties due to the six months' men, hired in June 1780, were paid them; and the nominal amount of the bounties paid by Woburn after 1776, would at once be reduced from £48,944 8*s.* to £5,283 4*s.* in lawful money. To this sum add the £1,500, paid before 1777, and the sum total of the bounties paid by Woburn in the war of the Revolution will be £6,783 4*s.*, lawful money.

The annexed schedule exhibits the numbers of the men employed by Woburn, in distinct companies, for various military services after 1776; the times and places when and where they served; the names of their respective *commanders*; the kind of service in which they were severally engaged; the nominal bounties they received for those services; and the annual amount, nearly, of those bounties in lawful money; so far as these several particulars can now be ascertained.

---

[18] History of Concord, p. 123.

[19] Zebadiah Wyman, Esq., Treasurer of Woburn in 1780, casually remarks on a loose paper left behind him, "1400 Paper Dollars, in the year 1780, Augt 4th. is £6:0:0 [or $20] in specie." In this proportion, $100 in silver would be equal to $7,000 paper at that time; and between August 4, and December 31, 1780, there would be ample room for $7,000 to sink five hundred dollars.

SCHEDULE.

	Nominal bounties	Value in lawful money
1777: \$100=\$105. Fourteen men, 3 months from Jany 1st., in a "tour of duty" at Boston, at 12/each	£8 :8 [20]	
Twelve men, 2 months, under Capt. Jesse Wyman, at Rhode Island	72 :0 [20]	
Twenty nine men, about 4 months, under Capt. Abraham Foster [of Wilmington?] at the Westward, [against Burgoyne]	491 :8 [21]	
Sixty four men in the "Fifteen Battalions" required of Massachusetts for the Continental Army, enlisted for three years, or during the War.	1558 :0 [22]	
Twenty men, 2 months from Septr 1st. at Cambridge, under Lieut. Joseph Johnson, "guarding Stores."	154 :8 [23]	
Twenty five men, 5 months from Novr 1st. under Capt. Cadwallader Ford of Wilmington, "guarding prisoners" at Cambridge.	283 :14 [24]	
Twenty six men, hired Decr 22d. to do military duty, for a bounty of £12.00 each; but service and commander not named.	312 :00 [25]	£2742 :00
1778: \$100=\$328. Twenty men, 3 months at Bunker Hill, under Capt. Jesse Wyman, by Order of Court, Feb. 7. 1778.	216 :10 [26]	
Eight men, 3 months from April 2d. under Lieut. Nathan Dix, guarding prisoners at or near Cambridge.	88 :8 [27]	
Four men, under Capt. Benja^{n} Edgell, in Rhode Island, till Jany 1. 1779, by Order of Court June 10. 1778.	129 :00 [28]	
Twenty seven men, by Resolve of Court June 25 [23d?] 1778, 15 days at the Lines, "to guard prisoners."	67 :10 [28]	
Eight men, by Order of Brigadier, June 26th to serve 5 months at the Lines, "to guard prisoners of Convention." [29]	108 :00 [29]	
Twelve men, hired April 20th. to join the Conti-		

[20] Documents, X., XVIII.

[21] Documents, XVIII. This document mentions twenty-four men only. But there are twenty-nine orders on file for paying twenty-nine distinct individuals, as engaged in the expedition under Capt. Foster.

[22] Documents, X., XVIII.

[23] Documents, V., VIII., X., XVIII.

[24] Documents, VI., VIII., X., XVIII.

[25] Documents, XII.

[26] Documents, VIII., X., XVI , XVIII.

[27] Documents, VII., VIII., X., XVIII.

[28] Documents, XV.

[29] The captured army of Burgoyne. The treaty of capitulation, by which it was surrendered to Gates, was called a "*Convention.*"

	Nominal bounties	Value in lawful money
nental Army at Fishkill for 9 months: bounty paid.	1190 :00 [30]	
Eight men hired to do duty at the North River, as Militia, for eight months: bounty	815 :00 [30]	
Six weeks men (number not stated) to serve in Rhode Island; by Order of Council July 1778.	335 :14 [31]	
Men (number not given) engaged Septr 6th. to serve in Rhode Island, and afterwards ordered to Boston, under Lieut. Joseph Winn, for 3½ months, ending Jany 1st. 1779.	339 :8 [31]	1003 :00
1779: $100=$742. Levies of fifty men in all made in January, April, June and October 1779, and bounty money paid them, amounting to £7976 :00; but to what place these men were ordered, and for what service is not stated [32]	7976 :00	1074 :18
1780. Twenty seven men, to serve 3 months in Rhode Island, under Capt. William Green of Reading. Their wages appear to have been paid them by the town, which was then reimbursed by the State. No bounty mentioned.[33]		
Twenty nine men were hired to serve in the Continental Army six months, for a bounty of £1200 :00 each, paper money.	34800 :00 [34]	464 :00
Amount of Bounties after 1776.	£48945 :08	£5283 :18

1781: $100=$7500. But it was not only men for the army, and bounty money to encourage them to enlist, that was required of Woburn. In the course of the War, in common with all the other towns in the State, this town was called upon to furnish her due proportion of meat for the sustenance of the soldiers, and of raiment for their wear, and of horses for cavalry or draught. And from numerous Documents, originally kept in the town treasurer's office, and still extant, there can be no doubt that the town fully answered all the demands made on her for these ends.

[30] Documents, X., XVIII.

[31] Documents, XII., XV.

[32] Documents, XII.

[33] Documents, IX.

[34] Document, XII., and orders on file for the payment of the men. £12 bounty per man appears to be the sum originally agreed upon. But in consequence of the continued depreciation of the paper currency, orders were eventually given many of the soldiers for their bounty, amounting to £1,650 and £1,800 currency. And yet, in paying two such orders in 1782, the treasurer allowed in lawful money only £12 2*s.* 8*d.* for £1,800, and only £12 for £1,650 currency, including in both instances, "expenses of travel home."

	Nominal or Depreciated,	Lawful Money.
1780: \$100=\$2934. By two Resolves of the State Legislature, passed in September and December 1780, Woburn was required to supply the Continental Army with 24078 pounds of beef; or if the town preferred, to furnish the worth of that quantity of provision in money. In these two instances, agents employed by the town raised a large proportion of the beef required; and two Beef Taxes were assessed in October and December of that year, amounting to £54927 currency, to pay for the whole.	£54927 :00	£1872 :01 :00
1781: \$100=\$7500. From the following Receipt on file, the Legislature appears to have passed a third Resolve on this subject Jany 4. 1781. "Woburn Feb. 20. 1781. Received of the town of Woburn, by the hand of Mr Zebadiah Wyman, treasurer for said town, the sum of five thousand pounds, in lieu of three thousand five hundred and three pounds & two thirds of a pound of beef, in part of said town's proportion of beef, agreeable to a Resolve of the General Court Jany 4. 1781; for which I have given duplicate Receipts. Reuben Kimball, Agent."	5000 :00	66 :13 :4
A fourth Resolve was passed by the Court June 22d. 1781, by which 9938 lbs. of beef was apportioned on Woburn for the supply of the Army. In regard to this requisition, the town at a meeting July 16. 1781 chose a committee of five, to purchase the proportion of beef now called for, at the town's expense. Several citizens advanced specie for the immediate purchase of the beef demanded; agents procured the meat asked for; and were eventually reimbursed by Orders on the town treasurer. If the charge per 100 lbs for the 9938 lbs was equal to that charged for a portion of that quantity mentioned in the annexed Order,[35] viz. 33/9*d* lawful money per 100 lbs, the whole cost was £167 :14 lawful money, equal to £12525 and upwards of depreciated currency that year.	12525 :00	167 :14 :0
Total expense of the town for beef	£72452 :00	£2106 :8 :4

[35] "To the Treasurer of the Town of Woburn: Sir, please to pay Col. Loammi Baldwin eight pounds in *specie*, in part for three thousand pounds of beef, he supplied the Town of Woburn for the use of the army, at 33/9 per hundred, in 1781. Woburn Feb. 11. 1782.

Zebh Wyman
Joseph Johnson &c } Selectmen of Woburn."

Again, Woburn was repeatedly called upon to furnish its due proportion of clothing for the army. A Resolve was passed by the State Legislature, March 13, 1778, requiring each town in the State to provide for the army as many shirts, pairs of shoes and pairs of stockings, as would be equal to one-seventh part of all its male inhabitants. These articles when collected in any town were to be delivered by its Selectmen or committee to the agent appointed for the county in which that town was situated. The agent, in his turn, was to provide wagons or other suitable carriages, at the public expense, for the conveyance of those articles to the State Commissary in the northern or in the southern department of the army, agreeably to directions of the resolve. And the commissioners were required to deliver without delay, in their respective departments, out of the articles of clothing thus put into their hands, by the several towns, one shirt, one pair of shoes and one pair of stockings, as "a present from the people of this State," to each non-commissioned officer, and to each private soldier, raised in this State, and enlisted in the service for three years, or during the war, towards filling up the State's quota of the continental army.[36] This Resolve was printed, and a copy was sent to each town, and one to each agent in the State. And Woburn, upon receiving a copy, showed no backwardness to comply with its requisitions. At town meeting, March 31st, soon after the Resolve was passed, it was voted to draw money out of the treasury, to buy stockings, shoes and shirts with, for Woburn's part of the continental army. And numerous orders on the town treasurer, still preserved on file, do show that in compliance with this Resolve of the Legislature, large supplies of every description of clothing mentioned in it, at a cost of above £650, were brought in to the Selectmen, to be transported under their care, to the state storehouse in Concord, kept by James Barrett, Esq., agent for

---

[36] "The Continental Journal, and Weekly Advertiser," Boston, March 19, 1778.

the county of Middlesex. See copies of a few of these orders in the notes.[37]

Moreover, a Resolve was passed by the State Legislature, June 22, 1781, "for collecting clothes for this Commonwealth's quota of the Continental army," etc., etc.[38] By this Resolve, there was apportioned upon the whole county of Middlesex nine hundred and ninety-three shirts, and as many pairs of stockings, and of shoes, and four hundred and ninety-six blankets; and of these articles, Woburn was required to supply forty-two shirts, forty-two pairs of stockings, forty-two pairs of shoes, and twenty-one blankets; the same apportionment as was set upon the adjoining town of Reading. To make sure of, or to facilitate Woburn's compliance with this requisition, a meeting, to be held August 13, 1781, was

---

[37] "To the Town Treasurer.

"Sir: Please pay Dea. David Blanchard forty one pounds and eight pence in full for Shirts and Hose, and making Shirts, and for collecting and carrying the store to Concord for the Continental Soldiers; and this shall be your Discharge for the same.

"£41 :0 :8.
"Woburn Sept[r] 10. 1778.

"William Tay
"Samuel Thompson
"Jed[n] Richardson
"Jona. Tidd
} Selectmen."

"Sir Please to pay to Sam[l] Leathe twenty seven pounds in full for fifteen pair Shoes he has supplied the Town with for the use of the Continental Soldiers.

"Woburn, May 4th. 1778.
"To Jona. Lawrence, Treasurer.

"William Tay
"Sam[l] Thompson
"Benja[n] Edgell
"Jed[n] Richardson
} Selectmen."

"To the Town Treasurer.

"Sir: Please to pay Col. Loammi Baldwin eighty seven pounds, six shillings & eight pence in full for Shirts he delivered to the Selectmen to turn into the State Store &c &c &c

"Woburn 11th Feb[y] 1780. [Signed] } Selectmen."

"To the Town Treasurer.

"Sir, Please to pay Zechariah Richardson twenty pounds for Hose he delivered to the Selectmen, to turn into the State Store; and this shall be &c &c &c

"Woburn 11th. February 1780.

"William Tay
"Sam[l] Thompson
"Benj[n] Edgell
} Selectmen."

[38] Vol. of Resolves at the State House; No. LXIV.

notified by the Selectmen, of such inhabitants as were disposed to give their assistance towards it. At that meeting, sundry individuals agreed to secure the complement of clothing for the soldiers that was demanded of this town; and there can be no question that their agreement was duly and faithfully fulfilled. Many individuals, both male and female, were now set on work, procuring cloth and making it up into shirts, knitting stockings, making shoes, and providing blankets; and upon finishing their work, they severally presented their bills, and obtained orders for payment out of the treasury of the town, which, in return, agreeably to provisions of the Resolve of Court above referred to, was reimbursed for its expense upon the articles of raiment supplied by it, out of the treasury of the State. Orders yet extant, obtained for articles of clothing for the army, furnished by inhabitants of Woburn under this Resolve of Court, amount to about £100. Copies of a few of these Orders are given in the notes.[39]

---

[39] "Sir, Please to pay Mr Saml Leathe one pound ten shillings two pence two farthings in part for fifteen pairs Shoes he supplied the Selectmen with in December 1781. Woburn Jany 28. 1782.

"To Mr Zeb^{h} Wyman
"Treasurer for s^{d} Town.

"Loammi Baldwin
"Paul Wyman
"Zeb^{h} Wyman
} Selectmen of Woburn."

"Sir, Please to pay Mr Saml Leathe five pounds, nineteen shillings & nine pence two farthings in full for fifteen pairs of Shoes, at 10/ a Pair, he supplied the Selectmen with in Decemb^{r} 1781; he having received an Order for the other part. Woburn Jany 28th. 1782.

"To Mr Zebadiah Wyman
"Treasurer for s^{d} Town."

"Loammi Baldwin
"Paul Wyman
"Zeb^{h} Wyman
} Selectmen of Woburn."

"Sir: Please to pay Mr Jacob Caldwell five Pounds two Shillings in full for four Blankets he supplied the Selectmen of Woburn for ye use of ye Army in 1781, at 25/6. Woburn Feb. 18. 1782

"To Mr Zeb^{h} Wyman, Treasurer for Woburn.

"Loammi Baldwin
"Joseph Johnson
"Zeb^{h} Wyman
"Ezra Wyman
} Selectmen of Woburn."

"Woburn February 19. 1782.

"Sir, Please to pay to Paul Wyman the sum of seven pounds, it being in part for his procuring the following parts of Clothing: Viz^{t} Shirts,

During the whole of the Revolutionary War, Woburn was excessively burdened with taxes, the larger portion of which that war had originated, and rendered necessary. In 1774, the year before the commencement of the contest, its province tax was but £75 18*s.* 5*d*; its county tax, £21 2*s.* 6*d.*; and its town rate only £150; making its taxes, of every description, for that year but little more than £247. But during the years the war continued, viz: from 1775 to 1783, inclusively, taxes in Woburn rose within a trifle to the enormous nominal sum of £300,000. Most of these rates, it is true, were made payable in the depreciated, ever declining currency of that day. But after making all due allowance for the depreciation of the paper they were payable in, they will be found, when added to the taxes that were expressly ordered, or evidently intended to be assessed in lawful money, or to be paid in silver or gold, to amount to a little more than £28,000, lawful money.[40] In the course of the nine years above referred to, there were assessed in Woburn, and ordered to be collected and paid over to the Town, County, or State Treasurer, twelve town and five county rates; twelve State taxes, three "Continental taxes," (as they were termed); two "War taxes," four "Silver" or "hard money taxes," and two "Beef taxes,"[41] making forty assess-

---

shoes, stockings and blankets he supplied the State for Woburn in 1781: and his Receipt &c

"To the Treasurer of the Town.

"Zebh Wyman
"Joseph Johnson
"Ezra Wyman } Selectmen of Woburn."

[40] In reducing sums in paper currency to their equivalents in lawful money, I have observed here and elsewhere the rule suggested by Lemuel Shattuck, Esq., in his History of Concord, and quoted above in this chapter.

[41] The reason of the distinction made in the records between "Continental" and "State" taxes is unknown. Taxes of both descriptions were made by order of the General Court of the State, and were payable alike to the State Treasurer, without naming any distinct object for either. The two "War taxes" were ordered by votes of the town in 1776 and 1777, expressly to enable the town to defray the charges incurred by it thus far in the war. Of the four "Silver," or "Hard money taxes," two were imposed by the town and two by the State. The "Beef Taxes" were to raise money for the purchase of beef for the army. All taxes assessed after 1780 appear to have been in "lawful money."

ments within nine years. That these public burdens must have weighed very heavily upon the people will be readily perceived. Especially must this have been the case in the year 1780, when, beside a tax of £376, to be paid in specie, no less than eight other taxes were assessed in Woburn, amounting, in all, to £230,889 currency, equal to £7,869 8*s*., lawful money, or to £8,245 8*s*., inclusively of the silver tax of £376, just referred to. Again, to pay the "large town tax," as it was called, assessed in July of that year, and amounting, nominally, to £60,190, equivalent to £2,051 9*s*., lawful money, there were only three hundred and seventy-seven residents, and fifty-six non-resident tax payers; of the residents, twenty-three were widows and unmarried females, and seventy-four paid only a poll-tax or less; and of the fifty-six non-residents, forty-nine paid less than a poll-tax, which, in that assessment, was £41 currency. Under such circumstances, how must these and the like burdens have ground some of those they fell upon to the very dust, as it were! And what could have sustained any under the load, but the persuasion, that the load of oppression which they must otherwise have borne, was still heavier; and that they were contending for a boon, which was more precious than houses, lands, money, or life itself could be without it?

The burdens of taxation which the war for Independence occasioned were vastly enhanced by the constant depreciation of the paper currency, which the government issued to pay the expense of the contest. For two or three years after the war broke out, the currency seems to have varied but little in value from lawful money. But in the fourth year (1778) that variation had become considerable, and was continually increasing. Wages for labor by the month, paid at the end of six months, in the nominal sum agreed upon, would not purchase for the laborer nearly so large a supply of necessaries for his family as they would when contracted for. Goods bought to be sold again seldom brought back to the trader a return of equal worth to his purchase money, though it might nominally exceed it. And a legacy devised to a widow in needy circumstances, kept back a year by the executor, as the law allowed, and then paid in the paper currency of the day, was sure to be of far inferior worth to the sum named and intended in the will. To remedy the grievous evils growing out of this state of things, and which were universally felt, a State convention was held at Concord, July 14, 1779, in which Woburn was represented by its delegate, Deacon Samuel Thompson. There were present at this convention one hundred and seventy-four delegates, who, "after passing some very spirited resolutions, fixing the prices of several articles of merchandise, and agreeing upon an address to the people, adjourned on the 17th, recommending another similar Convention to meet again in October."[42] The proceedings of the convention, "relative to the lowering the exorbitant prices of all and each of the necessaries of life," were accepted by the inhabitants of Woburn, at a meeting August 4th, and a committee of nine was chosen "to report to the town on this subject at the adjournment of the meeting to August 26th. The report of this committee, which was duly presented and accepted by the town, was as follows:

"West India Flip or Toddy at 12*s*. per mug or bowl: New England 10*s*. per mug.

"A common Dinner 15 / ; other meals in proportion.

"Keeping a horse at hay 15 / ; at grass 10 / per night.

"Oats 45 / per bushel; 5 / per mess.

"A yoke of Oxen 12 / per night at grass.

"Lodging 4 / per night.

"Day Labour 48 /, being found, until the last of August; after that, 36 / per day.

"A Team carrying a ton weight, 18 / per mile, not going more than 90 miles.

"Carpenters and Masons 54 / per day, being found.

"Horse shoeing all round, steeling the fore shoes at the toe, £3 12*s*.

"Shoeing Oxen, 16 dollars per yoke: other smith work in proportion.

"A Tailor 36 / per day.

"Green Hides 3 / per pound: Sole Leather 18 / per pound; and all other Leather in proportion.

[42] Shattuck's Concord, p. 122.

"Mens best Shoes 18 dollars per pair; women's best Leather Shoes 84/.

"For making mens shoes 48/: Womens, 40/ per pair: and other work in proportion.

"Cloth Shoes, finding the leather and heels, 54/.

"Sheeps Wool, 23/ per pound; Flax, 15/ per lb; Rough Tallow 9/ per pound.

"And all other mechanics that are not mentioned here, are to work in the same proportions as those that are here mentioned.

"Per Order of the Committee,

BENJ^{N}. EDGEL, Clerk."[43]

At the same adjourned meeting, (August 26th,) a committee of fifteen was chosen "to Inspect and see that the Resolves of the Convention begun and held at Concord on the fourteenth day of July last, and the Resolves of the Committee chosen by this Town at a General Town Meeting, August the 4th. 1779, be strictly adhered to in each and every particular."

A committee also of three was chosen at the same time, consisting of Dr. Samuel Blogget, Timothy Winn, Jr., and Isaac Johnson, which "should draw up something by way of Instructions" for the committee of inspection. This committee of three, after a short interval, made a report, which being read, was accepted and passed. Their report contained several very stringent resolutions, among which was substantially the following, namely: That if any person belonging to this town should violate the resolutions of the Concord Convention, or those of this town made in pursuance thereof, he should, upon conviction, [at a public trial before the committee of inspection] be accounted as an enemy of his country, have his name published in the newspapers of Boston, and be cut off from all intercourse and dealings with the other inhabitants of the town for such a term of time as the committee of inspection should appoint.[44]

But it was probably soon found by experience that it is easier to pass resolutions concerning such matters, than to enforce them. We read of no one being accused of a breach of these

[43] Town Records, Vol. IX., pp. 521, 522. [44] Town Records, Vol. IX., pp. 521, 522.

Orders of the town, or of suffering the penalty annexed to the transgression of them. At a town meeting, October 22, 1779, a new committee was chosen "to stipulate prices for the town of Woburn." At an adjournment of this meeting, November 1st, the report of this committee in regard to prices was recommitted, for the sake of making amendments and additions; and then it was voted to abide by it. But at a further adjournment, November 13th, this vote was reconsidered. Learning by experience doubtless, that there were insuperable difficulties in the way of carrying the resolutions they had passed on this subject into effect, nothing more was done about them, and they were all suffered to go to rest.

Amid the din of war, the attention of the people of Massachusetts generally was diverted, in 1780, to a very different subject.

A new constitution or form of government for Massachusetts, framed by the State Legislature of 1777, had been sent to Woburn, May 1778, for the consideration of its inhabitants. But this being read and deliberately considered in town meeting, June 8th following, had been unanimously disapproved. At the same time, the people had instructed their representative for that year, Col. Loammi Baldwin, to favor no plan for drawing up another constitution, except in a convention chosen by the people at large, expressly for that purpose.[45] The constitution now laid before them had been framed and sanctioned by such a convention, which had assembled at Cambridge in September 1779, and in which Woburn had been represented by Dr. Samuel Blogget, as its delegate.[46] At a legal meeting, May 15, 1780, a committee of fifteen was chosen to consider the proposed constitution, and to report to the town at its adjournment, June 5th. On the day appointed, this committee reported; and the town voted to pass upon the new constitution submitted to them, article by article.

The Bill of Rights was approved, except the third article, relative to provision by law for the support of public worship,

---

45 Town Records, Vol. IX., p. 451.

46 Town Records, Vol. IX., p. 521.

which met some opposition. The article, however, was finally accepted as it stood, by a vote of fifty-two to twenty-three.

The article of the constitution requiring in voters a property qualification was offensive to some; and an amendment was carried, allowing every freeman the privilege of voting, who was twenty-one years of age.

At an adjournment of this business to June 7th, votes were passed, that delegates to Congress should be qualified as were representatives to our own General Court, and that all ordained ministers of the gospel, and attorneys-at-law should be excluded from seats in the Legislature of Massachusetts.

It was voted, moreover, as the sense of the inhabitants of Woburn, that at the expiration of seven years from the ratification of the new constitution, a convention should be called to revise it.

And now, having finished the consideration of the proposed new constitution of Government for Massachusetts, Woburn voted its acceptance of it, excepting the articles objected to, and amended by twenty-two votes in the affirmative, to two in the negative.[47]

The Federal Constitution, or Form of Government for the United States, was drawn up in a convention of delegates from twelve States, assembled in Philadelphia; and was unanimously agreed to by all the States present, September 17, 1787. Agreeably to a Resolve passed by the Legislature of Massachusetts, October 1787, this constitution was submitted to the consideration of a convention chosen by the several towns and districts of this Commonwealth, which assembled in Boston, January 9, 1788, and which, after several weeks of careful deliberation, voted to adopt it. The delegates of Woburn to this convention, chosen at a town meeting, December 17, 1787, were Deacon Timothy Winn and Mr. James Fowle, Jr. Deacon Winn opposed the adoption of this constitution without some amendments; and prepared a speech to deliver before the convention upon the subject, when a motion was expected to be

---

[47] Town Records, Vol. X., pp. 24, 25.

made for the appointment of a committee which should endeavor to harmonize the conflicting views of different members of that body, and, by consenting to certain amendments of the constitution, to insure its acceptance by the unanimous or very general voice of its members. But it so happened, that the proposed conciliatory committee was appointed, and its report accepted at a time when Deacon Winn was absent from the convention. And being consequently disappointed in his intentions to deliver in person the speech he had prepared for the occasion, he submitted it for publication, as "a part of the debate" before the convention, in one of the newspapers of the day.—*See a copy of it in the Boston Independent Chronicle of March* 27, 1788.

During the Revolutionary War, two gentlemen, natives of Woburn, attained to great eminence in society, of whom it seems a matter of right, that some particular notice should here be taken.

To begin with the elder of the two, Colonel Loammi Baldwin. He was son of James and Ruth (Richardson) Baldwin, and a descendant of the third generation from Deacon Henry Baldwin, one of the first settlers of Woburn, and a subscriber to the "Town Orders," drawn up at Charlestown, for the regulation of the then projected new settlement, in December 1641.

His father was by trade a carpenter, of good repute; and is reported to have been the master workman in the erection of the precinct (Burlington) meeting-house in 1732, which is still standing.

He was born at "New Bridge," (North Woburn) January 10, 1744, O. S., or January 21, 1744-5, N. S. Discovering from early life a strong desire for acquiring knowledge, he was a constant attendant upon the instructions of Master Fowle, that noted teacher of the grammar school in Woburn, both in the centre of the town and at the precinct, many years in succession. And at a more advanced period of life, with a view to obtaining a thorough acquaintance with Natural and Experimental Philosophy, he was accustomed to walk from North Woburn to Cambridge, in company with his school-mate, Benjamin Thompson (afterwards Count Rumford), to attend the lectures of Professor Winthrop (for which liberty had been given them); and upon their return home on foot, they were wont to make rude instruments for themselves, with which to illustrate the principles they had heard laid down in the lecture-room at the college.

At the commencement of the war in 1775, he enlisted for the service of his country in the regiment of foot, commanded by Col. Samuel Gerrish. Here he was rapidly advanced to be Lieut.-Colonel: and upon the retirement of Col. Gerrish from the army, in August of that year, he was put at the head of the regiment, and was, not long after, commissioned to be Colonel.

His regiment was originally distinguished as the 38th, and consisted of eight companies, all of them stationed at Boston lines, viz: four at Sewall's Point, Brookline, three at Chelsea, and one (Capt. Wood's company of Woburn) at Medford. But upon the reorganization of the army at the close of 1775, it included ten companies, and was designated as the 26th regiment. Till the end of 1775, Col. Baldwin remained near Boston: but in April, 1776, he followed Washington to New York city;[48] and there we find him June 22d, at the "Grand Battery, in the command of the "Main Guard."

When Washington was compelled, by the superior numbers of the enemy, to evacuate New York, September 14, 1776, and to retreat to the west, or Pennsylvania side of the Delaware, about December 8th, Baldwin with his men followed him. And on the memorable night of December 25, 1776, when in face of a violent and extremely cold storm of snow and hail the Commander in Chief recrossed the Delaware to the Jersey side, and took by surprise at Trenton the next morning a body of about 1,000 Hessian troops, commanded by Col. Rahl, Col. Baldwin and his men[49] accompanied

[48] The following passages are extracts from the folio volume deposited at the State House by the Baldwin family, and containing his correspondence and various memoranda: —

"New York Apl. 19. 1776 Abstract for Non-Commissioned Officers & Soldiers . . . . in 26th. Regt commanded by Col. Loammi Baldwin for month of Feby 1776."

"A Report of the main Guard at the Grand Battery N. Y. June 13. 1776."

"A List of the Main Guard, under the command of Lt. Col. Baldwin [Col. Loammi Baldwin?] June 22. 1776."

[49] "A Return of the Officers and Soldiers belonging to the 26th. Regt commanded by Col. Loammi Baldwin, that went on the Expedition to Trentown the 26th. inst. December."

"Trenton Jany ye 2d. 1777.

"This will impower Corpl Caleb Simonds to receive all that I do not receive at my discharge, namely, wages, allowance money granted by the

the General in his daring enterprise, and partook of the honor and joy with which it was crowned; a victory most unexpected and disastrous to the British, but most reviving to the desponding minds of the friends of liberty and of the American cause.

Colonel Baldwin was honorably discharged from the continental army about 1777, on account of ill health. But his subsequent life, spent in his native place, though free from the hardships and dangers of the camp, was by no means a life of leisure and retirement. He still retained and cherished the enterprising spirit and active habits of his youth. And his fellow-citizens highly appreciating his talents and capacity for business, and confident of his integrity and zeal for the public good, took frequent opportunities for manifesting their respect for him, and found him ample employment the remainder of his days. We find him appointed on a large proportion of all the committees chosen for a long succession of years, on important town business; and of these, he was generally the chairman. In 1780, he was appointed High Sheriff of the County of Middlesex, being the first who held that office in this county, after the adoption of the State constitution. In 1778, 1779, and again in 1800 and the four immediately following years, he represented Woburn in the General Court. At the election of representative to Congress for Essex South District (to which Woburn was then attached) in 1794, he had all the votes cast in Woburn but one. In August and September 1796, he had all the votes; and in November of that year, at the third trial for the choice of the same officer, he had seventy-four votes out of the seventy-six that were then cast in Woburn. And at elections in other years, he was a prominent candidate among those held up in Woburn, for the office of State Senator, Lieutenant Governor of the Commonwealth, and Elector of President of the United States.[50]

General, and for arms, ammunition &c taken at Trenton the 26th. of Decr 1776. "Ebenezer ——?" [Ebenezer Lock?]

"Rowley, July 25th. 1778.

"Col. Baldwin: Sir, Be pleased to pay unto Jonathan Stickney my travel money from the Army at Trenton to Rowley in the year 1776, and my share of plunder money that was taken at Trintown, and his Receipt shall be your discharge. "Joseph Stickney."

[50] To the above it may be added, that Col. Baldwin, on account doubtless of his enlarged acquaintance with mathematics, and his familiarity with arts connected therewith, was chosen a member of the American Academy of Arts and Sciences; and received from Harvard College in 1785 the honorary degree of Master of Arts.

But though Col. Baldwin was deservedly a favorite with his fellow-townsmen and with his fellow-citizens generally, he was not an abject seeker of popularity — not one, who, for the sake of winning or prolonging the popular favor, stood ready to sacrifice his principles of duty to the public. Witness his protest with others against the action of the town in the time of Shays' Rebellion. In 1786, 1787, when the Executive was constrained to call out a military force to put that rebellion down, the town of Woburn, in a moment of high excitement, voted January 29, 1787:

"1. Not to give any encouragement to the men called out to go into the present Expedition.

"2. Not to aid or assist in the present Expedition."

But against this proceeding of the town, Col. Baldwin and thirty-six others immediately entered their protests; and, two days after, the town itself reconsidered the votes it had passed on this subject.

The prominent part taken by Col. Baldwin in the construction and establishment of the Middlesex Canal will be adverted to more particularly in a following chapter. To him also are the community indebted for the introduction to public notice, and for the earliest cultivation of the Baldwin apple. The history of this celebrated variety of fruit, as connected with his name, is understood, upon good authority, to be this: As Col. Baldwin was one day surveying land at a place called Butters' Row in Wilmington, near the bounds of that town, Woburn and Burlington, he observed one or more woodpeckers continually flying to a certain tree, growing on land of Mr. James Butters, hard by. Prompted by curiosity to ascertain the cause of their frequenting that tree, he at length went to it; and finding under it apples of an excellent flavor, and well worth cultivating, he returned to the tree the next spring, and took from it scions to graft into stocks of his own. Other persons in that vicinity, induced by his example or advice, grafted trees of theirs soon after with scions from the same stock. And, subsequently, whenever Col. Baldwin attended court, or went into different parts of the county, as High Sheriff, he was accustomed to carry scions of this variety of apple with him, and to distribute them among his friends; so that this species of fruit soon came to be extensively known and cultivated. The original tree, it is said, was blown down in the famous "September gale," in 1815.

At first, apples of this description were called by many, "Butters' Apples," from the name of the person upon whose land the original tree was found; and by others, "Woodpecker Apples," from the bird, whose constant flight to it attracted the notice of Col. Baldwin, and led to the discovery of the excellency of the fruit which grew on it. But, on a certain day, (it is reported) when Col. Baldwin had a party of gentlemen at his house to dine, he set before them a dish of these apples; and one of his guests, admiring their good qualities, asked him by what name they were known? "By no name in particular," the Colonel replied; "call them, if you please, Baldwin apples." And this has ever since been their common name.

Col. Baldwin's first wife was Mary, daughter of James Fowle, Esq: for many years Town Clerk of Woburn. His children by her were:

1. Cyrus, for many years the respected agent of the Middlesex Canal Company, residing at the head of the canal in Chelmsford.

2. Mary, who died young, of scarlet fever, May 13, 1776, when her father was absent in the war.

3. Benjamin Franklin, Esq., who died suddenly October 1821, as he was on his return to Woburn from the cattle show in Brighton.

4. Loammi, Esq., born in 1780, graduated at Harvard University, 1800, a well known and highly respected civil engineer; died in 1838.

5. Hon. James Fowle, born in 1782; settled in Boston as a merchant; sometime member of the Senate of Massachusetts, for the County of Suffolk; and prominent among the Commissioners for introducing pure water into Boston from the lake Cochituate. He died after a very short illness, May 20, 1862.

Col. Baldwin's first wife, Mary, dying September 27, 1786,[51] he married for his second wife, Margaret, daughter of Josiah Fowle, of Woburn. His children by her were:

1. Clarissa, wife of Thomas B. Coolidge.

2. George R., born in 1798, and now (1867) the only surviving child of Col. Loammi Baldwin. He is still the proprietor of the original farm of his ancestors, and the occupant of the spacious mansion of his father.

Col. Baldwin's second wife, Margaret, died August 8, 1799.[51] He himself deceased October 20, 1807.[51]

---

[51] Diary of Samuel Thompson, Esq.

Benjamin Thompson, Count Rumford, was a descendant of the fifth generation from James Thompson, who was born, in England probably, in 1593, emigrated to New England about 1630; took up his abode at Charlestown, Mass., was admitted with his wife Elizabeth into the church of Charlestown, July 31, 1633; became one of the earliest settlers of Woburn, being a subscriber with thirty-one others to the original Town Orders in December 1640; was a member of the first Board of Selectmen, chosen 1644; and died, 1682, aged eighty-nine years.

Benjamin Thompson, his father, was the son of Capt. Ebenezer Thompson and Hannah (Convers) his wife; was born November 27, 1729; and married, 1752, Ruth Simonds, daughter of Lieut. James Simonds, a worthy descendant of the third generation from William Simonds, another of the early settlers of Woburn. Lieut. Simonds served his country in the French and Indian wars; was an inhabitant of Woburn Precinct (now Burlington); dwelt in the house, recently of Capt. Ishmael Munroe, that stood where the road from the precinct meeting-house to Lexington intersects the ancient road from Woburn Centre to Hodge Hole Meadows in Burlington; was Precinct Clerk from 1733 to 1747; married Mary, daughter of James and Mary Fowle, of Woburn, June 17, 1714; and died July 30, 1775, aged eighty-nine.

Benjamin Thompson, the future Count of Rumford, and son of the above Benjamin and Ruth Thompson, was born March 26, 1753, in the west end of the house of his grandfather, Capt. Ebenezer Thompson, where his parents went to live immediately after their marriage. That house, an ancient two-story dwelling house, is still standing; recently, till her death, the home of the Count's first cousin, the widow of Willard Jones, and situate a few rods south of the meeting-house in North Woburn, at the corner of the road coming from Burlington, and of the road leading from Woburn Centre to Wilmington; and is distinguished by a huge willow tree growing directly in front of it.

In this humble dwelling, the child Benjamin continued to live with his mother and grandfather after the death of his father, who died November 7, 1754, when the boy was hardly one year and eight months old. But in March 1756, his mother married, for her second husband, Mr. Josiah Pierce, Jr., of Woburn,[52] and took her

[52] "Josiah Peirce junr entered his Intentions of Marriage with Ruth Thompson, both Woburn, Jany 1. 1756." (Woburn Records of Int. of Marriage.)

son Benjamin with her to her new home; a house, it is said, that once stood directly opposite the Baldwin mansion, but is now taken down, though the cellar of it is yet visible.

He was distinguished, while yet a boy, by quickness of apprehension, fondness for books, and a genius for mechanical invention. At a suitable age, he was sent (accompanied by his neighbor and school-mate, Loammi Baldwin) to that celebrated teacher in Woburn, Master John Fowle, a graduate of Harvard College, 1747; who kept the grammar school in his native town, some ten or twelve years in succession. By him he was taught reading, writing, arithmetic, and the grammar of his own language, through the medium of the Latin. After leaving Mr. Fowle at eleven years of age, he was put under the charge of a Mr. Hill of Medford, with whom he proceeded in the study of mathematics; and was also taught astronomy; of his proficiency in which, he gave evidence by calculating eclipses of the sun and moon.

At the age of thirteen, he was bound an apprentice to Mr. John Appleton, a respectable merchant in Salem; and while he was with him, he industriously improved his leisure moments in extending his acquaintance with mathematics and physical science. But this gentleman, having in consequence of the growing difficulties between Great Britain and her Colonies, entered into the non-importation agreement, his business became so contracted, that he no longer needed an apprentice; and young Thompson was allowed to return to his mother's in Woburn. From the same cause, he left the employ of Mr. Hopestill Capen, a dry goods dealer in Boston, in whose store, some time after he quitted Mr. Appleton, he was engaged in the Spring of 1770 as a clerk.

The leisure which these successive relinquishments of commercial pursuits gave young Thompson, was diligently employed by him either in school-keeping, or in the cultivation of his own mind. In the winter of 1768–9, we find him teaching a school at Wilmington. And in the summer of 1769, he applied himself to the study of anatomy and physiology, under the direction of Dr. John Hay, a physician then resident in Woburn, with a view to qualifying himself for the practice of medicine.

In the summer of 1770, after quitting Mr. Capen's store in Boston, he and his friend and school-mate, Loammi Baldwin, obtained liberty to attend Professor Winthrop's course of lectures upon Natural Philosophy, delivered in Harvard College. This was a privilege which was highly appreciated by them both. In their attendance upon these lectures, they were accustomed to walk from Woburn to Cambridge; and upon their return, they would employ themselves in attempts to illustrate the principles which they had heard laid down in the lecture-room, by experiments and rude instruments of their own contriving.

In the autumn of 1770, he took charge of a school at Concord, N. H., (then called Rumford); and while fulfilling this engagement, he became acquainted with Mrs. Sarah Rolfe, daughter of Rev. Timothy Walker, the first minister of the place, and widow of Col. Benjamin Rolfe, one of the early settlers of Concord, and a gentleman of influence there, who deceased in 1770. This lady he married, in 1772, and came into possession by her of a large property. And attending with her, not long after their marriage, a military muster at Portsmouth, N. H., he was introduced to Gov. Wentworth, who conceived such an esteem for him, that he quickly after conferred on him the office of Major, in one of the New Hampshire regiments.

But this sudden military promotion was deeply resented by the officers over whose heads he had been unexpectedly elevated. Henceforth, they omitted no opportunity of doing him an injury. At the commencement of the Revolutionary War, they but too successfully spread an insinuation that he was disaffected to the cause of his country; and that he held a criminal correspondence with Gov. Wentworth and Gen. Gage. To refute this latter charge, he solemnly averred that the correspondence he had holden with Gov. Wentworth was not of a political character, and was begun before the Governor avowed himself a tory, and while his administration was popular with all parties; and that his only letter to Gen. Gage consisted of six lines, requesting him to order that two deserters from the British army, in 1774, whom he had employed on his farm in Concord, N. H., and whom Gen. Gage had pardoned upon their return to their ranks, at the intercession of Maj. Thompson while in Boston, might not publicly reveal the name of their successful advocate with the General on their behalf.

But no defence he could make, no explanation he could offer of the charges alleged against him, could free him from public suspicion and obloquy. At Concord, he was not suffered to remain in safety and peace: and when he came to Woburn, he was on one memorable occasion in danger of personal violence, from which, probably, only the interposition of his friend, Baldwin, delivered him; and, on another occasion, he was arrested and tried in the meeting-house at Woburn, before the Committee of Correspondence, upon the charge of disaffection to the cause of his country. This trial resulted in his release from arrest, but a refusal on the part of the court to give him a full acquittal. Considering this refusal as unjust, he appealed to the Committee of Safety for the colony, which referred him to the Provincial Congress; and this body declined acting on the petition he presented them. Deeply resenting this treatment, and the insults to which he was constantly subjected, finding that the actual services he was occasionally enabled to render the popular cause were insufficient to secure him the public confidence, and that his repeated efforts to obtain a command in the army of his country were unavailing, he at length made up his mind to remove to a distance from this scene of trial. Accordingly, in a letter to his father-in-law, Rev. Timothy Walker, he assures him, that not being conscious of any feelings or acts in his political career that were inimical to the interests of the land of his birth, he could not conscientiously make any confessions to his opponents, (as that gentleman had proposed he might do, for the sake of appeasing their animosity); he assigns reasons why he deemed it imperatively necessary to retire to some place at a distance from his friends in this vicinity; and earnestly and affectionately commends his wife and daughter to his care.[53] And then collecting what money he could, from every resource at his command, and giving out, that having failed to obtain employment in the northern army, he was going south to find means of support, he left Cambridge, October 10, 1775; and going to the nearest post-town, accompanied by Josiah Peirce, Jr., (3d?) his half brother, he there dismissed him; and then went on his way, leaving his relatives and friends here in utter uncertainty where he was, how he was situated, and what he was doing, till the revolutionary struggle was over.

Maj. Thompson himself proceeded directly to Newport; and finding there the next day a boat belonging to the British Frigate Scarborough, he was conveyed in it to the frigate, which took him on board; and after remaining in it a few days, he was landed at Boston, which was still occupied by Gen. Gage, and his army.

---

[53] Renwick's Life, Appendix, pp. 210–216, in Sparks's Collection.

And when Gage's successor, Gen. Howe, evacuated Boston, in March following, he sent his despatches containing the news to England by Thompson, who re-embarked in the ship which had conveyed him to Boston, while Gen. Howe himself with his army sailed for Halifax.

The despatches borne by Thompson were directed to Lord George Germaine, Secretary of State for the department, to which the affairs of the colonies were intrusted. By this powerful minister, he was very graciously received, and immediately offered employment in his own department, which Thompson thankfully accepted, and entered at once on the discharge of his official duties. And in this employment he acquitted himself with so much ability and faithfulness, that within four years from his arrival in England, he was advanced to the dignity of "under Secretary of State."

Early in 1784, being on a tour to the continent, Col. Thompson received a flattering invitation from Charles Frederick, Elector and reigning Duke of Bavaria, to come and reside with him at Munich his Capital, with encouraging assurances of advantageous employment. Being inclined to accept this invitation, he went back to England shortly after receiving it, to obtain permission from the King to enter into the service of a foreign prince. Such permission was readily granted him. And, as a testimonial of the royal approbation of his labors while in England, the king conferred on him the honor of knighthood, accepted his resignation as a colonel of dragoons, (an office with which he had been recently invested,) and allowed him to retain the half pay of his military rank; a privilege which was continued to him through life.

Going from England to Munich, before the close of the year 1784, he found an honorable post assigned him near the person of the sovereign; and there he at once commenced a series of exertions and labors, which proved very successful, and highly beneficial both to the government and to the public. He effected very important reforms in the military establishment of the country. He brought about arrangements, by which the soldiers were better fed, clothed and paid; were encouraged in various industrial pursuits for the benefit of themselves and families: schools were founded, in which they and their children were instructed gratis in the rudiments of learning; and workshops were provided, in which their uniforms were made, and military equipments were wrought by their own hands and those of their wives, the State furnishing the raw materials.

He adopted measures likewise, by which mendicity, that had grown to be an enormous evil in Munich, was utterly abolished there. But while he put down beggary in Munich, he instituted means, by which, through the voluntary contributions of its inhabitants, and the countenance and aid of the principal officers of State, and by a council chosen by them from among the people, the poor were in all respects amply provided for, were trained and inured to habits of honest industry, and were led to cherish sentiments of self-respect, which fostered in them both the desire and the ability to get their own living, and to make themselves independent of the public aid. These benevolent, disinterested labors of Sir Benjamin Thompson for the poor of Munich kindled in them the warmest sentiments of veneration, gratitude, and love; sentiments of which they repeatedly gave public unmistakable tokens. On occasion of his being once seized with a dangerous illness, while he had the management of the workhouse established for their benefit, "its inmates," we are told, "went in procession to the cathedral, where, at their request, divine service was performed, and public prayers offered for his recovery: and four years afterwards, when the news of his being ill at Naples reached Munich, they voluntarily set apart an hour each evening, to join in supplications for his restoration to health."[54]

Nor was it by the poor only that he was honored, revered, and caressed. Many were the tokens conferred on him of the high esteem in which he was held for his abilities and worth by his noble friend, the Elector, and by the literati of Bavaria, and other countries of Germany. Among the numerous honorary distinctions awarded him, was his admission "as a member of the two academies of Munich and Manheim;" his election in 1787 as "a member of the Academy of Science at Berlin;" his appointment of "Councillor of State" to the Elector; Lieut.-General of the Army of Bavaria; "Commander-in-chief of the General Staff;" "Minister of War;" "Superintendent of the Police of the Electorate;" and to crown all, "in the interval between the death of the Emperor Joseph, and the coronation of his successor Leopold," his friend, the Elector, becoming Vicar of the empire, availed himself of the prerogatives of that office, to make him "a Count of the Holy Roman Empire." "In receiving the last dignity, he chose a title in remembrance of the country of his nativity, and of

[54] Renwick's Life, Chap. vi., p. 98.

the place endeared by recollections both of pleasure and pain; and was thenceforth known as Count of Rumford, from one of the names by which the residence of his wife had been distinguished."[55]

After a residence of about ten years in Bavaria, his health became impaired, and he sought relief in a journey to Naples. But this expedient proving ineffectual, he, on his return to Munich, obtained leave to visit England again, which he did in 1795, after an absence of eleven years. Here he received great attention from his former friends and associates, was consulted in almost all schemes for the promotion of public benevolent ends, and published his essays for the improvement of fireplaces, and the cure of smoky chimneys. And now having recovered his health, (his principal inducement for making this visit to England) he was enabled advantageously to pursue his philosophical inquiries and experiments both in England and in Ireland, when alarming intelligence from the Electorate hastened his departure from London to Munich. Arriving in that city early in 1796, he found it in a state of terror and consternation. The war between France and Austria, which followed the French Revolution, had brought an army of each of the contending parties into the neighborhood, or to the very walls of the city. And the Elector, alarmed for his own safety, fled from his capital, eight days after the arrival of Rumford, having first appointed him head of the Council of Regency, during his absence. Availing himself of the power conferred on him by this appointment, Rumford put himself at the head of the Bavarian forces, and by his resolute yet prudent management, he induced both the opposing armies to desist from their threatened hostile purposes, and to retire; thus averting the danger which threatened the city, and opening a way for the Elector's return. For this, his services, the inhabitants of Munich gave Rumford unequivocal tokens of their gratitude. And the Elector loaded him with new honors, and permitted him to settle one-half of the pension which he allowed him on his daughter, (who had accompanied him thither from England,) and extended its term to the duration of her life.[56]

To recover his health, which was again giving way, he was induced, with the elector's leave, to make another journey to England, accompanied by his daughter, in 1798. While there, the fame of his attainments in learning, philosophy and usefulness

[55] Renwick's Life, Chap. iv., pp. 69–71.

[56] Renwick's Life, Chap. ix., p. 156.

having spread far and wide, he received a formal invitation from the government of the United States to revisit his native land. This invitation, his daughter was very urgent with him to accept immediately. He himself was strongly inclined to do so; and wrote to his friend, Col. Loammi Baldwin, of Woburn, Mass., to secure for him a house and land in the vicinity of Cambridge, which he might make the place of his residence on his arrival, and leave to his daughter for a home, when he had done with it. But being, in the mean while, earnestly solicited to assist in the establishment of the "Royal Institution," an institution patronized by the King, aided by liberal contributions of the wealthy, and designed, according to its charter, for "diffusing the knowledge, and facilitating the general introduction of useful mechanical inventions and improvements, and for teaching, by courses of philosophical lectures and experiments, the application of science to the useful purposes of life," he was reluctantly persuaded, from motives of duty, to postpone his intended visit to the United States, and never afterwards found it convenient to resume it.[57]

The death of the Elector, Charles Frederic, Rumford's zealous patron, benefactor, and fast friend, in 1799, changed the whole future course of his life. For the Elector's nephew and successor, Prince Maximilian Joseph Deux Ponts, though the first to introduce Rumford to the notice of his uncle, and still friendly to him, was so wrought upon by his nobles, who were jealous of the fame and influence of Rumford, as to show himself indisposed to find him the employment which the old Elector had. This state of things, Rumford perceived upon his return from England to Bavaria. And, disappointed and mortified by the neglect he had to submit to, having first assisted in reorganizing "the Bavarian Academy of Sciences," he took his final leave of the Electorate.[58]

But he did not go from it without leaving behind, in the hearts of the people, a grateful remembrance of his benevolent exertions, not only for the correction of great evils existent among them, and for the advancement of their highest and best worldly interests, but also for the promotion of their pleasure, entertainment and comfort, in their leisure moments. To use the words of his biographer, "In the immediate vicinity of Munich was a large extent of waste land, which had formerly been a hunting ground of the Prince: and although the game had long since been extirpated,

[57] Renwick's Life, Ch. ix., pp. 157-161. [58] Renwick's Life, Ch. ix., pp. 164-166.

and the forest had disappeared, it was still the property of the Elector. Rumford, who had in England imbibed a taste for the art of landscape gardening . . . . proposed to render this profitable, by converting portions of it into a 'ferme ornee,' [an ornamental farm,] while other parts were laid out in walks and drives, for the recreation of the inhabitants of Munich. The circuit of the grounds was six miles, around which a road was constructed, embellished at intervals with picturesque cottages and dwellings, that were occupied by the tenants who cultivated portions of the ground, or by those employed in superintending and taking care of the grounds.

"To diversify the features of the ground, a space was excavated, which filled with water, formed a beautiful artificial lake, while the earth removed from it was employed to form a mount (mound ?). To accommodate the citizens in search of recreation, a public coffee-house was erected, and committed to the charge of a respectable keeper, while edifices intended for embellishment, afforded seats at the best points of view.

"After Rumford left Bavaria, the principal nobility and inhabitants of Munich chose to express their gratitude for his exertions in procuring them this place of recreation, by erecting a monument to commemorate his agency, on which they also caused to be recorded his services in rooting out mendicity, and founding institutions for education." [59]

---

[59] "This monument is of a quadrangular form, having two principal fronts opposite to each other, ornamented with basso relievos and inscriptions. On one side is an inscription in the German language, of which the following is a literal translation: —

"'Stay, Wanderer.
At the creative fiat of Charles Theodore,
Rumford, the Friend of Mankind,
By Genius, Taste, and Love inspired,
Changed this once desert Place
Into what thou now beholdest.'

"On the opposite side of the monument, under a bust of Count Rumford:

"'To him,
Who rooted out the greatest of public Evils,
Idleness and Mendicity,
Relieved and instructed the Poor,
And founded many Institutions
For the Education of our Youth.

After quitting Bavaria, having employed himself some time in travelling in Germany, Italy, and Switzerland, Rumford arrived at length in Paris, where he was received with all due honor and distinction. His daughter had now left him, having returned to America about the time he gave up his projected voyage to his native land. And the Count himself becoming acquainted at Paris with the widowed lady of Lavoisier, the celebrated chemist, a mutual attachment between them ensued, which terminated in their marriage, as soon as the requisite certificates of his own birth, and of the death of his first wife (which he had written his daughter in July 1804 to procure for him) could be obtained from the United States. He now took up his abode in the village of Auteuil (near Paris), which had belonged to his wife's former husband, and been the seat of many of his important discoveries in physical and chemical science. And here Rumford himself continued to pursue his philosophical inquiries and studies, till death removed him from the world. His decease, occasioned by a fever, occurred August 21, 1814, at his villa in Auteuil, in the sixty-second year of his age, "depriving mankind of one of its most eminent benefactors, and science of one of its brightest ornaments."[60]

Count Rumford left behind him many precious memorials of his filial affection, and of his general benevolence and largeness of heart.

In letters, written between 1795 and 1808, to his mother, who lived to an advanced age, he gave reiterated assurances of his warmest gratitude and love; and in proof of this, he transmitted to her ten thousand dollars in stocks of the United States, as a deed of gift, to be absolutely at her disposal. For his daughter Sarah, (known here as the Countess, who died lately at Concord, N.H.,) he made ample provision for her comfort and support. Nor did he forget, in the distribution of his bounty, an unfortunate sister-in-law, Ruth, a daughter of his mother by her second marriage. Learning that his mother had bequeathed by will, out of the moneys he had given her, a thousand dollars to his daughter Sarah, he

---

Go, Wanderer,
And strive to equal him
In Genius and Activity,
And us
In Gratitude.' "[a]

[a] Renwick's Life, Chap. vii., pp 123, 124.

[60] Renwick's Life, Chap. ix., pp. 166–168; Chap. xi., p. 201.

wrote to his mother, requesting her to make a new will, and to devise to Ruth the legacy she had intended for Sarah.[61]

Nor did he confine his beneficence to the narrow circle of his family connections and early friends. In the year 1796, being at that time in London, "he presented to the American Academy of Arts and Sciences at Boston, five thousand dollars, in the three per cent Stocks of the United States" . . . . "to the end that the interest of the same may be received from time to time forever, and the amount of the same applied and given, once every second year, as a premium to the author of the most important discovery, or useful improvement, which shall be made and published by printing, or in any way made known to the public, in any part of the continent of America, or in any of the American islands, during the preceding two years, on heat, or on light; the preference always being given to such discoveries, as shall, in the opinion of the academy, tend most to promote the good of mankind." [62]

"By his Will, Count Rumford bequeathed to Harvard College one thousand dollars annually, and the reversion of other sums, for the purpose of founding a professorship 'to teach, by regular courses of academical and public lectures, accompanied with proper experiments, the utility of the physical and mathematical sciences, for the improvement of the useful arts, and for the extension of the industry, prosperity, happiness, and well-being of society.' The amount of property which came into the hands of the corporation of the College, in 1815, after the death of Count Rumford, was about eleven hundred dollars annually, subject to a deduction of about two hundred dollars a year, payable to the Countess, his daughter, in case she should fail to receive her annuity of two thousand florins from the Court of Bavaria. The University was also to receive the reversion of about four hundred and forty dollars annually, after the death of certain annuitants.

"The Rumford professorship was accordingly established in the university, and went into operation in the year 1816. Dr. Jacob Bigelow was the first professor, who occupied the chair eleven years, and was succeeded by Mr. Daniel Treadwell. Hitherto this foundation has produced all the benefits which the liberal donor could have anticipated. A course of lectures is annually delivered to the undergraduates and other students of the university. The aggregate amount of the fund at this time, according to the Treas-

---

[61] Renwick's Life, Appendix, pp. 207–209. [62] Renwick's Life, Appendix, p. 202.

urer's last Annual Report is about twenty-nine thousand dollars. A valuable apparatus, consisting of machines, models and instruments, suitable for illustrating the topics embraced in the lectures, has been added to the department."[63]

In view of the literary studies, of the diversified labors and sacrifices of Count Rumford to benefit his fellow-men, as well as of the final disposal of his property, all must acknowledge him entitled to the highest praise, as a practical philosopher and philanthropist, an ardent lover of learning, and friend to the cause of humanity.

In respect to his religious sentiments, Rumford cherished apparently unshaken faith in the being and infinite perfections, the universal providence and government of God. In speaking upon this subject, his biographer observes,

" — — Above all, in his inquiries he never lost sight of the most important object of science, its bearing upon the evidences of natural theology; and, at every new step in his discoveries, pauses to show in what manner they illustrate the power and wisdom of the Deity. After dwelling upon this subject, he goes on to say, —

" 'But I must take care not to tire my reader by pursuing these speculations too far. If I have persisted in them, if I have dwelt upon them with peculiar satisfaction and complacency, it is because I think them uncommonly interesting, and also because I conceived they might be of use in this age of refinement and skepticism.

" 'If, among barbarous nations, the fear of a God, and the practice of religious duties, tend to soften savage dispositions, and to prepare the mind for those sweet enjoyments which result from peace, order, and friendly intercourse; a belief in the existence of a Supreme Intelligence, who rules and governs the universe with wisdom and goodness, is not less essential to the happiness of those, who, by cultivating their mental powers, have learnt to know how little can be known.' "[64]

It is truly refreshing to read the above passage, dictated, as it was, by one so eminent for learning and practical philosophy, as Count Rumford, and bearing his testimony, as it does, to truths lying at the foundation of all true religion. And it would have been exceedingly gratifying to have closed the foregoing brief sketch of him in this History of Woburn, his native place, with an additional statement upon good authority, that he was a pro-

[63] Renwick's Life, Appendix, p. 206. [64] Renwick's Life, Chap. xi., pp. 196, 197.

fessed Christian, an exemplary, consistent follower of the meek and holy Jesus. But such a statement, his biography, so often quoted above, does not, in any passage that has been observed, warrant to be made concerning him. It is true that Rumford is once or twice there presented, as calling himself a Protestant, in distinction from the Catholic population around him. Such an avowal is a sufficient proof that he preferred the Protestant to the Catholic understanding of the Christian religion. But it seems far from being equivalent to an express declaration of faith in the gospel of Christ, and a serious, habitual purpose to be governed by its principles and rules.

CHAPTER XIII.

Difficulties in which the Town was Involved at the Conclusion of the Revolutionary War. — Its Opposition to the Return of the Refugees. Its Stand in Shay's Rebellion. — Its Embarrassments by Debt. — Measures for Payment of Debt. — Middlesex Canal. — Schools from 1775 to 1866. — New Orders for School Districts. — New School-houses. — Warren Academy. — Incorporation of Burlington. — Public Solemnities at the Death of Washington.

THOUGH the peace agreed upon, 1783, between Great Britain and the United States had put a stop to the War of the Revolution, yet, the bitterness and animosity which that war had given rise to, were not at once allayed. In particular, the hard thoughts and inimical feelings, which the refugees (as they were termed) had excited in their former brethren and fellow-citizens, against themselves, by fleeing from their native country, and declining to take part with its defenders in their contest for liberty and independence, still rankled in the breasts of multitudes. Such feelings were manifested in Woburn, especially on the following occasion.

At a general town meeting, May 12, 1783, "Voted, that the Selectmen draw up a letter, as an answer to a letter received from the town of Boston, relative to the return of Absentees and Conspirators, dated April the 10th. 1783, and send it to said town."

"Unanimously Voted it as their opinion, that the Absentees and Conspirators or Refugees ought never to be suffered to return, but be excluded from having lot or portion among us."[1]

At the same time, a committee, consisting of Mr. William Scott, Col. Loammi Baldwin and Capt. John Wood, was appointed to draft instructions to their representative in General Court, upon this and other interesting subjects, and to submit them to

[1] Town Records, Vol. X., p. 293.

the town for its acceptance, on the day that meeting should be adjourned to.

Accordingly, such instructions were laid before the town by the committee at their adjourned meeting, May 26th; and were as follows:

"To Capt. Samuel Belknap.

"Sir,

"The inhabitants of this town, convinced of your integrity, uprightness, and warm attachment to the cause of liberty and interest of your country; and having experienced your fidelity, when you last filled that important office, have now elected you their representative in the Great and General Court.

"We hope you will still persist with that rectitude of conduct which you have hitherto pursued; and that you, neither being persuaded by flattery, intimidated by menace, or stimulated by sinister views or personal emoluments, will not deviate from that path of duty, or betray that confidence reposed in you by your constituents.

"The town you represent, have voted your being furnished with Instruction; and has unanimously voted against the resettlement in this State of all such men, as have, in our glorious contest for liberty, proved inimical to their country, let them be of whatever denomination; whether stigmatized by the name of Tory, Refugee, Conspirator, or Absentee.

"Although the crimes of some have been atrocious, and that [those] of others attended with less criminality; yet all, by their good offices, their cash, and counsel to our implacable enemies; [by] the bent of their inclination to betray their country, or the denial of that assistance which was their duty to perform in the time of danger, have forfeited their claim to our protection, and must frustrate their overtures to become citizens of the State. They chose their Party, they chose their King, and to their own Master let them stand or fall.

"Tho' we are (by the blessing of God) in the peaceable possession of a land flowing with milk and honey, yet the Land of Canaan will enjoy no rest, while the Philistines are suffered to dwell amongst us.

"When the British King (like Rehoboam of old) answered our Petitions with threats of whipping with scorpions, and the alarm was sounded, 'To your tents, O Israel: what portion have we in

David? Neither have we Inheritance in the Son of Jesse (or George) : ' the Whigs obey'd, but the Tories shrank from danger.

" Our burned towns, and the wanton destruction of property, the loss of our blood and treasure, must ever prove an insuperable barrier against such men being reinstated, as became devotees to the shrine of royalty.

" After delivering this compendium of our sentiments, we Instruct you to use every effort to prevent the return of men thus characterized, to their former possessions, whose aims will be, to sow the seeds of discord among us. A little leaven may ferment the whole mass. *Principiis obsta*, as to vice, is a maxim inculcated by theologists, and amongst physicians, for the early suppression of morbific qualities : the same maxim is applicable in politics injurious to the Commonwealth."

" You'll bear in mind, that Congress are obliged only to recommend, but they neither can nor will offer coercion.

" We recommend the framing of such Acts, as tend to encourage Learning, Commerce and Agriculture. Lest enormous grants, salaries, pensions, etc., should exceed our finances, comparative views are to be taken, and strict economy observed.

" An Application to Congress is highly expedient to recommend their Consolidating their old Emission, and rousing it from its present lethargic state, which causes so much discontent.

" The shutting the Continental Loan Office gives fresh alarm, and National Credit suffers reproach. Reputation, or National Faith once lost, is hard to be regain'd ; its preservation should be guarded with caution.

" You will sacredly observe the foregoing Instructions, provided they do not militate with our Definitive Treaty of Peace.

Signed by Order of the Town,

JAMES FOWLE Junr. Town Clerk.

"The Town voted to accept of the above Instructions; and ordered their Town Clerk to give a Copy of the same to Capt. Samuel Belknap, Representative for said Town, and attest the same in behalf of said Town." [2]

At the close of the war, the inhabitants of Woburn were in a depressed and straitened condition. The boon they had

---

[2] Town Records, Vol. X., pp. 294, 295.

fought for was won; but not without great sacrifices of property and life. During the war, heavy losses had been incurred; business had been much deranged; many hopes of worldly prosperity had been disappointed; numerous efforts for acquiring, and plans for securing worldly wealth, had failed, or been defeated. The town, likewise, was much in debt. To provide money for paying the bounties demanded, in making up its quotas of men that were at various times called for, to enlist in the public service, the town had been obliged to borrow considerable sums of money upon note;[3] of which, when payment was demanded, its narrow finances rendered it unable to refund: so that, in 1786, several executions were issued in court against it.

In view of the unhappy situation the people of Woburn were then in, may be plausibly conjectured the reasons of the part which they took in Shay's rebellion, in 1786–7. Oppressed with their own pecuniary burdens, and suffering the like public grievances, real or imaginary, which their brethren in the western parts of the State were complaining of, they felt more sympathy with them than was meet, when they rose up in resistance to the government that was set over them, and to the laws of the land. Hence, when called upon to assist by a military force to suppress the rebellion, the town voted, January 29, 1787,

"Not to act upon the second Article in the Warrant, which Article was, To see if the town will do any thing concerning the Training Band now sent for.

"Voted, not to give any encouragement to the men called for, to go into the present Expedition.

"Voted, not to aid nor assist in the present Expedition."[4] And though a protest was immediately made, and entered in the town book, against the last two votes, by thirty-seven prominent and highly respectable citizens; and though at an adjournment

---

[3] The principal due upon the notes against the town March 1, 1786, amounted to £1304 0*s*. 7½*d*. For interest on the same, £133 14*s*. 7*d*.

[3] Town Records, Vol. X., p. 484.

[4] Town Records, Vol. XI., p. 67.

of the meeting two days after, these same votes were reconsidered by the town itself; yet, at a town meeting, October 22d, following, " It was Voted not to act upon the Article relative to making any consideration to those persons that were draughted to go into the Government's service thirty days under Capt. William Blanchard in Jany last past."[5] And yet again, at a meeting of the town, May 5, 1788, it was " Voted Not to make any allowance to those persons that hired or went in the Expedition from this Town after Daniel Shays in January One Thousand Seven Hundred and Eighty Seven, agreeable to a Petition signed by William Carter and others."[6]

Notwithstanding the appearance of hostility to the government, and of favoring the rebel cause, which these votes manifest, it is not known that any inhabitant of this town ever openly joined the rebels in their outrageous attempts. The people of Woburn had always hitherto approved themselves as loyal to the government set over them, as those of any town in the State. The votes above referred to were passed in a moment of excitement, and under the pressure of difficulties, which the majority of them had been led, like the rebels, erroneously to ascribe to the government. But when the prudent measures which their rulers adopted had relieved them of those difficulties, and time had opened their eyes to their mistake, in supposing their government to have been the cause of them, their former sentiments of loyalty revived; and they probably would have been ashamed, within no long time after, to repeat the action referred to, on the occurrence of any similar occasion.

To extricate itself from its pecuniary embarrassments, the town had recourse, at different times, between 1783 and 1789, to various expedients.

The treasurer was authorized to put off all the paper money of the new emission in his hands, belonging to the town, to the best advantage; and to deliver all the paper money of the old emission belonging to the town, that was lying in his hands, to Mr. Isaac Johnson, who was to dispose of it in the best manner

---

[5] Town Records, Vol. XI., p. 108.

[6] Town Records, Vol. XI., p. 154.

he could; taking care *not to allow more than one hundred and fifty paper dollars for one hard one:* and both persons to be accountable to the town.[7]

He was authorized to call in all debts due to the town upon note, from persons he judged able to pay: and to sell, at public auction, certain parcels of real estate, supposed to belong to the town, as the Meeting-house Hill, and the School-house Pond, (so called) with land adjoining, and to give a title or deed of the same.[8]

The delinquent collectors were required to gather and to pay immediately the sums in which they were deficient; and were authorized to allow a liberal premium to all who would pay in advance, or within a short time, their taxes about to be assessed, in order "to satisfie the Executions" against the town.[9]

Finally, at a meeting, March 19, 1787, the town voted to raise a tax of £300 lawful money, to be paid in hard money only, to defray the town debts due out of town, and them only.[10]

By these and similar prudent means, the town was ere long cleared of debt, and began to flourish and prosper. The people were roused from their state of depression; and they began to pursue their wonted avocations with cheerfulness and success.

Among the effects of that spirit of enterprise and improvement, public and private, which the restoration of peace to the country, the clearing of the town from its embarrassments by debt, and the revival of business and mutual confidence had awakened or cherished, may be reckoned the Middlesex Canal. Its construction was authorized by an act of the Legislature passed June 22, 1793, by which "James Sullivan Esqr. of Boston, Oliver Prescott of Groton, James Winthrop of Cambridge, Loammi Baldwin of Woburn, Benjamin Hall, Jonathan Porter and others of Medford were incorporated, they and their successors, as a Corporation forever, by the name of the Proprietors of the Middlesex Canal.[11] It was at first contemplated to carry the canal only from the waters of the Merrimack River in

---

[7] Town Records, Vol. X., p. 329. [8] Town Records, Vol. X., p. 455; Vol. XI., p. 152.
[9] Town Records, Vol. XI., p. 152; Vol. XI., pp. 6, 7. [10] Town Records, Vol. XI., p. 77.
[11] Special Laws of Massachusetts, Vol. I., p. 465; Vol. II., pp. 26, 241, 342; Vol. III., p. 131.

Chelmsford to those of the Medford River, through Billerica, Wilmington, Woburn, and Medford. But subsequent acts allowed the proprietors to continue it to Charles River, and there to open a communication with Boston by boats; extended the time for completing it to three years, from June 22, 1803; and authorized them to demand forever a toll of one-sixteenth of a dollar per mile for every ton of goods conveyed in boats, and for every ton of timber floated on rafts.[11] As a considerable part of the canal lay within the bounds of Woburn, much, if not the chief portion of the care and responsibility in constructing it, rested upon that noted citizen of Woburn, and one of the principal proprietors of the canal, Col. Loammi Baldwin. With him, it was a favorite enterprise. He entered with a warm zeal upon the undertaking, and much of his time and care were spent upon the work. By vote of the directors, he attended Mr. Weston, a skilful English surveyor, whom he had procured from Philadelphia, in surveying the route of the canal from Chelmsford, in 1794. He was constantly with the numerous workmen employed upon it, overseeing and directing them. And highly was he gratified, doubtless, in seeing it become navigable from the Merrimack to Charles River, in 1803.[12] The facilities it afforded for the transportation of timber and country produce to Boston, and of merchandise from the city to its head in Chelmsford, rendered it a work of great and growing public utility, and for several years a source of increasing revenue to the proprietors. But railroads and steam-cars at length superseded it. The year the Lowell railroad went into full operation, the receipts of the canal fell off one-third. When the Lowell and Nashua road went into operation, the receipts of the canal were reduced another third. Shortly after, the dividends hardly sufficed to pay for current expenses and repairs: [12] and now (1867) a large proportion of the track of the canal through Woburn has been filled up with earth again; and over spots where rafts were once wafted, and boats were seen passing,

[12] Historical Sketch, etc., etc., by Caleb Eddy, Esq., agent of the corporation, pp. 4–6.

loaded with goods and persons, houses have been erected, and are inhabited, as on the solid ground by the way-side.

The history of the schools in Woburn, which was brought down in Chapter VII. to the year 1775, will now be resumed.

During the first seven years of the Revolutionary war, begun in 1775, £40 lawful money, or its equivalent in the depreciated paper of that day, was annually raised in Woburn for schooling. In 1775 and 1776, such a portion of that amount was laid out each of those years, as was sufficient to keep a grammar school in the two parishes nine months in the whole; and the remainder was appropriated to the instruction of children in the extreme parts of the town. But, under this arrangement, it is obvious that the advantages for schooling in the remote quarters of the two parishes must have been very small. To remedy this defect, the town speedily adopted a new method of appropriating its school money. For the fifteen years immediately succeeding 1776, a school committee to manage the affairs of the schools was but seldom chosen, and no provision was made expressly for a grammar school, except in 1778 and 1787. During that whole period, there was a gradual increase in the sum annually raised for schooling, from £40, to £60, £80 and £90, lawful money, a year. But the decision of the important questions, How shall the money be laid out? Who shall be employed to teach? When, and where, and how long, shall the schools be kept? seems to have been left to a committee for apportioning the money, or to the majority of the inhabitants of each parish, or of the several districts. This committee would first apportion the school money to each parish, "according to their pay," towards the town taxes, and then leave to each parish, or to the several districts in the First Parish, to determine what was to be done with the portion severally allotted them. The practice of the town on this subject seems, during all this time, to have been agreeable to its vote, March 1, 1779: "That the Second Parish should have their proportionable part of the money that is granted by the town for schooling the ensuing year, to be appropriated to that use, and no other; and that each parish may hire whom they please, and at any season of the year when they please." [13]

But in the year 1792, a new era commenced in Woburn, in regard to schools. At March meeting, of that year, a committee, consisting of the two clergymen of the town, Rev. Messrs. Sargeant and Marrett, and of five other prominent citizens, was chosen, "to examine into the government of the Schools, and to recommend some uniform system of instruction." [14] The report of this committee, which was submitted to the town May 7th, was as follows:

"The influence of Education on society, the advantages arising from it in advancing Religion and Morality, in distinguishing between the unlettered Savage and the refinement of civilization, will ever excite towns and other bodies corporate, to be particularly attentive to the System of Education pursued in the Instruction of the rising Generation.

"We have therefore, as a Committee of the Town of Woburn, chosen for the express purpose of forming a uniform System of Instruction in the respective Schools, unanimously agreed to recommend the following: Viz.

"1st. We recommend an exact attention to the Law of the Commonwealth, as to the choice, recommendation, and literary acquirements of each instructor, as first impressions are usually lasting. We think each Master ought to be a man of morality and education: and we would wish that the Town would be careful in the choice of their School Committee, so that none may be appointed to procure Masters, except such as are capable of judging of the abilities of the Masters, or will take measures to be informed of their characters and qualifications.

"2d. The School to be opened and closed with Prayers, which we think decent, and becoming creatures dependent on a Creator.

"3d. We also recommend that the Holy Bible should be read once each day by such Class as is capable of reading the same, and such parts selected, at the discretion of the Master, as may best suit the age and capacity of the children.

"We also recommend to the use of the Schools the following Books, Viz.—Perry's Spelling Book and Grammar; Webster's In-

---

[13] Town Records, Vol. IX., p. 498.

[14] Town Records, Vol. XII., pp. 66, 68.

stitutes, Third Part; The Children's Friend, Ladies' Accidence, Art of Speaking, Morse's Geography abridged, last edition: one or all of them, as can be made convenient to the Parents, Masters and Children: the mode of teaching them to be left with each Master.

"To such as study Latin we recommend the following Books: viz. Cheever's Accidence, or the Philadelphia Latin Grammar; Corderius' Colloquies; Æsop's Fables; Eutropius, Castalio's Latin Testament, Ward's Latin Grammar; Clark's Introduction to making Latin; Virgil, and Tully; Greek Grammar and Greek Testament. We also recommend Pike's, Fenning's, Fisher's, or Bonnycastle's Arithmetic; and to the upper Class, an attention to English Composition, once each week or fortnight, as may best suit the convenience of the Master.

"4. We also recommend Jenk's [Jenkin's?] Art of Writing, to be pursued as far as possible by each Master in his School, as being the most easy, concise and plain method ever published. We wish also due attention may be paid to the Paper, Pens and Ink of each Scholar; as 'tis of more consequence that they should be good at the commencement of their writing than when further advanced.

"5ly. We recommend the School to be Classed at the discretion of the Master. We also wish to shew our disapprobation of Corporal punishments; and recommend as a substitute, Public Admonition, degradation to the bottom of the Class; and if they continue refractory & stubborn, after all measures are used, we recommend a dismission of such Scholars from the School for such time as the Master may direct, and not [to be] again admitted, unless by a written confession in open School, and a promise of amendment.

"6ly. We recommend that the Catechism be taught in School once a week, especially the Commandments, with their several explanations.

"7ly. We also would recommend, that the Selectmen provide [for] the poor Scholars in each School, Paper, Pens, Ink and Books, at the charge of the Town, if they are poor Orphans, or Children of such Parents, who are unable to provide for them; so that each Child may have the advantage of a free School, and be made useful to himself and others.

"8ly. We recommend a visitation of the respective Schools by the Ministers of the Town, the School Committee, and the Selectmen, on the day previous to each Master's finishing his respective School; notice being given them by the respective Masters: at which time [there shall be] an Examination of the Scholars, and specimens exhibited of their several acquirements in knowledge, and a Journal of the behaviour of each Scholar shall be shewn by the Master, who shall keep a Book for that purpose: and the Visiting Committee shall give such marks of approbation and disapprobation as they shall think proper. . . We think a measure of this kind would have a good effect on Master and pupils.

"We earnestly wish the interest, welfare and happiness of the rising Generation: and submit the preceding recommendations to the consideration of the town.

"LOAMMI BALDWIN
JOSEPH BARTLETT
ZEB. WYMAN
REUBEN KIMBALL
JOHN WALKER
SAMUEL SARGEANT } Committee."

"The Town Voted to accept the above Report: and that the Town Clerk shall Record said Report in the Town Book of Records of Town Meetings; and that the Town Clerk furnish each School master with a copy of said Report at the opening of the Schools, and that each Master shall return said copy to the Town Clerk at the close of his School."[15]

On the same day that the above report was read and accepted. viz: May 7, 1792, there was likewise appointed a committee to divide the town into school districts. This committee reported May 28th, as follows:

REPORT, ETC.

"The Committee appointed to divide the Town of Woburn into School Districts, have attended that business, and Report as follows: viz.

"That the whole of the Grammar School be kept in the School house nigh the Meeting house in each Parish in said Town, and to be proportioned according to the sum that each Parish may pay towards the town taxes. Also that there be a School District,

[15] Town Records, Vol. XII., pp. 73, 75, 76.

agreeable to a Petition of Mr Josiah Walker and others, to consist of the following persons within the Lines of said District, here mentioned, Viz. James Walker, William Abbot, Isaac Marion, Dea. Timothy Winn, Ensign Timothy Winn, John Kendall, Lt. Joseph Winn, Timothy Winn 3d. William Young, John Bruce junr., Bill Center, Josiah Walker, Josiah Walker junr., Nathan Pierce, Jonathan Tyler, John Bruce, Reuben Johnson, Nathan Simonds, Ebenezer Cummings, Ezra Wyman, Thomas Gleason and Jeremiah Winn."[16] Also that the Districts called Richardson's Row, Button End, and New Bridge, extend and include the same as they formerly have done. Also the West District extend and include the same as formerly, excepting those who are included in Josiah Walker's District. Also that the Second Parish draw out of the Town Treasury their proportion of the money assessed for supporting the Schools, in the same proportion as they pay towards the Town Tax, and to be divided into two equal parts (all excepting that part which is or may be appropriated to keep the Grammar School, as aforesaid, and those who belong to Walker's District) ; said money to be laid out in the two School Houses proposed to be erected, one for the North District, near the South end of the lane leading to Wilmington by William Carter's ; the other at or near Joshua Kendall's, at a place called the Wood Market. Also that the other Districts draw their money out of said Town Treasury, according as they pay towards the town taxes, and lay said money out for Schooling, as the Law directs, and agreeably to the direction of the Town."

"ZEBEDIAH WYMAN
JOSEPH BROWN
JOHN WALKER
JOSIAH PARKER
JAMES REED
JESSE DEAN
SAMUEL THOMPSON } Committee.[17]

Woburn 28th. May, 1792."

Finally, to perfect its arrangements in regard to Schools, the town built in 1794 and the year following, nine new school-

[16] Town Records, Vol. XII., p 74. To this district it was voted, May 6, 1794, to add Mr. Samuel Walker, Benjamin Wyman, John Flagg, Jesse Russell, Robert Douglas, and David Cummings. Town Records, Vol. XII., p. 143.

[17] Town Records, Vol. XII., p. 74.

houses, one in each of the recently formed districts, at a cost of £580, or $1,933⅓ in all. At its meeting in March 1794, a committee of nine, or one for each district, was chosen for this purpose among others, to view the school-houses which then were, and to estimate the expense of repairing them, or of building new ones, in the several districts.[18] This committee, consisting of Capt. Joseph Bartlett, Mr. Josiah Parker, Lieut. Jeduthan Richardson, Mr. Elijah Leathe, Jr., Mr. Abijah Thompson, Mr. Timothy Winn, Jr., Capt. James Reed, Ensign Jesse Dean, and Col. John Walker, reported at May meeting that year as follows: "We recommend to the Town to raise the sum of one hundred and fifty pounds, in addition to the sum of one hundred and fifty pounds which was voted [for Schooling] at March meeting, to be appropriated to build School houses in the several Districts." They also recommended to the town, that each district should pay for its schooling that year by subscription; and that this sum of three hundred pounds, when raised, should be appropriated in the following manner, viz:

"The first Parish middle District to have			£55. 0. 0.
The second Parish middle District to have			45. 0. 0
The West Side	"	"	40. 5. 0
Richardson's Row	"	"	28:17:6
New Bridge	"	"	27:17:6
Button End	"	"	25: 0:0
Lt. Joseph Winn's [District]	"	"	25: 0:0
Capt. James Reed	"	"	26:10:0
Lt. Jesse Dean	"	"	26:10:0
			£300:00:0"[19]

In compliance with this recommendation, the town voted to raise the £300 for the purpose designated in the report. It also appointed the same gentlemen to be a committee to superintend the erection of the school-houses, each in his own district; to see that the work was completed; and that a deed to

[18] Town Records, Vol. XII., p. 137.

[19] Town Records, Vol. XII., pp. 143, 144. Supposing that the £300 raised in May 1795, to complete the school-houses, was appropriated in the several districts in the same proportion as the above, each school-house would cost just double what was first estimated it would.

the town of the land on which each school-house stood should be obtained.[19]

But the people, in their zeal and hurry for building the new school-houses, overlooked or neglected making provision by subscription, as the committee had recommended, for the support of schooling that year. In consequence of this neglect, the town was presented the next year (1795) by the Grand Jury for not complying with the requirements of the law on this head. To avert the penalty in such cases imposed, or to procure the remission or abatement of it, Capt. Joseph Bartlett was employed as agent for the town, to attend the Court at Concord, and there to plead the expense the town had incurred in building school-houses, etc., etc., during the time it was presented, in palliation of its neglect to fulfil the requirements of the law; but how he succeeded in his agency is not known.[20]

In the mean while, the building of the new school-houses went on. At May meeting, 1795, the building committee reported, that, in their estimation, it would cost £280 more than had been granted for the purpose in May 1794, to complete them. Whereupon, the town voted £300 "for the purpose of finishing said School houses." It was also voted, if any surplus remained of the £300, above the cost of finishing the school-houses, it should be appropriated to support schooling in them the present year (in addition to the £100 raised in April for the same use); and that the building committee should also be "the committee to provide schooling in the several districts the present year."[20]

And now the public schools in Woburn, being provided with every needful accommodation, and under the favorable influence of the new regulations, began to flourish as they never had before. And, although for a little while they were checked in their progress by the incorporation of the Second Parish as a distinct town, in 1799, yet they speedily surmounted that obstacle in their onward course. Parents have since showed a livelier interest for the education of their children than they

---

[19] Town Records, Vol. XII., p. 143.

[20] Town Records, Vol. XII., p. 195.

formerly exhibited, and have made more liberal grants of money for the promotion of this excellent end. Hence their schools have been multiplied in number; the terms of time which they were wont to be kept have been prolonged; and their children have enjoyed far superior advantages, and more enlarged means and opportunities for the acquisition of knowledge than they heretofore have been accustomed to. And as the town itself has of late years surprisingly increased both in population and in wealth, so there has been a marked and a very rapid progress in its schools, both in the number of their pupils, and in the privileges of instruction which they have afforded.

In this connection, while treating of the public schools of Woburn, it seems an appropriate time and place to give some account of *Warren Academy*, situate in the midst of it.

This important institution of learning derives its name as well as being from its munificent founder, Isaac Warren, Esq., of Charlestown. That benevolent gentleman, after much deliberation how he might bestow a portion of the wealth, which a kind Providence had put into his hands, so as best to promote the glory of the Giver, and the good of his fellow-men, came at length to the conclusion, that he could in no way do more for the advancement of these ends, than by making a donation for the establishment of an institution "for the Literary, Moral and Religious Instruction of Youth:" and Woburn was selected by him for the site of this institution, because it was then distinguished by a remarkable outpouring of the Holy Spirit of God, and an extensive, powerful revival of evangelical religion.

Under the influence of this conclusion, Mr. Warren was led to procure a meeting, February 21, 1827, at the house of his pastor, Rev. Warren Fay of Charlestown, where, in his own presence, and that of Rev. Messrs. Fay and Joseph Bennett of Woburn, the preliminaries of the designed institution were drawn up and agreed upon. After prayer to God, it was there determined to found an academy at Woburn, on the principles of the gospel, denominated "Orthodox or Calvinistic;" intending that it should always be under the instruction of pious Calvinistic teachers; and that no others should ever be employed.[21]

"A compact was then drawn up, including the form of a subscription paper, and stipulating that the three persons above named, Isaac Warren Esqr., Rev. Warren Fay, and Rev. Joseph Bennett, and also the Hon Samuel Hubbard [of Boston] should have the right and power of appointing such persons to be associated with them as Trustees, and forming such bye laws and regulations for the benefit of the Academy, as in the first instance they should think proper."[22]

Then, at the time and place above named, Isaac Warren, Esq., subscribed five thousand dollars, on condition that five thousand dollars more should be obtained; and this required sum was secured by the special exertions of Rev. Mr. Bennett, chiefly from among the inhabitants of Woburn.

The Trustees first organized, May 31, 1827, when they chose Isaac Warren, Esq., chairman, Rev. Warren Fay, secretary, and Rev. Joseph Bennett, treasurer. The same day, the Board of Trustees was enlarged by the choice of Benjamin Wyman, Esq., and Capt. Joseph Gardner, both of Woburn; and September 19, 1829, by the choice of Rev. Aaron Warner of Medford.

In pursuance of votes passed by the Trustees at several successive meetings, subsequently to the above, a building suitable for an Academy was erected on the eminence, since known as Academy Hill, and finished in 1827 or 1828; a preceptor was appointed for one year; the terms of tuition were fixed at four dollars per quarter, except in the case of beneficiaries of the American Education Society, who, it was voted, should receive instruction at the academy gratis; a system of by-laws, pro-

---

[21] To secure the future compliance with this vote more effectually, it was voted at the annual meeting, August 21, 1835, "That the Trustees intend to sustain the principles on which this Seminary was founded, and to employ none but 'pious Calvinistic Instructors;' and that it be understood as established in this Board for all future time, that its character shall be Evangelical or Calvinistic; and none but those of the above mentioned religious views shall be eligible to membership in this Board." — (Academy Records.)

[22] Academy Records.

posed by Rev. Mr. Fay, was adopted, and ordered to be recorded; and the Legislature of Massachusetts was petitioned for an act of incorporation, which was granted, March 10, 1830, and accepted by the Trustees, April 24th, of the same year.[22]

By the Act of Incorporation it was ordered, that the number of the trustees should never exceed eleven, nor be less than five, at any one time: and the trustees were empowered to fill their own vacancies; to choose their own officers; to hold funds, to a certain amount, for the benefit of the academy; and to make by-laws and regulations for their own government, and that of the institution under their care.

The by-laws and rules approved and adopted previously to the Act of Incorporation, or subsequently to it, provided

1. That there should be "four vacations in the academy annually, commencing on the Monday next preceding the last Wednesday of May, August, November, and February. The vacations commencing in May, August and November shall be two weeks each, and the one in February one week."

2. That there should be a stated meeting of the trustees annually, to be held in the town of Woburn; beside special meetings, that might be called by the Committee of Arrangements. The stated meeting was originally held at the close of the summer term: In 1850, it was ordered to be held at the close of the fall term; but in 1863, the old arrangement was reverted to.

3. That the officers of the institution should be elected annually at the stated meeting.

4. That there should be, at the stated meeting of the trustees, a public examination of the students of the academy, on which occasion, prayer was to be offered, and an address delivered by one of the trustees previously appointed. There were also to be examinations of the students by the examining committee before the vacation in May and November.

5. The students were required to attend the devotional exercises in the academy on week days, and public worship on the Sabbath.

6. They were forbidden to go out of town in term time without the consent of parent or preceptor; to enter into any enclosure without the permission of the owner; to frequent taverns, to use profane language, to practice games of chance, etc., etc.

7. The preceptor was directed to read the Holy Scriptures and to offer prayer in the academy morning and evening; to appoint, with the advice of the examining committee, the exercises of the school, and the books to be studied; to maintain over the students a constant supervision, in school and out; to give them kind and faithful advice for direction, or in forming their habits, manners, and deportment; and habitually to seek their highest intellectual improvement, their increase in "religious knowledge, and the advancement of their spiritual and immortal interests." [22]

On Wednesday, June 27, 1838, the academy building was consumed by fire. This at the time, was reputed to be the work of an incendiary. But though a reward of a hundred dollars was offered for the detection of the person or persons who perpetrated the crime, and though several individuals were examined in regard to it, yet no one was ever proved to have been concerned in the commission of it.

A committee was speedily appointed to examine the ruins, who reported it expedient to rebuild the old walls, as they stood, beginning a few feet from the top. This report was accepted; a building committee was chosen; and so rapidly, under its direction, did the work of reconstruction proceed, that the new building was ready for occupation by December following; and the academy, in the course of that month, was opened anew with appropriate exercises, especially with an address, by previous appointment, from Rev. Dr. Fay.[22]

In the mean while, Rev. Mr. Bennett, who had been appointed and requested to solicit donations in aid of the institution, (especially to replace the philosophical apparatus, destroyed by the fire,) was so successful in his efforts to this end, as to raise above $1,400 by subscription, besides books. Of the money thus generously contributed, it was voted to lay out five hundred dollars upon the purchase of a suitable philosophical apparatus; and a committee consisting of Rev. Dr. Fay, Rev. Joseph Bennett and George W. Warren, Esq., of Charlestown, was chosen for the purpose. The treasurer also was directed to procure a plain clock for the school-room.[22]

By the sale in 1857, of the boarding house, and of land attached to it, "the invested funds of the Institution were materially increased, and the means of its usefulness were proportionably enlarged." And hence the committee on lands, etc., chosen in 1856, and consisting of Gen. A. Thompson, Rev. E. W. Clark, Rev. J. Edwards, George W. Warren, Esq., and Deacon Thos. Richardson, took occasion to report at the annual meeting of the board, November 20, 1857, that "while the principal of the fund should be kept good, it is desirable that the income of the fund should be principally employed in putting the Academy building and Grounds around in complete order; in providing in the Building a Room for the Meetings of the Trustees; and also in making an annual addition to the Library and Philosophical Apparatus."

And bearing in mind, "that this new accession to the Fund of the Trustees has been almost wholly derived from the sale of the Boarding House and appurtenances, which was the donation of Isaac Warren Esq. the founder of the Institution, and in addition to his original subscription, both of which were made in his lifetime: It seems highly proper, that the Trustees should provide for a permanent memorial of him, to be placed in the proposed Trustees' room, as a mark of respect to his memory, and in token of his beneficence to this Institution.

"The Committee therefore unanimously propose the adoption of the votes herewith subjoined.

"For the Committee,

G. WASH[N]. WARREN."

"Voted, That this Committee be authorized, at such time as they may deem proper, to put the Academy Building in complete repair; to provide a cellar and furnace for the same; to provide and furnish a room for the use of the Trustees; and to grade and ornament the grounds about the building in a suitable manner.

"Voted, That in grateful recognition of the liberal endowment made by Isaac Warren, Esq., the founder of this Institution, the President be requested and authorized to procure on behalf of the Board, a Marble Bust of him, to be placed in the Trustees' room.

"On motion made, it was voted to accept and adopt the above Report and the accompanying Votes." [22]

List of Preceptors of the Academy.

1828. Mr. Alfred W. Pike.
1831. Mr. Jarvis Gregg.
1831, Sept. 23. Mr. Cyrus Holmes.
1836, Aug. 26. Mr. A. K. Hathaway.
1842. Rev. A. P. Chute.
1846. Mr. Abner Rice.
——. Mr. Osgood Johnson. Had resigned, Nov. 16, 1853.
1853. Mr. J. J. Ladd.
1859. Mr. E. W. Stone.
1861. Mr. D. W. Sanborn.
1865. Mr. William A. Stone, M. A.

At the Annual Meeting, August 4, 1865, the Board of Trustees was composed as follows:

Gen. Abijah Thompson, Esq.,	admitted	1834.	Treasurer.
George W. Warren, Esq.,	"	1835.	President.
Rev. Joseph L. Bennett,	"	1852.	
Dea. Thomas Richardson,	"	1854.	
Hon. Horace Conn,	"	1856.	
Rev. J. B. Miles,	"	1856.	
Rev. R. T. Robinson,	"	1856.	
Rev. Joseph C. Bodwell, D. D.,	"	1862.	
Ephraim Cutter, M. D.,	"	1863.	Secretary.
Dea. John R. Kimball,	"	1865.	
Rev. Elihu P. Marvin,	"	1865.	
Rev. Melancthon G. Wheeler,	"	1865.	

Several of the former Members of the Board (as Rev. Aaron Warner) have resigned in consequence of a change of residence; and to others who have deceased, merited tributes of respect have been paid, as follows: To Rev. Joseph Bennett, August 16, 1848. To Capt. Joseph Gardiner, November 19, 1858; and to Dr. Benjamin Cutter (for thirty years Secretary) June 18, 1864.

In 1799, an important division of Woburn was effected, viz: the separation of the Second Parish from the First, and its incorporation by the General Court as a distinct town, by the name of Burlington. Attempts for this end had been repeatedly made before, viz: in January, 1733–4, only three years after the incorporation of the parish; and, again, in 1774 and in 1782; [23] but they had all been defeated by the timely and decided oppo-

[23] Parish Records, Vol. I., p. 51; Vol. II., pp. 110, 170, 171.

sition of the First Parish. But the measure aimed at in these successive efforts was carried at last. The motion for this purpose commenced in this, as in all the preceding instances, in the precinct. At a parish meeting, May 29, 1797, it was

"1st. Voted unanimously, to take measures to obtain a division of the town of Woburn, so that the Second Parish in said town might be incorporated into a separate town.

"2ly. Voted, to choose a Committee of seven persons, who are directed to take such measures as shall appear to them reasonable and proper to obtain said separation. The Committee chosen were

"JOHN WALKER, ESQ.,	ENSIGN TIMOTHY WINN,
CAPT. REUBEN KIMBALL,	MR. EDWARD WALKER,
CAPT. JOHN WOOD,	MR. JOHN CALDWELL,

MAJ. JOHN RADFORD.

"3ly. Voted that the above persons be a Committee, and are directed to collect the minds of all the qualified voters in said Parish, respecting a separation of said town of Woburn."

At an adjournment of the meeting to June 1st, P. M., two more persons were added to the Committee above named, viz: Capt. James Reed and Mr. James Walker.

"4ly. Voted that the above Committee of nine persons be directed to petition the General Court of this Commonwealth jointly, or by any one or more of them, in behalf of said Parish, and to take and use all reasonable and lawful measures to obtain the object above mentioned. Also voted that the above mentioned nine persons be a Committee to make and receive in behalf of said Parish such proposals as they may judge proper and expedient respecting said separation.

"5ly. Voted to raise the sum of fifty dollars, to defray the expense that may arise in prosecuting the above object." [24]

The committee chosen by the parish to obtain, if possible, a division of the town, seem now to have drawn up a memorial on this subject, and to have presented it to the General Court at its next session. And at a precinct meeting, February 7, 1798:

---

[24] Parish Records, continuation of, pp. 4, 5.

"After having the proceedings of the Committee made known,

"Voted unanimously, that they approve thereof.

"Voted, that the Memorial presented to the General Court by them [the Committee] is perfectly agreeable to their minds, and that they are anxious to have the prayer thereof granted.

"Voted unanimously, that the Committee chosen in May last to petition the General Court for a division of the Town of Woburn, are empowered generally to act and agree in behalf of said Parish in every matter or thing that may come before the General Court respecting the division aforesaid."[25]

And at a still subsequent meeting, March 12, 1798, the parish "Voted, that the Committee already chosen, be requested to proceed agreeably to their Instructions, and to use all possible means in their power to obtain a separation of the town of Woburn, agreeably to their Memorial, or in any other way they shall think proper: and that all the powers that have heretofore at any legal meeting been granted them, are still continued in force."[26]

But the majority of the town was decidedly opposed to the contemplated division; and did not look with unconcern upon the zealous efforts of the people of the Second Parish to procure it. At a general meeting of the inhabitants of the town, at the meeting-house of the First Parish, December 18, 1797, in acting upon an article of the warrant, relative to setting off the Second Parish as a town, it was found that eighty-six were against such a separation, and thirty-nine in favor. Five agents were then chosen to attend the General Court at their next session, to oppose a division of the town, viz:

Col. Loammi Baldwin,
Samuel Thompson, Esq.,
Maj. Jeremiah Clapp,
Daniel Wyman,
Abijah Thompson,
} Agents.[27]

And at a town meeting, April 2, 1798, in relation to a memorial of the Second Parish in Woburn, respecting a division

[25] Parish Records, continuation of, p. 7. [26] Continuation of Parish Records, p. 14.

[27] Town Records, Vol. XII., p. 280.

of the town, "Voted a Committee of nine Persons to inquire into the grounds of uneasiness of the Second Parish, which has occasioned their application to the Legislature for a Division of this town, and report at the next meeting.

"COL. LOAMMI BALDWIN,
SAMUEL THOMPSON, ESQ.,
MAJ. JEREMIAH CLAPP,
CAPT. BENJAMIN WYMAN,
MR. BILL RUSSELL,
CAPT. JOSEPH BROWN,
MR. JAMES WALKER,
GEN. JOHN WALKER,
CAPT. JOHN WOOD,
} Committee."[28]

Mem. Fifty-eight votes for choosing a committee, thirty-five against.

At a town meeting, May 7, 1798, the committee reported as follows:

"The Committee appointed by the town of Woburn to inquire into the grounds of uneasiness of the Second Parish in Woburn, which has occasioned their application to the Legislature for a Division of this Town, have attended that service; and report, that your Committee held a meeting at the house of Capt. John Wood, Jun., in said Second Parish on 23d ultimo, and have previously notified the Committee who had been appointed by the 2d Parish to apply to the General Court for the division of the town, and to attend with such others as might be best capable of giving information respecting the grounds of uneasiness, as required by the town. And after diligent inquiry was made of the Committee of the Second Parish, and many others who attended, your Committee could not find as there were any real grounds of uneasiness existing, neither was there one word of complaint made, but what the Second Parish have had its full proportion of advantages equal and in common with the rest of the town: and it is the opinion of your Com-

---

[28] Town Records, Vol. XII., p. 307.

mittee, that there does not actually exist any real grounds for uneasiness at all; but we have great reason to fear that the present movements and attempts for a division of the town originated altogether in private views.

"LOAMMI BALDWIN,
SAMUEL THOMPSON,
JEREMIAH CLAPP,
BENJAMIN WYMAN, } Committee.[29]
JOSEPH BROWN,
BILL RUSSELL,

"ZEBADIAH WYMAN, Town Clerk."

The committee's report, as above, was accepted. Three agents were then chosen, viz: Maj. Jeremiah Clapp, Mr. Abijah Thompson and Capt. Joseph Brown, who should attend the General Court, at its next session, to oppose a division, and were directed to remonstrate in writing against it.

Voted, also, that the Representative of the town, Samuel Thompson, Esq., be instructed to use his influence in the Court in opposition to a division of the town.[29]

But at this stage of the proceedings in reference to a division of the town, the inhabitants of the Second Parish seem to have stolen a march upon those of the First. A general town meeting was called, to be held October 1, 1798, at the meeting-house of the Second Parish. One article of the warrant for this meeting was, "To see if the Town will choose a Committee to meet the Committee which is appointed by the General Court, on a Petition of General Walker and others to view the Town, in order to ascertain the expediency of a division of said Town into two Towns, or into a Town and District. Also to see if the Town will give their Committee, when chosen, any particular instructions respecting the matter, or do any thing in regard to the same, that they may think best when met together." From some cause or other, a large portion of the inhabitants of the First Parish appear to have been absent from this meeting:

---

[29] Town Records, Vol. XII., p. 309.

and the consequence was, that votes were then passed, which directly contravened the measures taken by the town in the two meetings next preceding. In acting upon the article above cited, a committee was chosen to meet the Court's committee, consisting of Lieut. Joseph Winn, Gen. John Walker and Mr. John Kendall; and a second committee was appointed to draft instructions for the first, which were accepted by the town, and were as follows, viz:

"That the Committee this day appointed to attend the Committee from the General Court be instructed to attend said Committee, and use their endeavours, in behalf of the Town of Woburn, to have the town divided, agreeable to the Prayers of the inhabitants of the Second Parish in said town, and that all just and equitable measures be taken by them to have the same accomplished as soon as may be; and that they appear in behalf of said town, at the next session of the General Court, and urge the necessity and utility of the measure in the most pressing manner they are able, or in any other way they may think most proper to accomplish a division of said town."[30]

But at a general town meeting, at the meeting-house of the First Parish, November 5, 1798, the action of the meeting, October 1st, in regard to a division of the town, was entirely reversed.

In answer to the petition of a number of the inhabitants "to see if the Town will dismiss the Committee which was chosen at their last town meeting to attend the Hon. Committee from the General Court upon a Division of the Town": the house was polled, and eighty-three were for acting on this article, and forty-three against.

"Voted, that the Committee, which was chosen on the 1st Oct. 1798, viz, Messrs. Gen. John Walker, Lieut. Joseph Winn and Mr. John Kendall, for the purpose of meeting the Hon. Committee from the General Court, by a vote of the town this day passed is dismissed from any further service for the town as a Committee.

---

[30] Town Records, Vol. XII., p. 311.

"Voted, to choose Agents to attend the General Court, or any Committee that is or may be appointed by the General Court, upon a Division of the Town."

Chose three agents by hand vote: to whom two more were presently added:

COL. LOAMMI BALDWIN,
MAJ. JEREMIAH CLAPP,
MR. ABIJAH THOMPSON, } Agents.
MR. NATHAN SIMONDS,
CAPT. JOSEPH BROWN,

Voted, that the instructions which Col. Loammi Baldwin has this day drawn up be the instructions for the above agents: which instructions were as follows:

Instructions:

"1. Voted, to choose a standing Committee of five persons to be Agents for the Town to oppose a Division of the Town, any three of which Committee shall constitute a quorum to do business, and no more than three are to attend at any one time, at the expense of the town. And the said Committee are requested and authorized to attend when it shall be necessary, at the General Court, or before any Committee that has been or that may hereafter be appointed, upon the Division of the Town, and in the name and in behalf of this town, to oppose any division thereof, and to remonstrate against the continuance of those expensive measures which are pursuing against it; and if necessary, to petition the Legislature, to be heard on the subject upon the floor of the House; and generally to do and transact every thing which they may think necessary for the interest of the town, to prevent a measure which appears pregnant with so many evils as that of the division of the town.

"2d. And it is also further Voted, that the numbers of Voters present at the appointment of said Committee be taken, and a Record thereof made; and the said Committee with the foregoing Commission shall continue and exist for the term of one year next ensuing this date, if the cause which has given rise for their appointment shall continue so long, unless in the mean time they shall be dismissed, or their commission altered, in legal Town Meeting, when there shall be as many Voters at least present as there are now at the appointment of said Committee.

"3d. Voted, that Samuel Thompson, Esq., who is appointed to represent this town in the General Court, the present year, be instructed, and is hereby instructed, to use his influence and utmost endeavors in the General Court to prevent a division of the town, and if possible, to put a speedy stop to the expensive measures which have been unreasonably pursued against the rights, the interest and happiness of the citizens thereof.

"Voted, that all the instructions and directions given to Messrs. Gen. John Walker, Lt. Joseph Winn and John Kendall, the Committee chosen at the last meeting to attend the General Court's Committee upon the Division of the Town be repealed, and made null and void."[31]

But all the strenuous efforts of the majority of the town to prevent the contemplated division of it did not avail. Such were the representations made to the Court, on the part of the Second Parish, or such the adroitness of its management for securing the end aimed at, that the Court came at last to the conclusion, that a division of the town was expedient; and on February 28, 1799, incorporated the Second Parish of Woburn as a distinct town, by the name of Burlington.[32]

By this act of the Legislature, Woburn lost 7,418 acres of territory, beside the Locke Farm, which was originally included in it, but which, after the incorporation of Burlington, was set off to Lexington.[33]

Of three hundred and fifty-three persons resident in Woburn, who were taxed there upon the town tax in 1798, there were ninety-six who belonged to the precinct.[34]

Of a town tax raised in Woburn, 1798, and amounting to $2,703.10, the Second Parish paid $795.20.[34]

The population of Woburn, Winchester and Burlington was

---

31 Town Records, Vol. XII., pp. 314, 315.

32 Special Laws of Mass., Vol. II., p. 283.

33 Plan of Burlington, by Bart. Richardson, 1831.

34 Town Records, Vol. XII., pp. 317-343.

as follows, according to the United States census, in the years named:

	1790.	1800.	1810.	1820.	1830.	1840.	1850.	1860.
Woburn,	1,727	1,228	1,219	1,519	1,977	2,993	3,956	6,287 [35]
Winchester,							1,353	1,937
Burlington,		534	471	508	446	510	545	606

N. B. Winchester was incorporated April 30, 1850, from parts of Woburn, Medford and West Cambridge.[36]

Burlington incorporated February 28, 1799, originally Woburn, Second Parish: part of it annexed to Lexington, January 10, 1810.[37]

The death of General Washington (deservedly called the Father of his Country) in December 1799, excited a universal and profound sensation of grief throughout the United States. At a town meeting in Woburn, January 8, 1800, called as soon as could be after the event was announced, it was voted:

"1. That a week day be assigned, on which the Town may pay their respects to the memory of the late General George Washington, who died on the 14th of December, A. D. 1799.

"2. That the Selectmen with three other Gentlemen, viz. Col. Loammi Baldwin, Major Jeremiah Clapp, and Dea. Josiah Convers, be a Committee to appoint said day, and concert a mode in which the town may proceed to pay their respects to the memory of their friend, Gen. George Washington deceased."

The Report of the Committee, rendered within an hour after, was:

"The citizens of the town of Woburn, being deeply affected at the death of his Excellency, George Washington Esq. late General of the Armies of the United States, who died the 14th Dec. last, do resolve that Thursday, the 16th instant, be set apart to testify their respect to the memory of their late beloved friend and patron, General George Washington.

"And that it be recommended to the Inhabitants of this Town to suspend the ordinary business of labour, and that an Eulogium adapted to the occasion be delivered at the Meeting House on said day.

---

[35] Public Documents, Annual Statistics, 1864, No. 1, pp. 30, 31.

[36] Public Documents, etc., 1864, No. 1, p. 15.

[37] Public Documents, 1864, No. 1, pp. 13, 14.

"Voted to recommend to all the male inhabitants to wear a black crape or ribbon on their left arm, and the females, black trimming on their head dresses, for the term of thirty days."

This report was accepted by the town, which then chose a committee of nine persons, to make and carry into effect the necessary arrangements for said day, viz:

COL. LOAMMI BALDWIN.
SAMUEL THOMPSON, ESQ.
DEA. JOSIAH CONVERS.
MR. ABIJAH THOMPSON.
CAPT. JOSEPH BOND.
LIEUT. JOSEPH LAWRENCE.
CAPT. BENJAMIN WYMAN.
MR. ELIJAH LEATHE, JR.
MAJ. JEREMIAH CLAPP.[38]

Finally, "Voted, in case that an Orator cannot be obtained to pronounce an Eulogium on the day appointed, the above Committee are authorized to appoint another time for said Solemnity, and to give seasonable notice to the Town of the time they may appoint." [38]

The services in commemoration of the death of Washington were held January 16th, (the day recommended by the Committee,) in the old meeting-house on the Common, which was so densely crowded with attendants, that it was found necessary to prop it up. An escort was formed by the military company under the command of Lieut. Stephen Richardson; and by the children and youth of the public schools. Prayer was offered by Rev. Daniel Oliver, then preaching in Woburn. An address, adapted to the occasion, was delivered by Rev. Dr. Morse of Charlestown, founded on the words Deut. xxxiv. 7. "And Moses was an hundred and twenty years old when he died; his eye was not dim, nor his natural force abated." Rev. Elias Smith, of the Baptist society, made the concluding prayer.[39]

---

[38] Town Records, Vol. XII., p. 358.

[39] Communication from Col. Leonard Thompson, by Nathan Wyman, Esq., town clerk.

CHAPTER XIV.

Ecclesiastical History from 1775. — First Church: Rev. Messrs. Sargeant, Chickering, Bennett.

To resume the ecclesiastical history of Woburn, which was brought down in Chapter XI., to 1775:

At the commencement of the present century, in consequence of the incorporation of the Second Parish as the town of Burlington in 1799, the old first congregational parish of Woburn comprehended all the inhabitants of the town, excepting the few connected with the Baptist Society, which had been then but recently formed. To preserve harmony with that society, however, the town entered into an engagement with it, September 28, 1801, to omit taxing its members for the support of Congregational preaching, or any other religious purpose, on condition of its returning every year, by the first of May, to the town assessors, a list of those who belonged to it.[1] And moreover, it forbore, after 1802, to enter in the town records (agreeably to previous custom) its proceedings relative to raising money for preaching, or to the settlement or maintenance of its ministers, but transferred them to a new volume, termed the "Parish Books" or otherwise "the Ministerial Book of Records."[2] The last tax for the support of preaching that is recorded in the town book was raised by the town September 21, 1801, and recorded in the Town Records, Vol. XIII., p. 62–66.

After the dismission of Rev. Mr. Sherman, in 1775, the First Parish was almost ten years without a settled minister. The friends of the dismissed pastor were too much soured and grieved at his removal, to be very ready to agree with his opponents in the choice of a successor. Upon two occasions, they manifested much solicitude to have Mr. Sherman invited back and resettled over them. Particularly, at a parish meet-

[1] Town Records, Vol. XIII., p. 47.
[2] Town Records, Vol. XIII., pp. 70, 126, 186, 188, 217, 254, 348, 379.

ing, December 8, 1778, in taking steps to determine how many were in favor of giving him such an invitation, the people were found to be very nearly equally divided.[3]

At a meeting, April 5, 1779, it was voted to set apart April 22d, as a day of fasting and prayer, " in order to the settlement of a Gospel Minister in this Parish;" and to apply to the following ministers in the vicinity, viz:

Rev. Messrs. MORRILL of Wilmington,
" " CLARK of Lexington,
" " THACHER of Malden,
" " PRENTISS of Reading,
" " MARRETT of Woburn, Second Parish,
" " OSGOOD of Medford,

" to assist the Parish, and carry on the work of the day."[4]

During the long period which elapsed that Woburn First Parish was destitute of a settled ministry, numerous candidates were employed, with a view to settlement over them. Among the more prominent of these were Messrs. Caleb Jewett, in 1779, William Greenough, in 1780, Jonathan Homer, in 1781, and Phinehas Wright, in 1784. Each of these gentlemen was successively called by the church to the pastoral office; and, in respect to the two named last, the parish voted concurrence with the church, and a salary. But they all declined continuing in Woburn. Mr. Jewett was afterwards settled, it is believed, in Maine; Messrs. Greenough and Homer in Newton; and Mr. Wright in Bolton.

December 8, 1784, the church made choice of Mr. Samuel Sargeant for their pastor. With this choice the parish concurred, at a meeting December 13th, when they voted to give him annually £150 salary, so long as he should do the whole work of the ministry in the parish, and £150 settlement. And at an adjournment of this meeting, January 3, 1785, it was voted to pay Mr. Sargeant his settlement one half in one year, and the other half in two years from that time; and to give him £50 annually for his maintenance, so long as he shall be the minister of the parish,

[3] Parish Records, Vol. II., pp. 219, 220. [4] Parish Records, Vol. II. Page not noted by clerk.

should he fail, by reason of age, etc., to do the whole work of the ministry.[5]

And at an adjourned meeting, January 24th, the parish voted, by forty votes to twenty, their continued satisfaction with their previous proceedings on this head; and appointed a committee "to complete a contract with Mr. Samuel Sargeant," who that day accepted the invitation given him to settle.[5]

February 14th, a committee of the parish was appointed to meet a committee of the church, to make provision for the ordination; and also with Mr. Sargeant to determine what churches to apply to, for their assistance on the occasion. The day appointed for the ordination is not named either in the church or in the parish records; but from the Precinct Church Records, it appears to have taken place March 14, 1785, Mr. Sargeant having been received into the fellowship of the Church a fortnight before.

At this time, there were, on the Parish tax lists for 1785, one hundred and twenty-seven resident persons on the west list, and one hundred and four resident persons on the east list, taxed for the minister's salary.[5]

But scarcely was Mr. Sargeant regularly inducted into the pastoral office, before those troubles commenced respecting him, with which the parish was agitated for nearly fourteen years. The choice of him by the parish, as their minister, was far from unanimous, as is evident from their proceedings at their meeting January 24, 1785, at which they confirmed their previous doings at his election; and subsequent acquaintance with him, and use to his ministrations did not allay the opposition to him, or increase the number of his friends. At a meeting of the parish May 1, 1786, Mr. Zachariah Richardson, a stanch friend of Mr. Sherman, and who seemed hardly willing to sit under the preaching of any other minister, brought forward a petition *that every one might be allowed to pay his parish tax wherever he attended preaching*: and though the parish refused, by forty votes to twenty-three, to act on this petition, yet another petition,

---

[5] Parish Records, Vol. II.

signed by the same individual and ten others, was presented at a meeting October 29th of the next year, urging that a committee might be chosen, to see if they can agree with the Rev. Samuel Sargeant, that he should quit the desk.[5]

Before the end of the year 1786, several members of Woburn First Parish had withdrawn from the public worship of their own town, and frequently attended the meetings of the Baptist society in West Cambridge: and though the assessors in Woburn were directed by the parish to assess the parish taxes, as they had been wont to, yet at several parish meetings in Woburn, in 1787 and 1788, it was a matter of debate, what should be done with the parish taxes of those persons; whether they should be paid to the Baptists, who demanded them of the parish treasurer, or not.

Alarmed by these contentions, and tokens of alienation from Rev. Mr. Sargeant on the part of many, several prominent citizens procured a parish meeting, to be called January 4, 1790, to see if the parish will act upon the following articles, agreeably to the petition of Bartholomew Richardson and others:

First, "To see if the Parish will take any measures to reconcile and heal the divisions and uneasiness that do now and have for some time past subsisted between a considerable number of the Parish and the Rev^{d} Mr Samuel Sargeant.

"Second, To choose a large committee to wait on the Rev. Mr Sargeant, to confer with him on the subject of a reconciliation and compromise between him and a great number of the Parish, and if possible, to lay a plan for obtaining peace and unity once more amongst us."[6]

At this meeting, January 4, 1790, a numerous committee, viz: Dr. Samuel Bloggett, Messrs. Jesse Richardson, Robert Douglas, Elijah Leathe, Deacon Zebadiah Wyman, Messrs. Joseph Winn, Josiah Convers, Lieut. Jeduthan Richardson, Maj. John Hastings, Mr. Paul Wyman, Capt. Joseph Bartlett, Samuel Thompson, Esq., and Mr. Daniel Wyman, thirteen in all, was chosen, to take part in the efforts proposed above; and also upon certain

[6] Parish Records, Vol. II.

papers communicated by Mr. Sargeant, and to report at adjournment, January 18th.

At the adjournment, the committee reported that they did not consider the proposals of Mr. Sargeant, contained in his letters communicated to the parish, as sufficient to calm the disaffection.

"That they had waited on Mr Sargeant, and had informed him, as far as was in their power, with regard to the existing uneasiness; that he expressed great grief thereat; had ever sought their welfare; was sensible of the burdens of his people; was willing to sustain an equal share with any of his brethren; and (with regard to his demands on the Parish) had never exacted interest on his Orders; on the contrary, had often settled them, after they had been due 15 or 20 months, without any compensation for delay, even when he was paying interest himself for money he had borrowed; that he had never in any year since his residence among them, received, on an average, more than £10 over and above a sufficiency to pay for his own board and horse keeping, at the rate he gave while a Candidate; and that he had never received a farthing of his settlement money since the day it was voted: finally, that if he were chargeable with rash or imprudent speeches, had injured any one, or done any thing inconsistent with the character of a Christian minister or gentleman, he was willing to make any proper satisfaction; and to submit all matters of uneasiness to a Mutual Council of Churches, and abide its decision."

The report, of which the above is an abstract of the principal particulars, is signed by Joseph Bartlett, the committee's clerk. And in perusing it, one cannot but perceive reason for Christian sympathy with Rev. Mr. Sargeant, in some of its statements, and in others just cause of complaint on his part against the parish for delinquency in not fulfilling their engagements with him.

But the report did not satisfy the parish, which decided not to accept it, by sixteen votes to thirty-three, and then referred the matter anew to the same committee, with some enlargement of their commission, to report further at an adjourned meeting, January 28th.[6]

At the adjournment, the committee added to their former report, that having inquired into and considered certain speeches reported to have been made by Rev. Mr. Sargeant, they had found one to be without foundation, and as to another, they had not been able to obtain satisfaction.

They further reported, that having endeavored impartially to acquaint themselves with the sentiments of the inhabitants of the Parish, with regard to Mr. Sargeant, " they had found 24 decidedly in his favor.

" 48 inclined to have the connection between Mr. Sargeant and his people dissolved.

" 50, who had not seen fit to manifest their wishes.

" 22 who had signed off to the Baptists.

" And a few remained, whom they had not seen, and whose sentiments, in regard to Mr. Sargeant, they had had no opportunity to ascertain."

This report was read and accepted; and then the meeting was dissolved.[6]

In the year 1790, Mr. Sargeant sued the parish at law, probably for his settlement money. No defence was attempted by the parish in this suit; but they agreed to be defaulted.

About the same time, Rev. Thomas Green, minister of the Baptist society in West Cambridge, sued the parish for recovery of the taxes of those inhabitants of Woburn, who attended worship in his society. Committees were successively appointed to defend the parish against Mr. Green. But eventually, the case was decided in Mr. Green's favor, who obtained an execution against the parish; and orders were given to the parish assessors, October 17, 1791, "to omit taxing those persons reputed to belong to Mr. Thomas Green's Society, whose names are returned to the [Parish] Committee, except Benjamin Fowle, Ephraim Tottingham, and such others, as the assessors may think best to tax or not, according to the assessors' discretion."

At a meeting of the Parish, September 27, 1792, an address to the church, drawn up by a committee chosen for the purpose, was submitted to the parish, in which it was stated, "that the disaffection to Mr. Sargeant had existed several years, was continually increasing, and disturbing not only their religious transactions, but the harmony of their social intercourse; and threatening, unless a remedy was speedily applied, the most injurious consequences:

that 'a new Religion, had been introduced among them, and the usual place of worship had been forsaken by a considerable number of valuable citizens; and that many who continued to attend, did it more from a sense of duty, and a love of good order, than from any expectation of benefit: that they did not now complain, on behalf of the parish, of the religious or moral character of Mr Sargeant; but that so unintelligible were his instructions, and so mysterious and dark his mode of communication, that the general complaint was, that neither profit nor advantage could be expected; and that they believed the general wish of the parish was for an amicable separation, such as would be honorable to Mr. Sargeant, and not injurious to them; and that unless a separation did take place, they had good reason to believe that a number of others, Mr. Sargeant's hearers, would withdraw." [7]

This address was accepted by the parish, and the committee which drew it up, soon after, at the request of the parish, presented it to the church. From the church records, it appears that the church met October 24th, to hear the address read; and appointed a committee of three, viz, Samuel Thompson, Esq., Deacons Obadiah Kendall and Zebadiah Wyman, to prepare an answer.

But their answer, whatever it was, did not satisfy the parish, or divert them from their purpose, which was to get rid of Mr. Sargeant. At their adjourned meeting, October 29th, they chose a committee of five, viz: Capt. Joseph Bartlett, Mr. Jeremiah Clapp, Capt. Joseph Brown, Ichabod Parker and Josiah Parker, to meet the church, and to request that a committee might be chosen from their body to join with the parish committee "to wait upon Mr. Sargeant, and see what agreement can be made with him, relative to his relinquishing his connexion over this Parish"; and report at the adjournment of this meeting, November 12th.

The above request of the parish was communicated to the church, November 2d, when it was voted to resolve the church into a committee of the whole, to join the committee from the parish. This joint committee met November 5th; but after calling Deacon Zebadiah Wyman to the chair, they came to no conclusion, and dissolved the meeting. (See Church Records.)

---

[7] Parish Records, Vol. II.

At a meeting of the parish, January 28, 1793, it was put to vote —

1. "To see if the Parish will submit the present difficulty existing between the Rev$^{d.}$ Samuel Sargeant and a number of the Parish (agreeably to the original Contract with Mr Sargeant at his settlement) to a Mutual Council of Churches.

2. "Then voted to choose a Committee of five persons, to Request Mr Samuel Sargeant to call a Church Meeting, to see if the Church will join in a Council; and Report to the Parish at their adjournment.

"Then made choice of Mr Abijah Thompson, Capt. Joseph Brown, Mr Paul Wyman, Capt. Joseph Bartlett, and Mr Jeremiah Clapp"; and voted to adjourn to the 18th of February next, at 2 of the clock, P. M.[8]

February 18, 1793, the parish met according to their adjournment, and called upon their committee for their report, who said they had none, although the church had met. But from the Church Records, we learn the proceedings of the church in regard to those of the parish, at their meeting January 28th, and upon other interesting matters, as follows: —

The church met February 18, 1793, and heard read the proceedings of the parish at their meeting, January 28th. When it was voted, after mature deliberation,

1. "Not to act at present on the request of the Parish."

2. Informed Mr. Sargeant that a number of persons appeared disposed to withdraw from the parish, and requested him to say, whether in case they should withdraw, he would relinquish the proportion of his salary, for which such persons would be liable? To which Mr. Sargeant replied as follows: —

"Should a number of persons relinquish their connexion with the Parish, and join any other denomination of Christians, the loss shall be mine, not the parish's. Pay me from year to year the same proportion on Polls, real and personal Estate, as you paid the last year in the sum of one hundred pounds and I will relinquish the deficiency."

These doings were sent to the parish, and the parish dissolved their meeting.[9]

In this unhappy posture of affairs, the First Church and Parish in Woburn continued, in relation to their pastor, Rev. Mr.

---

[8] Parish Records, Vol. III., p. 1.

[9] Parish Records, Vol. III., p. 2.

Sargeant, for five years more. A large number of the parish were earnestly desirous that the connection between them and their minister should be dissolved. But a majority of the church appear to have resolutely adhered to him, and been very unwilling to part with him. But in 1798, the church, alarmed at the then state of things, and apparently fearing that to retain Mr. Sargeant in the ministry among them any longer might be fatal to the peace of the parish, and to the interests of religion in it, came to the conclusion it would be best to carry into effect an agreement entered into by them and Mr. Sargeant just before his ordination. That agreement was as follows:

In the warrant for a parish meeting, March 19, 1798, one article was,

"To see what the Parish will do, respecting the uneasiness of a number of persons belonging to said Parish, relative to sitting under the Rev. Samuel Sargeant's preaching," etc. In acting at the meeting upon this article, "Voted to poll the House on the Question of the uneasiness under the Rev. Mr Samuel Sargeant's preaching: which was accordingly done. The Return was, that thirty-five were uneasy, and nine otherwise minded."[10]

The parish then proceeded to choose a committee of seven persons, viz: Maj. Jeremiah Clapp, Mr. Deacon Wyman, Capt. Joseph Brown, Mr. Jacob Peirce, Capt. Benjamin Wyman, Mr. Bill Russell, and Capt. Abijah Thompson, "to request the Rev. Samuel Sargeant and the Church to call a Church meeting for the purpose of choosing a Committee to meet the Parish Committee, to consult together respecting the uneasiness of a number of persons belonging to said Parish, relative to their sitting under the Rev^{d}. Mr Samuel Sargeant's Preaching."[10]

The committee of seven, chosen as above, proceeded to communicate the request of the parish to the church, who voted compliance with it, and at a meeting, April 9th, having heard the doings of the parish, March 19th, chose from their own body Samuel Thompson Esq., Deacon Jeduthan Richardson, Deacon Obadiah Kendall, Abijah Thompson and Joseph Lawrence, as a committee, to join with the committee from the parish. At a parish meeting, July 2d, this joint committee reported as follows, viz:

[10] Parish Records, Vol. III., pp. 40, 41.

"We the Subscribers, a joint Committee chosen from the Church and Parish to consider the present uneasiness subsisting between the Rev. Samuel Sargeant the Church and Parish, have attended that business agreeably to their instructions, and report as follows: viz. that after waiting upon Mr. Sargeant at his house, and consulting with him, find he will not come to any agreement, nor make any proposals respecting the terms of a Separation; but does not object to a Council agreed upon by him and the Church: and we recommend to the Parish to leave it with Mr. Sargeant and the Church to agree upon a Council, and that the uneasiness together with all matters of dispute be submitted to their determination.

"JEDUTHUN RICHARDSON } per Order." [11]
"July 2, 1798. JEREM^h^. CLAPP. }

The parish voted to accept the above report; and also to join with the church in a council; and that their committee should unite with the committee from the church in making the necessary provision for receiving the council.

Hitherto, the church seems to have entertained a lingering hope, that an accommodation on some terms might be effected between Rev. Mr. Sargeant and the parish, and thus save the necessity of calling a council. But the result of the conference between him and the joint committee, related in the report just given, convinced them it was useless to cherish such an expectation any longer.

Accordingly, at a meeting July 9th, they voted with Mr. Sargeant's concurrence, to call a mutual council of five churches, viz: the church in Chelsea, the church in Billerica, two churches in Reading, and the church in Salem, of which Rev. Messrs. Payson, Cumings, Stone, Prentiss and Barnard, D. D., were pastors.

2. Appointed Tuesday, 25th September next, 10 o'clock, A. M., for the Council to convene; and the pastor and deacons to be the committee to send the letters missive.

The following is the form of a letter missive agreed upon at a church meeting:

"Woburn 23d. July 1798.

"To the Church in Billerica:

"Revd. Hon^b.^ and Beloved.

"The first Church of Christ in Woburn, sendeth Greeting.

"Earnestly requesting your Presence with us on Tuesday 25th Septr. next, at 10 o'clock A. M. by your Pastor and Delegate,

---

[11] Parish Records, Vol. III., p. 43.

"To consider 'The uneasiness of those Persons belonging to this Parish relative to their sitting under the Rev. Samuel Sargeant's preaching'; and to judge of the expediency of his continuing his pastoral relation to this Church. And if it be expedient to dissolve the pastoral Relation, to judge on what Terms and Conditions it shall be dissolved; according to the mutual agreement between Mr Sargeant and the Church dated 28th. Febr. 1785.

"Wishing Grace, Mercy and Peace to be multiplied unto you, We subscribe ourselves Yours in the Faith and Fellowship of the Gospel of Jesus Christ:

"The other Churches sent unto are

"The Church in Chelsea, Two Chh[s] in Reading
The Church in Salem, of which
Rev. Mr Payson, Stone, Prentiss and Barnard D.D.
are Pastors."

"The Rev. Mr Henry Cummings.
To be communicated."

SAMUEL SARGEANT, Pastor.
SAMUEL THOMPSON, JEDUTHUN RICHARDSON, } Deacons.
} Committee of the Church.

At a legal parish meeting, September 17, 1798:

"Voted to instruct their present Committee to join the Committee from the Church and Parish; and for the Joint Committee to proceed to lay all complaints, difficulties or grievances subsisting between the Rev. Mr Sargeant, the Church and Parish that they may think proper, before the Council, which is mutually chosen by Mr Sargeant and the Church, to be assembled at Woburn on Tuesday the 25th. instant, and that they furnish the Rev[d]. Samuel Sargeant with a Copy of the same as soon as may be.

"The Names of the Joint Committee:

"The Joint Committee	Dea. SAMUEL THOMPSON Dea. OBADIAH KENDALL Dea. JEDUTHUN RICHARDSON JOSEPH LAWRENCE ABIJAH THOMPSON	"On the part of the Church."
	JEREMIAH CLAPP ICHABOD PARKER JOSIAH PARKER OBADIAH KENDALL Jun[r]. JOSEPH BROWN	"On the part of the Parish."
"The Parish then Voted to add two more to the Committee, viz:	DANIEL WYMAN BENJAMIN WYMAN	"Added two more."

"Voted to dissolve the Meeting.

"SAMUEL THOMPSON, Parish Clerk."[12]

[12] Parish Records, Vol. III., p. 44.

Address of the joint Committee of the Church and Parish to the Mutual Council.

Prepared agreeably to instructions of the Parish, at a meeting, September 17, 1798.

"To the Venerable Council, to be assembled at Woburn 25th of September 1798.

"A statement of the following Grievances and Difficulties subsisting between the Rev. Samuel Sargeant and the First Church and Parish in Woburn, [is] submitted to them for their consideration and decision by the Joint Committee chosen by the Church and Parish for that purpose.

"It appears that the uneasiness originated at or about the time of Mr. Sargeant's settlement A. D. 1785, and notwithstanding the opposition that was then made against him by a large number of the inhabitants, it was thought best by the Council to ordain him.

"We further state that ever since Mr. Sargeant was ordained, the opposition has increased. Several attempts at different times have been made to dissolve the connexion, as may appear by the Parish Records.

"A Baptist Society has been formed, principally consisting of Inhabitants that have left the first Parish, in consequence (as we apprehend) of their being dissatisfied with Mr Sargeant. And we sensibly feel the loss of so large a number who have already withdrawn from us; and have great reason to fear, that a very considerable number more will soon leave us, unless some measures be speedily taken to prevent it.

"We further say, that the mysterious and unintelligible manner of Mr. Sargeant's communicating his ideas is the general complaint of his hearers: and it is further alleged that he has neglected Catechising the children; nor has kept up Lectures, according to the practice of other churches; and that his Visits have been few and partial. For these and other reasons there is such a general uneasiness in the Parish, that we do believe his usefulness is near at an end in this place; and that a dissolution of his Ministerial Relation will be most for the peace, happiness and interest of both him and the Parish.

"As it will be too tedious (if not impossible) to exhibit on paper all that may be necessary to lay before the Council, we wish to reserve the liberty to offer all such other matters as may be expedient for them to hear relating to the premises; and that Mr Sargeant have liberty to do the same.

"As there is provision in the Contract made between Mr. Sargeant and the Church, that either party being dissatisfied with the Result of a mutual Council, may have a right to appeal to the Association, and should there be an Appeal, we expect the Church and Parish will have the liberty to offer any new matters to the Association that they may think proper, provided they furnish Mr. Sargeant seasonably with a Copy of the same." [13]

"*Result of Council.*

"WOBURN, 27th. Sept. 1798.

"An ecclesiastical Council, consisting of the following Churches, viz. The Church in Chelsea, the Church in Billerica, the North Church in Salem, the first and second Church in Reading, being convened agreeable to Letters Missive from the Rev. [Samuel] Sargeant and the church of Christ in the first Parish in Woburn, to consider their circumstances, and the expediency of dissolving his pastoral Relation, as stated in said Letters Missive: Having addressed the Throne of Grace for Light and Direction, and having attended to the discussions and state [statements?] of the parties in said Parish, particularly to the uneasiness of a large number of the Church and people under the pastoral care of the Rev. Mr Sargeant, who wish to have his ministerial connexion with them dissolved.

"And having viewed and compared the probable consequences, both of his continuing in the ministry among them, and of a dissolution of his pastoral relation, are clearly of opinion, that circumstances are such, as make it expedient that his said relation should be dissolved, provided they shall be willing to make him any reasonable compensation. And, accordingly, the Council *do unanimously advise* him the said Mr Sargeant to ask a dismission from the church and people of his charge, on condition that they shall pay him nine hundred dollars, that sum being judged no more than a reasonable compensation for his relinquishing his contract.

"We do not advise to this measure on account of any culpability which we have found in Mr Sargeant. For justice and charity to him oblige us to say that his moral character as a Man, as a Christian, and as a Minister, stands fair and unimpeached; no charges having been offered of any immoral Conduct, false Doctrine or criminal delinquency in office.

---

[13] Parish Records, Vol. III., p. 45.

" We find ourselves therefore constrained to observe, that it cannot but be a painful consideration to all sincere Christians, and particularly discouraging to the ministers of the Gospel to reflect, that any of the sacred order, after having spent the best part of their days in the service of the Sanctuary with a fair character, maintained through the whole of their ministry, should in consequence of divisions and uneasinesses, which do not implicate them in criminality, be reduced to the disagreeable alternative of taking a dismission, or living in a most uncomfortable and perplexing controversy with a great part of their parishioners.

" Mr Sargeant, so far as we are able to get acquainted with the circumstances of his case, falls under the above predicament.

" And being ourselves persuaded of his integrity and uprightness, and the goodness of his heart and character, We can, and do with the greatest sincerity, recommend him to any people who may see fit to employ him as a minister.

" Though unfeignedly grieved at the separation which may now take place between their Pastor and this Church and People, yet we have been highly pleased with the honorable manner in which they have conducted the whole hearing before us.

"We have earnestly wished this temper might have issued in your Order and happiness, still united together. But our wishes in this respect are not gratified. The Relation between you being dissolved, according to our advice, cherish that humility and penitence, which become you upon an event so serious and affecting.

" We humbly trust, as a Council, we have heard you with patience and impartiality; and have decided in the integrity of our hearts.

" All that remains for us to do is to commend you to the blessing of Almighty God, which is more valuable than any thing else.

" Wherever the Pastor of this Church goes, may he prosper, and finally receive a Crown of Life which shall never fade away!

" May the Church and People have peace and be edified, and be continually under His guidance, who is able to preserve them from falling, and to present them faultless before the presence of his glory with exceeding joy.

" Phillips Payson, Moderator.

" Caleb Prentiss, Scribe."

" The above is the Result of a mutual Council of Churches,

chosen by Mr Sargeant and the Church in the first Parish in Woburn 9th. July 1798, and convened 25th. Septr. 1798.

"True Copy: Attest. SAMUEL SARGEANT, Pastor."

But the difficulties with Rev. Mr. Sargeant were not yet ended. The compensation awarded him by the council for relinquishing his contract seems to have been considered by the parish as excessive. At a parish meeting, October 10, 1798, the Result of Council having been read, a committee of seven was chosen, which was empowered "to make such agreement with the Rev. Mr. Samuel Sargeant on such terms of separation as they may think expedient." At an adjournment of this meeting, November 7th, the committee reported verbally to the parish, "that they had applied to Mr. Sargeant, but could not come to any agreement with him, which they thought would be satisfactory to the Parish." Whereupon it was voted, after some consultation, "That the Parish do not comply with the Result of the Council."[14]

At a meeting, April 8, 1799, in compliance with an article in the warrant, "to see if the Parish will take any measure by a committee or otherwise to make a final settlement with the Rev. Samuel Sargeant," the parish chose a committee of five for this purpose, viz: Mr. Abijah Thompson, Mr. Daniel Reed, Lieut. Joseph Lawrence, Maj. Jeremiah Clapp, and Mr. Bartholomew Richardson, Jr., which reported at an adjournment of that meeting, April 29, 1799, that they "had agreed with the Rev. Samuel Sargeant to quit his Ministerial connection, together with all contracts heretofore entered into by him with the Church and Parish, and to receive from the Parish the sum of four hundred dollars together with his salary up to the twenty-eighth day of May next, as specified in the Memorandum of Agreement made between Mr Sargeant and the Committee authorized for the above purpose, Woburn April 9th. 1799.

"ABIJAH THOMPSON
DANIEL REED.
JOSEPH LAWRENCE
JEREMIAH CLAPP
BARTH^{W}. RICHARDSON."

[14] Parish Records, Vol. III., pp. 48, 49.

The report was accepted: and the committee was directed, with the treasurer, to complete the settlement with Mr. Sargeant, in the way and manner above reported, as soon as possible, and then report to the parish.[15] And when this arrangement was carried into effect, the connection between Rev. Mr. Sargeant and the people of Woburn doubtless ceased.

Rev. Samuel Sargeant was born at Worcester, November 6, 1755; graduated at Dartmouth College, 1783, where he studied divinity under the direction of Rev. Professor Ripley. Dismissed from Woburn, he removed to Chester, Vt., and was never resettled in the ministry. At different times, however, he made several missionary tours in the employment of the Connecticut and Massachusetts Missionary Societies; particularly in the northern parts of Vermont, in Wayne and Luzerne counties, Pennsylvania, and in Oneida county, New York. He also had the charge of the church in Chester, and at times preached in the town by contract for a longer or a shorter period, as occasion offered; but without settlement. He died at Chester, June 2, 1818, aged sixty-three.[16]

During his ministry at Woburn, there were sixty-two admissions to the church; one hundred and eighty infants and one adult were baptized; and one hundred and twelve marriages on record were solemnized, inclusively of his own.[17]

After the withdrawal of Rev. Mr. Sargeant, May 27, 1799, agreeably to the advice of a Mutual Council convened at Woburn in September of the year before, the Church remained destitute of a settled pastor several years.

July 14, 1801, the church gave a call to the pastoral office to Mr. Joshua Lane, a graduate of Harvard College, in 1799. In this choice, the town concurred in September. It also voted to give him six hundred dollars as a settlement, and an annual salary of four hundred and fifty dollars, so long as he should continue their Gospel minister.[18] And at a subsequent town

---

15 Parish Records, Vol. III., pp. 56, 57.

16 Phineas O. Sargeant, Esq., his son; Am. Quarterly Register, Vol. XI., pp. 176, 188.

17 Church Records.

18 Town Records, Vol. XIII., pp. 46, 60, 61. Church Records, Vol. I., p. 81.

meeting, December 21st, it was stipulated, that if Mr. Lane should be taken off from preaching by infirmity or old age, he should "*relinquish* one half of his salary"; thus virtually promising to pay him, through life, under the circumstances supposed, the other half if he continued in his pastoral relation.

Upon these terms, Mr. Lane accepted the invitation given him to settle in Woburn. December 28th, committees of the church and town met with Mr. Lane to make some necessary arrangements preliminary to his ordination. But not being able to finish them then for want of time, they adjourned the completion of them for a few days. But before the day of adjournment arrived, Mr. Lane altered his mind, and requested the town in writing, without assigning his reasons, to release him from his engagement to settle with them as their minister.[18]

At a meeting, May 17, 1802, the church gave a call to Mr. Humphrey Moore, another son of Harvard, of the class of 1799, to become their pastor. With this call, the town concurred, by a very full vote. But Mr. Moore's answer was in the negative. He was subsequently settled in the ministry at Milford, N. H. where (August 19, 1867) he still continues.

At a meeting, December 5, 1803, the church, by an unanimous vote of all the brethren present, made choice of Mr. Joseph Chickering for their pastor. In this choice the town concurred unanimously, December, 22, 1803; and voted, December 29th, to give him an annual salary of six hundred and fifty dollars, and fifteen cords of good hard wood; and eight hundred dollars within a year from his ordination, as a settlement: and furthermore the town voted, January 26, 1804, "That when by reason old age, or other infirmity, Mr Joseph Chickering shall be unable to perform the work of the Gospel Ministry, he shall then receive one half of the aforesaid Annual Salary, to be equally apportioned on the Money and Wood, during the time he shall stand in the connection of a Gospel Minister in the Town of Woburn.[19]

This invitation Mr. Chickering accepted, February 12, 1804.

---

[19] Parish Records, Vol. III., pp. 96, 98.

The ordination was appointed to be on Wednesday, March 28th; and the following churches with their respective pastors were requested to assist in the solemnity: viz.

Lexington, under the pastoral care of			Rev. JONAS CLARK.
Reading, North Church,	"	"	Rev. ELIAB STONE.
Medfield,	"	"	Rev. THOMAS PRENTISS.
Andover, South Church,	"	"	Rev. JONATHAN FRENCH.
Medford,	"	"	Rev. DAVID OSGOOD.
Billerica,	"	"	Rev. HENRY CUMINGS.
Burlington,	"	"	Rev. JOHN MARRETT.
Dedham, First Church,	"	"	Rev. JOSHUA BATES.
Dedham, South Church,	"	'	Rev. JABEZ CHICKERING.
Dedham, West Church,	"	"	Rev. THOMAS THACHER.
Cambridge, West Church,	"	"	Rev. THADDEUS FISKE.
Brookline,	"	"	Rev. JOHN PIERCE.
Bedford,	"	"	Rev. SAMUEL STEARNS.
Medway,	"	"	Rev. LUTHER WRIGHT.
Milford, N. H.	"	"	Rev. HUMPHREY MOORE.

On the day set for the ordination, delegates from all the afore-named churches, and all the pastors except Rev. Messrs. Prentiss and French, appeared at the place appointed, and formed in council choosing Rev. Jonas Clark for Moderator, and Rev. Thaddeus Fiske for Scribe. Having gone through with the usual preliminary inquiries and examination, the council expressed unanimously their satisfaction, and voted they were ready to proceed to ordination.

To Rev. Mr. CLARKE the Council assigned The Charge.
To Rev. Mr. STONE " " The Ordaining Prayer.
To Rev. Mr. MARRETT " " The Right Hand of Fellowship.
To Rev. Dr. CUMINGS, " " The Introductory Prayer.
To Rev. Mr. THACHER " " The Concluding Prayer.

At the meeting-house, all the parts were performed agreeably to the above appointments of the Council. Rev. Jabez Chickering, father of the pastor elect, by previous request, preached the sermon. "The exercises were performed and attended to with becoming solemnity; and perfect order and regularity marked the proceedings of the whole day."[20]

In 1808, the third meeting-house in Woburn, erected on the southeast side of the common, finished in 1752, and in which Rev. Mr. Chickering was ordained in 1804, was burnt down. This catastrophe is noticed as follows, in a note to his dedication sermon. "On the night of the 17th of June, 1808, at about half past eleven o'clock, the meeting house was discovered to be on fire, and in less than an hour was reduced to ashes. Several circumstances evinced design, and caution to prevent other damage. There is only one considerable opening from the common where the house stood, which is to the southwest; and a night was chosen, when the wind blew from the northeast. Had it blown from any other quarter, other buildings must inevitably have been consumed. Most of the powder in the tower of the house, amounting to near 200 pounds, must also have been removed, as the explosion was so inconsiderable, that many persons who were awake, and within a mile of the spot, did not notice it. The west door was also observed to be open, when the fire was first discovered. Notwithstanding design was so evident, no circumstance has transpired to justify a suspicion of any individual."[21] A reward of five hundred dollars was offered by the town, and advertised in two of the public newspapers, to any who would detect the person or persons who perpetrated the crime[22]; but no discovery was ever made public, and the incendiary or incendiaries escaped with impunity.

At several town meetings previous to the fire, it had been a question for consideration, whether to repair the old meeting-house or build a new one?[23] At an adjourned meeting, June 5th, especially, it was at one time decided by thirty-four votes to thirty-three, to repair. But this decision was presently reconsidered; and a committee was appointed to examine the meeting house, to see what partial repairs might be made to save the timbers from their present decaying condition, and to report at an adjournment of the meeting for one fortnight, viz: on June

---

[20] Church Records, Vol. I., pp. 82–85.
[21] Dedication Sermon, note (a), p. 24.
[22] Town Records, Vol. XIII., p. 274.
[23] Town Records, Vol. XIII., pp. 269, 271.

19th. Hence, there was obviously cause for suspecting that the author of the conflagration was some one who was opposed to repairing the meeting-house, and who hence took this effectual method to prevent it.

The town met June 19th, at the Centre school-house, and decided by sixty-seven votes to three to build a new meeting-house; and chose a committee to draught a plan for the same, and to estimate the quantity of materials requisite to build it, either of wood or brick.[24] This committee made report to the town at its next meeting, June 27th, when their plan for the new house was accepted; and then, and at a subsequent adjournment, it was determined to build it of wood, and to erect it on the spot where the centre school-house then stood; a committee was chosen, consisting of Maj. Benjamin Franklin Baldwin, Lieut. Willard Jones and Lieut. Bartholomew Richardson, Jr., as agents for contracting for the materials and workmanship; the sum of $6,000 was raised for the purpose of building, to be assessed according to the direction of the Treasurer; and the Treasurer himself was authorized to hire that sum, as it might be demanded for use.[25] Such was the abundant preparation made by the town for the erection of its fourth meeting-house, to supply the place of the third, which had been burnt. And such was the zeal and expedition with which the above-named agents, as a building committee, discharged their trust, that within one year from the time the old one was destroyed by fire, the new one was ready for occupation. It stood on the site afterwards occupied by its successor, the fifth congregational meeting-house, now owned, enlarged and adorned by the Unitarian Society; "was a building fifty-five feet wide, and sixty long, exclusive of a projection, six feet by thirty in front, and ornamented with a handsome steeple. The entry on the gallery floor afforded a convenient hall for public meetings on business, and was finished with accommodations for that purpose."[26] It was solemnly dedicated, June 28, 1809, when an appropriate and interesting discourse was delivered to the large

[24] Town Records, Vol. XIII., p. 272. [25] Town Records, Vol. XIII., p. 275.
[26] Dedication Sermon, note (h), p. 28.

audience assembled on the occasion, by Rev. Joseph Chickering, the pastor, from Acts VII. 48. "The Most High dwelleth not in temples made with hands." This discourse, with very valuable historical notes appended to it, was afterwards published by request.

Previously to the dedication, it had been decided in town meeting, May 25, 1809, and subsequently, not to pay the expense of building the new meeting-house by a tax on the town, but by the sale of the pews at public auction.[27] In pursuance of this plan, the building committee was directed to number and appraise the pews; and according to the report of this committee (enlarged by the addition of four other persons) made June 8th, and accepted, each pew was to be appraised in proportion to its value and situation in the house; the sum total was to amount to $8,000; no pew was to be sold for a sum less than the appraisement; the town clerk was to make a record of all the pews sold, together with the purchasers' names and prices paid; and pew No. 51 was to be reserved for the use of the town.[26] The auction was held in the meeting-house on Monday, June 19th; and the proceeds of the sale, including the choice money, amounted to $10,911, which exceeded the cost of the building by $3,000.[24]

In regard to this surplus, arising from the sale of pews in the meeting-house, a committee chosen by the town to devise the best method of appropriating it, recommended in their report, to make of it, and of all other moneys that might be given for the same end, "a perpetual fund, towards the support of the Regular Ordained Minister of the Congregational Society" in Woburn; and that when the interest of the whole fund should amount to two hundred dollars per annum, "to apply the interest of the whole Fund, annually, towards the support of the said Congregational Minister."[28] This report was accepted: and agreeably to its recommendation, the town voted October 16, 1809, "to choose a Board of Trustees, to be incorporated into a body politic for the

[27] Town Records, Vol. XIII., p. 317.

[28] Town Records, Vol. XIII., p. 320. For the clerk's record of the pews sold, names of purchasers, etc, see Town Records, Vol. XIII., pp. 435–437.

purpose of superintending and taking care of any Money, Moneys, Lands or Donations, appropriated or established as a Fund for the purpose of supporting the Gospel Ministry in the Congregational Society in the Town of Woburn." The gentlemen chosen as trustees of this fund on this occasion were:

Maj. BENJAMIN FRANKLIN BALDWIN,
Lieut. BARTHOLOMEW RICHARDSON, Jr.
Lieut. WILLARD JONES,
Mr. JACOB PEIRCE,
Mr. DANIEL WYMAN.[29]

The Legislature was petitioned to incorporate these trustees and their successors for the end mentioned, by a committee of the town's appointment: and the desired act of incorporation was granted, February 24, 1810.[30] But by an act of Court, passed April 1, 1861, the trustees were authorized to apply the fund in their hands, which had been designed for the support of the Congregational minister in Woburn, to the payment of the debts of the First Congregational Society. See Acts and Resolves, 1861: p. 444.

At the commencement of Rev. Mr. Chickering's ministry in Woburn, circumstances bade fair that it would be long and successful, and very acceptable to the people. Attendance upon his public services on the Sabbath was unusually full and constant. The young manifested, it is understood, an unwonted concern in spiritual and divine things. Through the exertions of the pastor, a warm interest had been excited in the breasts of the people in several of the benevolent and religious societies got up at that day; as the Middlesex County Bible Society, and the Middlesex Evangelical Society. And as his ministry progressed, there were, previously to 1811, large accessions to his church, of members both male and female, young and old.

But at the expiration of about seven years from his settlement, a cloud arose, which darkened the fair prospect which had hitherto presented itself. About that time, an unhappy variance took place between Rev. Mr. Chickering and a prominent pa-

[29] Town Records, Vol XIII., pp. 324, 326. [30] Special Statutes of Mass., Vol. IV., p. 255.

rishioner, a gentleman of high standing and extensive influence. It respected (as it is understood) a piece of land belonging to Mr. Chickering, which the gentleman referred to wished to purchase, that he might avail himself of a brook running through it for manufacturing purposes. Mr. Chickering was willing to sell it; but requested some security to be given, that seemed to him necessary, that the use to be made of it might not damage his other property in the vicinity. The security demanded, that gentleman was unwilling to give. Mr. Chickering still insisted upon it, as an indispensable condition of selling his land. But the other persisted in declining to give it. Hence the negotiation between them was broken off; and an alienation ensued which was never healed. Mutual friends to them both looked on with sad concern, and made repeated attempts to effect a reconciliation; but in vain.[31] Neither party would yield what the other insisted on, to make up the breach between them. And though the church continued to increase, especially during a season of revival in the year 1817, yet, through the influence of some opponents doubtless, the minds of many of the people were soured, and they no longer appreciated Mr. Chickering's services as they once did. At length, at a meeting of the parish, held January 8, 1821, such votes were passed, as induced Mr. Chickering to make the following communication, first to the society, and then to the church.

"A. D. 1821, Jan. 28. The church was requested to stop after public worship, and the following communication was made by the pastor.

"Dear brethren,

"You all know, that the following communication has been made to the parish, and accepted by them in a regular parish meeting."

---

[31] One such effort is referred to in Article 16th, of Warrant for Town Meeting, March 4, 1811, as follows: "To see if the Town will by a Committee or otherwise take any measures to settle the unhappy difficulty existing between the Rev. Joseph Chickering and Major Benj. F. Baldwin; or do any thing whereby the peace, unity and happiness of the Congregational Society in said Town may be restored and preserved." — (Town Records, Vol. XIII., p. 378.)

"To the Congregational Parish in Woburn.

"Brethren & Friends:

"It was long my expectation and the wish of my heart to spend my days in your service. I would still cherish this wish, were there such a degree of union among you, as might encourage a reasonable hope, that my labors might be useful. But the result of your last parish meeting is in my view, and in view of most of those I have consulted, a decisive indication that my removal has become expedient, and that any further effort to prevent it would be injurious to your peace and to the interests of religion. I hope therefore, that those who have been most attached to my ministry, will acquiesce, with Christian condescension, in an event painful alike to themselves and to me. To avoid unnecessary delay and discussion, I propose that my pastoral and ministerial relation to this church and people be dissolved on the following conditions:

"1. That the church shall consent to my removal.

"2. That an ecclesiastical council be called to look into our proceedings, dissolve the relation, and give me such a recommendation as they may think proper.

"3. That the relation be dissolved in six months, from the time when these proposals shall be accepted and recorded by the parish; during which time I shall supply the pulpit, and perform such pastoral duties, as under existing circumstances may be convenient.

"4. That my salary for the present year be paid with the usual punctuality; and the proportion of it which may be due for the next year, ten days before my removal; the wood being commuted to money, as for several years past.

"5. I am willing that these proposals, when accepted by the parish and church, should be laid before a council for their sanction, as soon as the parish may choose.

"6. If any of them be thought objectionable, they shall be submitted to the council for their decision.

"When it is considered, that I have voluntarily relinquished all claim of indemnification for the pecuniary loss which I must inevitably sustain in disposing of my property, I trust that none will think these proposals unreasonable. And, Brethren and Friends, let me intreat that neither unchristian irritation or resentment may be indulged on the one hand, or unbecoming exultation on the other. The event is solemn. It must be reviewed at the judgment day; and so must the feelings with which it is effected.

God grant, that you may now, and at all future times, follow after the things which make for peace, and things wherewith one may edify another; that your self command, mutual forbearance, harmony and Christian feelings, on this trying occasion, may be a presage of the manner, in which you will seek, and settle another minister: And may the great Shepherd give you a pastor, who shall be more prudent, more useful, and more happy in retaining your affection, than

"Your humble, afflicted, but affectionate Servant in the Lord,

"Woburn Jan. 22, 1821. "JOSEPH CHICKERING."

"As one condition of my being dismissed is the consent of the church, I now ask your consent, dearly beloved brethren, to this measure. None will doubt, that such a request must be painful to me, as the granting of it will be to most of you. But I am fully satisfied, after the most mature and prayerful deliberation, that such an event has become expedient; and therefore hope, that you will *unitedly* acquiesce in it, and seek the continuance of Christian ordinances, after the period above specified, by such instruments as God in his good Providence may provide."

"Whereupon voted,

"1. That a meeting to consider and act on this communication be holden on Saturday next, one o'clock, P. M.

"2. That the meeting be at the centre school-house.

"3. At the request of the Pastor, that the Rev. Mr Emerson of South Reading, be invited to attend and moderate the meeting."[32]

"Feb. 3, 1821, the church met according to appointment.

"The Rev. Reuben Emerson being present, agreeably to the request of the church, moderated the meeting.

"The record of the last meeting was read; after which the Moderator led in prayer.

"After free conversation,

"Voted, that a committee of three persons be chosen to prepare, and lay before the church, votes on the subject now under consideration.

---

[32] Church Records, Vol. I., pp. 176–179.

"Voted, that the committee consist of three persons.

"Chose Deacon Wyman, Brother Calvin Richardson and Jonathan Tidd.

"The committee reported the following resolutions:

"1. Resolved, as the expression of the feelings of the members of the church, that it is not their wish and desire that the Rev. Joseph Chickering should be dismissed from his pastoral relation to them, could he continue in that relation with a prospect of future usefulness.

"2. Resolved, as the sense of this church, that under the existing circumstances of the parish, and in consequence of the proposals made by the Rev. Mr Chickering to said parish, and accepted by them at their last meeting, the members of the church view it to be their duty (though with the deepest feelings of regret) to yield their consent, that the pastoral relation between them and their pastor should be dissolved, agreeably to the proposals made by him.

"The first Resolution was passed unanimously.

"The second Resolution was passed, *nemine contradicente.*

"Voted thanks to the Rev. Moderator for his kind services.

"Voted, that after prayers this meeting be dissolved.

"The meeting was concluded with prayer by the Moderator.

"REUBEN EMERSON, Moderator.

"JOSEPH CHICKERING, Scribe."[33]

"Feb. 11, 1821. The church being requested to tarry after the close of public exercises:

"Voted, To choose a committee of four, to join with the Pastor and a committee already chosen by the parish, in agreeing on and assembling a council for the purposes specified in the communication acted on at our last meeting: also to appear before the Council in behalf of the church, to give any information, and make any communications that may be requested.

"Chose Deacon Benj. Wyman, and Bros. Calvin Richardson, Uriah Manning and Josiah Walker.

"Feb. 15, 1821. The above named Committee met, on the 15th of February, with the parish committee and the pastor,

[33] Church Records, Vol. I., pp. 179-181.

and agreed on the churches and time named in the following *letter missive*, which was sent to each pastor to be communicated:

"The Congregational Church and Parish in Woburn to the Church in ——— under the pastoral care of Rev.———

"Reverend and beloved:

"It has pleased God to permit such opposition to arise against the Rev. Joseph Chickering our Pastor, that he has judged it expedient to propose to us the dissolution of his ministerial relation. His proposal, with the terms annexed to it, have been accepted by the parish. The Church has also deemed it 'their duty, though with the deepest feelings of regret, to yield their consent.' The parties have mutually agreed to request an ecclesiastical Council, to consist of the following pastors and churches. Rev. Dr. Ripley, Concord; Rev. Dr. Holmes, Cambridge; Rev. Freegrace Raynolds, Wilmington; Rev. Samuel Stearns, Bedford; Rev. Reuben Emerson, S. Reading; Rev. Samuel Sewall, Burlington; and Rev. Justin Edwards, Andover; to meet, according to our Pastor's request, 'look into our proceedings, dissolve the relation, and give him such a recommendation as they may think proper.' This is therefore to request your assistance, by your Rev. Pastor and a delegate, on Wednesday, the 11th day of April next, for the purposes above specified.

"Wishing you grace, mercy and peace, and requesting your prayers to God for his blessing, direction and support under our trials, we subscribe ourselves very respectfully.

"Yours in the Lord.

"Signed by the Pastor, Benj. Wyman for the church, and Bill Russell for the Parish." [34]

"*Result of Council.*

"A Council, convoked by the Congregational Church and Parish in Woburn, in concurrence with their Pastor, to look into their proceedings, with a view to the dissolution of the pastoral relation, met at Woburn on the 11th day of April, 1821.

"Present:

"The Church in Concord, Rev. Ezra Ripley, D. D., Pastor.

"The first Church in Cambridge: Rev. Abiel Holmes, D. D., Pastor; Bro. Abel Whitney, Delegate.

"The Church in Wilmington: Rev. Freegrace Raynolds, Pastor; Dea. Benj. Foster, Delegate.

"The Church in Bedford: Rev. Samuel Stearns, Pastor; Bro. Amariah Preston, Delegate.

"The Church in So. Reading: Rev. Reuben Emerson, Pastor.

"The Church in Burlington: Rev. Samuel Sewall, Pastor; Bro. Ebenezer Cummings, Delegate.

"The South Church in Andover: Rev. Justin Edwards, Pastor; Bro. Solomon Holt, Delegate.

---

[34] Church Records, Vol. I., pp. 181, 182.

"Rev. Dr. Ripley was chosen *Moderator*, and Rev. Mr. Edwards, *Scribe.*

"The Council, having attended to the subject before them with that serious deliberation which its importance required, and with prayer to the Father of lights for direction, came unanimously to the following Result:

"That the pastoral relation between the Reverend Joseph Chickering and the Congregational Church and Society in Woburn be, and hereby is dissolved, on the conditions to which they have mutually agreed.

"In arriving at this result, the Council have been highly gratified to find nothing alleged, or insinuated against the moral, or Christian, or ministerial character of the Pastor: yet this fact could not but render the measures for his dismission the more mysterious, and this act of the Council the more difficult and reluctant. Taking into view however past occurrences and the prospect of the future, the Council are united in approving the measure proposed by the Pastor and People; a measure, which, although "deeply regretted" by the Church and many others, appears to be best adapted to the interests and happiness of the whole.

"The spirit which has marked the proceedings of the Church and Society during the sitting of the Council has been honorable to both; and is considered as a favorable indication of future union and peace. For that peace and union the Council devoutly pray; and unitedly commend the Church and Society to the care and benediction of the Divine Head of the Church.

"With the knowledge of the respectable talents, the moral and Christian character, and the ministerial qualifications of the Rev. Mr. Chickering, and in the belief that his past success in the ministry is a good pledge of his future usefulness, the Council very cordially recommend him to the Christian community, as a pious, able and faithful minister of Jesus Christ, wherever the Providence of God may call him.

"Attest. JUSTIN EDWARDS, Scribe, EZRA RIPLEY, Moderator.

"ABIEL HOLMES. ABEL WHITNEY.
FREEGRACE RAYNOLDS. BENJAMIN FOSTER.
SAMUEL STEARNS. AMARIAH PRESTON.
REUBEN EMERSON. EBENEZER CUMMINGS, Jun.
SAMUEL SEWALL. SOLOMON HOLT."[35]

[35] Church Records, Vol. I., pp. 183-185.

1821, July 17, the church met, agreeably to appointment on the previous Sabbath, and voted to choose a Moderator, and a clerk, to serve during the pleasure of the church, after the pastoral relation of Rev. Mr. Chickering shall cease.

Chose for Moderator, Deacon Benjamin Wyman.

" Clerk, Deacon Benjamin Wyman.

"Voted, That a Committee of five persons be chosen to form a vote expressive of the affection of this church towards their Pastor, the Rev. Joseph Chickering; containing such a recommendation as may be proper in such a case; and to lay the same before the church. Chose Deacons Josiah Wright, Ebenezer Lawrence and Benjamin Wyman; and Brothers Jonas Hale and Uriah Manning."

September 9th, (Sabbath) the church being stopped after the exercises of the day, the above committee submitted to them the following vote for their acceptance, viz:

"That the Rev. Joseph Chickering has been the pastor of this church more than seventeen years last past; during which time he has conducted himself as a diligent, faithful and affectionate pastor, and one whose labors (we believe) have been blest to the good of many souls in this place; and they do hereby express their united and most cordial affection for him, as their late pastor; and do most deeply lament the occasion of his pastoral relation to them being dissolved.

"With the knowledge they have of his respectable talents, his moral and Christian character, and his ministerial qualifications, and in the full belief that his past success is a good pledge of his future usefulness, [they] do most cordially recommend him to the Christian community as a pious, able and faithful minister of Jesus Christ, wheresoever the providence of God may call him.

" Woburn, Sept. 4th, 1821.

"Josiah Wright,
Ebenezer Lawrence,
Benjamin Wyman,
Jonas Hale,
Uriah Manning. } Committee.

" Voted unanimously by the Church." [36]

[36] Church Records, Vol. I., pp. 186, 187.

During the ministry of Rev. Mr. Chickering, one hundred and sixty-four were admitted to the church, viz: Fifty-five males, and one hundred and nine females; and two hundred and seventy were baptized, viz: Two hundred and thirty children, and forty adults.

Of the one hundred and sixty-four admissions, sixty-six were during a season of revival, in 1817; and of these, twenty-four were in one day, viz: June 1st.

One hundred and eighty-seven couples were united by him in marriage.

Rev. Mr. Chickering was son of Rev. Jabez Chickering, pastor of the church in the South Parish of Dedham. He was born in that parish, April 30, 1780; graduated at Harvard University, 1799; studied theology at Cambridge under the direction of Rev. Professor Tappan; ordained at Woburn, March 28, 1804; dismissed at his own request, with the sanction of a Council, April 11, 1821; and after retiring from Woburn, was installed over the church in Phillipston, Worcester County, Mass., July 10, 1822; dismissed at his own request, in consequence of bodily infirmity, July 16, 1835; but continued to reside at Phillipston till his decease, January 27, 1844, where also his widow died shortly after him.

Mr. Chickering married twice: first, Miss Betsey, daughter of the venerable Deacon John White of Concord; and she dying, November 3, 1815, he married, secondly, Miss Sarah Abbot Holt, of Albany, Me. By his first wife, he had five children, of whom the three youngest (one an infant) died within about a fortnight of their mother's decease, before or after. By his second wife, he had a daughter and two sons, Betsey, Henry and Abbot, born at Woburn; and one or more children, it is believed, born at Phillipston. Of his two surviving children by his first wife, the elder is Rev. John White Chickering, D. D., recently pastor of a church in Portland, Me.; now an agent in the temperance cause, a resident in Boston: the younger is Mr. Joseph Chickering, a very successful and highly respected mechanic at the west.

After the dismission of Rev. Mr. Chickering, in 1821, the

church took some steps, in September following, towards settling in the ministry Mr. Hutchins Taylor, with whose preaching, they expressed themselves satisfied.[37] But not succeeding in this attempt, they gave an unanimous call, November 19, 1821, to Mr. Joseph Bennett, to become their pastor. In this choice, the parish unanimously concurred; and offered him a salary of seven hundred dollars per annum.[38] Mr. Bennett communicated to the people his acceptance of the invitation given him, on Thanksgiving day, December 6th; and, subsequently, committees of the church and parish agreed with him on the day for the ordination, and the churches to be invited to assist in Council on the solemn occasion. The result of the Council was as follows:

"At an Ecclesiastical Council holden at Woburn, January 1st, 1822.

"Present:

"Andover, Theological Seminary: Rev. Dr. JAMES MURDOCK, Pastor; LEWIS DWIGHT, Delegate.

"Andover South Parish: Rev. JUSTIN EDWARDS, Pastor; NATHANIEL SWIFT, Delegate.

"Tewksbury: Rev. JACOB COGGIN, Pastor; OLIVER CLARK, Delegate.

"Wilmington: Rev. FREEGRACE RAYNOLDS, Pastor; Dea. BENJ. FOSTER, Delegate.

"Reading, West Parish: Rev. SAMUEL GREEN, Pastor; TIMOTHY WAKEFIELD, BENJ. PRATT, Delegates.

"South Reading: Rev. REUBEN EMERSON, Pastor; JAMES GOULD, Delegate.

"Burlington: Rev. SAMUEL SEWALL, Pastor; Dea. JONATHAN SIMONDS, Dea. NATHL. CUTTER, Delegates.

"Stoneham: Rev. JOHN H. STEVENS, Pastor; Dea. JABEZ LYNDE, BRO. THADDEUS RICHARDSON, Delegates.

"Bedford: Rev. SAMUEL STEARNS, Pastor; BENJ. SIMONDS, JUN., MATTHEW HAYWARD, Delegates.

"Charlestown: Rev. WARREN FAY, Pastor; Dea. ISAAC WARREN, MATTHEW SKELTON, Delegates.

---

[37] Church Records, Vol. I., p. 188.

[38] Parish Records, Vol. III., pp. 366, 367.

"Dorchester: Rev. JOHN CODMAN, Pastor; BRO. NATHANIEL SWIFT, Delegate.

"Framingham: Rev. DAVID KELLOGG, Pastor; Dea. LUTHER HAVEN, Delegate.

"West Cambridge: Rev. THADDEUS FISKE, D.D., Pastor; Dea. EPHRAIM FROST, EPHRAIM CUTTER, Delegates.

"Tyngsborough: Rev. NATHL. LAWRENCE, Pastor; Dea. JOHN FARWELL, JEREMIAH HOWARD, Delegates.

"Chose Rev. Mr. David Kellogg, Moderator: Chose Rev. Samuel Sewall, Scribe.

"The Council opened with prayer by the Rev. Moderator.

"The proceedings of the Church and Parish in regard to the choice of Mr. Joseph Bennett as their Gospel Minister were then read by the Scribe, and were voted by the Council to be regular and satisfactory.

"Certificates of Mr. Bennett's church membership, and of his Approbation and License to preach by the Marlborough Association, were then produced and read, as likewise his answer to the call of the Church and Society; acceptance of all which documents was voted by the Council.

"The Candidate then read his Confession of Faith. The members having put such questions as they pleased to the Candidate, voted themselves satisfied, and that they were ready to proceed to the Ordination.

"Voted that the Rev. Mr. CODMAN make the Introductory Prayer.
" " Rev. Mr. FAY preach the Sermon.
" " Rev. Dr. MURDOCK make the Ordaining Prayer.
" " Rev. Mr. KELLOGG give the Charge.
" " Rev. Mr. GREEN give the Right Hand of Fellowship.
" " Rev. Mr. COGGIN address the Church and People.
" " Rev. Mr. LAWRENCE make the Concluding Prayer.

"The Council then adjourned to the Meeting House.

"DAVID KELLOGG, Moderator.

"Attest. SAMUEL SEWALL, Scribe."[39]

---

[39] Church Records, Vol. I., pp. 200, 201.

"Previous to the Ordination, the Church were requested to assemble for a few moments; when, they having received Mr Bennett's Dismission and Recommendation from the Church in Framingham, voted unanimously to receive him as a member in full communion with this church.

"Moved by Dea. Wright, that the thanks of this Church be presented to Benjamin Wyman for his faithful service as Moderator & Clerk of the Church. Voted unanimously.

"Attest, BENJAMIN WYMAN, Clerk.[40]

The ministry of Rev. Mr. Bennett was distinguished by large accessions to the church, especially in the year 1827, (a year of revival,) when two hundred and twenty-six were added to its numbers, two hundred and twelve by profession, and fourteen by letter. During the same period, too, the discipline of the church was enforced with more than usual strenuousness;[41] the Sabbath school was diligently promoted and numerously attended; and various societies, both of the town and State, for the advancement of Christian knowledge and charity, were liberally encouraged. For all these tokens of spiritual and moral growth and prosperity, the town and the public were largely indebted to the zealous labors and kind efforts of Rev. Mr. Bennett.

But in 1840, the increase and prosperity of the church sustained a temporary check by the dismission of the members of the South Village. It was in this quarter, probably, that the first dwelling-house in the town was erected, viz: at the Convers' mill. And yet, for a long succession of years, the settlements there had been so slow, and the inhabitants so few and scattering, that no school-house appears to have been built in the place till 1790; and though a public school was some years appointed to be kept there, it could be accommodated only in some private house, and that only for a few weeks in the course of the season. Other years, the children who attended school must be provided with a private one at the cost of their parents,

---

[40] Church Records, Vol. I., p. 201.

[41] Between 1823 and 1841, thirty-two cases of discipline are recorded in Church Records, Vol. I., of which twenty resulted in excommunication.

or travel to the centre of the town, which is from one to two miles distant.

But, from the operation of various causes, especially the location of the Lowell Railroad through the centre of the village, it began, about 1830, rapidly to increase both in business and in population; and at length, feeling themselves competent to sustain public worship among themselves, the inhabitants commenced a series of measures to obtain for themselves the privilege. The first step taken to this end was the following resolution, submitted to the church by Deacon Benjamin F. Thompson, at a meeting, March 21, 1839: "Resolved as the sense of this church, that there ought to be another orthodox church and society established in this town, when, in the opinion of this church, the necessary funds shall be obtained to carry the same properly into effect."[42] But the discussion to which this resolution, and another offered in its stead, gave rise, occasioning delay, they were both withdrawn by the mover; and the following letter was read to the church after Communion, November 2, 1840.

"To the Congregational Church, Woburn, Mass.

"Dear Brethren and Friends:

"We, the subscribers, deeming it our duty, as well as our convenience, to colonize and congregate in the South Village of this town for the purpose of worshipping the God of our fathers in the way we have been taught, request that you would give us a dismission from the body with which we are still happily united, to the end that we may be constituted the South Congregational Church in Woburn. And we ask it, not from any dissatisfaction as it respects Pastor, Church, or Congregation; for no dissatisfaction exists, as we hope there never may, but love, concord, and reciprocal kindness. But we make the request, because we are persuaded that the advancement of truth and righteousness will be promoted by the means, as more will be induced to attend the public worship of God, and can attend it more conveniently: Because the church is so large and efficient, that we can well be spared, and a large and flourishing church still remain: Because

[42] Church Records, Vol. I., p. 245.

the growing population of the town demands another place of worship, and the place we have chosen is suited to accommodate such increasing population: Because we think we can sustain the regular administration of the word and ordinances, and have ample means to sustain the same here: and Because we think that both you and we can to better advantage enjoy the stated means of grace.

" On these principles, we present the preceding request: hoping and expecting, that it will not only be kindly and cheerfully granted, but that Christian love, brotherly kindness, fellowship and good-will, which we trust we now feel, will henceforth be reciprocated.

[Subscribed by]

" N. B. JOHNSON.
B. F. THOMPSON.
MARSHALL WYMAN.
STEPHEN CUTTER.
OLIVER R. CLARK.

[and by ninety-seven others, male and female.]

The request presented in the foregoing letter was immediately granted. The result was, the dedication in South Woburn, December 30, 1840, of a new house of worship, which had been some time, apparently, in process of erection; the speedy gathering of the brethren and sisters dismissed as above from First Church of Woburn, into a distinct Congregational Church; the ordination of Rev. George P. Smith as its pastor, June 17, 1841; and the incorporation by the Legislature of the village of South Woburn, together with portions of Medford and West Cambridge, as the town of Winchester, April 30, 1850.[43]

The day next after the dedication in South Woburn, viz: December 31, 1840, the fifth meeting-house of the First Congregational Society in Woburn was dedicated. Its fourth house of public worship had stood only thirty-one years. But upon examination, in order to some repairs, it was ascertained that the timber used in its construction had become so far decayed and rotten, in consequence probably of having been cut at a wrong season of the year, that it was judged safest and best to take it down

---

[43] Massachusetts Special Laws, Vol. IX., pp. 234, 235.

entirely, and to build anew. Accordingly, a handsome and convenient edifice, seventy feet by sixty, was erected on the site of the former meeting-house, with a vestry in the basement, which had for some time been finished and occupied as the place of worship, before the main building was completed. The dedication services, December 31, 1840, were, 1st. Invocation, and reading of portions of the Scriptures by Rev. Mr. Sewall, of Burlington; 2d. Introductory prayer by Rev. Mr. Baker, of Medford; 3d. Sermon, by the pastor, Rev. Mr. Bennett, from Haggai ii. 9. "The glory of this latter house shall be greater," etc., etc.; 4th. Consecrating prayer, by Rev. Mr. Coggin, of Tewksbury; 5th. Address to the people, by Rev. Mr. Albro, of Cambridge; and 6th. Concluding prayer, by Rev. Mr. Norwood, of Wilmington.

For many years, Rev. Mr. Bennett continued to be very popular and successful in his ministry. His pulpit services were highly acceptable both to his own people, and to all the churches in the vicinity. But he was naturally of a very nervous temperament, and easily excited; and hence at times he would be very elevated in his spirits, and at others deeply depressed. Over this, his natural predisposition, his excellent lady exerted a powerful influence; and so long as her life was spared to him, she generally managed so as to keep it from running into either extreme. But after her decease, February 11, 1846, there was nothing left to check and regulate it. Causes comparatively trifling would often raise his spirits so far, as that he would unawares become quite eccentric both in speech and in action; and then again his spirits would flag and sink so low, that he would apparently begin to think that his usefulness was gone, and that his life was no longer desirable to himself or others. And hence, in one of these deplorable turns of melancholy depression, he was left to take his own life, November 19, 1847. His funeral was very largely attended at the meeting-house by his brethren in the ministry, and by the inhabitants of Woburn and the neighboring towns. A sermon was preached on the solemn occasion by Rev. Dr. John W. Chickering, of Portland, who happened to be on a visit to Rev. Mr. Bennett at the time of his decease. This sermon was published at the expense of the church; and at a parish meeting, December 6th following, it was voted to pay a full year's salary to the heirs of Rev. Mr. Bennett.[44]

Rev. Joseph Bennett was born at Framingham, May 13, 1798; was graduated at Harvard University, 1818: studied theology at the institution in Andover; was ordained at Woburn, January 1, 1822, and was married in February following to Miss Mary Lamson, "his ever-discreet counsellor, as well as affectionate and beloved friend." By her he had two children, viz: 1. Rev. Joseph Lamson Bennett, minister first at East Cambridge, now at Lockport, N. Y.; and 2. Mary Lamson Bennett, married to Rev. Thomas Morong, of Gloucester, Mass.

During his ministry in Woburn, seven hundred and sixty persons, (including himself,) were admitted into the church, viz: five hundred and ninety-six by profession, and one hundred and sixty-four by letter; and six hundred and nine were baptized, viz: three hundred and seventy-one infants and children and two hundred and thirty-eight adults. Also, two hundred and forty-two marriages are recorded, as solemnized by him to January 1, 1843, inclusively. Marriages solemnized by him subsequently to that date, were not recorded by him on the church book.

---

[44] Parish Records, Vol. III., p. 523.

CHAPTER XV.

First Church: Rev. Messrs. Edwards, March, and Bodwell. — Congregational Church, North Woburn. — Baptist Church. — Independent Baptist Church. — Universalist Church. — Unitarian Church. — Methodist Episcopal Church. — Roman Catholic Church. — Protestant Episcopal Church.

AFTER the decease of Rev. Mr. Bennett, the church took speedy action for the settlement of another pastor. It gave, March 17, 1848, an unanimous invitation to Mr. Jonathan Edwards, of Andover, to become their pastor. In this measure of the church, the parish concurred, March 20th, and voted a salary to Mr. Edwards of a thousand dollars per annum, payable semi-annually, with this proviso, "That either party might dissolve the connection by a mutual Council, after giving six months' notice of its intention."[1] And at a meeting, May 22d, in compliance with a wish expressed by Mr. Edwards, the parish voted to allow him the privilege of an annual vacation of four Sabbaths; and added, to his salary before stipulated, fifty dollars, to enable him to supply the pulpit during his vacation.[2] The invitation given him thus qualified, Mr. Edwards accepted May 26th. In the interval which elapsed before his ordination, the church voted as follows: "Resolved that we do not consider the relation of Pastor and Church to be complete, without the pastor becoming a member of the particular church of which he is the overseer."[3] Agreeably to this vote, Mr. Edwards was admitted into the First Church of Woburn, September 3d, and ordained its pastor, September 7, 1848.

The ordaining council consisted of pastors and delegates from eleven churches, and of Rev. Justin Edwards, D. D., father of the candidate. The public services on the interesting occasion were as follows, viz:

---

[1] Parish Records, Vol. III., pp. 528, 529. [2] Parish Records, Vol. III., pp. 530–532.
[3] Church Records, Vol. III., p. 213.

Reading of the minutes, by the scribe, Rev. William Ives Burdington of Charlestown.

Introductory Prayer, by Rev. J. L. TAYLOR, Andover.

Reading the Scriptures, by Rev. ALEXANDER J. SESSIONS, Salem.

Sermon, by Rev. E. N. KIRK, Boston.

Ordaining Prayer, by Rev. REUBEN EMERSON, South Reading.

Charge, by Rev. JUSTIN EDWARDS, Andover.

Right Hand, by Rev. GEORGE RICHARDS, Central Church, Boston.

Address to the People, by Rev. JOHN W. CHICKERING, Portland.

Concluding Prayer, by Rev. JACOB COGGIN, Tewksbury.

Rev. BROWN EMERSON, D. D., Salem, Moderator.[4]

During the eight years of Rev. Mr. Edwards' continuance in Woburn, entire harmony and mutual confidence prevailed between him and his people. In discharging the duties of his sacred office, his heart was often gladdened and encouraged in perceiving that his labors were not in vain in the Lord; and the people on their part repeatedly manifested their satisfaction with him, and respect for him, by various tokens of kindness and affection; and especially by complying, virtually, with the following vote of the church, passed February 20, 1854. "Voted unanimously, that we recommend to the Parish, to raise the salary of Rev. Jona. Edwards to a sum not less that fifteen hundred dollars." [5]

But suddenly this fair prospect of a long, as well as successful ministry by Rev. Mr. Edwards, was broken up. January 2, 1856, he requested the church to unite with him in calling a mutual council for his dismission, he having received, as he stated to them, a pressing call to go elsewhere "to engage in a new and highly important church enterprise in an unoccupied field;" expressing at the same time the pleasure he had derived from his present connection; his regret at leaving, his best wishes and prayers for the church, etc., etc. The church, with

---

[4] Church Records, Vol. III., pp. 216, 217.

[5] Church Records, Vol. III., p. 227.

expressions of regret, acceded to his request for calling a council; and voted to unite with the parish committee, if they saw fit, to carry this measure into effect.[6] Accordingly, a council was called; and agreeably to its decision, Rev. Mr. Edwards was dismissed from Woburn, January 21, 1856.[6]

Rev. Jonathan Edwards was son of Rev. Justin Edwards, D. D., of Andover, and Mrs. Lydia (Bigelow) Edwards; was born at Andover, July 17, 1820; graduated at Yale College, 1840; studied theology at New Haven and at Andover; was graduated at Andover Theological Seminary, 1847, but continued there a year longer as "Abbott Resident." Upon his leaving Woburn, he took charge of Plymouth congregational church in Rochester, N. Y., as its first pastor, February 14, 1856; removed from Rochester on account of health, November 1862, came to Dedham, Mass., and was there installed, as successor to Rev. Ebenezer Burgess, D. D., January 1, 1863, over the First Congregational Church in that ancient town, which was gathered in 1638. Upon February 26, 1865, he sailed on a voyage for health; and after visiting England, Scotland, France, and other countries on the continent of Europe, he returned to his charge in Dedham, August 1865.[7]

During his ministry in Woburn, fifty-nine were received into his church by profession, and ninety-nine by letter: total, one hundred and fifty-eight.

There were seventy-eight baptisms of infants, and thirty-one of adults: total, one hundred and nine.[8]

Marriages solemized by him, during his ministry, were fifty-two.[8]

1856, August 18, the church voted unanimously to extend a call to Rev. Daniel March, of Brooklyn, N. Y., to become their pastor.[9] The parish concurred with the church in this choice, and offered Rev. Mr. March a salary of $1,600 annually, in case he should accept the call given him to become their gospel minister. Mr. March accepted the call given him, and October 1st was appointed as the day for his installation. On that day, a

[6] Church Records, Vol. III., pp. 229–231.

[7] Letter of Rev. Mr. Edwards, June 8, 1866.

[8] Church Records.

[9] Church Records, Vol. III., p. 235.

council of fourteen churches assembled in the vestry of the church, and after the usual examination and inquiries were gone through with to their satisfaction, the council voted they were ready to proceed to installation. The public services on this occasion were:

1. Introductory Prayer by Rev. DANIEL R. CADY, West Cambridge.
2. Reading of the Scriptures, by Rev. J. I. M. MANNING, of Mystic Church, Medford.
3. Sermon, by Rev. A. L. STONE, Park Street Church, Boston.
4. Installing Prayer, by Rev. L. Thompson, West Amesbury.
5. Charge, by Rev. J. W. CHICKERING, D. D., Portland.
6. Right Hand, by Rev. R. T. ROBINSON, Winchester.
7. Address to the people, by Rev. E. B. FOSTER, John Street Church, Lowell.
8. Concluding Prayer, by Rev. J. L. BENNETT, East Cambridge.

Rev. David T. KIMBALL, (Ipswich,) Moderator.
Rev. E. P. MARVIN, Medford 2d Church, Scribe.[10]

The connection of the First Church and Society in Woburn with Rev. Mr. March, as their pastor and minister, was prosperous and happy; but not destined to be of long duration. 1862, February 7, the church met to consider the request of the pastor, communicated the preceding Sabbath, to accept his resignation of the pastoral office. Voted, to accept his resignation.

Voted, to choose a committee of the church to unite with a committee of the parish, and with the pastor, in calling an ecclesiastical council to effect his dismission.[11]

1857, February 17, a council at the joint invitation of the First Church, society and pastor, met in Woburn, in which six churches by pastors and delegates were represented; Rev. William Barrows, Moderator, and Rev. R. T. Robinson, Scribe.

Papers were presented to the council, containing Rev. Mr. March's letter of resignation, a certified copy of the action of the church, and the record of the doings of the parish.

---

[10] Church Records, Vol. III., pp. 236, 237. [11] Church Records, Vol. III., p. 247.

Verbal statements also were made by Rev. Mr. March, and by the respective committees; after which, the council voted to be by themselves, and came to the following result, which was unanimously adopted.

Result.

"The Rev. Mr. March having resigned his office of Pastor of the First Congregational Church and Society in Woburn, and the Church and Society having voted unanimously to accept his resignation, the Council convened see no other course for them to pursue, than to complete the dissolution of the Pastoral Relation; and the same is declared to be, and it hereby is dissolved.

"In coming to this Result, the Council cannot but regret, while they feel and would bear testimony to the fact, that Rev. Mr. March has acted conscientiously in this thing, and with a sincere desire to know and do the will of God, that a pastoral connection so recently and happily formed, one too which has proved so harmonious and productive of good, should be broken up. They deeply sympathize with the Church and Society in their severe disappointment in the loss of their chosen and much loved Pastor: and express the hope, that blessed of God as they have been in their history hitherto, and united as they still are, — having always shown a high appreciation of the Pastoral relation and office, — the Great Head of the Church will speedily guide them to the selection and settlement of another Pastor, under whose ministry they shall continue to prosper in the future, as in the past.

"The Council also would give expression to their high estimation of, and undiminished confidence in, the Rev. Mr March, both as a sincere and devoted Christain man, and an able and faithful minister of the Gospel. It is their united and fervent prayer, that in whatever station he may be placed, he may still show himself approved unto God, a workman that need not be ashamed, and may ever receive largely of that grace, which is alone sufficient for the great and responsible work committed unto his hand.

"W. Barrows, Moderator.
"Woburn, Feb. 17, 1862. R. T. Robinson, Scribe."[12]

Rev. Mr. March was born at Millbury, Mass., July 21, 1806; graduated at Yale College, 1840; studied theology at the sem-

[12] Church Records, Vol. III., pp. 247–249.

inary in Yale College two years (having previously studied privately) and received license to preach; was ordained over the church in Cheshire, Conn., April 29, 1845; installed over First Church in Nashua, N. H., January 3, 1849; installed over the South Congregational Church in Brooklyn, N. Y., January 16, 1855; at Woburn, October 1, 1856; and over the Clinton Street Presbyterian Church in Philadelphia, February 23, 1862.[13]

During Rev. Mr. March's ministry in Woburn, two hundred and fourteen were admitted to the church, viz: one hundred and thirty-seven by profession, and seventy-seven by letter; one hundred and twenty-four were baptized, viz: sixty-three infants, and sixty-one adults, and forty-three marriages were solemnized by him.

At a meeting of the church, October 6, 1862, it was voted unanimously, (seventy-five votes in the affirmative, and none in the negative,) "That the First Congregational Church in Woburn extend an invitation to Rev. J. C. Bodwell of Framingham, Mass., to become its Pastor." In this measure the parish concurred; and also voted to give Mr. Bodwell an annual salary of $1,600, (which was afterwards increased to $2,000,) if he should settle over them. The invitation thus given him was accepted by Rev. Mr. Bodwell; and a council of ten churches (including Saxonville, Rev. B. G. Northrop) convened for his installation at the vestry of First Church, Woburn, November 11, 1862; of which Rev. E. P. Marvin was chosen Moderator, and Rev. Charles R. Bliss, Scribe.

The council listened to communications stating proceedings of the church and parish in extending a call to Rev. J. C. Bodwell to settle over them; to the letter containing their call; to the reply of Mr. Bodwell, in evidence of his church membership; and to a report of the council, dismissing him from his former charge: all which being satisfactory, they proceeded to examination.

After attending to a very full and clear written statement of the theological views of the candidate, — a statement of his reli-

[13] Letter from Rev. Mr. March.

gious experience, and motives in entering the ministry, — council being by themselves, voted they were satisfied, and ready to proceed to installation. Services on this occasion, were as follows:

Invocation, Rev. CHARLES R. BLISS.
Reading of the Scriptures, Rev. B. G. NORTHROP.
Introductory Prayer, Rev. J. S. KENNARD, Baptist.
Sermon, Rev. J. G. TUCKER, Holliston.
Prayer of Installation, Rev. DANIEL R. CADY.
Charge, Rev. W. BARROWS.
Right Hand, Rev. R. T. ROBINSON.
Address to the People, Rev. E. P. MARVIN.
Benediction, the PASTOR.

E. P. MARVIN, Moderator.
C. R. BLISS, Scribe.

Rev. Mr. Bodwell commenced his ministry in Woburn under very favorable auspices. His people were attentive at his public services; a very large majority became warmly attached to him; and in evidence of this attachment, they not only paid him punctually his stipulated salary from year to year, but at the beginning of the year 1866, they presented him with $1,400 as a free gift.

But in view of an invitation given him to become the principal of the Theological Institute at Hartford, Conn., he thought proper to request a dismission from his pastoral charge in Woburn. This request was granted by his church and people; and his dismission was sanctioned by an Ecclesiastical Council assembled in Woburn, August 3, 1866, as appears by the annexed authentic record of its proceedings:

Result of Council.

"Pursuant to letters missive, an Ecclesiastical Council convened on Friday, August 3d, 1866, in the lecture room of the First Congregational Church in Woburn, to consider and act upon the request of their pastor, Rev. Jos. C. Bodwell, D. D., for a dismission from his pastoral relation to them. The following churches were represented:

"North Congregational church, Woburn: Rev. M. G. WHEELER, pastor, Dea C. R. THOMPSON, delegate.

"1st Trinitarian Congregational church, Medford: Rev. JAMES T. McCOLLUM, pastor, Dea. HENRY L. BARNES, delegate.

"1st Congregational church, Winchester; Dea. O. R. CLARK, delegate.

"Congregational church, Stoneham; Dea. SILAS DEAN, delegate.

"1st Congregational church, Middletown, Ct., Rev. J. TAYLOR, D. D., pastor.

"Old South church, Reading; Rev. WILLIAM BARROWS, pastor, D. T. H. SWEETSER, Dea. H. WHEELER, delegates.

"Congregational church, Billerica, Rev. J. G. D. STEARNS, pastor.

"Congregational church, West Killingly, Ct., Rev. W. W. DAVENPORT, pastor.

"Rev. E. P. MARVIN, D. D., of Medford.

"The Council was organized by the choice of Rev. William Barrows, Moderator, and Rev. W. W. Davenport, Scribe.

"The Moderator opened the Council with prayer. The letter of Rev. Dr. Bodwell, asking a dismission in order that he may accept a professorship in the Theological Seminary at Hartford, Ct. was read to the Council, together with the action of the church and society thereon, uniting with him in calling the Council. Remarks were made by Dr. Taylor, Dr. Marvin, Mr. Davenport, Mr. W. A. Stone of the committee of the Church, and by Dr. Bodwell.

"The Council being by itself, Dr. Marvin offered the following resolution: 'Resolved, That in the opinion of this Council, it is expedient that the request of Dr. Bodwell for a dismission, should be granted, in order that he may accept the professorship to which he has been elected in the Theological Seminary at Hartford: and his pastoral relation to the First Church in Woburn is hereby dissolved, the dissolution to take effect on the first day of September next.'"

The Resolution was unanimously adopted.

The scribe, the moderator, and Dr. Marvin were appointed a committee to prepare a result of council. The committee reported the following, which was unanimously adopted.

"The Council have come to this result with much sorrow, both on account of the great personal loss which we feel in the removal of so able a preacher, so cultivated and genial a man, and so true a Christian friend; and also on account of the heavy sacrifice which this church and people are called to make. The deep affection cherished by the society for their minister; his superior abilities as a preacher and pastor; the marked success which has crowned his labors in this broad and difficult field; the steady accessions by profession to the church; the removal of a burdensome debt of $40,000 from the society; the constant growth of the congregation; the unusual influence of the pastor upon the schools of the town, and upon the community in general, all convince us that it is no ordinary loss which this church and society must now sustain.

"Nevertheless, the call which comes from another field of the highest importance to the cause of Christ, as presented so forcibly to this Council, constrains us, as it has the church and parish, to feel that it is the clear and imperative voice of the Head of the church, which calls Dr. Bodwell away from his successful labors here. The peculiar interest which he has excited in the young men of the Theological Seminary at Hartford, and the unanimity and earnestness of the call from the Board of Trustees and the generous benefactors of the institution, are unmistakable indications that God has, in his providence, even a more important field for him to occupy.

"The Council also desire to express their unqualified confidence in Rev. Dr. Bodwell, as an able and faithful minister of the Gospel, sound in the faith, apt to teach, and wise to win souls. They tender to him their sympathy in this rupturing of the ties of affection that bind him to his people.

"They also tender to the church and society their sincere and affectionate sympathy in the trial to which they are subjected in the providence of God, which takes from them a pastor to whom they cling with the warmest attachment and unwavering confidence; and our trust is, that the Great Head of the church will care for them in their bereavement, and will soon send them a faithful and acceptable pastor, to feed them with knowledge and understanding. We trust that they may be comforted by the consideration, that he whom they surrender at the Master's call, is to be useful to them and to many other churches, in the new form of service in which he is now to be engaged.

"The minutes were read and approved; and, after prayer by the Moderator, the Council was dissolved.

"Attest. W. Barrows, Moderator.

"William W. Davenport, Scribe."[14]

"Rev. Joseph Connor Bodwell, D. D., was born at Sanbornton, N. H., June 11, 1812, a son of Rev. Abraham Bodwell, a gradu-

[14] Church Records; Minutes of Council.

ate of Harvard College, 1805, and pastor of the Congregational church in Sanbornton, from 1806 to 1852.

"Joseph C. Bodwell, his son, was fitted for college, at the academy in his native place; was graduated at Dartmouth College, 1833; was a teacher of youth three years in Haverhill, N. H., and in Sanbornton. In 1836, he went to London, and pursued his theological studies at Highbury College, under the venerable Dr. Henderson. On the 3d of April, 1839, Mr. Bodwell was ordained as pastor of the Independent Church, worshipping in St. Nicholas Street, Weymouth, a beautiful watering place in the South of England, and a favorite resort of King George III. and the lamented princess Charlotte. On the 15th of May, 1839, he was married to Catharine, only daughter of John Sykes, Esq., of Highbury Park, London. On the 22d of June, 1847, he was installed pastor of the Independent Church in Northgate Street, Bury St. Edmund's, famous in former ages for its magnificent Norman tower, and for its large and wealthy abbey. In the autumn of 1850, Mr. Bodwell returned to the United States with his wife, two sons and two daughters, having buried a son and a daughter in England. On the 30th of June, 1852, he was installed at Framingham; whence he was dismissed November 5, 1862, that he might accept a call to the pastoral office in Woburn. In 1864, the degree of Doctor in Divinity was conferred on him by Dartmouth College."[15]

During the ministry of Rev. Dr. Bodwell in Woburn, there were one hundred and three admissions to the church, viz: fifty-five by profession, and forty-eight by letter; sixty-three baptisms, viz: thirty-six of infants, and twenty-seven of adults,[16] and forty-two couples were united by him in marriage.

During the same period, too, there was erected, and in October 1863 dedicated by his society, a new church, an elegant and stately edifice, said to be one of the largest, if not the largest Congregational church in the State, being, in its extreme length, one hundred and fifty feet, its extreme width, eighty feet, its steeple one hundred and ninety-six feet in height, and capable

[15] Letter from Rev. Dr. Bodwell. [16] Certificate of Dr. Ephraim Cutter, clerk.

of seating fifteen hundred persons. The cost of the organ was $4,000, the cost of the building, in round numbers, was $62,000; all which has now been paid for.[17]

This ancient church, left destitute of a pastor by the dismission of Dr. Bodwell, contains now (October 1, 1866) five hundred and thirty-four members, viz: one hundred and eighty-one males, and three hundred and fifty-three females.[17]

Congregational Church in North Woburn.

Previously to 1846, the inhabitants of North Woburn had been attached to one or other of the religious societies in the centre of the town, and there resorted on the Sabbath for public worship. But that year, a number of gentlemen, inhabitants of that village, formed the plan of setting up a meeting on the Sabbath among themselves; by which they would not only procure to themselves and families the privileges of public worship nearer home, but might also encourage such of their neighbors to attend, as had become negligent of the duty, on account of their distance from the centre. In pursuance of this plan, they, in September of that year, fitted up the chamber of the village school-house, as a place of assembly on the Sabbath for public worship; and then invited Rev. Samuel Sewall of Burlington, at that time without pastoral charge, to preach on Sabbath days in the room they had provided, for a year. Mr. Sewall accepted the invitation; and preached for the first time in North Woburn school-house, October 11, 1846. The experiment proved a successful one, and very gratifying to those who initiated it. Meetings on Lord's days were well attended; one or two miles' travel was saved each day to those who had hitherto been accustomed to worship in the centre; and many were induced to attend with them divine service, who from one cause or another had become careless or indifferent about attending elsewhere. Hence, Mr. Sewall's first engagement with them was prolonged from year to year. In March 1849, a regular religious society, upon evangelical principles, was formed in the village. In

[17] Communication of Dr. Ephraim Cutter, clerk.

June 1849, the foundations were laid for a new meeting-house, which was completed and dedicated, October 11th, of that year. On November 22d, of the same year, an orthodox church was gathered in the place, consisting of twelve males and twenty-eight females, of whom thirty-three had been dismissed and recommended by First Church, Woburn, and seven by several other churches. This solemn transaction was performed in the presence and with the advice and sanction of the following churches by their pastors and delegates, viz: First Church, Woburn, Rev. Jonathan Edwards, pastor, and Deacon Stephen Richardson, delegate; Wilmington, Rev. Barnabas M. Fay, pastor, and Deacon Benjamin Foster, delegate; Burlington, Rev. Harrison G. Park, pastor, and Deacon John Marion, delegate; and South Woburn (Winchester) Church, Mr. Sumner Richardson, delegate. The public services of the occasion were held in the meeting-house, P. M., when Rev. Mr. Fay offered the introductory prayer; Rev. Mr. Park propounded the articles of faith and church covenant agreed upon, to the persons to be embodied, for their public assent; and then offered the consecrating prayer; and finally, Rev. Mr. Edwards, in the name of his own church, and of the other churches here represented, gave the right hand of fellowship to Deacon Thompson on behalf of the church gathered and now solemnly recognized. A handsome set of communion and other church furniture, consisting of five plated cups, two tankards and a baptismal basin, was now presented this new church by Rev. Mr. Edwards, on behalf of individual members of his own church and society, in an address to Rev. Mr. Sewall; to which, at the request of the church, he made a brief response, expressing thanks in their name. Here, also, the church voted unanimously, that as the society in this place had given Rev. Mr. Sewall an invitation to preach to them another year, they approved that choice, and requested him to officiate at the communion, and to perform all other pastoral acts that might be called for during that time. The exercises of the solemnity were closed with the administration of the communion to the newly organized church, and to all other professing Christians assembled on the interesting occasion, by Rev. Mr. Sewall, assisted by Rev. Mr. Fay; Deacons Charles Thompson and Richardson, Foster and Marion, distributing the elements.

Rev. Mr. Sewall continued to minister to the society in North Woburn, as their stated supply, and as the acting pastor of the church, till January 1852; when, in view of his advanced age, and of the distance between the village and his home, he announced his intentions of declining any further engagement to preach there, when his present engagement expired.

In June 1852, Rev. George T. Dole, who had previously been settled as a minister in Beverly, but was then residing in Lowell, commenced preaching as a candidate for settlement in North Woburn. In August following, a call was given him to the pastoral office and to the gospel ministry in this place. This call was accepted, and he was installed October 12th. The churches convened in council on the occasion were, church in North Danvers, Rev. Milton P. Braman; First Church, Charlestown, Rev. William I. Budington; South Reading, Rev. Messrs. Reuben and Alfred Emerson; Lowell, Rev. Amos Blanchard, D. D.; Reading, South Parish, Rev. Lyman Whiting; Wilmington, Rev. Joseph E. Swallow; Woburn, First Church, Rev. Jonathan Edwards; Burlington, Rev. Samuel Sewall, delegate. Also Rev. Leander Thompson, returned missionary from the East; and Rev. Mr. Thompson, of Dracut, were present. The public services of the solemnity were, (1) Invocation and reading of the scriptures, by Rev. Mr. Edwards; (2) Prayer, by Rev. L. Thompson; (3) Sermon, by Rev. Mr. Braman, from 1. Cor. xii. 4. "Now there are diversities of gifts, but the same Spirit:" a very ingenious discourse; full of instruction, and well adapted to the occasion, and to the times. (4) Installing prayer, by Rev. Mr. Sewall; (5) Right Hand of Fellowship, by Rev. A. Emerson; (6) Charge, by Rev. Mr. Budington; (7) Address to the people, by Rev. Dr. Blanchard; (8) Concluding prayer, by Rev. Mr. Whiting.

After laboring in the ministry with this church and people three years, Rev. Mr. Dole was dismissed at his own request, with the sanction of a council, October 3, 1855. During the two years which immediately followed his dismission, the pulpit was supplied part of the time with preaching by students from the Theological Seminary at Andover, and part of the time the house was closed.

In October 1857, Mr. Alpheus S. Nickerson, a student of Andover Theological Seminary, was engaged to supply the pulpit a year; and in December following, the church offered by vote to invite a council to ordain him, though *without a legal settlement.* This offer was accepted by Mr. Nickerson: and a council was accordingly convened, December 16th, for this purpose, consisting of the following churches, viz: First Church in Woburn, Rev. Daniel March; Winchester, Rev. R. T. Robinson; Mystic church in Medford, Rev. E. Marvin; Melrose, Rev. A. H. Sessions; West Cambridge, Rev. D. Cady; Wilmington, Rev. S. H. Tolman; South Reading, Rev. J. B. Johnson; Burlington, Rev. S. Sewall, delegate.

This council, however, after a long and patient examination, decided not to ordain Mr. Nickerson immediately; but to give him opportunity, after an interval of eight weeks, to come before them once more, and be examined anew. But this decision did not satisfy the church, which called another council, to meet February 2, 1858, composed of the following churches, viz: Tewksbury, Rev. R. Tolman; Pine Street, Boston, Rev. H. M. Dexter; Plymouth church, Chelsea, Rev. E. H. Nevins; South Reading, Rev. J. B. Johnson; Chestnut Street, Chelsea, ———; Park Street, Boston, Rev. A. L. Stone; Dighton, Rev. C. Sanford; First, Woburn, Rev. Daniel March; Winchester, Rev. R. T. Robinson; Wilmington, Rev. S. H. Tolman; Bedford, Rev. H. Patrick; South Dennis, Rev. W. H. Sturtevant; East Bridgewater, ———. This second council, "after a careful and protracted consideration of the whole subject, decided to ordain Mr. Nickerson;" which accordingly they did the same day.

In the month of April following, "Mr. Nickerson being without a legal settlement, left the society of his own choice." For several months afterwards, the meeting-house was not opened for regular worship, though the Sabbath school organization was kept up, and regular sessions maintained. From October 1858, till May 1860, with the exception of short intervals, the pulpit was supplied by students from the seminary in Andover. In May 1860, Rev. Henry Kimball, of New York city, was engaged to preach for one year. He was succeeded by Rev. Swift Byington, whose services were so acceptable, that at the expiration of his engagement for a year, the arrangement was continued almost another year; that is, "as long as the society furnished the means to pay his salary."

"After Mr Byington left, the house was closed for several months, but was re-opened in the fall of 1863, and the pulpit was supplied for more than a year by Rev. Mr. Harding, agent of the Plymouth Monument Association."

In July 1865, an invitation was extended to Rev. Melancthon G. Wheeler to become the stated pastor of the church and society. This invitation was accepted, and he was accordingly installed July 26, 1865, by a council then convened, consisting of pastors and delegates from the following churches:

First Church Woburn, Rev. J. C. Bodwell, pastor; Deacon Stephen Richardson, delegate.

Church in Stoneham, Deacon J. Dunlap, delegate.

Bethesda Church, Reading, Rev. W. H. Wilcox, pastor; Deacon S. E. Park, delegate.

Church in West Amesbury, Rev. Leander Thompson, pastor; Bro. Andrew Frye, delegate.

Church in Winchester, Rev. R. T. Robinson, pastor; Deacon S. Abbott, delegate.

South Church, Reading, Rev. William Barrows, pastor; Bro. Nathan Bancroft, delegate.

Church in Wilmington, Deacon C. Morrill, delegate.

Church in Burlington, Deacon John Marion, delegate.

Church in South Reading, Rev. Charles R. Bliss, pastor; Bro. J. G. Aborn, delegate.

Rev. Mr. Wheeler still (November 20, 1866) continues pastor of the church in North Woburn, where his services are highly acceptable to the church and society. He was born in Charlotte, Vermont; graduated at Union College, Schenectady, N. Y., and at Andover Theological Seminary; settled at Abington Centre,

Conway, Williamsburgh, and South Dartmouth, previously to his installation at North Woburn.

The number of members in the North Woburn church, July 12, 1866, was fifty-nine.[18]

Baptist Church and Society.

Notice was taken, it will be remembered, in Chapter V., of this history, of certain citizens of Woburn, some of them men of distinction in the town, who withdrew from the worship of the congregational society, embraced and practised the peculiarities of the Baptist denomination, and were prosecuted therefor, in 1671, before the civil courts. But their meetings for distinctive worship soon ceased. Most of them rejoined their congregational brethren; some of them became officers in the old Congregational Church and Society in Woburn; and in the next generation, all visible tokens of their former separation ceased to exist.

The present highly respectable Baptist Church in Woburn originated in the disaffection towards Rev. Mr. Sargeant, which sprang up in his society soon after his ordination in 1785. Before the close of the year, 1786, several members of the Congregational Parish, dissatisfied with Mr. Sargeant's preaching, had begun to frequent the meetings of the Baptists in West Cambridge, (then the northwest parish in Cambridge,) where a small Baptist Church had been organized in 1781, and was then under the pastoral care of Rev. Thomas Green. In 1790, the number of those who had thus withdrawn from Mr. Sargeant's society amounted to twenty-two;[19] and as the assessors of Woburn still persisted in taxing them for the support of the congregational worship, Rev. Mr. Green commenced a lawsuit, in 1790, for the recovery of their parish taxes. In this suit, he was successful: and thenceforth, the assessors of Woburn were directed, October 17, 1791, "to omit taxing those persons

---

[18] The above account of North Woburn Church has been derived partly from minutes of my own, taken at the time, and partly from statements of Dea. Josiah Linscott, kindly furnished me from his own recollection, and from the Records of the Church.

[19] Report of Committee of First Parish, at adjourned meeting, January 28, 1790.

reputed to belong to Mr. Thomas Green's society, whose names were returned to the parish committee, except Benj. Fowle, Ephraim Tottingham, and such others, as the assessors think best to tax or not, according to their own discretion."[20]

In the mean while, several who had withdrawn from the public worship in Woburn to attend meeting in West Cambridge, had joined the Baptist Church in that place; and at their request, an arrangement was made in 1790, with Rev. Mr. Green, its pastor, to preach once a month in Woburn. Not long after, it was agreed that he should preach half the time in Woburn; the name of the church was altered from "the Baptist Church in Cambridge" to the "Cambridge and Woburn Baptist Church."[21] And so much more rapidly did the branch of this church in Woburn gain in numbers and strength, than the mother church in Cambridge, that "Cambridge" was, in a few years, dropped from its title, and it was thenceforth styled and known, as the "Woburn Baptist Church."[21]

The first meetings of this church in Woburn were held in a house belonging to Capt. John Edgell. This was a large unfinished building erected on the spot, where a new house of Mr. Henry Flagg now stands. "The whole of the second floor was in one unfinished room, (with a great chimney stack running up in the middle,) and furnished with plain benches. It was accessible by a narrow stairway in the rear of the house; and would seat perhaps a hundred people. To this spot, the fathers and mothers of this church resorted each Sabbath day," when they held meeting in Woburn; "and climbing those stairs, filled the rude benches with perhaps threescore lowly worshippers."[21]

In 1793, much to the regret of his people, Rev. Thomas Green removed his residence to another place. He was succeeded by Elder Simon Snow, who remained but about a year. In the early part of 1794, Elder Peak was called to preach half the time in Woburn and in Newtown, N. H., alternately. He is described as "a tall, slim man, dignified in appearance, and of considerable intellectual power. His influence was felt at once

[20] Record of First Parish. The reason of the distinction here made is unknown.
[21] First sermon of Rev. Mr. Kennard.

upon the church; the congregation grew, till the room where they met seemed too small to accommodate them; and the church resolved to arise and build a house unto the Lord. This was in the spring of 1794. This was a brave resolution, for so feeble a band. Yet the favor of God was manifested, as it always is, when his people attempt great things for him. No sooner had the building been begun, than the Spirit of God was poured out upon the church, through the labors of Elder Peak; and while the temple of wood was being erected, the Holy Ghost was building up the spiritual temple of lively stones. The work of revival embraced both the Woburn church, and that in South Reading; the church in Woburn was greatly refreshed; and as a result, thirty-five persons were baptized and added amidst much rejoicing."[21]

The meeting-house, which the Baptist Society commenced building in the spring of 1794, was ready for occupation in July of that year.[22] It was erected on the spot very near the dwelling-house of the late Col. William Winn; "The frame of it is still standing, though very much altered in appearance, at the corner of Main and Church streets, and has been for many years used as a manufacturing establishment. When the church first met there, it was a plain frame building without finish or ornament. It was about forty feet square, and consisted of one floor only, (the walls and ceiling being left for several years much in the style of a barn,) furnished with rude benches." But uninviting as the appearance was which it presented, both within and without, yet here Elder Peak, Drs. Baldwin, Stillman and others, in visiting the weak churches, would stop and preach."

Meetings of the church still continued to be held in West Cambridge and Woburn, alternately, till 1797; but very soon after, the church voted to hold the services altogether in Woburn, it being most convenient for a majority of the members.[23]

After worshipping in the house just described some five or six years, the brethren resolved to improve it: "which they did by ceiling and plastering it, and putting in pews, which were square

[22] "1794. July 20. Baptists met at new meeting house first time." — *Diary of Samuel Thompson, Esq.*

[23] Rev. Mr. Kennard's first sermon.

and panelled, with the seats made to turn up in prayer time; there were two blocks of these, making in all thirty-five pews, and an aisle running up the middle, and another round the walls. They also put up a gallery, which was reached from a porch in the west end, where also was the main entrance. The pulpit was very high, with a sounding-board over it, as was the fashion in those days; and was reached by two short flights of stairs. In front of the pulpit was the Deacon's Seat, where these elders in the church sat facing the congregation, and apparently supporting the minister, and overlooking the flock."[23]

The church continued to worship in this meeting-house "from 1795 till 1825 [1794 till 1828 ?] or about thirty years." During this period, they were served in the pastoral office by Elder Peak, who left in the latter part of 1795.[24]

"He was followed by Rev. Elias Smith; 'a man of singular traits of character.' He remained two years, and then withdrew from the church and the denomination, to enter upon a somewhat erratic course, so far as theological opinions and church relations are concerned."[24]

Rev. Mr. Smith was followed by Elder E. Nelson, who was pastor from 1802 till 1804; and was succeeded by Elder Isaiah Stone, and he in 1809 by Elder S. Wydown.

"In the year 1804, the Rev. Thomas Paul, a colored preacher, visited the church, and supplied it for a number of months. He was a man of more than ordinary genius and originality of mind, independence of spirit, joined to deep humility before God. His preaching was attended by the demonstration of the Spirit and with power. A precious revival appeared in the church; and as a result, thirty-nine souls were brought to Christ, and baptized into the fellowship of the church."

"In 1811, Rev. Thomas Waterman took the pastoral charge. He was a man small of stature, like Paul, but with a manly intellect. He had been educated in an English College, and was eminent among a race of ministers, who had most of them but very limited literary culture, for the extent of his attain-

[23] Rev. Mr. Kennard's first sermon.

[24] Rev. Mr. Kennard's second sermon.

ments. . . . . In addition to his pastoral work, he . . . . kept a school of a superior character, and was much respected in the community, as a gentleman of refinement, and an able Christian minister. He died suddenly, probably in a fit of apoplexy, after having served the church to great acceptance about three years. His remains lie in our cemetery, where a neat shaft, erected through the exertions of a prominent member of this society, still living, commemorates in modest terms his virtues. His companion, who long outlived him, and who is well remembered for her womanly and Christian character, has lately been laid by his sleeping dust.

"In 1817, Rev. Herbert Marshall was ordained pastor. He was a man of respectable, not of shining abilities as a preacher; but distinguished for his simple-hearted faith, his fervor and industry in his work, and especially by his power in prayer. In answer to his fervent prayers, the Spirit descended with wonderful power upon the church and congregation, and a remarkably deep and permanent work of grace was wrought in the church. It seemed to reach every member, and is still remembered and often referred to, as the great revival of 1817. Seventy persons were baptized in one year; and among them some of the most valuable members the church has ever had."

"Rev. George Phippen became pastor in 1818; and was succeeded by Rev. Adoniram Judson, father of the Missionary, a venerable and highly esteemed servant of God: who was followed, 1823, by Rev. James N. Seaman. During these pastorates, the church seemed under a cloud, and experienced some trials. Very few were added to the church; and the membership on the whole diminished.

"With the settlement of Rev. Samuel Malory, in 1826, the cloud seemed to break, and the sunshine of prosperity cheered the church. An extensive revival of religion was sent from on high, and seventy were received into the church by baptism, of whom the same may be said as of those received during the revival of 1817. In the increase of the church (which now numbered over two hundred) and of the congregation, the meeting-house began to be too small for them: and they must either enlarge, or build a new house. From an account of the movement contained in the 'Old Book of the Treasurer's Accounts,' we learn, that Mrs. Rebecca Tottingham, who owned the land adjacent to that on which the church stood, and which it was necessary to purchase, if the house was enlarged, was asked by a committee to sell it to the church for that purpose: but that she, after due deliberation, (as the old Record goes) gave a lot of land sufficient to enlarge the house, build sheds, and a parsonage house, for the *love, affection and esteem* she had for the Baptist Church and Society in this place. Let it be spoken of for a memorial of her.

"Upon subsequent consideration however, it was thought best to procure a lot in the centre of the town, and build a new house." . . . . Accordingly, "a lot was procured; and upon it was a bakery, which was removed to make way for a place where the Bread of Life might be held forth for the hungry. It was begun in May 1827; was planned and superintended by Brother Samuel Abbot, and finished and dedicated in the spring of 1828. The original dimensions were fifty-eight by sixty feet, with a porch of six feet in front. Its whole cost, including the land, was about $8,000. It has since been enlarged. The Record at the time appropriately says, 'We have abundant reason to bless God for all our efforts to build an House of Worship; and if we will but view the hand of Providence, we shall see that all and every move has been overruled for the best under the guidance of Heaven. To God be all the glory!'

"From 1829 to 1833, Rev. B. C. Wade was pastor; and from 1833 to 1835, Rev. T. B. Ripley. Rev. N. Hooper followed from 1837 to 1840. During his time, there was quite a division in the church. Forty-five of the members withdrew. While some of these were such as had caused much dissension, others were brother and sisters beloved and honored. Some of them still survive, and still possess the confidence and esteem of those who know them best. It is believed that in the case of most if not all of the survivors of those sad days, the feelings that were then kindled have long ago died away."

"Mr. Hooper was succeeded by Rev. S. B. Randall, from 1844 to 1847, when Rev. J. C. Stockbridge became pastor. During his ministry, a gracious work of conversion was enjoyed, and about forty added in one year to the church. His ministry and that of Brother Ricker and Brother Bronson being within the memory of you all, I need not dwell upon them. You know better than I, my hearers, their faithfulness, their ability and their success. During Brother Ricker's time, this house was enlarged and improved; and during Brother Bronson's, the debt incurred was paid off.

"The church has been blessed in its deacons: Thaddeus Davis, Daniel Brooks, Josiah Converse, Jacob Richardson, Jesse Converse, John Fowle, Samuel Tidd, all of whom have gone to their rest. The deaths of Brothers Richardson and Tidd were a peculiarly heavy blow. They fell suddenly and in their prime; cut down in the midst of most important services they were rendering the church. She was plunged in deepest sorrow; their loss seemed irreparable. But their death was blessed to the spiritual good of the church: and in regard to them, and the other names mentioned, as well as those who have succeeded them, we may say, how much does the church owe of gratitude to God for giving them!

"The total number added to those connected with the church since its organization is about nine hundred. Of these about six hundred and fifty have been received by baptism. Surely God hath done great things for us, whereof we are glad.

"During all these years, the doctrines of the church have remained unaltered. There may have been, indeed, during the early part of her history, a large development of what are called the high Calvinistic doctrines, in regard to Sovereignty, Election, etc., etc. These have not been withdrawn in their *essence*; but there has been a development also of other doctrines, which supplement and limit those, so as to present a symmetrical system."[25]

To the above account of the Baptist Church in Woburn, taken almost entirely from two historical discourses concerning it

[25] Rev. Mr. Kennard's second sermon.

preached by Rev. Mr. Kennard, the immediate predecessor of its present pastor, Rev. Mr. Townley, may be added the following brief notices of several of the more recent ministers of this church and people, kindly furnished by Rev. Dr. Stockbridge and Mr. John D. Tidd.

Rev. J. C. Stockbridge was born, June 8, 1818, at Yarmouth, Maine; received his academic education at the academy in his native town; was graduated from Brown University, 1838; studied theology at the Institution in Newton, where he was graduated in 1844; and was installed as pastor of the Baptist Church in Woburn, January 27, 1848. This relation he sustained, "the happy pastor" of a people beloved by him, till October 1852, when he was dismissed from Woburn, that he might assume the pastoral charge of the First Baptist Church in Providence, R. I. to which he had been invited, during the absence of its minister, Rev. Dr. Granger, who had been appointed as one of a deputation from the Missionary Union, to visit the Baptist missionary stations in Burmah.

At the close of the year, he was called to the pastoral office of the Charles Street Church, Boston, over which he was installed October 23, 1853. In this position, he remained nearly eight years; and during this time, viz: at commencement, in 1859, he received from Harvard University the honorary degree of D. D.

His health beginning to fail him, that he might preserve that invaluable blessing, as well as fulfil a long cherished purpose, he gave up all ministerial labor early in 1865, and embarked for Europe. Landing in Sicily, he went thence to Greece, and made a visit of much interest at Athens. Returning to Sicily, he commenced travelling extensively in Italy and Switzerland, and over some portions of France and Germany; and in passing along in these several countries, he remained some time at Rome and Paris, and visited Naples, Florence, Bologna, Venice, Milan, and Geneva. Sailing down the Rhine, he came to Cologne. He then went to Holland, spent a few days at Amsterdam, visited the Hague and Rotterdam, and crossing the sea from Holland he came to England, where he spent several weeks, making tours in various directions through the country; took a short trip to Scotland, and then coming back to Liverpool, he embarked in the steamer for New York, where he arrived in safety, after an absence abroad of about eight months.

Soon after his return to this country, he took charge of the Free Street Church, Portland, where he remained till recently; when the situation of Principal of a literary institution in Providence being offered him, he accepted it, and his present residence is in that city.

Rev. Joseph Ricker was installed February 14, 1853; dismissed April 1, 1858, and afterwards appointed chaplain of the State Prison in Charlestown. He then became pastor of the Baptist Church in Milford, Mass.; and is now settled in Augusta, Me.

Rev. B. F. Bronson entered upon his pastoral labors in this church, June 1, 1858, without any public services of installation; was dismissed April 27, 1862, and settled in Roxbury, receiving an appointment, in connection with his pastorate in Roxbury, as Secretary of the Massachusetts Baptist State Convention. He is now settled at Southbridge, Mass.

Rev. J. Spencer Kennard was installed October 31, 1862; dismissed December 15, 1865; took charge of the Calvary Church, Albany, N. Y.; and is now settled in Philadelphia, Pa., succeeding his honored father, who was removed by death from a pastorate over the same church of more than twenty-five years.

The present pastor of this church, and immediate successor of Mr. Kennard, is Rev. H. C. Townley, who was installed July 17, 1866.

In connection with his labors, there has been enjoyed by his people an interesting season of revival. Since his settlement, thirty-three persons have been baptized by him and added to the church. And although for two or three months past there has been no observable special interest, yet, during this interval, a measure of interest has been kept up, which is at present on the increase; and the members of this church "are confidently expecting to be permitted soon to witness displays of divine power in the conversion of the impenitent."

INDEPENDENT BAPTIST CHURCH.

The church in Woburn, thus denominated, originated in a secession from the First Baptist Church. On the 22d day of June, 1838, Leonard Fowle, Jesse Convers, George Flagg, John Edgell, with thirty other members of the Baptist Church, thirty-four in all,[26] requested letters of dismission from that church. Their request was granted to each petitioner severally, in letters after the following form:

"To all whom it may concern; This may certify, that A. B. is a member in good standing in the Baptist Church in Woburn, Mass.; and as such is hereby dismissed at his (or her) request, and recommended to any church of the same faith and order. Done at a regular meeting of the church:

"Woburn, June 22d, 1838. A. A. NEWHALL, Clerk."

The reasons assigned by these brethren and sisters for requesting dismission from the church to which they had hitherto belonged were:

1. First, "The admitting into the pulpit of others than the professed ministers of the gospel, and the discussion of other subjects than the gospel, from the pulpit, against the expressed wish of the injured brothers and sisters."

2. Secondly and principally, "the seeming letting down of the doctrines of grace, as found in the Word of God, and embodied in the Church Covenant."

Having made repeated efforts for an adjustment of the difficulties above suggested, without success, "they felt it a duty to go out, however trying, not knowing whither they went."

These withdrawing brethren and sisters from the First Baptist Church do not appear to have formed themselves into a separate church by any new organization, but to have considered themselves as already such by mutual consent, and united by the bonds of the covenant into which they had formerly entered.

By the courtesy of the First Baptist Church, they were allowed the use of their old meeting-house, then unoccupied, at a mere

---

[26] Forty-five, according to Rev. Mr. Kennard's second sermon.

nominal rent, till the chapel they now assemble in, was erected for them by a member of their own body, Mrs. Sarah Convers.

Since their establishment as an Independent Church, they have been favored successively with the pastoral services of Elders Hartwell Osburn and Lemuel Cox, Jr., who labored among them more than fourteen years, "much to their edification and comfort." Since the year 1861, they have been without a stated minister, but do not forsake the assembling of themselves together; but meet semi-monthly, "and enjoy a good degree of harmony, although by frequent removals and deaths, their number is now much reduced; being at this date (May 7, 1866) but about thirty." [27]

First Universalist Society.

About 1828, a number of Christians of the Universalist persuasion formed themselves into a society, and erected a meeting-house, which was dedicated December 23, 1829, and was improved by them as their house of worship several years. For their first minister, they had Rev. Otis A. Skinner. His successors in office (the dates of whose respective settlements have not been preserved on record) were Rev. Messrs. Daniel D. Smith, A. L. Balch, John Gregory and J. C. Waldo.[28] But this society at length ceased to have preaching, and after retaining possession of their meeting-house for some time, they eventually sold it to the town, and it is now occupied, with various alterations, as the Town Hall.

Second Universalist Society.

A Second Universalist Society was formed, and a constitution adopted by it, early in 1841. At a meeting held in the meeting-house of the First Universalist Society, April 5, 1841, and continued by adjournment to April 19th, this Second Society was organized by the choice of Joshua V. Peirce as Clerk, John Johnson, Jr., Moderator, Messrs. John Johnson, Jr., John Knight, 2d, and William Winn, Jr., as Standing Committee, Joshua V. Peirce, as Treasurer, and Timothy Winn, as Collector.

---

[27] Letter of May 7, 1866, from a member of the Independent Church.

[28] John Johnson, Esq., communication from.

At a meeting, June 27, 1844, it was voted that they would hold their meetings in the Town Hall, with the consent of the "Unitarian Society" to release it to them a part of the time.

At a meeting held in the Town Hall, April 4th, 1845, one article of the warrant was, "To see what measures they would take to build a meeting-house the ensuing season," and a committee of three was then chosen to ascertain "how many pews could be sold in a new house, and to report at the adjournment of that meeting." The meeting-house which the society thus appears to have contemplated building in the spring of 1845 was built and finished before winter that year, and from certain minutes seems to have been dedicated November 21st. It is the same house as that afterwards occupied by the Unitarian Society, and more recently by the Methodists.

May 18, 1845, the society accepted the proposal of Rev. W. B. Randolph to come and preach for them for what money they could raise for his support, and voted him their thanks for his offer.[29] But at a meeting, March 16, 1846, they voted not to hire Mr. Randolph another year, and instructed their treasurer, April 14th, "to hire money sufficient to pay him what was due to him to that date."

Rev. Mr. Randolph was the first and the last minister whom the Second Universalist Society appears to have statedly employed. No other subsequently to him is mentioned on their records. At a meeting, March 29, 1847, called "to see if they would close up their affairs,"[30] they seem to have dissolved their connection with one another, as a distinct religious society, and to have yielded up the disposal of their meeting-house, upon some terms, to the Unitarians, who thenceforth had the charge of providing the preacher employed in it, and of paying for his services.

First Unitarian Society.

Reference is made in the records of the Second Universalist Society, 1844, to Unitarians, as being at that time accustomed to assemble for worship in the Town Hall. No regular legally

---

[29] Memoranda, by John Johnson, Esq.

[30] Letter of Rev. Eli Fay.

constituted society, however, of this denomination appears to have existed in Woburn, till 1847. By a warrant issued by Albert H. Nelson, Esq., March 31, 1847, the members of a religious association, not named therein or incorporated, were warned to assemble in the vestry of the Universalist meeting-house that day, at a given hour.[31] In compliance with this notice, several gentlemen of the Unitarian belief came together at the time and place appointed, some of whom had had apparently no previous connection with the Universalist Society, and the first act of their proceedings on that occasion was, to organize the gentlemen present into "The First Unitarian Society in Woburn."[31]

At a parish meeting, held May 20, 1848, Rev. Henry F. Edes, an alumnus of Bowdoin College, 1828, and of the Theological School, Cambridge, 1831, was invited to become the pastor. He accepted the invitation; but resigned March 18, 1850.[31]

January 10, 1853, Mr. George F. Simmons was unanimously called to the pastoral office; but declined.[31]

March 7, 1853, Rev. John M. Masters, a graduate, 1847, and a tutor, 1850, of Harvard University, was chosen and accepted. During his ministry, the church building was remodelled, and the society prospered greatly. But, March 25, 1855, he tendered his resignation, on account of ill health.[31]

April 15, 1857, Rev. Rufus P. Stebbins, D. D., was elected pastor. The office to which he was thus chosen, he accepted; and continued to fill it till November 28, 1863. The society prospered under his labors.[31]

Rev. Dr. Stebbins is a native of Wilbraham, Mass.: was a graduate of Amherst College, 1834; an alumnus of Cambridge Theological School, 1837; settled in Leominster, September 20, 1837–44. President of the Meadville Theological School, Meadville, Pa., 1844–56; and received the honorary degree of D. D. from Harvard University, 1851.

Rev. Eli Fay was chosen his successor, April 16, 1864,[32] and still (1867) continues in office.

---

[31] Letter of Rev. Eli Fay.

[32] Letter of Rev. Eli Fay.

Before the ministry of Rev. Dr. Stebbins in Woburn was completed, his society had taken measures to provide themselves with a larger and more commodious house of worship. Thus far, since their organization as a society, they had met on sabbath days in the church built by the Second Universalist Society, in 1845, and which had been remodelled and enlarged by them, during the ministry of Rev. Mr. Masters. But now, the more fully to answer their wishes in this respect, they had purchased, enlarged and adorned, at the cost of about forty thousand dollars, the comparatively new church erected by the First Congregational Society of Woburn, in 1841; and having finished their labors upon this stately, elegant church edifice, they dedicated it anew, April 16, 1865.

Methodist Episcopal Church.

Methodist preaching was commenced in Woburn, at the town house, 1850, by brethren of that denomination, Stephen M. Vail, D. D., Leonard P. Frost, and J. W. Merrill, D. D. Previously, there had been a few Methodists in the town, a portion if not all of whom belonged to the Methodist Episcopal Church in Medford, and had for some time been organized as a class, nearly all the members of which attended very punctually.

In February 1851, a church was organized by Amos Binney, presiding elder, consisting of ten members in full communion, and several probationers.

In May 1851, Brother H. Kendall, a local preacher, was appointed by the presiding elder to supply the people regularly with preaching. He is characterized, as "earnest, laborious and successful" in his vocation; and at quitting the place, in 1852, he left to the charge of his successor twenty-seven members in church fellowship, and twelve probationers.

In 1852, he was followed by Brother J. B. Holman, a local preacher, who made the earliest permanent church record.

In 1853, Brother Cary succeeded, the first appointed by the Conference; but left before the close of the year; and was followed by Brother H. R. Parmenter from the Biblical Institution at Concord, N. H.

In 1854, Brother George Sutherland was stationed at Woburn by the Conference; preached there two years, and was very successful in his labors. During his ministry, the chapel was moved from the site now occupied by Lyceum Hall, and placed where it now stands; was bought of the parties that built and owned it, paid for, and "filled to overflowing with an attentive congregation, most of whom loved God and each other."

In 1856, Brother Sutherland was followed by Brother Treadwell; and he, in turn, in 1857, by Brother J. A. Ames, "who was very successful. More persons were received on probation, more baptized, and more married by the pastor of the Methodist Church in Woburn during his two years' service, than in any other equal length of time, during the first fourteen years of its history."

Brother Ames was followed, in 1859, by Brother M. P. Webster; and he, in 1860, by Brother Otheman; and he, in 1862, by Brother Atkinson; and he, in 1863, by Brother Barney, a student from Concord, N. H.

During the years 1862, 1863, "many were ready to give up the organization; and but for a very few determined spirits, the church must have broken up. For a long time, the Records show no conversions, no baptisms, and no marriages. In fact, the church seems to have been crippled socially, financially and spiritually."

During 1864, the church was supplied, under the presiding elder, by Rev. N. D. George, who, with the church, succeeded in obtaining pledges for nearly enough to meet the cash payment ($5,000) on the church building we[33] now occupy. About one-half of such pledges were collected, when Brother George was succeeded, in 1865, by [the] present pastor, (Rev. M. M. Parkhurst.) Between the 1st of April and 17th of May, the building was purchased, the balance of subscription ($2,500) was collected and paid over, and a deed obtained. The church building was thoroughly repaired, carpeted, cushioned. Gas

[33] The foregoing account is copied chiefly from communication of Rev. Mr. M. M. Parkhurst, May 1866, the present pastor of this church.

pipes were brought into the audience room; a new pulpit, altar rail and chairs purchased, and the house was re-opened May 17, 1865, with all the bills paid, but the small balance ($1,000) of the purchase money of the church."

During the time from the 1st of April, 1865, to the present [May 1866], the congregation has increased greatly; the sabbath school has doubled in numbers; the church has enlarged in financial ability and social power; and has increased its pastor's salary, and its membership about four-tenths.[33]

Roman Catholic Church.

In 1847, the Roman Catholics commenced holding meetings at Woburn, in the Town Hall. A house of worship was erected by them, in 1852, under the supervision of Father Carroll, who then officiated among them as priest, and who was succeeded in office by Father Brannigan. In 1862, Father McCarthy became a resident priest in the town, and remained until 1864, when Father John Qually became pastor.[34]

The church erected in 1852 for the public worship of this denomination of Christians, is now, it is understood, found too strait for them, and strenuous efforts are now being made, under the direction of Father Qually, and with the aid of several citizens of the town, to build them a larger and more convenient house for this purpose.

The present average attendance upon their Sunday services is about eight hundred. A sabbath school of about two hundred and fifty meets in the afternoon at the church.[34]

Protestant Episcopal Society.

Zealous efforts are now being made to establish an Episcopal Society in Woburn. Numbers, it is understood, regularly meet on the sabbath in Lyceum Hall, who make use there of the Liturgy of the Protestant Episcopal Church of the United States in their worship, and who hope ere long to see a church erected, and a society legally formed, for the benefit of their denomination. And here it seems not inappropriate, and may be accept-

---

[34] Communication of Father Qually, April 21, 1866.

able to the good people of Woburn, to remind them that the worship of God, according to the forms and usages of the Church of England, is no new thing in their town.

In 1751, immediately after the ordination of Rev. Thomas Jones as pastor of the Second or Precinct Church in Woburn, twelve dissatisfied persons out of the one hundred and three, who were that year ratable inhabitants of the parish, signed off, as was said, to the Church of England.[35] Most of them, it is believed, joined the Episcopal Church in Cambridge; but a few of them appear to have connected themselves with one or other of the three Episcopal Churches then in Boston. In the course of the three next succeeding years, 1752, 1753, 1754, two others joined them, and they were all rated each year by the Second Parish Assessors for their minister taxes; and those taxes were severally paid over (as the Province law of 1742 then required) to the Episcopal clergyman, upon whose services the Assessors were certified, that they "usually and frequently attended." But after 1754, they do not appear from the Parish Records to have been rated at all by the Second Parish Assessors for their parish taxes.

Shortly after the individuals above referred to had withdrawn from the worship of the Second Precinct in Woburn to that of the Church of England, they were joined by Benjamin Simonds,

---

[35] "Profess'd or Pretended members of the Church of England, Inhabiting this Parish: rated for Salary only.

"William Smith	7 :8 :
Robert Reed	6 :0.
Swithin Reed	18 :11.
Ebenezer Reed	18 :6.
George Reed jun^r	9 :9.
Eliphaz Reed	9 :9.
James Perry	9 :2
Thomas Skelton jun.	16 :0
Caleb Simonds	18 :1 :2
Caleb Simonds jun.	11 :0 :0
Seth Johnson	16 :0 :0
John Cutler	16 :5 :0."

Second Parish Records for 1752, *Vol. II., p.* 18.

of the First Parish,[36] who proved a very important man among them. His house is still standing, having its back to the road at the north, but a magnificent elm growing in the yard on the south side in front; and is the same house as that now occupied by Mr. Jesse Cutler on the road from Burlington to Cummingsville. At this house, these professed Episcopalians met on ordinary sabbaths for public worship, when the liturgy of the church of England was read to them, and not improbably a printed sermon likewise, by Mr. Thomas Skelton, Jr., one of their number. But on extra occasions, when an Episcopal clergyman from Cambridge or Boston came to minister to them, they would, as often as the weather allowed, meet in the yard under the shade of the wide-spreading elm, no room in the house being large enough to hold them, and there the minister would preach to them, and celebrate the ordinances. The late Mrs. William Kendall, of this town, once showed me an octavo English prayer book, from which she said her grandfather, Mr. Thomas Skelton, Jr., was accustomed to read the church of England prayers on sabbath days in the Episcopal meeting at Mr. Simonds'; and Mr. Gideon Simonds, deceased, a son of Mr.

---

36 Copy of certificate, yet extant, of membership from Christ Church, Boston, to Benjamin Simonds: —

"This may Cartify the treasurer of the first precinct in Wooburn, that Mr Benjamin Simonds of said precinct is a professed member of the Church of England, and that he atends the publick worshep of God on Sundays at Christ Church in Boston as frequently as he can, and as is useuel at his Distance.

his
"TIMOTHY X CUTLER, minister of Christ Church in Boston
mark

"Boston September ye 10. 1759.

"Witnes the signing of Docter Cutler,
" Caleb Simonds juner,
" Sarah Cutler."

"John Pigen
"Thomas Ivers } Church wardins."

This certificate is accompanied by another on the same page, in the same words, to the treasurer of the *second* precinct in Woburn; and it bears indubitable marks of being a transcript, taken by some ignorant and careless person from a genuine certificate of Rev. Dr. Cutler, signed by him and his church wardens at the given date, except writing "his mark," which must be deemed an expedient of the transcriber, adopted for some purpose of his own.

Caleb Simonds, Jr., a member of that meeting, once told me, that he, and (I think I may confidently add) his brothers Calvin and Jesse, were baptized by an Episcopal clergyman under that venerable elm.

But at the commencement of the revolutionary war, this Episcopal meeting in Woburn, like several others of that denomination in various parts of New England, appears to have been broken up. Its connection, however, with the Episcopal churches in Boston, by which it had been patronized, was not at once dissolved, as the annexed certificate, still extant, seems to indicate.

Dec. 4, A. D. 1781. Then was married Mr Ebenezer Page to Miss Susanna Simons [daughter of the above named Benjamin Simons] by the Rev. Mr. Samuel Parker of Boston."

Nor was the attachment to the royal government of England, which the use of its established forms of public divine worship had nurtured and strengthened in this band of Episcopalians in Woburn, at once renounced or cast off. The late Capt. James Reed, Sen. of this town, once told me, that being collector one year for Woburn, he presented a tax bill to Mr. Thomas Skelton, Jr., the Episcopal reader mentioned above, for payment. "I wont pay it," said Mr. Skelton; "the government that ordered the tax, is no lawful government; and I wont submit to any tax of its imposing." After repeatedly applying to Mr. Skelton to pay the bill, Capt. Reed was peremptorily commanded by the assessors of Woburn, to collect the tax, or to take the body. Upon Capt. Reed's communicating the orders he had received, Mr. Skelton instantly replied, "Well, take the body, if you will; but I suppose you will give me time to go up stairs, and shift my clothes before you take me off." The liberty asked was readily granted; but Mr. Skelton was gone to his chamber so long, that Capt. Reed began to be seriously alarmed, lest his debtor had given him the slip. At length Mr. Skelton returning to him, said, "Capt. Reed, will you sign a paper I shall give you, if I will pay you them taxes?" "Sign!" replied Capt. Reed; "Why, Mr. Skelton, I'll sign anything, if you will only pay that demand." Mr. Skelton then produced a receipt to be signed, expressed as follows: "Received of Thomas Skelton Jr., he being threatened with imprisonment, his taxes due for such a year." The receipt was quickly signed, and Mr. Skelton was let off in peace.

At another time, the same Mr. Skelton sold a piece of land to Mr. Swithin Reed, the Captain's father; and, drawing up a deed of it himself, gave it to the Captain to deliver. Upon reading it, the old gentleman said to his son, "Jim, I don't know but this deed is all right; yet it seems to me, it don't read exactly as other deeds do. Here, take it to Cambridge, and show it to "Mr. Deany," [Hon. Judge Francis Dana] "and he'll tell you at once whether it be as it should be." Accordingly, the Captain took it to Cambridge as directed, and the moment the judge read it, he threw it aside, saying, "it was not worth a farthing." "Why, what is the matter with it?" inquired the Captain. "Matter!" said the Judge: "Why, don't you see? Instead of dating it in such a year of the United States Independence, he writes, "In such a year of His Majesty's Reign!"

The prime movers of this Episcopal meeting have all of them long since gone the way of all the earth. Their children, too, are all dead. Those of them who continued in town, at the time the war of the Revolution put a stop to their assembling on the sabbath for Episcopal worship, joined to a man, it is believed, the Precinct Congregational Society; and nothing more was heard in Woburn or its precinct, of meeting to worship according to the liturgy of the Church of England, till the present attempt to establish an Episcopal Society was commenced.

P. S. On Tuesday, October 29, 1867, the corner-stone of an Episcopal Church, to be called Trinity Church, was laid in Woburn, in due form. The principal services of the occasion were conducted by Rev. Dr. Huntington, rector of Emmanuel Church, Boston. In consequence of the unfavorableness of the weather, the persons who were to take part in, or to witness the exercises of the solemnity, fifty or sixty in number, assembled at the house of Mr. Oliver W. Rogers, adjoining the church, where appropriate lessons from the Scriptures were read, prayers were offered, and the hymn, Te Deum Laudamus, was sung by the choir. Then the whole company moved in procession to the church, where a list was read by the Rev. H. D. Nicholson, the rector, of the articles previously deposited in a metallic box let into the stone, which lay ready to be set in its place. This list comprehended an "historical sketch of the parish, names of the officers, by-laws, names of building committee, architect, builder, copies of Middlesex Journal, Christian Witness, order of service for the day, etc., etc."

"Rev. Dr. Huntington then taking a hammer, and striking the stone three blows, in the name of the Father and of the Son and of the Holy Ghost, pronounced,

"'I lay the corner-stone of an edifice to be here erected by the name of Trinity Church, to be devoted to the service of Almighty God, according to the doctrine, discipline, and worship of the Protestant Episcopal Church in the United States of America.

"'Other foundation can no man lay than that which is laid, even Jesus Christ, who is God over all, blessed for evermore, in whom we have redemption through His blood, even the forgiveness of sins. Amen.'

"On their returning to the house, Dr. Huntington addressed those assembled, in a most eloquent and masterly manner. The exercises then concluded with a hymn."—*Middlesex Journal, Woburn, Nov.* 2, 1867.

CHAPTER XVI.

Progress of Woburn since 1800, in population, business, wealth, buildings, schools, and other means of promoting the public welfare.

GREAT and rapid, during the last sixty years, have been the advances of Woburn in numbers, business and wealth; in all the means of literary and social progress, and of spiritual prosperity and enjoyment. It is the design of this last chapter of its history, to contrast the present condition of the town, in respect to the above-named and other particulars, with what it was at the commencement of this century, and in other previous portions of its history.

POPULATION. — Within the last twenty years, the number of the inhabitants of Woburn has surprisingly increased. The total population of the town in 1765, was 1,575.[1] According to the colonial census in 1776, it had advanced only to 1,691.[1] By the first census under the United States government in 1790, the sum of the white and colored inhabitants was but 1,750. By the second census in 1800, it had diminished to 1,246, in consequence of the detachment of Burlington from Woburn the year before. In 1810, the population was still further reduced in number to 1,219, which is less by twenty-seven than it was in 1800. In 1820, it was only 1,579, which is but four more than it was in 1765, fifty-five years before. But since 1820, the increase has been very rapid. In 1830, the whole number of inhabitants, according to the census taken that year, was 1,977; in 1840, it was 2,994; and although by the incorporation of Winchester as a separate town April 30, 1850, Woburn lost a large number of people who previously belonged to it, yet by the census of 1860, the sum total of its inhabitants had increased to 6,295, which is more than double the number it contained in

[1] Town Report, March 1865, pp. 31, 32.

1840, only twenty years before; and even this large number, according to a State census of 1865, had advanced still further on May 1st of that year to 7,003, an increase of 708 in five years.[2]

To accommodate its 1,575 inhabitants with dwellings, Woburn was provided in 1765 with 228 houses; but in 1860, with 1,126 houses for its 6,295 inhabitants.[1]

Principal Business. — The principal employment of the original inhabitants of Woburn was doubtless the cultivation of the soil, for which they all had larger or smaller grants of land given them by the town. But at the present day (1867), the employment pursued in the town more than any other is work upon leather. For in a town report for the year ending March 1, 1866, it appears that of two hundred and forty-one children whose births are registered in 1865, the fathers of ninety-four were curriers, of twenty-four were tanners, of fourteen were cordwainers, and of six were leather and shoe mauufacturers, making a total of one hundred and thirty-eight employed upon leather, and leaving only one hundred and three of all other occupations.[3]

The leather business was followed in Woburn from the beginning, upon a small scale. John and Francis Wyman, brothers, and among the first settlers of the town, were tanners; and, as tradition affirms, had their tanyard in the Wyman Lane, near where the late Dea. Benjamin Wyman (a descendant from Francis) had his dwelling. Gershom Flagg, too, another early inhabitant, who came a young man, from Watertown, and married in Woburn in 1668, was a tanner by trade, and had his "dwelling hows, bark hows, mill hows, and bearne hows, tann fats, with an acre of land more or less thereunto belonginge, being or situate in High Street nere the meetting hows, bounded West by Mr Thomas Carter, and East by the burying place, South by the trayning feild."[4] And during Philip's war, Woburn taxes at one time were partly paid in shoes, manufactured

[2] Communication from Nathan Wyman, Esq., town clerk.
[3] Town Report, March 1866, pp. 3–7.
[4] Town Records, Vol. I., p. 21, inverted.

probably from leather prepared by one or all of the citizens above named.[5]

But it is not likely that either of them carried on the business very extensively, or employed about it many hands. For Lieut. John Wyman, having his eldest son killed by the Indians in the swamp fight, December 1675, petitioned the General Court in May following, that his servant, Robert Simpson, a tanner by trade, whom he had "*bought* on purpose for the management of his tan yard," but who had been long in the war, needed clothes, and was then a garrison soldier in Hadley, might be allowed to come home to him, that "so his lether now in the fatts may not be spoyled;"[6] which looks as though Mr. Wyman was not sufficiently provided with help to conduct his business, or that the servants he had then with him were not well skilled in the trade they worked at.

The Messrs. Wyman appear to have been succeeded in their business, in the same vicinity where they had wrought, by Jonathan Wyman, a grandson of John; and also at a later period (about 1768), by Mr. David Cummings, originally from Topsfield, who is styled in sundry papers he left behind him, a tanner, and who was an ancestor of the present John Cummings, Jr., Esq. But tanners in Woburn were then few and scarce; and it has recently been told me by a middle-aged gentleman of Burlington, that he could remember the time when it used to be said, that "old Mr Jonathan Tidd, of New Bridge, was the only tanner in Woburn."

But since Gen. Abijah Thompson entered into the business of tanning, etc., about the year 1814, it has astonishingly and with great rapidity increased in Woburn. According to the statistics of the "Industry of Massachusetts," for the year ending May 1, 1865, p. 419, and published with the sanction of the Secretary of the Commonwealth, there were that year in active

---

[5] "Paid in to the Treasurer [1675] by John Richison, Constable, in silver and debenters all advanced, the full sum of - - - - £68 :16 :3
"paid more by shoose and barly - - - - - - 08 :11 :6"
Town Records, Vol. I., pp. 64, 65.

[6] Extract from Colony Records, by Rev. Joseph B. Felt.

operation in Woburn twenty-one tanning and currying establishments, which tanned and curried leather to the value of $1,723,450, and employed five hundred and fifty-four hands. There were also four establishments for making patent and enamelled leather, estimated at $285,550, and finding employ for fifty-eight hands. At the same time, there were manufactured in the town 758 pairs of boots of all kinds, and of shoes of all kinds 160,145 pairs, the making of which boots and shoes employed two hundred and three males and one hundred and five females, and the total value of which was estimated to be $254,190. And although in this latter branch of business,—the manufacturing of boots and shoes,—Woburn was excelled in 1865 by two or three towns in Middlesex County, as Holliston and Hopkinton, yet there was no town in the county which then equalled it in the extent and value of its tanning and currying.[7]

WEALTH.—An almost uninterrupted increase of the population and business of the town, since the present century commenced, has vastly increased its wealth. Some judgment of this increase may be formed by comparing the taxes of 1800 and of 1865. In 1800, the sum assessed for town purposes was only $2,205, and for State and county taxes, $613.50, making a total of $2,818.50.[8] But in 1865, the sum total assessed for all purposes, State, county and town, was $87,432.37.[9]

Again, in 1865, the personal property assessed in Woburn was	$2,068,021 00
The real estate	3,144,455 00
Total valuation	$5,212,476 00
Whereas the total valuation in 1860, was	4,504,341 00
Showing a gain in five years, of	$708,135 00

WOBURN BRANCH RAILROAD.—Another great improvement made in the condition of Woburn during the present century

[7] Industry of Massachusetts, May 1, 1865, p. 419.
[8] Town Records, Vol. XIII., pp. 26, 29, 30.
[9] Town Report, 1866, p. 51.

has resulted from the establishment of the Woburn Branch Railroad. This road was chartered in 1843, and was opened for travel December 30, 1844. And it has unquestionably been the means of greatly enlarging both the business and the wealth of the town. Such are the facilities it affords for the speedy transportation both of persons and of freight, that gentlemen of Woburn who have business in Boston, or goods to be conveyed to or from there, may, by means of the cars, go to the city in the morning, transact their business, and return to Woburn at noon or night, if they please; and thus may share in the advantages of Boston for trade, combined with the almost uninterrupted enjoyment of domestic intercourse and the comforts of home.

The following estimate, kindly furnished me by Mr. Alvah Wood, ticket-master on this road, of the business and travel done upon it for one year between Woburn and Boston, or between Woburn and some or other of the towns between, shows that the citizens of Woburn have not been slow to perceive and improve the privileges which this road afforded them.

"The amount received at Woburn Centre for tickets, for the year 1866, was - - - - - - -	$21,185 46
"The amount received for local freight - -	19,486 11
" " " " through freight - -	70,952 14
"Total collections for 1866 - -	$111,623 71

"The above amount is exclusive of commutation tickets, of which there are about 130, which at $72 per year, would add to the total $9,360.

"Number of passengers [in 1866?] from Woburn Centre, 136,000."

Buildings. — Since the present century came in, the vast increase of wealth in Woburn has effected a marked improvement in its buildings of every description. In 1800, the only considerable public edifice was the church on the training-field; and that, though then capacious enough to accommodate the people in their weekly worship, was erected close to the road from Wilmington to Medford, was without porch, without steeple, and had nothing of elegance to recommend it. And as to the private dwelling-houses of the town at that period, though, generally speaking, they were substantially built, neat and convenient, yet (if we may except the Baldwin mansion) there was nothing beautiful or attractive about them. But now we see scattered in all parts of the town, and quite thickly in the centre, large and costly dwelling-houses, beautiful to look to, and some even approaching magnificence. We see a convenient town-house, instead of a contracted school-house, or a small chamber over the church porch, to hold town meetings in. We see a Lyceum Hall, intended for large gatherings of the people on secular occasions, unsurpassed in capaciousness and elegance by few if any buildings in the neighborhood, of the like design. We see a lofty High School House, which is an ornament and an honor to the town; and we see four houses for public worship, all of them highly respectable in appearance, and well adapted to their intended use; and two of them in particular, stately, imposing (as well as costly) structures, calculated in a measure to excite in a spectator from abroad those sentiments of pious awe, which the exercises within are professedly designed to cherish and promote. And ere many months have passed away, an additional church to the above four may be expected to be seen in Woburn, viz: a new Catholic church, which is now in process of erection, and which promises to be an elegant house of worship, and sufficiently large to accommodate the numerous worshippers of that denomination in the town.

Poor Farm. — During the latter half of the last century, the question was often agitated in town meeting, What shall be done with the helpless poor, instead of boarding them out in private families? and resolves were repeatedly passed to build or procure a workhouse, in which the poor might be employed and maintained.[10] In particular, it was voted at a general town meeting, April 7, 1794, 1. To have the poor of the town supported in a workhouse; 2. That the selectmen be a committee

---

[10] Town Records, Vol. VII., pp. 56, 59; Vol. VIII., pp. 104, 147; Vol. XI., p. 153.

to procure a house for that purpose. 3. That the selectmen should not support or assist any of the poor, except those who live in the workhouse.[11] Nothing effectual however was then done to this end; and the above and other numerous Resolves on this subject all came to nothing. But since 1800, a Poor Farm of suitable extent, with the requisite buildings thereon, has been purchased by the town; and the poor are there comfortably provided for; and the old matter of discussion and debate on this subject has been put to rest.

CEMETERY.— The original Woburn burying-ground was situate, it is well known, on the hill in the centre of the town. But this revered spot, where the remains of the honored fathers of the town were committed to the dust, having long since been filled, a place for a new burying-ground was purchased not far from the railroad station, about the close of the last century. But this too, in process of time, proving inadequate for the purpose intended, a large tract of ground conveniently situated for a public Cemetery for a town like Woburn, has been purchased for this use since 1800. This tract, now enlarged to about twenty-eight or thirty acres, has been securely fenced, and laid out into lots, which have been taken up by a large proportion of the families in the place; and many of them are now distinguished by suitable ornaments, and exhibit impressive tokens of the respectful remembrance cherished by the living in Woburn for their honored and beloved dead. And for its future enlargement, the sum of five thousand dollars has been recently left by Mr. Sewell Flagg, a citizen of the Town, who died June 17, 1866.[a]

---

[11] Town Records, Vol. XII., p. 141.

[a] Town Report for 1867, p. 61. The town voted, April 7, 1845, that the selectmen be a committee to purchase, for a burial place, eight or ten acres of Mr. Choate (Hon. Charles Choate?) which had been offered for the purpose, at $75.00 per acre. At the same time, a committee of three was appointed by the chair, to nominate a committee of five, to lay out the new burial ground. Agreeably to its instructions, the committee of five chosen, viz: Gen. Abijah Thompson, Col. Moses F. Winn, Messrs. Oliver C. Rogers, Samuel T. Richardson and Nathaniel A. Richardson, laid out the ground which was purchased by the selectmen, into lots, appraised

SCHOOLS.—Since the commencement of the present century, great progress has been made in the public schools in Woburn, and in measures for securing a good education therein. In 1795, the town erected within its then bounds, nine school-houses, buildings of contracted dimensions and scanty accommodations, at an expense of about £600, or $2,000.[12] In 1799, at the incorporation of the Second Parish, as Burlington, five only of those school-houses, estimated as worth £350, or $1,126, were retained by Woburn;[12] and in each of them was kept a separate school. But in 1865, the town had twelve school-houses, most of them new, large and handsome, and all of them convenient for their intended use; viz, the High School House, the Central Advanced, and ten others beside, in which are kept twenty-two schools, Primary, Intermediate, Advanced or Mixed,[13] and the whole twelve, with their fixtures and the land they stand upon, are valued at $55,500.[13]

---

the lots, and advertised them for sale at auction, October 30, 1845. Previously to the auction, however, this burial ground was solemnly consecrated to its intended use as follows:

"The Order of the Ceremonies at the Consecration of the Woburn Cemetery on Tuesday, October 30, 1845, was as follows, viz:

"1. Invocation by Rev. Webster B. Randolph.

"2. Voluntary by the Marion Band.

"3. Reading of the Scriptures, by Rev. Silas B. Randall.

"4. An Original Hymn, composed for the occasion, by Mrs. Mary L. Bennett.

"5. Address by Rev. Joseph Bennett.

"6. Consecrating Prayer, by Rev. Luther Wright.

"7. Old Hundred.

"8. Benediction by Rev. Silas B. Randall.

"The day was fine, and the ceremonies were very interesting. They commenced at one o'clock, P. M., and continued for about an hour. It has been estimated there were above one thousand people present on the occasion."—*Notice of Nathan Wyman, Jr., town clerk, in Town Records, Vol. XVI., p.* 378.

[12] Town Records, Vol. XII., pp. 143, 144, 195. By the terms of separation, Woburn was entitled to six of the nine school-houses. But as one which belonged to it stood within the bounds of Burlington, it was either sold to Burlington at auction, according to order of the town, or by some mutual agreement Burlington was allowed to keep it in possession.—*Town Records, Vol. XIII., pp.* 21, 44, 45.

[13] Town Report, 1866, pp. 18, 50.

In 1799, after the separation of Burlington, $300 was voted for the support of schooling in Woburn.[14] In 1800, this sum was increased to $350,[15] and gradually in subsequent years, to $400, to $500, to $600, etc., etc., and April 20, 1839, the town voted to raise $1,200 for the support of schools. But in 1865, the town was at the cost of $10,500 and upwards, for school purposes; from which, after deducting $400 paid for the care of school-rooms, there will remain $10,000 and upwards, appropriated to the compensation of teachers.[16]

Nor is the progress of the schools in Woburn more conspicuous than the increased number and accommodations of its school-houses, and in the liberal sums latterly granted by the town for the payment of able teachers therein, than in the increased variety of studies pursued in them, the improved method of taking those studies in orderly succession, and the standard character of some, (at least) of the books that are used.[17]

The books introduced into the Woburn schools in 1792, by the committee appointed "to recommend some uniform system of instruction," formed by no means a contemptible list.[18] At that that day, for instance, "Perry's Spelling Book," and "Child's Friend," were used not only in Woburn, but very extensively and successfully elsewhere, for teaching children to read and spell; "Pike's Arithmetic" was a text-book in Harvard College, as late as 1800; "Cheever's Accidence" was in such high repute for beginners in Latin, that it passed through twenty editions from the press, — and was still further recommended by the long and eminently successful experience of its venerable author, Master Ezekiel Cheever, who spent nearly seventy years of his life, in teaching at New Haven, Ipswich, Charlestown and Boston, and who died, head master of Boston Latin School, in 1708, aged ninety-three. And as to "Corderius," "Eutropius," and "Castalis," they were in general if not universal use, in academies and classical schools, as suitable introductions to Virgil and Cæsar's Commentaries.

---

[14] Town Records, Vol. XII., pp. 353–355. [15] Town Records, Vol. XIII., pp. 13, 40.

[16] Town Report, 1866, pp. 18, 21.

[17] Town Report, 1866, pp. 43, 44, compared with Town Records, Vol. XII., p. 75.

[18] Town Records, Vol. XII., p. 75.

But what gives the common, public schools of Woburn of the present day the superiority over those which were kept there sixty years ago, is not that all the books used in them now are decidedly preferable to all the school-books of former days; but it is the orderly, thorough system of study now established in them, and by the aid of which, gradual yet sure advances are now made from the lower and easier branches of learning to those which are higher, but more intricate or difficult.

In the public schools of Woburn, according to present arrangements, there is a regular progressive course of study, calculated to employ each scholar who goes through it, fourteen years; viz, three years in the primary school, till he be eight years old; three years in the intermediate; four years in the advanced or grammar school, and four years in the high school, where his education is completed. Beginning with the first rudiments of learning in the primary school, he is there taught Sargent's Charts, Primer and First Reader; Robinson's Progressive Primary Arithmetic, and Cornell's Primary Geography; with exercises on the slate and black-board. After remaining three years in the primary school, he enters the *intermediate school*, where he abides three years more, continuing his attention to reading and spelling, in the use of Sargent's Second Reader and Spelling Book; pursues the study of Robinson's Progressive, Intellectual, and Rudiments of Written Arithmetic, and Cornell's Intermediate Geography; and at the same time exercising himself in writing, singing, and drawing maps, etc., on the slate and black-board. Three years afterwards, he is admitted into the advanced or grammar school, where, in addition to continued attention to reading, spelling and writing, and to Robinson's arithmetics, and to Cornell's Geography, he takes up the study of familiar science, English Grammar, and Lossing's History of the United States. Finally, after being connected four years with the grammar school, he enters the high school, where for four years more he enjoys the privilege of learning Latin or French, and, at the selection of his parents, algebra, geometry, chemistry, or botany; ancient or modern history; natural, moral or mental philosophy; astronomy, Constitution of the United

States; rhetoric, and miscellaneous exercises in arithmetic, surveying, geography, book-keeping, declamation, English language, reading, composition.[19]

Public Town Library.—This important and valuable Institution, unknown to the inhabitants of Woburn in the last century, originated in the suggestion of one of the citizens of the town, Jonathan Bowers Winn, Esq., in 1854. At town meeting, in November, that year, he offered to give towards a Free Public Library the money he had received, as a member of the Constitutional Convention of 1853, provided the town would give a like sum for the same purpose. At March Meeting, 1855, the town voted to accept Mr. Winn's offer; and appropriated the sum of three hundred dollars, to be expended, with Mr. Winn's donation, in the purchase of books for a public library. It likewise authorized the Selectmen to draw from the treasury such additional sums as might be found necessary to providing a room for the proposed library, and fitting it up with suitable conveniences. It also chose a committee of seven persons, and gave them full powers, on the town's behalf, to provide and furnish a room, to purchase books, to appoint a librarian, and to establish all necessary By-Laws, Rules and Regulations for the observance of those who should make use of the library.[20]

Thus empowered, the Library Committee, consisting of J. B. Winn, Albert H. Nelson, Esq., Joshua P. Convers, Esq., Dr. Truman Rickard, Messrs. Lewis L. Whitney, Josiah Linscott and Albert Thompson, proceeded promptly to fulfil the objects of their appointment. They purchased books, which they had selected with great care, for the library; they prepared a room in the Town Hall for its reception; and they successfully exerted their influence to increase their means for enlarging the library, in procuring donations both of money and books. And thus,

[19] Town Report, 1866, pp. 43, 44. It is not expected that each scholar in the high school should engage in the study of all the branches of learning here enumerated, but only of such as their respective parents should select, and prefer to have them pursue.

[20] Catalogue of 1856, pp. 3, 4.

within three years from the time that the subject was first mentioned, they had the satisfaction of publicly announcing that a valuable library of more than 1,700 volumes was open, without cost or charge, to all the resident citizens of the town, whether poor or rich, who were twenty-one years of age, and who would subscribe the By-Laws of the Institution, and conform to their requirements.[20]

In 1865, the library was removed to a locality more commodious and desirable than the room which it had occupied hitherto in the Town Hall. There a new library room was fitted up for it, and opened in October; the books were arranged anew; an addition was made to them of fifty volumes by purchase; of three hundred and seventy-five volumes which had once belonged to the Young Men's Society, but which now, with the consent of the surviving owners, were incorporated with the town library; and of one hundred and fifty volumes more, belonging to the Agricultural Library, which, with the consent of the proprietors, were now deposited in the town library, under the care of the town.[21]

With these additions, the whole number of books belonging to the town library, according to the catalogue recently prepared, is 3,298:[21] and to provide for its future increase, a generous legacy of five hundred dollars, bequeathed for its benefit in the Will of the late Hon. Bowen Buckman, Esq., who died November 16, 1864, has been placed in the hands of the Selectmen. This bequest the present Library Committee recommend, should be allowed to remain as a permanent fund, of which the interest only should be annually expended.[21]

Beside the town library, Woburn has three other institutions of the kind: viz.

1. *The Charitable Religious Library*, connected with the First Congregational Church, which was founded, 1807, under the auspices of Rev. Mr. Chickering, and which now contains about eight hundred volumes.[22]

2. *North Woburn Library*, founded November 1840, and containing at this present time seven hundred and five volumes.[23]

---

[21] Town Report of 1866, pp. 55–61.

[22] Dr. Ephraim Cutter.

[23] Communication of N. Wyman, Esq., town clerk.

3. *Woburn Academy Library*, containing three hundred or four hundred volumes.[22]

To the above excellent institutions, and a few others of a similar character that might be named, which have all originated since the present century commenced, may be added,

1. *The Woburn Agricultural and Mechanic Association*, incorporated March 5, 1830: J. B. Winn, President; John Johnson, Secretary.[23]

2. *The Young Men's Literary Association*, organized November 7, 1855: E. F. Wyer, President; H. A. Carter, Secretary.[23]

3. *Irish Literary Association*, organized 1857. Timothy Corcoran, President; Patrick Murphy, Secretary.[23]

4. *Natural History Society*, organized 1859. John Cummings, Jr., President; J. F. Frisbie, Secretary.[23]

SABBATH SCHOOLS.—With this popular and laudable means of imparting and widely diffusing religious instruction among the young, Woburn is well provided. In former days, heads of families in this as well as in other towns throughout New England appear to have been very diligent and conscientious in teaching their children the great principles of the Christian religion and morality by frequently exercising them in the catechism then in use. And, accordingly, an aged minister in this vicinity (now I trust in heaven) observed some years ago, in conversing with me upon Sabbath Schools, "Why, the fact is, sir, that in my boyhood, every family was a Sabbath School." Pastors of churches, too, at that day, were accustomed to consider themselves as under indispensable obligations to hear and examine the children and youth of their respective charges, at stated times, in the catechism. And hence, when Rev. John Fox, the third minister of Woburn, became totally blind, as he was for several years the latter part of his life, he used, it is said on good authority,[24] to have the young people of his flock come at times to his chamber, and there to catechise them, and address to them

[24] Alden's Epitaphs, Vol. I., p. 229, No. 238.

his pious counsels.[a] And on the other hand, one of the charges alleged (with what justice I cannot say) against Rev. Mr. Sargeant, of Woburn, before the Council that dismissed him in 1798, was, that he had neglected to catechise the children of his people.[25] But since the introduction and establishment of Sabbath Schools in this town, at a period subsequent to the commencement of the present century, they seem to have been welcomed here and elsewhere as a means much preferable to the catechism for instructing the young in the knowledge of Christian truth and duty, and to have displaced, in very considerable measure at least, the public catechetical exercises of former years.

Woburn contains at the present day (1867) seven distinct Sabbath Schools, viz:

1. Baptist,	organized	May 1818.	No. of Scholars,	339[26]
2. First Congregational,	"	June 17, 1818.	"	575[27]
3. North Woburn Congl.,	"	November 1846.	"	150[26]
4. Methodist,	"	August 1, 1850.	"	141[26]
5. Unitarian,	"	May 1853.	"	165[26]
6. Protestant Episcopal,	"	June 1866.	"	40[26]
7. Roman Catholic,			"	200[28]
	Making a total of			1,610

children and youth, who enjoy the inestimable privilege of weekly instruction in the all-important truths and duties of religion and

a Such too, apparently, was the custom of Rev. Mr. Jackson, junior colleague to Rev. Mr. Fox. He used the Catechism in teaching the children and youth of his congregation the great truths of religion and morality. Prince, a negro slave, (belonging to Rev. Timothy Walker, first minister of Penacook, now Concord, N. H.),[a] who originated in Woburn, and who eventually returned to Woburn again, and died here in the almshouse, September 6, 1825, aged 115 years, once told Col. Leonard Thompson of this town, that he remembered Mr. Jackson's hearing him repeat his catechism.[b]

a Bouton's History of Concord, N. H., pp. 252, 253. b Col. Leonard Thompson.

25 Address to the Council by the Joint Committee of the Church and Parish. See Parish Records, Vol. III., p. 45.

26 Communication of N. Wyman, Esq., town clerk.

27 Congregational Quarterly, January 1867, page 73.

28 Communication of Rev. Father Qually, May 1867.

morality, of whom a considerable proportion derive no benefit on these topics from parental teachings and example, and who, destitute of the advantage in these respects which the Sabbath Schools afford them, might be left to grow up in heathenish ignorance, the pests of civil society, and the grief of any Christian community in which they reside.

Bank.— No public institution for furnishing money upon loan existed in Woburn previously to 1800. The Bank of Woburn was incorporated in 1853, with a capital stock of $100,000. It has since, viz, in January 1865, been changed to "First National Bank" of Woburn, with its capital stock increased to $300,000.[29] It is a prosperous institution; affords a safe and profitable investment for money; and proves a great accommodation to the business men of the town. Abijah Thompson, President; E. J. Jenks, Cashier.[29]

Woburn Five Cents Savings Bank; Incorporated, April 1854: Amount of deposits, $90,379.57. Abijah Thompson, President; James N. Dow, Secretary.[29]

An excellent though recent institution; affording the poor, the fatherless and the widow, a means of saving a portion of their scanty earnings, which might otherwise have been thoughtlessly wasted and scattered to the winds; and of gathering in time, by little and little, a sum, which in some unforeseen exigency, may prove a source to them of unspeakable comfort and advantage.

Woburn Gas Light Company.— Incorporated 1854: Gas works built, 1855. Commenced making gas, January 10, 1856. D. D. Hart, President in 1867; Aaron Thompson, Treasurer.[29]

A most useful association, though of modern origin; which, by the gas its managers produce, renders the streets of Woburn passable with comfort and safety by night, as well as by day; and furnishes the means of lighting up halls, and places of popular resort in the evening with a brilliant light, which largely contributes to the ease and pleasure with which public speakers

[29] Communication of N. Wyman, Esq., town clerk.

may be heard on various interesting occasions, by the crowds who assemble to listen to their addresses.

MASONIC INSTITUTIONS.

Mount Horeb Lodge.— Instituted in 1856: contains at present (1867) about eighty members. T. G. DAVIS, Master; C. K. CONN, Secretary.[30]

Good Samaritan Lodge. — Instituted October 17, 1865; No. of members, two hundred and fifty. GEORGE H. WOODSIDE, C. T.; FREDERIC W. ELLIS, Secretary.[30]

FIRE DEPARTMENT.

An Act of the Legislature, 1851, establishing a Fire Department in Woburn, was accepted April 7, 1851.[31]

"The Woburn Fire Department is organized as follows:

"Chief Engineer and four assistant engineers.

"Steam Fire Engine, 'Woburn No. 1,' built by the Amoskeag Manufacturing Company, Manchester, N. H.; in charge of an engineer, fireman and driver.

"'Independent' Hose Company, No. 1, consists of twenty members. They have charge of a beautiful four-wheeled hose carriage, built by Button, of New York, and 1,200 feet serviceable hose.

"Hook and Ladder Company, No. 1, consists of fifteen members. They have a serviceable truck, well supplied with hooks, ladders, ropes, rakes, axes, etc. These three companies are located on Railroad Street.

"'*Jacob Webster*' Engine Company, No. 2, consists of thirty-nine members. They have a very good Howard & Davis hand engine, and all the apparatus usual with such machines. This company is at North Woburn.

"Washington Engine Company, No. 3, consists of one hundred and seventeen members. They have a machine the exact counterpart of No. 2. This company is at Cummingsville.

---

[30] Communication of N. Wyman, Esq., town clerk.
[31] Town Records, Vol. XVII., p. 332.

"Niagara Engine, No. 1, is at present without a company; but is kept in good order, and can be used in an emergency. It is kept in the basement of the First Congregational Meeting-house."

"From JOHN L. PARKER."[32]

CHARITABLE READING SOCIETY.

Lastly (though it be not the least of the numerous benevolent associations in Woburn), must be noticed the "Charitable Reading Society of Woburn, connected with the First Congregational Church." This society originated with a young lady, who, conceiving a strong desire to see established in Woburn an association for self-improvement and doing good to others, similar to one whose good fruits she had witnessed in Boston during the winter of 1814–15, communicated her desire on her return to another young lady of Woburn, of a kindred spirit. These two combined, and drew up a skeleton constitution for such a society as they wished for, which they submitted to their pastor, Rev. Mr. Chickering, for his revision; and when they received it from his hands amended and approved, they immediately put it in circulation through the town for signatures. It was speedily returned to them, with the addition of thirty names besides their own. And then, agreeably to an article of the constitution, they met at the Town Hall, on Wednesday P. M., June 21, 1815, to organize. At that meeting, they elected their pastor's wife, Mrs. Betsey Chickering, for their President; and chose all the other requisite officers in due form: and though within five months from their organization, they and the whole community were afflicted with poignant grief by the death of their lovely and beloved President, yet they did not give way to discouragement. The society still lived; the vacancy caused by their President's death was in due time filled by the election of Mrs. Mary B. Wyman; and before the first year of the society had expired, thirty-three new members were added to their list.

The rules and customs of this society were, to meet once a

[32] Communicated by Nathan Wyman, Esq., September 24, 1867.

month either at the house of some member, or in the room over the porch of the Congregational meeting-house, then used as a Town Hall; to open each meeting with reading a portion from the Scriptures, and to offer prayer from a prayer-book procured for them by Rev. Mr. Chickering: but this form of devotional exercise was at an early period exchanged for extempore prayer. Then followed the appointment of committees to search out and to visit the poor, sick and infirm; the hearing of reports of committees previously appointed for this purpose; and the granting of needed relief from funds raised principally, at first, from a monthly contribution by each member of sixty cents each. Next followed reading, by one or more of the members, portions of some interesting and instructive publications, such as Blair's Sermons, Hunter's Sacred Biography, Mason on Self Knowledge, Mary Lundie Duncan, Lady Huntington, Parsons Cooke on Benevolence, and occasionally extracts from the Boston Recorder or Panoplist, the Missionary Herald, and "various magazines and reports, calculated to raise the standard of benevolence by apprising us of the world's want and wretchedness."

This society celebrated its fiftieth anniversary, 21st June, 1865, in the First Congregational Church, with the mutual friendly greetings of its members both resident and from abroad, and with appropriate exercises and addresses. From the proceedings on that occasion, which were afterwards published, it appears, that during the fifty years of the society's existence then completed, a total of $2,500 had been raised in money, and paid out for various benevolent objects. Of this sum, $817 had been bestowed on the poor about home, beside clothing and other necessaries not counted; a large share had been used in fitting out children for the Sunday School; several promising young men had been assisted in their efforts to obtain a liberal education; ministers, churches and colleges in straitened circumstances had been helped; contributions had been made to several Missionary Societies, both domestic and foreign; and certain missionaries in foreign lands had received benefactions; the Christian Commission, the Sanitary Commission, Sabbath School Missions, the Freedman's Aid Society, and the Congregational Aid Society, had all tasted the bounty of the Charitable Reading Society of Woburn. Nor must it be forgotten or overlooked that this society was the immediate instrument, under God, of getting up the sabbath school in the First Congregational Society within three years from its own organization. At a meeting, May 6, 1818, several members expressed themselves as anxious to establish a sabbath school, but no vote was taken. June 3d, it was voted to establish one. A special meeting for this purpose was called, to be held June 17th, at the Town Hall. A Constitution, which had been prepared, was then read twice, adopted, and a board of managers (three of whom were living at the late anniversary meeting) and a board of twelve lady teachers were chosen.

Presidents of this Society for the first fifty years.

1815. Mrs. BETSEY CHICKERING.
1816. Mrs. MARY B. WYMAN.
1818, 20. Mrs. SARAH CHICKERING.
1819. Miss SUSAN CLAPP ?
1821. Mrs. E. LEATHE.
1822–Feb. 1846. Mrs. MARY BENNETT.
1846–47–48. Mrs. CELINDA THOMPSON.
1849–50–51. Mrs. ANNA B. THOMPSON.
1852–53–54. Mrs. N. B. GRAMMER.
1855. Mrs. A. G. CARTER.[33]

In reviewing the statements presented in this chapter, showing the advances which Woburn has made this century thus far, in matters pertaining to the present comfort and respectability, and to the future happiness of all her inhabitants, well may her aged citizens exclaim, What hath God wrought for us! How many, and how beneficial have been the changes which He in his kind Providence has accomplished for this place! Be thankful, my friends, if in any measure he has employed you as his instruments for effecting so much for the cause of humanity, and for the promotion of your own benefit, and that of your children, and

---

[33] Proceedings at celebration of fiftieth anniversary, 1865.

children's children, yet unborn. Ascribe praise and thanksgiving to him for the honorable distinction He has thus bestowed on you. While life is spared, and your opportunities are lengthened out, still labor to be continuing and multiplying and increasing the benefits conferred by you on this place of your nativity or long continued residence. Encourage those, who are rising up to take the places you have so creditably filled, to pursue a course like to that which you have followed, and which, with the smiles of Heaven, has resulted in so much good to yourselves and to them: that when you quit this stage of action, others whom you leave behind may call you blessed; may praise God for you, and for others of a like spirit who have gone before you, and say, Behold the men by whom Woburn has been built up!

Young men of Woburn, allow an old man who wishes you all well, for your fathers' sake as well as your own, to address you with a few words of congratulation and advice. You are about to enter on the cultivation of fields in which others have wrought before you; to reap the fruits of their toil, and to enjoy the privileges and advantages which they have labored to procure or prolong to you. I rejoice in the happy lot which has fallen to you, and which, it may be truly said, far exceeds that of hundreds, nay thousands of others, even in this favored land. But remember that of them to whom much is given, much will be required.

Be thankful then to God for the auspicious circumstances under which you enter upon the duties and cares and labors of life. Resolve, in his strength (which daily implore), that the choice favors you inherit shall not diminish or turn to no account in your hands. Improve well the means of enlarging your knowledge, which your predecessors have so liberally provided. Accustom yourselves to the active, industrious habits which you have observed in them. In transacting the business of your several callings, and in all your dealings with others around you, use those methods only which the wise and good before you have sanctioned by their instructions and example. Imbibe and cherish that public spirit which they have manifested in aiming at the good of others, as well as their own, in the various sacrifices and generous exertions they have made. In a word, assured of the intimate, inseparable connection there is between religious, virtuous principle and action, with all real, lasting prosperity, both private and public (a truth which you have seen illustrated and proved in so many instances of actual fact, in the foregoing history), make it your habitual concern to shun what is base and dishonorable, to practise whatsoever things are pure, just, lovely and of good report; and to seek to prosper in your several worldly employments in those ways only which are enjoined by the precepts and recommended by the example of the meek and lowly Jesus, and by the gospel of his grace. So may you confidently expect that the God of Heaven, the God of your fathers, your own God, will guide and keep, prosper and bless you in all your affairs and concerns; will make all things work for your good; will give you the satisfaction, as you proceed in your earthly course, of seeing the continued and increasing prosperity of this place of your abode, as being the result, in some good degree, under God, of your benevolent efforts; and before you pass away, will impart to you joy unspeakable in reflecting that you have not lived in vain; that you have employed your time and talents and means for good, in promoting the designs of their Divine Author, and so as to secure through the Saviour his everlasting approbation and reward.

APPENDIX

TO

HISTORY OF WOBURN.

APPENDIX, No. I.

Town Orders for Woburn, agreed upon by the Commissioners at their first Meeting, December 18, 1640.

[Omitting the Preamble.]

"It is required that all persons admitted to be Inhabitance in the said Towne shall by voluntary Agreement subscribe to these Orders following; upon which Condistion, they are admited.

"*First Order for Sixpenc an Acre.*" "For the caring one [carrying on] Common Charges, all such persons as shall bee thought meete to haue land and admittance for Inhabitance, shall paye for every Acre of land formerly layd out by Charlestowne, but now in the limmets of Woburne, six pence; and for all hereafter layd out, twelve pence.

"*Second Order: to returne their lotts, if not improved in* 15 *months.*" "Every person taking lott or land in the said Towne shall within fiueteen monthes after the laying out of the same, bulde [build] for dwelling therone, and improve the said land by planting ether in part or in whole; or surrender the same upp to the towne againe: also they shall not make sale of it to any person but such as the Towne shall approve of."

"*Thurd Order: about fencing.*" "That all manner of persons shall fence their Catell of all sorts ether by fence or keeper: only it is Required all garden plots and orchards shall bee well inclosed ether by pale or otherwayes."

"*ffourth Order about Inmats.*" "That Noe maner of person shall entertayne Inmate, ether married or other, for longer time than three days, without the consent of fower [four] of the Select-men: Every person ofending in this perticqler [particular] shall paye to the use of the Towne for every day they offend herein six pence."

fiuft Order: about timber." "That noe person shall sell or cutt any younge Oake lyke to bee good timber, under eaight inches square, upon forfitur [forfeiture] of fiue shillings for euery such offence."

"*These Persons subscribed to these Orders.*"

"Edward Johnson	John Carter
Edward Conuars	Jams Conuars
John Mousall	Danill Bacon
Ezekill Richison	Edward Winne
Samuwell Richison	Henery Bolden
Thomas Richison	ffrances Kendall
William Lernedt	John Teed
James Thomson	Henery Tottingham
John Wright	Richerd Lowden
Michall Bacon	Will. Greene
John Seers	Benjamen Butterffeild
John Wyman	Henery Jefts
ffrances Wyman	Jams Parker
Mr Thomas Graues	John Russell
Nicholas Dauis	Jams Britten
Nicholas Treerice	Thomas ffuller." [1]

APPENDIX, No. II.

Lines in Verse by Capt. Edward Johnson,

Referring to the difficulties encountered by him and the other Commissioners for the Settlement of Woburn, and prefixed by him to the Town Records, Vol. I., p. 1.

"Records For The Towne of Woburne,

ffrom the year 1640 : the 8 : day of th : 10 month :

Paulisper Fui."

In peniles [pennyless] age I Woburne Towne began :
Charls Towne first mou'd the Court my lins to span :
To vewe my land place, Compild body [to] reare,
Nowell, Sims, Sedgwick, thes my patrons were.
Sum fearing I'le grow great upon these grounds,
Poore I wase putt to nurs among the Clownes;
Who being taken with such myghty things
As had bin work of Noble Queeins and Kings,

---

[1] Woburn Records, Vol. I., p. 2.

Till Babe gan crye and great disturbance make,
Nurses Repent they did her undertake.
One [1] leaues her quite; another [2] hee doth hie
To foren lands free from the Baby's crye:
To [two] [3] more of seauen, seeing nursing prou'd soe thwarte,
Thought it more ease in following of the Carte.
A naighbour by, [4] hopeing the Babe wold bee
A pritty Girle, to rocking her went hee.
Too [two] [5] nurses less undanted then [than] the rest
ffirst howses ffinish: thus the Girle gane drest.
Its' rare to see how this poore Towne did rise
By weakest means: two [too] weake in great ones Eys:
And sure it is, that mettells' deere Exstraction
Had neuer share in this poore Town's Erextion;
Without which metall and sum fresh supplys [supplies]
Patrons conclud she neuer upp wold rise.
If ever she mongst ladys haue a station,
Say 'twas ffrom Parents, not her education.
And now conclud the Lord's owne hand it was,
That with weak means did bring this work to pass;
Not only Towne, but Sister Church to [too] ade [add]
Which out of dust and ashes now is had.
Then all inhabit Woburne Towne, stay make
The Lord, not means, of all you undertake.

[Woburn Records, Vol. I., p. 1.]

APPENDIX, No. III.

Old and New Style.

The distinction between Old Style and New owes its origin to the difference in length between the *Julian year* and the *Solar.* The Julian year (so named from Julius Cæsar, who instituted this way of reckoning time) consisted of 365 days and 6 hours; making three consecutive years of 365 days each, and the one next following of 366 days, to be equivalent to four years of the above denomination. The Julian year was in general use throughout Christendom, in the computation of time, from the sitting of the Nicene Council, A. D. 325, till A. D. 1582. It

---

1 Ezekiel Richardson. 2 Thomas Graves.
3 Samuel and Thomas Richardson? 4 Edward Johnson.
5 Edward Convers, built at the Mill; and John Mousall, on "Hilly Way."

was then ascertained by accurate observation, that it exceeded the Solar year (or that which was measured by the apparent annual motion of the sun from one point till his return to the same point again) a little more than eleven minutes. This excess, amounting to a day in about 131 years, or to three days in 400 years, had arisen, in 1582, to about ten days since the Nicene Council, A. D. 325, when the vernal equinox was on March 21st, but was now thrown back to March 11th. As this change had caused derangement in the computation of Easter day, that great festival of the Church, which was regulated by the day on which that equinox occurred, Pope Gregory XIII., the then Roman pontiff, ordered that ten days should be omitted in the Calendar reckoning, thus restoring the vernal equinox to its old place in the Calendar, the 21st of March. And to prevent a recurrence of the error, he further directed, that the Bissextile or Leap year should be omitted thrice every four hundred years, viz: in each centennial year, the two first figures of which could not be divided by four without a remainder, as A. D. 1700, 1800, and 1900, and be reckoned only in those centennial years which could bear such division, as A. D. 1600 and 2000. This method of computing time was called, from its author, the Gregorian, or otherwise, the New Style; and was speedily adopted in all or most Catholic countries. But in Great Britain, the Julian or Old Style was still retained; and the year 1700 being considered there as a Leap year, the difference between the Old and the New Style was now increased to eleven days. But in 1752, New Style was adopted in Great Britain and its American dependencies; and the Calendar was corrected by dropping eleven days in September; thus bringing it into conformity with the Gregorian Calendar. But in Russia, Old Style is still continued; and the year 1800 having consequently been accounted there as a Leap year, the difference in that empire between Old Style and New is grown to be twelve days. From the above statements, it is plain, that to reduce dates in England and this country from Old Style to New, ten days must be added for events that occurred between 1600 and 1700; and eleven days for such as took place between 1700 and the adoption of New

Style in Great Britain and its American Colonies in 1752. The landing at Plymouth, for instance, was on December 11, 1620, Old Style, answering to December 21st, New Style. And the birthday of Washington occurring February 11, 1732, Old Style, its date in New Style is February 22d.

Moreover, in countries which adopted the New Style at its introduction in 1582, the year began with January 1st; whereas, in Great Britain and its American colonies, March was anciently regarded as the first month of the new year, and January and February as the eleventh and twelfth months of the year preceding. For instance, the first choice of Selectmen in Woburn is recorded to have taken place on the 13th of the 2d month, (April 13th,) 1644; the second choice on the 19th of 12th month, "1644" (viz: 19th of February, 1644–5); and the third choice, on the 3d of the 1st month, (3d of March,) 1646. [1]

But though March was then called in England and its dependencies the first *month* of the year, yet in the eye of the law the first *day* of the year was not till March 25th, or Lady Day. Accordingly, Governor Winthrop, in writing to his wife from aboard the Arbella, as he was about to sail for New England, dates his letter March 22, 1629; and yet dates another letter, written to her from aboard the same ship only six days after, March 28, 1630.[2]

Again, events that took place before 1752, between March 1st and March 25th, were designated in England and this country by a double date, as March 10th, $\frac{1745}{1746}$; for though they happened in the first month of the new year, yet the law regarded them as having taken place in the old year; so that they were practically accounted as belonging to a period of time that was common to both years. And for a like reason, the custom of double dating came, at length, to be extended to events in January and February, as occurring in the year preceding, according to Old Style, and in the year following, according to the New.

---

[1] Woburn Records, Vol. I., pp. 6–8.

[2] Winthrop's History, by Savage, Vol. I., Appendix, pp. 440, 441.

APPENDIX, No. IV.

Church Covenant.

The Covenant agreed upon by the founders of the Church of Woburn in 1642, and copied from Johnson's Wonderworking Providence, in the account given of the gathering of this church in Chapter I. of this History, appears to have continued unchanged till 1756, when the following was adopted, probably on the recommendation of Rev. Mr. Sherman, the junior pastor: the Records containing the original covenant being then unaccountably missing or lost.

The Covenant of the Church of Christ in Woburn, April the 6th 1756.

"We whose names are hereunto subscribed, apprehending ourselves called of God into a Church State of the Gospel, do first of all confess ourselves unworthy to be so highly favoured of the Lord, and admire that rich & free grace of his that triumphs over so great unworthiness, and with an humble reliance upon the aids of grace therein promised to those who, through a sense of their own inability to do any good thing, do humbly wait on him for all, we do thankfully lay hold on his Covenant, and chuse the things that please him.

1. "We avouch the Lord to be our God, and give up ourselves and our Seed after us in their generations to be his people, in the truth and sincerity of our hearts.

2ly. "We give up ourselves to the Lord Jesus Christ, to be ruled and guided by him in the matters of his worship, and in our whole conversation; acknowledging him not only our alone Saviour, but our King to reign and rule over us, and our Prophet and teacher by his word and Spirit; forsaking all other teachers and doctrines which he has not commanded; and we do wholly disclaim our own righteousness in point of Justification, and depend alone upon him for righteousness and Life, Grace and Glory.

3ly. "We do profess ourselves to be Congregational in our Judgment, and do purpose to practise upon Congregational principles, as far as they are agreeable to the doctrines of God's word, looking upon the Platform of Discipline in general, as gathered out of the word of God, and agreeing therewith.

4ly. "We do further promise, by the help of Christ, to walk with our brethren and sisters of this Congregation [1] in the spirit of brotherly love, watching over them, and caring for them; avoiding all jealousies, suspicions, backbitings, censurings, quarrelings and secret risings of heart against them; forgiving and forbearing, and yet seasonably admonishing and restoring them by a spirit of meekness, and setting them in joynt again that have been overtaken in any fault amongst us.

5ly. "We further promise and bind ourselves in the strength of Christ to labour how we may advance the Gospel and Kingdom of Christ; how we may win and gain them that are without, how we may settle grace and peace amongst ourselves: and seek as much as we can the peace of all the Churches; seeking the help, counsel and direction of other churches, if need be; not putting a stumbling block before any, but will labour to abstain from all appearance [of evil].

6ly. "We do hereby promise to behave and demean ourselves obediently in all lawfull things to those that God hath or shall place over us in the Church or Commonwealth; knowing that it is our duty not to grieve them, but to encourage them in their places, and in the administration of the charge which God hath committed unto them.

7ly. "We Resolve, by the help and strength of God, to approve ourselves in our particular callings as becometh saints: shunning idleness, not sloathfull in business, knowing that idleness is the bane of any Society: Neither will we deal h[ardly] or oppressingly with any wherein we are the Lord's stewards. And further? [finally] we promise to dedicate our Children to God, and to teach them the good knowledge of God the Lord, according to the best of our abilities, and to fear and serve him with us, that it may be well with them and us forever.

"These things we solemnly promise, as in the presence of the omniscient Jehovah."

Entered here by Jabez Richardson." Chh. Rec. Vol. I., p. 3.

On the page of the Records next following the above Covenant is the annexed List of subscribers to it, or otherwise, of the male members of the Church at the time of its adoption.

---

[1] That is, "*of this Church.*" Anciently, the word Congregation was often used, as synonymous with Church.

" The Rev^{d}. Mr John Fox
The Rev^{d}. Mr Josiah Sherman
Deacon Josiah Peirce
Deacon Samuel Eames
Samuel Neauards [Nevers]
David Wyman
Nathan Wyman
Jacob Richardson
John Holdwin [Holden]
William Tay
Samuel Kendall
Edward Walker
Nathan Richardson
Benjamin Richardson
Isaac Snow
Joseph Wright
John Wright
Thomas Richardson
Thomas Wright
Ebenezer Brooks
Josiah Parker
Josiah Johnson."

Church Records, Vol. I., p. 4.

Covenant of Admission into the Church of Woburn.

At a meeting of the Church, 1768, November 13th, " Voted that the following Covenant, or Confession of Faith, should be made use of, and consented to, by all who are received as Members of this Church.

The Church Covenant.

" You do now solemnly and sincerely give up yourself and yours to God in the Lord Jesus Christ, according to the Covenant of Grace, to be for him, and him only; resolving and engaging to make the Word of God the rule of your faith and practice [as it is explained in our well-known Catechism composed by the Assembly of Divines at Westminster]. You do take the ever blessed Jehovah for your chief good and last End. You do take the Lord Jesus Christ for your Prophet, Priest and King; the Holy Ghost for your Sanctifier, Leader and Comforter: promising, by the help of God, to walk before him in holiness and righteousness all your days. You do also put yourself under the care and watch of this Church, and the government of Christ herein; and promise to attend duly on the holy Ordinances of Christ here administered for your edification in faith and holiness. This you solemnly engage and promise before God, Angels, and this Assembly.

"Then I signify to you, in the name and with the concurrence of this Church, that we receive you into our sacred Fellowship and Communion; and do promise, through Christ's assistance, to watch over you, and carry ourselves towards you with such brotherly affection and Christian regard, as the Rules of the Gospel demand and enjoin in such a relation. This we do, imploring our Lord Jesus Christ, that both we and you may be found faithful in his Covenant, and may have grace to serve him with that holiness which becomes his House forever.

"I now declare you to be a member of this Church in full Communion —" *Church Records, Vol.* 1, *p.* 70.

The words enclosed in brackets in the above Covenant were erased by vote of the Church, June 27, 1785. See Church Records, p. 34. And in this altered form, it continued to be used at admissions as late as 1809.[1] Previously to admission and entering into Covenant, however, candidates, it is understood, were required in 1838, and before, to give their assent to the following Confession of Faith, which is of more recent adoption in this Church, viz:

Confession of Faith.

"You believe there is but one God, the Creator, Preserver, and Governor of the Universe; a Being self-existent and immutable, infinite in power, wisdom, justice, goodness, mercy, and truth.

"You believe that the Scriptures of the Old and New Testament were given by the inspiration of God, and are a perfect rule of faith and practice.

"You believe that God is revealed in the Scriptures as the Father, the Son, and the Holy Ghost; and that these three are one, and in all divine attributes equal.

"You believe that God made all things for himself; that known unto him are all his works from the beginning; that he governs all things according to the counsel of his own will; and that the principles and administration of his government are perfectly holy, just, and good.

"You believe that God created man holy, and that he fell from his happy state by sinning against God; that, in consequence of the fall, mankind are born without holiness, and continue alienated from God, until renewed and reconciled by the Holy Spirit.

"You believe that God, as an act of pure mercy, gave his Son to die for the sins of the world, and that Jesus Christ, by his sufferings and death, has made an atonement sufficient for the redemption of all mankind; so that God can be just and the justifier of him that believeth; and that upon condition of repentance and of faith in our Lord Jesus Christ, pardon and eternal life are sincerely offered to all.

"You believe that mankind do, of their own accord, refuse to

---

[1] Chickering's Dedication Sermon, Appendix, p. 27.

comply with these conditions, to the aggravation of their guilt and condemnation; but that God, notwithstanding he perceived how mankind would treat the Gospel of his Son, did always purpose to save from deserved ruin, great multitudes of the human race, through sanctification of the Spirit and belief of the truth.

"You believe that without a change of heart by the special agency of the Holy Spirit, no one can be an heir of eternal life.

"You believe in the necessity of such repentance for sin, as arises from supreme love to God; and of such faith in Jesus Christ, as includes an affectionate submission to him and reliance upon him for pardon and eternal life.

"You believe that men are dependent upon God to give repentance and faith, because they are voluntarily and obstinately opposed to their duty; and that the influence of the Holy Spirit is bestowed, not as a reward of antecedent merit, or well doing on the part of him who receives it, but as a free gift of God; and yet that this influence of the Spirit is ordinarily so inseparably connected with the careful use of means by the sinner, as creates entire obligation and ample encouragement to attend upon them, and renders all hopes of conversion in the neglect of means eminently presumptuous.

"You believe that there will be a resurrection of the dead, both of the just and of the unjust, when all must stand before the judgment seat of Christ, and receive a sentence of retribution, according to the deeds done in the body; and that the wicked will go into punishment, and the righteous into life, both of which will never end.

"Moreover you believe, that in this world the Lord Jesus Christ has a visible Church, the terms of admission to which are a public profession of faith in Christ, sustained by credible evidence; that Baptism and the Lord's Supper are ordinances to be observed in the Church to the end of the world; that none but members of the visible church, in regular standing, have a right to partake of the Lord's Supper.

All these things you truly confess and cordially believe.

(Those who have not been baptized, here receive the ordinance of Baptism.)

You will now enter into Covenant with God, and with this Church.

(For Covenant, see above.)

APPENDIX, No. V.

Whence Woburn Derived its Name.[1]

Curiosity may prompt the inquiry, Why was the town at its incorporation called Woburn? Was it not (it may be asked in reply) from respect for Hon. Richard Russell, who came to Charlestown in 1640, from Herefordshire, England, and quickly took rank among the prominent and most influential citizens not only of Charlestown, (which he represented in the General Court, in 1643,) but throughout the Colony, of which he was many years an assistant, and the treasurer from 1645 till his death in 1676? This distinguished gentleman, it may be plausibly supposed, was a relative of the noble family of the Russells, in Bedfordshire, England, who had long been settled at Woburn, in that County, and were proprietors of Woburn Abbey, or of a palace built on its site, which they made their home. If this conjecture be correct, the giving to this town of the name it bears admits of an easy explanation. When Charlestown Village was to be incorporated, in 1642, and it was asked by the Court, What name it should be known by? the members from Charlestown, viz: Hon. Increase Nowell, of the Assistants, Capt. Robert Sedgwick and Mr. Francis Willoughby, Deputies for the September Session, or either of them, may be readily conceived to have proposed the name of Woburn, out of regard to their newly arrived but highly valued fellow-citizen, Richard Russell, and also with a view to perpetuate in this town the name of the favorite residence of his noble relatives in the mother country.

Woburn, in England, is described as follows in the "Complete System of Geography," London 1747:

"Woburn in the Hundred of Manshead is of chief Note for the Palace of the Duke of Bedford, where stood the ancient Abbey, which was founded Anno 1145; and for a Canal before it, that carries a Yacht of thirty or forty Tons, and several smaller pleasure Boats. The 19th. of June 1724, above a hundred of its Houses were burnt down, which are since neatly rebuilt, and a fine Market place erected, intirely at the Expence of the Duke of Bedford; so that the Town makes a handsome Appearance. Here is a Free-school founded by Francis [Russell] Earl of Bedford; and a Charity School for thirty Boys, who are both cloth'd and taught, founded and maintain'd by Wriothesley late Duke of Bedford and his Duchess."

Vol. I. Bedfordshire, p. 132, folio.

---

[1] Chap. 1, Note 26.

APPENDIX, NO. VI.

Land of Nod.

See History, Chapter I., Note 38.

The 3,000 acres given up by Woburn, in exchange for land received from Charlestown, according to the final agreement between the two towns, concluded upon July 29, 1650, lay at the northern extremity of the four miles square, adjoining Andover, and within the limits of what is now Wilmington. Though the rights of property in it were yielded to Charlestown, yet for all municipal control and regulations, it was considered as still within the bounds of Woburn. It was called "the land of Nod;" a name probably suggested, (as Hon. Richard Frothingham happily conjectures in his History of Charlestown, No. 3, p. 111) "by a comparison of its forlorn condition, so far remote from Church ordinances, with the Nod to which Cain wandered, when he went from the presence of the Lord, Genesis IV." And by this name it was long known, and still is, by many of Wilmington, at the present day.

This tract of land continued for years in a neglected, uncultivated state. Its precise location, by suitable metes and bounds, was not determined till June 1671; and it was not till September 1674, that Woburn formally resigned her propriety in it, according to the following certificate in Woburn Records:

"The 21 of September, Seventy fower, Charlstowne men, Mr William Sims and Edward Wilson, in the behalfe of the propryetors of the land of Node, did goe with Woburne Committee, and resaiue their three thousand Acres in the land of Nod, according to bounds giuen under their hands upon Record, bearing date the 20: of the 4 mo. [20 June] 71; with which bounds they were fully sattisfied."—*Woburn Records, Vol. I., p.* 54.

But how happened it that these 3,000 acres were surrendered, not to Charlestown, to which it was given in exchange by Woburn in 1650, but to the proprietors of the land of Nod? and who were these proprietors? It seems that in 1643, one year only after the incorporation of Woburn, and seven years before the mutual agreement between Charlestown and Woburn, in regard to their respective bounds, etc., etc., was entered into, Charlestown, considering the land of Nod as already her own, (in consequence, probably, of some previous understanding between the two towns,) parcelled it out among twelve of her prominent citizens, in the following proportions, viz:—

To Robert Sedgwick	was granted	300	acres.
Zechariah Symmes	"	300	"
Thomas Allen	"	300	"
Richard Russell	"	300	"
Francis Willoughby	"	300	"
John Allen	"	300	"
William Stitson	"	250	"
William Phillips	"	200	"
Ralph Woory	"	200	"
Robert Cooke	"	250	"
Thomas Graves	"	250	"
Mr. Barnard	"	200	"[1]

But these gentlemen held the land thus given them but in low estimation. Several of them surrendered back their respective grants to the town again. And of the grants thus relinquished, Charlestown in 1652 bestowed five hundred acres upon Francis Norton. Subsequently, Francis Willoughby bought the shares of Francis Norton and John Allen, which, added to his own, made 1,100 acres. In 1683, May 1st, Lawrence Hammond, who had married Francis Willoughby's widow, sold these 1,100 acres to John Hull, of Boston; who dying in September of the same year, his rights in Nod fell to Samuel Sewall, (afterwards Judge Sewall,) who had married Hull's daughter and only heir; and who, for some years, was accustomed to lease a portion of the meadow in Nod, and to receive rent for it. Hearing of this, Charlestown appointed a committee to examine into its rights in Nod. In their Report, dated December 25, 1704, this committee say: "We are informed that there are several per-

[1] Frothingham's Charlestown, No. 3, p. 112.

sons that claim part of that tract of land (Nod) which we cannot allow of: for we are very well satisfied, that this tract of land was originally the land that Woburn exchanged with Charlestown for lands then belonging to Charlestown; and we cannot find any record that this land was ever legally conveyed to any particular person." The town accepted this Report; and conceiving itself agreeably to it to be the rightful owner of all the territory in dispute, leased to two individuals the whole of the meadow contained in it. This assumption by Charlestown was resisted by Judge Sewall, who wrote as follows to one of the lessees above referred to:

"BOSTON, June 6. 1705.

"Friend: I am informed that some Charlestown Gentlemen have lately Lett to you and Henry Holt of Andover all the Meadow belonging to the Land of Nod. These are to acquaint you that I have a good Right to above a third part of the said Meadow, and am in the actual Improvement of it. I made a Lease of it to Thomas Asten of Andover the 28th. of August last for eleven years. I Lett it before to Oliver Holt by Lease in writing; and for many years before, I Lett it out to others, and received the rent. My Interest in that Land cost a great deal of Money. My Deed is Acknowledged, and has been upon Record above Twenty Year. I have an honest and legal Right: which I acquaint you with, to prevent your giving my Tenant any disturbance: and Rest

"Your loving friend, S. S.

"Let your partner in the Lease see what I say to you."

" Sent by Peirson Richardson."[2]

In consequence, apparently, of this step taken by Judge Sewall, Charlestown commenced an action at law against him. The case was tried at Cambridge, before a Special Court, September 18, 1705; and again, upon the appeal of Charlestown, before the Superior Court of the Province at Cambridge, July 29, 1706; and on both occasions, the decision was in Sewall's favor.[3] Thus the rights of individual proprietors to portions of the land were legally confirmed; and Charlestown was found to be entitled to only a part of Nod, and not the whole, as it had recently claimed. At a meeting of the Proprietors, at Charlestown, April 14, 1718, it was voted to divide

[2] Sewall's Letter Book, p. 174.

[3] Sewall's Diary.

the whole 3,000 acres; and Capt. Joseph Burnap, of Reading, a noted Surveyor, was employed to do it.[3] The work was accomplished by him November 10, 1718; and on November 25th, Capt. Burnap presented to the Proprietors at Charlestown a Plan of the whole, divided into Shares.[3] Lot No. 1 of 300 acres fell to Judge Sewall, who sold it to Samuel Dummer, Esq., a brother or near relative of Lieut.- Gov. William Dummer, Esq.; and acknowledged the deed of it March 9, 1726-7.[3] Other proprietors doubtless parted with their interest in it from time to time in a like way. And "a vote of Charlestown May 10. 1742 indicates that a part of the town's share of it has been sold; and a Committee was then authorized to sell the remainder." [1]

APPENDIX, No. VII.

1. Letter of Major Convers to Governor Joseph Dudley.

[Superscription.]

"For His Exc^{y}. Joseph Dudly, Esqr. Captn. Gen^{ll}. Gou^{r}. In Chiefe, &c.

"These.

"Woob^{n}. August 14th, 1704.

"May it pleas Your Exc^{y}.

"I Received Your Excel^{s}. Order of y^{e}. 10th, Courrant, I Rec^{d}. it y^{e}. same day about 4 in y^{e}. afternoone, for the detaching 45 Soldiers &c: and to post y^{m}. in 3 squadrons under y^{e}. Comand of a Sarg^{t}. to Each, viz. Groaton, Lanchester & Malburow. I forthwith sent out my Warrants to all y^{e}. touns in y^{e}. Lower Regam^{t}; the Soldiers were all Impress^{d} y^{t}. night and y^{e}. 11th day and began to March, the 12 day I went and posted them according to Order, Giueing the sarg^{ts}. written Orders to obserue till further Orders, directing them to take advice of the Capt^{s}. of the Respectiue touns:

"At Malburow, John Benjamin sarg^{t}. 15 men }
"Lanchester, Benjamin Wilson sarg^{t}. 14 men } 45.
"Groaton, Joseph Child, sarg^{t}. 16 men }

here is y^{e}. whole Number Your Excelencey sent for, posted according to order. I think there are too many garrasons in every toune. If these men be Reposted, one at a garrason, and two at another, I shall account my labour lost, and y^{e}. men next to thrown away, Saving alwayes, what is in Obedience to Your Exc^{s}. Comand there is nothing lost or thrown away.

"Exc^{t}. S^{r}. I pray for a gracious pardon, and am

"Your Very Humble Ready and Obedient Servt.

JAMS. CONVERSE."

2. LETTER OF MAJOR JAMES CONVERS TO JOSEPH DUDLEY, ESQ., GOVERNOR, &C.

[Superscription.]

"To His Excel^{y}. Joseph Dudley, Esqr. Captn. Gen^{ll}. and Govern^{r}. in Chief &c These.—

"For her Maj^{ts}. Service."

"Woobourne: Jan: 27th. 1704. [1704–5.

"May it pleas Your Excel^{y}.

"I Rec^{d}. Your Exc^{s}. Letter to Coll. Ting on tuseday last about ten, and [with] much a-doo I found a Snow-Shoo man, and posted it away, and it got to Coll. Tings (as I understand) about one of y^{e}. clock y^{t}. night, my meaning is, about one of y^{e}. Clock in the morning. I also Rec^{d}. your Exel^{s}. order about mustering of Sixty men to be in a Readiness at an hours Warning to march to y^{e}. assistance of y^{e}. frontiers &c: this I Rec^{d}. y^{e}. 25th. in y^{e}. night, y^{e}. 26. I prosecuted it as far as I could: I haue not been so far as y^{e}. next Neighbours hous this fortnight, we cannot goe on horsback nor a foot, the snow is so exseeding deep, but I writ Warrants and sent by my lad to Capt. Johnson and other officers to Rais about sixty, but knowing y^{t}. there was not one third of y^{t}. number of Snow shoos in toune, and most of y^{m}.

troopers y^t. liue at the farms, I sent therefore to y^e. troop officers that are in our toune to muster y^m. and I hope Your Exc^y. will exscuse me, I sent to Maj^r. Sweyne to provide 35 or 40 more, to be Comanded by Lt. Thos. Nichols of y^t. toune [Reading ?] If any thing could be done on horsback, I am Ready, but not else — I am not able. I doubt all these will not make aboue 20 or 30 Snow shoo men. I do not know what there is at Malden and $Charlst^n$. farms and Mistick: I know there are som at Cambridg farms and Watter towne, and they liue Neerer y^n. we, If your Exc^y. pleas to Order Coll. Phillips to look after y^m. Your Exc^y. pro [promised ?] Coll. Phillips and Coll. ffoxcroft y^t. I should be a perpetual drouge [drudge] to y^m. and so I am, I am Willing to do what I can, but not all. Wattertoune and Cambridge farms exspect a Call, pleas to let y^m. haue it. So Craueing pardon, I Humbly subscribe Your Exc^s. poore and old, but very Ready Willing Servant

"to y^e. utmost of my abillety,

"Jam^s. Converse."

APPENDIX, NO. VIII.

Writ of Mandamus.[1]

"Province of the Mass[a] Bay. Suffolk sc. } George, by the Grace of God of Great Britain, France & Ireland King, Defender of the ffaith, &c.

"To Eleazer Flegg Esqr. Joseph Wright John Fowle Josiah Converse James Peirce Yeomen all of Woburn in our County of Middlesex, Selectmen of the s^d Town, and to the said John Fowle Clerk of the said Town, Greeting.

"Whereas on the sixth day of July last past Timothy Walker of Woburn $afores^d$ $Gent^n$ was hired by you the Select men $afores^d$, to keep the Grammar School in the Town $afores^d$, for one quarter of a year, to Commence on Monday the nineteenth of the same July, at Eleven pounds money for the s^d quarter, and accordingly Entered upon y^e s^d service; and afterwards

[1] Copy of the original writ, kindly lent me by its present owner, J. Wingate Thornton, Esq., of Boston.

differences arising in the s^{d} Town concerning his appointment to ye s^{d} Office, Upon the 27th day of August last past, the s^{d} Town being convened to make their Election, and settle what schoolmaster they thought proper Elected and Voted ye s^{d} Timothy Walker to be ye School Master for the present year, he being before that approved according to Law for the afores^{d} service, And ye Moderator accordingly declared his Election, and Ordered you the Town Clerk aforesaid to Record ye Warrant for the s^{d} Meeting, and ye Election of the s^{d} Timothy Walker as afores^{d}. Whereupon ye s^{d} Timothy Walker offered to keep ye s^{d} School, Yet you the s^{d} John Fowle, to whom of right it belongs to Record ye Election afores^{d}, tho' often desired, have refused and still do refuse to do it. And you the Selectmen afores^{d}, to whom it belongs to admit the s^{d} School Master, tho' often requested have refused & still do refuse to admit ye s^{d} Timothy Walker to keep ye s^{d} Grammar School, tho' he has often offered himself to you to that End. But you have admitted and put into ye s^{d} office one Ebenezer Flegg, of Woburn afores^{d} Gent^{n} to ye great damage & grievance of the said Timothy Walker, as we have perceived by his Complaint. Whereupon he has supplicated us that we would provide him suitable Remedy in this behalf. We, therefore, willing as is just to provide for the afores^{d} Timothy Walker due & speedy Justice in this behalf, Command you, ye s^{d} John Fowle to Record ye Warrant and Election afores^{d} without delay; and you the s^{d} Selectmen to Remove ye s^{d} Eb^{r} Flegg and admit the s^{d} Timothy Walker to ye place and office of Grammar School Master of ye s^{d} Town of Woburn, without delay, or signify to us the Cause why you do not, least by your Defaults repeated Complaints come to us: And Certify to Us how you have Executed this Precept, Remitting this Writ to Us at Boston before our Justices of our Superior Court of Judicature, Court of Assize, and General Gaol Delivery at Boston within our County of Suffolk on ffriday the 15th day of October next at Eleven of the Clock in ye forenoon of ye s^{d} day. Witness Samuel Sewall, Esqr. at Boston this ninth day of September In the Twelfth year of our Reign, Annoq. Dom. 1725.

BENJ^{N} ROLFE, *Clerk*."

APPENDIX, No. IX.

Diary of Lieut. Samuel Thompson of Woburn,

A Soldier in the French War, during the year 1758.

1758 May 24. Set out from home, and went to Concord. Received the Bounty, and went to Bolton, and lodged at David Alexander's,[1] Thursday night.

25. Went to Worcester, and received our Blankets and lodged.

26. Marched to Leicester: lodged.

27. Saturday, went to Brookfield.

28. Sunday: went to Cold Spring meeting house, and lodged there.

29. Monday: march to old Hadley: lodged.

30. Tuesday afternoon; went over y^e^. ferry and lodged.

31. Wednesday: Election: took out our provision and ammunition at Northampton and lodged. A rainy storm stopped us 3 or 4 days.

June 1. Thursday: loitered all day at Northampton.

2. Friday: lazing at Northampton & lodged.

3. Saturday. Marched from Northampton into the woods for Pantoocick Fort, where we come to a tavern about ten miles from Northampton, and camped.

4. Sunday: marched all day in the woods over several Rivers.

5. Monday: bad marching, sloughs and mountains, rivers, stumps: very weary, and so camped.

6. Tuesday: marched to Pantoosick Fort about 11 o'clock, and took out bread for four days, and then went to Fort Conectecaw and camped.

7. Wednesday, marched to a Dutch place, where we got at 12 o'clock. Stopped 3 hours: then marched over several bad rivers; and poplar[2] was almost cast away. Camped in ye. wood; and Mr. Crosby's arm was put out &c.

8. Thursday: marched to the half way house by 10 o'clock, where we stopped some hours, and then marched till we came over against Albany, one mile East of the River, or thereabouts.

9. Friday: marched on the East side of Hudson River, and lost in ye. wood; but we came to ye. River again: we made but one mile good, and went seven miles as we judged; and had to creep up the banks, and had like to have lost our horse: but at last we came to....by ye. River, and lodged at Flat bush.

10. Took out store for one week 5 miles above Albany, and lodged in a barn.

11. Sunday: two sermons preached to the Soldiers. Abijah [3] had a sore throat: and we lodged in the said barn, which was every night full of Soldiers.

---

[1] A son of Philip and Joanna Alexander, born at Woburn, 7 September, 1716.

[2] "Mare named Popler."

[3] His brother Abijah, afterward Sheriff.

12. Went over to Albany, and spent the rest of ye. day, and lodged in the barn again &c &c.

13. Tuesday: Spent all day again at Flat bush, and lodged in the said barn.

14. Wednesday: drawed up in the forenoon in order to march, and marched. In the afternoon; but I went up ye. River in a battow to the Half Moon, and camped very weary.

15. Thursday: marched from the Half Moon to Stillwater, and lodged.

16. Friday, marched from Stillwater to Salletoag,[4] and camped: a mile or two beyond: we took stores for three days, and Abijah was some better. So went in Fort. . . . .

17. Saturday: from thence we went to Fort Miller, where we stayed one hour or two; and then we marched to Fort Edward by 5 oclock afternoon, and we camped in the woods.

18. Sunday: we stayed where we camped ye. night before; and we had two Sermons; and between Sermons I went over ye. river, and viewed Fort Edward, which was exceeding strong, commanded with a numerous artillery; and I returned and heard a sermon, Sun 2 hours high. At night I went down to Fort Miller with 8 men, with a packet to Major Gage. And with 8 men came up in the battow. In the same evening by 11 o'clock came to my old Camp.

19. Monday: kept at our Camp still, and lodged.

20. Took out stores at Fort Edward, and divided some of them; and camped.

21. Wednesday; divided the rest of ye stores: a smart thunder shower.

22. Thursday, I went out in a Scout of three hundred after Indians, but we found none: so we returned after 4 or 5 hours scout at seven in ye. evening. A man whipt 10 lashes.

23. Friday, at our old encampments. 24. Saturday, Still at our encampments.

25. Sunday: marched from Fort Edward to the Half Way Brook and camped. This morning, as we got to ye. Fort Edward, we heard a very smart firing half a mile in ye. wood. We thought yt. Major Rogers had found a party of ye. enemy; we expected a very smart fight: but ye. General had given leave for four or five hundred Rangers to go out and hold a bush fight for ¼ of an hour.

26. Monday; rainy morning. Camped at the Half way Brook.

27. Tuesday. Some rain. Camped at the Half way Brook.

28. Wednesday. For these some days past we have much marching; and the men keep passing along for ye. engagement every day great numbers. And this day I received a letter which caused me much joy. I had a letter from Mr. Snow that all was well; and Mr. Alexander came this day to the Half way Brook; and we camp'd within ye. Fort.

29. Thursday, three of my Mess went to ye. Lake with Capt. Jones: we camped in the Fort.

30. Friday, all day on guard in the Fort. Forces still on ye. march up to the Lake: great preparations every day. I sent a letter home.

---

[4] Saratoga.

July 1. Saturday we camped in the Fort of Pickets: again I sent a letter home.

2. Sunday, I marched up to ye. Lake with 10 men, and came back to the Halfway Brook, and right back to ye. Lake again: and on our march there was a smart thunder shower, and we were all very wet; and when we came to camp, it rained; but we made a fire, and dryed us as well as we could, and camped about half a mile this side of the Lake.

Monday, In ye. morning, we marched down to the Lake, and fetched our men; and Col. Cummings had orders to stay with 500 men to keep at the Lake, and many of our men were uneasy and sorry: we camped where General Johnson had a fight with ye. enemy; and I went to see the ruins of ye. Fort, and all ye. entrenchments that the French dug; and I see where the bombs and bullets had cut down trees and dug holes.

4. Tuesday, camped where Genl. Johnson had his fight.....

Wednesday, our Army set sail in battows for the Narrows; and the army consists of 25000 & 400 and odd men.

5. At 5 in the morning they mustered and set off as fast as they could; and we saw them till noon, and when they had got off, we struck our tents, and removed into the Fort William Henry, and set up our tents there and camped.

6. Thursday, in ye. afternoon, the Mohawks came in, and I was on guard all day. Saml. Tay took a vomit, and was ill with a bloody Flux; and I was full of business all day.

7. Friday: The Mohawks set sail for the Narrows. Abijah was sick and took a vomit. I had scarcely time to cook, as the Hampshire forces came to us in the afternoon.

8. Saturday, Post came from the Narrows; and they brought Lord How[5] to ye. Fort, who was slain at their landing; and in ye. afternoon there came in 100 and odd men, French prisoners, into the Fort.

9. Sunday morning, In a surprise by bad news from the Narrows, and all day in a Concern; for sometimes we heard that our army was defeated, and then that they did prosper and gain ground; but on the whole, our army was forced to give over their trial for the Narrows, and return to our great astonishment & amazement, and with a great loss, among the old Countrymen in a special manner, and till our army came and landed at Fort William Henry, and brought in many wounded men, and so camped that night in confusion; and the Mohawks brought in some scalps: yet our Provincials did not lose so many men as we feared we had lost. The Highlanders lost many men, and the Regulars lost many: the Jersey Blues lost many, and the Yorkers suffered in the loss of many men.

---

[5] "Howe, George, lord viscount, was the eldest son of Sir E. Scrope, second lord viscount Howe in Ireland. He commanded five thousand British troops, which arrived at Halifax in July, 1757. In the next year, when Abercrombie proceeded against Ticonderoga, in an attack on the advanced guard of the French in the woods, Lord Howe fell on the first fire, in July 1758, aged 33. In him, says Mante, 'the soul of the army seemed to expire.' By his military talents and many virtues he had acquired esteem and affection. Massachusetts erected a monument to his memory in Westminster Abbey, at the expense of 250 pounds." Allen's Biog. Dict.

10. Monday in the morning I went and viewed the wounded men; and some of them were dead, and some were taking on and complaining with pain: a wofull sight indeed, and all lay in confusion: and just at night we struck our tents, and moved out of ye Fort, and pitched where General Johnson had his fight.

11. Tuesday, unloaded all ye. Battows, and piled up the Stores, and camped.

12. Wednesday, took out five days allowance, and divided it to the Company; flour, pork, beef and rice, and butter, and camped.

13. Thursday, struck our tents in ye. morning, and went with all our luggage about one mile (to the South West of the Fort) from where we camped, and could not find our ground where it was laid out; and we took out one day's allowance of fresh beef, and divided it to the Company, and camped ? at random here and there.

14. Friday, struck our tents in the morning, and went back to the Halfway Brook, and carried exceeding heavy packs.... ; was uneasy with moving so often; and when we came there, Capt. Tay's son was dead and was buried this evening; and we camped within the stockades.

15. Saturday, Fixed up our Fort, and uncle Josiah Wright [6] was exceeding bad, and he died about four o'clock afternoon, and was buried about dusk, and I followed him to his grave as the nighest Relation he had there, and saw the last respects paid, and thanked them all for their service, and returned to our camps.

16. Sunday, Mr. Morrill preached two Sermons, (1.) from Psalm 37 & 7 verse, and (2.) Luke 16, v. 31. two fine sermons: and Col. Gates' Regiment march by Half-way Brook to day to Fort Edwd: so we camped.

17. Monday forenoon we went out in a scout with 9 men; but we see nothing and returned: scouted in ye. afternoon, & see nothing. I was not well; I had a bad spell. This night we were alarmed by ye. watch.

18. Tuesday, divided some stores: Mr. Ephraim Kendall [7] died: and there was a very smart thunder shower; 3 or 4 as hard claps as ever I heard; and a rainy afternoon: and Mr. Kendall was buried: myself not well.

19. Wednesday: some poorly, yet I went about and camped.

20. Thursday, in the morning, 10 men in a scout waylaid by the Indians, and shot at and larmed the Fort, and a number of our men went out to assist them, and the enemy followed our men down to our Fort, and in their retreat, Capt. Jones and Lieut. Godfrey were killed, and Capt. Lawrence and Capt. Dakin, and Lieut. Curtis and Ensn. Davis, and two or three non-commissioned officers and privates, to the number of fourteen men, who were brought into the Fort, all scalped but Ensn. Davis, who was killed within 20 or 30 rods from the Fort: and there was one grave dug, and all of them were buried together, the officers by themselves at one

---

[6] Josiah, son of Josiah and Ruth Wright, born 2 December, 1701. Esquire Thompson's mother, Ruth Wright, was a sister of the Josiah here mentioned as sick and dead.

[7] Ephraim Kendall and Ruth Peirce, both of Wilmington, married 24 February, 1737. Woburn Records of Births, Marriages, etc.

end, and the rest at the other end of the grave; and Mr. Morrill made a prayer at the grave, and it was a solemn funeral: and Nath[l] Eaton died in the Fort and was buried; and we kept a very strong guard that night of 100 men. Haggit [and] William Coggin wounded.

A List of Men's names that were killed in this fight.

Capt. Ebenezer Jones of Wilmington
Capt. Dakin of Sudbury
Lieut. Samuell Curtice of Ditto.
Private Grout of do
Lieut. Simon Godfrey of Billerica
Capt. Lawrence of Groton
Corp[l] Gould of Groton Gore
Private Abel Satle [Sawtell] of Groton
Private Eleazer Eames of Groton
Do Stephen Foster Do.
Serg[t]. Oliver Wright, Westford
Private Simon Wheeler Do
Ens[n]. Davis of Methuen
Serg[t]. Russel of Concord
Private Abraham Harden [Harnden?] of Pembroke.
Private Payson of Rowley
Private Patterson ———

We have also an account that there are seven of our men carried into Ticonderoga, which make up the number of those that were missing.

21. Friday, in y[e]. forenoon, a party of about 150 went out to find more men that were missing, and we found 4 men who were scalped, and we buried them, and so returned: and at prayer this evening we were Laromed by a false outcry. Nicholas Brown died and was buried; and Moses Haggit died.

22. Saturday, This morning Moses Haggit was buried: and we trenched half round y[e]. Fort this day a small trench. Our men are very poor, and we scarce could get men for work and for guard; but for my own part, I am very well.

23. Sunday: no preaching, for Mr. Morrill was very poor: and about one or two oclock, all our Camp got in an uproar, and some had slung their packs in order to march right off; and for my own part, I thought that they would have risen and marched right off; but our Colonels understood it, and went about in the Regiment, and spoke very sharp, and put them all to silence, and ordered them all to work again, in the afternoon; and so they left the flurry.

24. Monday, we had an eighteen pounder come to our Fort, and I worked. In y[e] afternoon we set another row of pickets round the Flanker. Nicholas Noyes died this night in the Fort.

25. Tuesday, all the fires are ordered out of fort, ovens excepted; and Nicholas Noyes was buried; and about noon order came to march right off from y[e]. Halfway Brook to the Lake, and we got up to the Lake at dark, and set up our tent, and lay warm, altho' it was a very rainy night.

26. Wednesday: loitering all ye. forenoon: a little thunder shower; and we moved our tents, and set them up in a regular form, and so camped.

27. Thursday; worked all day making breast work; and all the Regiments move under arms at 9 and 5. that forenoon and afternoon.

28. Friday we went up 13 of us to peal bark about 8 miles toward the Narrows, and we got a considerable quantity for to make camp. And in the evening there came news that the Indians had killed a number of teams and their guard below ye. Halfway Brook; and there was a scout fitting to go after them, and that made a great confusion in the minds of men, for we knew not what was the reason of so great a noise in ye. camp.

29. Saturday: Flying news about ye. Scout that was gone out after those Indians that did the mischief: and in the night there came in a Post from Rogers.

30. Sunday, before day they did muster, and sent out seventy five men out of our Regiment, eleven out of our Company, who went a little after sunrise down the Lake, and what the News was, we could not tell; yet all sorts of camp news was *brief*[8] about. But when our men were gone, they set [sent?] eleven more at one minute's warning, with 3 days provision, as those who were gone before, which did amount to 75 more out of our Regiment, and the number of men already gone is guessed to be nigh 1000 men, and ye. same number to be at one minute's warning with 3 days provision; yet there was but about 200 that went off about 2 oclock. 80 in Col. Nichols Regiment.

31. Monday, very rainy, and nothing but camp news all the forenoon; but fair in the afternoon, and in the evening there came in some of the men that went down the Lake.

August 1. [Tuesday]. Early in ye morning those men were ordered right down the Lake again: and about 80 of Col. Nichols' Regiment were ordered right down to ye Half way Brook, and I among the rest, and the whole number was about 800 men, who were stationed at the Half way Brook for a spell. Took 3 days provision: bread, pork.

2. Wednesday at the Half way Brook, a Post came and told us that Cape Breton was taken; and Gershom Flegg came up, and brought me a letter that all was well at home, which caused me much joy.

3. Thursday, orders that no man should ease himself in ye. Fort; and that the Roll must be called over, morning and evening; and a Scout of three or four hundred sent out after the Indians; and the duty is very hard for the men.

4. Friday. Took out 2 days stores, and divided it to the men: pork, bread, flour.

5. Saturday, a Scout sent out, but see nothing; duty very hard: and Colonel Fitch went down to Fort Edward with his Regiment: and some of our men were on duty twice in a day.

---

8 "Brief;" "a provincialism, in the sense of *rife, common,* or *prevalent,* in England, and the United States." Worcester's Dictionary.

6. Sunday: took out 3 days stores and divided it: pork, bisket, butter, peas: and the rest of Col. Fitch's men went down to Fort Edward.

7. Monday, 20 odd men came from y[e] South Bay who were poor [poorly]; and said that Major Rogers will come away in a day or two.

8. Tuesday: all our men and [on ?] duty; and news came from Major Rogers, and we sent 400 men to him, and 200 from above Fort Edward who were at work, 600 in all; and Capt. Brewer came down from y[e] Lake about 10 o'clock at night with 100 men.

9. Wednesday: about 10 o'clock we had more men come from Rogers, and he beat the enemy, and lost about   men, and got 52 scalps, and came to Fort Edward, and brought in his wounded into Fort Edward.

10. Thursday: not much news. 11. Friday, about forty teams for the Lake from Fort Edward.

12. Saturday: fixed our things, and marched to Lake George, and camped there.

13. Sunday: 2 fine Sermons: and at noon Order for a Scout to go to the South Bay, and our men that were in the height [fight?] with Rogers, came in to us at the Lake from Fort Edward.

14. Monday: a large Scout of five or six hundred men sent out after the enemy; some say, 1000 men: and just at night, a picquet guard raised, 50 men, in our Regiment.

15. Tuesday: I was on the picquet guard, and went to Half way Brook, and was wet.

16. Wednesday: a cold storm; and I worked to build me a house; and nothing remarkable.

17. Thursday; nothing remarkable. 18. Friday, we sold Beer; and nothing remarkable. 19. Saturday: nothing remarkable.

20. Sunday: I was on guard, and could not go to meeting: and it rained almost all day. 21. Monday: nothing remarkable.

22. Tuesday: the Scout came in, and a great number of teams just at night.

23. Wednesday: not well; nothing remarkable. 24. Thursday, not well, but kept about. Our Company was filled out.

25. Friday. A party drawed up to send out to the Half way Brook, and I went there, and was stated there; and the same day went half way to Fort Edward, and came back to Half way Brook.

26. Saturday; on guard at the Half way Brook; 14 men went up to y[e]. Lake alone, and came back well, all of them.

27. Sunday. On guard till 8 oclock in the morning; and a number of teams, about 20, which went from Fort Edward to the Lake.

28. Monday, certified that Cape Breton was taken, and 63 cannon shot at Fort Edward and small arms. In joy we made a great fire, and every soldier had a jill of Rum at the Half way Brook: and it was a very rainy night.

29. Tuesday: 140 of us went and made a breast work; and we had a jill of rum; and we had a remarkable drink of flip this evening: a very cold night. 30. Wednesday: nothing remarkable.

31. Thursday: full of camp news about going home.

September 1. Friday: Quite the reverse: for there came up two brass 24 pounders, and 21 teams loaded with shot, and other teams, to the number of 70 teams; and all the news is, go forward.

2. Saturday: I on guard; and the teams went up from here to the Lake; and a Scout went out for 7 days of 700 men.

3. Sunday: on guard till 8 oclock in the morning; and about noon Mr James Wyman came here, and we sent letters home by him: and there were 8 teams went up to the Lake this day.

4. Monday: nothing extraordinary only camp news, that the French are coming to take us: rainy night.

5. Tuesday: I on guard; and we earned half a jill of rum by making a great many bonfires.

6. Wednesday: on guard till 8 o'clock: news of a great scout of Indians.

7. Thursday: on escort down towards Fort Edward; and a great number of teams up to the Lake. Joseph Russel[9] died yesterday.

8. Friday: the Scout came in, and we were relieved from the Half way Brook, and went up to the Lake, and came [camped?] there.

9. Saturday: the picquet guard went to meet the teams; a Sergeant and four men went forward to tell Half way Brook guard that the picquet was coming; and the Indians shot the Sergeant and scalped him before one man got to him; and then the Indians ran away.

10. Sunday: on guard all day, the Quarter guard: and nothing remarkable.

11. Monday: on guard till 8 o'clock; and certified that Cateraguea was taken; and in token there were great fires made upon the high mountains round y^e. Lake, a mile or two distant from Fort William Henry, and there was above 100 Cannon fired, and all the army fired 3 times round with small arms, and huzza'd, and threw up their hats; and it was a great day in y^e. army.

12. Tuesday, we built up our chimney and . . . . 13. Wednesday: not very well, but keep about. . . . Abijah is poor.

14. Thursday: both of us not well, but I keep about: and I heard it was Thanksgiving at the Bay. It was a rainy night, and we were all very poor &c.

15. Friday: I was very poor, but just keep about, and I took physick: Abijah was poor, and Jesse Wyman was poor, and Lieut. Fassett died this night.

16. Saturday: Lt. Pearson, and his brother, and Serj^t. Nichols got a pass home; and I was poorly. Lt. Fassett was buried: and this night I took pills for physick.

17. Sunday: not well, but keep about a little. Mr Morrill came up from Albany, and preached two sermons this day.

18. Monday: some better: pretty cold weather. Camp news about going home in 3 weeks; but all uncertain.

---

[9] Joseph Russell, son of Joseph and Jane Russell, and grandson of John, Jr., and Elizabeth Russell, born at Woburn, 22 September, 1713. Woburn Records.

19. Tuesday: walked about down to the Lake, and see 'em fit up the battows; and great preparations, and what it will amount to I know not: some better.

20. Wednesday: much better; and our Sutler had stores come up for the Regiment. Camp news.

21. Thursday: I was on the picquet guard, but went no where, and no remarkables: pretty warm weather for the season of the year.

22. Friday. Received 3 letters, that all was well at home: and this evening, two of Capt. Parker's [company) died very sudden, Mansfield and Eben^r. Knight: and the Half way Brook was relieved this day.

23. Saturday. I was on guard all day. Camp news brief. 70 or 80 teams come up. Jeremiah Blanchard, and John and Moses (Barns?) came from Fort Edward &c.

24. Sunday: on guard till 8 o'clock; and Mr. Joshua Tompson set out for home. Mr. Morrill preached 2 sermons from 2. Cor. 4 & 18 all day: and just at night a Scout of 150 went down the Lake.

25. Monday: a party went to get hay; but we did not know where. John Richardson, James Wright, Salem Scipio [10] went; but we heard they went about 4 miles from the Lake; and there were 70 odd teams came up. Sam. Tidd took a vomit.

26. Tuesday: I on the picquet, but went no where.

27. Wednesday, the picquet went to Half way Brook, and our haying party came home. Sam Tidd poor &c and five teams and 7 or 8 wagons came up.

28. Thursday. I sawed some boards for to make me a house; and nothing remarkable. Camp news very brief. Sam. Tidd poor.

29. Friday: yesterday all the fires in the Camps ordered out of the Breast work from 8 oclock till sun down; and obeyed generally yesterday: and at night the Scout came in, who went out last Sunday.

30. Saturday: on the main guard on [L ?] Hill all day, and I kept time in the evening till 1 o'clock, and the Captain & the other Lieutenant the rest of the night; and a number of our men that were sick were viewed, and are to go away.

October 1. Sunday: on the main guard till 8 oclock: and Sam. Tidd poor; and I heard Mr Morrill preach in the afternoon [from] 97 Psalm, 1st verse: and much Camp news; and a Flag of Truce set out for the Narrows; and a number of our sick were sent off to day; and Abijah was something poor.

2. Monday: Saml. Tidd poor; and a rainy afternoon; and Camp news very brief about going home &c and Mr Saml. Abbot died.

3. Tuesday: Mr Abbot buried; and Abijah and Sam. Tidd very poor. I worked on my house.

4. Wednesday: 'bijah and Sam. Tidd poor: I worked on my house: and very cold weather.

5. Thursday: very cold morning; and I worked on my house; and much Camp news; and a party detached for Half way Brook to morrow.

---

[10] A slave, often mentioned in Woburn Records by this name; *from Salem*, I suppose.

6. Friday: a raw day; and our men went to relieve those at Half way Brook; and General Amherst came up yesterday, and our army was drawed up all round the Breast work for the new General to view this day, every Regiment by themselves. Sam. Tidd very poor.

7. Saturday: a pleasant day: Samll. Tidd very bad, and myself some poor & 'bijah; and some wagons came up.

8. Sunday. Samll. Tidd no better; 'bijah and I some better. Mr. Morrill preached this day [from] John 8. & 9 verse forenoon, and 2d Peter, 3 chapt. 10, 11, 12 verses afternoon.

9. Monday: Sam. Tidd very bad, and some of our men viewed, and Capt. Osgood and Wm. Coggin got a pass; and Thomas Blanchard died this evening.

10. Tuesday: Capt. Osgood and Bill Coggin set out for home; and Sam. Tidd[11] died; and Thomas Blanchard and Sam. Tidd buried: a rainy night: on duty in the forenoon.

11. Wednesday: some poor for some days past, but I kept about: nothing remarkable.

12. Thursday: about 35 viewed, and got a pass to go home: and no remarkables.

13. Friday: on the main guard at the old Picquet Fort, and a regular Captain, both of us fifty men, 25 each: a rainy night, but I lay dry and warm by a good fire at night.

14. Saturday: on guard till eight o'clock in the morning: much camp news about going home next week &c.

15. Sunday: pretty cold weather. Mr. Morrill's text, 1 Kings, 8 chapter, 57, 58, 60 & 61st. verses [in the forenoon] 26 Isaiah, 8, 9 verses, afternoon: and Mr. James Wyman came up and brought letters, that all was well at home.

16. Monday: about 30 of our Regiment got a pass to go home, and about 100 teams came up this day. . . .

17. Tuesday: the teams carried the artillery down to Fort Edward, and a great number of waggons came up to carry away the Battows.

18. Wednesday, 100 Battows went down in ye morning, and Col. Worcester's regiment went down, and the teams and more waggons came up and loaded.

19. Thursday: the teams and waggons went down again loaded, and seven of our Company and Jesse Wyman went home, and late in ye night, the waggons come and loaded again.

20. Friday: on the main guard, and a number of battows carried down, and teams and waggons come up and loaded.

21. Saturday: the teams and waggons went down: we drawed 4 days provision: and Lieut. Joshua Walker & Serjt [McCord?] set out for home: and they were unrigging the Sloop, and she haled up about 30 or 40 whale boats down ye Lake to sink them; and the waggons came up again.

---

[11] Samuel, son of Samuel and Phebe Tidd, born 17 May, 1741; died, under age, in the army at Lake George, October 10, 1758. [See State Muster Roll.]

22. Sunday: the waggons went down again with battows, and they haled a number of battows down the Lake to sink; and they knocked down the barracks within the new Picket Fort, and they bury the guns belonging to the Sloop, and the boards of the barracks, and the Sloop irons, and many other things: and Mr. Morrill preached; his text, 1 Thessalonians 2, 12 forenoon: no preaching in the afternoon; for Orders came, that our Regiment with 2 more Regiments, and every 20 men to draw battows down to Fort Edward tomorrow.

23. Monday: we drawed out a number of battows down to Fort Edward, and camped 94 [by?] a Store house: very cold night.

24. Tuesday; Set out from Fort Edward in a battow, and we had a very bad spell at the Falls at Fort Miller. We haled our battow out on the land forty rod, and put it in the River again, and we got stuck in the Falls. I got out and lifted in the River one hour in y^e. dark, and we got off, and went on shore, and set up three tents, and put our Sick in one; and it was a rainy night, and we made a great fire.

25. Wednesday, I went on land part of the day, and part by water; and we camped three miles below Stillwater in a house: a rainy night, and a very bad snow storm all the fore part of the next day.

26. Thursday: I marched all day, and crossed the River at Half Moon at one or two o'clock, and went to Flatbush, and lodged in a house. I bought a good supper.

27. Friday: went in a battow to Green Bush, and got into a barn with our Sick. And I went to Albany and drawed provision for ye Company, and lay in ye barn at Green Bush; and I had a very bad cold.

28. Saturday: very bad cold; and Abijah and the rest of our Company set out for home in the morning; and I went about to take care of the Sick, and felt pretty poor. Sam^ll. Hutchinson and Danl. Holt sick. I put Sam^ll. Hutchinson into Hospitall, and Camped in Barn.

29. Sunday: Set out from Green Bush about 10 o'clock, and came to half way house about noon, and rid in a waggon to Canterhook[12] mills before sundown, and Camped in a barn.

30. Monday: Set out from Kenderhook before sun rise, and went to Goodaneers, and eat chocolate, and went to Stone house 11 o'clock. Set out from thence to Lovejoy's, and eat beef and turnips, and paid for it; and went to Roberts', and lodged in his barn, &c.

31. Tuesday: eat —— and milk at Roberts' ; paid for it, and set out from thence, and came to Sheffield about 10 o'clock at ye meeting house we marched to Davis's, and I eat beef and potatoes about 2 oclock: then we set out from thence, and went to Mr. Brewer's about 3 o'clock, where we eat supper and breakfast on Province cost, and I lodged in a bed.

November 1. Wednesday set out from Brewer's, sun ½ hour high; went into Green woods to a house 11 miles from Brewer's: eat a dinner on the Province cost. Set out from thence about noon, and came to Glascow meeting house at 3 o'clock. Stopped there a few minutes, and went one

---

[12] Kinderhook.

mile to a tavern and lodged in a barn. I see Mr. Zorobabel Snow at this place. I eat on the Province cost.

2. Thursday: Set out from the tavern at break of day, and came to Westfield; Sun hour high. I eat chocolate at my own cost. Set out from there, and came to Springfield about 2 oclock to the River, and went over to a tavern one mile this side, and eat on the Province cost. Then I went 5 mile further, and lodged in a barn; eat supper on the Province cost.

3. Friday: Set out before sunrise, and went ten mile, before breakfast to Graves's; eat on the Province cost, and then went to Brimfield to uncle James Tompson's,[13] and got there 4 oclock, and lodged there in a bed.

4. Saturday: stayed at uncle James Tompson's till 3 oclock, and set out and went 4 mile: met Daniel[14] and went back to uncle's, and lay there and Daniel.

5. Sunday. Set out from uncle's, and got lost; but we came to uncle Hartwell's about 1 oclock, and eat a good dinner. Set out from thence, Sun ½ hour high, and rode to Worcester to Brown's, and lodged there.

6. Monday. Set out from Brown's, and came to Agar's [Hagar's?] and went to breakfast; poor chocolate: then rode as far as Deacon Rice's; went to dinner; poor beef: then rode to Roes [Munroe's?] of Concord; drinked some cherry, and then rode home to my own house, where I found them all well, &c., on Monday night, about 9 oclock the 6th of November seventeen hundred fifty-eight.

APPENDIX, No. X.

French Neutrals.

During the war, which commenced in 1755, between England and France, frequent references are made in the Woburn Treasurer's Records to the *Neutral French.* These originally were inhabitants of Nova Scotia, about seven thousand in number, "mild, frugal, industrious and pious" in their character; Colonists of France, but who, upon the cession of that Province by France to England, at the treaty of Utrecht, in 1713, became rightfully subjects of Great Britain. But such was their attachment to their native country, its government and religion, that though they were allowed to hold their lands upon condition of taking the oath of allegiance to the Sovereign of England, yet they refused to do this, except with this qualification, that they should not be obliged, in case

---

[13] James, son of Jonathan and Frances Thompson, born 14 November, 1696; a brother of Esquire Samuel Thompson's father.

[14] Daniel Thompson, brother of Esquire Samuel; killed eventually at Concord fight, April 19, 1775.

of any future war between France and England, to take up arms in defence of the British Province they now inhabited, against their own countrymen. By this qualification to their oath of allegiance, these French Colonists took the *position*, and acquired the *name* of Neutrals between the French and English: and had their conduct afterwards been always answerable to the name and position they had so assumed, they would, not improbably, have been suffered to remain unmolested, both as to their property and their persons. But during the war between France and England, which commenced in 1755, it was alleged against them by the English, that they had abandoned their neutral character and position; that they "furnished the French and Indians with intelligence, quarters, provisions, and assistance in annoying the government of the Province; that three hundred of them were actually found in arms at the taking of Fort Beau-sejour; and that notwithstanding an offer was made to such of them as had not been openly in arms to be allowed to continue in possession of their land, if they would take the oath of allegiance without any qualification, they unanimously refused it." [1]

In view of these charges (which were probably just, as to many individuals among them), the Lieut.-Governor of the Province and his Council, when met together to consider what was best to be done with this people, decided that it would not be consistent with the public safety that they should remain any longer in the Province; and that if they were allowed to remove to Canada, the result would be, to replenish the armies of France. Hence they resolved to remove them all by force, and to distribute them among the several British Colonies, "where they could not unite in any offensive measures, and where they might be naturalized to the government and country." [1]

The execution of this plan was intrusted principally to the Massachusetts forces, headed by Lieut.-Colonel Winslow. [2] A convenient time having arrived, the inhabitants, who had hitherto been kept in entire ignorance of their destiny, "were called into the different ports to hear the King's orders, as they were termed. At Grand Pré, where Col. Winslow had the immediate command, four hundred and eighteen of their best men assembled. These being shut into the church (for that too had become an arsenal) he placed

---

[1] Minot's History of Massachusetts, Vol. I., pp. 220, 221, 222.

[2] Lieut.-Colonel John Winslow of Marshfield.

himself with his officers in the centre, and addressed them thus: 'Gentlemen: I have received from his Excellency, Governor Lawrence, the King's commission which I have in my hand; and by his orders you are convened together, to manifest to you his Majesty's final resolution to the French inhabitants of this his Province of Nova Scotia; who for almost half a century have had more indulgence granted them, than any of his subjects in any part of his dominions. What use you have made of it, you yourselves best know.

"'The part of duty I am now upon, though necessary, is very disagreeable to my natural make and temper, as I know it must be grievous to you, who are of the same species.

"'But it is not my business to animadvert, but to obey such orders as I receive; and therefore, without hesitation, shall deliver you his Majesty's orders and instructions; namely,

"'That your land and tenements, cattle of all kinds, and live stock of all sorts, are forfeited to the crown, with all other your effects, saving your money and household goods; and you yourselves to be removed from this his Province.'

"Thus it is peremptorily his Majesty's orders, that the whole French inhabitants of these districts be removed; and I am, through his Majesty's goodness, directed to allow you liberty to carry off your money and household goods, as many as you can without discommoding the vessels you go in. I shall do everything in my power, that all those goods be secured to you, and that you are not molested in carrying them off; also, that whole families shall go in the same vessel; and make this remove, which I am sensible must give you a great deal of trouble, as easy as his Majesty's service will admit; and hope that in whatever part of the world you may fall, you may be faithful subjects, a peaceable and happy people.

"I must also inform you, that it is his Majesty's pleasure that you remain in security, under the inspection and direction of the troops that I have the honor to command." "And he then declared them the King's prisoners."

"The whole number of persons collected at Grand Pré finally amounted to 483 men and 337 women, heads of families, and their sons and daughters to 527 of the former, and 576 of the latter, making in the whole 1,927 souls. Their stock was upwards of 5,000 horned cattle, 493 horses, and 12,887 sheep and swine.

"As some of these wretched inhabitants escaped to the woods, all possible measures were adopted to force them back to captivity. The country was laid waste to prevent their subsistence. In the district of Minas alone, there were destroyed 255 houses, 276 barns, 155 out-houses, 11 mills, and 1 church; and the friends of those who refused to come in were threatened, as the victims of their obstinacy. In short, so operative were the terrors that surrounded them, that of twenty-four young men who deserted from a transport, twenty-two were glad to return of themselves, the others being shot by sentinels, and one of their friends, who was supposed to have been accessary to their escape, having been carried on shore to behold the destruction of his house and effects, which were burned in his presence, as a punishment for his temerity, and perfidious aid to his comrades. Being embarked by force of the musquetry, they were dispersed, according to the original plan, among the several British Colonies. One thousand arrived in Massachusetts Bay, and became a public expense, owing in a great degree to an unchangeable antipathy to their situation, which prompted them to reject the usual beneficiary but humiliating establishment of paupers for their children."[3]

Of the thousand French Neutrals brought to Massachusetts, to be distributed among its towns, we learn from Gage's History of Rowley, that "Rowley had fourteen to provide for & . . . . that Bradford had eleven as their proportion. Boxford had fifteen a part of the time, but in March (1758) six of them were removed to Middleton."[4] "The selectmen of the several towns were authorized by law to bind them out to service. It is not known that any of those in Rowley were bound out. The Province was charged with the expense of their board. After the peace of 1763, the town [Rowley] March 17, 1767, made a grant of £13 6*s*. 8*d*. to aid them in returning to the place of their nativity."[4]

From the following Memoranda in the Records of the Treasurer of Woburn of that day, it appears that a number of these unfortunate people were placed in this town, under the care of different families:

1756 May 10. "Paid to Benjan. Wyman for provisions for the French family now maintained by the Town . . £1.3.0."

" June 20. Paid to Dr. John Prince for his doctoring the French in this town to this day . . . . . . 1.15.8."

[3] Minot's History, Vol. I., pp. 224, 227.

[4] Gage's Rowley, p. 208.

1756 July 15. Paid to Mr. Thomas Reed for beef, pork, meal, wood, and sundries for the French family in Woburn .	£3.09.0."
" Decr. 29. Paid to Mr. Isaac Snow for provisions to the French People in our town in full to this day . .	3.02.0."
1757 March 4. "There is a Note in the Hands of Josiah Johnson Esqr. of about twenty six Pounds from the Province, to pay this Town for keeping the French people taken from Menis and sent here." p. 122	
" June 1. Paid to James Thompson for three loads of wood he found for the French	0 :10 :0."
" July 29. Paid to Dea. Timothy Winn for provisions for the French people in our town.	0 :10 :11."
" Aug. 17. Paid to Oliver Richardson for beans for ye. French family	0 :2 :1½."
1758. Febr. 23. "Paid to Dea. Timothy Winn for keeping the French ye. fore part of ye. year.	0 :10 :8."
" March 9. "Paid to Dea. Timothy Winn for service done ye. Town respecting the French	0 :4 :0."
" May 23. "Paid to Benjn. Richardson for taking care of the French	0 :4 :0 :"
" Decr. 4. "Paid to Joseph Wright for time and trouble spent about ye. French	0 :4 :0 :"
" " "Paid to Benjn. Flagg for Clothing for the French Nuters	1 :4 :0."
1760 Jany. 13. "Paid to Mr. Benjn. Flagg in full of an Order of sixteen shillings for keeping the French in the year 1758	0 :16 :0."
" Oct. 13. "Paid to Mr. Benjn. Brooks in *full* for keeping the French Family one year	28 :5 :7.1"
" " "Paid to Benjn. Brooks in *part* of an Order for keeping the French family	0 :19 :8 :3."
1761. Jany. 16. "Paid to Mr. Isaac Snow [for] a Coffin for Abraham French [for Abm. a Frenchman? see March 30]	0 :7 :4 :0."
" March 30. " Paid to Mr. Isaac Brooks for digging a *grave* for *the Frenchman*, and keeping a woman stranger	0 :8.0.0"
" March 30. " Paid to Dr. John Prince in full for doctoring the French family in the years 1758 & 1759. . . .	0 :9 :6 :0
" Aug. 29. Received of Mr. James Fowle, which he received of ye Province Treasurer for keeping the French in Woburn	5 :13 :4 :0."
" July 6. " Paid to Mr. Joshua Walker in full for going to Wilmington to divide the french family [to carry part of them there?]	0 :4 :0 :0"
" Oct. 4. "Paid to Mr. Joshua Harnden in full for moving the French family from Wilmington to Charlestown	0 :8 :0 :0."
" " "Paid to Mr. Joseph Harnden in part of an Order for house rent for the French family in Wilmington	0 :16 :0 :0."

1764. Oct. 12. "Paid Capt. Zach[a] Flagg in full for a part of a load of wood he found for the French . . . . 0 :2 :0 :0.
1764. Dec[r] 29. "Paid John Lappidore in full for what the Selectmen agreed to give him for maintaining the French for one year . . . . 1 :12 :0 :0"
1766 Jany. 8. "Paid to John Labedore for him and his family (Was not Lappidore himself one of the French?) . 1 :12 :0.0."
" August 28. "Paid to John Labedore[5] . . . . . 1 :12 :0 :0."

APPENDIX, No. XI.

Bounty for Killing Blackbirds and Squirrels in 1741, etc.

About 1740, the fields in Woburn appear to have been greatly infested, in planting and harvest time, with blackbirds and squirrels. To get rid of these pests, the inhabitants in town meeting March 30, 1741, passed the following vote:

"Voted, that the Town Treasurer is directed to pay unto the Fathers and Masters of Children and Servants three pence per head for Crow Black-birds, Jebirds [Jaybirds?] and Mouse Squirrels that they their Children or Servants shall or may kill and destroy within the said Town of Woburn from the twelfth day of April next to the last day of June next, provided that the heads of said birds and squirrels be brought into the Treasury by said Fathers and Masters on the General Town meeting in May next, or on the first Monday of July next ensuing, which are the times appointed by the Town for the Treasurer to receive and pay for the same: Always provided that the General Court does not make an Act of Law upon that account." [1]

And now all the boys in Woburn, stimulated by the promise of a bounty to a work of destruction, which they are always ready enough from mere wantonness to perform, entered with alacrity into the warfare which they had now been encouraged to undertake. Through a large portion of the years 1741, 1742 and 1743, they were employed in this business: nor did they confine themselves to the times for their bloody work to which the vote of the town restricted them, but readily engaged in it whenever the

[5] The last entry in the treasurer's book that I find, respecting the French. I have observed no mention there of any money given them, to aid them to return to their own country, as was done in 1767 at Rowley.

[1] Town Records, Vol. VII., p. 363.

prospect of success invited them to stir in it. Nor did the Treasurer himself appear to feel limited in the bounty he paid them, but increased it as he pleased, as though the amount of it were a matter left to his own discretion to determine; and hence we find him giving four pence instead of three pence for every squirrel's head that was brought to him, three pence for every old blackbird's head, and a penny for the head of every young one.

The results of the crusade against these little mischievous creatures, which the above vote of the town initiated, may well fill us of the present day with surprise, now that their number is so vastly diminished. Within a twelvemonth from April 28, 1741, the treasurer paid bounty upon 5,200 squirrels' heads that were brought to him, and upon 2,015 blackbirds' heads, young and old.[2] And the expense incurred by the town for this purpose was reimbursed from the State Treasury, as appears by the annexed Certificate of the treasurer of Woburn:

"March y^{e}. 13th. 1741–2. Received from the Country Treasurer, of the bounty we paid for birds and squirrels last year, the sum of one hundred and twenty seven Pound and five Shillings and three Pence. £127 :5 :3."[3]

Subjoined are a few specimens of the activity and diligence of the boys in their work of destruction, as are recorded in the Treasurer's book of accounts:

"May y^{e}. 4. 1741. Paid Mr. Zachariah Snow for 29 Black Birds heads	£0 : 7 : 3."
"May y^{e}. 25. 1741. Paid Amos Kendall for one hundred and two Black birds heads and twenty eight Squirrels. . .	1. 14. 10."
"June y^{e}. 6. 1741 Paid Jedidiah Leathe for one hundred and four Squirrels, and three old Black Birds, and twelve young Black Birds Heads.	1 : 16 : 5."
"June y^{e}. 8. 1741. Paid Joshua Jones for fifty eight Black Birds and thirty Squirrels heads.	1 : 4 : 6."
"June y^{e}. 16. 1741. Paid Jonathan Proctor for 75 old and 5 young Black Birds heads, and 44 Squirrels heads. . .	1. 13 : 10."
"August y^{e}. 5. 1741. Paid John Tottingham for 94 Squirrels, and 6 old and 4 young Blackbirds heads	1 : 13 : 2."
"August y^{e}. 5. 1741. Paid Amos Kendall for 114 Squirrels', and 15 old Blackbirds and 4 young ones heads . . .	2 : 2 : 1.
"December y^{e}. 25. 1741. Paid Farrar [for] 73 Squirrels' Heads	1. 4. 4."

[2] Treasurer's Book of Accounts, from 1739 to 1772, pp. 14–24, and p. 31.
[3] Treasurer's Book, p. 32.

February 1. 1741–2. "Paid Samll. Nevers for 33 old and 13 young black birds' and 58 Squirrels' heads. . . . 1. 8. 8"
"February 26. 1741–2. Paid Jacob Peirce for 318 Squirrels and 4 old and one young blackbirds' heads . . . 5. 7. 1."
" Paid Joshua Kendall for 150 Squirrels heads . . . . 2. 10. 0"
"February 27. 1741–2. Paid Jacob Richardson ye. 3d. for 189 squirrels and 12 old black birds and 7 young ones [heads] . . . . 3. 6. 7."

In the Treasurer's Book, there are registered upon 7 folio pages, 173 entries of payments made by him for the heads of blackbirds and squirrels killed between 1741 and 1742, and brought to him, and amounting severally from four pence to upwards of five pounds.[4] Nor did this work of destruction then cease. It was resumed in August 1742; four pages more of the Treasurer's Book are occupied with recording its results[5]; and November 30, 1743 there was paid out of the Province Treasury £103 : 9*s*. 10*d*. for what had been done in Woburn in this way.[6]

APPENDIX, No. XII.

List of Men, who served for Woburn in the War of the Revolution:

Comprehending:

(1.) Known Citizens of Woburn, and others, who on plausible grounds are presumed to have been Inhabitants of the town when the War began, or soon after; and all of whom, being drafted, rendered personal service in it, or procured others who did it in their stead.

(2.) Strangers from a distance, and persons belonging to other towns, who were hired from time to time by Woburn to fill up its quota, or by private individuals to act for them as substitutes. Soldiers of this latter class are distinguished by prefixing a (†) to their names in the List; and though originating elsewhere, yet several of them, it is to be observed, made Woburn eventually their permanent place of residence.

---

4 Treasurer's Book, pp. 14–21. 5 Treasurer's Book, pp. 31, 38–41.
6 Treasurer's Book, p. 44.

Documents in the Archives of the Town or State, referred to in the List as Authorities, or Sources of Information.

I. Orders for the payment of individual Soldiers.

At the commencement of the Revolutionary War, there were in Woburn three companies of militia commanded respectively by Capts. Samuel Belknap, Jesse Wyman, and Joshua Walker of the Precinct. Original Muster Rolls or Lists of these companies are still preserved. They each give the names of the soldiers belonging to it; and annexed to their names, in appropriate columns, is the valuation of the services respectively assigned them during the first two years of the war, 1775, 1776.

When the terms of their enlistments had expired, at the end of 1776, compensation was made them by Orders on the town treasurer for the payment of the bounties which the town had voted to give for each service performed by them respectively. These Orders, which are (most of them) still preserved, and are very numerous, generally bear date from March 20, 1777; they have all been numbered; the number of each of them is set in the List here presented against the name of the person in favor of whom it was drawn; and they all (with scarcely an exception) are receipted on the back by the persons who severally took from the treasurer the amount of them, in their own proper hand. They do not specify, however, on the face of them the particular services for which payment is directed in them to be made, but only signify in general, that they were given for "Service in the present War"; or for "Service done in the present War before 1777," or "January 1st, 1777."

To these Orders may properly be added selections from returns made at stated times of drafts or enlistments for special services, by Samuel Nevers, sworn clerk of the Precinct Company, under Capt. Walker.

II. Town Reports and Orders (numbered on the Town Files of Documents by V., VI., VII., etc. to XX.), respecting the payment of whole companies of men (or of the several individuals composing them), which were sent out subsequently to 1776 on various military expeditions, or "tours of duty;" and which are distinguished on the following List by the names of their respective commanders, and by the times and places of their mission.

III. Names of the "Eight months' Men," in the Continental

army in 1775, obtained from the original Muster Rolls in Woburn, or from the Register of the same in the State House, Boston.

IV. Names of the men who enlisted for Woburn, 1777, for three years, or "during the War," in the Continental service, as exhibited in the Town Document No. XIX., or in the State House Records, or in both.

V. Names of the men belonging to Woburn, or serving for it, in the 37th, afterwards the 26th Regiment in the United States service, commanded by Col. Loammi Baldwin, of Woburn, collected from his numerous manuscript papers; which papers having been deposited by his heirs in the Archives of the State, have there been bound up together in a large folio volume, known as the *Baldwin Volume.*

VI. Names of the men who constituted a reinforcement of the United States troops required of Woburn to furnish for six months in 1780; and which have been preserved in Orders for the payment of their respective bounties, and other authentic papers belonging to the town.

VII. *Worcester Rolls*, so called; viz: one or more manuscript volumes preserved in the State House, and containing soldiers' names, etc., etc.

Abbreviations used in the following List:

(1.) "S." for "Service." (2.) "S. p. W."; Service in the present war; that is, before 1777. (3.) "St. H. L."; the State House List of the persons or soldiers referred to. (4.) "C. A."; Continental Army. (5.) "Bn's Regt."; the regiment commanded by Col. Baldwin, of Woburn. (6.) "Bn. Vol."; Volume of Baldwin papers, correspondence, etc., etc. (7.) "Woods Co."; The company in the Baldwin Regiment, commanded by Capt. John Wood, of Woburn Precinct, and consisting principally of Woburn men. (8.) I., II., III., IV., to XIX., XX., inclusively, denote Documents distinguished by one or other of those numbers in the Town Files. (9.) No. of Order for payment preserved by the Treasurer, and signified by 1, 2, 30, 100, 400, etc., etc., etc.

WOBURN MEN IN THE REVOLUTIONARY WAR.

1775 – 1783.

Abbot: William. C. A. Bn's. Regt. Pettingell's Co. 1775. Bn. Vol.
†Adams: John. C. A. 1777, 3 years, xix.
Alexander: Abra. C. A. 8 mos. 1775. St. H. L.
Alexander: Abram. C. A. Bn's Regt. Wood's Co. 1775. Bn. Vol.
Alexander: Abram. Expedition to Ticonderoga,[1] July 1776. Nevers' Returns.
Alexander: Giles. S. p. W. March 28, 1777: date of Order. 373.
Alexander: John. S. p. W. before Jan. 1777. 140, 265.
Alexander: John, jun. C. A. 6 mos. for Wob. 1780. 286, 310, 320. 357, 361, 431.
Alexander: Philip. C. A. 3 years, 1777–1779. xix. St. H. L.
Alexander: William. At the lines fifteen days, guarding prisoners of Convention. 475.
Alexander: William. C. A. 6 mos. 1780. 224.
†Allen: Ezekiel. C. A. 8 mos. 1775. for Woburn. St. H. L.
Allen: Ezekiel. C. A. 8 mos. Bn's Regt. Wood's Co. 1775. Bn. Vol.
Andrews: Lt. Abm. C. A. Whitney's Regt. for Wob. Worc. Rolls.
†Austin: David. C. A. 1777. 3 years. xix.
†Bachelor: Wm. C. A. 1777. 3 years enlisted for. xix.
†Barbadoes: Isaac. C. A. 1777. 3 years. xix.
Baldwin: Cyrus. S. p. W. Order dated March 20, 1777. 207.
Baldwin: James. S. p. W. March 20, 1777. 36.
Baldwin: Col. Loammi. S. p. W. before Jan. 1777. 260.
†Beard: Abel. C. A. 6 mos. 1780. 232, 437.
Belknap: Josiah. Rhode Island. Capt. Wyman, 1777. 360, 423, 453.
Belknap: Capt. Samuel. S. p. W. Order dated March 20, 1777. 57.
Belknap: Capt. Samuel. C. A. Brooks's Regt. Worc. Rolls.
Bennett: James. C. A. 3 years. 1777–79. xix. St. H. L.
Bennett: James. C. A. Bn's Regt. Wood's Co. 1775. Bn. Vol.
Bennett: John. C. A. Bn's Regt. Wood's Co. 1776. Bn. Vol.
Bennett: John. C. A. 6 mos. 1780. 241.
Bennett: Sergt. C. A. 8 mos. 1775. St. H. L.
Stephen: C. A. Bn's Regt. Wood's Co. 1775. Bn. Vol.
Bennett: Thomas. C. A. Bn's Regt. Wood's Co. 1775. Bn. Vol.
Bennett: Thomas. Capt. Wm. Green, R. I. 3 mos. 1780. ix. 313.
†Biscoe: Sergt. George. C. A. 8 mos. 1775, for Woburn. St. H. L.
Biscoe: Sergt. George. C. A. Baldwin's Regt. Wood's Co. 1775. Bn. Vol.
Blackman: Kemer. C. A. for Woburn. Worc. Rolls.
Blanchard: Dea. David. S. p. W. before Jan. 1777. 20.
Blanch.: David, jun. Lt. Jos. Johnson, Cambridge, 1777. v. viii. 64.
Blanch.: David, jun. Guarding prisoners of Convention, 1778. 309.
Blanchard: Benj. Bunker Hill, 5 weeks, 1779. 290.
Blanchard: Benj. C. A. Bn's Regt. Wood's Co. 1775. Bn. Vol.
Blanchard: Josiah. C. A. 6 mos. 1780, for Woburn. 219, 422.
Blogget: Amos. R. I. 6 mos. 1779, for Woburn. 454.
Blogget: Dr. Samuel. S. p. W. before 1777. 10.
Blogget: Mr. Thomas. S. p. W. before 1777. 201.
Brewster: William. S. p. W. before 1777. 47.
Brooks: Jabez. C. A. 3 years 1777 enlisted for; but died before end of engagement. 222.
Brooks: John. Lt. Dix, near Cambridge, 3 mos. 1778, guarding prisoners. vii. viii.

[1] Where he died in the autumn of 1776. Rev. Mr. Marrett's List of Deaths in 1776.

Brooks: Jonathan. S. p. W. before 1777. 147.
Brooks: Joseph. Cont. Army. Worc. Rolls.
Brooks: Lt. Nathaniel. S. p. W. before 1777. 316.
Brooks: Ens. Timothy, jun. S. p. W. before 1777. 5.
Brooks: Timothy, 3d. S. p. W. before 1777. 379.
Brooks: Lt. Zachariah. S. p. W. before 1777. 84.
Brown: Dan. Green. S. p. W. before 1777. 102.
Brown: Joseph. Lt. Jos. Johnson, Cambridge, 1777. v. viii. 124, 257.
Brown: Josiah. S. p. W. before Jan. 1777. 189, 290.
Bruce: Mr. John. S. p. W. before 1777. 166.
Bruce: John, jun. S. p. W. before 1777. 41.
Bruce: Lewis. C. A. 6 mos. 1780. 439,457.
Bruce: Thomas. S. P. W. before Jan. 1777. 27, 327, 384.
Bruce: Thomas, jun. S. p. W. before Jan. 1777. 271.
Bucknam: Jacob. Capt. Ford, Cambridge, 1777-78. vi. viii.
Burton: Lt. Isaac. S. p. W. before 1777. 254.
Burton: Lt. Isaac. Exped. to Ticonderoga, 5 mos. 1776. Nevers' List.
Caldwell: Jacob. S. p. W. before 1777. 99.
Caldwell: John. C. A. at the North: a recruit for 1777. xi.
†Carrel: [Caryl?] John. C. A. 1777 for 3 years. xix.
Carter: Jonas. Lt. Jas. Johnson, at Camb. 2 mos. 1777. v. viii.
Carter: Jonathan. Capt. Ford, at Camb. 5 mos. 1777-8. vi. viii. 171.
Carter: Samuel. S. p. W. before 1777. 315.
Carter: Simon. S. p. W. before 1777. 44.
Carter: William. Capt. Foster, at the Northward, against Burgoyne. 1777. 155.
Center: Bill. S. p. W. before 1777. 353.
Cheever: John. C. A. at the North, a recruit for, 1777. xi.
†Cheney: Samuel. C. A. 1777, for 3 years. xix.
Convers: Benjamin. S. p. W. before 1777. 145.
Convers: Josiah, jun. S. p. W. before 1777. 177.
Convers: Josiah. Capt. Foster, at the Northward, 1777, against Burgoyne. 274.
Convers: Robert. S. P. W. before 1777. 200.
†Cornell: John. C. A. 1777, for 3 years. xix.
Cummings: David. S. p. W. before 1777. 93, 336.
Cummings: Ebenezer. Lt. Jos. Johnson, Cambridge, 2 mos. 1777. v. viii.
Cutler: Nathaniel. S. p. W. before Jan. 1777. 402.
Cutler: Nath. jun. S. p. W. before 1777. 355.
Cutler: Nath. Capt. Wyman, Bunker Hill, 1778. viii. xvi. 106.
Cutler: Samuel. Capt. Ford, Camb. 1777-78. vi. vii. 108, 382.
Cutter: John, jun. S. p. W. before 1777. 76.
Cutter: Seth, jun. Capt. Wyman, Bunker Hill, 1778. viii. xvi. 406.
Dean: Jesse.[2] C. A. 8 mos. 1775. St. H. L.
Dean: Jesse. C. A. Bn's Regt. Wood's Co. 1775. Bn. Vol.
Dean: Lemuel. Capt. Ford, Cambridge, 1777-78. vi. viii. 107.
Dean: Samuel. S. p. W. before 1777. 103.
Dean: Supply. S. p. W. before 1777. 159, 389.
Dean: Thomas. C. A. 8 mos. 1775. St. H. L.
Dean: Thomas. C. A. Bn's Regt. Wood's Co. 1775. Bn. Vol.
Dean: Sergt. Thomas. S. p. W. before 1777. 206.
†Ditson: Samuel. C. A. 8 mos. 1775. St. H. L.
Dix: Lt. Nathan. C. A. Bn's Regt. Wood's Co. 1775. Bn. Vol. S. p. W. before 1777. 199.
Douglas: Barnard. Capt. Green, R. I. 3 mos. 1780. ix. 72.
Douglas: John. C. A. 3 years, 1777-79. St. H. L.

[2] Jesse Dean was in Woburn in 1775, and was taxed there in the province tax for that year. In 1776, 1777, he was taxed in Woburn among the non-residents of *Wilmington*. But, eventually, he became a constant inhabitant of Woburn Precinct.

Douglas: Robert. S. p. W. before 1777. 210.
Douglas: Robert. Capt. Foster, at the Northward, 1777. 242.
Dodge: Andrew. S. p. W. before 1777. 125.
Dodge: Andrew. Capt. Foster, at the Northward, 1777. 112.
†Dow: Nathan. C. A. 1777, for 3 years; discharged. xix. St. H. L.
Eames: Jacob. S. p. W. before 1777. 63.
Eames: Samuel. C. A. 6 mos. 1780. 318, 456.
Eaton: Jonathan. Capt. Ford, Cambridge, 1777-78. vi. viii. 62.
Eaton: Noah. S. p. W. before 1777. 284.
Edgell: Capt. Benjamin. S. p. W. before 1777. 37.
Edgell: Capt. Benjamin. R. I. 1778. 351.
†Edwards: John. C. A. 1777, for 3 years. xix.
Evans: Andrew. S. p. W. before 1777. 294, 328.
Evans: Andrew, jun. C. A. 6 mos. 1780. 247, 369.
Evans: Andrew, 3d. Lt. Dix, Cambridge, 1778. vii. viii.
Evans: Jonas. S. p. W. before Jan. 1777. 296, 329.
Evans: Silas. C. A. 1777, for 3 years. St. H. L. xix.
†Fairfield: Elijah. C. A. for Woburn. Worc. Rolls.
Farmer: Thomas. S. p. W. before 1777. 338.
Farrington: Matthew. C. A. Bn's Regt. Wood's Co. 1775. Bn. Vol.
†Finch: Simeon. C. A. 1777, for 3 years for Woburn. xix.
Finch:
Fisk: Robert. C. A. Bn's Regt. Pettingell's Co. 1775. Bn. Vol.
Fisk: Robert. C. A. 1777, during the War. xix. St. H. L.
†Fitzgerald: John. C. A. 8 mos. 1775, for Woburn. St. H. L.
†Flagg: Gershom.[3] C. A. 6 mos. 1780, for Woburn. 408.
Flagg: Hiram. Capt. Green, R. I. 3 mos. 1780. ix. 313, 352.
Flagg: John. Capt. Foster, at the Northward, 1777. 297.

†Forbes: John. C. A. 1777, 3 years, for Woburn. xix.
†Foam: Abijah. C. A. 1777, 3 years, for Woburn. xix.
Fowle: Benjamin. S. p. W. before 1777. 137, 314.
Fowle: James, jun. S. p. W. before 1777. 184, 196.
Fowle: James, 3d. S. p. W. before 1777. 270.
Fowle: James, 4th. C. A. 1777, for 3 years. xix.
Fowle: John [3d?]. Capt. Wyman, Bunker Hill, 1778. viii. xvi.
Fowle: Josiah. S. p. W. before 1777. 31.
Fowle: Josiah, jun. S. p. W. before 1777. 28.
Fowle: Leonard. S. p. W. before 1777. 266.
Fowle Leonard, Capt. Foster, at the Northward, 1777. 377.
Fowle: William. Capt. Green, R. I. 3 mos. 1780. ix. 252, 367.
Fox: Adj. William. Lt. Jos. Johnson, Cambridge, 1777. v. viii. 404.
Fuller: Silas. Capt. Foster, at the Northward, 1777. 212.
†Gardner: James.[4] C. A. 6 mos. 1780. 221, 302, 456.
Giddings: Joseph. S. p. W. before 1777. 98, 194.
Gleason: Benjamin. Capt. Wyman, Bunker Hill, 1778. xvi. viii. 121.
Gleason: Thomas. S. p. W. before 1777. 33, 398, 445.
Gleason: Thomas. C. A. 3 years. 419.
Gloyd: Benjamin. C. A. 8 mos. 1775. St. H. L.
Gloyd: Benjamin. S. p. W. before 1777. 378.
Goodwin: Uriah. Continental Army. Worc. Rolls.
†Greaton: Col. Robert. C. A. 1777, during the War. xix. St. H. L.
†Hadley: Benjamin. C. A. Bn's Regt. Wood's Co. 1775. Bn. Vol.
Hadley: Benjamin. Capt. Green, R. I. 3 mos. 1780. ix. 230, 272, 462.
Hardee or Hardy: Asher. S. p. W. before 1777. 325. C. A. 1777, for 3 years. xix.
Hay: Dr. John. S. p. W. before 1777. 283.

---

3 Gershom Flagg is the name of a noted inhabitant of Woburn in former times. But the person here referred to, though a descendant of his, lived and died in Wilmington.

4 James Gardner was not taxed in Woburn; and is presumed to have been an inhabitant of "Gardner Row," just within the bounds of "Charlestown End."

Heywood: Jonathan. Capt. Ford, Cambridge, 1777–78. vi. viii.
†Hodge: Ebenezer. C. A. 1777, for 3 years, for Woburn. xix. St. H. L.
Holden: Jonathan. S. p. W. before 1777. 16.
†Hopkins: Jesse. C. A. Bn's Reg. Wood's Co. 1775. Bn. Vol.
Ingraham: Elijah. C. A. 1777, for 3 years, for Woburn. St. H. L.
Jaquith: Isaac. S. p. W. before 1777. 259.
Johnson: Abijah. C. A. 8 mos. 1775. St. H. L.
Johnson: Abijah. Capt. Edgell. R. I. 6 weeks. 1778. 354.
Johnson: Azel. Capt. Foster at the Northward, 1777. 113.
Johnson: Azel. C. A. 6 mos. 1780. 251.
Johnson: Daniel. S. p. W. before 1777. 347.
Johnson: Francis. Capt. Foster at the Northward, 1777. 132
Johnson: Ichabod. C. A. 8 mos. 1775. St. H. L.
Johnson: Ichabod. Capt. Ford, Cambridge, 1777–78. vi. viii.
Johnson: Ichabod. C. A. 6 mos. 1780. 244, 415.
Johnson: Isaac. Capt. Edgell, R. I. 6 weeks. 1778. 348.
Johnson: James. S. p. W. before 1777. 198, 300, 442.
Johnson: James. Lieut. Dix, Cambridge, 1778. vii. viii.
Johnson: John. C. A. Bn's Regt. Wood's Co. 1776. Bn. Vol.
Johnson: Jonathan. S. p. W. before 1777. 264, 267.
Johnson: Lt. Joseph. At Cambridge 2 mos. 1777. v. viii. 25.
Johnson: Jotham. S. p. W. before Jan. 1777. 176, 278.
Johnson: Reuben. S. p. W. before 1777. 149.
Johnson: Samuel. S. p. W. before 1777. 324.
Johnson: Ensign Seth. S. p. W. before 1777. 146.
Johnson: Shubael. S. p. W. before 1777. 158, 337.
Johnson: William, jun. S. p. W. before 1777. 169.
Johnson: William. Capt. Ford, Cambridge, 1777–78. vi. viii.
†Jones: Sergt. John. C. A. 1777. 3 years. xix. St. H. L.
Jones: Jonathan. Capt. Wyman. R. I. 1777. 249.
Jones: Jonathan. Capt. Ford, Cambridge, 1777–78. vi. viii.
Jones: Jonathan. C. A. 6 mos. 1780. 331, 413.
Jones: Joshua. S. p. W. before 1777. 400.
Kendall: Benjamin. C. A. 8 mos. 1775. St. H. L.
Kendall: Benjamin. C. A. Bn's Regt. Wood's Co. 1775–76. Bn. Vol.
Kendall: Benjamin. C. A. 1777, for 3 years. St. H. L.
Kendall: Jonathan. Lt. Jos. Johnson, Camb. 1777. v. viii. 133.
Kendall: Joseph. Capt. Foster at the Northward, 1777.
Kendall: Joseph. Capt. Dix, R. I. 1778. 463.
Kendall: Joshua. S. p. W. before 1777. 8.
Kendall: Nathan. S. p. W. before 1777. 9, 388.
Kendall: Nathan. Capt. Wyman, Bunker Hill, 1778. viii. xvi.
Kendall: Obadiah. S. p. W. before 1777. 92.
Kendall: Obadiah. Lt. Jos. Johnson, Cambridge, 1777. v. viii. 323.
Kendall: Oliver. C. A. Bn's Regt. Woods' Co. 1776. Bn. Vol.
Kendall: Oliver. C. A. 1777 for 3 years. St. H. L.
†Killgore: Trueworthy. C. A. 1777. 3 years. xix. St. H. L.
Kimball: John. S. p. W. before 1777. 101.
Kimball: John. Capt. Foster at Northw. 1777. 151.
Kimball: Joseph. S. p. W. before 1777. 181.
Kimball: Lt. Reuben. Capt. Foster at Northward, 1777. 114.
Kimball: Reuben. C. A. 1777. 3 years. xix.
†Knox: James. C. A. 8 mos. 1775. St. H. L.
Knox: James. Col. Greaton's Regt. Knox's Artificers. Worc. Rolls.
Larrabee or Leatherby: Thomas. Capt. Foster at Northw. 1777. 317.
Lawrence: Ebenezer. Capt. Ford, Cambridge, 1777-78. vi. viii. 115.
Lawrence: Jonathan [jun.]. Capt. Foster at Northward, 1777. 61.
Lawrence: Joseph. S. p. W. before 1777. 2.
Leathe: Elijah. S. p. W. before Jan. 1777. 97, 248.
Leathe: Elijah, jun. Capt. Foster at Northw. 1777. 122, 370.

Leathe: James. Capt. Dix, R. I. 6 weeks, 1778. 375.
Lenox: Cornelius. [A Mulatto.] C. A. 8 mos. 1775. St. H. L.
Lenox: Cornelius. C. A. Bn's Regt. Wood's Co. 1775. Bn. Vol.
Lock: Benjamin. C. A. 8 mos. 1775. 335, 434.
Lock: Ebenezer. C. A. 8 mos. 1775. St. H. L.
Lock: Ebenezer. C. A. Bn's Regt. Wood's Co. 1775-76. Bn. Vol.
Lock: Ebenezer. C. A. 1777. 3 years enlisted for. xix. St. H. L.
Lock: Ebenezer, jun. C. A. Bn's Regt. Wood's Co. 1775-6. Bn. Vol.
Lock: Jonathan. S. p. W. before 1777. 230.
Lock: Jonathan. Capt. Green, R. I. 3 mos. 1780. ix. 417,435.
Lock: Josiah. S. p. W. "since 1774." 458.
Lock: Thomas, Capt. C. A. Bn's Regt. Wood's Co. 1775-76. Bn. Vol.
Lock: Thomas, jun. Capt. Foster at Northward, 1777. 195.
Lock: Thomas, jun. Lt. Dix, near Camb. 3 mos. 1778. vii. viii.
Lock: William. Expedition to Ticonderoga, July, 1776.[5]
†McDowell: William. C. A. 1777. 3 years. xix.
McGill: Robert. Capt. Foster at Northward, 1777. 60, 120.
McLean: Uriah. C. A. 1777. 3 years. St. H. L.
Mallet: Isaac. Capt. Ford, Cambridge, 1777-78. vi. viii. 298.
Marion: Ebenezer. C. A. 8 mos. 1775. St. H. L.
Marion: Ebenezer. C. A. Bn's Regt. Wood's Co. 1775. Bn. Vol.
Marion: Ebenezer. C. A. 1777: enlisted for 3 years, but died. St. H. L.
Marion: Isaac. S. p. W. before Jan. 1, 1777. 64, 344
Marion: Isaac. Capt. Ford, Cambridge, 1777-78. vi. viii. 5.
Mason: Aaron. C. A. 1777. 3 years. xix. St. H. L. 460.
Mason: Charles. C. A. 1777. 3 years. [died]. xix. St. H. L.
†Merow: Prince. [a Mulatto servant.] C. A. 1777. 3 years. xix.
Miller: Job. C. A. 6 mos. 1780. for Woburn. 220, 438.
Munroe: Andrew.[6] C. A. 1777. 3 years. St. H. L.
Munroe: Andrew. C. A. 6 mos. 1780. for Woburn. 234.
†Neal: Edward. C. A. 1777. 3 years. [an Invalid.] St. H. L.
Nevers: Samuel, jun. Capt. Foster at Northward, 1777. 105.
Newman: Ebenezer. C. A. 8 mos. 1775. St. H. L.
Newman: Ebenezer. C. A. Bn's Regt. Wood's Co. 1775. Bn. Vol.
Newman: Josiah. Lt. Jos. Johnson at Cambridge, 1777. v. viii.
Newman: Josiah. Bunker Hill, 5 weeks from Jan. 25, 1779. 441.
Newman: Josiah. Capt. Green, R. I. 3 mos. 1780. ix. 416, 470.
Newman: Thomas. S. p. W. before 1777. 89.
Newman: Thomas. C. A. 1777. 3 years. xix.
‡Organ: [al. Morgan] Thomas. C. A. 1777. 3 years. xix. St. H. L.
†Osburn: James. C. A. 1777. 3 years. xix. St. H. L.
Osburn: Fife Major. C. A. 1780. 6 mos. Col Greaton's Regt. 421, 474.
Parker: Edmund. Capt. Green, R. I. 3 mos. 1780. ix. 430.
Parker: Josiah. Capt. Wyman, Bunker Hill, 1778. viii. xvi. 130.
Parker: Josiah. Lt. Jos. Johnson, Cambridge, 1777. v. viii. 134.
Peirce: Benjamin. Continental Army. Worc. Rolls.
Peirce: Joshua. C. A. 8 mos. 1775. 255.
Peirce: Josiah. S. p. W. before 1777. 32.
Perry: John. C. A. Bn's Regt. Wood's Co. 1776. Bn. Vol.
Perry: John. Capt. Edgell, R. I. 6 weeks. 1778. 468.
Perry: Jonathan. C. A. 6 mos. 1780. Worc. Rolls.
Perry: Lt. Joseph. Lt. Dix, near Cambridge Lines, 1778. vii. viii.
Perry: Lt. Joseph. Capt. Green, R. I. 3 mos. 1780. ix. 49, 165.
Peters: Philip. S. p. W. before Jan. 1777. 51.

---

[5] In Rev. Mr. Marrett's List of Deaths, 1776, William Lock is said to have died at Ticonderoga in the autumn of that year.

[6] Andrew Monroe, a native of Lexington, but taxed as an inhabitant of Woburn in the State tax for 1780, '81, '82.

†Phipps: Elijah. Capt. Green, R. I. 3 mos. 1780. ix. 414.
†Pike: Ebenezer. C. A. 8 mos. 1775. for Woburn. St. H. L.
†Pitts: Michael. C. A. 8 mos. 1775. for Woburn. St. H. L.
Pomp: Blackman. C. A. 8 mos. 1775. St. H. L.
Pomp: Blackman. C. A. Bn's Regt. Pettingill's Co. 1775. Bn. Vol.
Pomp: Blackman. Capt. Green, R. I. 3 mos. 1780. ix. 292, 319, 430.
Poole: Eleazar Flagg. S. p. W. 1776. 3, 192.
Pool: Eleazar F. jun. C. A. 6 mos. 1780. 214.
Porter: Dudley. S. p. W. before Jan. 777. 80, 346.
Porter: Lt. Jonathan. C. A. 3 years. 1777–9. xix. St. H. L.
Porter: Josiah. Continental Army. Worc. Rolls.
Porter: William. S. p. W. before 1777. 42.
Porter: William, jun. Capt. Wyman, Bunker Hill, 1778. viii. xvi. 135.
Phillips: Thomas. Exped. to Ticonderoga 1776. S. Nevers' Return.
Rainger: Nehemiah. S. p. W. before 1777. 341.
†Rand: Jack. C. A. 1777. 3 years. xix. St. H. L.
Rand: Jack. C. A. 6 mos. 1780. 461.
Randall: Josiah. C. A. Bn's Regt. Wood's Co. 1775. Bn. Vol.
Reed: Amos, S. p. W. before 1777. 301.
Reed: Daniel. Capt. Foster at Northward, 1777. 383.
Reed: Ebenezer. S. p. W. before 1777. 40, 70.
Reed: Ezekiel. Continental Army. Worc. Rolls.
Reed: George. S. p. W. before 1777. 394.
Reed: George, jun.[7]
Reed: Isaac. Capt. Ford, Cambridge, 1777–78. vi. viii.
Reed: Israel. C. A. 8 mos. 1775. St. H. L.
Reed: Jacob. S. p. W. "before Jan. 1777." 35, 403.
Reed: James, jun. C. A. 8 mos. 1775. St. H. L.
Reed: James jun. Capt. Green, R. I. 3 mos. 1780. ix. 410, 465.
Reed: Lt. James. Capt. Ford, Cambridge, 1777–78. vi. viii. 172.
Reed: Joel. C. A. Bn's Regt. Woods' Co. 1776. Bn. Vol.
Reed: Joel. C. A. 1777. 3 years. St. H. L.
Reed: John. C. A. 8 mos. 1775. St. H. L.
Reed: Jonas. Capt. Foster, at Northward, 1777. 153.
Reed: Capt. Joshua. S. p. W. before Jan. 1777. 17, 349.
Reed: Joshua [jun.?]. S. p. W. before 1777. 90, 256.
Reed: Joshua, jun. C. A. 1777, 3 years. xix.
Reed: Joshua. C. A. Drummer. Worc. Rolls.
Reed: Micah. S. p. W. before 1777. 342.
Reed: Micah. Capt. Foster at Northward, 1777. 109.
Reed: Micah. Capt. Ford, Camb. 1777–78. vi. viii. 161.
Reed: Newhall. S. p. W. before 1777. 127, 197.
Reed: Newhall. C. A. 8 mos. 1775. St. H. L.
Reed: Reuben. C. A. 1777. 3 years. St. H. L.
Reed: Dea. Samuel. S. p. W. before 1777. 45.
Reed: Swithin. S. p. W. before 1777. 50.
Reed: Thomas. C. A. 8 mos. 1775. St. H. L.
Reed: Ward. Capt. Green, R. I. 3 mos. 1780. ix. 436.
Richarson: Abel, jun. S. p. W. before Jan. 1777. 46, 126, 128.
Richarson: Abijah. Lt. Jos. Johnson, Cambridge, 1777. v. viii.
Richarson: Alford. Capt. Wyman, R. I. 1777. 433.
Richardson: Barnabas. Capt. Wyman, R. I. 2 mos. 1777. 330.
Richardson: Barnabas. Lt. Joseph Johnson, Camb. 2 mos. 1777. v. 341.
Richardson: Bartholomew. S. p. W. before 1777. 162.
Richardson: Barth. jun. S. p. W. before 1777. 208.

---

[7] "June 26, 1775. Attended the funeral of George Reed, jun. who died of a fever, which was occasioned by a surfeit or heat he got in Charlestown fight, the 17th inst." Rev. Mr. Marrett's Interleaved Almanac for 1775.

Richardson: Charles. Capt. Green, R. I. 3 mos. 1780. ix. 426, 455.
Richardson: Ebenezer. S. p. W. before 1777. 261.
Richardson: Ebenezer, jun. S. p. W. before 1777. 407.
Richardson: Edmund. S. p. W. before 1777. 48.
Richardson: Edmund. C. A. 8 mos. 1775. St. H. L.
Richardson: Edward. S. p. W. before 1777. 238.
Richardson: Eleazer. S. p. W. before 1777. 285.
Richardson: Jacob. C. A. 8 mos. 1775. St. H. L.
Richardson: Jacob.[8] C. A. 6 mos. 1780. 215, 226, 227, 472.
Richardson: James. C. A. 8 mos. 1775. St. H. L.
Richardson: Lt. Jeduthun. S. p. W. before 1777. 321.
Richardson: Lt.Jeduthun. Capt.Ford, Camb. 1777–78. vi. viii. 104.
Richardson: Lt. Jeduthun. Fifer. Capt.Green, R. I. 3 mos. 1780. ix. 425.
Richardson: Jesse. S. p. W. before 1777. 55, 278.
Richardson: Jesse, jun. Capt. Green, R. I. 3 mos. 1780. ix. 427.
Richardson: Jesse, [son of Zechariah] Guarding prisoners of Convention 15 days in July 1778. 73.
Richardson: Gideon. C. A. 8 mos. 1775. St. H. L.
Richardson: Gideon. C. A. 1777. 3 years. xix. St. H. L.
Richardson: Ichabod. C. A. 8 mos. 1775. St. H. L.
Richardson: Lt. John. S. p. W. before 1777. 448.
Richardson: John, jun. C. A. 8 mos. 1775. St. H. L.
Richardson: Capt. Jonas. S. p. W. in 1775.
Richardson: Jonas. C. A. 1777, during the War. St. H. L.
Richardson: Jonathan. S. p. W. before 1777. 391.
Richardson: Jonathan. Capt. Ford, Cambridge, 1777–78. vi. viii. 172.
Richardson: Josiah. S. p. W. before Jan. 1777. 157.
Richardson: Sergt. Luke. Captain Green, R. I. 3 mos. 1780. ix. 275, 362.
Richardson: Leonard. C. A. 1777, 3 years. xix.
Richardson: Matthew. C. A. 8 mos. 1775. St. H. L.
Richardson: Matthew. Capt. Ford, Cambridge, 1777–78. vi. viii.
Richardson: Nathan. S. p. W. "before Jan. 1777." 17, 349.
Richardson: Partridge. Lt. Joseph Johnson, Cambridge, 1777. v. viii.
Richardson: Paul. Lt. Dix, Cambridge, 1778. vii. viii. x. xviii.
Richardson: Peter. Capt. Green, R. I. 3 mos. 1780. ix. 424.
Richardson: Reuben, Ensign. S. p. W. before 1777. 85.
Richardson: Samuel. S. p. W. before 1777. 24.
Richardson: Samuel. Capt. Foster, at Northward, 1777. xi. 312.
Richardson: Silas. S. p. W. before 1777. 386.
Richardson: Silas, Sergt. Lt. Jos. Johnson, Cambridge, 1777. v. viii. 178, 179.
Richardson: Stephen. S. p. W. before 1777. 26.
Richardson: Stephen. C. A. 1777. 3 years. xix. Worc. Rolls.
Richardson: Stephen, Lieut. S. p. W. before 1777. 185.
Richardson: Mr. Zachariah.S. "p. W. before Jan. 1777." 12, 187.
Richardson: Zachariah, jun. S. p. W. before 1777. 245.
Richardson: Zadok. S. p. W. before 1777. 29.
Richardson: Zadok. Capt. Ford, Camb. 5 mos. 1777–78. vi. viii.

---

[8] "The Bearer hereof, Jacob Richardson, a Soldier in the Seventh Massachusetts Regiment, having served as a faithful good Soldier in the said Regiment, the Term of Six Months, being the full Term for which he inlisted, is hereby discharged from the same.

"Given under my hand at West Point this Ninth Day of January, 1781.

Moses Knap, Maj[r] Com[t].

"Agreeable to General Orders, the Commissaries are directed to issue Provisions sufficient to carry the Bearer to Oborn in the Massachusetts Bay State. Moses Knap, Major Com[t]."

Other discharges like the above are on the Town Files.

Richardson: Zebulon. S. p. W. "before Jan. 1777." 175, 299.
Richardson: Zebulon. Guarding prisoners of Convention 15 days in July 1778. 381.
Robbins: Jonathan. S. p. W. "before 1777." 420.
Robbins: Jonathan. Capt. Wyman, Bunker Hill, 1778. viii. 246.
Ross: Alexander McLean. C. A. Bn's Regt. Wood's Co. 1776. Bn. Vol.
Russell: Bill. Capt. Green, R. I. 3 mos. 1780. ix. 22, 430, 444.
Russell: Jesse, jun. Capt. Ford, Camb. 1777–78. vi. viii.
Russell: Samuel. C. A. 8 mos. 1775; killed at Bunker Hill, June 17, 1775. St. H. L.
Scott: Mr. William. S. p. W. before 1777. 142.
Scottow: John. Capt. Wm. Green, R. I. 1780. ix. 446, 471.
Scottow: John. Continental Army. Worc. Rolls.
†Sergeant: Reuben. C. A. 1777, 3 years. xix.
Simonds: Caleb, jun. C. A. 8 mos. 1775. St. H. L.
Simonds: Caleb, jun. C. A. Bn's Regt. Wood's Co. 1775. Bn. Vol.
Simonds: Caleb, jun. C. A. 6 mos. 1780.
Simonds: Calvin. S. p. W. "before Jan. 1, 1777." 150, 277.
Simonds: Jesse. S. p. W. before 1777. 86.
Simonds: Jonathan. S. p W. before 1777. 139, 345.
Simonds: Jonathan. Capt. Ford, Cambridge, 1777–78. vi. viii.
Simonds: Luther. S. p. W. before 1777. 269.
Simonds: Silas. S. p. W. before 1777. 182.
Skelton: Daize. S. p. W. "before Jan. 1777." 278, 289, 363.
Skelton: Daize. Capt. Foster at Northward, 1777. 174.
Skelton: Matthew. S. p. W. "before Jan. 1, 1777." 281, 306.
Skelton: Thomas, jun. S. p. W. before 1777. 163.
Skelton: Thomas, jun. Lt. Dix, Cambridge, 1778. vii. viii. 152.
Skinner: Abraham. S. p. W. before 1777. 350.
Skinner: Abraham. Capt. Ford, Cambridge, 1777-78. vi. viii. 123.
Skinner: John. S. p. W. before 1777. 23.
Skinner: Joseph. S. p. W. before 1777. 237.
Smith: Abijah. S. p. W. before 1777. 358.
†Smith: Edward. C. A. 1777. 3 years for Woburn. xix.
†Smith: James. C. A. 1777. 3 years for Woburn. xix.
Smith: Jonathan. S. p. W. before 1777. 279.
Smith: Snow James. C. A. 3 years. 1777-79. xix. St. H. L.
Smith: Jesse. S. p. W. 1776. 340.
Smith: Jonathan. C. A. 1777. 3 years. xix. St. H. L.
Sutton: Prince [a black?]. C. A. 8 mos. 1775. St. H. L.
Sutton: Prince. C. A. Bn's Regt. Wood's Co. 1775. Bn. Vol.
Sutton: Prince. C. A. 1777. 3 years. xix.
Sutton: Prince. Capt. Green, R. I. 3 mos. 1780. ix. 365.
†Swett: Cicero. [a black or mulatto?] C. A. 1777. 3 years. St. H. L.
Symmes: Samuel. S. p. W. before 1777. 205.
Symmes: William. Capt. Ford, Cambridge, 1777-78. vi. viii.
Symmes: William. Cont. Army. Worc. Rolls.
Symmes: Zachariah. S. p. W. before 1777. 56.
Stratton: William. Exped. to Ticonderoga[9] 1776. Nevers' List.
Tay: Aaron. S. p. W. before 1777. 303.
Tay: John. S. p. W. before 1777. 18.
Tay: John, jun. C. A. 6 mos. 1780. 240.
Tay: William, sen. S. p. W. before 1777. 393,397.
Tay: William, jun. Lieut. Capt. Foster at Northw. 1777. [" by his servant."] 117.
Tay: William, 3d. S. p. W. before 1777. 77.
Tay: William, 3d. Capt. Wyman, Bunker Hill, 1778. viii. xvi. 116.
Tay: Samuel. Capt. S. p. W. before 1777. 34,193.
Thompson: Abijah. Capt. Foster at Northward, 1777. 250.
Thompson: Jabez. S. p. W. before 1777. 75.

[9] Where he died in the autumn of that year. Rev. Mr. Marrett's List of Deaths in 1776.

Thompson: Jonathan. ["Musician."] C. A. 8 mos. 1775. St. H. L.
Thompson: Jonathan. C. A. Bn's Regt. Pettingell's Co. 1775. Bn. Vol.
Thompson: Samuel, Esq. S p. W. before Jan. 1777. 34, 193.
Tidd: Benjamin. Lt. Jos. Johnson, Cambridge, 1777. v. viii.
Tidd: Benjamin. Bunker Hill, 5 weeks from Jan. 25, 1778-9. 440.
Tidd: Jonathan, jun. Lt. Jos. Johnson, Cambridge, 1777. v. viii. 295.
Tidd: Lt. Jonathan. C. A. 8 mos. 1775. St. H. L.
Tidd: Lt. Jonathan. C. A. Bn's Regt. Wood's Co. 1775. Bn. Vol.
Tidd: Samuel. S. p. W. before 1777. 343.
Tidd: Samuel. Lt. Jos. Johnson, Cambridge, 1777. 118.
Tottingham: David. Capt. Green, R. I. 1780. ix. 364.
Tottingham: Elisha. S. p. W. before 1777. 129.
Tottingham: Ephraim. S. p. W. before 1777. 96.
Tottingham: Jonathan. S. p. W. "before Jan. 1777." 334.
Trask: David. C. A. 8 mos. 1775. St. H. L.
Trask: David. C. A. 6 mos. 1780. 218, 411.
Trask: John. S. p. W. "before Jan. 1777." 13, 100, 180.
Trask: John. C. A. 1777, 3 years. St. H. L.
Trask: Jonathan. C. A. 8 mos. 1775. St. H. L.
Trask: Jonathan. C. A. 1777, 3 years. St. H. L.
Trask: Joseph. Lt. Jos. Johnson, Cambridge, 1777. 119, 262.
Trask: Joseph. Capt. Wyman, Bunker Hill, 1778. viii. xvi.
Trask: Nathaniel. C. A. Bn's Regt. Wood's Co. 1775. Bn. Vol.
†Tufts: Ebenezer. C. A. 8 mos. 1775. for Woburn. St. H. L.
†Tufts: Zachary. C. A. 8 mos. 1775. for Woburn. St. H. L.
Tweed: David. C. A. 6 mos. 1780. 218, 411.
Tweed: James. Exped. to Ticonderoga, 1776. Never's Returns.
Twiss: Edward, jun. S. p. W. before 1777. 190, 287.
Twiss: James. Cont. Army. Worc. Rolls.
Twiss: Solomon. C. A. Bn's Regt. Wood's Co. 1775. Bn. Vol.
Twiss: Stephen. C. A. 8 mos. 1775. St. H. L.
Twiss: Stephen. C. A. Bn's Regt. Wood's Co. 1775. Bn. Vol.
Twiss: Stephen. C. A. 1777. 3 years. St. H. L.
Twiss: Stephen. } War in R. I. Enlisted for, July 6, 1781. 469.
Twiss: Stephen, jun. }
Twiss: Timothy. S. p. W. before 1777. 304, 395.
Twiss: Timothy. Capt. Wyman, Bunker Hill, 1778. viii. xvi.
Tyler: Jeremiah. C. A. 1777. 3 years. xix. St. H. L.
Tyler: Jeremiah. Capt. Green, R. I. 3 mos. 1780. ix. 366.
Tyler: Jonathan. Capt. Green, R. I. 3 mos. 1780. ix. 447, 459.
Tyler: Moses, jun. C. A. 1777. [3 years?] 332, 466.
Tyler: Moses, jun. C. A. 6 mos. 1780. 333.
Wade: Ebenezer. S. p. W. before 1777. 211.
Walker: Edward. C. A. Bn's Regt. Pettingell's Co. 1775. Bn. Vol.
Walker: James, Corp. C. A. 8 mos. 1775. St. H. L.
Walker: James, Corp. C. A. Bn's Regt. Wood's Co. 1775. Bn. Vol.
Walker: James, Corp. Bunker Hill, 5 weeks from Jan. 25, 1779. 443.
Walker: John. C. A. Bn's Regt. Pettingell's Co. 1775. Bn. Vol.
Walker: John. C. A. 6 mos. 1780. 217.
Walker: Joshua, Capt. S. p. W. before 1777. 399.
Walker: Joshua, Capt. C. A. 1777, 3 years. xix.
Walker: Joshua, jun.
Walker: Joshua, jun. Lt. Jos. Johnson, Camb. 2 mos. 1777. v. viii.
Walker: Joshua, jun. Capt. Wyman, Bunker Hill, 1778. viii, 67.
Walker: Josiah. S. p. W. before 1777. 235.
Walker: Josiah [jun?]. Lt. Joseph Johnson, Cambridge, 1777. v. viii. 15.
Walker: Timothy? C. A. Bn's Regt. Pettingell's Co. 1775. Bn. Vol.
Watts: Nathaniel. S. P. W. before 1777. 88.

Watts: Samuel. S. p. W. before 1777. 156.
†White: Luther. C. A. 8 mos. 1775. for Woburn. St. H. L.
†Willis: John. C. A. 8 mos. 1775. for Woburn. St. H. L.
Wilson: Samuel [jun?]. C. A. 8 mos. 1775. St. H. L.
Wilson: Samuel, [jun?]. C. A. Bn's Regt. Pettingell's Co. 1775. Bn. Vol.
Wilson: Timothy. S. p. W. before 1777. 186.
Wilson: Timothy. Capt. Foster at Northward, 1777. 305.
Wilson: Timothy. Capt. Green, R. I. 3 mos. 1780. ix.
Winn: David. Capt. Edgell. R. I. 6 weeks. 1778. 231.
Winn: Increase. S. p. W. before 1777. 280.
Winn: Jacob. C. A. 8 mos. 1775. St. H. L.
Winn: Jacob. C. A. Bn's Regt. Pettingell's Co. 1775. Bn. Vol.
Winn: Jacob. Lt. Jos. Johnson, Cambridge, 1777. v. viii. 164.
Winn: Joseph, Lt. S. p. W. before 1777. 204.
Winn: Joseph, Lt. Capt. Ford, Cambridge, 1777-78. vi. viii. 53.
Winn: Jeremiah. C. A. 8 mos. 1775. St. H. L.
Winn: Jeremiah. C. A. Bn's Regt. Pettingell's Co. 1775. Bn. Vol.
Winn: Samuel. S. p. W. before 1777. 94.
Winn: Samuel. Capt. Wyman, Bunker Hill, 1778. viii. xvi. 263.
Winn: Dea. Timothy. S. p. W. before 1777. 138.
Winn: Timothy, jun. Ensign: S. p. W. before 1777. 78, 371.
Winn: Timothy, 3d. Capt. Green, R. I. 3 mos. 1780. ix. 376, 380.
Wood: Benjamin. C. A. 8 mos. 1775. St. H. L
Wood: Edward. C. A. 8 mos. 1775. St. H. L.
Wood: Edward. C. A. Bn's Regt. Wood's Co. 1775. Bn. Vol.
Wood: Edward. Capt. Foster at the Northw. 1777. 111, 385.
Wood: Edward. C. A. 6 mos. 1780. 216.
Wood: Capt. John. S. p. W. before Jan. 1, 1777. 191.
Wood: Capt. John. C. A. 1777, 3 years. xix.
Wood: Capt. John. C. A. Bn's Regt. 1775. Bn. Vol.
Wood: Lt. Silvanus. C. A. 8 mos. 1775. St. H. L.
Wood: Lt. Silvanus. C. A. Bn's Regt. Wood's Co. 1775, Lt. 1776. Bn. Vol. 308.
Wood: Solomon.[10] S. p. W. before 1777. 141, 188.
Wright: Jesse. Capt. Wyman, Bunker Hill, 1778. viii. xvi.
Wright: Jonathan. S. p. W. "before Jan. 1777." 356.
Wright: Jonathan. Capt. Wyman, Bunker Hill, 1778. viii. xvi.
Wright: Joseph. S. p. W. before 1777. 83.
Wright: Josiah. Capt. Wyman, Bunker Hill, 1778. viii. xvi.
Wright: Philemon. Capt. Wyman, R. I. 2 mos. 1777. 405.
Wright: Philemon. C. A. Bn's Regt. Wood's Co. 1776. Bn. Vol.
Wright: Thomas, jun. Lt. Jos. Johnson, Camb. 2 mos. 1777. v. viii. 131.
Wright: Thomas, jun. Guarding prisoners of Convention, 15 days. July 1778. 39.
Wright: Timothy. S. p. W. "before January 1, 1777." 339.
Wyman: Abel. Capt. Jesse Wyman, Bunker Hill, 1778. viii. xvi.
Wyman: David. Capt. Ford, Cambridge, 1777-78. vi. viii.
Wyman: Elijah. S. p. W. before 1777.
Wyman: Eliphaz. S. p. W. before 1777. 372.
Wyman: Eliphaz. Capt. Foster at Northward, 1777. 110.
Wyman: Ezra. S. p. W. before 1777. 293.
Wyman: Ezra, jun. Capt. Wyman, Bunker Hill, 1778. viii. xvi.
Wyman: Francis. C. A. Bn's Regt. Wood's Co. 1776. Bn. Vol.
Wyman: Hezekiah. S. p. W. before 1777. 167.
Wyman: Lt. James. S. p. W. before 1777. 288.

---

[10] Solomon Wood "died of the small pox in the Army at the Jerseys, March 16, 1777." Rev. Mr. Marrett's List of Deaths.

Wyman, James, jun. C. A. 1777, 3 years. xix. St. H. L.
Wyman: James, jun. C. A. 1780. 6 mos. 233.
Wyman: Capt. Jesse. S. p. W. before 1777. 66.
Wyman: Capt. Jesse. S. in R. I. 1777. 2 mos. 223.
Wyman: Capt. Jesse. S. at Bunker Hill, 3 mos. 1778. viii. xvi.
Wyman: Jesse, jun.[11]
Wyman: Jonas.[12] S. p. W. [deceased] Order paid to Administrator. 38.
Wyman: Jonathan. S. p. W. before 1777. 95.
Wyman: Joseph. C. A. 6 mos. 1780. 6, 429, 464.
Wyman: Joseph, [son of Sam. Esq.] Bunker Hill, 5 weeks from Jan. 25, 1779. 225.
Wyman: Joshua. S. p. W. before 1777. 19, 21.
Wyman: Nathan. S. p. W. before Jan. 1777. 136, 148.
Wyman: Nathan, jun. C. A. 8 mos. 1775. St. H. L.
Wyman: Nathan, jun. C. A. Bn's Regt. Pettingell's Co. 1775. Bn·Vol.
Wyman: Nathan, jun. Lt. Jos. Johnson, Cambridge, 1777. v. viii.
Wyman: Nathan, jun. Capt. Green, R. I. 3 mos. 1780. ix. 428.
Wyman: Nathaniel. Capt. Foster at Northward, 1777. 183.
Wyman: Nathaniel, jun. S. p. W. before 1777. 203.
Wyman: Paul. S. p. W. before 1777. 30.
Wyman: Samuel, Esq. S. p. W. before 1777. 326.
Wyman: Stephen. C. A. Bn's Regt. Wood's Co. 1776. Bn. Vol.
Wyman: Thomas. S. p. W. before 1777. 11.
Wyman: Zebadiah. S. p. W. before 1777. 68.
†Yew, [Yow?] Oliver. C. A. 1777, during the War. St. H. L.

The Compiler of the above List has spared no pains to make it as correct and complete as possible. But he dares not flatter himself that there are no deficiencies in it, no errors in its details.

By counting the individuals in the foregoing list, it will be found, that there were 376 inhabitants of Woburn who enlisted in the War of the Revolution, and 46 strangers who were hired by it for the same service; making a total of 422 who served for it in that contest with Great Britain.

APPENDIX, No. XIII.

Lists of Town and Church Officers, School Teachers, &c.

Selectmen.

From 1644, *when the first choice was made, to* 1860.

Edward Johnson, 1644, 5, 6, 7, 9, 50, 51, 2, 3, 4, 5, 6, 7, 8.
Edward Convers, 1644, 5, 6, 7, 9, 50, 51, 2, 3, 4, 5, 6, 7, 8, 9.
John Mousall, 1644, 5, 6, 7, 9, 50, 51, 2, 3, 4, 5, 6, 7, 8, 9.
William Learned, 1644, 5.
Ezekiel Richardson, 1644, 5, 6, 7.
Samuel Richardson, 1644, 5, 6, 9, 50, 51.
James Thompson, 1644, 6, 9, 50, 51, 2, 3, 4, 5, 6, 7, 8.

---

11 "1775 Jnne 22. Attended the funeral of Jesse Wyman, aged 21, living in the Old Parish, mortally wounded in the battle at Charlestown." Rev. Mr. Marrett's Interleaved Almanac.

12 Jonas Wyman died in the autumn of 1776, in the army at New York. Rev. Mr. Marrett's List of Deaths in 1776.

John Wright, 1645, 6, 7, 9, 50, 51, 2, 3, 4, 5, 6, 7, 8.
Miles Nutt, 1647, 9, 50, 52, 3, 4, 5, 6.
John Tidd, 1647.
No Record of choice for 1648.
Ralph Hill, 1651.
John Russell, 1652, 3, 4, 5, 6.
Only five Selectmen chosen for 1657.
Michael Bacon, 1659.
Francis Kendall, 1659.
Édward Convers, 1660, 1, 2, 3.
John Mousall, 1660, 1, 2, 3, 4.
Thomas Peirce, 1660, 1, 2.
John Wright, 1660, 1, 2, 3, 4.
James Thompson, 1660, 1, 2, 7, 9.
Edward Johnson, 1661, 7, 9.
Thomas Fuller, 1663-4.
Francis Kendall, 1663, 5, 6, 7, 8.
Lieut. John Carter, 1664.
William Johnson, 1664.
Josiah Convers, 1664.
James Convers, 1664.
Michael Bacon, 1665, 6, 8.
Thomas Peirce, 1665, 6.
Bartholomew Peirson, 1665, 6.
Robert Peirce, 1665.
John Wyman, 1666, 7, 8.
John Seirs, 1667, 8.
John Mousall, jun., 1668.
Samuel Walker, 1668.
Henry Brooks, 1669.
Edward Winn, 1669.
John Wright, 1670.
Francis Kendall, 1670, 3, 4, 5, 6, 7, 8.
Michael Bacon, 1670.
Isaac Cole, 1670.
Joseph Wright, 1670.
Edward Johnson, 1671.
James Thompson, 1671.
Henry Brooks, 1671, 2.
John Mousall, jun., 1671.
Matthew Johnson, 1671, 2, 6, 7, 8.
John Carter, 1672, 3, 4, 5, 6, 7, 8, 9.
Ensign James Convers, 1674, 5, 6 declined for 1676, chosen 1677, 8, 9.
William Johnson, 1672, 3, 4, 5, 6, 7, 8, 9; declined serving 1676.
Josiah Convers, 1672; declined; and in his stead was chosen
Serg. James Convers, 1672.
John Wyman, 1673.
Joseph Wright, 1673.
Francis Wyman, 1674, 5.
Mr. Samuel Carter, 1679.
Samuel Walker, jun., 1679.
Lt. William Johnson, 1680, 82, 83, 4, 5, 6, 7, 8.
Ens. James Convers, 1680, 82, 3, 4, 5, 6, 8.
Serg. Matthew Johnson, 1680, 81, 2, 3, 4, 5, 6, 8.
John Wright, 1680, 81.
Francis Kendall, 1680, 82, 3, 7, 8.
Henry Baldwin, 1681.
Mr. Samuel Carter, 1681, 2, 3.
Samuel Blogget, 1681.
Serg. James Convers, 1684, 86.
Corp. Saml. Walker, 1684, 85, Sarg. 1686, 7.
Sarg. Thos. Fuller, 1685.
William Locke, 1687.
Increase Winn, 1687, 8.
N. B. Only 4 Selectmen chosen in February, 1686-7. The same rechosen in March 7, 1686-7.
P. S. Wm. Johnson Selectman for 1687, beside the 4 recorded.
The choice by the people at the usual time in Feb. annulled, and a new choice ordered by Justices of the Peace.
No Meeting for choice of town officers in 1689.
Sarg. Samuel Walker, 1690.
Samuel Blogget, sen., 1690.
Lt. John Richardson, 1690.
John Wright, sen., 1690.
John Peirce, sen., 1690.
Capt. William Johnson, 1691.
Lt. James Convers, jun., 1691.
Ens. Saml. Walker, 1691.
Sarg. Matthew Johnson, 1691.
Saml. Blogget, sen., 1691, 93, 95, 6, 7.
Lieut. John Richardson, 1692.
Ens. Joseph Winn, sen., 1692, 93.
Joseph Wright, sen., 1692.
John Burbean, sen., 1692.
Lt. Joseph Peirce, 1692, 93, 95.
Josêph Richardson, sen., 1693, 4.
James Fowle, 1693, 4.
James Convers, jun., [Capt.] 1694.
Jonathan Wyman, 1694.
Joshua Sawyer, 1694.
Lt. Josiah Parker, 1695.
Jacob Wyman, 1695.
James Simonds, 1695.
William Locke, sen., 1696.
Lt. Matthew Johnson, 1696.
Sergt. Israel Walker, 1696.
Benjamin Simonds, 1696, 97.
Ens. John Peirce, 1697.
Lt. Josiah Convers, 1697. 8; chosen 1701, but did not accept.
Sergt. John Tidd, 1697, 1701, 1709.
Lt. Joseph Wright, 1698.
James Convers, jun., 1698, 99.
Corp. Benj. Simonds, 1698, 9.
Jacob Wyman, 1698.

Sergt. Eben. Johnson, 1699.
Sergt. Sam. Blogget, 1699.
Nath. Richardson. sen., 1699.
Capt. Edw. Johnson, 1700, 01, 02, 03, 04, 07, 08.
Sergt. James Fowle, 1700, 01, (1702, declined,) 03, 04, 05, 07, 08, 09.
Lieut. Joseph Peirce, 1700.
Lieut. John Carter, 1700, 1710.
Sergt. George Reed, 1700,1705, 06.
Thomas Peirce, 1701.
Jos. Richardson, sen., 1702.
Lt. Josiah Convers, 1702, 03, 04, 05, 06, Capt. 1707, 09.
James Simonds, 1702.
Samuel Blogget, sen., 1703.
Dea. Sam. Walker, 1703.
William Locke, jun., 1704.
Joshua Sawyer, jun., 1704, sen., 1707.
Major James Convers, 1705, 06.
Ens. John Peirce, 1705, 06, 08, 10.
Sergt. Saml. Wilson, 1706.
Corn. Benj. Simonds, 1707: Lieut. 1709, 1711.
Capt. Seth Wyman, 1707.
Saml. Walker, 1708, Dec. 1711, 12, 14, 15, 18.
Sergt. Eben. Johnson, 1709, 13, 16.
James Fowle, 1710, 11, 12, 13, 14; died March 19, 1714.
John Brooks, 1710.
Josiah Johnson, 1710.
Joshua Sawyer, 1711, 12.
Capt. Edw. Johnson, 1711, 12, 13, 14, 15; Dea. 1718.
Capt. Josiah Convers, 1712, 13, 15, 17.
Ens. Samuel Blogget, 1713.
Lt. Eleazar Flagg, 1714, 15; Capt. 1718, 19.
Qr. Mast. Jos. Richardson, 1714, 16.
John Fowle, 1714, 15, 16, 17, 18, 19.
Jacob Wyman, 1716.
Sergt. Benj. Johnson, 1716.
Sergt. John Tidd, 1717.
Sergt. Benj. Peirce, 1717, 18.
Samuel Richardson, 1717.
Sergt. George Reed, 1719.
Capt. John Coggin, 1719.
Corn. Peirson Richardson, 1719.
Dea. Edward Johnson, 1720, 22, 23, 24.
John Fowle, 1720, 21, 22, 23, 24, 25, 26, 27, 28, 29.
Samuel Richardson, 1720, 22, 23, 26, 27, 28.
Dea. George Reed, 1720, 22, 23, 29.
Dea. Saml. Walker, 1720, 27, 28.
James Peirce, sen., 1721, 24; Sergt. 25.
James Thompson, 1721.
Ens. Stephen Richardson, 1721.
Joseph Wright, 1721, 22, 24, 25, 27, 28, 29.
John Brooks, 1723.
Ens. Josiah Convers, 1724, 25.
Col. Eleazar Flegg, 1725, 26.
Josiah Johnson, 1726.
Dea. James Thompson, 1726.
Capt. Robert Convers, 1727.
Dea. James Thompson, 1728.
Ens. Samuel Blogget, 1729.
Jacob Wyman, 1729.
Josiah Johnson, 1730, 31, 32, 33, 34, 35, 36.
John Fowle, 1730, 31, 32, 33, 34, 35, 36, 37, 38.
Joseph Wright, 1730, 32.
Dea. George Reed, 1730, 31.
Saml. Richardson, 1730, 31, 32, 35, 36
Jacob Wyman, 1731.
Dea. William Locke, 1732.
Corp. James Simonds, 1733, 34, 35, 36, Lieut. 1742, 49, 50.
Lieut. Joshua Thompson, 1733.
John Russell, 1734, 35, 36, 37, 38, 39, 40, 41, 42, 43, 45.
Jacob Richardson, 1734.
Jona. Poole, Esq. 1737, 38, 39, 40, 44.
Josiah Peirce, 1737, 38, 39, 40.
James Proctor, 1737, 38, 39, 40, 41, Lieut. 44, 47, 48, Capt. 49.
Edward Walker, 1739, 40, 45.
Mr. Roland Cotton, 1741, 42, 43.
Capt. John Fowle, jun., 1741.
Dr. Jonathan Heywood, 1741.
David Wyman, 1742, 43, 45, 46, 47, 48, 49, 50.
Benj. Richardson, 1742, 1744.
Josiah Johnson, 1743, 44, 46, 47, 48, 50, 51.
Ebenezer Convers, 1743.
William Tay, 1744, 46, 47, 48, 50, 51.
William Locke, 1745.
Nathan Wyman, 1745, 49.
Lt. Samuel Kendall, 1746, 47, 48.
Joshua Jones, 1746, 50.
Francis Johnson, 1749.
Lieut. Eben. Thompson, 1751.
Benjamin Johnson, 1751.
Capt. John Reed, 1751.
Ebenezer Thompson, 1752.
David Wyman, 1752.
John Reed, 1752.
Oliver Richardson, 1752, 53, 54, 55.
James Fowle, 1752, 53, 54, 55, 59, 60, 61, Esq. 62.
Ebenezer Convers, 1753.
Joshua Jones, 1753, 58, 59, 62, 63, 69, 70, 71, 72.

Thomas Reed, 1753, 54, 55.
Samuel Reed, 1754, 55.
Samuel Wyman, jun. 1754, 55.
Josiah Johnson, Esq. 1756, 58, 66.
Lieut. William Tay, 1756, 59, 60, 61, 62, 63, 64, 65, 67, 70, 71.
Deacon Timothy Winn, 1756, 57.
Mr. Isaac Snow, 1756, 58.
Mr. Ichabod Richardson, 1756.
Capt. Timothy Brooks, 1757.
Mr. Benja. Richardson, 1757, 64.
Mr. Joseph Wright, 1757.
Mr. Jonathan Fox, 1757, Capt. 1763, 64, 65, 67, 68, 69.
Mr. James Baldwin, 1758, 59.
Mr. Jacob Richardson, jun., 1758.
Mr. Nathan Richardson, 1759, 60, 61, Dea. 62, 63.
Mr. Joshua Walker, 1760, 61, Lt. 1773, 74, 75, Capt. 1776, 77.
Mr. Samuel Tidd, 1760, 61.
Capt. Benj. Johnson, 1762, 64, 65, 66, 67, 68.
James Fowle, Esq., 1763, 65, 66, 67, 68, 69, 70, 71, 72, 73, 74, 75.
Mr. Ebenezer Convers, 1764.
Mr. Jacob Wright, 1765, 66.
Dea. Samuel Wyman, 1766, 68, 69, 70, 71, 72, 73, 74, 75, 80.
Mr. James Wyman, 1767, 68, 69.
Mr. Oliver Richardson, 1770, 71, 72.
Lieut. William Tay, 1772, 73, 74, 75, 76, 77, 78, 79.
Dea. Timothy Winn, 1773, 74, 75.
Mr. Thomas Wright, 1776, 77.
Lt. Samuel Thompson, 1776, 77, Dea. 1778, 79.
Dea. David Blanchard, 1776, 77.
Capt. Benjamin Edgel, 1778, 79, 80, 82, 83.
Lt. Jeduthun Richardson, 1778, 79, 80, 82, 83, 84, 85.
Lt. Jonathan Tidd, 1778, 79.
Nathan Richardson, 1780.
Ens. Timothy Winn, 1780, 82, 83, 84, 88.
Col. Loammi Baldwin, 1781.
Paul Wyman, 1781.
Dea. Joseph Johnson, 1781, 89, 90.
Zebadiah Wyman, 1781, 82, 83, 84, 85, 88, 89, Dea. 1790, 91.
Ezra Wyman, 1781.
Lieut. Joseph Winn, 1782, 83, 91, 92, 93.
Mr. Sam. Wyman, jun. 1784, 85, 87, 88, 89.
Mr. James Walker, 1784, 85, 87, 88.
Capt. John Wood, 1785, 87.
Major Samuel Tay, 1786.
Mr. Josiah Johnson, 1786.
Capt. Reuben Kimball, 1786.
Mr. Benjamin Convers, 1786.
Lieut. James Reed, 1786, 89, 90, 91.
James Fowle, jun., 1787.
John Flagg, 1787, 88, 89, 90.
Daniel Reed, 1790, 91.
Isaac Marion, 1791, 92, 93.
Capt. Joseph Brown, 1792, 93.
Ensign John Walker, 1792, Col. 1793.
Mr. Josiah Parker, 1792, 93.
Abijah Thompson, 1794, 95, 96, 97, 98, 99, 1800.
Benjamin Simonds, 1794, 95, 96.
Edward Walker, 1794, 95, 96.
Daniel Wyman, 1794, 95, 96, 97, 98, 99.
Abel Wyman, 1794, Lt. 95.
Jesse Dean, 1796, 97, 98.
Elijah Leathe, jun., 1797, 98, 99.
Samuel Walker, 1797, 98.
Nathan Simonds, 1799, 1800, 1803, 04.
Benjamin Wyman, 1799, 1800, 1801, 02, Major, 03, 04.
Bill Russell, 1800, 1801, 02, 1805, 06, Col. 07.
Reuben Johnson, 1800.
Abijah Thompson, 1801, 02.
Jacob Pierce, 1802, 03, 04.
John Fowle, 1802, 03, Dea. 1805, 06.
Jacob Richardson, 1803, 04.
James Leathe, 1804.
Lt. Jonathan Tidd, 1805, 1806.
Capt. Nathan Harrington, 1805, 06, 07, 08, 09, 10.
Joseph W. Beers, 1805, 06, 07, 08, 09, 10, 11.
Luke Reed, 1807, 08, 09, 10, 11.
John Tidd, 1807.
Nathan Simonds, 1808, 09, 10, 11.
Col. Bill Russell, 1808, 09, 10, 11.
Capt. William Fox, 1811, 12, 13.
Benj. F. Baldwin, 1812, 13.
Jacob Richardson, 1812, 13.
John Wade, Esq. 1814, 15, 16, 17, 18, 19, 20, 21, 22, 23, 24, 25.
Josiah Parker, 1814, 15, 16, 17, 18, 19.
Capt. Isaac Richardson, 1814, 15, 16, 17.
Jonathan Tidd, jun., 1818, 19, 20.
Dr. Sylvanus Plympton, 1819.
Marshall Fowle, 1820, 21, 22, 23, 24, 25, 26, 27.
Joseph Parker, 1821, 22.
Samuel Tidd, 1823, 24, 25.
Joseph Gardner, 1826, 27, 28, 29, 30.
Samuel T. Richardson, 1826.
Samuel Abbot, 1827, 28, 29, 30, 31.
Samuel I Richardson, 1828.
Stephen Nichols, 1829, 30, 31.

Abijah Thompson, 1831, 32, 33.
John Tidd, 1832, 33.
Jason Richardson, 1832, 33.
John Wade, 1834, 35.
Stephen Nichols, 1834, 35, 36.
Charles Carter, 1834, 35, 38, 39.
John Edgell, 1836.
Augustus Plympton, 1836, 38, 39.
John Cummings, 1837.
Loring Emerson, 1837, 42, 43.
Barth. Richardson, jun., 1837, 44.
Leonard Fowle, 1838, 39.
Albert Thompson, 1840, 41, 44.
Oliver Tay, 1840.
Samuel R. Duren, 1840.
Leonard Thompson, 1841, 42, 43.
Luke Tidd, 1841, 42, 43, 44.
Benjamin F. Thompson, 1845, 1846.
James Tweed, jun. 1845, 46, 47, 48, 49.
Gen. Abijah Thompson, 1845.
John Tidd, 1846, 47, 48, 49.
Cyrus Thompson, 1847, 48, 49, 50.
Nathan B. Johnson, 1850.
Bowen Buckman, 1850.
Saml. R. Duren, to fill a vacancy in the board, 1850.
Stephen Nichols, jun., 1851, 52.
Horace Conn, 1851, 52, 53, 55.
Samuel R. Duren, 1851.
Horace Collamore, 1852, 53.
Alfred G. Carter, 1853.
Joshua E. Littlefield, 1854.
John Johnson, jun., 1854.
John Flanders, 1854, 55.
Moses F. Winn, 1855, 56.
Albert Thompson, 1856.
Elisha Burbank, 1856, 57, 58.
Horace Collamore, 1857.
John Cummings, jun., 1857.
Parker L. Convers, 1858.
F. K. Cragin, 1858.
Horace Conn, 1859.
William T. Grammer, 1859.
Joseph Kelly, 1859.
Ebenezer N. Blake, 1860.
Horace Conn, 1860.
Joseph Kelly, 1860.

Commissioners "to end Small Causes."

Edward Johnson, 1649, 50, 1, 2, 3, 4, 5, 6, 7, 8, 9, 1660, 64.
Edward Convers, 1649, 50, 51, 2, 3, 4, 5, 6, 7, 8, 9, 1660.
John Mousall, 1649, 50, 51, 2, 3, 4, 5, 6, 7, 8, 9, 1660, 64.
John Carter, 1664, 1674.
William Johnson, 1674.
James Convers, 1674.

Commissioners "of the Rate."

John Wright, 1646.
Ensign John Carter, 1653.
John Tidd, "Commissioner for the Country Rate," 1655.
John Wyman, "Commissioner for the Country Rate," 1656.
John Carter, 1658.
William Johnson, 1659.
James Convers, 1660.
Edward Johnson, 1661.
Josiah Convers, 1662.
Edward Johnson, 1663.
Thomas Peirce, 1664.
Allen Convers, 1666.
James Convers, 1667.
John Carter, 1668.
William Johnson, 1669.
Thomas Peirce, 1670.
John Wright, 1671.
John Wyman, 1672.
Ensign James Convers, 1673.
Josiah Convers, 1674, 5, 6, 8.
James Convers, [jun?] 1677.
Mr. Samuel Carter, 1680.
Joseph Richardson, 1681.
Lt. John Wyman, 1682.
Capt. Saml. Walker, 1683.
Dea. Josiah Convers, 1684.
Sergt. James Convers, 1685.
Mr Samuel Carter, 1686.
Lt. James Convers, (jun.?) 1688.
Lt. Gershom Flagg, 1690.
Sargt. Matthew Johnson, Aug. 20, 1690.
Ensign Joseph Winn, 1691.
Saml. Blogget, sen., 1692.
Joseph Wright, sen., 1693.
James Fowle, "Comm." 1703, to aid in making the Province Tax, according to Act of Court, March 1703.

Recorders or Town Clerks.

Edward Johnson, chosen in 1640.
William Johnson, chosen in 1672.
Lt. James Convers, jun., chosen in 1688.
Mr. Sam. Carter, chosen in 1690.
Capt. James Convers, jun., chosen in 1691.
Capt. James Convers, jun., chosen in 1693, 94, 95, 96, 97, 98, 99, 1700.
Serg. James Fowle, chosen in 1701, 02, 03, 04, 05, 06, 07, 08, 09, 10.
Serg. James Fowle, chosen in 1711, 12, 13, 14: died March 19, 1714.
John Fowle, chosen in 1714, 15, 16, 17, 18, 19, 20, 21, 22, 23, 24, 25.
John Fowle, chosen in 1726, 27, 28, 29, 30, 31, 32, 33, 34, 35, 36, 37, 38.
John Russell, chosen in 1739, 40, 41, 42, 43: declined serving 1744.
John Fowle, 3d, chosen in 1744.
John Russell, chosen in 1745.
James Fowle, chosen in 1746, 7, 8, 9, 1750, 1, 2, 3, 4, 5, 6, 7, 8, 9, 1760.
James Fowle, chosen in 1760, 1, 2, Esq. 1763, 4, 5, 6, 7, 8, 9, 1770.
James Fowle, chosen in 1771, 2, 3, 4, 5, 6, 7, 8, 1779.
James Fowle, jun., chosen in 1779, Aug. 26, 1780, 1, 2, 3, 4, 5, 6, 7, 8, 9, 1790.
Zebadiah Wyman, chosen in 1791, 1792.
Isaac Brooks, chosen in 1793.
Zebadiah Wyman, chosen in 1794, 5, 6, 7, 8, 9, 1800, 01, 02, 03, 04.
Zebadiah Wyman, chosen in 1805, 06, 07, 08, 09, 1810, 11, 12, 13.
Marshall Fowle, chosen in 1814, 15, 16, 17, 18, 19, 20, 21, 22, 23, 24.
Marshall Fowle, chosen in 1825, 26, 27, 28, 29, 30, 31, 32, 33.
Died suddenly June 14, 1833.
Oliver B. Coolidge, chosen in 1833, 34, 35, 36, 37, 38, 39.
Martin L. Convers, chosen in 1840, 41, 42, 43.
Nathan Wyman, chosen in 1844, 45, 46, 47, 48, 49, 50, 51, 52, 53, 54.
Nathan Wyman, chosen in 1855, 56, 57, 58, 59, 1860.

Treasurers.

John Tidd, 1695: no one chosen, 1696.
The Selectmen supplied the Treasurer's place, 1697-1718.
Sergt. George Reed, 1719; Dea. George Reed, 1720, 21, 22.
John Fowle, 1724, 25, 26, 27, 28, 29, 1730.
John Fowle, 1731, 32, 33, 34, 35, 36, 37, 39.
John Russell. 1738.
Mr Isaac Snow, 1740, 41, 42, 43, 44.
Mr. Eleazar Carter, 1745, 46, 47.
Mr. Benjamin Wyman, 1748, 49.
Mr. Benjamin Brooks, 1750, 51.
Mr. Benjamin Wyman, 1752, 53, 54, 55, 56, 57, 58.
Mr. Zebadiah Wyman, 1759, 1760, 61.
Eleazar Flagg Poole, 1762, 63, 64, 65, 66; Ensign, 1767.
Eleazar Flagg Poole, 1768, 69, 1770, 71, 72; Lieut. 1773.
Capt. Benjamin Wyman, 1774.
Dea. Samuel Wyman, 1775, 76.
Mr. Jonathan Lawrence, 1777, 78.
Mr. Zebadiah Wyman, 1779, 80, 81, 82, 83, 84.
Lt. Joseph Winn, 1785, 86, 87.
Mr. Zebadiah Wyman, 1788, 89; Dea. 1790, 91, 92.
Mr. Benjamin Wyman, 1793, 94; Lt. 95, 96, 97; Capt. 1798, 99.
Joseph Lawrence, 1800, 1801.
Zebadiah Wyman, 1802, 03, 04.
Dr. John Page, 1805.
Zebadiah Wyman, 1806, 07, 08, 09, 1810, 1811, 12, 13.
John Wade, Esq., 1814, 15, 16, 17, 18, 19, 20, 21, 22, 23.
John Wade, Esq., 1824, 25.
John Fowle, 3d, 1826, 27, 28, 31.
Bowen Buckman, 1829, 30, 32.
John Edgell, 1831, 35, 36, 38, 39.
Joel F. Thayer, 1833, 34, 37.
Joshua V. Pierce, 1840, 41; resigned, and removed from Town.
William Woodbury, 1841, 42, 43, 44, 45, 46.
Gawin R. Gage, 1847, 48, 49, 50, 51, 52, 53, 54, 55, 56.
Gawin R. Gage, 1857, 1858, 59.
Gawin R. Gage, 1860.

Deputies to General Court.

Edward Johnson, 1646, 47, 9, 1650, 1, 2, 3, 4, 5, 6, 8, 9.
Edward Convers, 1660.
Edward Johnson, 1661, 2, 3, 7, 8, 9.
Mr. Humphrey Davie, Capt. Edw. Johnson, } 1670, 71.
Mr. Humphrey Davie, Capt. Edw. Hutchinson, } of Boston, 1672, 73.
Mr. Humphrey Davie, William Johnson, } 1674.
"Mr. Humphrey Davie was chosen Deputy for *the whole yeare* 1675."
Mr. Humphrey Davie, Lieut. Wm. Johnson, } Deputies *the whole year*, 1676.
Mr. Humphrey Davie, Lieut. Wm. Johnson, } 1677, 78, 79.
Ensign James Convers, deputy in Feb. Session, 1679–80.
Lieut. Wm. Johnson, Ensign James Convers, } 1680.
Lieut. Wm. Johnson, 1681, 82, 83, [chosen "*Assistant*" at May Session, 1684.
Ens. James Convers, Nov. Session, 1683: May Session, 1684, 85, 86.
Sergt. Matt. Johnson, 1686.
Ens. James Convers, 1689.
Sargt. Matt. Johnson, 1689, 90, 91, 92.
Ens. Saml. Walker, Sargt. John Peirce, } Members of Convention, 1689.
Lt. James Convers, 1691, 92.
Saml. Blogget, sen., 1693.
Dea. Samuel Walker, 1694.
James Convers, jun., 1695, 96, 97, 98, 99.
James Wright, 1696: disallowed.
Capt. Edw. Johnson, 1700.
Major James Convers, 1701, 02, 03, 04, 05, 06.
Ens. John Peirce, 1706, Aug. 13, in room of Major Convers, deceased.
Ens. John Peirce, 1707, 08, 09, 12, 13, 14, 16, 17, 1718.
Joshua Sawyer, sen., 1710, 1711.
Capt. Josiah Convers, 1715.
Dea. Saml. Walker, 1719, 20, and for Court, June 13, 1720.
Daniel Peirce, 1721, and for Court 23d Aug., 1721.
Daniel Peirce, 1722, 23, 24, 25, 26.
John Fowle, 1727, 28, 30, 31, 35.
Ens. Samuel Blogget, 1729.
Samuel Richardson, 1732, 33; voted 1734 to choose, but name not recorded.
Mr. Josiah Peirce, 1736.
M. Roland Cotton, 1737, 38, 39, 40, 41, 42, 43; Esq. 1744.
Mr. Edward Walker, 1745.
Dea. Josiah Peirce, 1746, 47, 48, 49.
Voted not to send, 1750.
Mr. Edward Walker, 1751, 52, 53, 54; chosen for 1756, but declined.
Josiah Johnson, Esq., 1756, 57, 58, 1766.
Mr. James Fowle, 1759, 1760, 61: Esq. 1762, 63, 64, 65, 67, 68.
Mr. Oliver Richardson, 1769, 70, 71, 72, [1773?].
Dea. Saml. Wyman, 1773,? 74; do. for Court at Salem, Oct. 5, 1774.
Dea. Saml. Wyman, for Provincial Congress, Feb. 1775.
Josiah Johnson, Esq., 1775; May 31, at Watertown.
Josiah Johnson, Esq., to Genl. Court at Watertown, July 19, 1775.
Samuel Wyman, Esq., at Watertown, 1776; at Boston, 1777.
Col. Loammi Baldwin, 1778, 79, 1780.
Capt. Saml. Belknap, 1781, 1783.
Dea. Joseph Johnson, 1782.
Saml. Thompson, Esq. 1785, 86, 89, 90.
Dea. Timothy Winn, 1787, 1788, 1791.
Capt. Timothy Winn, 1790.
Samuel Thompson, Esq. 1792, 93.
Col. John Walker, 1794, 95, 96.
1797, Voted not to send.
Samuel Thompson, Esq. 1798.
1799, Voted not to send.
Hon. Loammi Baldwin, Esq. 1800, 01, 02, 03, 04.
Samuel Thompson, Esq. 1805, 06.
Col. Bill Russell, 1807, 1808.
Dr. Sylvanus Plympton, 1809.
Mr. Luke Reed, 1810, 11.
Dr. Sylvanus Plympton, Major John Wade, } 1812.
Major John Wade, Lieut. Jona. Tidd, } 1813.
Major John Wade, 1814, 15, 16, 17, 18, 19, 20, 21, 22.
Dr. Sylvanus Plympton, 1816.
John Wade, Esq., 1823, 26.
Marshall Fowle, 1823, 1824, 25.
John Wade, Joseph Gardner, } 1827.
Marshall Fowle, & Joseph Gardner, } 1828.
Marshall Fowle, & John Wade, } 1829.

Hon. Wm. C. Jarvis, 1830.
Marshall Fowle, John Wade, Stephen Nichols, } 1831.
Stephen Nichols, Samuel Abbot, Joseph Gardner, } Nov. 14, 1831.
Marshall Fowle, Samuel Abbot, Joseph Gardner, } 1832.
John Wade, Stephen Nichols, Oliver B. Coolidge, } 1833, 34.
Oliver B. Coolidge, 1835.
John Convers, 1835.
William Tidd, 1835.
Stephen Eames, 1836.
Henry Flagg, 1836.
Leonard Thompson, 1836.
John Cummings, 1837.
Augustus Plympton, 1837.
Leonard Fowle, 1838.
William Flanders, 1838.
Calvin A. Wyman, 1838.
Henry Parker, 1839.
Thomas Poole, 1839.
Bowen Buckman, 1840.
Nathaniel A. Richardson, 1841, 42, 43.
1844, Nov. 24. Voted not to send this year.
John C. Brackett, 1845.
No choice 1846, none 1847, no choice 1849.
Nov. 27, 1848. Voted not to send.
Nov. 11 & Nov. 25, 1850, no choice.
Timothy Winn, 1851.
Joseph Dow, 1852.
No choice, 1853.
Wm. T. Grammer, 1854.
Ebenezer N. Blake, 1855.
William T. Grammer, 1856.
Charles S. Convers, 1857.
Nathan Wyman, 1858.
Nathan Wyman, 1859.
Franklin Smith, 1860.

TEACHERS OF GRAMMAR SCHOOL, WOBURN, TILL 1771.

NAMES.	When engaged.	For how long.	Terms per annum, or money paid.
Mr. Samuel Carter	1685	A year	£5 per an. [no scholars.
	1686	A year	1.10 only paid, having
Rev. Jabez Fox	1694	A year	Nothing promised, appa-
	1699	do.	rently, and nothing pd.
Mr. John Fox	1700	4 months	£9 paid.
"	1701	1 year	28 per annum.
"	1702	do.	18 per annum.
Mr. Dudley Bradstreet[1]	1704	No time set	
Mr. Samuel Burr[2]	1704	6 months	15 and horse keeping.
Mr. Gershom Rawlins[3]	1705	6 months	15 paid.
Mr. William Rawson[4]	1705	3 months	7.10 paid.
Mr. Samuel Mighill[5]	1706	6 months	15 and a horse.
	1707	10 months	20.
Mr. John Tufts[6]	1708	8 months	20 paid.
"	1708	3 months	7.10 paid.
"	1709	12 months	30 and horse kept.
	1710	3 months	7.16 paid.
Mr. Recompense Wadsworth[7]	1710	6 months	12 and board 11 weeks.
	1711, '12	13 months	
Mr. Peter Clark[8]	1712	6 months	11 and board.
Mr. Urian Angier[9]	1713	10 months	22 per an. and board.
	1714	1 year	21.15 paid and board.
Mr. John Gardner[10]	1715, '16, '17	29 months	40 per an. 96.13.8 paid.
Mr. Nathaniel Prentice[11]	1718, '19	9½ months	40 per an. for 6½ mos.
			50 per an. for 3 mos.
Mr. (Nathaniel?) Cotton[12]	1719	7 months	21.16.3 paid.
Mr. Nathaniel Prentice[11]	1720	2 months	7.05 paid.
Mr. John Hancock[13]	1720, '21, '22		49.6.8 paid.
Mr. Nathaniel Hancock[14]	1722, '23		51.1.4 paid.
Mr. Josiah Convers[15]	1723, '24, '25		69.11.8 paid.
Mr. Ebenezer Flagg, jun.[16]	1725	4 months	12.5 paid.
Mr. Timothy Walker[17]	1725		27.10 recovered by law.
Mr. Samuel Jennison[18]	1725	3 months	11 paid.
Mr. Habijah Weld[19]	1725–26	7 months	50 per annum.
"Mr. (Nathaniel?) Saltonstall"[20]	1727	3 months	12.10 paid.
Mr. Isaac Richardson[21]	1727–28	3 months	12.10 paid.
Mr. Jabez Fox[22]	1728	11 months	50 per annum.

1 Mr. Bradstreet was of Andover, a grandson of Gov. Bradstreet; H. C. 1698; came to Woburn at the time agreed on: stayed there through March Court, to save the town from a presentment by the grand jury; but having no scholars, he then withdrew, having expenses paid, and receiving eighteen shillings as "a gratuity." Town Records, IV., p. 255.

2 Mr. Burr was graduated at H. C., 1697.

3 Mr. Rawlins was a graduate of H. C. 1705.

4 Mr. Rawson of H. C., 1703.

5 Mr. Mighill, H. C., 1704; kept the school only part of the time agreed on in 1707, and received £6.00 in full.

6 Mr. Tufts was of H. C., 1708; and afterwards ordained over Second Church in Newbury.

7 Mr. Wadsworth, born in Boston; of H. C., 1708.

8 Mr. Clark, of H. C., 1712; minister of Danvers, 1717.

9 A son of Rev. Samuel Angier, of Rehoboth, and a grandson of Rev. Urian Oakes, President of Harvard College.

10 Mr. Gardner, of Charlestown End, H. C., 1715; minister of Stow, 1718.

11 Graduate of H. C., 1715.

12 "Mr. Cotton" (if Rev. Nathaniel) was of H. C., 1717; and afterwards minister of Bristol, R. I.

13 Of H. C., 1719; minister of Braintree, 1726; father of Gov. Hancock.

14 Rev. Nathaniel Hancock, H. C., 1721.

15 A native of Woburn, H. C., 1723; a son of Capt. Josiah Convers, and a grandson of Deacon Josiah.

16 A native of Woburn, son of Ebenezer Flagg, sen., H. C., 1725; minister of Chester, N. H., 1736.

17 Mr. Walker, son of Dea. Samuel Walker, 2d, of Woburn, H. C., 1725; minister of Concord, N. H., 1730.

18 Mr. Jennison was of H. C., 1720; afterward a preacher and settled minister.

19 Mr. Weld, H. C., 1723; ordained at Attleborough, Mass., 1727.

20 "Mr. (Nathaniel?) Saltonstall," of H. C., 1727.

21 Mr. Isaac Richardson, a native of Woburn, of H. C., 1726.

22 Mr. Fox, son of Rev. John Fox, of H. C., 1727.

TEACHERS OF GRAMMAR SCHOOL, WOBURN, TILL 1771.

(Continued.)

NAMES.	When engaged.	For how long.	Terms per annum, or money paid.
Mr. Ebenezer Flegg [23]	1729, '30, '31	31 months	£131 paid.
" "	1732	3 months	12.10 paid.
Mr. Jabez Richardson [24]	1732	3 months	12.10 paid.
Mr. Thomas Balch [25]	1732	½ month	2 paid.
Mr. Ebenezer Wyman [26]	1732	2 months	9.5.11 paid.
" "	1733	12 months	50 paid.
Mr. James Fowle [27]	1734	12 months	50 paid.
Mr. Isaac Richardson [21]	1735	9¼ months	38.10 paid.
Mr. James Fowle [27]	1736	6½ months	26.18.6 paid.
Mr. Ebenezer Wyman [26]	1736	11 weeks	10 11.8 paid.
" "	1737	12 months	50 paid.
Mr. James Fowle [27]	1737	. . . .	60, bills of credit.
" "	1738	12 months	70 paid.
" "	1739	10½ months	70 paid.
" "	1740, '41, '42	36 months	210, bills of credit.
" "	1743, '44	19 months	85, bills credit, per an.
Mr. Isaac Richardson [21]	1745	3 months	21.10, old tenor, paid.
" "	1746	8 months	100, old tenor, per an.
" "	1747	3 months	100, old tenor, per an.
Mr. Adam Richardson [28]	1747	2 months	100, old tenor, per an.
" "	1748, '49	10 months	220, old tenor, per an.
Mr. Jonathan Sewall [29]	1750	. . . .	28 8.10, lawful money.
Mr. Ebenezer Thompson [30]	1752	3 months	300, old tenor, per an.
" "	1753	3 months	10, law. mon., p. order.
Mr. Jabez Richardson [31]	1754	3 months	9.6.8, law. money. paid.
" "	1754	2 months	250, old tenor, per an.
" "	1755	1 month	270, old tenor, per an.
Mr. Jacob Eliot [32]	1756	. . . .	16.13.4 paid, per order.
Mr. Jabez Richardson [33]	1757	. . . .	27.3.1, law. money, pd.
" "	1759	. . . .	4.19.9 paid.
Mr. John Fowle [34]	1758	. . . .	6.2.2 paid.
" "	1759	. . . .	40 law. money, per an.
" "	1760, '61	. . . .	
" "	1762	11 months	40 per annum.
	1763, '64, '65		
	1766, '67, '68		
	1769		
Mr. Jacob Coggin [35]	1770, '71		

[23] See 16.

[24] Mr. Jabez Richardson, a graduate of H. C., 1730.

[25] Mr. Balch, of H. C., 1733; first minister of Second Parish, Dedham, 1736.

[26] Mr. Wyman, son of Jacob Wyman, Woburn; of H. C., 1731; and minister of Union, Conn.

[27] Mr. James Fowle, son of Capt. John Fowle, of Woburn, graduate of H. C., 1731, and Town Clerk of Woburn from 1746 to 1779, inclusively.

[28] Mr. Adam Richardson, a native of Woburn, and graduate of H. C., 1730.

[29] Mr. Jonathan Sewall, a graduate of H. C., 1748, and Attorney General at the commencement of the revolutionary war.

[30] A native of Woburn, son of Ebenezer and Hannah (Convers) Thompson, and graduated at H. C., 1752.

[31] See 24. A school teacher, apparently, by profession.

[32] Jacob Eliot, a graduate of H. C., 1755.

[33] See 24. Mr. Jabez Richardson was probably a native, certainly an inhabitant, of Woburn, in 1756. See Church Records, Vol. I., page 3.

[34] Mr. John Fowle, or "*Master Fowle*" as he was called many years, was a native of Woburn, a son of John and Mary (Convers) Fowle, and a graduate of H. C., 1747.

[35] Mr. Jacob Coggin, a native of Woburn, graduate of H. C., 1763, a schoolmaster by profession, and occasionally preached.

N. B. The pay per annum engaged to Master Fowle, for teaching, is not stated in the Records, except in 1759 and 1762. From the sums paid by the Treasurer at divers times for his services, he appears to have had a little more, some years, than £40 per annum. As the town voted to raise £40 for schooling in 1771, 1772, (See Town Records, Vol. IX., pp. 128, 165,) it is inferred that that sum was the annual pay of Mr. Coggin in those years.

PASTORS OF FIRST CHURCH, WOBURN.

NAMES.	Where born.	When.	Where educated.	When ordained, or installed.	Dismissed, or resigned.	Where died.	When.	Age.
Thomas Carter	England	About 1610	St. John's College, Cambridge, Eng.	Nov. 22, 1642	. . . .	Woburn	Sept. 5, 1684	74 years.
Jabez Fox	Concord, Mass.	About 1647	Har. College, 1665	Nov. 1679	. . . .	Boston, while on a visit.	February 28, 1702–3	56 years.
John Fox	Cambridge	About 1678	H. College, 1698	Nov. 17, 1703	. . . .	Woburn	Dec. 12, 1756	78 years.
Edward Jackson	Newton	April 3, 1700	H. College, 1719	Aug. 1, 1729	. . . .	Woburn	Sept. 24, 1754	55 years.
Josiah Sherman	Watertown	April 2, 1729	Princeton, N. J., 1754	Jan. 28, 1756	Apr. 11, 1775	Woodbridge, Ct.	Nov. 24, 1789	61 years.
Samuel Sargeant	Worcester	Nov. 6, 1755	Dart. College, 1783	Mar. 14, 1785	Apr. 29, 1799	Chester, Vt.	June 2, 1818	63 years.
Joseph Chickering	Dedham	Apr. 30, 1780	H. College, 1799	Mar. 28, 1804	Apr. 11, 1821	Phillipston, Mass.	Jan. 27, 1844	63 years.
Joseph Bennett	Framingham	May 13, 1798	H. College, 1818	Jan. 1, 1822	. . . .	Woburn	Nov. 19, 1847	49 years.
Jonathan Edwards	Andover	July 17, 1820	Y. College, 1840	Sept. 7, 1848	Jan. 9, 1856			
Daniel March	Millbury, Mass.	July 21, 1806	Y. College, 1840	Oct. 1, 1856	Feb. 17, 1862			
Joseph C. Bodwell, D.D.,	Sanbornton, N. H.	June 11, 1812	D. College, 1833	Nov. 11, 1862	Aug. 3, 1866			

N. B. Rev. Josiah Cotton, first and only Pastor of the Third Church in Woburn, was born at Sandwich, in June 1702; graduated at Harvard College, 1722; installed at Woburn, July 15, 1747; dismissed in 1756; installed at Sandown, N. H., November 28, 1759; and there died, May 27, 1780, aged 78.

DEACONS OF THE FIRST CHURCH, WOBURN.

NAMES.	Chosen, or (†) styled Deacon in T. Records.	Resigned.	Died.	Age.
Edward Convers	Probably in 1642	....	1663	75
John Mousall		....	1665	70
John Wright	† Nov. 10, 1664	....	1688	
John Russell	† Nov. 10, 1664	....	1676	
Josiah Convers	1674	....	1690	72
Henry Baldwin	1686	....	1698	
Samuel Walker, 2d	1692	....	1704	61
Joseph Wright	† 1698	....	1724	85
William Locke	1700	....	1720	91
Samuel Walker, 3d [1]	1709	1735	1744	77
William Locke, jun.	1709	....	1738	80
Edward Johnson	† 1720	....	1725	67
George Reed, jun. [1]	1719	1735	1756	96
James Thompson [2]	1725	1733	1763	84
Josiah Wright	† 1736	....	1747	73
Joseph Hartwell	1736	....	1743	63
Josiah Peirce	1742	....	1759	68
Stephen Richardson	1745	....	1752	79
Samuel Eames	1745	....	1775	84
John Wright	1758	....	1763	55
John Leathe [3]	1759	....	1775	80
Nathan Richardson	1761	....	1775	74
Samuel Wyman	1764	....	1787	70
Obadiah Kendall	1777	....	1811	86
Samuel Thompson	1777	1812	1820	89
Zebadiah Wyman	1789	....	1793	52
Josiah Richardson	1789	....	1795	48
Jeduthan Richardson	1796	1812	1815	78
Josiah Wright	1805	1825	1830	80
Ebenezer Lawrence	1812	1828	1842	84
Benjamin Wyman	1812	....	1836	68
Calvin Richardson	1825	1849	1866	89
Uriah Manning	1828	1837	1862	76
Henry Gardner	1828	....	1837	50
Nathan B. Johnson	1828	1840		
Luther Eames	1828	1836	1857	55
Benjamin F. Thompson	1836	1840	1863	64
Stephen Richardson	1836			
Marshal Wyman	1838	1840		
Charles Thompson	1838	1849		
Ezekiel Johnson	1841	....	1866	84
Luke Wyman	1841	1842		
Thomas Richardson	1841			
Jonas Hale	1843	....	1858	77
Abner Rice	1850	1852		
Uriah Manning	1849	....	1862	76
Willard J. Pearsons	1852			
John R. Kimball	1858			
Eckley Stearns	1863	1867		
Nathan H. Richardson	1863	1867		
Gawin R. Gage	1863			
Ephraim Cutter	1864			

[1] Samuel Walker and George Reed, jun., being chosen deacons, 1735, of the Church of the Second Precinct, where they lived, they transferred to it their relation to the First Church.

[2] James Thompson became deacon of the Church of Wilmington, where he lived, after the incorporation of the town, 1730.

[3] John Leathe was deacon of the Third Church, Woburn, till the reunion of the First and Third, in 1759.

College Graduates who were Natives of Woburn.

Baldwin, Loammi, Esq.; H. U. 1800.
Bennett, Rev. Joseph L.
Burbeen, Mr. Joseph; H. U. 1731.
Burbeen, Paul; H. U. 1743.
Carter, Mr. Samuel; H. U. 1660.
Chickering, Rev. John White, D. D.
Coggin, Mr. Jacob; H. U. 1763.
Coggin, Rev. Jacob; H. U. 1803.
Convers, Josiah; H. U. 1723.
Convers, Joshua P. Esq.; B. U.
Convers, Sherman; Y. C. 1813.
Cutter, Ephraim; Y. C. 1852. M. D. H. U. 1856. M. M. S. S.
Fox, Hon. Jabez; H. U. 1727.
Flagg, Rev. Ebenezer; H. U. 1725.
Flagg, John; H. U. 1761.
Fowle, James, Esq.; H. U. 1731.
Fowle, John, Master; H. U. 1747.
Hayward, Jonathan; H. U. 1756. He was son of Dr. Jona. Hayward, (or "Heywood,") who died in Woburn, Aug. 13, 1749, aged "45," [Gravestone]. This son of his died in Woburn a pauper, May 19, 1812, æt 73.
Kendall, Rev. Samuel; H. U. 1731.
Lawrence, Rev. Nathaniel; H. U. 1787.
Lock, Samuel; H. U. 1755. He was son of Samuel and Rebekah (Richardson) Lock of Woburn; born Nov. 23, 1731; settled in the Ministry at Sherborn; was made President of H. U. 1770, resigned 1773, and died at Sherborn, 1778.
Plympton, Sylvanus, M. D. H. U. 1818.
Plympton, Augustus, M. D. at H. U. 1824.
Plympton, Henry Sylvanus, M. D.; at H. U. 1860.
Reed, William; H. U. 1811.
Richardson, Adam; H. U. 1730.
Richardson, Isaac; H. U. 1726.
Richardson, Jabez; H. U. 1730.
Richardson, Gideon; H. U. 1749.
Richardson, Luther, Esq.; H. U. 1799.
Richardson, Wyman, Esq.; H. U. 1804.
Richardson, John; H. U. 1813.
Thompson, Ebenezer; H. U. 1752.
Thompson, Jonathan; H. U. 1803.
Thompson, Rev. Leander; was sent as Missionary to Syria by A. B. F. M., in and since his return from there has been settled in the ministry at West Amesbury. Mass.
Wade, John; Amherst College, 1830. LL. B. 1834, at H. U.
Walker, Rev. James, D. D.; H. U. 1814. President of the University from 1853 to 1860.
Winn, Timothy; H. U. 1795.
Winn, Abel Theodore; H. U. 1859.
Wyman, John; H. U. 1721.
Wyman, Rev. Ebenezer; H. U. 1731.
Wyman, Rufus; H. U. 1799, M. D.
Add to the above Col. Loammi Baldwin, who rec'd 1785 from H. U. the Honorary degree of M. A.

GENEALOGICAL NOTICES

OF THE

Earliest Inhabitants of Woburn and their Families,

COMPREHENDING:

I. SUBSCRIBERS AT CHARLESTOWN, DECEMBER 1, 1640, TO THE TOWN ORDERS INTENDED FOR WOBURN.

II. MEN TAXED IN THE FIRST FOUR TAXES IN WOBURN UPON RECORD,

VIZ:

1. THE RATE FOR THE COUNTRY, 8 SEPTEMBER, 1645.
2. THE TOWN RATE, 22 DECEMBER, 1646.
3. THE COUNTRY RATE, 26 AUGUST, 1666.
4. THE RATE FOR THE "NEW MEETING HOUSE," 1672,

AND FINALLY,

III. THE MEN WHO WERE DEEMED, IN 1668, TO HAVE EXCLUSIVE RIGHT IN THE COMMON LANDS OF WOBURN.

GENEALOGICAL NOTICES.

BACON. *I.* Michael, son of Michael Bacon, of Dedham, 1640, who is said to have come from Ireland, bringing with him wife and four children; viz: Michael, Daniel, John and Sarah. These children are named in their father's will, 14 Apr. 1648. His wife, their mother, died 1647. [Savage's Genealogical Dict.]

Michael, eldest son of Michael of Dedham, was of Charlestown, 1640, where he subscribed, 18 Dec. 1640, "Town Orders" for the then projected town of Woburn. He became, shortly after, one of its original inhabitants; and had born to him there two daughters, viz: Elizabeth, born 4 Jan. 1642: and Sarah, b. 24 Aug. 1644. His wife Mary dying 26 Aug. 1655, he md. Mary Richardson, 26 Oct. 1655; and after her death 19 May, 1670, he took to him a third wife, Mary Noyes, 28 Nov. 1670. He died 4 July, 1688.

BACON. *II.* Michael, jun., only son of the preceding, born probably at Charlestown, before his father settled in Woburn, md. Sarah Richardson, 22 March, 1660,[a] by whom he had three daughters, Mary, Sarah and Abigail; and also a son Michael, whom he recognizes in a deed, dated 4 Oct. 1696, as his "loving son, Michael Bacon, jun., of Billerica, shoemaker." (a) [Wob. Records of Births, Marriages, etc. (a) MSS. of Mr. John A. Boutelle, Wob.]

BACON. Daniel, son of Michael of Dedham, born in Ireland, and another of the original settlers of Woburn. He md. Mary Reed of Bridgewater, by whom he had six sons, Thomas, John, Isaac, Jacob, Daniel and John; and two daughters, Rachel, and Lydia. About 1669, he removed to Cambridge Village, now Newton; and died 7 Sept. 1691. [Savage's Geneal. Dict.]

BAKER. John, was of Charlestown, 1636.[a] His name appears in the Country Rate assessed in Woburn, 26 Aug. 1666. He md. Susanna Martin, 28 May, 1654. By her, he had (1) John, born 25 March, 1654. (2) Mary, b. 22 Feb. 1655-6 (3) Joseph, b. 15 June, 1657, and died soon after. (4) Joseph, b. 1 Feb. 1659-60. (5) Susanna, b. 15 March, 1662, and died soon. (6) Susanna, b. 12 April, 1663; md. to John Cutler, 1682. (7) a son b. 8 March, 1664, and died within a week. (8) Samuel, b. 21 April, 1665. (9) Benjamin, b. 24 May, 1667. (10) James, b. 10 June, 1670. (11) Jonathan, b. 2 Apr. 1674. (12) William, b. 18 Aug. 1679.

John Baker died 6 Nov. 1695. "Old Goody Baker died Dec. 3, 1714." [Woburn Rec. Woburn Records of Births, Deaths, etc.[a] Frothingham's Charlestown, p. 85.]

---

[a] Memoranda of Saml. Thompson, Esq.

BALDWIN. *I.* Henry, said to be from Devonshire, England; a subscriber in Charlestown to the "Town Orders" for Woburn, in 1640, and after that, a distinguished citizen of the latter town, and freeman of the Colony, 1652. His place of residence was at "New Bridge," or North Woburn, where some of his descendants in each succeeding generation have had their abode, and been large proprietors of land. He was of the Board of Selectmen for Woburn, 1681; and a deacon of the Church from 1686 to his death. He md. 1 Nov. 1649, Phebe, eldest daughter of Ezekiel Richardson, born probably on the other side of the Atlantic. By her, he had eleven children: (1) Susanna, born 30 Aug. 1650, and died soon. (2) Susanna, b. 25 July, 1652. (3) Phebe, b. 7 Sept. 1654, md. to Samuel Richardson, 7 Nov. 1676, and died 20 Oct. 1679. (4) John, b. 28 Oct. 1656. (5) Daniel, 15 March, 1659; md. to Hannah, probably daughter of Joseph Richardson, 6 Jan. 1684-5. (6) Timothy, b. 27 May, 1661. (7) Mary, b. 19 July, 1663, and died soon. (8) *Henry*, b. 15 Nov. 1664. (9) Abigail, b. 20 Aug. 1667; md. to John Reed, 1705? (10) Ruth, b. 31 July, 1670. (11) Benjamin, b. 20 Jan. 1672-3. [Wob. Rec. of Births, etc., Savage's Geneal. Dict.]

Dea. Henry Baldwin died 14 Feb. 1697-8. Widow Phebe Baldwin died 13 Sept. 1716. [Wob. Rec. of Births, etc., etc.]

BALDWIN. *II.* Henry Baldwin, jun., md. Abigail Fisk, 4 May, 1692; and had 8 children. (1) Henry, b. 12 Jan. 1692-3. (2) David, b. 9 Apl. 1696. (3) Isaac, b. 20 Feb. 1699-1700. (4) Abigail, b. 13 Feb. 1701-2; died 4 Sept. 1704. (5) James, b. 11 July, 1705; died 12 June, 1709. (6) Abigail, b. 19 Nov. 1707. (7) *James*, b. 19 Oct. 1710. (8) Samuel, b. 31 Aug. 1717.

II. Henry Baldwin died 7 July, 1739. [Wob. Rec. of Births, etc.]

Isaac, son of *II* Henry Baldwin, md. Mary Flegg, (Flagg) both of Woburn, 24 March, 1726. Their children were: (1) Luke, b. 23 Dec. 1728. (2) Jeduthan, b. 13 Jan. 1731-2. (3) Nahum, b. 3 May, 1734. (4) Isaac, b. 12 Dec. 1738.

BALDWIN. James, son of *II* Henry Baldwin, md. Ruth Richardson, 29 May, 1739, and had 4 children. (1) Cyrus, b. 5 Nov. 1740. (2) Reuel, b. 9 May, 1742; died 21 Feb. 1745-6. (3) Loammi, [Col. Baldwin: See Chapt. XII.,] b. 10 Jan. 1744-5. (4) Reuel, b. 30 June, 1747.

James Baldwin died 28 June, 1791, æt. 81. His wife, Ruth, died 13 May, 1791, aged 78 years.[a]

BLOGGET. Samuel, son of Thomas, who came in the "Increase" from London, 1635, at the age of 30 years, with his wife Susanna, aged 37 years, and two sons, Daniel and Samuel. He (Thomas Bloggett) was a glover by occupation; settled at Cambridge, where he had a daughter Susanna born to him in June 1637; and a son Thomas, who died 7 Aug. 1639. In his will, made 10 Aug. 1641, and proved 8 July following, he provides for his wife and three children, viz: Daniel, Samuel and Susanna. After his decease, his *widow* Susanna was md. to James Thompson, sen., of Woburn, 15 Feb. 1643-4; and his *daughter* Susanna md. Jonathan Thompson, son of James Thompson, sen., and Elizabeth, his first wife, 28 Nov. 1655.

BLOGGET. *I.* Samuel Blogget was born in England; brought by his parents to this country when 1½ year old; came to Woburn early to reside; md. Ruth Iggleden ["Eggleden" County Records] of Boston, 13 Dec. 1655; had (1) Ruth, born 28 Dec. 1656. (2) Samuel, b. 10 Dec. 1658. (3) Thomas, b. 26 Feb. 1661; md. Rebecca Tidd, 11 Nov. 1685. (4) Susanna, b......md. to James Simonds, 29 Dec. 1685. (5) Sarah, b. 17 Feb. 1668. (6, 7) Martha and Mary, twins, b. 15 Sept. 1673. Martha md. to Joseph Winn, 1696.

I. Samuel Blogget died 3 July, 1687: his widow Ruth died 14 Oct. 1703.

BLOGGET. *II.* Samuel Blogget, son of *I* Samuel, married Huldah, daughter of William Simonds, 30 Apr. 1683; and had (1) Samuel, born 21 Dec. 1683; (2) Daniel, b. 24 March, 1685. (3) William, b. 11 Jan. 1686-7. (4) Huldah, b. 9 Feb. 1688-9; md. to Ebenezer Reed. (5) Caleb, b. 11 Nov. 1691. (6) Joshua, b. 26 Feb. 1693-4. (7) Josiah, b. 27 March, 1696. (8) John, b. 19 Apr. 1699. (9) Benjamin, b. 4 March, 1701. (10) Nathan, b. 15 March, 1704. The following records of his and of his wife's death are from the manuscripts of the Simonds family: "Ensign Samuel Blogget deceased November fifth 1743." "Widow Huldah Blogget deceased March the fourteenth 1745-6." N. B. *II.* Samuel Blogget represented Woburn in the General Court, 1693. [See Woburn Town Records. Records of Births, etc. Savage's Geneal. Dictionary.]

"BRITTEN," ["BRITTON," OR "BRITTAINE."] James, came not improbably in the "Increase" from London, 1635, aged 27, "if the custom record of the embarkation of James Bitton lost a single letter, which is not improbable." He subscribed the Town Orders for Woburn, in 1640, at Charlestown; came to Woburn to dwell soon after; was taxed there, 1645, in the first tax upon Record; and died 3 May, 1655. His widow, Jane, md. Isaac Cole, 1 Feb. 1658-9.

[Savage Geneal. Dict.: Town Rec. of Births, etc., etc.]

BROOKS. Henry, of Woburn, may have been the same as Henry Brooks of Concord, made freeman 14 March, 1639 [a]. He is noticed in the Town Records as an inhabitant of Woburn, and a proprietor of land there, near Horn Pond, 10 Jan. 1652 [b]. He was one of the Selectmen, 1669. His wife, Susanna, dying 15 Sept. 1681, he married Annis Jaquith, [a sister of Abraham Jaquith?] 12 July, 1682; and died 12 April, 1683. In his Will, dated 18 July, 1682, he names wife Annis, and children John, Timothy, who was of Billerica, Isaac, and Sarah, wife of John Mousall, who were then living [a].

BROOKS. John Brooks married Eunice, dr. of Dea. John Mousall, 1 Nov. 1649. Their children were: (1) John, b. 23 Nov. 1650, died in 1653. (2) Sarah, b. 21 Nov. 1652; md. to Ephraim Buck. (3) Eunice, b. 10 Oct. 1655. (4) Joanna, b. 22 March, 1659; md. to David Roberts, 1678. (5) John, b. 1 March, 1664. (6) Ebenezer, b. 9 Dec. 1666. (7) Deborah, b. 20 March, 1669. (8) Jabez, b. 17 July, 1673. Eunice Brooks dying 1 Jan. 1684, John Brooks md. Mary Richardson, [widow of

---

[a] Savage's Geneal. Dictionary. [b] T. R., vol. I., p. 17.

Theophilus?] 25 Feb. 1683-4. By Inventory of Will, he died 29 Sept. 1691. His widow died 28 Aug. 1704. [a]

Timothy Brooks md. Mary, dr. of John Russell, sen., 2 Dec. 1659. Their children were: (1) Timothy, born 10 Nov. 1660, and died soon. (2) Timothy, b. 9 Oct. 1661. (3) John, b. 16 Oct. 1662. [c] (4) Mary, born . . . . and died 2 July, 1670, at Billerica, [b] to which town, subsequently to her birth, her parents had removed. Other daughters they had born to them at Billerica, one of whom married —— Mason of Swansea.

Mary, wife of Timothy Brooks, died at Billerica, 15 Sept. 1680.

BROOKS. Isaac Brooks married Miriam Daniels, 10 Jan. 1665-6. Their children were: (1), Sarah, born 14 May, 1667; died soon. (2) Miriam, b. 29 May, 1668; died young. (3) Isaac, b. 13 Aug. 1669. (4) Henry, b. 4 Oct. 1671. (5) Miriam, b. 16 Dec. 1673. Isaac Brooks died 8 Sept. 1686. Descendants from the above three sons of Henry Brooks have been numerous. [Wob. Rec. of Births etc., etc.]

BRUSH or BRUCE. George Brush (whose descendants have long since spelt their name Bruce) is said to have been a Scotchman. He married Elizabeth, daughter of William Clark, 28 Dec. 1659; and had by her: (1) William, b. 21 Nov. 1660, and died Jan. following. (2) William, b. 20 Oct. 1661, and died 3 Nov. 1661. (3) Elizabeth, b. 26 Jan. 1663. (4) Mary, b. 15 June, 1665; married to Walter Cranston, 4 June, 1683. (5) William, b. 28 April, 1667. (6) John, b. 18 June, 1670. (7) Elizabeth, b. 24 Aug. 1672. (8) George, b. 18 Jan. 1674, and died the same day. (9) Joseph, b. 11 Jan. 1674-5, and died 28 Feb. 1675-6. (10) Joseph, b. 29 Dec. 1676. (11) Samuel, b. 28 March, 1680. (12) Margery, b. 24 April, 1684; md. to Isaac Walker, 1705. (13) Lydia, b. 10 April, 1687. George Brush died 18 Aug. 1692. "Elizabeth *Bruce*, widow of George Bruce," died 13 Aug. 1700. [Savage's Genl. Dict. Town Recs. of Births, etc., etc.]

"BERBEANE" or BURBEEN. John came, it is said, from Scotland; was a tailor by occupation; and married Sarah Gould, 16 April, 1660. Their children were: (1) Mary, born 2 July, 1661; died 20 July, 1733? (2) John, b. 9 Aug. 1663. [c] (3) James, born 15 May, 1668. "Old John Burbeen died 8 Jan. 1713-14, aged about 86 years [Gravestone]. Sarah, his wife, died 14 May, 1670." [Wob. Records of Births, etc: Gravestone.]

BURBEEN. *I*. James, son of John Burbeen, married Mary ——. Their children were: (1, 2) Mary and Sarah, twins, born 6 March, 1694: Sarah died 17 March, 1694. (3) James, b. 21 Aug. 1696. (4) John, b. 12 March, 1699; died 25 Aug., 1700. (5) Sarah, b. 17 June, 1701; married Rev. Timothy Walker, of Concord, N. H. [d] (6) Ruth, b. 28 March, 1708; md. to Mr. Jonathan Heywood, 1735. (7) Joseph, b. 3 March, 1712.

Mary, wife of James Burbeen, died 14 Oct. 1724: "Mr. James Berbeane" died 4 September, 1729.

---

[a] Rec. of Births, etc., etc. [b] Rec. of Births at Billerica.

[c] John Burbeen slain by the Indians near Dunstable, with B. Carter, and D. Baldwin, 5 Sept. 1724. Fox's Hist., p. 108.

[d] Bouton's Hist. Concord.

BURBEEN. *II.* James, son of James and Mary Burbeen, md. Mary Richardson, 5 Sept. 1721. Their children were: (1) James, son of Mary (Richardson) Burbeen, born 11 July, 1722. (2) Paul, b. 6 Apl. 1724. (3) John, b. 9 Feb. 1725-6. (4) Mary, b. 6 July, 1729. (5) Sarah, b. 7 March, 1733.

BURBEEN. Mr. Joseph, son of *I* James and Mary Burbeen, was graduated at Harvard College, 1731; occasionally preached, but was never settled in the Ministry; by his wife Esther had: (1) Esther, born 29 May, 1738; md. to Jesse Wyman, 1760. (2) Bridget, b. 17 July, 1742. (3) Susanna, b. 11 Apr. 1746; md. to Hon. Timothy Walker, Judge, Concord, N. H.[a] Mrs. Esther Burbeen died about 30 March, 1776.[b] Mr. Joseph Burbeen died 1794.[c]

BURBEEN. Paul, son of *II* James and Mary Burbeen, was graduated at H. C. 1743: died 1795.[c] [Wob. Records of Births, etc., etc.]

BUCK. Ephraim, son of Roger Buck of Cambridge, who came to this country in the "Increase," 1635, aged 18 years, settled at Cambridge, and had born there, by his wife Susanna, the above Ephraim, with five other children. His wife Susanna dying Sept. 10, 1685, he removed to Woburn, and there died Nov. 10, 1693.

BUCK. His son, Ephraim Buck, was born at Cambridge, July 26, 1646; removed to Woburn, and was taxed there in the Meeting House Rate, 1672: married at Woburn, Sarah, daughter of John Brooks, Jan. 1, 1670-1, and had by her: (1) Sarah, b. Jan. 11, 1673. (2) Ephraim, b. July 13, 1676. (3) John, b. 1678-9, and died within a month after. (4) John again, b. Feb. 7, 1679-80. (5) Samuel, b. Nov. 13, 1682. (6) Eunice, b. July 7, 1685. (7) Ebenezer, b. May 20, 1689. (8) Mary, b. Oct. 28, 1691. Ephraim Buck died Jan.... 1720-21. His descendants now living reside principally in Wilmington. [Woburn Records of Births, Marriages, etc. Savage's Geneal. Dict.]

BUTTER (OR BUTTERS). *I.* William was an inhabitant of Woburn, 1666, where he was taxed in the Country Rate, 26 Aug. of that year. He appears to have died 13 Nov., 1692. "Widow Butter died at Watertown, —— 1701." *II.* William Butter or Butters, his son, by his wife Rebekah, had (1) William, born 18 Sept. 1689; died soon. (2) William, b. 24 May, 1691; died 1711. (3) Rebekah, b. 10 Oct. 1693; died ——. (4) Lydia, b. 11 June, 1695; md. to Ebenezer Carter, 1719. (5) Rebekah, b. 30 Aug. 1698; md. to William Hamblett, 1720. (6) Samuel, b. 21 June, 1703. (7) Mary, b. 28 July, 1705; md. to Samuel Johnson, Feb. 1725. (8) John, b. 22 Oct. 1708. (9) . . . . daughter of William and Rebekah Butter, died 1711. (10) William, b. 8 April, 1713.

Samuel, son of *II.* William Butter, married Sarah Jaquith, 25 Jan. 1726. Their children were: (1) Sarah, b. 4 Nov. 1726. (2) Samuel, born 3 Nov. 1728.

The families of this name resided principally in those quarters of Woburn now known as Wilmington and Burlington. They were formerly

---

a Bouton's Hist. Concord.

b Memoranda of Samuel Thompson, Esq.

c Coll. Catalogue.

considerably numerous; and many descendants still remain in both towns.

BUTTERFIELD. Benjamin, a subscriber at Charlestown to the Town Orders for Woburn, 1640; an inhabitant of Woburn shortly after; was taxed there in 1645; and by his wife, Ann, had several children born there; as (1) Nathaniel, b. 14 Feb. 1642–3. (2) Samuel, b. 17 May, 1647. (3) Joseph, b. 15 Aug. 1649. In 1654, he removed to Chelmsford, where his wife, Ann, died 19 May, 1660; and he md. a second time, 3 June, 1663, Hannah, wid. of Thomas Whittemore of Malden. [Wob. Rec., Savage's Geneal. Dict.]

CARTER. Rev. Thomas. See Chap. IV.

CARTER. Mr. Samuel, eldest son of Rev. Thomas [see Chap. IV.] married Eunice, daughter of John Brooks, 1672; by whom he had: (1) Mary, born 24 July, 1673. (2) Samuel, b. 27 Aug. 1675; died 10 Sept. 1676. (3) Samuel, b. 7 Jan. 1677–8. (4) John, b. 14 March, 1680. (5) Thomas, b. 3 Apr. 1682. (6) Nathaniel, b. 7 Apr. 1685. (7) Eunice, b. 29 March 1687. (8) Abigail, b. May 1689. (9) Abigail, again, b. 30 May, 1690. He died 1693. His widow married John Kendall, for his 3d wife, subsequently to 1701. [Woburn Records of Births, etc., etc.]

CARTER. Timothy, third son of Rev. Thomas Carter, [See Chap. IV.] married, 3 May, 1680, Anna Fiske, daughter of David Fiske, of Cambridge Farms, i. e. Lexington; and by her had: (1) David, b. 17 Oct. 1681, died 22 May, 1736. (2) Timothy, born 12 July, 1683, and died the same year. (3) Anna, b. 17 July, 1684. (4) Timothy, b. 17 Oct. 1686. (5) Theophilus, b. 20 Oct. 1688. (6) Thomas, b. 14 Aug. 1690. (7) Abigail, b. 18 March, 1692. (8) Sarah, b. 24 Nov. 1694. (9) Elizabeth, b. 27 Aug. 1696; died 26 June, 1709. (10) Benjamin, b. 22 March, 1699; died soon. (11) Mary, b. 23 June, 1700; md. to Jasher Wyman 1721. (12) Martha, b. 22 July, 1702; md. to John Bruce 1721? (13) Benjamin again, b. 8 Nov. 1704.

Anna, wife of Timothy Carter, died 27 Jan. 1715–16. He died 8 July, 1727. [Town Records of Births, etc., etc.]

CARTER. Thomas, youngest son of Rev. Thomas Carter, married 1682, Margaret or Margery Whitmore, daughter of Francis Whitmore, of Cambridge. Their children were: (1) Mary, born 5 Oct. 1683; md. to Joshua Sawyer, jun., of Charlestown, 22 May, 1706. (2) Thomas, b. 13 June, 1686. (3) Eleazar, b. 20 Apr. 1689. (4) Daniel, b. 10 Aug. 1691. (5) Ebenezer, b. 24 Sept. 1695. (6) Ezra, b. 22 June, 1701.

"Margery, wife of Thomas Carter, died 5 Oct. 1734."

Descendants of Rev. Thomas Carter, bearing his name, were formerly very numerous, particularly in Wilmington, and in "Carter Row," so called, Burlington. And though, in the towns just mentioned, their number is now considerably diminished, they have not yet become extinct. By the following account of the family of the minister's grandson, Ebenezer, son of Thomas, and of the family of his great-great-grandson, William, son of Ebenezer, many, probably, in Wilmington and Burlington will be reminded of individuals of his posterity of whom they have heard, and of some whom they have seen and known.

Ebenezer Carter and Lydia "Butter," both of Woburn, married 15 Apr.

1719. Children were: (1) Ebenezer, born 25 May, 1720. (2, 3) Lydia & Abigail, twins, b. 4 Jan. 1721–2. (4) Ezra, b. 2 May, 1723. (5) William, b. 28 Apr. 1725. (6) Nathan, b. 2 Jan. 1727–8.

William Carter of Woburn entered his intentions of marriage with Abigail "Butter" of Wilmington, 18 Jan. 1754. Children were: (1) William, b. 11 Sept. 1754. (2) Benjamin, born 2 May, 1756. (3) Jonas, b. 17 April, 1758. (4) David, b. 20 May, 1761. (5) Jonathan, b. 2 Nov. 1763. (6) Joshua, b. 22 Sept. 1765. [Wob. Records of Births, etc.]

CARTER. *I.* John Carter, usually distinguished in Woburn Town Book, as "Captain John," or "the Captain," was an early inhabitant of Woburn, having been a subscriber to the "Town Orders" in 1640. By his wife, Elizabeth, he had children as follows: (1) Elizabeth, b. 8 Aug. 1643, and died 20 Dec. 1653, or as the County Records have, 23 Feb. 1654. (2) Mary, born 8 March, 1646. (3) Abigail, b. 21 Apr. 1648. (4) Hannah, b. 19 Jan. 1650–51; md. to James Convers, jun. (5) John, b. 6 Feb. 1652–3. Elizabeth, wife of Capt. John Carter, died 7 May, 1691, [aged 78 years, Gravestone.] Capt. John Carter and Elizabeth Groce were md. . . . . 1691. He died 14 Sept. 1692."

CARTER. *II.* John Carter and Ruth Burnham md. 20 June, 1678. Their children were: (1) Elizabeth, born 18 Sept. 1680; md. to Ebenezer Flagg, 1700. (2) Ruth, b. 18 Oct. 1681; md. to Josiah Wright, 1700. (3) Mary, b. 17 July, 1683. (4) John, b. 8 Aug. 1685; died 21 May, 1705. (5) Thomas, b. 3 July, 1687. (6) Abigail, b. 30 March, 1689; md. to Ralph Kendall, 1707? (7) Phebe, b. 11 June, 1691. (8) Joseph, b. 16 Feb. 1692–3. (9) Samuel, b. 31 Oct. 1694. (10) Esther, b. 21 Aug. 1696. (11) Josiah, b. 3 Aug. 1698. (12) Jabez, b. 17 Sept., 1700. (13, 14) Nathaniel and Benjamin, twins, b. 4 March, 1702. Benjamin, slain by the Indians near Dunstable, N. H., 5 Sept. 1724. (a)

Ruth, wife of Lieut. John Carter, died 11 Jan. 1723-4, (aged 55 years: Gravestone.)

Lieut. John Carter died 13 April, 1727, [aged 75 years: Gravestone.]

Descendants in the male line of Capt. John Carter, once a numerous race, living in Woburn and Burlington, seem now to be almost extinct in both these towns. One of the 7th generation, William, a grandson of the late Mr. Jonathan Carter, yet lives in Burlington; and there may be one or more living in Woburn; but if any remain there, it is apprehended they must be very few. [Wob. Records of Births, etc. (a) Fox's Dunstable, p. 108.]

CARTER. Joseph Carter, sen., was of Newbury, 1636; removed to Woburn, as Mr. Savage conjectures, (a) before 1659; was taxed there in the Country Rate, 26 Aug. 1666; lived with his son Joseph, jun., in Wyman's Lane (so called), Woburn, on the old Billerica Road; and died in Charlestown, 30 Dec. 1676. (b)

Joseph Carter, jun., of Woburn, son of the preceding, currier, married Bethiah......and had (1) Bethiah, b. 8 June, 1671; md. to Roland Jones, 1695. (2) Susanna, b. 24 Feb. 1672-3. (3) Joseph, b. 28 Nov. 1674. (4) John, b. 26 Feb. 1676-7. (5) Abigail, b. 1 Feb. 1678-9. (6) Henry, b. 4

Oct. 1683. (7) Faith, b. 28 Apr. 1688. (c) Joseph Carter, jun., of Woburn, currier, was deceased 29 May, 1706, leaving Bethiah, his widow. (c) [(a) Geneal. Dict. (b) Charlestown Records. (c) Wyman Papers, No. 66, Wob. Records.]

CHALKLEY. Robert Chalkley was of Woburn, 1645, where he was taxed in the Country Rate, 8 Sept. of that year; but as his name is not on the List for the town rate assessed 22 Dec. 1646, he had doubtless before that time returned to Charlestown. He was made freeman 1647, and died in Charlestown, 2 Sept. 1672. By his Will, made 27 Aug. preceding, he gave all his estate to his wife Elizabeth, who died at Charlestown, 13 Oct. 1678. [Woburn Rec. Colony Rec. Savage's Geneal. Dict.]

CHAMBERLAIN. Thomas Chamberlain, freeman, 29 May, 1644; taxed in Woburn, in the Country Rate, 8 Sept. 1645. By wife, Mary, he had borne to him: (1) Thomas, born elsewhere, possibly in England. (2) Samuel, born in Woburn, 7 Oct. 1645. (3) Mary, b. 30 Jan. 1649. He then removed to Chelmsford. [Col. Rec., Woburn Rec., Savage's Geneal. Dict.]

CLARK. William, a weaver by occupation, was of Watertown, 1631; made freeman, 1639; removed to Woburn not far from 1654, reference being made there by the Selectmen, 27 May, 1654, to a grant of land made to him by the town. He was taxed in Woburn in the Country Rate 26 Aug. 1666. By his wife, Margery, who accompanied him from England, he had borne to him in Watertown:

(1) Mary, born Dec. 10, 1640; md. 27 Dec. 1655 to William Locke, of Woburn.

(2) Elizabeth, b. 26 Nov. 1642; md. 1659 to George Brush [Bruce] of Woburn.

(3) Hannah, b. 13 Feb. 1646; md. 1667 to William Frissell, of Concord, who died 1684.

(4) Lydia, married and left a widow with two daughters.

William Clark died 15 March, 1682, aged 87; and his widow died 11 Oct. 1694, aged 95.

[Bond's Watertown, p. 159, Savage's Geneal. Dict., Mass. Colony Rec., Woburn Town Rec. Vol. I.]

CLEAVELAND. *I.* Moses Cleaveland (or Cleveland, as the name is now more usually spelled, in conformity, it is understood, to the mode of spelling it in England,) came to this country (says family tradition) with his master, a joiner, from Ipswich, in the county of Suffolk. He early took up his permanent abode in Woburn, as appears by the Town Records, which, under date of 3 Feb. 1648-9, mention a committee appointed to lay out the portion of land which had been promised him. He married Ann, daughter of Edward Winn (born in England) 26 Sept. 1648; and had by her the following children, viz: (1) Moses, born 1 Sept. 1651. (2) Hannah, b. 4 Aug. 1653; married to Thomas Henshaw (pronounced at that day Hincher) 1677. (3) Aaron, b. 10 Jan. 1654-5. (4) Samuel, b. 9 June, 1657. (5) Miriam, b. 10 July, 1659; md. a Fosdick, or rather Foskett,[a] of Charles-

[a] Savage, in Geneal. Dict.

town. (6) Joanna, b. 19 Sept. 1661, died 2 July, 1667. (7) Edward, b. 20 May, 1663. (8) Josiah, b. 26 Feb. 1666–7. (9) Isaac, b. 11 May, 1669. (10) Joanna, b. 5 Apr. 1670; md. a Keyes, of Chelmsford. (11) Enoch, b. 1 Aug. 1671. Moses Cleaveland, sen., died 9 Jan. 1701–2. No record of his wife's death has been observed.

II. Moses Cleaveland married Ruth Norton, 4 Oct. 1676; and had by her: (1) "Annah" [Anna, or Hannah?] b. 7 Nov. 1677. (2) Joseph, b. 31 March, 1686.

I. Aaron Cleaveland md. Dorcas Wilson, 26 Sept. 1675. Their children were: (1) Dorcas, b. 29 Oct. 1676; md. John Knight, 12 March, 1699.[a] (2) Hannah, b. 18 Dec. 1678, died 13 June, 1679. (3) Aaron, b. 9 July, 1680. (4) Hannah, b. 2 June, 1687; md. a Beard.[b] (5) Moses, b. 24 Feb. 1689–90. (6) Sarah, b. 5 March, 1692; md. to Job Richardson, 1718? (7) Miriam, b. 9 July, 1694. (8) Isabel, b. 6 April, 1697; died 7 Dec. 1714. (9) Benjamin, b. 16 May, 1701.[c] (10) Ann, daughter of Aaron and Dorcas, b. . . . . . . [b]

Dorcas, wife of Aaron Cleaveland, died 29 Nov. 1714. Soon after her death, he md. a second wife, Prudence, ... [b]; and died 14 Sept. 1716, aged, according to Gravestone, 62 years.

CLEAVELAND. *II.* Aaron, son of Aaron and Dorcas Cleaveland, a carpenter by trade, md. Abigail, ... and resided in Woburn till after the birth of his second child. He then removed; and took up his residence, first, apparently, in Medford, then in Cambridge, after that, in Medford again; and subsequently in Charlestown. He was admitted 7 Oct. 1711, into the Church at Cambridge; and his mother, Dorcas, dying in his house there, in 1714, and his eldest son in 1716, they were both buried in Cambridge Graveyard. [See epitaphs on mother and son in Harris's Collection.] In 1720, his Church relationship was transferred from Cambridge to Medford church. But, even after that, he had one child at least, baptized in the church at Cambridge. He continued to reside in Medford or Charlestown, till 1738, when he removed with his family to East Haddam, Ct., where he bore the title of "*Captain*," and traded largely in land. Whether he remained there or not till his decease has not been ascertained.

His children by his wife Abigail having been born in different places, their births are not all recorded in one place. These were (1) Aaron, born at Woburn, 20 Oct. 1702, died at Cambridge, and was buried there in 1716. (2), Samuel, b. at Woburn, 17 May, 1704. In Vol. XLIII. p. 517, Registry of Deeds [for Suffolk?], under date of 23 May, 1743, is a deed from "Samuel Cleaveland," of Boston, mariner, in which he calls Aaron Cleaveland his father. (3) *Abigail*, "daughter of Aaron & Abigail Cleaveland," born at Medford, 10 May, 1706. [Medford Town Records.] (4) *John*, "son of Aaron & Abigail Cleaveland," was baptized 7 Oct. 1711, in the First church of Cambridge, the same day his father was taken

---

[a] Cambridge Records. [b] Rev. O. A. Taylor, from papers in Probate Office.
[c] Removed from Woburn, 1722. Compare Woburn Records, Vol. V. p. 138, 143, 155.

into that church. (5) Josiah, son of Aaron Cleaveland & Abigail his wife, was baptized in infancy, at Cambridge, 1 Nov. 1713. [Cambridge Ch. Records.] He md. 1 Jan. 1735 [1735-6?], Joanna Porter, daughter of Rev. Aaron Porter, of Medford; owned the Halfway Covenant in 1736; and had a son born to him 12 Dec. 1736, whom he called Aaron. This Josiah Cleaveland removed to Haddam, Ct., about the same time his father did. In a paper in the Registry of Deeds, dated 28 Nov. 1738, he styles himself "Josiah Cleaveland, now of Millenton, in East Haddam, in the Colony of Connecticut and County of Hartford, late of Charlestown, in the County of Middlesex, Mass., Housewright," etc., etc. As late as 10 Feb. 1748-9, he had removed to Boston. (6) Aaron, born at Cambridge, 29 Oct. 1715, [Cambridge Town Records.] Of him, see more below. (7) *John*, son of Aaron and Abigail Cleaveland, was baptized in infancy, 18 July, 1717. (8) "*Moses*, son of Aaron and Abigail Cleaveland, was baptized, being an infant, 19 July, 1719." (9) "7 Jan. 1724, was baptized in infancy . . . . . . of Aaron & Abigail Cleaveland his wife." [Cambridge Ch. Records.] The child then baptized, whose name was not recorded, may have been his daughter *Mary*, who married Elisha Clark, of Haddam, 17 Sept. 1741; and had four children by him, viz: (1) "Waterius," [Waters, or Waterhouse?], b. 30 June, 1742. (2) *Elisha*, b. 23 Apr. 1744. (3) *William*, b. 19 Aug. 1746. (4) Mary, b. 4 Apr. 1749.

Samuel, 3d son, 4th child of Moses and Ann Cleaveland, first settlers of the name in Woburn, married, 17 May, 1680, Jane, daughter of Solomon Keyes of Chelmsford, and this, his first wife dying 4 Nov. 1681, he md. for his 2d wife, 23 May, 1682, Persis, dr. of Richard Hildreth of the same town. He resided there several years, and had several children born to him.[a] About 1693, he seems to have gone back to Woburn, where, 26 June, 1693, his dr. Elizabeth was born;[b] and very soon after, he removed with his family to Canterbury, Connecticut, and there had other children. He died probably 1736.[a]

Josiah, brother of the above Samuel Cleaveland, served in the Indian War: was of Chelmsford, 1691; and there, by his wife, Mary, he had several children born to him, as also afterwards at Canterbury, Ct., to which he removed.[a] According to Mr. Savage, he died 26 April, 1709.[a]

In 1699, Samuel and Josiah Cleaveland, sons of Moses and Ann, were inhabitants of Plainfield, Ct., on the West Side of Quinabaug River, now Canterbury. Between 1699 and 1703, they were joined by their brother Isaac; [and doubtless, too, by their brother Edward.] In 1716, there were only 63 taxable inhabitants in all Canterbury, and of these 63 nine were Cleavelands; viz: (1) Samuel, whose property was estimated at £84: 00. (2) Samuel, jun., [son of Samuel?] at £48: 06. (3) Joseph [son of Samuel?] at £40: 00. (4) Edward, sen., [brother of Samuel and Josiah?] at £35: 00. (5) Edward, jun., [son of Edward, sen.,?] at £24: 00. (6) Widow Cleaveland [supposed to be Isaac's widow] at £100: 00. (7)

[a] Savage's Geneal. Dict. [b] Woburn Records of Births, etc.

Josiah, [son of Josiah, then deceased?] at £44 : 00. (8) Joseph, jun.,? [who?] at £36 :10. (9) Moses [son of Samuel, born, according to Mr. Savage, in 1695] estimated at £22 : 00. These nine made one-seventh of all the inhabitants of the town, and owned one-eighth of all the taxable property.[a]

Enoch, youngest son of Moses and Ann Cleaveland, was a tailor by trade; lived successively at Sudbury, Framingham, and Concord, at which last-mentioned town he died, 1729, leaving a widow and three children. His widow, Elizabeth, died before 5 April, 1731; and his eldest son, Jonathan, of Acton, a tailor by occupation, administered on his father's estate. [Letter of Rev. Oliver A. Taylor, Manchester, Mass.]

Many have been the descendants of "Moyses Cleaveland," who came to New England, the humble apprentice of a joiner, in 1635, and established himself in Woburn about 1648, that have done worthily in their day; have been distinguished not only by their position in society, but by their weight of character and influence, and by the usefulness of their lives. And although a place cannot be claimed for them here, as inhabitants of Woburn; yet it will be gratifying, it is presumed, to the present people of the town, to see some notice taken of them in this work, as descendants of one of the early settlers of the place.

1. Rev. Aaron Cleveland, great grandson of Moses and Ann, and son of Aaron and Abigail Cleveland, successively inhabitants of Woburn, Medford, Cambridge, Medford again, and Charlestown, and finally of East Haddam, Ct. was born 29 October, 1715. As this record of his birth is from Cambridge Town Records, and as the record of his baptism the next day, 30 Oct. 1715, is from the Records of the Church of Cambridge, it may be confidently presumed that Cambridge was the place of his birth; though it has been said by some that he was born in Medford. He entered Harvard College at sixteen years of age; was graduated, 1735; was settled over the church and people of Haddam, Ct., in July 1739; married, 4 Aug. 1739, Susannah, daughter of Rev. Aaron Porter, of Medford, born 1 March, 1716, and sister of Joanna Porter, born 22 March, 1719, whom his brother, Josiah Cleveland, had married, 1 Jan. 1735 [1735–6?]. Rev. Mr. Cleveland was dismissed from Haddam, 1746; installed over the South Church in Malden, about June 1747, and dismissed about Oct. 1750. We next hear of him at Halifax, Nova Scotia, whence he sailed for England; received Orders in the Church of England at London, 1755, and was commissioned, 1 July, 1757, by the Society for Propagating the Gospel in Foreign Parts, to take charge of the Episcopal Church in Newcastle, Delaware, in compliance with the request of that people. On his way to Boston, to make arrangements for conveying his family to Newcastle, he stopped at the house of Dr. Franklin, in Philadelphia; was there taken sick, and died 11 Aug. 1757. His remains were interred in Christ's Church, Philadelphia. His widow died at Salem, 1788. The Pennsylvania Gazette of 18 August, 1757 contained an obituary notice, in which was a warm eulogium upon him, written by the editor, Dr. Franklin.

[a] Letter of Silvester Judd, Esq., Northampton.

2. Rev. Aaron Cleveland of Norwich, son of the preceding, was born at Haddam, Ct. 3 Feb. 1744. His father dying when he was only thirteen years of age, the plan for giving him an education at college was defeated; and he was put by his friends in Connecticut to learn the hatter's trade, and followed that business many years. In 1779, he was a member of the Legislature of Connecticut; was ordained soon after to the Congregational ministry; and continued to perform his clerical functions in various places till his death. He was for some time resident in Norwich, Weathersfield, and West Hartford; but never had a settlement in any congregation. He performed missionary services in Hartford County and vicinity, and preached frequently as a supply in almost all its towns; and long afterwards was spoken of with profound respect by those who had heard him. And his wit, too, and agreeableness in company, became proverbial. He published in 1775, a "Poem against Slavery;" and two sermons against *War*, preached just after the news of the battle of Waterloo, 1815. In the "Poets of Connecticut," were published in 1844, two poems of his "which show what he might have been with better advantages." He died of dysentery in New Haven, 21 Sept. 1815, at the house of a relative, Mrs. Porter; and lies buried in New Haven. [Allen's Biography; Letters of Professor C. D. Cleveland, 1846; and of Rev. A. Cleveland Coxe, 1847.]

N. B. The mother of Rev. Mr. Coxe, just referred to, was Abiah Hyde, daughter of Rev. A. Cleveland, of Norwich, by his second wife, a Clement, of Norwich.[a] The father of Professor C. D. Cleveland is the venerable Rev. Charles Cleveland of Boston, son of Rev. Mr. Cleveland of Norwich, who, people of Woburn will remember, was present there on a late memorable occasion, 22d February, 1867; and who, though upwards of 95 years of age, still paces the streets of Boston in his pious and benevolent labors.

3. Rev. John Cleveland of Chebacco. He was a great-grandson of Moses and Ann of Woburn, a grandson of Samuel and Persis Cleveland of Chelmsford and Canterbury, Ct., and a son of Josiah Cleveland of Canterbury, and of Abigail (Paine) Cleveland, his wife. He was born at Canterbury, 22 April, 1722; was graduated at Yale College, 1745; and settled over Chebacco Parish in Ipswich, now the town of Essex, 1747. He married for his first wife Mary Dodge (Choate?) daughter of Parker Dodge, by whom he had 4 sons and 3 daughters. And she dying in 1768, he next md. widow Mary Neal Forster, of Manchester, with whom his connection, as also that with his first wife, was eminently happy.

In the French war, 1758, he went as Chaplain, and at the commencement of the Revolutionary struggle he served as a Chaplain at Cambridge; and with him at that time were two of his brothers and all four of his sons. In 1763, he was rejoiced to witness a powerful revival among his people. In his preaching, he was not confined to written sermons. It was said of him by Rev. Dr. Emmons that "he was a pattern of piety, and an ornament to the Christian and clerical profession." His faithful labors were

---

[a]Letter of Rev. A. Cleveland Coxe, 1847.

crowned with great success; at one period in about six months, one hundred persons were added to his church. He died in peace and hope, 22 April, 1799, on his seventy-seventh birth-day.

4. Rev. Ebenezer Cleveland, brother of the preceding, was born in Canterbury, 1725; received a degree at Yale College, 1748; married Abigail Stevens of Canterbury, 1746; commenced preaching at *Sandy* Bay, Gloucester (now Rockport), in 1751 or 1752, and was ordained their first minister, 1755. During much of his time in the Revolutionary War, he was absent from his people, as a chaplain in the army. In 1780, he left the army, and removed to Coos, N. H., on some land he had received, and also as superintendent of the Dartmouth College lands. While he resided here, his daughter Mary was married to Professor John Smith, of Dartmouth College; and he spent seven or eight years, preaching as he could, part of the time in a barn. Subsequently, he was for a year or two employed as an evangelist in Maine. Returning from Maine, he was settled in the ministry at Amesbury, where he remained four or five years. He then went back to Rockport, and there spent the remainder of his days. Rev. Dr. Allen observes of him, "His lot was cast in hard places, and in hard times; and he had a large family and domestic causes of uneasiness, so that his life was that of a worthy man struggling with adversity." He died 4 July, 1805, in the 79th year of his age, in the hope of immortal glory. His wife deceased 25th Dec. 1804, æt. 77. A monument has been erected to their memory in Rockport, upon which appropriate epitaphs have been inscribed to them both. [Allen's Biog. Dict., Letter from Rev. O. A. Taylor, 23d April, 1846.]

5. Rev. John Cleveland, eldest son of Rev. John Cleveland, of Chebacco, was born in 1750, and was fitted for College, but prevented by ill health from entering. At the commencement of the Revolution, he enlisted in the army, obtained a lieutenant's commission, and continued in the service during the war. Having had from his youth a strong inclination for the Christian ministry, his wishes in this respect were at length gratified. He was called to the pastoral office in Stoneham, 1785; and being dismissed from there in 1794, he was re-rettled in 1798, over the North Parish in Wrentham, where, after a faithful and exemplary discharge of ministerial duty, he died, 1818, aged 68. [Allen's Biography.]

6. Parker Cleveland, M. D., son of Rev. John Cleveland, of Chebacco, born 1751, settled as a physician in Byfield at the age of 19; and during the first year of the war of the Revolution was the surgeon of a regiment.. He was skilful as a physician; often represented Rowley (to which Byfield belonged) in the Legislature; and was eminently pious, devout, and benevolent, as a Christian. He married, for his first wife, E. Jackman, in 1772, by whom he had Parker Cleveland, a graduate 1799, and subsequently a tutor of Harvard College, and an eminent professor of natural philosophy, chemistry, etc., etc., for many years in Bowdoin College. For his second wife, he md. Abigail Cleveland of Canterbury, Ct., by whom he had Rev. John P. Cleveland, D. D., successively of Salem, Cincinnati, Providence, Northampton, Mass., and Lowell.

Dr. Parker Cleveland died in Feb. 1826, aged 74. [Letter of Rev. O. A. Taylor. Allen's Biog. Dict.]

7. Nehemiah Cleveland, youngest son of Rev. John Cleveland, of Chebacco, was born 1760. He accompanied his father, at the age of 16, during the siege of Boston, and enlisted in the army for about a year. Having studied medicine with his brother, and with Dr. Manning, of Ipswich, he entered on the practice in Topsfield, 1783. He was also much employed in his day in various honorable public offices. For his first wife, he md. Lucy, daughter of Dr. Manning, of Ipswich, who died 1791, leaving no children. By his second wife, Experience Lord, daughter of Dr. Elisha Lord, of Pomfret, Ct., he had nine children; (1) Nehemiah, who died soon. (2) Experience, who died young, (3) Nehemiah, of Brooklyn, N. Y., late preceptor of Dummer Academy, Byfield, born 1796. (4) William, b. 1798, now [1846] in Topsfield. (5) Lucy, born 1800, died 1838. (6) Mary, born 1802, wife of Rev. Oliver Alden Taylor, of Manchester, Mass. (7, 8) twins, born 1804, of whom one died; the other, John, the present John Cleveland, Esq., of New York city. (9) Rev. Elisha Lord Cleveland, of New Haven, born in 1806.

Dr. Nehemiah Cleveland died 26 Feb. 1837, aged 76, sustained by the consolations of the religion which he had professed and adorned. His widow, Experience, died at the house of her son-in-law, in Manchester, Rev. Mr. Taylor, (who has himself since deceased) 21 Jan. 1845, in the 81st year of her age. [Allen's Biog. Dict. Letter of Rev. Mr. Taylor, 23 Apl. 1846.]

COLE. Isaac, son of Isaac, of Charlestown, who came to this country 1635, with wife Joanna and two children, in the Hercules, from Sandwich, County of Kent, England.[a] This son of his was born in 1637, at Charlestown, came to Woburn to reside, and had granted him by the town, 25 April, 1662, a lot of land in the centre, 50 poles, bounded by the high way [High Street] on the east, and by the high way to the burying place on the north.[b] He married Jane, widow of James Britten, or Britton, 1 Feb. 1659, but had no children. He was one of those eight members of Woburn church who were presented by the grand jury in Oct. 1671, for refusing to commune with the church on the ground of certain alleged scruples of conscience, and whose case was commended by the court to the consideration of a council of neighboring churches, to assemble March, 1672, before the court should come to a final decision. [See Chapt. V.] What the result of the council was, and what the decision of the court, is not known.

Isaac Cole died 10 June, 1674: his widow, Jane, died 10 March, 1687.[c]

CONVERS. Edward, Deacon. See Chapt. II.

CONVERS. James, Ensign. See Chapt. V.

CONVERS. Josiah, Deacon, eldest son of Dea. Edward Convers; born in England; came with his father to New England in 1630; abode awhile at Charlestown, and came with his father to Woburn to dwell, about 1641. He

[a] Savage's Geneal. Dict. [b] Town Rec. Vol. I., p. 51. [c] Rec. of Deaths.

married, 26 March 1651, Esther Champney, daughter of Richard Champney, of Cambridge, a ruling elder of the church there, in 1658.[a] By his wife Esther, Dea. Convers had a son Josiah, born 15 March, 1660, who married, 8 Oct. 1685, Ruth Marshall, and had children by her. In after times, this son of his was much employed in town business, was familiarly known by the title of "Captain Josiah," and died 15 July, 1717, aged 58.[b]

Deacon Josiah Convers was a deacon of the Church of Woburn in 1674, and died 3 Feb. 1689–90, aged 72 years.[b] [Woburn Records of Births, Marriages and Deaths; Savage's Geneal. Dict. [a] Cambridge Ch. Records. [b] Gravestone.]

CONVERS. Samuel, Son of Dea. Edward Convers, born in Charlestown; baptized in the church there 12 March, 1637–8,[a] settled at Woburn; made freeman 1666; married Judith, daughter of Rev. Thomas Carter, 8 June, (14 Oct.?) 1660; by whom he had a son Samuel, born 4 Apl. 1662. [Wob. Rec., Savage's Geneal. Dict.,[a] Charlestown, Ch. Records.]

CONVERS. Allen Convers, called by Dea. Edward in his Will a "kinsman," and made an overseer thereof. He is supposed on his arrival in this country to have gone first to Salem; and is said by Felt to have had land granted him there in 1639. He was in Woburn as early as 1642; was taxed there in the Country Rate of 1645; and was made freeman in 1644. He was appointed Commissioner of the Rate in Woburn, 1666; and taught school there in 1676. By his wife, Sarah, he had borne to him 11 Oct. 1642, a son Zechariah; and after him several other children. He died 19 Apl. 1679. His wife died only three days after him, (it is supposed) of the small-pox, which was then spread in the town, and among its victims there is numbered "Goodwife Conuars."[a] [Savage; Town Records. [a] Town Rec., Vol. II., inverted, p. 163.]

CONVERS. James, jun., Major. See Chapt. V. and Woburn Records of Marriages and Deaths.

Two of his sons, Robert and Josiah, were men of distinction and influence in their day. Robert, born 29 Dec. 1677, married Mary Sawyer, 19 Dec. 1698, and by her had twelve children; but his male posterity in Woburn, it is believed, are now extinct. "Capt. Robert Conuarse" died 20 July, 1736.

Josiah, his son, born 12 Sept. 1684, md. Hannah, daughter of Joshua Sawyer of Woburn, 30 Dec. 1706; and by her, and by Dorothy, a second wife, he had 8 children.

Josiah, son of Josiah and Hannah Convers, born 2 March, 1710, md. Sarah Evans, of Reading, about 1732, had 4 children, and died 17 June, 1748.

Josiah, son of Josiah and Sarah Convers, born 27 Jan. 1733, [1733–4?] md. Hephzibah Brooks, 28 March, 1758, and had issue as follows: (1) Josiah, born 14 March, 1759. (2) John, b. 3 March, 1761. (3) Jesse, born 9 Feb. 1765. (4) Joshua, born 20 Jan. 1767. (5) Luther, born 26 Jan. 1777, died 11 March, 1861.

Of the sons of Josiah and Hephzibah Convers, two were instances of very remarkable longevity. Jesse died in 1864, when he lacked but a few months of being 100 years old. Joshua completed his century of existence 20th Jan. 1867; and there were highly interesting services performed in his presence (and in which he himself took part) in celebration of the event, 22d Feb. 1867, in Lyceum Hall, Woburn.

"CRAGGIN," or CRAGIN. John, was taxed in the Country Rate, made 26 Aug. 1666; and is numbered 3 April, 1668, with those who had right in the common lands of Woburn [a]. He married Sarah Dawes, 4 Nov. 1661; and by her had 8 children; two of whom, twins, Rachel and Leah, were born 14 March, 1680, and both died 4 days after. He died 27 Oct. 1708; his widow, Sarah, died 23 Dec. 1725.

"CRAGGIN, or CRAGIN. John Craggin, jun., his son, entered his intentions of marriage with Deborah Skelton, 13 April, 1700: and to them were born twins, John and Anna, 25 March, 1701; and, secondly, Benjamin, born 27 Nov. 1702. John Craggin, jun., died 26 Jan. 1703-4. [Woburn Records of Births, &c. [a] Town Records, Vol. I., pp. 43, 44.]

CUTLER. John was probably one of three brothers, Robert, James and John, who are supposed to have emigrated from Hingham, Norfolk County, England; and to be the ancestors, one or other of them, of all, or most of their name in New England. *James*, dwelt first at Watertown, then at "Cambridge North Farms," now Lexington; Robert, was of Charlestown, a deacon of the church there, and ancestor of that distinguished scholar and divine, Rev. Dr. Timothy Cutler, President of Yale College, 1719; and afterwards, becoming an Episcopalian, Rector of Christ's Church, Boston, where he died, 17 Aug. 1765, æt. 82.

John Cutler was in Woburn 1646, being taxed there for the first time in December of that year. He married in Woburn, 3 Sept. 1650, Olive Thompson, born probably in England, a daughter of James Thompson, one of the original settlers of Woburn, and a member of the first Board of Selectmen, chosen in 1644. His first wife dying, he married a second, the widow of Mr. John Lewis, of Lynn, who also had deceased in 1666. In the mean while, becoming providentially deranged, he was, by order of the County Court, 3 April, 1666, put under the guardianship of the Selectmen for the disposal of him and his property for his own benefit and that of his children. In a suit at law, in 1678, against his trustees, judgment was obtained in favor of the town, in satisfaction of the expense the town had been at for his maintenance the twelve years previous. But the Selectmen agreed to give up by deed to his son John, a large portion of the lands which had once belonged to his father, for a very moderate consideration; he promising not to sell, except to his sisters to live on, or to the town; in which latter case, he was to receive back from the town as much as he had paid for them. [Wob. Records.]

I. John Cutler died of the small-pox in 1678-9. The dates of the death of his two wives are not known. His children, who were probably all by his first wife, were: (1) Mary, born 7 Aug. 1651; died 3 May, 1655. (2) Susanna, b. 22 March, 1653-4. (3) John. (4) Mary (or "Marah,") b. 5 May, 1663; married to Matthew Smith of Woburn as his second wife, 20 June, 1684. [Woburn Town Rec.; Wob. Rec. of Births, etc., etc.]

II. John Cutler, only son of John & Olive (Thompson) Cutler, was born about 1656; married for his first wife Anna ———, who died 24 July, 1681, having borne him a daughter, Susanna, who seems likewise to have died young. For his second wife, he married Susanna, daughter of John and Susanna (Martin) Baker, in 1682, by whom he had: (1) John, born 15 Jan. 1682–3, and died the 2d day from his birth. (2) John, born 7 Dec. 1684, and died the same day. (3) John, born 4 Jan. 1685–6; married, first, Lydia Burnap, who died 27 Apr. 1743; secondly, Rachel Poodney of Wilmington, 24 Nov. 1743. He lived, much respected, within the limits of Woburn Precinct; died 10 Jan. 1767, aged 81, and lies buried (as does also his widow Rachel, who died 22 Aug. 1784, in her 84th year) in the Precinct, or Burlington burying ground. By neither of his two wives, does this *III.* Mr. John Cutler appear to have had children. (4) Susanna, born 8 Nov. 1687. Susanna, the second wife of *II.* John Cutler, being dead, he married, 14 Oct. 1692, for his third wife, Elizabeth Reed, daughter of the first Deacon George Reed of Woburn, and Elizabeth (Jennings, or Jennison) Reed, his wife, born 29 July, 1653; by whom he had children as follows: (1) *Hannah*, or *Anna*, born 5 July, 1694, and died, a single woman, apparently, 6 Feb. 1737–8. (2) Rebekah, born 8 Aug. 1697. (3) Nathaniel, born 23 May, 1700. (4) Sarah, born 22 Apr. 1702.

II. John Cutler died 25 Nov. 1709: Elizabeth, his widow, died 9 Jan. 1709–10. [Wob. Rec. of Births, etc., etc.]

CUTLER. *III.* Nathaniel, only son of *II.* John Cutler and Elizabeth his wife, married Abigail Bruce of Woburn, 21 March, 1723. Their children were: (1) *Nathaniel*, born 26 May, 1724. (2) John, b. 21 July, 1726. (3) Sarah, b. 26 May, 1729. (4) Abigail, b. 6 Sept. 1731. (5) Elizabeth, b. 30 Nov. 1735. (6) *William*, born 7 Feb. 1737–8; married Mary Trask, 17 Apl. 1760. (7) Mary, born 26 Feb. 1739–40; married to Shubael Johnson, 1760. (8) Silas, born 30 May, 1743; married Ruth Johnson, 31 Oct. 1765; removed to Templeton, Mass., and there died. (9) Ruth, born 9 Jan. 1745, (1745–6?) "*Lieut.* Nathaniel Cutler," in his 49th year; died 25 Aug. 1748. Gravestone in Precinct Bur. Ground.

Of the posterity of John Cutler, the first settler of the name in Woburn about 1646, four entire generations have passed away from this stage of existence; one or two individuals of the fifth generation still linger behind, and from the numerous ranks of the sixth and seventh generations, a considerable number upon reckoning are found missing; but a goodly remnant is left, resident in Burlington, Chicopee, and various other places in New England, and in the West.

DAVIS. Nicholas came in "*the Planter*," early in 1635, aged 40, with his wife Sarah, 48, and his "cossen" (cousin), meaning, probably his nephew, William Locke, aged 6, and others, his servants.[a] His wife Sarah dying 24 May, 1643, he married, 12 July following, Elizabeth, widow of Joseph Isaacs, of Cambridge. He was active in promoting the settlement of Woburn, the Town Orders for which he subscribed at Charlestown in

[a] Savage's Geneal. Dict.

Dec. 1640; was taxed there in the first "Country Rate," levied 8 Sept. 1645; and also in the first Town Rate, assessed 22 Dec. 1646. But his name is not found in any subsequent tax list in Woburn. He probably removed to York, and was there in 1652. "His will of 27 April, 1667, proved 12 March, 1670," refers not to any son, but presents the names of many remote relations.

DEAN or "DAINE." William, "married at Billerica, 1 Sept. 1670, Martha Bateman, of Concord," by whom he had: (1) Martha, born 17 Aug. 1671. (2) William, born 5 July, 1673. (3) Samuel, born 26 July, 1675. (4) John, b. 25 June, 1677. (5) Sarah, b. 1687, died 6 March, 1688. His name appears for the first time on any recorded Tax List for Woburn, in the new Meeting Rate, 1672. [Town Rec. Vol. I, pp. 38, 39.] His death is not on record. Martha Dean [wife or daughter?] died 1711.

[Woburn Rec. of Births; Savage's Geneal. Dict.]

In a list of soldiers stationed [about 1695?] at Fort Mary, Saco Falls, where John Hill was Captain, are recorded "William Dean, Woburn," and "Samuel Dean, Woburn." These were doubtless the sons by those names of William and Martha Dean, above mentioned. There is evidence to make it probable that one of these two brothers was taken prisoner and carried off. One or both of them probably settled in that region.[a]

John, son of William and Martha Dean, had by his wife Mary: (1) John, born 10 Jan. 1704-5. (2) William, born 7 May, 1706. (3) Edward, born 14 Sept. 1707. (4) Ebenezer, born 28 Jan. 1708-9; embarked at Boston about 1739, and was never heard of afterwards. By his wife Mary, he had a son Ebenezer, and a daughter. The son, born 7 Oct. 1733, was a shoemaker, removed to Maine, and died at Lincolnville, 1810, æt. 77; had 15 children, a numerous posterity in Maine and at the West.[a] (5) Thomas, born 23 Nov. 1712. (6) Molly, born 16 Apl. 1715, died 20 July, 1739. (7) Samuel, born 24 Feb. 1716-7.

Mr. John Dean died February 1751. All his sons had families of children.

Edward, son of John and Mary Dean, married for his first wife Patience, daughter of Jacob and Elizabeth Wyman, 1 May, 1740; and she dying, 15 June, 1741, he entered his Intentions of Marriage with "Sarah Robie" of Billerica, 14 Ap. 1753; by whom he had (1) Jesse, that well known citizen of Burlington, born 17 Feb. 1754: and (2) Sarah, born 3 June, 1756, wife of Major John Radford.

EAMES. Robert, was of Charlestown (1651)[b]; but removing to Woburn, he was taxed there, 1666, and had right in the common lands of Woburn allowed him in 1668.[c] By his wife Elizabeth, he had born to him in Woburn, (1) Samuel, 7 Apr. 1653, and died 14 Apr. same year. (2) John, born . . . . . and died 18 Jan. 1654. (3) Elizabeth, born 4 June, 1659. (4) Mary, 11 June, 1661; married to Abraham Cozzens, 1684. (5) Priscilla, 2 May, 1663. (6) Samuel, 2 Sept. 1664. (7) Abigail, 22 Sept. 1666. (8) John, 9 May, 1668.[d]

---

[a] Letter of John Dean, Esq., Boston.

[b] Savage's Geneal. Dict.. [c] Wob. Town Records. [d] Wob. Rec. of Births, etc., etc.

Elizabeth, wife of Robert Eames, died 22 March, 1710. Robert Eames died 30 July, 1712.[a] But Mr. Savage remarks in Geneal. Dict. of this Robert Eames, "I suppose he removed to Chelmsford, in the part called Dracut, and died, 25 Apr. 1671. His will, made 3 days before, names "brother John and cousin Richard, son of sister Dorothy Newman, of Farnham, in Co. Surrey; and adds no more to our knowledge."

EAMES. Samuel, married Mary ——, by whom he had: (1) Samuel, born 8 Sept. 1692. (2) Lydia, b. 28 Oct. 1692 [1694?]; m. to Ebenezer Buck, 1713. (3) Daniel, b. 10 Jan. 1696 (1696–7?) (4) Jacob, b. 11 July, 1699, "Jacob, son of Samuell Eames, died of the small pox," Jan. 1721 (1721–2?) (5) Hephzibah, b. 7 March, 1702. (6) Joshua, b. 8 May, 1705. (7) Caleb, b. 17 March, 1708. (8) Elizabeth, b. 26 March, 1711. (9) Robert, b. 6 Oct. 1712; died the same day. (10) Abigail, b. 11 Apr. 1714. (11) Jonathan, b. 18 Aug. 1716. N. B. Samuel and Mary Eames appear, by deed of land in Woburn to Daniel Fisk, 14 Oct. 1740, to belong at that date, to Wilmington, set off from Woburn 1730. [Rec. of Births, etc.]

EAMES. Samuel, son of Samuel and Mary Eames, married Judith Simonds, both of Woburn, 2 July, 1717. To them were born: (1) Judith, 22 March, 1718; md. to Zach. Symmes, 1741. (2) Samuel, 13 Feb. 1719 (1719–20); died 13 April, 1727. (3) Jacob, 10 Aug. 1723. (4) Samuel, 28 June, 1727. "Deacon Eames' son Samuel died 12 Dec. 1756." (5) Rebekah, a daughter, died 21 Apr. 1728. (6) Huldah, b. 4 March, 1733, m. to Elijah Wyman, 1765. Dea. Samuel Eames died 20 Jan. 1775, [aged 84. Gravestone: 83d year.] Judith, wife of Dea. Samuel Eames, died 10 Jan. 1766, [aged 71: Gravestone.]

Daniel, son of Samuel and Mary Eames, md. Abigail Nourse of Reading, 8 March, 1720. Had a son Daniel born at Reading, 30 March, 1721. (2) Mary, b. 12 Apr. 1723. (3) John, b. at Woburn, 19 Apr. 1727. (4) Jonathan, b. at Wilmington, 9 Nov. 1730; graduated at Harvard College, 1752; minister of Newtown, N. H. (5) Jacob, b. 12 June, 1732, at Wilmington. (6) Samuel, b. at Wilmington, 24 Jan. 1734–5. Afterwards, Capt. Daniel Eames removed to Haverhill, and md. for a second wife, Mary Chadwick, of Bradford, 9 Aug. 1748; and for a third wife, Priscilla Kimball, widow, 2 Feb. 1756.[b]

EAMES. Caleb, son of Samuel and Mary Eames, md. Sarah, daughter of John and Sarah Simonds, both of Woburn, 5 Apr. 1732. Their children were: (1) Caleb, born 7 Nov. 1732. (2) Jonas, b. 15 March, 1734; died 10 Feb. 1736–7. (3) Caleb, b. 26 Dec. 1737. (4) Jonas, b. 2 Feb. 1742–3. (5) John, b. 25 Oct. 1746; md. Abigail, daughter of Samuel Thompson, Esq.[c]

EAMES. Jacob, son of Dea. Samuel and Judith Eames, entered his Intentions of Marriage with Rachel, daughter of Nathan and Huldah Wyman, both of Woburn, 15 March, 1748. Their children were: (1) Rachel, born 5 Nov. 1749. (2) Jacob, b. 6 June, 1751. (3) Nathan, b. 11 April, 1753; died 21 July, 1773, æt. 21; Gr. St. (4) Ruth, born 28 May, 1758. [Rec. of Births, etc.]

N.B. Of late years, the name of Eames is written and spelled by some Ames.

---

[a] Wob. Town Records. [b] Mr. John A. Boutelle, Woburn.
[c] Wob. Rec. of Births, etc. Mem. of Saml. Thompson, Esq.

FARLEY. George, an early inhabitant of Woburn, his name being on the List of the Country Tax assessed there 8 Sept. 1645, the first on record. He there married Christian Births, 9 April, 1641; by whom he had: (1) James, born 23 Nov. 1643; died 10 Dec. following. (2) Caleb, born 1 Apr. 1645. (3) Mary, born 27 Feb. 1646–7. [a] Not long after, he removed to Billerica, where he had: (1) Samuel, born the "last weeke" in Sept. 1654. (2) Mehetabel, born the "last weeke" in Apr. 1656, "and departed this life" 1 Feb. 1672–3.[b] On the 19th of Nov. 1656, George Farley, "of Billerica," sold his house and land, 20 acres, in Woburn, to Richard Snow.[c]

"George Farley, sen., departed this life" 27 Dec. 1693. "Christian Farley, widdow of Georg Farley," died 27 March, 1702. [b]

N. B. The name Farley is sometimes spelt Farlow, and Farlo. *See* Savage's Geneal. Dict.

FARRAR. John, was admitted an inhabitant of Woburn, at Town Meeting (February 1655–6?), to choose town officers for 1656.[d] He is presumed to have been a brother of Jacob Farrar, of Lancaster, who appears, from the following record in Woburn Town Book, to have died at Woburn: "Jacob Ffarer, sen., died 14 August, 1677." His widow, Ann, was married to John "Seirs," of Woburn, as his second wife, 2 Nov. 1680.[e] To John Farrar were born: (1) Mary, 10 Apr. 1656. (2) Jacob, 22 Oct. 1657; died of the small-pox June 1679.[a] (3) Isaac, 16 Dec. 1659, and died in a fortnight after. (4) Joanna, 9 Apr. 1661; married to Robert Dayle, 1680. (5) Mercy, 1 April, 1663. (6) Hannah, 22 Jan. 1667–8; married to John Wyman, wheelwright, 14 Dec. 1685. (7) Isaac, 1 July, 1671.

John Farrar died 11 July, 1690. His wife's name, and the date of her death are not known.

FARRAR. Isaac Farrar, his son, had by his wife Mary: (1) Mary, born 6 Dec. 1699. (2) Isaac, b. 2 Apr. 1702. (3) John, b. 7 Jan. 1703–4. (4) Jacob, b. 11 June, 1705. (5) Anne, b. 13 Aug. 1707. (6) Jonathan, b. 28 Apr. 1709. (7) Joanna, b. 17 March, 1711. " . . . . daughter of Isaac Farrar, died ye. . . . . March 1713."

Isaac Farrar's name not occurring on the Woburn Province Tax Lists for 1714, 1715, he is supposed to have previously removed from the town.

FLAGG. Gershom, was born at Watertown, 16 April, 1641, the eldest son of Thomas and Mary of Watertown, where the name was originally spelled *Flegg.*[f] He came to Woburn about 1668, where he married Hannah Lepingwell, 15 April, 1668, a daughter of Michael "Lepingwell." He was a tanner by trade; and in 1673 had his dwelling-house, and tanning establishments, with about an acre of land attached, in High Street, near the site of the first meeting-house, having Rev. Mr. Carter's house on the West, the Old Burying Place on the East, and the Training Field on the

---

[a] Woburn Records of Births, etc. [b] Billerica Records. [c] Wyman Papers.
[d] Town Records, Vol. I., p. 23. [e] Rec. of Births, etc., etc.
[f] Dr. Henry Bond's Letters; also Bond's Watertown.

South.[a] His children were: (1) *Gershom*, born 10 March, 1669. (2) Eleazer, b. 1 Aug. 1670. (3) John, b. 25 May, 1673. (4) Hannah, b. 12 March, 1675; married to Israel Walker, 1696? (5) Thomas, b. 22 June, 1677; died the next day. (6) Ebenezer, b. 21 Dec. 1678. (7) Abigail, b. 8. Jan. 1681-2; md. to David "Cuttler," 12 Dec. 1700; 2dly, to Stephen Wright, 12 Apr. 1704. (8) Mary, b. 2 Feb. 1682-3. (9) Thomas, b. 19 Apl. 1685. (10) Benoni, b. 19 Aug. 1687; and died the same day.

Lieut. Gershom Flagg was killed, with Wiswall his captain and others, by the Indians at Wheelwright's Pond, in the town of Lee, N. H., 6 July, 1690.[b] His widow was married, Dec. 10, 1696, to Ensign Israel Walker.[c] Descendants from Gershom Flagg have been numerous and respectable, both in Woburn and in Wilmington. Col. Eleazer Flagg, (or, *Flegg*, as he preferred to write his name,) a gentleman of note and influence in Woburn in the early part of the last century, was his second son. Rev. Ebenezer Flagg, a graduate of Harvard College 1725, was a grandson, by his son Ebenezer. He was born 18 Oct. 1704; ordained at Chester, N. H., in 1736; and died there, 14 Nov. 1796, aged 92. Dr. John Flagg of Lynn was son of Rev. Ebenezer.

FOSTER. Hopestill; was in Woburn 1672, where his name is on the Tax List for building the new meeting-house that year.[d] He md. Elizabeth, widow of the second Thomas Whittemore, 15 Oct. 1670,[e] by whom he had: (1) Thomas, b. 17 Apr. 1672; died 1st May following. (2) Abigail, b. 12 March, 1673; md. to Timothy "Farlow" [Farley] of Billerica. (3) John, b. 14 Feb. 1676-7. (4) Mercy, b. 26 Feb. 1677-8. Time of Mr. Foster's decease is not on record in Woburn. [Wob. Rec. of Births, etc.]

FOWLE. *I.* James was taxed in Woburn 1666; and is registered as one of those who had right in the common lands of the town in 1668.[f] He was a cordwainer by trade; and had liberty granted him by the town, 26 Feb. 1678, "to take in a little piece of land [to set a shop on, not improbably] behind the Bell Hill," provided it should be laid out by the Selectmen.[b] Bell Hill was probably the elevation West of the old Fowle Tavern stand, near the centre of the town; and appears to have been so called because the bell that called the people to public worship in the first meeting-house was hung on its top.

James Fowle is supposed to have been a son of George, of Concord. By his wife Abigail, he had: (1) James, born 4 March, 1667. (2) Abigail, b. 15 Oct. 1669; md. to Jonathan Wyman 1689. (3) John, b. 12 March, 1671. (4) Samuel, b. 17 Sept. 1674. (5) Jacob, b. 3 Apl. 1677. (6) Elizabeth, b. 28 Sept. 1681; md. to Timothy Walker 1699. (7) Hannah, b. 23 Jan. 1683-4; md. 1705 to Samuel Trumbull, of Charlestown. (8) Mary, b. 18 July, 1687.

---

a Woburn Records, Vol. I., inverted, p. 21.
b Belknap's N. H., one vol., p. 134.
c Savage's Geneal. Dict.: Wob. Records of Marriages.
d Town Records, Vol. I., pp. 38, 39, 40.
e Savage's Geneal Dict.
f Town Records.

"Lt. James ffoull" died 17 Dec. 1690, [aged 49 years. Gravestone.] His widow, Abigail, married to Ensign Samuel Walker, 18 Apr. 1692, as his second wife.[a]

FOWLE. *II.* James Fowle, son of Lieut. James, married Mary, (daughter of Joseph Richardson), 2 Oct. 1688. Their children were: (1) Mary, born 18 June, 1689; m. to James Simonds, 1714. (2) James, b. 20 July, 1691; died 11 Oct. 1706. (3) Abigail, b. 22 Aug. 1693. (4) John, b. 11 Nov. 1695. (5) Hannah, b. 13 Sept. 1697. (6) Elizabeth, b. 9 Aug. 1699. (7) Ruth, b. 16 Apr. 1701; d. 3 March, 1713, [aged 11 years. Gravestone.] (8) Sarah, b. 29 July, 1703: m. to James Richardson, 1728? (9) Samuel, b. 10 June, 1705. (10) Esther, b. 29 May, 1707; md. to Nathan Simonds, 2 Nov. 1726. (11) Martha, b. 12 March, 1709; md. to Rev. Supply Clap, of Woburn Precinct, 1737. (12) Catharine, b. 20 Sept. 1711; md. to Josiah Whittemore, of Charlestown, 1730. Capt. James Fowle d. 19 March, 1714, [aged 47 years & 14 days. Gravestone.] His widow was afterwards md. to *II.* Samuel Walker, deacon, first of Woburn Church, and then, in 1735, of the Precinct Church, now Burlington. She died his widow, at Charlestown, [23 Oct. 1748, aged 80. Gravestone.]

FOWLE. *I.* John, son of Lieut. James and Abigail Fowle, married Elizabeth Prescott, of Concord, 1 July, 1696. Their children were: (1) Elizabeth, b. 19 Sept. 1698; died 4 March, 1699. (2) John, b. 7 Jan. 1699–1700. (3) Elizabeth, b. 16 Dec. 1701. (4) Dorothy, b. 9 Aug. 1703; died 28 May, 1704. (5) Dorothy, b. 14 March, 1705; d. 14 Sept. 1732. (6) Rebecca, b. 21 Nov. 1706; m. to Phineas Richardson, 1728? (7) Abigail, b. 15 Dec. 1707. (8) Hannah, b. 30 Aug. and d. 3 Oct. 1710 [1709?] (9) James, b. 16 July, 1710. (10) Jonathan, b. 29 Aug. 1712; d. 21 Nov. 1714. (11) Mary, b. 14 Dec. 1713; md. to Alexander Cochran of Boston, 1736? (12) Hannah, b. 10 Aug. 1715. (13) Ruth, b. 9 Feb. 1716–17; d. 18 Feb. 1720–21. (14) Lucy, b. 28 July, 1720; md. to Henry Gardner. (15) Ruth, b. 10 Apr. 1722. Capt. John Fowle d. 13 June, 1744. His widow, Elizabeth Fowle, died 14 May, 1753.

FOWLE. *I.* Jacob, son of Lieut. James Fowle, md. Mary Broughton, [granddaughter of first Rev. John Rayner of Dover, N. H.,] 3 Nov. 1701. Their children were: (1) Jacob, born 12 June, 1703, died soon. (2) Mary, b. 28 Nov. 1704. (3) Jacob, b. 24 Feb. 1706–7. (4) Abigail, b. 6 March, 1709. (5) Dorothy, b. 5 Feb. 1710–11. (6) Timothy, b. 28 Aug. 1713; died 5 July, 1741. (7) Elizabeth, b. 3 Feb. 1715–16. (8) Judith, b. 14 Jan. 1718–19. (9) Ruth, b. 2 July, 1721.

FOWLE. *II.* John, son of Capt. James and Mary Fowle, married Mary Convers, both of Woburn, 25 Dec. 1718. Their children were: (1) James, b. 13 June, 1720. (2) John [Master Fowle], b. 1 Feb. 1726–7; died 15 Oct. 1786, æt. 61. (3) Josiah, b. 14 July, 1731. (4) Mary, b. 12 May, 1734; md. to Joshua Wyman, jun., 1760. (5) Leonard, b. 8 Jan. 1737–8.

Major John Fowle died 28 Sept. 1775. [Memorandum of Samuel Thompson, Esq.]

---

[a] Rec. of Births, Marriages, etc., etc.

The Fowles of Woburn have always been a highly distinguished family: and the office of Town Clerk, they seemed for many years to hold by prescription. Capt. James Fowle was chosen Clerk in 1701, and was annually re-chosen till 1714, when he died in office. His brother, Capt. John Fowle, was immediately appointed his successor, and served the town in that capacity twenty-five years. In 1744, Cornet John Fowle, apparently Capt. John's son, was chosen Clerk; but his death, in 1745, prevented his being re-chosen. From 1746, James Fowle, Esq., was chosen Clerk every year, without interruption, for 34 years; and died in office, 1779. His son, James Fowle, jun., immediately succeeded him in his labors for 11 years more. And in 1814, Marshall Fowle, Esq., son of James Fowle, jun., was chosen Clerk, and was uniformly re-chosen for 19 years more, when he died in office, in 1833. So that during the 132 years which elapsed between the election of Capt. James Fowle, in 1701, and the death of Marshall Fowle, Esq., in 1833, Woburn had a Fowle for its Clerk 103 years, or more than three-fourths of the time.

FULLER. Thomas: a subscriber to the Town Orders for Woburn drawn up at Charlestown in Dec. 1640; was a smith by trade; and had meadow granted him in Woburn at Ragg Rock, 1648; and also 4 poles square of swamp "next his shop," Dec. 28th. He bore the title of "Sargeant" in 1656, and of Lieutenant in 1685. He was a Selectman in 1663, 1664, and again in 1685; and a petitioner with others to the General Court, 1664, for an additional grant of land to the town.

He married, 13 June, 1643, Elizabeth Tidd, by whom he had: (1) Thomas, born 30 April, 1644. (2) Elizabeth, b. 12 Sept. 1645. (3) Ruth, b. 17 May, 1648. (4) Deborah, b. 12 May, 1650; md. to Isaac Richardson. (5) John, b. 1 March, 1653. (6) Jacob, b. 14 May, 1655. (7) Joseph, b. 8 Aug. 1658. (8) Benjamin, b. 15 Apr. 1660. (9) Samuel, b. 9 May, 1662.

His wife Elizabeth dying, he appears to have left Woburn for Salem Village (Danvers) about 1664; whence (leaving his sons, it is likely, to spread into Wills Hill, or Middleton,) he returned to Woburn in 1684; married Sarah, widow of Lieut. John Wyman, and daughter of Miles Nutt, 25 Aug. 1684: and she dying, 24 May, 1688, he seems to have again removed from Woburn to Danvers, married Hannah ——, and to have died abroad. After his death, his widow came to Woburn, to reside with her married daughters, wives of James Proctor, Aaron Cleveland, John Wilson, etc., etc., whom the Selectmen compelled to give bonds for her maintenance, 21 June, 1697. [Town Records, Vol. III., p. 97; also, Records of Births, Marriages, etc., etc., and letter of Henry H. Fuller, Esq., Boston.]

GARDNER. Richard, came, says family tradition, from the County of Surry, England; settled first within the bounds of Woburn, having his house nearly opposite to the mansion of the late Luke Reed, Esq., in Woburn West End, about 40 rods from the road, where remains of the cellar and well were still discernible in 1857[a]; but between 1661 and 1667, he removed into "Charlestown End," to the spot where the two maiden ladies,

[a] Capt. Joseph Gardner of Woburn, now deceased.

Miss Patience Gardner and her sister, had their habitation. And hence the births of his last four children are not recorded in Woburn Records, but must be looked for in those of Charlestown. He married Anna Blanchard, of Acton, (Savage says of Charlestown, widow of Thomas, of Mystic, or Malden side,) 18 Oct. 1651, by whom he had: (1) *John*, born 14 Aug. 1652. (2) Anna, b. 17 Jan. 1654–5; died before her father. (3) Benjamin, b. 26 Dec. 1656; died also before his father. (4) Henry, b. 12 Feb. 1657–8. (5) Esther, b. 15 Oct. 1659; md. William, eldest son of Major William Johnson and Esther his wife; and died 17 Dec. 1706, æt. 48. (6) Ruth, b. 1 Apr. 1661, and md. to John Gypson [Gibson?]. (7) Hannah, born md. Coddington. (8) Abigail, born md. to James Thompson. (9) Rebecca, born m. Samuel Whittemore, of Cambridge, 13 (?) Feb. 1686. (10) Mehetabel, born md. [John] Connett. Richard Gardner died 29 May (al. March 4), 1698, aged about 79 years. Gravestone.

I. Henry Gardner married, first, Elizabeth ——, by whom he had: (1) John, born 22 July, 1695. (2) *Henry*, b. 2 Aug. 1698. (3) Samuel, b. 10 Sept. 1700; died unmarried, 3 March [al. 3 Dec.], 1723. (4) Elizabeth, b. 25 Dec. 1702; md. ——, Sawyer. (5) Mary, b. 28 May, 1705; "Do. of Charlestown," md. to Zechariah Flagg, of Woburn, 2 Jan. 1733. After the death of his first wife, Elizabeth, who died 3 June, [1703, aged 43, Gravestone.] Henry Gardner md. Hannah Prescott, who survived him. He died 20 Feb. 1713–14, æt. 57, while his son John was in college.

GARDNER. *II.* John, son of Henry and Elizabeth Gardner, was graduated at Harvard College, 1715; ordained at Stow, in 1718; and died, the minister of that town, 10 Jan. 1775, æt. 80. He was the father of Hon. Henry Gardner, treasurer of Massachusetts in the time of the Revolution; and of Rev. Francis Gardner, minister of Leominster. [Wob. Rec. of Births, etc., etc.]

GRAVES. Mr. Thomas: See Chapt. II.

GLAZIER. John was in Woburn, 1663; was taxed here in 1666; and, to encourage him to remain in the town, fourteen inhabitants, at a general meeting, 8th August, 1672, agreed to give him an acre of land each, one gave two acres, and eight gave half an acre each, twenty acres in all, to be deducted from their several proportions of the common lands about to be divided, and to be laid out at the Wyman Bridge, some on each side of the brook.[a] By his wife, Elizabeth, (daughter of John George, of Charlestown;[b]) John Glazier had: (1) *John*, born, ——, 1663. (2) *Zechariah*, b. 20 Apr. 1666. (3) *Elizabeth*, b. 4 Aug. 1668. (4) *John*, b. 15 Dec. 1669. (5) *Ruth*, b. 30 May, 1671. (6) *Samuel*, b. 5 July, 1672. (7) *George*, b. 3 June, 1676.[c]

GREEN. *I.* William was of Charlestown, 1640, and a subscriber that year to "Town Orders" for Woburn, and among its earliest inhabitants. He was made freeman 1644. By his wife Hannah, he had: (1) Mary, born 20 Jan. 1644. (2) Hannah, born 7 Feb. 1646–7; married to Joseph

---

[a] Town Records, Vol. I., p. 40. [b] Savage's Geneal. Dict. [c] County Records. See also Wob. Records of Births, etc., etc.

Richardson. (3) John, b. 11 Oct. 1649. (4) William, b. 22 Oct. 1651. William Green, sen., died 7 Jan. 1653–4. By him, or by one of his sons, was probably owned the lot in the centre of Burlington known as the Green Lot; and the ruins of the house once attached to it are still to be seen.

John Green, a *brother* probably of the above William, taxed with him at Woburn in 1645; but was not taxed there in 1646, and seems to have soon left the town.

GREEN. John, *son* of the above William Green, married, 3 July, 1671, Sarah, daughter of John Bateman, of Boston; by whom he had: Sarah, born 6 June, 1672. (2) Samuel, b. 29 Jan. 1673–4. (3) John, b. 6 Jan. 1676–7. (4) Hannah, b. 4 March, 1679. He was taxed in a Town Rate, 22 Dec. 1679; and in 1680 he was numbered among those who were appointed by the Selectmen, 5 July, to be under the inspection of Sergeant Matthew Johnson, as tythingman[a]. But in a tax made for the minister for 1687 his name does not occur; whence it is concluded, that at the last mentioned date he was dead, or removed from the town.

GREEN. *II.* William Green, jun., son of William Green, sen., had, by his wife Mary, William, born 9 Aug. 1675. His first wife dying, 3 June, 1676, he married for his second wife Hannah, daughter of Francis Kendall, by whom he had: (1) Francis, b. 30 Nov. 1678. (2) Ebenezer, b. 18 July, 1680. (3) Mehetabel, b. 30 June, 1682; died 27 March, 1698. (4) Hannah, b. 7 Oct. 1684. (5) Mary, b. 1 Nov. 1686. (6) Samuel, b. 18th July, 1689. (7) Jacob, b. 14 Oct. 1691. (8) Joseph, b. 14 Apr. 1694. (9) Abigail, b. . . . . . 1699. William Green, jun., died 1 Dec. 1717. [Woburn Rec. of Births, etc., Savage's Geneal. Dict.]

HALL. Thomas: (or *Hale*, in County Records) taxed in the Meeting-House rate, 1672[a]. By his wife ——, he had: (1) Elizabeth, born 14 Dec. 1674; died a fortnight after. (2) Abigail, b. 20 Aug. and died 30 Oct. 1681.

HENSHAW. *I.* Thomas: His name occurs in the List for the Meeting-house Rate, 1672; but not in the Tax List for 1666, nor among those who had right in the common lands of Woburn, 1668.[c] He was married 24 Sept. 1677, to Hannah, daughter of Moses Cleaveland. Their children were: (1) Elizabeth, born 30 July, 1678; md. to John "Manser," Charlestown, 3 June, 1701. (2) Thomas, b. 17 Nov. 1680. (3) Hannah, b. 21 May, 1683. (4) William, b. 25 Nov. 1685. (5) Samuel, b. 13 March, 1688. (6) Ebenezer, b. 1 March, 1691; died a pauper, 28 Feb. 1756. (7) Josiah, b. 1 March, 1695.

Thomas "Hensher" died 16 Jan. 1699, [1699–1700.]

HENSHAW. *II.* Thomas "Hincher," son of the preceding, and Mary Brooks, married 26 May, 1712. By her he had: (1) Thomas, born 1 Sept. 1713. (2) William, b. 21 Dec. 1715. (3) Isaac, b. 22 Aug. 1719.

---

[a] T. R., Vol. II., p. 153–4. [b] T. R. Vol. I., pp. 38, 39, 40.
[c] Woburn Records, Vol. I., pp. 38, 39, 40.

"Mr. Isaac Hincher died Jan. 3, 1756." (4) Joshua, b. 1 Oct. 1751. (5) Mary, b. 7 Feb. 1723, (1723-4). (6) Oliver, b. 14 March, 1726.

Thomas Hincher died 11 Sept. 1726. [N. B. The name *Henshaw* but seldom occurs in Woburn Records: it is there almost invariably spelt "Henshow," "Hensher," or "Hincher."]

HILL. Ralph: was originally of Plymouth, where he married Margaret Toothaker, probably a widow, 1638. Removing to Woburn, he was taxed there as an inhabitant, 1645, 1646: and there had a son born to him, viz: Jonathan, 20 Apl. 1646. He was made freeman, 1647; was Selectman of Woburn, 1651; but in 1653, he removed to Billerica, and became one of its earliest settlers; and in 1659 he sold his house and land in Woburn to Richard Snow. He died at Billerica, 29 Apl. 1663. His widow died there 22 Nov. 1683, aged "about 88." In his Will, 10 Nov. 1662, he names his son Nathaniel, (born probably at Plymouth) Jonathan, Ralph, Martha, Rebecca, his widow Margaret, his son-in-law, Roger Toothaker, etc., etc., etc. [Savage's Geneal. Dict., Woburn Records, Billerica Records, Wyman Papers, No. 53.]

HOLLAND. Christopher was one of the earliest settlers of Woburn, being taxed there in the "Rate for the Country," levied 8 Sept. 1645. But he soon removed, being of Boston, in 1652. [Wob. Town Records, Vol. I., p. 8, Savage's Geneal. Dict.]

Nothing more is found of him in Woburn.

IVONS. Edward was taxed as an inhabitant of Woburn, in 1666[a]; had once a grant of land made to him in the centre of the town, near the Training Field[b]; and at the general distribution of land and timber among the proprietors, in 1668, he had a share assigned him in the "4th Eighth."[c] But becoming deranged, and rendered poor thereby, and incapable of taking care of himself, the Selectmen took him under their protection, and provided for his comfort.[d] He died about 1683, and was buried at the town's expense.[e]

JOHNSON. Capt. Edward: See Chapter II. Major William: See Chapt. V.

JOHNSON. Matthew, son of Capt. Edward, and brother of Major William: born in England: came from Charlestown to Woburn to reside; was taxed there in Country Rate of 26 Aug. 1666; and had a share in the common lands of Woburn assigned him, 1668, in the "8th Eighth."[e] He m. Hannah, daughter of Peter Palfrey, 12 Nov. 1656; and, she dying, 1 Aug. 1662, he took for his second wife, 23 Oct. 1662, Rebekah, daughter of John Wiswall, of Dorchester, then of Boston, and ruling elder of First Church there. By her he had: (1) Rebekah, b. 1 March, 1665; m. to Samuel Wyman, 1692. (2) Matthew, b. 18 March, 1667. (3) Hannah, b. 23 Apr. 1669. (4) Samuel, b. 28 April, 1672. (5) Ruth, b. 1

---

[a] T. R., Vol. I., pp. 43, 44. [b] T. R., Vol. I., p. 31. [c] T. R., Vol. I., p. 46. [d] T. R., Vol. I., p. 113; Vol. II., p. 150; Vol. III., pp. 3, 36. His name is spelt by Mr. Savage, in his Geneal. Dict., *Ines.*

[e] T. R., Vol. I. p. 47.

Jan. 1674-5; m. to John Reed, 2d, 1697? (6) Sarah, b. 14 April, 1677; md. to Daniel Reed, 1699. (7) Henry, b. 7 Apr. 1683.

Lieut. Matthew Johnson was a carpenter by trade; and was employed in building the house erected by the town for Rev. Jabez Fox, in 1680. He represented Woburn in the General Court, 1689, 1690, '91 and 92'; and died 19 July, 1696, aged 62 [Gravestone.] His widow, Rebekah, died 25 Dec. 1709. [Wob. Rec., Savage's Geneal. Dict.]

JOHNSON. John, brother of Matthew, was a miller, and proprietor of a saw-mill in Woburn; married Bethiah Reed, daughter of William and Mabel Reed, 28 Apr. 1657; had: (1) John, born 24 Jan. 1657-8. (2) Bethiah, b. 20 Jan. 1659-60; m. to ———, Wolcott, Cambridge. (3) William b. 29 Sept. 1662; removed to Plainfield (Canterbury), Ct. (4) Obadiah, b. 15 June, 1664; removed to Canterbury, Ct. 1690.[a] (5) Samuel, b. 29 Oct. 1670. (6) Nathaniel, b. 15 May, 1673.

John Johnson, becoming sick, enfeebled and poor in his latter years, he and his wife Bethiah were taken by their sons, William and Obadiah, in 1712, to Canterbury, Ct., and there maintained by them during life at the charge of Woburn.[b] Mrs. Bethiah Johnson died about 1717.[c] Her husband survived till 1720.[c] [Woburn Rec. of Births, etc. Savage's Geneal Dict.]

JEFTS. Henry, a subscriber to the "Town Orders" for Woburn in 1640; taxed in the Country Rate of Sept. 1645; had grants of land made to him in Woburn. He married "Anna Stowars" (Ann Stowers) 13 Sept. 1647; and she dying, he md. for his 2d wife, Hannah Births, 21 May, 1649; by whom he had John, born 11 May, 1651. In 1653, he had become an inhabitant of Billerica, where a daughter Hannah died in "the first weeke" of May, 1653. His children, born afterwards, were: (1) Hannah, b. 4 Feb. 1654-5. (2) Joanna, b. 24 May, 1656. (3) Henry, b. 21 March, 1658-9, Hannah, his wife, dying 15 Sept. 1662, he md. for his 3d wife, 3 Oct. 1666, Mary Bird, widow; and after her decease, 1 April, 1679, he married a 4th wife, Mary Baker, of Concord, widow, 5 May, 1681.

"Henry Jefts, sen., departed this life, aged about 94 years, 24 May, 1700." [Billerica Rec., Woburn Rec., Savage's Geneal. Dict.]

JAQUITH. *I.* Abraham, son of Abraham Jaquith, of Charlestown, and of Ann, his wife, a daughter of James Jordan, of Dedham. He was born 19 Dec. 1644; took up his residence in Woburn (viz: that part of it which is now Wilmington); was taxed there 1666; md. Mary Adford, 13 March, 1671; had: (1) Abraham, born 17 Feb. 1672-3. (2) Elizabeth, b. 19 May, 1675. (3)Sarah, b. 21 Sept. 1677.

JAQUITH. *II.* Abraham, son of the preceding, married Sarah Jones 26 Dec. 1700. To them were born; (1) Abraham, 30 Dec. 1701. (2) Sarah, 8 March, 1703; md. to Samuel Butter, Jan. 29, 1726-7? (3) John, 7 Oct. 1704. (4) Mary, 1 Sept. 1706. (5) Elizabeth, 5 June, 1708. (6) Adford, 15 Apl. 1710. (7) Abigail, 10 June, 1712. (8) Ebenezer, 3 June, 1714. (9)

---

[a] Letter from Rev. E. R. Johnson, New Carlisle, Clark Co., Ohio, Sept. 1852, a descendant from Obadiah Johnson. [b] Town Records, Vol. V., p. 220. [c] Town Rec., Vol. VI., pp. 44, 133.

Benjamin, b. 27 June, 1716. (10, 11) William and Lydia, twins, b. 1 May, 1718: both died the same month. (12) Hannah, 19 July, 1719. (13) Ruth, 10 April, and died 30th Apl. 1722. (14) Susanna, 23 June, and died 5 July, 1723. (15) Seth, 5 June, and died 16 July, 1724.

[Woburn Records of Births, etc., etc.; Savage's Geneal. Dict.]

Kendall is a family name of local derivation, borrowed from Kent-dale, that is, a dale in the County of Kent, England; or, as may be thought by some, from Kendal, a noted town in Westmoreland County, on the borders of the river *Ken.* From one or the other of these sources, the Kendal's or Kendall's in England probably derived their origin and their name.

KENDALL. Francis, born in England, is supposed to have been the common ancestor of all of his name in New England. He was in Charlestown, 1640, where he subscribed the "Town Orders" for Woburn in December of that year; and was taxed among the earliest inhabitants of Woburn, 1645. The record of his marriage there reads thus: "Ffrances Kendall, alias Miles, and Mary Tedd, [Tidd] maryed 24th. of 10 mo. [24 Dec.] 1644;" which lends support to a family tradition, communicated many years ago by Rev. Dr. Kendall, of Weston, that in order to conceal from his parents his intentions to emigrate to this country, he embarked in England under a feigned name. His children by his wife Mary were: (1) John, born 2 July, 1646. (2) Thomas, b. 10 Jan. 1648–9. (3) Mary, b. 20 Jan. 1650–1; married to Israel Reed about 1669. (4) Elizabeth, b. 15 Jan. 1652–3; md. to James Peirce. (5) Hannah, b. 26 Jan. 1654–5; md. to William Green, jun., as his second wife. (6) Rebekah, b. 2 March, 1657; md. to Joshua Eaton; deceased in 1706. (7) Samuel, b. 8 March, 1659. (8) Jacob, b. 25 Jan. 1660–1. (9) Abigail, b. 6 Apr. 1666; md. to William "Read," 24 May, 1686.

Mary, his wife, died in 1705. "Francis Kendall, sen., died . . . . 1708," when, according to a testimony given by him in Court, 1700, he must have been 88 years old. He was a gentleman of great respectability and influence in the place of his residence. He served the town, at different times, 18 years on the Board of Selectmen; and was often appointed on important committees, especially on one for distributing the common lands of the town, 1664;[a] and on another, respecting the erection of the second meeting-house, 1672[a].

In his Will, dated 9 May, 1706, when he was "stricken in years," (he writes), "and expecting daily his change," he styles himself a miller; and gives one-half of his mill, with a proportionate interest in the streams, dams and utensils thereto belonging, to his son John; one-quarter to Thomas, and one-quarter to Samuel. This mill has ever since been in the possession of his posterity. Its present owner and occupant, Mr. Joseph R. Kendall, a descendant from Thomas, second son of Francis, is of the 6th generation from its original proprietor. [Kendall Family Papers.]

Francis Kendall remembers likewise in his Will the eight children of his brother Thomas, (one of the first settlers of Reading, and a deacon of

---

[a] T. R., Vol. I., pp. 24, 36.

the church there) who were living, when he, his said brother died. It seems that this brother of Francis Kendall, of Woburn, Deacon Thomas Kendall, of Reading, and Rebecca, his wife, had had ten daughters, but no son that lived. But these daughters, in order to preserve their maiden name, Kendall, among their posterity, directed, each of them, when married, that her first born son should have the given name, Kendall, prefixed to his surname; as Kendall Peirson, Kendall Boutwell, Kendall Eaton, Kendall Briant, etc., etc., etc., which gave occasion to the following lines respecting these daughters in a Poem written by Lillie Eaton, Esq., of South Reading, and published with Flint's Historical Address upon the 200th Anniversary of the founding of Reading. In mentioning the venerable matron, their mother, he observes:

"She had ten daughters; and each one,
When married, christened her first son
Kendall; and thus we may infer
Why 'tis these names so oft occur."

Flint's Address, p. 64.

The children of John, Thomas, Samuel, and Jacob Kendall, the four sons of Francis the first, were as follows:

John, eldest son of Francis Kendall, married, 29 Jan. 1668, Hannah, daughter of Thomas Bartlett. Their children were: (1) Mary, born 1 Sept. 1671. (2) Lydia, b. 23 Apr. 1674. (3) Francis, b. 4 Dec. 1678; died soon. His first wife, Hannah, dying, John Kendall md. Elizabeth Comey, 29 March, 1681, and had by her: (1) Francis, b. 11 Apr. 1682. (2) John, b. 7 Oct. 1684; died young. (3) David, b. 14 Nov. 1686. (4) Elizabeth, b. 23 Feb. 1688-9; md. to Amos Knight, 1720? (5) Jonathan, b. 28 Nov. 1690. (6) Rebekah, b. 22 March, 1693. (7) Nathaniel, b. 27 Feb. 1694-5. (8) John, 2d, b. 8 July, 1699. Elizabeth, wife of John Kendall, died in December 1701. After her death, he married, for his 3d wife, Eunice, widow of Mr. Samuel Carter, and daughter of John Brooks. She was living in 1706. [Wob. Rec. of Births, etc., etc. Savage's Geneal. Dict.]

Thomas, second son of Francis Kendall, married Ruth———,1673. Their children were: (1) Ruth, b. 17 Feb. 1674-5; married to John Walker, jun., son of first Dea. Samuel Walker. (2) Thomas, b. 19 May, 1677. (3) Mary, b. 27 Feb. 1680; md. to Joseph Whittmore, 1698-9. (4) Samuel, b. 29 Oct. 1682. (5) Ralph, b. 4 May, 1685. (6) Eleazer, b. 16 Nov. 1687. (7, 8) Jabez and Jane, twins, b. 10 Sept. 1692. Jane md. to Joseph Russell, 1712. (9) a still-born son, born 16 Dec. 1695. Ruth, wife of Thomas Kendall, died 18th of the same month and year. Thomas Kendall md. for his 2d wife Abigail Broughton, March 30, 1696, who died 31 Dec. 1716. He died himself, 25 May, 1730.

Samuel, third son of Francis Kendall, married 13 Nov. 1683, Rebekah, daughter of Isaac Mixer. Their children were: (1) Samuel, born 13 Aug. 1684. (2) Isaac, b. 13 Sept. 1686. (3) Joshua, b. 14 March, 1689. (4) Rebekah, b. 6 July, 1691; died 25 Nov. 1691. Rebekah, wife of Samuel Kendall, dying 25 Oct. 1691, he married, for his second wife, Mary, daughter of William Locke, 30 March, 1692. By her he had: (1) Mary, b. 3 Feb. 1692–3; who died 14 Aug. 1727. (2) Rebekah, b. 26 Jan. 1694–5; wife of Samuel Russell. (3) Abigail, b. 31 March, 1697; md. to William Nichols, of Reading, 1719–20. (4) Ebenezer, b. 16 May, 1700. (5) Ruth, b. 23 Apr. 1703; md. to —— Bancroft. (6) Tabitha, b. 22 Jan. 1706–7; md. to Nathan Richardson, 1729, and died 25 Nov. 1739. Samuel Kendall finally removed, we are told, to Lancaster.[a] He probably remained in Woburn till the summer of 1742, being taxed there in a Parish tax assessed Jan. 28, 1741–2, but not in one assessed in February, 1742–3.[b] His Will, written 6 Dec. 1742, when he was "advanced in years," is subscribed with his own hand, "Samuel Kendal."[c] But it is said not to have been proved till 1749.[a] [Woburn Records of Births, etc., etc.]

Jacob, youngest son of Francis Kendall, married Persis "Heywood," or "Hayward," 2 Jan. 1683–4. Their children were: (1) Persis, born 24 Aug. 1685. (2) Jacob, b. 12 Jan. 1686–7. (3) Joseph, b. 7 Dec. 1688. (4) Jonathan, b. 2 Nov. and died 11 Nov. 1690. (5) Daniel, b. 23. Oct. 1691. Persis, wife of Jacob Kendall, died 19 Oct. 1694, and he married for his second wife Alice Temple, 10 Jan. 1694–5. By her he had: (1) Ebenezer, b. 9 Nov. 1695; died young. (2) John, b. 19 Jan. 1696–7; died 17 Oct. 1697. (3) Sarah, b. 18 July, 1698. (4) Esther, b. 20 Nov. 1699. (5) Hezekiah, b. 26 May, 1701. (6) Nathan, b. 12 Dec. 1702. (7) Susanna, b. 27 Oct. 1704. (8) Phebe, b. 19 Dec. 1706. (9) David, b. 28 Sept. 1708. (9) Ebenezer, again, b. 5 Apr. 1710. (10) Alice, b. 31 Jan. 1711–12. (11) Abraham, b. 26 Apr. 1712. [This, or the preceding record, or both, obviously erroneous.] (12) Jacob, again, b. 22 Apr. 1714; died 1 June, 1714. (13) Persis, again, b. 23 Aug. 1715.

[Woburn Records of Births, etc., etc. Savage's Geneal. Dict.]

Descendants of these four brothers, who made Woburn their place of permanent residence, were formerly very numerous. Individuals of the name and connection still remain in the town, but have much dwindled of late in respect to numbers. But multitudes of Kendalls have gone forth from Woburn, to replenish other towns of the Commonwealth. Tewksbury and Sherborn, in Middlesex County, and Athol, Lancaster, Leominster, and Sterling, in Worcester County, have all been more or less indebted to Woburn for her many sons and daughters, Kendalls by name or birth, whom she has contributed to help settle those towns, or when settled already, to increase their number of inhabitants.[d] And no family of Kendalls in Woburn has done more to swell the tide of emigration towards the towns above mentioned than that of Samuel Kendall, grandson of Francis, and son of Thomas and Ruth Kendall, born in Woburn, 29 October, 1682. He was a carpenter by trade; and formerly known far and wide beyond his native place as Lieutenant Kendall, from having received a Lieutenant's commission from Governor Belcher, 5 Oct. 1732.[e] He was a very active, enterprising, public spirited man, often employed in town

[a] Savage's Geneal. Dict. [b] Rec. of First Parish, Woburn. [c] Will, among Kendall Papers. [d] Mr. Calvin Kendall of Athol, son of Mr. Jesse of that town, 1846. [e] Kendall Papers;

business, and much engaged in promoting both the civil and the religious prosperity of Woburn. He was an original proprietor of North Town, or Townsend, and as such, became involved in a controversy with the heirs of Major Hathorne, of Salem, who claimed a portion of the lands in that town, under a prior grant from the General Court.[a] He was also a principle settler of *Paguaige*, or Athol; in the settlement of which he and several of his sons suffered much from floods, and from the depredations of Indians during the French wars between 1744 and 1760.[a] By his wife Elizabeth, Lieut. Kendall had fifteen children, as follows:

1. Samuel, born 30 June, 1708. Minister of New Salem.
2. James, " 28 April, 1710. Lived and died in Sterling, once a part of Lancaster.
3. Josiah, " 1 September, 1712. Lived and died in Sterling.
4. Ezekiel, " 14 March, 1715. An inhabitant of Sterling; lived and died there.
5. Timothy, " 23 March, 1717. Lived and died at Leominster.
6. Elizabeth," 3 September, 1719. Wife of John Brooks, of Sterling, then Lancaster.
7. Jonas, " 10 March, 1721. Leominster.
8. Sarah, " 16 April, 1723. Wife of John Kendall of Leominster, a son of *II.* Francis, born 11 April, 1682, a grandson of *I.* John, and great grandson of *I.* Francis Kendall.
9. Susanna, " 5 July, 1724. Lived single.
10. Obadiah," at Woburn, 3 September, 1725. Occupant of the paternal mill: deacon of the church of Woburn.
11. Jesse, " 15 May, 1727. Lived at Athol, a husbandman and miller; one of the first settlers of Athol: married Elizabeth, daughter of Andrew and Mary Evans, of Woburn, about 1751, and had by her twelve children.
12. Seth, " 4 January, 1728-9. Lived at Athol.
13. Abigail, " 27 February, 1730-1. Wife of Jacob Peirce, of Woburn.
14. Ephraim," 9 November, 1732. Died 16 February, 1732-3.
15. Jerusha, " 13 February, 1734-5. Wife of Reuben Richardson, jun., of Woburn.[b]

Elizabeth, wife of Mr. Samuel Kendall, died 10 January, 1741-2. He appears then to have married a second wife. The following probably is a record of his Intentions of Marriage: "Samuel Kendall entered his Intentions of Marriage with Mehitabel *Asmore* [Hosmer?] of Concord, July 6, 1751."[b]

"Lt. Kendall's wife died" 24 August, 1755. "Lieut. Samuel Kendall" died 13 December, 1764.

Among the descendants of the Kendalls who went from Woburn and set-

---

[a] Kendall Papers. [b] Woburn Records of Births, etc., etc.

tled in other places were several gentlemen of distinction and great respectability of character, of whom it seems proper here to give a passing notice.

1. Rev. Samuel Kendall (or Kendal, as he preferred to spell his name), D. D., son of Elisha Kendall, of Sherborn, who was the 12th son of *II.* Thomas and Sarah (Cheever) Kendall of Woburn and Sherborn, a grandson of *I.* Thomas and Ruth Kendall, of Woburn, and a great grandson of Francis Kendall, the first settler of the name. He was born at Sherborne, 11 July, 1753; graduated at Harvard College, 1782; ordained at Weston, 5 Nov. 1783; and died there, 16 Feb. 1815, æt. 62. Elisha Kendall, his father, who spent his latter days with him at Weston, outlived him, dying 1824, aged 99. [Rev. Dr. Kendall's Century Sermon, pp. 44, 45: Allen's Biog. Dict.]

2. Rev. Samuel Kendall, eldest son of Lieut. Samuel, was born at Woburn, 30 June, 1708; graduated at Harvard College, 1731; ordained at New Salem, Franklin County, Mass. at the gathering of the church there, 15 Dec. 1742; dismissed, 1776; and died, 31 Jan. 1792, aged 84. [Woburn Records of Births, etc. Allen's Biog. Dict.]

3. Rev. James Kendall, D. D., of Plymouth. He was the youngest son of Major James Kendall, of Sterling, Worc. County, Mass., whose father, James Kendall, was the second son of Lieut. Samuel Kendall, of Woburn; married Sarah Richardson of Woburn, 21 July, 1735, and removed to Sterling (then Lancaster) to reside. Rev. James, his grandson, was born at Sterling, 3 Nov. 1769; grd. at H. C., 1796; ordained at Plymouth, 1 Jan. 1800; and died there, 17 March, 1859, aged 89 years, 4 months, 14 days; and in the 60th year of his ministry. [Mr. Calvin Kendall of Athol, Funeral Sermon of, etc.]

4. Hon. Jonas Kendall. He was son of Jonas, 6th son of Lieut. Samuel Kendall, of Woburn, and an early settler in Leominster. He was born at Leominster, his father's residence, 27 Oct. 1757; was largely engaged, it is believed, in the manufacturing business at Leominster; was sometime member of the Senate of Massachusetts; and at death was nearly 80 years of age. [Mr. Calvin Kendall of Athol: Letter of Hon. Joseph G. Kendall, his son, etc., etc.]

5. Hon. Joseph Gowing Kendall, son of the preceding, was a native of Leominster; a graduate, 1810, and subsequently a tutor of Harvard College; was a lawyer by profession; a Clerk of the Courts, resident at Worcester; and once represented that district in the Congress of the United States. He died in 1847. [Letter from him, 1846: College Catalogue, etc., etc.]

6. Rev. David Kendall was a son of Jesse Kendall, of Athol, who was the 8th son of Lieut. Samuel Kendall of Woburn. He was grd. at H. C., 1794; was minister of Hubbardston from 1802 to 1809. He then removed to Augusta, Oneida County, N. Y., where he continued in the pastoral office till his death, 19 Feb. 1853, at the age of 85. [Mr. Calvin Kendall of Athol: Allen's Biog. Dict.]

KNIGHT. *I.* Joseph, sen., was originally of Watertown. He sold his house there, Dec. 10, 1649; and soon after, with his wife, Hannah, removed to Woburn.[a] He was made freeman 1652, was taxed in Woburn, 1666; and was numbered among those who had right in the common lands of Woburn, 1668. At Woburn, he had born to him, by his wife, Hannah: (1) Sarah, born 8 March, 1651. (2) Samuel, b. 8 Sept. 1652, and died, 26 Dec. 1653. (3) Hannah, b. 25 March, 1654. (4) John, b. 16 Jan. 1665-6. (5) Elizabeth, b. 7 Apr. 1658. (6) Mary, b. 6 June, 1660; died, 10 Apr. 1661. (7) Dinah, b. 4 July, 1661; md. to John Morse, of Watertown, 1686. (8) Samuel, again, b. 18 March, 1663. (9) Mary, b. 12 Dec. 1672; died, 1 March, 1673. (10) Joseph, b. 12 Dec. 1673. (11) Edward, b. 31 Aug. 1677. (12) Isaac, b. 24 Feb. 1679-80; died, 4 March, 1679-80. (13) James, b. 22 Apr. 1681, and died the next day.

Joseph Knight [" Sen." County Records] died 13 Aug. 1687." "Hannah, relict of Joseph Knight, sen., died 13 Jan. 1694-5."

II. "Joseph Knight, jun." Among those made freemen at the Court in May, 1675, and "re-admitted to freedome, 21 Feb. 1675-6," is found "Joseph Knight, Wob."[b] He was taxed in the rate for the second Meeting-house in Woburn, 1672; married Martha Lilley, 4 Apr. 1699; and in his will, 16 Jan. 1733, names wife Martha and six daughters.

I. John Knight was taxed in Woburn, 1666; married there, 2 March, 1681, "Abigail, daughter of John and Sarah Craggen;" and had by her: (1) Abigail, born 27 Dec. 1681. (2) John, b. 31 Jan. 1683-4; died 21 June, 1685. (3) John, b. 3 March, 1686. (4) Benjamin, b. 20 March, 1688; died Sept. 1697. (5) *Samuel*, b. 27 Sept. 1690. (6) Mercy, b. 3 Feb. 1692-3. (7) Ebenezer, b. 20 Aug. 1695. (8) Rebekah, b. 14 May, 1698. (9) Benjamin, b. 20 Oct. 1700. (10) Joseph, b. 9 Nov. and died 19 Dec. 1702. (11) Amaziah, b. 14 Dec. 1703. Abigail, wife of John Knight, died 17 June, 1707. "John Knight, sen." died 9 Nov. 1735. [Woburn Records.]

II. John, his son, born 3 March, 1686, is probably the John Knight who sold his homestead, 3 Feb. 1735-6, in Woburn Precinct, to Rev. Mr. Supply Clap; vacated the house 19 May, 1736; and seems to have removed from the town, as no further mention of him has been observed. [Woburn Records. Rev. Mr. Clap's papers, etc.]

Michael Knight had right in common lands of Woburn assigned him, 1668; was admitted freeman, 1654; married Mary Bullard, 20 Oct. 1657; and had: (1) Mary, born 14 Oct. 1658; md. to George Polly, jun., 1677. (2) Jonathan, b. 23 March, 1662. (3) Joseph,[c] b. 10 Jan. 1664-5. (4) Lydia, b. 29 Sept. 1674. [Woburn Rec. Colony Rec.]

LEARNED. William, born in England; admitted freeman of the Colony, 1634; received with Goodeth, his wife, into the present First Church, Charlestown, 6 Dec. 1632; subscribed at Charlestown the "Town Orders" for Woburn, 1640; was one of the first seven members of the

---

[a] Bond's Watertown, pp. 328, 816. Col. Records. Woburn Town Records, and Records of Marriages, etc., etc. Savage's Geneal. Dict.

[b] Col. Rec. Wob. Rec. Rec. of Births, etc., in Wob. Savage's Geneal. Dict.

[c] "Joshua" according to Savage, b. 20 Jan. 1664-5.

church of Woburn at its gathering, in 1642, and one of the first Board of Selectmen in Woburn, chosen 1644. He died, 1 March, 1646.

LEARNED. Isaac, apparently an only child of William Learned, was born in England; married, 9 July, 1646, Mary Stearns, eldest child of Isaac and Mary Stearns, of Watertown. He settled first in Woburn; but, April 2, 1652, he sold his house and lands in Woburn to Bartholomew Peirson, of Watertown, and removed to Chelmsford, where he was at one time Selectman, and where he died, 27 Nov. 1657. He had born to him at Woburn: (1) Mary, b. 7 Aug. 1647. (2) Hannah, b. 24 Aug. 1649. (3) William, "eldest son," birth not recorded, but probably born in Woburn; died, 1684, unmarried.[a] At Chelmsford, were born: (1) Sarah, 28 b, Oct. 1653.[a] (2) Isaac, b. 16 Sept. 1655.[a] (3) Benoni, born 2 days after his father's death, 29 Nov. 1657.[a] [Bond's Hist. Watertown; Colony Records, Charlestown First Ch. Records; Woburn Town Records; Woburn Records of Births, Marriages, etc., etc.]

LEPINGWELL. Michael was an early inhabitant of Woburn, and taxed in the first rate levied there for the Country, 8 Sept. 1645. By his wife, Isabel, he had: (1) Hannah, born 1 Sept. 1642; died 10 Feb. 1642-3. (2) Hannah, b. 6 Jan. 1645-6; md. Gershom Flagg. (3) Sarah ["Mary," County Records], b. 10 March, 1647. (4) Thomas, b. 13 Jan. 1648-9. (5) Ruth, b. 2 Jan. 1649-50. (6) Michael, b. 8 June, and died 15 June, 1651. (7) Rachel, b. 4 March, 1653. (8) Abigail, b. 24 May, 1655. (9) Esther, b. 16 May, 1657. (10) Tabitha, b. 8 May, 1661. Isabel Lepingwell died 17 Nov. 1671. Michael Lepingwell died 22 March, 1687.

[Wob. Rec. of Births, etc., etc. The Lepingwells have been extinct from Woburn a century, or more. Descendants or relations, apparently, are found elsewhere; but they spell their name Leffingwell. See Savage's Geneal. Dict.]

LITTLEFIELD. Francis. His name first appears in Woburn in the Town Rate assessed 22 Dec. 1646; but not in any subsequent List. By his wife Jane, he had a daughter Mary, born 14 Dec. 1646; but the mother died, 20 Dec. 1646, within a week from the daughter's birth; and the father himself probably soon removed from the town. [Records of the Town. Wob. Rec. of Births, Deaths, etc.]

LOWDEN. Richard was of Charlestown, 1638, and there subscribed the "Town Orders" for Woburn, Dec. 1640; but it does not appear that he ever changed his residence for Woburn. [Savage: Town Records of Wob.]

LOCKE. William Locke, sen., was probably born in London, 13 Dec. 1628; came from there in the "Planter," 1635, being then a child 6 years old, with Nicholas Davis, who calls him in his Will "cossen," meaning probably, his nephew. He doubtless lived at first with his uncle at Charlestown, where his uncle subscribed the Town Orders for Woburn, Dec. 1640, and became one of the first planters of this new settlement. Locke seated himself down with him at Woburn; married 27 Nov. 1655,

---

[a] Bond's Watertown, p. 334.

Mary, daughter of William Clark, of Watertown; lived in Woburn, at the place well known as Capt. Fox's place; was chosen deacon of the church of Woburn about 1700; and died 16th of June, 1720. His wife, Mary, died before him, 18 July, 1715. His children were: (1) William, born 27 Dec. 1657, and died 9 Jan. following. (2) William, b. 18 Jan 1658-9. (3) John, b. 1 Aug. 1661. (4) Joseph, b. 8 March, 1664; to whom his father gave by deed lands in "Cambridge ffarmes" (now Lexington) 26 March, 1695, and who was doubtless the founder of the numerous families named Locke in that town. (5) Mary, b. 16 Oct. 1666; md. to Samuel Kendall, 30 March, 1692. (6) Samuel, b. 14 Oct. 1669. (7) Ebenezer, b. 8 Jan. 1673-4. (8) James, b. 14 Nov. 1677. (9) Elizabeth, b. 4 Jan. 1680-1; md. to James Markham, 14 Oct. 1700. [Wob. Town Records: Wob. Rec. of Births, etc., Savage's Geneal. Dict.]

LOCKE. *II.* William Locke, jun., lived at the Thos. Locke place, so called, formerly in Woburn, now in Lexington. He md. 29 May, 1683, Sarah, daughter of Francis and Isabel Whitmore, of Cambridge, who was born 2 March, 1662[a]; by whom he had: (1) William, b. 28 June, 1684, buried 29 Jan. 1767, aged 83[b]. (2) Francis, b. 25 July, 1690; lived in West Cambridge, a tanner[c]. (3) Daniel, b. 9 July, 1693, of Woburn, a weaver[c]. His wife, Sarah, dying, he md. Abigail Heywood (Hayward) 8 June, 1698; by whom he had: (1) Ebenezer ——, who md. Elizabeth ——. (2) Abigail, b. 22 June, 1710; md. to Jonas Merriam, of Lexington, housewright. William Locke, jun., was deacon of the church of Woburn, 1709, and died 8 July, 1738. His widow survived him, and died, probably, 1748 or '49.

LOCKE. John, son of William Locke, sen., md. 31 May, 1683, Elizabeth Plympton, a daughter of Thomas Plympton, of Sudbury, who was an emigrant from England, and was killed by the Indians in fight at Sudbury 18 [21st.] April, 1676. She was born 23 Dec. 1658, and by her he had: (1) Thomas, b. 20 March, and died 23 March, 1684. (2) Marah [Mary, County Rec.] b. 1 April, 1685. (3) John, b. 14 May, 1686; died 15 Feb. 1709-10. (4) Thomas, b. 5 April, 1688; died 27 Nov. 1717. ("aged 29" Gravestone.) (5) A daughter, b. 11 June, 1693. (6) Abigail, b. 2 April, 1694; md. to Nath. Kendall, 1720. (7) Peter, b. 10 Sept. 1678; died 25 Dec. 1709. Elizabeth, wife of John Lock, dying 23 Feb. 1719-20, he married Mary Wyman, widow of Nath. Wyman, and daughter of Increase Winn, 30 Nov. 1720. He died April 1756; and his widow about the same time. [Woburn Rec. of Births, etc. Savage's General Dict.]

LOCKE. *I.* Samuel, son of William Locke, sen., lived in Lexington; had a wife Ruth, who died 14 Dec. 1714; and for a second wife he took Mary Day, of Ipswich, by whom he had an only child, Samuel, b. 5 July 1718, of whom it is only told, "that he had good estate from his father, and spent it." [Savage's Geneal. Dict.]

LOCKE. Ebenezer, son of William Locke, sen., md. Susanna, daughter of Israel Walker, 18 Oct. 1697: by whom he had: (1) Ebenezer, b. 28 April, 1699. His wife Susanna dying, 13 June, 1699, he married, 14 Oct. 1701,

---

[a] Book of the Lockes. [b] Lexington Ch. Rec. [c] Old Deed, 1738.

Hannah Mead, daughter of David Mead, by whom he had: (1) Samuel, b. 24 Aug.1702. (2) Josiah, b. 15 March, 1705. (3) Joshua, b. 21 Aug. 1709. (4) Nathan, b. 20 March, 1713. (5) Hannah, born 11 April, 1716, md. to Asa Richardson, 1739.

Ebenezer Locke, sen. died 24 Dec. 1723: Hannah, his widow, died 24 July, 1739. [Woburn Rec. of Births, etc. Savage's Geneal. Dict.]

LOCKE. *II.* Samuel Locke, eldest son of Ebenezer and Hannah Locke, md. Rebecca Richardson, both of Woburn, 2 March, 1730. Their eldest son, Samuel Locke, born 23 Nov. 1731, graduated at Harvard College, 1755; early called to be President of that Institution in 1770; "was a fine scholar, but by untoward circumstances required to resign his office," in 1773; returned to Sherborn, where he had been previously settled in the ministry, and died there, of apoplexy, 15 Jan. 1778. [Woburn Records of Births, etc. Savage's General Dict.]

MOUSALL. Deacon John Mousall: See Chapt. II.

II. John Mousall, his son, married Sarah Brooks, 13 May, 1650: died 2 April, 1698. [Woburn Recds. of Births, etc., etc.]

NEVERS. Richard Nevers (or *Neverds*, as his name is often written) is first mentioned as an inhabitant of Woburn in the Country Rate of 26 Aug. 1666.[a] By his wife Martha, he had three children: (1) Samuel, born 16 Dec. 1689. (2) Mary, b. 9 July, 1694. (3) Martha, b. 20 July, 1698.

Richard "Neverds" died the . . . . Nov. 1709. "The widow Neuards" died 15 March, 1720.

NEVERS. *I.* Samuel Nevers, his son, had by his wife Deborah: (1) Samuel, born 20 June, 1715. (2) William, b. 16 Aug. 1716. (3) Hannah, b. 4 Feb. 1717-18: md. to David Evans, of Reading, 1740. (4) Richard, b. 29 Dec. 1719. (5) Joshua, b. 13 June, 1721. (6) Deborah, b. 27 April, 1723. (7) Mary, b. 24 Oct. 1728.

NEVERS. *II.* Samuel Nevers, jun., son of Samuel, married Susanna Williams, 2 August, 1739. To them was born "Samuel Williams," son of Samuel and Susanna Nevers, born 2 Nov. 1741, died 22 Jan. 1741-2.

NEVERS. *III.* Samuel Nevers, whom *II.* Mr. Samuel Nevers adopted for his own, shortly after the death of his son, Samuel Williams, was originally named Thomas Marshall, son of William Marshall, a seafaring man of Scotch descent, and was born March 2, 1741-2. When taken into the family of Mr. Nevers, he grew up under his care, and went into the French War in 1758, and was present at the death of Gen. Wolf before Quebec. He was twice married; and died May 24, 1826, leaving a very numerous family of children.

NUTT. Myles was made freeman, 1637; was a proprietor of Watertown 1636-7, and in 1642. In Woburn, he was taxed in the first *town* rate on record, levied 22 Dec. 1646; and order also was given about the same time for enlarging his house lot. He was Selectman in Woburn, in 1647, and during seven of the nine years immediately succeeding. In 1644, November 5th, his daughter Sarah, whom he had brought with him from England,

---

[a] Town Rec. Vol. I., pp. 43, 44.

was married to Lieut. John Wyman; and after Mr. Wyman's death, May 1684, she was md. to Thomas Fuller 25 Aug. of the same year. Mr. Nutt died at Malden, 2 July, 1671, aged about 73 years. [Bond's Watertown: Woburn Town Records, Vol. I., p. 97. Records of Marriages, etc., etc., in Woburn.]

PARKER. Abraham; early settled in Woburn, being taxed there 8 Sept. 1645, the first tax for the *Country* on record. He married, 18 Nov. 1644, Rose Whitlock, by whom he had: (1) Hannah [Anna, County Records,] born 29 Oct. 1645. (2) John, b. 30 Oct. 1647. (3) Abraham, b. 8 March, 1650, died 20, 1651. (4) Abraham, again, b. Aug. 1652. About this time, he removed to Chelmsford, where he had other children born to him. He was made freeman 1645; and died 12 Aug. 1685. His widow died 13 Nov. 1691. [Woburn Records: Savage's Geneal. Dict.; Col. Records.]

PARKER. James: freeman 1644; a subscriber at Charlestown to the "Town Orders" for Woburn, 1640; and taxed in Woburn, 1645 and 1646. He married, 23 May, 1643, Elizabeth, daughter of Robert Long of Charlestown. By her he had: (1) Elizabeth, born 12 March, 1645. (2) Ann, b. 5 Jan. 1646-7. (3) John, b. 18 Jan. 1648-9. (4) Sarah, b. 29 Aug. 1650; died 15 Oct. 1651. (5) Joseph, b. 1651. (6) James, b. 15 Apr. 1652, and killed by the Indians, 27 July, 1694. About 1652, he removed from Woburn to Chelmsford, where he had other children born to him; and from Chelmsford to Groton. He died, 1701, in his 84th year. [Woburn Town Rec. and Records of Births, etc. Savage's Geneal. Reg.]

PEIRCE. John was taxed in Woburn, in the rate for the country in 1645, and in the town rate, 1646. His children recorded in Woburn are: (1) John, born 23 Nov. 1644. (2) Joseph, b. 12 Sept. 1646. (3) Thomas, b. 3 May, 1649. [Records of Births, etc., etc., in Wob. Town Records. N. B. This name is spelt *Peirce* with great uniformity in Wob. Rec., till a recent date.]

PEIRCE. *I.* John, son probably of the John preceding, married, 1 July, 1663, Deborah, daughter of Ensign James Convers; had: (1) Deborah, born 30 Oct. 1666. (2) John, born 26 Jan. 1670-1. (3) Thomas, b. 23 Dec. 1672. (4) James, b. 6 Aug. 1674; died when 11 years old. (5) Daniel, b. 7 Oct. 1676. (6) James, again, b. 8 Oct. 1686. (7) Joseph, b. 24 Aug. 1688. (8) Josiah, b. June, 1691. John Peirce represented Woburn in General Court, 1706; chosen 13 Aug. to succeed Major James Convers, deceased; and 9 years afterward, between 1707 and 1718, inclusively. [Wob. Records of Births, etc., etc. Savage's Geneal. Dict.]

Thomas Peirce, not improbably son of Thomas "Peerce," admitted into Charlestown Church 21 Feb. 1634-5.[a] He, (the son,) was born in England; was in Woburn as early as 1643; was taxed there, 1645; is often styled in the Records there, "Sargent Thomas Peirce; was Selectman of Woburn, 1660, and repeatedly afterwards; of the committee for dividing the common lands in Woburn among "the right proprietors," chosen 28 March, 1667; and also of the General Court's committee appointed for the

[a] Charlestown Ch. Records.

same purpose in 1668. By his wife, Elizabeth, there were born to him in Woburn: (1) John, born 7 March, 1643. (2) Thomas, b. 21 Jan. 1644-5. (3) Elizabeth, b. 25 Dec. 1646. (4) Joseph, b. 22 Sept. 1648; died 27 Feb. 1648-9. (5) Joseph, again, b. 13 Aug. 1649. (6) Stephen, b. 16 July, 1651. [Of Chelmsford, a tailor, 1678.[a]] (7) Samuel, b. 20 Feb. 1653-4; died 27 Feb. 1655-6. (8) Samuel, b. 7 Apr. 1656. (9) William, b. 7 March, 1657. (10) James, b. 7 May, 1659. "Old Mr James Peirce died 20 Jan. 1741-2." (11) Abigail, b. 20 Nov. 1660; md. to George Reed, 1684-5.

"Thomas Peirce, sen." died 6 Nov. 1683. "Widow Elizabeth Peirce died the 5th of March, 1688."

PEIRCE. Robert, not improbably a son of John and Elizabeth Peirce, of Watertown; freeman 1642; removed to Woburn about 1650, where he was taxed in the Country Rate for 1666, and was numbered among those who were entitled to an interest in the common lands of the town in 1668. By his wife, Mary, he had born in Woburn: (1) Judith, 30 Sept. 1651; died 30 May, 1689. (2) Mary, b. 21 Jan. 1653-4; md. to John Walker, (a brother of Samuel, jun., and Israel Walker,) 14 Oct. 1672. (3) Nathaniel, b. 4 Dec. 1655; md. Hannah Convers, 27 Dec. 1677. (4) Elizabeth, b. 6 March, 1658; md. to Samuel Wilson, 1681-2. (5) Jonathan, b. 2 Feb. 1662-3. (6) Joseph, b. 1 May, 1672.

Mary, wife of Robert Peirce, died 18 March, 1701. "Old Robert Peirce" died 10 Sept. 1706.

[Bond's Watertown; Col. Records; Woburn Town Rec.; Woburn Rec. of Births, Marriages, etc., etc.]

PIERSON. Bartholomew, was of Watertown 1640; admitted freeman 1648: bought of Isaac Learned his house and land in Woburn, 2 Apr. 1652; moved there the next year; was taxed there in the Rate for the Country, assessed 26 Aug. 1666; and was Selectman 1665 and 1666. By his wife, Ursula, he had born to him in Watertown: (1) Bartholomew, b. Sept. 1640; died next month. (2) Bartholomew, again, 26 Feb. 1641-2; died, in Woburn, 23 Feb. 1661-2. (3) Martha, b. 17 Sept. 1643. (4) Jonathan, b. 12 Aug. 1648. (5) Joseph, b. 8 Nov. 1650. After he removed to Woburn, he had born to him a daughter, viz: Sarah, b. 7 May, 1653. Another daughter probably of his, though her birth is not found on record, viz: Mary Pierson, was married in Cambridge to John Richardson, of Woburn, 28 Oct. 1673; and they had a son called by the well known name of Pierson Richardson.

Bartholomew Pierson died 12 March, 1687. His widow, Ursula, died 28 May, 1694. The name Pierson is variously spelt Pearson, Persune, and Person.

[Bond's Watertown, pp. 406, 910; Colony Records; Savage's Geneal. Dict.; Woburn Town Rec. and Rec. of Births, etc., etc.]

POLLY. George, a carpenter by trade; land ordered to be laid out to him in Woburn Feb. 3, 1648-9; chosen a Surveyor of Fences 1665; was taxed in the Rate for the Country 1666; and his right to share in the com-

---

[a] Wyman Papers, No. 13. Woburn Town Records, Records of Births, etc., etc.

mon lands of the town was acknowledged 1668. Married in Woburn Elizabeth Winn, daughter, probably, of Edward Winn, 21 May, 1649, by whom he had: (1) John, born 16 Dec. 1650. (2) Joseph, b. 25 Dec. 1652. (3) George, b. 4 Jan. 1655–6. (4) Elizabeth, b. 14 Apr. 1657; md. to John Brown, 1682. (5) Samuel, b. 24 Jan. 1660–1, and died the next month. (6) Hannah, b. 6 Apr. 1662, and died the same day. (7) Hannah, again, born 28 June, 1663; md. to J. Baker, jun., 1682.

George Polly died, 22 Dec. 1683. Elizabeth "Polle, widow," died 2 May, 1695.

POLLY. *I.* George Polly, jun., md. Mary Knight, 24 Oct. 1677; was a carpenter, like his father; had a family of ten children; and being pressed, 1692, into the public service, his family was helped by the town. [Town Records, and Rec. of Births, etc.]

POST. Richard, an early inhabitant of Woburn, being taxed there on the list for the Country Rate, 1645; and had grant of meadow made to him in 1648. He married Susanna Sutton, 27 Feb. 1649–50. For his second wife, he md. Mary Tyler, 18 Nov. 1662; and by her had: (1) Mary, b. 29 Sept. 1664. (2) Susanna, b. 13 Sept. 1666. (3) John, b. 14 Apr. 1669. He was taxed in the Rate for the Second Meeting-house, erected in 1672; but as his name is not mentioned in the tax lists for the town, 1679, 1680, it is presumed that he had then moved away. His house, according to a reliable tradition, stood a little north of the road leading from Mr. Caleb Richardson's, to the East School-house in Burlington, where it meets the ancient road from Woburn to Billerica, which passed west from the present great road and of Mr. Samuel Walker's house. There, remains of Mr. Post's house and his well are still to be seen. [Woburn Town Records; Records of Births, etc.]

REED. George Reed was son of William and Mabel Reed, who embarked from England in the "Defence," 4 July, 1656, for New England, bringing with them three of their children, viz: George, aged 6 years, Ralph, aged 5 years, and "Justice" or Justus, 18 months old.[a] They took up their abode in Woburn, upon land sold Mr. Reed by Nicholas Davis. Their dwelling-house stood in a pasture, called the Baldwin Pasture, on the road from Kendall's mill to the Messrs. Duren. The pasture is now owned by them; and remains of Mr. Reed's cellar and well are still to be seen there.[b] But, ere many years, William Reed and his wife Mabel returned to England. He died at Newcastle, upon Tyne, æt. 69; and not having appointed executors in his will, letters of administration were granted by Oliver Cromwell, the Protector, 31 Oct. 1656, to his widow, Mabel, who speedily returned with her four youngest children to New England; married Henry Summers, sen., of Woburn, 21 Nov. 1660; and, outliving him, died at the house of her son George, 5 [15?] June, 1690, aged 85 years.[c] [Wob. Rec. of Births, etc.]

---

[a] Hon. James Savage. [b] Letter of Jacob W. Reed, Esq., of Georgetown, Sept. 1856.
[c] Rev. Lucius R. Paige.

REED. William and Mabel Reed appear to have had 9 children, viz: George, Ralph, and "Justice" or Justus, who came with them to New England in 1635; "Michaell" and Israel, Abigail, Bethiah, Sarah and Rebekah.

Of "Justice," or Justus, nothing is known, after he came to this country. Of "Michaell," nothing is known, except that his father speaks of him in his Will, as married in New England. *Abigail* was married, 2 Oct. 1650, to Francis Wyman; but the date of her death is not on record. *Bethiah* was md. to John Johnson, 28 Apl. 1657; and was living, 1712, with her husband at their son Obadiah's, in Canterbury, Ct., where she died about 1717. *Sarah* was md. to Samuel Walker, jun., (afterwards Dea. Walker,) 10 Sept. 1662, and died 1 Nov. 1681. *Rebekah* was md. to Ensign Joseph Winn[a] about 1664: "Widow Rebekah Winn died the . . . 1734."

REED. *I.* George Reed, sen., was born in England; came to this country with his parents in 1635, when he was six years of age: settled at Woburn, where orders were given a Committee, 9 Nov. 1653, to lay out to him 6 acres of land, in consideration of a house lot which had been previously granted him, but which he had surrendered again to the town.[b] He was made freeman 1684; married, 4 Oct. 1652, Elizabeth Jennison [not "Ginnings," as the Records give the name], daughter of Robert Jennison, of Watertown; to whom were born: (1) Elizabeth, 29 July, 1653; md. 15 Dec. 1675, to Daniel Fiske. (2, 3) *twins*, sons, died 14 Nov. 1654, but a few hours old. (4) *Samuel*, b. 29 Apr. 1656. (5) *Abigail*, b. 27 June, 1658; md. to Nathl. Richardson, 1694. (6) *George*, b. 14 Sept. 1660. (7) *William*, b. 22 Sept. 1662. (8) *Sarah*, b. 12 Feb. 1664-5. Elizabeth, first wife of George Reed, dying 26 Feb. 1664-5, he md. 9th of Nov. 1665, Hannah Rockwell, of Charlestown,[c] by whom he had: (1) Hannah, b. 18 Feb. 1669-70. (2) *John*, b. 18 March, 1672. (3) *Mary*, b. 15 June, 1674; md. to Matthew Johnson, jun. (4) *Timothy*, b. 20 Oct. 1678. (5) *Thomas*, b. 15 July, 1682.

George Reed, sen., died 21 Feb. 1705-6, æt. 67. His second wife survived him.

REED. *II.* George Reed, jun., was born in Woburn, 14 Sept. 1660; married Abigail Peirce, daughter of Thomas, 18 Feb. 1684-5, by whom he had: (1) Abigail, b. 6 Feb. 1685-6. (2) Ebenezer, b. 6 March, 1690, (1691, County Records.) (3) George, b. 2 Aug. 1697; died 6 Oct. 1697. (4) Elizabeth, b. 14 June, 1700; md. 23 May, 1720, to Christopher Paige of Billerica, now Bedford; ancestor of Rev. Lucius Reed Paige, formerly of Cambridgeport.

II. George Reed was a deacon in First Church, Woburn, from 1719 till 1735, when, at the gathering of the Church in the Precinct, now Burlington, he was chosen one of its first two deacons. His first wife, Abigail, dying 9 Sept. 1719, he married, for his second wife, Sybil Rice of Sudbury, probably widow of Isaac, 24 May, 1721. He died at the very

---

a Mr. John A. Boutelle. b Town Rec., Vol. I., pp. 18, 19.
c Rev. Lucius R. Paige. Rec. of Births, etc. Savage's Geneal. Dict.

advanced age of 95 years and 4 months, 20 Jan. 1756. [Woburn Rec., Rev. Mr. Paige, Savage's Geneal. Dict.]

REED. Ralph, son of William and Mabel Reed, was brought by them in 1635 to this country from England, when a child of 5 years of age. He settled in Woburn, where a grant of land was made to him by the town in 1654,[a] and where he was taxed in 1666. He married Mary, daughter of Anthony Peirce, of Watertown, by whom he had: (1) William, born 1658. (2) John, b. 1660. (3) Joseph. (4) Daniel. (5) Timothy, b. 14 Feb. 1664-5. (6) David. (7) Jonathan.[b] A memorable fatal accident happened to William, the eldest son of Ralph, which is stated in the Records of Deaths as follows:[c] "William Read dyed by a shott November ye 7th, 1688: his brother Timothy at unawares in the Woods shot him in stedd of a dear."

Mary, wife of Ralph Read, died 15 Feb. 1701. Ralph Reed dyed 4 Jan. 1711-12.

REED. Israel, son of William and Mabel Reed, was brought with his sisters from England to this country by his mother, after the decease of his father; and when about 17 years of age was put under the guardianship of his brother George, till he should be 21 years old.[d] He was taxed in the rate for building the new meeting-house in 1672; followed, apparently, the business of a butcher; had land granted him "near the burying place," to set a barn on, 1683-4,[e] and had liberty given him by the town, 22 Feb. 1685-6, to erect a slaughter house near his house by the Rocke, at the discretion of the Selectmen.[f] He married, about 1669, Mary, daughter of Francis Kendall; by whom he had: (1) Mary, born 15 Oct. 1670; md. to Matthew Johnson, jun. (2) *Sarah*, b. 29 Aug. 1673. (3) a daughter, b. 2 Jan. 1678-9. (4) *Elizabeth*, b. 22 Dec. 1681; md. to Richard Snow, Jan. 1706-7. (5) *Ruth*, b. 6 Jan. 1683-4. (6) *Israel*, b. 17 March, 1687. (7) *Jemima*, b. 23 July, 1689. (8) Patience, b. 3 Dec. 1697; md. to Jeremiah Whittemore, of Charlestown, 15 March, 1722.

"Israel Reed died 29 June, 1711." "The widow Mary Reed died ye 17th of January, 1721" [1721-22].

It was to Israel Reed, jun., son of the above Israel Reed, to whom the grant to Woburn of 2000 acres was sold in 1734, by the town's committee.

RICHARDSON. Ezekiel Richardson, apparently the eldest of the three brothers of this name engaged in the settlement of Woburn, was born in England; came with his wife, Susanna, to Charlestown, probably in the fleet with Winthrop, in 1630. Both joined the church which was gathered there in 1630, and which afterwards became the First Church in Boston; and both were dismissed from it, 11 Oct. 1632, with others, in order to form the present First Church in Charlestown, which was gathered in November following. He was Representative of Charlestown in General Court, 1635; Selectman, in 1640; and one of the seven Commissioners appointed

---

[a] Town Records. [b] Savage's Geneal. Dict. [c] Wob. Rec. of Births, Deaths, etc.
[d] Rev. Lucius R. Paige. [e] Rec. of Town, Vol. I., p. 124. [f] T. R., Vol. III., p. 93; Rec. of Births, etc., etc.

that year by the church of Charlestown to effect the settlement of Woburn. Of the church of Woburn, he was one of the original members. By his wife, Susanna, he had: (1) *Phebe*, baptized in Boston, 3 June, 1632, and married, 1 Nov. 1649, to Henry Baldwin. (2) *Theophilus.* (3) *Josiah.* (4) *John*, who died at Woburn, 7 Jan. 1642-3. (5) *Jonathan*; died young. (6) *James.* (7) *Ruth*, born at Woburn, 23 Aug. and died 7 Sept. 1643. Ezekiel Richardson died 21 Oct. 1647.

RICHARDSON. *I.* Theophilus, eldest son of Ezekiel and Susanna Richardson, was baptized in the church of Charlestown, 22 Dec. 1633;[a] married, 2 May, 1654, Mary Champney, daughter of John and Joanna Champney, of Cambridge;[b] by whom he had: (1) *Ezekiel*, born 28 Oct. 1655. (2) *Mary*, b. 15 Jan. 1657-8. (3) *Sarah*, b. 23 Apr. 1660. (4) *Abigail*, b. 21 Oct. 1662. (5) *Hannah*, b. 6 Apr. 1665; md. to Daniel Baldwin, 1684-5. (6) *John*, b. 16 Jan. 1667-8; died 29 Oct. 1749, æt. 81 years. [Gravestone.] (7) *Esther*, b. 25 June, 1670. (8) *Ruth*, b. 31 Aug. 1673; md. to William Russell, of Salem Village [Danvers], 20 Jan. 1703-4.

Theophilus Richardson died 28 Dec. 1674. His widow, Mary, probably married John Brooks, sen., 30 Jan. 1683-4.

RICHARDSON. *II.* Ezekiel Richardson, son of Theophilus, and grandson of first Ezekiel, married, 27 July, 1687, Elizabeth Swan, of Cambridge; by whom he had: (1) *Theophilus*, born 4 July, 1688; died, 3 Aug. 1688. (2) *Elizabeth*, b. 20 Oct. 1689 [1690, County Records.] (3) *Theophilus*, b. 7 Jan. 1691-2. (4) *Ezekiel*, b. 22 Apr. 1694. (5) *Abigail*, b. 15 Jan. 1696-7. (6) *Aaron*, b. 16 Dec. 1701.

Ezekiel Richardson died 13 March, 1734.

RICHARDSON. *II.* John Richardson, son of *I.* Theophilus, and brother of *II.* Ezekiel, married Deborah ———, by whom he had: (1) *Mary*, born 10 Aug. 1689. (2) *John*, b. 29 Dec. 1692. (3) *Deborah*, b. 8 March, 1695; md. to John Kendall, 1718. (4) *Sarah*, b. 12 March, 1698; died 20 Feb. 1703-4. (5) *Josiah*, b. 14 Feb. 1700-1. (6) *Nathan*, b. 24 Jan. 1701-2. (7) Eunice, b. 3 Jan. 1703-4. Deborah, wife of John Richardson, died 12 Feb. 1703-4. [Record of Births, etc., in Woburn.]

RICHARDSON. Samuel Richardson, brother of the first Ezekiel, was born in England; was admitted into the church of Charlestown 18 Feb. 1637-8; and at dismission from that, he became one of the original members of the church in Woburn, gathered in August 1642. By his wife Joanna he had: (1) Mary, baptized in the church at Charlestown 25 Feb. 1637-8, and married probably to Thomas Mousall of Charlestown. (2) *John*, born at Charlestown, and baptized in the church there 12 Nov. 1639. (3) *Hannah*, b. at Woburn 8 March, and died there 8 April, 1642. (4) Joseph, b. 27 July, 1643. (5) Samuel, b. 22 *May*, 1646. [*April*, Gravestone.] (6) Stephen, b. 15 Aug. 1649. (7) Thomas, b. 31 Dec. 1651, died 27 Sept. 1657. Also a daughter *Elizabeth*, mentioned about 1666 in her mother's Will. Samuel Richardson died 23 March, 1658; His widow Joanna died in 1666.

---

[a] Charlestown Church Records. Savage's Geneal. Dict. Wob. Town Records. [b] Cambridge Ch. Rec.

[Charlestown Ch. Records: Savage's Geneal. Dict. Woburn Town Rec. of Births, etc., etc.]

RICHARDSON. John, eldest son of Samuel Richardson, married Elizabeth Bacon, daughter of Michael, of Woburn, 22 Oct. 1658; and had by her: (1) *John*, b. 24 Jan. 1660-1. (2) *Joseph*, b. 3 Jan. 1666-7. His wife Elizabeth dying, he md. 28 Oct. 1673, Mary Pierson, daughter of Bartholomew Pierson, by whom he had: (1) *Pierson* Richardson, b. 29 Sept. 1674. (2) *Jacob*, b. 15 Feb. 1675-6. (3) William, b. 29 June, and died 1 Aug. 1678. His 2d wife being dead, John Richardson "sen.," and Margaret Willing md. 25 June, 1689; and had: (1) *Willing*, a son, b. 5 Oct. 1692: died 14 March, 1704. (2) *Job*, b. 30 Apr. 1696.

Lieut. John Richardson died 1 Jan. 1696-7, aged 58 years [Gravestone] "Widow Margaret Richardson died 28 Oct. 1726." [Rec. of Births, etc., etc. Savage's Geneal. Dict.]

RICHARDSON. Joseph, second son of first Samuel Richardson, married Hannah Green, 5 Nov. 1666; by whom he had: (1) Hannah, born 22 Oct. 1667. (2) Mary, b. 22 March, 1669; md. to James Fowle 1688. (3) Elizabeth, b. 28 June, 1670; md. to John Coggin, 1692. (4) Joseph, b. 19 May, 1672. (5) Stephen, b. 7 Feb. 1673-4. [Afterwards known as *Dea. Stephen*, who died Feb. 1752, aged 79. Gravestone.]

Joseph Richardson, "sen.," was admitted freeman 1672; and died 5 March 1718. "The widow Hannah Richardson died 20 May, 1721. [Wob. Rec. of Births, etc. Savage's Geneal. Dict.]

RICHARDSON. *II.* Samuel, 3d son of first Samuel Richardson, and brother of John and Joseph above, had by his wife Martha, 5 Nov. 1670: (1, 2) *Samuel* and *Thomas*, twins, of whom Thomas was slain by the Indians, 10 April, 1676. (3) Elizabeth, born about 1672. (4) *Martha*, b. 20 Dec. 1673: Martha, the mother of this child, died the day of its birth. Samuel Richardson md. Hannah Kingsley, 30 Sept. 1674. This 2d wife Hannah, and an infant, *Hannah*, slain by the Indians, 10 Apr. 1676. He then md. Phebe, daughter of Henry Baldwin, 7 Nov. 1676, by whom he had: *Zechariah*, b. 21 Nov. 1677. Phebe Richardson, his 3d wife dying 20 Oct. 1679, he md. for his 4th wife, 8 Sept. 1680, Sarah Hayward; by whom he had: (1) *Thomas*, born 18 Aug. and died 9 Sept. 1681. (2) Sarah, b. 20 Aug. 1682. (3) *Thomas*, again, b. 25 Sept. 1684. (4) *Ebenezer*, b. 15 March, 1687. (5) . . . . son of Samuel and Sarah Richardson, b. 17 Aug. 1689, and died the same day. (6) *Hannah*, b. 11 Aug. 1690. (7) Eleazer, b. 10 Feb. 1692-3. (8) Jonathan, b. 16 July, 1696. (9) David, b. 14 Apr. 1700. Samuel Richardson died 29 Apr. 1712 [aged 66 years. Gravestone.] The widow Sarah Richardson died 14 Oct. 1717 [aged 62 years. Gravestone.] Wob. Records of Births, etc., etc. Savage's Geneal. Dict.]

RICHARDSON. *I.* Stephen Richardson, 4th son of first Samuel, and brother of the above John & Joseph, married, 2 Jan. 1674-5, Abigail Wyman, a daughter, probably, of Francis Wyman; by whom he had: (1) *Stephen*, born 20 Feb. 1675-6. (2) *Francis*, b. 19 and died 27 Jan. 1677-8. (3) *William*, b. 14 Dec. 1678. (4) *Francis*, again, b. 15 Jan. 1680-1. (5) *Timothy*, b. 6 Dec. 1682; died 18 Jan. 1682-3. (6) *Abigail*, b. 14 Nov. 1683. (7)

Prudence, b. 17 Jan. 1685-6. (8) *Timothy*, again, b. 24 Jan. 1687-8. (9) *Seth*, b. 16 Jan. 1689-90. (10) *Daniel*, b. 16 Oct. 1681. (11) *Mary*, b. 3 May, 1696. (12) *Rebekah*, b. 10 June, 1698; died 6 Dec. 1711. (13) *Solomon*, b. 27 March, 1702. (14) *Henry*, b. 1704.

Stephen Richardson, sen., died 22 March, 1718 ["abt. 67 years old:" Gravestone]. Widow Abigail Richardson died 17 Sept. 1720 [aged 60 years: Gravestone].

[Wob. Rec. of Births, etc., etc. Savage's Geneal. Dict.]

Thomas Richardson, born in England; doubtless came to this country with his brothers Ezekiel and Samuel above named, in 1630; was admitted into the church of Charlestown 18 Feb. 1638; and by his wife Mary had: *Mary*, who was baptized there 17 Nov. 1638; and (2) Sarah, baptized at Charlestown, 22 Nov. 1640.[a] His other children by his wife Mary were born in Woburn, and were: (1) *Isaac*, b. 24 May, 1643. (2) *Thomas*, b. 4 Oct. 1645. (3) *Ruth*, b. 14 Apr. 1647. (4) *Phebe*, b. 24 Jan. 1648-9. (5) Nathaniel, b. 2 Jan. 1650-1. Thomas Richardson died 28 Aug. 1651.

[Savage's Geneal. Dict. Wob. Rec. of Births, etc.]

RICHARDSON. *I.* Isaac Richardson, son of Thomas and Mary, married Deborah, daughter of Thomas Fuller, 19 June, 1667, and had by her: (1) *Jonathan*, born 12 Dec. 1669. (2) *Deborah*, *b.* 22 Jan. 1671-2. (3, 4) Joseph and Benjamin, twins, b. 25 June [al. January], 1674. (5) *Mercy* [*Mary*, County Records], b. 27 Oct. 1676; died 13 May, 1678. (6) *David*, b. 4 Feb. 1678-9. (7) Phebe, b. 14 Feb. 1680-1; married to Joseph Rice, Reading, 20 May, 1703? (8) *Mary*, b. 14 July, 1683. (9) *Elizabeth*, b. 8 Nov. 1685. (10) *Edward* [Samuel?], b. 2 Feb. 1687-8. Isaac Richardson died 2 Apr. 1689. [Savage's Geneal. Dict. Woburn Records of Births, etc., etc.]

RICHARDSON. *I.* Thomas, son of first Thomas Richardson, and brother of Isaac, born 4 October, 1645, settled in Billerica, and died there, 25 Feb. 1721, [1721-2?]; leaving numerous descendants. [Farmer's Geneal. Register.]

RICHARDSON. *I.* Nathaniel, son of first Thomas Richardson, and brother of Isaac, had by his wife Mary: (1) *Nathaniel*, born, 27 Aug. 1673. (2) *James*, b. 26 Feb. 1675-6. "Capt. James Richardson died 24 March, 1721-2, (aged 46 years & 23 days." G. S.) (3) *Mary*, b. 10 March, 1679; md. to Thomas Wyman, 1696; and to Josiah Winn, 1733. (4) *Joshua*, b. 3 June, 1681. (5) *Martha*, b. ——, 1683. (6) *John*, b. 25 Jan. 1684-5. (7) *Thomas*, b. 15 Apr. 1687. (8) *Hannah*, b. —— May, 1689. (9) *Samuel*, b. 24 Sept. 1691. (10) *Phineas*, b. ye. —— of February, 1693-4. (11) *Phebe*, b. 4 March, 1696; md. to David Wyman, 1716. (12) Amos, son of Nathl. and Mary Richardson, b. 10 Aug. 1698. (13) Benjamin, son of Nathl. and Mary Richardson, b. 27 Aug. 1700; died 5 Sept. 1700.

Nathaniel Richardson, sen., died 4 Dec. 1714. Mary Richardson, widow of Nathaniel Richardson, died 22 Dec. 1719. [Wob. Rec. of Births, etc., etc. Savage's Geneal. Dict.]

The Richardsons have always been the most numerous family in Woburn. On the Province Tax List for both Parishes, in 1769, of 330 resident males taxed, there were 42 Richardsons, 27 Wymans, 16 Reeds, and 24 Johnsons, making 109 persons of those four names; a number which, within a trifle, is equal to one-third of all the males then taxed. See T. R., Vol. IX., pp. 83–91.

Again, in 1760, the Province and County Tax (assessed in Woburn together) amounted to £641 17s. 6d. 1qr.

In the assessment of this Tax, there were:

On the East List,	160	resident persons assessed.			
On the West List,	166	"	"	"	
Making	326	"	"	"	in all.

T. R., Vol. VIII., pp. 295–302.

Of the resident persons taxed, there were of

Johnsons on the East List,	3 :	on the West List,	18=21
Reeds on the East List,	3 :	" " West List,	14=17
Richardsons on the East List,	42 :	" " West List,	2=44
Wymans on the East List,	14 :	" " West,	14=28
	62		48=110

equal to more than one-third of all the resident persons in town, that were taxed that year.

And of the 326 residents taxed that year in Woburn, 44, or nearly 2-15ths of the whole number, were Richardsons.

RUSSELL. John, sen. See Chap. V. Concerning his family, however, it may here be added, that his first wife, Elizabeth, he doubtless married in England. She dying at Woburn, 16 Dec. 1644, he married for his second wife Elizabeth Baker, 13 May, 1645. She died his widow, 17 Jan. 1689–90. His daughter Mary md. Timothy Brooks, 21 Dec. 1659. [Wob. Rec. of Births, etc. Savage's Geneal. Dict.]

RUSSELL. *II.* John Russell, jun., son of John Russell, sen. See Chapt. V.

He married Sarah Champney, of Cambridge, 31 Oct. 1661. Their children were: (1) John, born 1 Aug. 1662. (2) Joseph, b. 15 Jan. 1663–4. (3) Samuel, b. 3 Feb. 1667–8; died 1 Dec. 1668. (4) Sarah, b. 10 Feb. 1670–1. (5) *Elizabeth*, b. 19 Feb. 1672–3. ["Widow Elizabeth Peirce dyed June y^e. 5th, 1743, in the 71st. year of her age. Her maiden name, Eliza Russell." Rec. of Deaths, etc.] (6) *Jonathan*, b. 6 Aug. 1675; died June 20, 1708, ["aged 32 years & 10 mos." Gravestone.] (7) *Thomas*, b. 5 Jan. 1677–8. Sarah Russell, widow, died y^e. 25th of Apr. 1696.

RUSSELL. *III.* John, son of John Russell, jun., married Elizabeth Palmer, 21 Dec. 1682; by whom he had: (1) *John*, born 20 Sept. 1683. (2) *Joseph*, b. 3 Oct. 1685. (3) *Stephen*, b. 25 Aug. 1687. (4) *Elizabeth*, b. 21 June, 1690. (5) *Samuel*, b. 16 July, 1692. (6) *Sarah*, b. 15 Oct. 1694. (7) *John*, [name mistaken by Town Clerk] born 19 Aug. and died 12 Sept. 1697. (8) *Ruth*, b. 16 Jan. 1698–9; married to Sam. Eaton, 20 March, 1722. (9) *Jonathan*, b. 7 Nov. 1700. (10) *Mary*, b. 2 March, 1703; died 27 Nov. 1709. (11) Thomas, b. 26 June, 1705. John Russell died 26th July, 1717.

"Widow Elizabeth Russell," named in Province Tax, 1723, but not in 1724. She died about 1723. [Wob. Records of Births, etc., etc. Savage's Geneal. Dict.]

RUSSELL. *IV.* John Russell, son of *III.* John, and grandson of John Russell, jun., md. Joanna Winn, 27 Nov. 1711. Their children were: (1) *Mary*, b. 3 Oct. 1712; md. to Thomas Richardson, 1735; and died 11 Jan. 1741-2. (2) *Elizabeth*, b. 18 Dec. 1714. (3) Anne, b. 10 Feb. 1715-6; md. to John Coolidge, 1739. (4) *John*, b. 16 July, 1717. (5) *Abigail*, b. 22 Sept. 1719. (6) *Edward*, b. 7 April, 1722. (7) James, b. 22 Feb. 1723-4. (8) Daniel, b. 5 Apr. 1726.

Mr. Russell was Town Clerk, 1739, 40, 41, 42, 43 and 1745; and also chosen Clerk of First Parish at first Parish Meeting, 3 March, 1731-2, and constantly re-chosen every year till March 1741-2: but the date of his death, and that of his wife are not found in the Records. [T. Records, and Records of Births, etc.]

SEIRS. John Seirs (as the name is spelled in Woburn Records) was in Charlestown in 1639; subscribed there the "Town Orders" for Woburn, Dec. 1640; was admitted into the church at Charlestown, 28 March, 1641; made freeman the same year; was among the first who settled in Woburn; taxed there in 1645; and chosen Selectman, 1667, 1669. His first wife, Susanna, dying 29 Aug. 1677, he married Esther Mason, 20 Nov. 1677; and quickly after the decease of this, his second wife, 14 Aug. 1680, he married Ann Farrar, widow of the first Jacob Farrar, 2 Nov. 1680. He died, leaving no children, 5 Oct. 1697. [Woburn Records. Charlestown Ch. Records. Savage's Geneal. Dict.]

SHELDON. John Sheldon was taxed in Woburn, in the rate for the second Meeting-House, 1672; which shows he was then an inhabitant of Woburn. He had previously, viz: 1 Feb. 1658-9, married, at Billerica, Mary Thompson, widow of Simon Thompson, of Woburn, who deceased in May, 1658. By her he had a son, John, born 24 April, 1660, who at his death, 27 Aug. 1724, was a deacon in the church of Billerica. John Sheldon, sen., died 24 May, 1690, aged about 63 years. [Woburn and Billerica Records.]

SIMONDS. William Simonds, sen., settled in Woburn about 1644, near a place still known by the name of Dry Brook. He married, 18 Jan. 1643-4, Judith Hayward, widow of James Hayward, who had married her, when Judith Phippen, a fellow passenger, and a fellow servant, on board the "Planter," from London, 1635. By her, Simonds had: (1) *Sarah*, born 28 July, 1644. (2) *Judith*, b. 3 March, 1646. (3) *Mary*, b. 9 Dec. 1647. (4) *Caleb*, b. 16 Aug. 1649. (5) *William*, b. 15 Apr. 1651. (6) *Joseph*, b. 18 Oct. 1652. (7) Benjamin, b. 18 March, 1654. (8) Tabitha, b. 20 July; died 20 Aug. 1655. (9) Joshua, b. ——; died 16 July, 1657. (10) James, b. 1 Nov. 1658; married to Susanna Blogget, 29 Dec. 1685. (11) Bethiah, b. "9: 3 mo," 9 May, [3: 9 mo: 3 Nov.?] 1659; md. to John Walker, sen., 13 August, 1696. (12) Huldah, b. 20 Nov. 1660; md. to Samuel Blogget, jun., 1683.

William Simonds, sen., died 7 June, 1672: Judith Simonds, widow, died

3 Jan. 1689-90. [Woburn Records of Births, Marriages, etc., etc.; Savage's Geneal. Dict.]

SIMONDS. Caleb, eldest son of William and Judith Simonds, married Sarah Bacon, 25 Sept. 1677. To them were born: (1) *Samuel*, b. 30 June, 1678; died a pauper in 1757? [See Treasurer's Book, 29 July, 1757.] (2) James, b. 15 Jan. 1683-4. (3) Sarah, b. 11 Nov. died 16 Nov. 1687. Caleb Simonds died 4 Nov. 1712. "Widow Sarah Simonds died 11 Apr. 1627." [Woburn Records of Births, etc., etc.]

SIMONDS. *I.* James, son of the above Caleb and Sarah Simonds, had, by his wife Lydia: (1) *James*, born 22 April, 1714. (2) *Caleb*, b. 27 May, 1716. (3) *Sarah*, b. 2 March, 1718; died 25 Feb. 1745-6. (4) Lydia, b. 25 June, 1720; m. to Samuel Chamberlain 1744? (5) Abigail, b. 30 July, 1722; wife of James Thompson, of Wilmington, and mother of Mrs. John Flagg. (6) Susanna, b. 11 Sept. 1724. James Simonds died 28 Dec. 1733. Widow Lydia Simonds died 29 June, 1744. [Woburn Records of Births, etc., etc.]

SIMONDS. *II.* James Simonds, eldest son of James and Lydia, and once the owner, it is believed, of the "Jemmy Pasture," so called, in Burlington, now the property of Mr. Caleb Richardson, married Ann Convers, about Aug. 1745. To them were born: (1) *Anne*, 30 July, 1746; md. to Ebenezer Whitney, 1767. (2) *Jude*, b. 9 Jan. 1748-9. (3) *Esther*, b. 2 March, 1750. (4) *Hazael* [Asahel], b. 28 Dec. 1752. (5) *Ebenezer*, b. 4 March, 1755. (6) *Keziah*, b. 28 Jan. 1758. [Wob. Records of Births, etc.]

SIMONDS. *II.* Caleb Simonds, second son of the above James and Lydia, married Lydia Robinson, of Lexington, 1751. Their children were: (1) *Jonathan*, born 1 Jan. 1752; a farmer, and a deacon of the church in Burlington; died 27 May, 1827, æt. 76. (2) *Caleb*, a farmer, born 17 Feb. 1755; died 15 June, 1819, æt. 65. (3) *James*, b. 5 Dec. 1758. (4) *Lydia*, b. 28 Jan. 1761; md. to Amos Reed, butcher, of New Salem, 7 Oct. 1781; died at Salem, July or Aug. 1850, æt. 89.

Widow Lydia Simonds died 29 Jan. 1778, aged about 60. [Wob. Records of Births, etc. Rev. Mr. Marrett's Record of Deaths.]

SIMONDS. William Simonds, second son of William and Judith Simonds, it is presumed, removed from Woburn early, the records giving no information concerning him that has been observed, except the date of his birth, as presented above.

SIMONDS. Joseph Simonds, third son of William and Judith, was a carpenter. In 1679, he gave by deed to his brother James certain lands he owned in Woburn, on the road to Concord, with a new unfinished house thereon, barn, and land about it; and James gave to him in return, lands he owned in Cambridge Farms or Lexington, upon which Joseph Simonds soon settled, and became the father of the numerous families of his name, which in successive generations have been inhabitants of Lexington. [Original deed of Joseph Simonds.]

SIMONDS. *I.* Benjamin, fourth son of William and Judith Simonds, had by his wife Rebekah: (1) *William*, born 14 Feb. 1678-9; married

Elizabeth ——, and lived in Billerica. [a] (2) Benjamin, b. 14 Jan. 1680–81. (3) *Joseph*, b. 1 March, 1683. (4) *John*, b. 22 March, 1685. (5) *Rebekah*, b. 6 June, 1687. (6) *Daniel*, b. 21 Feb. 1689–90. (7) *Jacob*, b. 26 May, 1692. (8) *Judith*, b. 5 Oct. 1695; married to Samuel Eames, 1717. (9) Huldah, b. 25 Oct. 1700; md. to Nathan Wyman, 1723.

Rebekah, wife of Benjamin Simonds, died —— April, 1713. Lieut. Benjamin Simonds died 21 Sept. 1726.

SIMONDS. *II.* Benjamin, jun., son of Benjamin and Rebekah Simonds, married Abigail, daughter of Josiah Wood, 7 Aug. 1723. Their children were: (1) *Benjamin*, born 1 June, 1724. (2) *Abigail*, b. 6 Nov. 1725; md. to Samuel Wood, 22 Oct. 1747. (3) *Ruth*, b. 14 May, 1727; md. to Zebedee Simonds, 30 May, 1749. Abigail, wife of Benjamin Simonds, died 1 Nov. 1739, aged 48 years. Mr. Benjamin Simonds, sen., died 13 Jan. 1748–9, " aged sixty-nine years wanting one day." [Manuscripts of Simonds' family. Wob. Rec. of Births, etc., etc.]

SIMONDS. *III.* Benjamin, son of Benjamin and Abigail Simonds, was married to Susannah Simonds, daughter of *III.* James and Mary, and son of *II.* James and Susanna, 29 March, 1748. Their children were: (1) Susannah, born 11 Feb. 1749–50. (2) Benjamin, b. 30 Dec. 1751; died 24 Dec. 1753. (3) Benjamin, b. 20 May, 1754. (4) Zebedee, b. 23 Feb. 1756. (5) Nathan, b. 23 Oct. 1757. (6) Abigail, b. 31 May, 1759. (7) William, b. 6 March, 1761. (8) Mary, b. 5 Sept. 1762. (9) Martha, b. 5 Aug. 1764. (10) Lucy, b. 6 Apr. 1766. (11) Katharine, b. 16 Aug. 1769. Mr. Benjamin Simonds deceased 10 Dec. 1783, aged 59 years. Susanna Simonds, his widow, died 15 Nov. 1816, in her 91st year. Concerning their children, it may be added, that Zebedee died 2 July, 1778; William died 9 Apr. 1776; Mary died 18 June, 1776; Lucy died 15 Dec. 1792; and Katharine died 23 Aug. 1769. Susanna was married, 4 Dec. 1781, by Rev. Samuel Parker, of Boston, to Ebenezer Page, who died 10 June, 1784, when he was 47 years of age. [Wob. Rec. of Births, etc., etc. Manuscripts of Simonds' family.]

SIMONDS. *I.* James, fifth son that lived to maturity of William and Judith Simonds, married Susanna, daughter of Samuel and Ruth Blogget, 29 Dec. 1685. Their children were: (1) *James*, born 1 Nov. 1686. (2) *Susanna*, b. 2 May, 1689. (3) *Abigail*, b. 17 Jan. 1691–2. (4) *Sarah*, b. 13 Dec. 1694: md. to Samuel Wilson, 1719? (5) *Nathan*, b. 12 June, 1697. (6) *Ruth*, b. 12 Dec. 1699; md. to John Fowle, 3d, 1723.

Susanna, wife of James Simonds, died 9 Feb. 1714–5. James Simonds, sen., died 15 Sept. 1717. [Wob. Rec. Births, etc.]

SIMONDS. *II.* James Simonds, son of *I.* James and Susanna, married Mary, daughter of James and Mary Fowle, 17 June, 1714. Their children were: (1) *Mary*, born 27 Dec. 1715; md. to John Lawrence, 1736. (2) *James*, b. 10 March, 1717; md. Anna Lawrence, 12 May, 1740. (3) *Joshua*, b. 17 Oct. 1718. (4) *Caleb*, b. 27 Aug. 1720. (5) *Zebedee*, b. 4 Sept. 1723. (6)

---

[a] Billerica Rec. of Births, etc., etc. Woburn Rec. of Births, etc. Deeds of the Simonds' family.

Susanna, b. 20 June, 1725: md. to Benjamin Simonds, jun., 1748. (7) *Nathan*, b. 26 June, 1728. (8) *Ruth*, b. 10 Oct. 1730. Count Rumford's mother. (9) *Abigail*, b. 9 June, 1733; md. to Daniel Reed, jun., about 1754. Mary, wife of Lieut. James Simonds, died 9 March, 1762, "in her *seventy-fourth* year." [Gravestone.] Should be *seventy-third* year. Lieut. James Simonds died 30 July, 1775, in his 89th year.

[Precinct Ch. Rec. of Marriages, and Wob. Rec. of Births. Simonds' Manuscripts.]

SIMONDS. *III.* Caleb Simonds, son of Lieut. James and Mary Simonds, married Susanna Convers, daughter of Capt. Robert and Mary Convers, 26 March, 1746; and had: (1) *Jesse*, b. 13 Oct. 1747; lived in Billerica. (2) *Luther*, b. 2 Oct. 1749: killed by the rolling of a log upon him at mill, 2 April, 1792. (3) *Calvin*, b. 16 Oct. 1752; died at Burlington, 30 July, 1840, æt. 88. (4) *Achsah*, b. 12 March, 1755. (5) *Gideon*, b. 24 June, 1757; died at Burlington, suddenly, 12 June, 1835, æt. 78. (6) *Sarah*, b. 22 May, 1759. (7) *Ruth*, b. 13 Apr. 1763.

Mrs. Susanna Simonds, first wife of Mr. Caleb Simonds being dead, he married for his second wife, 6 Dec. 1774, Mrs. —— Munroe, widow of Andrew Munroe, of Lexington. She was instantly killed by a horse, which ran over her, while standing by her own door, 3 Sept. 1783, aged 58. Mr. Caleb Simonds died of old age, 4 Jan. 1811, in his 91st year. [Woburn Rec. of Births, etc. Lexington Ch. Rec. Rev. Mr. Marrett's Records of Deaths, etc.]

The Simonds family were formerly very numerous in Woburn and Burlington, and had spread much in Billerica, Bedford, and Lexington: and living representatives of it are yet to be found in most if not all of these towns.

SMITH. Matthew, supposed to be a son of Matthew Smith, cordwainer, who came from Sandwich, Kent County, England, 1637, with wife Jane and four children, to Charlestown, and was that year admitted an inhabitant.[a] Matthew, jun., was in Woburn, 1658; was taxed there in 1666, and is numbered among those who had right in the common lands of the town in 1668. There were born to him in Woburn: (1) Elizabeth, born 15 Sept. 1658. (2) Matthew, 2 Sept. 1659. (3) John, b. 19 Jan. 1661; died 18 Oct. 1663. (4) Samuel, b. 29 April, 1662. (5) Samuel, b. 26 July, 1663. (6) Hannah, b. 21 Oct. 1664. (7) John, again, b. 28 March, 1667.

II. Matthew, son of the above? married Mary Cutler, 20 June, 1684. [Savage's Geneal. Dict. Wob. Records.]

SNOW. Richard Snow was the earliest inhabitant of Woburn bearing his name. He was taxed there in the Rate for the Country, assessed 8 Sept. 1645, which was the first tax in Woburn upon record. In 1647-8, land was granted him by the town. He bought, 19 Nov. 1656, a house and 20 acres of land of George Farley, one of the original inhabitants of Woburn, then recently removed to Billerica; and in the general distribu-

[a] Frothingham's Charlestown, p. 88.

tion of common lands and timber, made in 1668, he had a due proportion assigned him in the "fifth Eighth." He seems to have been an industrious, thriving husbandman, and to have maintained a respectable rank in society; but not being ambitious of honor and distinction, he never attained to any considerable office either in the church or town. He died 9 Nov. 1711. Beside John and James Snow, sons apparently his, born before he came to Woburn to reside, he had born to him afterwards: (1) Daniel, b. 4 Feb. 1644-5; died 18 July, 1646. (2) Samuel, b. 28 May, 1647. (3) Zechariah, b. 29 March, 1649; was wounded in the Swamp or Narraganset Fight with the Indians, 19 Dec. 1675,[a] and died 14 April, 1711. His (Zechariah's) homestead in Wyman Lane was sold after his death, July 11th, 1711, to Benj. Wyman, tanner.[b]

I. John Snow, referred to above, as being probably a son of Richard Snow, born before his father took up his residence in Woburn, had: (1) John, b. 13 May, 1668. (2) Zerubbabel, b. 14 May, 1672. (3) Timothy, b. 16 Feb. 1674-5. (4) Hannah, b. 6 June, 1677. (5) Mary, b. 4 Aug. 1680. (6) Ebenezer, b. 6 Oct. 1682; died 11 Feb. 1703-4. (7) Nathaniel, b. 17 Nov. 1684. John Snow died 25 Nov. 1706. [Wob. Rec. of Births, etc., etc.]

I. Zerubbabel Snow, son of John, married Jemima Cutler, Sept. 22, 1697. Their children were: (1) Zerubbabel, b. 19 July, 1698. (2) Josiah, b. 24 Jan. 1699-1700. (3) Jabez, b. 12 March, 1701; died 9 Dec. 1715. (4) Jemima, b. 19 Aug. 1702; md. to Abraham Josselyn, of Marlborough, 1728. (5) Ebenezer, b. 26 Apl. 1744. (6) John, b. 30 March, 1706. (7) William, b. 25 Jan. 1707-8? (8) Abigail, b. 29 March, 1711. (9) Jabez, again, b. 16 March, 1716. *I.* Zerubbabel Snow died 20 Nov. 1733.

II. Zerubbabel Snow, his son, married Elizabeth Wyman, Aug. 11, 1721; had by her 8 children, and died Sept. 1747. His widow, Elizabeth, died May, 1776.[c] [Wob. Rec. of Births, etc.]

I. Timothy, son of *I.* John Snow, md. Lydia Peirce, 16 Jan. 1705-6. Their children were: (1) Timothy, b. 19 Feb. 1706-7, and died Sept. 20, 1775, æt. 69.[d] (2) Isaac, b. 26 Feb. 1708-9. (3) Lydia, b. 20 Feb. 1710-11; md. to Jabez Thompson, 1735? (4) Jacob, b. 5 Sept. 1714. (5) Mary, b. 13 Apl. 1717. (6) Zachary, b. 15 Aug. 1719; died Sept. 21, 1754, aged 36.[d] (7) Abraham, b. 28 Dec. 1721; died at Charlestown, March 9, 1772.[e] Mr. Timothy Snow died 4 March, 1747-8, aged 74 years.[f] His widow died Apl. 27, 1764, æt. 81.[f] [Rec. of Births, etc.]

Isaac, son of Timothy Snow, md. Esther Convers, July 8, 1732; and she dying, May 30, 1737, he md. for his second wife, Phebe Richardson, 18 Apl. 1738. Their children were: (1) Phebe, b. 5 Jan. 1738-9; md. to Daniel Thompson, 1760. (2) Bridget, b. 17 July, 1742; md. to Hiram Thompson, 1767. (3) Anne, b. 19 March, 1744; md. to Ebenezer Reed, June 23, 1777. (4) Mary, b. 26 Apl. 1747; died Dec. 8, 1753. Mr. Isaac Snow died March 31, 1776, æt. 67.[g] [Wob. Rec. of Births, etc.]

---

[a] Hist. Chap. IV. [b] Wyman Papers, No. 52. [c] Mem. of S. Thompson, Esq.
[d] Gravestone. [e] Mem. of Saml. Thompson, Esq. [f] Gravestone.
[g] Gravestone.

I. Samuel, son of Richard Snow, had by his wife Sarah: (1) Samuel, b. 8 Feb. 1669–70. (2) Sarah, b. 28 May, 1672. (3) Daniel, b. 9 July, 1674. (4) Abigail, b. 4 April, 1677. (5) Richard, b. 10 Dec. 1683. (6) Hannah, b. 8 June, 1686. Sarah, wife of Samuel Snow, dying, probably in child-bed, 15 June, 1686, one week after her daughter Hannah's birth, he married, 9 August, of the same year, Sarah Parker, of "New Cambridge," or Newton.[a] By her he had: (1) Deborah, b. Oct. 1687; died 30 Dec. 1687. (2) Joanna, b. 10 Feb. 1688–9. (3) Ebenezer, b. 7 Oct. 1691.

Sarah, wife of Samuel Snow, died 28 Jan. 1694–5. "Samuel Snow, sen.," died 28 Nov. 1717. [Records of Births, etc., etc., in Wob.]

SNOW. *II.* Samuel Snow, son of *I.* Samuel, and grandson of Richard, the first settler in Woburn by the name of Snow, and often distinguished in after years by the title of Lieut. Samuel Snow, had born to him by his wife Abigail: (1) *Samuel,* born 24 Aug. 1692. (2) *Abigail,* b. 18 Nov. 1694. (3) *Sarah,* b. 14 Sept. 1697. (4) *Ruth,* b. 8 May, 1700. (5) Rebekah, b. 11 Feb. 1702–3. (6) Elizabeth, b. 29 Dec. 1705. (7) Benjamin, b. 29 Aug. 1708. (8) Joseph, b. 18 May, 1713.

SNOW. *III.* Samuel, son of Lieut. Samuel Snow, born 24 Aug. 1692, married, 10 June, 1718, Sarah Lock, of Lexington; and by her had: (1) *Samuel,* born 7 Dec. 1719. (2) Oliver, b. 28 Aug. 1721. (3) Sarah, b. 24 Jan. 1723–4.

In 1724, Lieut. Samuel Snow and his son Samuel Snow, jun., bought, each of them, a tract of land in Ashford, Ct., and immediately removed their residence thither from Woburn. At Ashford, Lieut. Snow became one of the principal men; was generally Moderator at their town meetings, a Selectman, Town Treasurer, etc., for many years. He died 19 Dec. 1743. His widow Abigail died 12 Jan. 1747.[b]

His son also, Samuel Snow, jun., became a prominent character in Ashford, and held there some of the more important town offices several years. His daughter Sarah, born in Woburn, died at Ashford, 17 May, 1726. By his wife Sarah, he had after his removal to Ashford: (1) *Sarah,* b. 29 April, 1726. (2) *Stephen,* b. 5 July, 1730. (3) *Sylvanus,* b. 17 March, 1732. (4) *Elizabeth,* b. 11 July, 1734; died 1 Apr. 1737. (5) *Timothy,* b. 20 Sept. 1737; died 9 Apr. 1749. (6) Elizabeth, b. 28 Sept. 1739. Mr. Samuel Snow, jun., died 24 Dec. 1756, æt. 65. Sarah, his widow, died 16 Nov. 1790, æt. 95.[a] [Wob. Town Records. Wob. Records of Births, etc.]

SUMMERS. Henry "Summers," [Somers?] sen., is recorded as chosen, 23 Feb. 1663–4, as a Surveyor for Woburn; was taxed there in the Rate for the Country, 26 Aug. 1666; and is numbered with those who had right in the common lands of the town, 1668.[c] He married, 21 Nov. 1660, Mabel Reed, widow of William and mother of George Reed. She died, the widow of Summers, 15 June, 1690.

---

a County Records.

b Letter of Rev. Frederick P. Tracy, Williamsburg, Mass., 1845, descended from Lt. Snow, of Ashford.

c Town Records, Vol. I. pp. 43, 44.

SUMMERS. Henry Summers, jun., son of the preceding, was taxed in Woburn, 1666 and 1672; and was allowed by the Selectmen "to keepe ordinary for the Towne of Wobourn from the first of May, 1682, he forthwith getting a license."[a] He died 6 March, 1724. [Wob. Rec. of Births, etc.]

SUTTON. Lambert was first of Charlestown, where he was admitted into the church, 4 Apr. 1641; became soon after an inhabitant of Woburn, and was taxed there in the Rate for the Country, 8 Sept. 1645, and chosen a Surveyor, 1646. He was made freeman 1644, and died in Woburn, 27 Nov. 1649. [Charlestown Ch. Records: Colony Rec. Wob. Records of Births, etc.]

THOMPSON. James Thompson: born in England, probably in 1593; came with his wife to New England; was in Charlestown, 1632; and was admitted with her into the church of Charlestown in the autumn of 1633. He was made freeman 1634; subscribed at Charlestown, Dec. 1640, "Town Orders" for Woburn; and coming to Woburn to reside, he was chosen one of the first Board of Selectmen, 1644. His wife, Elizabeth, dying 13 Nov. 1643, he married for his second wife Susanna Blogget, widow of Thomas Blogget, of Cambridge, 15 Feb. 1643-4. This his second wife died 10 Feb. 1660-1: James Thompson himself died in 1682. By his first wife, Elizabeth, he had three sons, all probably born in England, viz: Simon, the eldest, James, jun., who died in Woburn, 24 Jan. 1646-7; and Jonathan. [Savage's Geneal. Dict. Charlestown Ch. Rec. Col. Rec. Wob. Town Rec. and Records of Births, etc.]

Simon Thompson, the eldest son of the first James Thompson, married 19 Dec. 1643, Mary, daughter of Deacon Edward Convers; by whom he had: (1) *John*, born 4 Apr. and died 12 Apr. 1645. (2) *Sarah*, b. 20 Feb. 1646-7. (3) *James*, b. 20 March, 1649. (4) *Mary*, b. 25 Jan. 1651-2; died 2 Feb. 1661-2. (5) *Ann*, b. 30 July, 1655. (6) *Rebecca*, b. May 1658. He was made freeman, 1648; and became a purchaser of Chelmsford; but his plans were cut short by death, which arrested him when in early life, May 1658. In his will, made that month, he makes provision for his children; names his father and his wife, and her father and her two brothers, James and Josiah Convers. His widow married John Sheldon, of Woburn and Billerica. [Wob. Rec. of Births, etc., etc. Savage's Geneal. Dict. Colony Records. Billerica Records of Births, Marriages, etc., etc.]

I. Jonathan Thompson, youngest son of first James and Elizabeth Thompson, married, 28 Nov. 1655, Susanna, daughter of Thomas and Susanna Blodgett, of Cambridge, and born there in June 1637. By her, he had issue, as follows: (1) *Susanna*, born 4 July, 1661. (2) *Jonathan*, b. 28 Sept. 1663. (3) *James*, b. 1666; died soon. (4) *James*, again, b. 27 June, 1667. (5) *Sarah*, b. 1 June, 1670. (6) *Simon*, b. 15 June, 1673. (7) Ebenezer, b. 18 Aug. 1676; died 19 Feb. 1697-8. Jonathan Thompson died 20 Oct. 1691. Susanna, his widow, died 6 Feb. 1697-8?

THOMPSON. *II.* Jonathan Thompson, jun., son of *I.* Jonathan and Susanna Thompson, born 28 Sept. 1663, married Frances Whittemore; by

[a] Town Records, Vol. I., p. 118.

whom he had: (1) *Jonathan*, born 9 Feb. 1689–90. (2) Hannah, b. 28 Jan. 1691–2. (3) Joseph, b. 20 Oct. 1694. (4) *James*, b. 14 Dec. 1696; was living in Brimfield, 1758. (5) *Susanna*, b. 6 July, 1699; md. to Benjamin Mead, 1722? (6) Ebenezer, b. 30 March, 1701. (7) *Mary*, b. 18 Aug. 1703. (8) *Samuel*, b. 8 Sept. 1705. (9) Patience, b. 25 Oct. 1713; md. to Timothy Lamson, of Concord, 1734?

Ebenezer, son of *II.* Jonathan and Frances Thompson, born 30 March, 1701; married Hannah Convers, 27 Sept. 1728; and had: (1) *Benjamin*, born 27 Nov. 1729. (2) *Ebenezer*, b. 15 Sept. 1731. (3) *Hannah*, b. 21 Sept. 1734. (4) Hiram, b. 17 May, 1743.

I. Benjamin, son of Ebenezer and Hannah Thompson, born 27 Nov. 1729, entered his Intentions of Marriage with Ruth Simonds, both of Woburn, 30 May, 1752. Being married shortly after, he had by her the next year:

II. Benjamin Thompson, born 26 March, 1753, who in after years gained a world wide reputation under the titles of Sir Benjamin Thompson, and Count Rumford. For account of him, see Chap. XII.

Benjamin Thompson, father of Count Rumford, died 7 Nov. 1755, in his 26th year. [Wob. Rec. of Births, etc.]

I. Samuel Thompson, 5th son, 8th child, of *II.* Jonathan and Frances Thompson, born 8 Sept. 1705, married Ruth Wright, daughter of Josiah and Ruth Wright, 31 Dec. 1730. To them were born: (1) *Samuel*, 30 Oct. 1731. (2) *Daniel*, 9 March, 1734. (3) *Ruth*, 9 March, 1737; md. to Noah Wyman, 1755. (4) *Abijah*, 11 April, 1739. (5) *Mary*, 24 May, 1741. (6) *Phebe*, 5 Feb. 1743–4. (7) Lois, b. 12 Aug. 1746. (8) Jonathan, b. 10 Sept. 1748.

Samuel Thompson died 13 May, 1748, in his 43d year. His widow, Ruth Thompson, died in Oct. 1775, aged 69 years. [Wob. Rec. of Births, etc. Diary of Samuel Thompson, Esq.]

II. Samuel, eldest son of *I.* Samuel and Ruth Thompson, born 30 Oct. 1731, was a gentleman of note and influence in his day. In 1758, he went in an expedition against the French to Lake George. Of this expedition, he has left a minute and interesting account in manuscript; and when he returned from it at the close of the year, he had been advanced to be a lieutenant in the military service. See Appendix No. IX. For a long succession of years afterwards, he was much employed as a Justice of the Peace, and as a Deacon of the Church, in the civil and ecclesiastical affairs of the town. He was chosen Selectman in 1776, 77, 78, 1779; he represented Woburn in the General Court in the years 1785, 86, 89, 92, 93, 98, 1805, 1806; and there were but few committees upon important town business, upon which, for many years, he was not appointed to serve. This highly respected citizen was thrice married. His first wife was Abigail Tidd, whom he married 15 May, 1753, and by her he had: (1) *Samuel*, born 7 April, 1754, and died at New York, a lieutenant in the military service of his country, of a putrid fever, 12 Aug. 1776, in his 23d year. (2) *Abigail*, b. 29 Dec. 1755; married to John Eames. (3) Mary, b. 13 Jan. 1758; died 6 Apr. 1759. (4) *Jonathan*, b. 26 Apr. 1760, father of the present Cyrus Thompson, Esq. (5) Arphaxad, b. 7 March, 1763; died 15 Dec. 1771. (6) *Leonard*, b. 1 Dec. 1764, the father of the present Col. Leonard Thompson.

Abigail, first wife to Samuel Thompson, Esq., dying 21 Sept. [2 Sept.?] 1768, aged 35 years, he next married Lydia Jones, of Concord, 26 Feb. 1770, by whom was born to him Lydia, 31 Jan. 1771.

Lydia, his second wife, dying 19 Oct. 1788, aged 54 years, he married for his third wife, Esther Wyman, 22 Oct. 1789.

Samuel Thompson, Esq., died Aug. 17, 1820. His wife Esther died before him, Aug. 5, 1818. His brother, Abijah Thompson, sheriff, father of Dea. Charles Thompson, died Jan. 16, 1811. Major Abijah Thompson, the sheriff's son, and father of General Abijah Thompson, died Oct. 27, 1820. [Woburn Town Records. Rec. of Births, etc., etc. Thompson's Diary, or Memoranda of Interesting Occurrences.]

TIDD. John Tidd (or as the name was otherwise once spelled, Tead, or Teed, or Ted) embarked, 12 May, 1637, at Yarmouth, England, aged 19, as servant of Samuel Greenfield, of Norwich; was of Charlestown that year; subscribed there in December 1640 "Town Orders" for Woburn; was taxed at Woburn in the Country Rate, 8 Sept. 1645; and chosen a Surveyor of Fences there in 1646. His wife Margaret died 1651. He died 24 April, 1657. By his Will, made 15 days before, it appears that he had a second wife, Alice; daughters, Mary and Elizabeth, and a son of his own name.[a] His daughter Mary was doubtless the wife of Francis Kendall, md. 24 Dec. 1644; and Elizabeth, the wife of Thomas Fuller, md. 13 June, 1643.

TIDD. *II.* John Tidd, jun., son of John, sen., and Margaret Tidd, born in England; married, 14 April, 1650, Rebekah Wood. By her he had issue: (1) *Hannah*, born 21 Sept. 1652. (2) *John*, b. 26 Feb. 1654–5. (3) *Mary*, b. 13 Nov. 1656. (4) *Samuel*, b. 16 Jan. 1658–9. (5) *Joseph*, b. 18 Jan. 1660–1; died 1 Feb. 1660–1. (6) Joseph, again, b. 20 Jan. 1661–2. (7) Rebekah, b. . . . . . . md. to Thomas Blogget, 11 Nov. 1685. The death of John Tidd, jun., and that of his wife Rebekah, are not found on Record. [Woburn Records of Births, etc., etc.]

TIDD. *III.* John Tidd, son of John Tidd, jun., and Rebekah Tidd, b. 26 Feb. 1654–5; married Elizabeth Fifield, 12 June, 1678; and had by her: (1) *Elizabeth*, born 19 Sept. 1679. (2) *John*, b. 2 Nov. 1681. (3) *Joseph*, b. 8 March, 1684. (4) "*Rebekah*, daughter of John and Elizabeth "Tedd," b. 4 Aug. 1687. (5) *Mary*, b. 25 Apr. 1690. (6) *Ebenezer*, b. 31 Aug. 1693.

"Elizabeth, wife of Sergt. John Tidd, died 6 Oct. 1732." "Old Mr. John Tidd died 3 Aug. 1743." [Wob. Rec. of Births, etc.]

TOTTINGHAM. Henry Tottingham, (or *Tottman*, as formerly often written and pronounced in Woburn) was born in England; was of Charlestown in 1640, when and where he subscribed the "Town Orders" for Woburn. He removed shortly after to Woburn; was taxed there in 1645, 1646, 1666; and had a right assigned him, 1668, in the common lands of the town.

---

[a] Savage's Geneal. Dict. Wob. Town Records. Records of Births, etc., etc.

By his wife, Anna, he had: (1) *Nehemiah*, born 23 Aug. 1646; died 28 March, 1714. (2) *Eliah*, ["Elijah," County Records] b. 28 Feb. 1651-2. Anna, wife of Henry Tottingham, died 23 Feb. 1653-4.

Henry Tottingham and Alice Alger, ["Allice Eager," County Rec.] married 13 July, 1654.

[Wob. Town Records: Rec. of Births, etc., etc.]

TOTTINGHAM. *I.* Eliah Tottingham, son of Henry and Anna, had by his wife Mary: (1) *Anna*, b. 24 Sept. 1685. (2) *Mary*, daughter of "Eliah and Mary Tottingham," born 18 Apr. 1688; married to Thomas Lane, 1721? (3) *Sarah*, b. 13 July, 1690; md. to Nath. Cutler, of Reading, 1715. (4) *Henry*, b. 29 Aug. 1692. (5) *Elisha*, b. 22 July, 1696. (6) Elizabeth, b. 8 Feb. 1698-9. (7) Alice, b. 10 June, 1701. (8) "Arminell," a daughter of Eliah and Mary, b. 30 July, 1707.

Eliah "Tottman," died 27 Nov. 1717.

TOTTINGHAM. *II.* Elisha, or Eliah Tottingham, son of *I.* Eliah and Mary, born 22 July, 1696, had by his wife Rebecca: (1) "Rebekah," b. 4 Aug. 1710; died 28 Apr. 1733. (2) *Elisha*, son of Eliah and Rebekah Tottingham, born 18 Oct. 1713. (3) *Elizabeth*, b. 4 May, 1722. (4) *John*, b. 9 Aug. 1724. (5) *Phebe*, b. 30 June, 1728. (6) *Abigail*, daughter of Eliah and Rebekah Tottingham, b. 30 Dec. 1737.

Eliah Tottingham died 29 March, 1743.

TOTTINGHAM. *III.* Elisha, son of *II.* Eliah and Rebekah Tottingham, born 18 Oct. 1713; md. Sarah Lawrence, of Woburn, 27 May, 1736, and had issue: (1) *Elisha*, b. 8. Feb. 1736-7. (2) *Sarah*, b. 21 Nov. 1738; md. to John Williams, of New Marlborough, 1765. (3) Nathaniel, b. 10 June, 1740. (4) *Ephraim*, b. 9 Apr. 1743. (5) *Moses*, b. 22 July, 1746. (6) *Jonathan*, b. 17 Dec. 1748. (7) James, b. 14 July, 1751. (8) Rebekah, b. 15 Nov. 1753. (9) Abigail, b. 15 July, 1755. (10) David, b. 24 Sept. 1758.

TOTTINGHAM. *II.* Henry "Tottman," son of *I.* Eliah and Mary Tottingham, married Eunice Wyman, both of Woburn, 7 Sept. 1721. Their children were: (1) Mary, born 6 March, 1724. (2) Alice, b. 6 May, 1727. Henry "Tottman" died 5 Apr. 1728.

TRERICE. Nicholas Trerice, or Trarice, was in 1634, 1635, a noted master of the ship Planter, in which he had brought many persons from London to New England. In 1636, he was admitted to be an inhabitant of Charlestown.[a] Here, by his wife Rebekah, he had a son John, who was baptized in the church of Charlestown 3 June, 1639. In Dec. 1640, he subscribed the "Town Orders" for Woburn: removed his residence to Woburn soon after; and here had a son, *Samuel*, born 7 May, 1643. He was taxed in Woburn, 1645, in the rate for the country, but not in the town rate for 1646; whence it is concluded, that, previously to 1646, he had removed back to Charlestown; and there his daughter Rebekah was married, in 1655, to Thomas Jenner; and his widow, Rebekah, in 1665, to Thomas Lynde. [Savage's Geneal. Dict. Woburn Town Records. Rec. of Births, etc., etc.]

WALKER. Samuel Walker, sen. See Chap. V.

---

[a] Frothingham's Charlestown, p. 86.

His children (the given name of his wife is unknown) were Samuel, jun., Israel, and probably, John, sen., of Woburn; Hannah, wife of James, son of Simon Thompson, of Woburn; and (in the opinion of John Farmer, Esq.) Joseph Walker, of Billerica. Isaac Walker, too, of Woburn, according to the following record of his birth, was also a son of his. "Isaac, son of *Samuel Walker, sen.*, born ye 1st of 9th mo. [November] 1677." But it is not improbable, that *sen.* was inadvertently written here for jun. This Isaac Walker married Margery Bruce, of Woburn, 20 Feb. 1704-5; and he, and his sons by her, Isaac, jun., Ezekiel and Timothy, were sometime of Pennacook, now Concord, N. H. See Bouton's History of Concord.

WALKER. Samuel Walker, jun., otherwise known as Ensign Walker, and Deacon Walker. See Chap. V. To the notice there given of Samuel Walker, jun., it may be added, that he married, 10 Sept. 1662 [23 Oct. County Records], Sarah Reed, daughter of William and Mabel Reed, and sister of George Reed. Their children were: (1) *Edward*, born 12 Oct. 1663: killed with others by the Indians at Lamprey River, N. H., 6 July, 1690.[a] (2) *John*, jun., b. 2 July, 1665. (3) *Samuel*, b. 25 Jan. 1667-8. (4) *Sarah*, b. 6 March, 1670; married to Capt. Edward Johnson, grandson of first Capt. Edward, founder of Woburn, and son of Major William, 1686-7. (5) *Timothy*, b. 16 June, 1672; died 19 June, 1706, leaving a wife and 3 children. (6) *Isaac*, b. 1 Nov. 1677? See above Samuel Walker, 1st. (7) *Ezekiel*, b. 5 March, 1679. Lived in Boston? Sarah, wife of Samuel Walker, jun., died 1 Nov. 1681.

"Ensign Samuell Walker & Abigail Foull" married 18 April, 1692.

"Deacon Sam^{ll} Walker" died 18 Jan. 1703-4 (aged 61 years. Gravestone.) [Records of Births, etc.]

Israel Walker, son of Samuel, sen., and brother of Samuel Walker, jun., was taxed, as being an inhabitant of Woburn, in the Rate for the Second Meeting-house, 1672. By his wife Susanna, he had born to him: (1) *Israel*, b. 29 Sept. 1672; died 1 Nov. 1683. (2) *Susanna*, b. 1 March, 1674; md. to Ebenezer Lock, 1697? (3) *Phebe*, b. 11 March, 1676. (4) *Henry*, b. 1 Feb. 1678-9. (5) *Hannah*, b. 26 Apr. 1681; died 8 May, 1681. (6) *Elizabeth*, b. ———, died 21 Jan. 1681-2. (7) *Nathaniel*, b. 15 Apr. 1682. (8) *Israel*, again, b. 26 July, 1684. (9) Hannah, again, b. 24 Sept. 1686; md. to Isaac Kendall, Oct. 1706. (10) Abigail, b. 26 Sept. 1688. (11) Edward, b. 6 Nov. 1690. Susanna, wife of Israel Walker, died 7 March, 1694. "Ens. Israel Walker and Hannah ffiagg" married 10 Dec. 1696.

Ensign Israel Walker died 20 April, 1719. "Widow Hannah Walker" died 29 March, 1724.

John Walker, sen., supposed above to be a son of Samuel Walker, sen., and a brother of Israel Walker, is found taxed in the Rate for the Second Meeting-house in Woburn, 1672. He married Mary, daughter of Robert Peirce, 14 Oct. 1672, and by her had: (1) *Benjamin*, born 25 Jan. 1673-4; died 17 Nov. 1675. (2) *Mary*, b. 27 Dec. 1675; died 24 Jan. 1675-6. (3)

---

[a] Belknap's Hist.

John, b. 27 Dec. 1677. "Mary, wife of John Walker, sen.," died 8 Nov. 1695.

John Walker and Bethiah Simonds, [daughter of William Simonds] married 13 Aug. 1696; to whom were born: (1) *Bethiah*, daughter of John and Bethiah Walker, b. 4 Nov. 1697. (2) *Benjamin*, b. 7 July, 1699. John Walker, sen., died 3 Jan. 1723-4.

I. Benjamin Walker and Grace Tay, both of Woburn, md. 24 Dec. 1724. To them were born: (1) Mary, born 4 Oct. 1725. (2) Elizabeth, b. 17 March, 1728. [Wob. Rec. of Births, etc., etc. Town Records.]

WATERS. Joseph Waters was taxed, as an inhabitant of Woburn, in the rate for the Second Meeting-house, 1672, and served in Philip's War, 1675-6.[a] Nothing is found concerning his family connections. Not improbably he was a relative, perhaps a brother, of Samuel Waters, an inhabitant of Woburn in 1675; to whom and his wife Mary were born 12 children between 1675 and 1696. She died 11 Dec. 1721, and he died 2 May, 1728. [Wob. Rec.]

WHITTEMORE. Thomas Whittemore was taxed in the Rate for the Country, assessed in Woburn 26 Aug. 1666, and is reckoned among those who were entitled to a share of the common lands of the town in 1668;[b] but not being taxed in the Rate for the new Meeting-house in 1672, he appears to have previously removed to some other place; or, more probably, as Mr. Savage[c] thinks, to have died in March 1670, for "5 of April that year his wife Elizabeth had administered." He married, 9 Nov. 1666, Elizabeth Peirce, daughter of Thomas Peirce, b. 25 Dec. 1646? and by her had: Joseph, born 14 Aug. 1667.

WILSON. *I.* John Wilson, sen., first appears upon the tax lists in Woburn, in the Rate for the Country, assessed 26 Aug. 1666; and is numbered among those who had right in the common lands of the town in 1668.[d] He appears by his wife ——— to have had two children born to him before he came to Woburn, viz: John, jun., and Dorcas; md. to Aaron Cleaveland, 26 Sept. 1675. In Woburn he had: (1) Samuel, b. 29 Dec. 1658. (2) Abigail, b. 8 Aug. 1666. (3) Elizabeth, b. 6 Aug. 1668. (4) Benjamin, b. 15 Oct. 1670. (5) Hannah, b. 31 May, 1672; md. to Jonathan Peirce, 1689.

I. John Wilson, sen., died 2 July, 1687. [Wob. Rec. of Births, etc.]

WILSON. *II.* John Wilson, jun., had born to him by his wife ———: (1) John, b. 3 Jan. 1672-3. (2) Hannah, d. of "John Wilson, jun.," b. 28 Dec. 1674; died 5 May, 1676. (3) Hannah, again, b. 11 March, 1677. (4) Susanna, b. 11 March, 1679. [Rec. of Births, etc., in Wob.]

I. Samuel Wilson, son of John Wilson, sen., above named, married Elizabeth, daughter of Robert Peirce, 24 Feb. 1681-2. Their children were: (1) *Elizabeth*, b. 28 Jan. 1682-3. (2) *Mary*, b. 10 Apr. 1685. (3) *Samuel*, b. 2 Feb. and died 7 Feb. 1687-8. (4) *Hannah*, b. 24 Dec.

---

a List by Thos. B. Wyman, Esq.

b Rec. of Wob., Vol. I., pp. 38, 39 - - - 44.

c Savage's Geneal. Dict.

d Town Rec., Vol. I., pp. 43, 44.

1688. (5) *Rebekah*, b. 5 March, 1693; died 29 Nov. 1694. (6) *Samuel*, again, b. 21 Nov. 1695. (7) *Rebekah*, b. 5 July, 1698. Sargeant Samuel Wilson died 21 Nov. 1729. [Wob. Rec. of Births, Marriages, etc., etc.]

WILSON. *II*. Samuel Wilson, son of *I*. Samuel and Elizabeth Wilson, born 21 Nov. 1695; md. Sarah Simonds, daughter of *I*. James and Susanna Simonds, "both of Woburn," 29 Oct. 1719. To them were born: (1) *Samuel*, b. 22 July, 1720; died 21 June, 1750, aged 29 years and 11 months.[a] (2) *Sarah*, b. 13 July, 1722; married to Jonathan Johnson, 1748. (3) *Susanna*, b. 28 March, 1725; md. a Haywood or Howard, that removed to Maine. (4) *Ruth*, b. 26 March, 1729; md. to Jona. Proctor about 1748. (5) Rebekah, b. 15 March, 1732; died 31 Oct. 1734.[b] (6) *Rebekah*, again, b. 27 July, 1734; md. to Azel Johnson, 1757. Mr. Samuel Wilson died Oct. 11, 1750, aged 55 years.[a] After his decease, Dea. Edw. Johnson md. Sarah Wilson, his widow, 19 Feb. 1755; that is, he md. the mother of his son Jonathan's wife. [Rec. of Births in Woburn.]

WINN. Edward Winn was of Woburn, 1641; made freeman, 1643; and taxed in Woburn, in the rate for the country, 8 Sept. 1645. By his wife Joanna, he had, 5 Dec. 1641, a son Increase, which was the first born child recorded in Woburn; but probably his son Joseph, and his daughters Ann and Elizabeth, had their birth in England before. Joanna, wife of Edward Winn, dying 8 March, 1649, he married a second wife, Sarah Beal, 10 Aug. 1649. And she also dying, 15 March, 1680, he took yet a third wife, Ann, or Hannah, widow of Nicholas Wood, who survived him, apparently, till 1686. He died 5 Sept. 1682. In his Will, made 6 May of that year, he names his son Increase, his son Joseph's daughter Sarah, the three youngest children of his daughter Ann, wife of Moses Cleaveland; and the three youngest of his daughter Elizabeth, wife of George Polly. His widow likewise made her Will, 9 Sept. 1685, which being proved, 1 Nov. 1686, is an indication that she was then deceased. [Wob. Records of Births, etc. Savage's Geneal. Dict.]

I. Increase Winn, son of Edward and Joanna, married Hannah Sawtell, 13 July, 1665. Their children were: (1) *Hannah*, born 11 Apr. 1666; md. to Samuel Baker. (2) *Edward*, b. 15 June, 1668. (3) *Mary*, b. 1 May, 1670; md. to Nathl. Wyman, 1692. (4) *Abigail*, b. 8 Jan. 1677–8. (5) *Rebekah*, b. 5 Nov. 1679. (6) *Jacob*, b. 4 Oct. 1681. (7) *Joanna*, b. 24 June, 1683. (8) *Increase*, b. 9 Feb. 1684–5; died 1 July, 1713, [aged 28 years and 4 months. Gravestone.]

"Sargent Increase Winn" died 14 Dec. 1690. Widow Hannah Winn died 18 Feb. 1722–3.

WINN. *II*. Jacob, son of Increase and Hannah Winn, married Prudence Wyman, 28 June, 1704; and by her had: (1) *Prudence*, born 28 July, 1705. (2) *Elizabeth*, b. 29 Sept. 1707. (3) *Hannah*, b. 1 March, 1711. (4) *Increase*, b. 24 Jan. 1716–17. (5) *Joshua*, b. 14 Apr. 1719. (6) *Abigail*, b. 25 Jan. 1722–3. Prudence, w. of Jacob Winn dying, he md. for his second wife, Phebe Palfray, 14 July, 1737.

---

[a] Gravestone.

[b] The first person buried in Wob. Precinct (Burlington) Burying-Ground.

WINN. *III.* Increase Winn, son of Jacob and Prudence Winn, married Elizabeth Knight, 5 Oct. 1742. Their children were: (1) *David,* ——, md. Hannah Twiss, 11 June, 1765. (2) *Elizabeth,* born 9 Dec. 1745; md. to Timothy Twiss, 12 July, 1768. (3) "*Annah*" or *Hannah,* b. 31 Oct. 1747. (4) *Jacob,* b. 16 July, 1751; md. Molly Twiss, and removed to Hollis, N. H. (5) *Molly,* b. Jan. 1753.

WINN. *III.* Joshua Winn, son of Jacob and Prudence Winn, married Mary Center, about Oct. 1645; and had by her: (1) *Joshua,* born 17 May, 1747. (2) *Jeremiah,* b. 29 Apr. 1749. (3) *Molly,* b. 5 Apr. 1751. (4) *James,* b. 7 Apr. 1753. (5) *Jonathan,* b. 18 Oct. 1755.

WINN. Joseph Winn, son of Edward and Joanna, among the first settlers of Woburn, was born in England; married Rebekah, daughter of William and Mabel Reed, and sister of first George Reed of Woburn, about 1664. Their children were: (1) *Rebekah,* born 25 May, 1665; and died 6 Apr. 1679. (2) *Sarah,* b. 9 Nov. 1666; md. to Ebenezer Johnson. (3) Joanna, b. ——; md. to Edward Knight, 13 July, 1699. (4) *Abigail,* b. 18 June, 1670; died 25 June, 1670. (5) *Joseph,* b. 15 May, 1671. (6) Josiah, b. 15 March, 1674. (7, 8) *Rebekah* and *Hannah,* twins, b. 14 Feb. 1678-9. Rebekah m. to Timothy Spaulding of Chelmsford, 5 March, 1700. No mention of Hannah in his Will.[a] (9) *Timothy,* b. ——; died 22 March, 1678. (10) *Anne,* b. 1 Nov. 1684; died 13 Sept. 1686. (11) Timothy, b. 27 Feb. 1686-7.

"Ensign Joseph Winn" died 22 Feb. 1714-15. Widow Rebekah Winn died ——, 1734. [Wob. Rec. of Births, etc., etc.]

WINN. *I.* Timothy Winn, son of Joseph and Rebekah Winn, married Elizabeth Brooks. Their children were:

II. Timothy, born about July 1712.

Elizabeth, born 1 Sept. 1719; md. to Nehemiah Wyman, 7 Dec. 1742.

Elizabeth, wife of Timothy Winn, died 14 May, 1724 [aged about 34: Gravestone].

Timothy Winn and Jane Belknap, both of Woburn, married 18 Feb. 1729-30. To them were born: (1) *Ruth,* 6 Aug. 1732. (2) *Joseph,* b. 3 July, 1734. (3) Jerusha, Aug. 4, 1740. *I.* Timothy Winn died 5 Jan. 1752 [aged 65: Gravestone].

Widow Jane Winn died of small-pox May 1775.[b] [Rec. of Births in Woburn.]

WINN. *II.* Timothy Winn, better known as Dea. Timothy Winn, was a gentleman of note and of much influence in his day. He was the son of *I.* Timothy and Elizabeth (Brooks) Winn, and was born in Woburn about July 1712. His place of residence falling within the bounds of Woburn Precinct, he joined the Precinct Church, May 4, 1740; and was chosen a deacon of that church Dec. 26, 1752; an office which he held during life. He was a man noted for his industry, economy, and success in amassing wealth. He was chosen one of the Selectmen of the town in 1756, '57; and

---

[a] Mr. Boutelle, from inspection of the Will. [b] Mem. of Samuel Thompson, Esq.

again in 1773, '74, '75. He represented Woburn in the General Court 1787, '88, and 1791. And in December 1787, he and James Fowle, jun., were chosen delegates for Woburn to the convention which met in Boston Jan. 9, 1788, respecting the ratification of the Constitution of the United States.

In all the early attempts to set off Woburn Precinct as a separate town, he was opposed, it is said, to the measure. But he favored, it is understood, the last attempt, which proved successful. But he did not live long to enjoy the success of it. He died March 3, 1800, aged 87 years and 8 months, a few days more than a year after the act of Court incorporating the Second Precinct as a town, by the name of Burlington. By his wife Mary (Bowers) Winn, Dea. Winn had two children that lived to mature age, viz: Timothy, born Dec. 20, 1740; and Mary, born June 21, 1743, and married, Jan. 2, 1777, to Col. John Waldron, of Dover, N. H. Dea. Winn's son Timothy, distinguished in Woburn Records as Timothy Winn, jun., and Ensign Timothy Winn, was a gentleman highly respected and esteemed. He married Sarah Reed of Woburn, Jan. 23, 1766; and she dying, in January of the following year, he married for his second wife Mary Bridge, daughter of Rev. Ebenezer Bridge, of Chelmsford. By her he had, among other children, the late Col. William Winn, of Burlington and Woburn, who was the father of the present William Winn, Esq., of Burlington, and Messrs. Jonathan Bowers Winn and Timothy Winn, of Woburn, gentlemen well known in all this vicinity.

II. Joseph Winn, son of *I.* Timothy and Jane Winn, and half brother of Dea. Timothy Winn, was a respected and influential citizen in his day. In the war of the Revolution, he served his country in the military line, and acquired the title of Lieutenant Winn; and at the first Town Meeting in Burlington, after the act incorporating it as a town, he was chosen chairman of the Board of Selectmen and of the Overseers of the Poor. He died Apr. 30, 1817, aged 82 years and 9 months. The late Abel Winn, Esq., of Burlington, was a son of his.

WRIGHT. John Wright. See Chap. V.

Joseph Wright. See Chap. V. add:

By his wife Elizabeth, he had issue as follows: (1) *Elizabeth*, born 2 July, 1664; married Eleazar Bateman, 2 Nov. 1686. (2) *Joseph*, b. 14 March, 1667; md. Elizabeth Bateman, 7 July, 1692. (3) *Sarah*, b. 25 Feb. 1669-70. (4) *John*, b. 2 Oct. 1672. (5) *Joanna*, b. 18 April, 1675; died 17 Feb. 1690-91. (6) *James*, b. 10 March, 1677. (7) *Timothy*, b. 3 Apr. 1679. (8) *Stephen*, b. 22 Jan. 1680-81. (9) *Jacob*, b. 22 June, 1683. (10) *Ruth*, b. 10 Oct. 1685. (11) Benjamin, b. 14 March, 1688. Elizabeth, wife of Dea. Joseph Wright, died 28 June, 1713. Deacon Joseph Wright, died 31 March, 1724.

WYMAN. *I.* John Wyman, a subscriber at Charlestown to Town Orders for Woburn, Dec. 1640, was taxed at Woburn in tax for the Country, 8 Sept. 1645; married 5 Nov. 1644, Sarah Nutt, whom her father, Myles Nutt, had brought with him from England. The children of John and Sarah Wyman were: (1) Samuel, born 20 Sept. and died 27 Sept. 1646. (2) *John*, b. 28 March, 1648. (3) *Sarah*, b. 15 Apr. 1650; md. 15 Dec. 1669, to Joseph Walker, of Billerica; died 26 Jan. 1729. (4) *Solomon*, b. 26 Feb.

1651-2; died 22 Sept. 1725. (5) *David*, b. 7 Apr. 1654. (6) *Elizabeth*, b. 18 Jan. 1655-6; died 21 Nov. 1658. (7) *Bathsheba*, b. 6 Oct. 1658; md. Nathaniel Tay, of Billerica, 30 May, 1677; died 9 July, 1730. (8) *Jonathan*, b. 13 July, 1661. (9) *Seth*, b. 3 Aug. 1663. (10) *Jacob*, b. ———, the youngest son of Lieut. Wyman.

Lieut. John Wyman died 9 May, 1684. His widow, Sarah, married after his death, Thomas Fuller, 25 Aug. 1684. [Wob. Rec. of Births, etc.]

WYMAN. *II.* John Wyman, jun., married Mary, daughter of Rev. Thomas Carter, about 1671. Their children were: (1) *John*, b. 23 Apr. 1672. (2) *Mary*, b. 25 June, 1674; md. to Thomas Peirce, jun., son of Sergt. Thomas, 27 Feb. 1693. John Wyman, jun., being one of Capt. Prentice's troop, was slain by the Indians in the Narraganset Fight, 19 Dec. 1675. His widow, Mary, was married 31 Oct. 1676, to Nath. Batchelder, of Hampton. [Wob. Rec. Births, etc. Savage's Geneal. Dict.]

WYMAN. David, son of *I.* John and Sarah Wyman, was a tanner; married 27 Apr. 1675, in Charlestown, Isabel Farmer, daughter of John Farmer, of Concord, by whom he had two children, viz: (1) David, b. 29 May, died 15 June, 1676. (2) *Isabel*, b. 5 July, 1677; md. 1700, in Malden, to John Green, of that town, and died 9 Aug. 1765, "in her 88th year." [Gravestone.]

David Wyman died of the small-pox in Woburn, 1678; and his widow married in Concord, James Blood, 19 Nov. 1679. [Wob. Rec. of Births, etc., etc. Manuscript Genealogy of Thomas B. Wyman, Esq. Savage's Geneal. Dict.]

WYMAN. Jonathan Wyman, son of *I.* John and Sarah Wyman, md. Abigail Fowle, daughter of Lieut. James Fowle, 29 July, 1689, who died 3 Jan. 1689-90. For his second wife, he md. Hannah, a daughter of Peter Fowle, 31 July, 1690. Their children were: (1) *Abigail*, b. 1 June, 1691; md. to Sam. Buck, and died 2 Dec. 1720. (2) *Hannah*, b. Nov. 1694; md. 1 June, 1717, to Israel Reed. (3) *Mary*, b. 26 Jan. 1696-7; md. prior to 1718 to Jeremiah Center. (4) *Elizabeth*, b. 15 Feb. 1700-1; md. 11 Aug. 1721, to Zerubbabel Snow. (5) *Jonathan*, b. 13 Sept. 1704. (6) *Sarah*, b. 18 Aug. 1706; md. —— to Nathan Brooks; and died 21 Feb. 1747. (7) *Zachary*, b. 19 July, 1709: a soldier in French War, 1748.

Cornet Jonathan Wyman died 15 Dec. 1736. [Wob. Rec. of Births, etc., etc. Wyman's MSS. Genealogy. Savage's Geneal. Dict.]

WYMAN. Seth Wyman, son of *I.* John and Sarah Wyman, md. Esther Johnson, daughter of Major Wm. Johnson, 17 Dec. 1685: by whom he had: (1) Seth, b. 13 Sept. 1686; killed at Lovewell Fight, 1725. (2) "*Hesther*," b. 25 Oct. 1688. (3) *Sarah*, b. 17 Jan. 1690-1; md. to Caleb Blogget. (4) *Jonathan*, b. 5 Nov. 1693; died 19 Jan. 1693-4. (5) *Susana*, b. 30 June, 1695. (6) *Abigail*, b. 6 Feb. 1698-9; md. 19 Jan. 1725, to Timothy Brooks; and died 16 March, 1780. (7) *Love*, b. 14 Feb. 1701-2; md. to Josiah Wyman? Lieut. Seth Wyman died 26 Oct. 1715. His widow, Esther, died 31 March, 1742.

[Wob. Rec. of Births, etc. Savage's Geneal. Dict. Wyman MSS. Genealogy.]

WYMAN. Jacob Wyman, youngest son of *I.* John and Sarah Wyman, a tanner; freeman, 1690; md. 23 Nov. 1687, Elizabeth, daughter of Samuel Richardson; and had: (1) *Jacob*, b. 11 Sept. 1688. (2) *Samuel*, b. 7 Feb. 1689–90. (3) *Elizabeth*, b. 7 Jan. 1691–2; md. to Josiah Waters; and died prior to 1742. (4) *David*, b. 14 Apr. 1693. (5) *Martha*, b. 13 Oct. 1695; md. to Major Joseph Richardson. (6) *Mary*, b. 8 July, 1698; died prior to 1742. (7) *John*, b. 11 Dec. 1700; died 9 July, 1721, a graduate of Harvard College the same year. (8) *Solomon*, b. 24 Apr. 1703; died aged 22 years. (9) *Patience*, b. 13 Apr. 1705. (10) *Ebenezer*, b. 5 May, 1707; H. C. 1731; minister of Union, Ct.; md. at Woburn, Mrs. Mary Wright, 22 May, 1739; died Feb. 9, 1746. (11) *Isaiah*, b. 28 Feb. 1708–9; died 9 Feb. 1746–7. (12) *Peter*, b. 27 Sept. 1711; md. Abigail Russell, about 1744, in Boston? (13) *Daniel*, b. 27 May, 1715; a saddler in East Sudbury, now Wayland; md. first, Rebecca ——, who died 10 Feb. 1744; 2dly, Dorothy Jennison, or Johnson, who died 30 Sept. 1806. Daniel Wyman died 29 Dec. 1766; had 8 children by his two wives.

Elizabeth, wife of Mr. Jacob Wyman, died 21 Nov. 1739. Mr. Jacob Wyman md. Mrs. Elizabeth Coggin, 4 Feb. 1739–40. Mr. Jacob Wyman died 31 March, 1742. Widow Elizabeth Wyman died 2 May, 1752. [Wob. Rec. of Births, etc. Savage's Geneal. Dict. Wyman MSS. Genealogy.]

Francis Wyman married 30 Jan. 1644–5, Judith Peirce, of Woburn, born at Norwich, England, daughter of John; died without issue. For his 2d wife, he md. Abigail Reed, daughter of William and Mabel, and sister of first George Reed, 2 Oct. 1650. Their children were: (1) Judith, born 29 Sept. and died 22 Dec. 1652. (2) *Francis*, born about 1654; died during Indian War, 26 Apr. 1676, about 22 years old. (3) *William*, b. about 1656. (4) Abigail, b. about 1659; married to Stephen Richardson, 2 Jan. 1675–6; died 17 Sept. 1720, aged 60. Gravestone. (5) *Timothy*, b. 15 Sept. 1661; died 1709. (6) *Joseph*, b. 9 Nov. 1663, lived a tailor, unmarried, and died 24 July, 1714. (7) *Nathaniel*, b. 25 Nov. 1665. (8) *Samuel*, b. 29 Nov. 1667. (9) *Thomas*, b. 1 April, 1671. (10) *Benjamin*, b. 25 Aug. 1674. (11) *Stephen*,[a] b. 2 June, 1676; died 19 Aug. 1676. (12) *Judith*, b. 15 Jan. 1678–9; md. to Nath. Bacon, of Billerica; living in 1714. Francis Wyman, sen., died 30 Nov. 1699, aged, per stone, about 82. [Wob. Rec. of Births, etc. Savage's Geneal. Dict.

WYMAN. *III.* William, son of Francis and Abigail Wyman, married Prudence ——. Their children were: (1) *William*, born 18 Jan. and died 20 Jan. 1682–3. (2) *Prudence*, b. 26 Dec. 1683; md. to Jacob Winn. (3) *William*, b. 15 Jan. 1685–6. (4) *Thomas*, b. 23 Aug. 1687; lived, in his latter days, and died in Pelham, N. H. (5) *Elizabeth*, b. 5 July, 1689, died 25 June, 1690. (6) Francis, b. 10 July, 1691. (7) *Joshua*, b. 3 Jan. 1692–3: a blacksmith: innholder, 1722; m. (1) Mary Pollard, (2) Mary Green, in Woburn, 14 July, 1747. (8) Edward, b. 10 Jan. 1695–6. (9) *Elizabeth*, b. 16 Feb. 1697–8. (10) *Deliverance*, b. 28 Feb. 1700–1; md. to Ezekiel Gowing, jun.,

---

[a] Wyman's MSS. Genealogy.

of Lynn, 1732. (11) *James*, b. 16 March, 1702; taxed in Woburn, 1723. William Wyman died 1705. [Woburn Rec. of Births, etc. Savage's Geneal. Dict. Wyman's MS. Genealogy.]

WYMAN. *V.* Timothy Wyman, son of Francis and Abigail Wyman, married Hannah ——; by whom he had: (1) *Hannah*, born 7 July, 1688. (2) *Timothy*, b. 5 April, 1691. (3) *Solomon*, b. 24 Oct. 1693; md. in Medford, 9 June, 1725, Mary Peirce, daughter of John Peirce of Woburn; which Mary, when afterwards a widow, md. Benjamin Johnson, 14 Feb. 1765. Solomon's Will dated 2 Jan. 1760. (4) *Joseph*, b. 1 Nov. 1695. (5) *Eunice*, b. 24 Feb. 1697-8; md. to Henry Tottingham, 1721; died prior to 1748. (6) *Anne*, b. 26 March, 1700: of Andover, and died unmarried 1774. (7) *Judith*, b. 16 June, 1702; md. to John Wright *III.* 1725, of Ashford, Ct.; living 1748. (8) *Eli*, b. 11 March, 1704; died 22 Aug. 1728. (9) *Ebenezer*, b. 21 March, 1706: of Townsend, Mass.; md. in Woburn, 24 Feb. 1736, Rebekah Johnson, daughter of Dea. Edward Johnson; and, secondly, in Billerica, 2 April, 1745, to Dorcas Wilson. Living in 1764. (10) *Hesther*, b. ——. (11) *Elizabeth*, ——. (12) Prudence, b. 8 March, 1709; md. to Thomas Phelps. Living 1748, 1772.

Timothy Wyman died 1709.

[Wob. Rec. of Births. Genealogy of the Wymans in Manuscript, by Thos. B. Wyman, Esq. Savage's Geneal. Dict.]

WYMAN. *VII.* Nathaniel Wyman, son of Francis and Abigail, married Mary, daughter of Increase Winn, 28 June, 1692. Their children were: (1) *Nathaniel*, b. 23 May, 1693; died 13 Dec. 1715. (2) *Mary*, b. 28 May, 1694; died insane, 1728. (3) *Abigail*, b. 5 Oct. 1695; md. to Benjamin Gowen. (4) *Ruth*, b. 17 Apr. 1697; md. to Thomas Gould, Charlestown, 1721. (5) *Hannah*, b. 28 Apr. 1699; md. to *II.* Timothy Wyman. (6) *Elizabeth*, b. 11 Nov. 1700; md. 12 March, 1723, to John "*Geary*," of Charlestown. [Stoneham?] (7) Phebe, b. 11 June, 1702; md. prior to 1729 to Thomas "Geary," [Gerry] Stoneham. (8) Rebekah, b. 14 April, 1704; md. 7 March, 1723, to Thomas Holden. (9) *Johanah*, [Joanna?] b. 25 July, 1705; md. to Jonathan Holden, 1731; died 11 Nov. 1786. (10) *Increase*, b. 1 March, 1707. (11) *Sarah*, b. 21 Aug. 1710; md. 6 July, 1732, to Ezekiel Walker; died prior to 1756. (12) *Keziah*, b 5. Apr. 1713; md. to John Reed, 1735; died 14 Jan. 1756.

Nathaniel Wyman died 8 Dec. 1717. His widow, Mary Wyman, md. to John Locke, of Woburn, 30 Nov. 1720. [Wob. Records of Births, etc. Savage's Geneal. Dict. Wyman's MSS. Genealogy.]

WYMAN. *VIII.* Samuel Wyman, son of Francis and Abigail; md. Rebekah, daughter of Mathew Johnson, —— 1692. Their children were: (1) *Rebekah*, born 11 Nov. 1693; married at Watertown to Thomas Richardson, of Woburn, 29 Sept. 1713; died 11 April, 1771. (2) *Abigail*, b. 5 Feb. 1694-5; md. prior to 1726 to Jonas Richardson. (3) *Hannah*, b. 10 Dec. 1696; md. 10 May, 1725, to Samuel Parker. (4) *Sarah*, b. 2 Feb. 1698-9; md. probably 31 Aug. 1726, to John Coggin. (5) *Samuel*, b. 18 March, 1700. (6) *Oliver*, b. 5. Sept. 1701; a soldier of Leominster in 1758, '59, and died 1759. (7) *Lydia*, b. 1 Jan. 1702-3; md. 24 July, 1729, at Reading, to Oliver Richardson, of Woburn. (8) *Patience*, b. 11 Jan. 1705-6;

md. to Edward Dean. (9) *Matthew*, b. 3 Aug. 1707: of Lancaster, a laborer; married 8 March, 1738-9, to Abigail Willard, by whom he left issue. He served in Willard's Comp., Nova Scotia, 1755. (10) *Esther*, b. 25 Feb. 1709-10. Samuel Wyman died 17 May, 1725. His widow, Rebekah, living 1735. [Records of Births, etc. Wyman's MSS. Genealogy. Savage's Geneal. Dict.]

WYMAN. *I.* Thomas, sen., son of Francis and Abigail Wyman, md. Mary Richardson, a daughter of Nathaniel, 5 May, 1696. Their children were: (1) *Thomas*, born 12 May, 1697. (2) *Josiah*, b. 18 March, 1700. (3) Phineas, b. 1701; living, insane, 1747. (4) *Timothy*, b. 1 March, 1702. (5) *Benjamin*, b. 12 June, 1704. (6) *John*, b. 6 July, 1706; died 26 March, 1729; a housewright, taxed from 1725 to 1728. (7) *Mary*, b. 10 March, 1708; md. 13 June, 1726, to Nath. Clark, Watertown. (8) *Aaron*, b. 6 Dec. 1709. (9) *Eleazer*, b. 13 Apr. 1712; died 16 July, 1747. (10) *Nathaniel*, b. 18 May, 1716. (11) Elizabeth, b. 19 Dec. 1718; md. to —— Blogget; issue by whom, and *Elizabeth* Wyman.

Thomas Wyman, sen., served in Sir Charles Hobby's troop at Annapolis, 10 Oct. 1710, to 10 Oct. 1711. He died 4 Sept. 1731. His widow Mary md. Josiah Winn, 17 Aug. 1733, and died 7 June, 1743.

Benjamin, son of Francis and Abigail Wyman, was a "maltster;" and married 20 Jan. 1702-3, Elizabeth Hancock, of Cambridge. Their children were: (1) *Elizabeth*, born 1 May, 1705; md. 11 June, 1724, to Jacob Richardson. (2) *Benjamin*, b. 13 Dec. (al. Nov.) 1706. (3) *Lucy*, b. 17 Apr. 1708; died 25 Oct. 1730: wife of Richard Davenport, of Shrewsbury. (4) *Zebadiah*, b. 26 June, 1709. (5) *Eunice*, b. 16 Nov. 1710; md. to Robert Peirce, 1736; died 15 Apr. or May, 1774 or 1775. (6) *Jerusha*, b. 23 July, 1712; md. to Edw. Richardson, 1730; died 10 Apr. 1784. (7) *Tabitha*, b. 7 Apr. 1714; md. to Josiah Kendall, 1736; died 24 Apr. 1800. (8) *Abijah*, b. 20 Sept. 1715. (9) *Katharine*, b. 6 May, 1717; md. 28 Feb. 1732-3? to William Tufts, of Medford; died, per stone, 20 Feb. 1749. (10) *Nathaniel*, b. 26 Jan. 1718-19. (11) *Abigail*, b. 26 Aug. 1720; m. 8 Apr. 1740, to Jacob Snow; died 31 Oct. 1771. (12) *Martha*, b. 7 May, 1722; md. 6 Sept. 1739, to Samuel Dean. (13) *Noah*, b. 30 July, 1724; died 10 Dec. 1726. (14) *Jonas*, b. 26 July, 1725; a blacksmith; died at Louisburg, 20 Jan. 1746. (15) Reuben, b. 9 Nov. 1726. Benjamin Wyman died 19 Dec. 1735. His widow m. 22 Aug. [al. Sept.] 1739, to Jonathan Bacon of Bedford; and died March 2, 1749, æt. 63. [Wob. Rec. of Births, etc. Savage's Geneal. Dict. Wyman MSS. Genealogy.]

Messrs. John and Francis Wyman were brothers, and original settlers of the town of Woburn. By occupation, they were both tanners; and had their dwellings and their tanning establishments near the late Dea. Benjamin Wyman's, in the Wyman Lane. They were also joint proprietors of extensive tracts of land in other parts of the town. About 1669, they united in the purchase of the "Coitmore Grant," so called, in Woburn, containing 500 acres, for which they paid £25 or £30 sterling each, to Mr. Joseph Rock, executor of the will of Martha (Coitmore) Coggan, who had been the widow of Capt. Coitmore, the grantee. This grant was laid out in the northwest part of Woburn, now Burlington; and upon it numerous descendants of both brothers were living a century ago, though now not a person by the name of Wyman is an inhabitant of that portion of the town. They also owned a large farm, with houses thereon, adjoining the Coitmore grant, situate in the west part of Woburn, and extending within the bounds of Billerica, upon which, by order of Court, they were taxed equally for some years, both in Billerica and in Woburn.

The descendants of these two brothers by the name of Wyman have been a multitude. In a genealogy of their families, prepared with great industry and untiring research by Thomas Bellows Wyman, Esq., of Charlestown, a descendant from John Wyman of the 6th generation, there were numbered, Nov. 6th, 1844, of the posterity of John Wyman, in the male line, 5 children, 31 grandchildren, 54 great-grandchildren, 91 of the 4th generation, 106 of the 5th, 147 of the 6th, and 8 of the 7th,—442 in all; and of the posterity, in the male line, of Francis Wyman, 9 children, 71 grand children, 152 great-grandchildren, 213 of the 4th generation, 188 of the 5th, 41 of the 6th,—674 in all; making a total, in 1844, of 1116 descendants, from the males, in each generation, from the two patriarchs, John and Francis Wyman.

Of the posterity of these two noted primitive settlers in Woburn, numbers may be referred to who were prominent men in their day; persons distinguished not only by their official relations, but by their ability and care to fulfil them with usefulness to society. Of this description, among the descendants of John Wyman, was Dea. Samuel Wyman, the revolutionary patriot, repeatedly chosen in those trying times to represent Woburn in the General Court, and in the Provincial Congress assembled at Watertown. And among the descendants of Francis Wyman answering to the above character, may be reckoned Capt. Benjamin Wyman, the faithful treasurer of the town from 1752 to 1758 inclusively, seven years in uninterrupted succession: Dea. Zebadiah Wyman, his successor in that important office, and at a very trying period, ten years out of the thirteen which elapsed from 1780 to 1792 inclusively: the late Dea. Benjamin Wyman, the judicious and upright magistrate, as well as exemplary officer of the First Church in this town; and Dr. Rufus Wyman, a native of Woburn, "the beloved physician," while at Chelmsford, the skilful, successful Superintendent of the McLean Asylum for the Insane at Somerville, honored in life, and lamented at his death.

WYMAN. John Wyman, 2d, distinguished as Sergeant John Wyman, and supposed by some to have been a near relative, perhaps a nephew, of John and Francis Wyman, had land granted him in Woburn, 25 Feb. 1679.[a]

He was a wheelwright by occupation, and married Hannah, daughter of John Farrar, of Woburn, 14 Dec. 1685. Their children were: (1) *John*, born 16 Nov. 1686. He settled in Wilmington, and died prior to 6 Jan. 1748.[a] (2) *Thomas*, b. 25 March, 1689, and died insane prior to 1749.[a] (3) *Jasher*, b. 6 Jan. 1691-2. (4) Nathan, b. 8 Jan. 1695-6. (5) *Hannah*, b.

---

[a] Woburn Records of Births, etc. Wyman's Manuscript Genealogy.

8 Aug. 1703. (6) *Anne*, b. 10 Apr. 1705; md. 5 May, 1739, to Samuel Bathrick, of Portsmouth, N. H.[a] (7) *Rachel*, b. 24 Oct. 1707.

Sergt. John Wyman died 19 April, 1728.

WYMAN. *I.* Nathan, son of Sergt. John Wyman and Hannah, married Huldah Simonds, daughter of Benjamin and Rebekah, both of Woburn, 29 Jan. 1723. Their children were: (1) *Nathan*, born 28 June, 1723. (2) *Rachel*, b. 31 July, 1724; md. to Jacob Eames, in 1748.[a] (3) *Elijah*, b. 22 Feb. 1727-8.

Nathan Wyman, wheelwright, died 4 Feb. 1773. Huldah, his wife, died 28 May, 1768, æt. 68, per stone.[a]

WYMAN. *II.* Nathan Wyman, jun., son of Nathan and Huldah, md. Rebekah Russell, daughter of Saml. and Rebekah, of Woburn, 11 June, 1749, and had issue: (1) *Nathan*, born 21 May, 1754. (2) *Rebekah*, b. 7 Aug. 1757; died 15 Sept. 1759. (3) *Zadok*, b. 20 [10?] Aug. 1760. (4) *Rebekah*, b. 7 Aug. 1762. (5) *John*, b. 26 Feb. 1765.

Rebekah, widow of Nathan, died 9 Oct. 1811, aged 85.[a]

WYMAN. *III.* Nathan Wyman, son of Nathan and Rebekah, m. 21 Nov. 1778, Mary Convers, daughter of Samuel and Mary, who had a son, *Nathan*, born 11 Sept. 1783.

III. Nathan Wyman died 30 April, 1821; his wife Mary died 3 Sept. 1817, æt. 51.

IV. Nathan Wyman, son of Nathan and Mary, md. Esther Wilder, and at his decease left two sons, viz: (1) Herbert, born May 7, 1818; md. Lydia Kimball, and lives respected at North Woburn. (2) *V.* Nathan, born 16 Feb. 1821; chosen Town Clerk of Woburn 1844, and by constant re-election still (1867) continues in that office.

---

[a] Woburn Records of Births, etc. Wyman's Manuscript Genealogy.

INDEX.

BY GEO. M. CHAMPNEY.

G.

H.

I.

N.

O.

P.

S.

T.

INDEX TO NAMES.

INDEX TO APPENDICES.